THE
New Humanities
READER

Second Edition

Richard E. Miller

RUTGERS UNIVERSITY

Kurt Spellmeyer

RUTGERS UNIVERSITY

HOUGHTON MIFFLIN COMPANY   Boston   New York

Acknowledgments

This project has been a long time in the making. It has been helped along by the hard work and dedication of the assistant and associate directors of the Rutgers Writing Program, the writing program's teaching faculty and staff, and the undergraduates at our university. We are fortunate to work in an environment where so many people are willing to innovate and to give curricular change a try. We are grateful, as well, for Houghton Mifflin's commitment to this project: the folks in custom publishing, our editors for the national edition of this volume, and the sales reps have all helped us fine-tune our vision for the new humanities. Now, all that remains to do is what always remains: to think connectively, to read creatively, and to write one's way to new ways of seeing.

Publisher: Pat Coryell
Editor-in-Chief: Suzanne Phelps Weir
Assistant Editor: Anne Leung
Senior Project Editor: Bob Greiner
Editorial Assistant: Robert Woo
Senior Art and Design Coordinator: Jill Haber
Senior Composition Buyer: Sarah Ambrose
Manufacturing Coordinator: Chuck Dutton
Senior Marketing Manager: Cindy Graff Cohen
Marketing Associate: Wendy Thayer

Cover credit: Background image of ripe wheat © by Robert Glusic/Photodisc Green
Neon Signs in Shanghai © John Hicks/CORBIS
Muslim Women in the town of Taroudannt © by Martin Harvey/CORBIS
(Back cover) Prehistoric Cave Painting, Ennedi Plateau, Tschad © Digital Vision/Veer.com

Permissions and credits are found in the Acknowledgments beginning on page 709. This Acknowledgments section constitutes an extension of the copyright page.

Printed in the U.S.A.

Library of Congress Control Number: 2005921389

ISBN: 0-618-56822-0

4 5 6 7 8 9-MP-09 08 07 06

CONTENTS

free market in which parents have the right to enhance their progeny in any way they want—and can afford.

The term "divided consciousness" refers to those times when we withdraw mentally from the world around us. Daydreams and others forms of subjective escape often help us to keep our mental balance by shutting out events when they threaten to be overwhelming. But when does our power to shut things out begin to close the door on sanity itself?

Anyone who watches the presidential debates or listens to talk radio can see that Americans love to argue. But the truth is that the "winner" in any debate may prove to be mistaken, while the loser may fail to communicate information that everyone could benefit from hearing. According to linguist Deborah Tannen, there has to be a better way.

Technological innovations happen in response to problems, but each innovation ends up producing a series of new problems in turn—which require new innovations, which produce new problems once again, apparently ad infinitum. Is all of this change self-defeating? While admitting that technology has "revenge effects," Edward Tenner makes the case that progress is no illusion.

Most people imagine losing one's self or having an empty self as a fate worse than death. But Robert Thurman, an expert on the Buddhism of Tibet, argues that we have misjudged the experience of "no self," which is not a dark corridor to oblivion, but the road to what he calls "infinite life."

Everyone knows that nature is ruled by the principle of "the survival of the fittest." The only problem is, this principle doesn't tell the whole story. If competition plays a part in biological life, cooperation and altruism do as well. In fact, evolution seems to push many species toward increasing degrees of altruism.

THEMATIC CONTENTS

What should a college or university ask beginning students to think and write about? Our idea is to let them deal with the most pressing problems of our time—problems that resist easy answers and that need to be explored in ways that move across the boundaries separating conventional fields of knowledge. In the process of crossing these boundaries, each of us has to invent our own ways of thinking and writing, but we offer the following thematic combinations to illustrate how this creative work might be done.

Art and the Making of Meaning

Culture and Performance

Democracy in the Age of Globalization

Economics and Justice

Education: Learning, Conforming, and Knowing

The Future of the Environment: Evolution and Human Ingenuity

Gender

Medical Practice and the Arts of Healing

Making Sense of Violence

World Religion and World Secularity

PREFACE

This book probably differs from most you have encountered, at least those that you have encountered in school. Generally, the books taught in school tell students how to think, but ours has a different purpose. We wanted to put in your hands a book that would require you to make connections for yourself as you think, read, and write about the events that are likely to shape your future life.

Although the articles and essays assembled here deal with subjects as diverse as the global increase in ethnic violence and the practice of Tibetan meditation, the book is not really "about" violence or meditation or any of the other subjects explored by the readings we have selected. Instead, this book is about the need for new ways of thinking, and it does not pretend that those ways of thinking are widely practiced today. Our world has seen more change in the last hundred years than it had seen in the previous thousand. From the media we get daily reports on subjects that our great-grandparents might have found incomprehensible: breakthroughs in cloning; mergers of U.S. firms with Japanese or German partners; a global treaty on biological weapons; a new account of the universe in the first seconds after the Big Bang; the melting of the polar icecaps; legislation to extend health-care benefits to same-sex couples. Such events are truly without precedent.

Never before have people faced uncertainty in so many different areas. Will the Internet be a negative influence, contributing to the forces that have pulled apart the family unit, or will it strengthen our neighborhoods and communities? Will the global economy create widespread unemployment and environmental decline, or will it usher in an era of undreamed-of prosperity and peace? Will encounters between different cultures, long separated by geography, lead to a new renaissance, or must such meetings always end in balkanization and violence? Unlike the questions posed by the standard textbook, the answers to these questions aren't waiting for any of us in the teacher's edition. Not even the best educated and the most experienced among us can foresee with certainty how the life of our times will turn out. If our problems today are much more sweeping than those encountered by humankind before, they are also more complex. Globalization is not just an issue for economists, or political scientists, or historians, or anthropologists: it is an issue for all of them—and us—together. The degradation of the biosphere is not just an ecological matter, but a political, social, and cultural matter as well.

The uniqueness of our time requires that we devise new understandings of ourselves and of the world. One purpose of this book is to provide a forum for these understandings to emerge. It may seem strange, perhaps, that we would have such lofty goals in a course for undergraduates. Surely the experts are better equipped to respond to issues of the sort our world now confronts than are beginning students in our colleges and universities. But this assumption may be unjustified. While the forms of expertise available today clearly have great value, most of the current academic disciplines were created more than a century ago, and the divisions of knowledge on which they are based reflect the needs of a very different society. It is worth remembering, for example, that in 1900 cars were a new technology, and airplanes and radios had yet to be invented. Scientists still debated the structure of the atom. The British Empire dominated three-fourths of the globe, and "culture" meant the traditions of Western Europe's elite, never more than one-tenth of one percent of the population of that region. In a certain sense, the current generation of college students, teachers, and administrators needs to reinvent the university itself, not by replacing one department or methodology with another, but by forging broad connections across areas of knowledge that still remain in relative isolation.

New Humanities for New Times: The Search for Coherence

Some readers of this book will be surprised by the absence of material from the traditional humanities: poems and plays, photographs of paintings and statues, excerpts from great works of philosophy such as Plato's *Republic* and Descartes's *Discourse on Method*. Clearly, no one should leave Aristotle or Shakespeare or Toni Morrison unread. And anyone unfamiliar with Leonardo da Vinci, Frida Kahlo, Thelonious Monk, and Georgia O'Keeffe has missed a priceless opportunity. Yet this book has grown out of the belief that the humanities today must reach farther than in centuries past. Without intending to do so, traditional humanists may have contributed to the decline of their own enterprise. One could even argue that the humanities have seen their principal task as the preservation of the past rather than the creation of the future. Humanists have often left real-world activities and concerns to other fields, while devoting themselves to passive contemplation, aesthetic pleasure, and partisan critique. Consequently, most people outside the university have come to consider the humanities as something closer to entertainment, wish fulfillment, or a covert form of politics, while regarding the sciences as the only real truth.

The humanities today must be understood in a new way: not as a particular area of knowledge but as the human dimension of *all* knowledge. Engineering may lie outside the traditional humanities, but it enters the domain of the New Humanities when we begin to consider the unexpected consequences of technological innovation, as Edward Tenner does in his observations on the consequences of the automobile. When we define the humanities in this way, it may come as a surprise that some of our society's foremost humanists work in fields quite far removed from the traditional humanities. Stephen Jay Gould, one of the writers in this collection, was a distinguished paleontologist who played a leading role in American cultural life. Well-versed in Western arts and letters, he also brought to his writing the knowledge and insight of a highly accomplished scientist. Marcia Angell, a pathologist and the former editor-in-chief of the *New England Journal of Medicine,* has helped to safeguard our society as a whole by challenging the way that drug companies do business.

The New Humanities, as represented by this book, bring change in another way as well: they invite us to take knowledge obtained at the university beyond the confines of the university itself. In a certain sense, this means that we all must become our own best teachers: we must find in our own lives—our problems, values, dreams, and commitments—an organizing principle we will not find in a curriculum which is bound to seem disorganized. The great, unspoken secret of the university is that the curriculum has no center: specialization makes sure of that. Historians write primarily for historians; literary critics for other critics. As we shuttle back and forth between these specialized disciplines, the only coherence we gain is the coherence we have constructed for ourselves. Under these conditions, what the New Humanities can teach us is a different way of using knowledge, a way of thinking that synthesizes many different fields of study.

Specialized learning in the disciplines typically deals with the "how," but it often leaves unanswered the "why." There has never been a course called "Life 101," and given the complexity of our world, such a course seems unlikely. But something important will be missing if we leave the "why" questions unexplored. Should we continue to pursue a technological utopia? Does modern science mean the end of religion? Is social inequality an acceptable price to pay for economic growth? Any attempt to answer these questions requires specialized knowledge, yet knowledge alone is not enough. Because a cogent, well-informed case can be made on either side of almost every issue, the source of our ultimate commitments must reach deeper. We might say that the "why" questions shape these commitments because they address our most basic and most personal relations to other people and to the world. In different ways, these questions ask us how we choose to live. No expert can choose on our behalf, because no expert can live our lives for us or define what our experiences should mean to us.

The coherence missing from the curriculum is not a quality of knowledge but of our own lives. In itself, no amount of learning can produce a sense of coherence. That sense arises, instead, from a creative and synthetic activity on our part as we interact with the world. Again and again, we need to make connections between discrete areas of knowledge and between knowledge and our personal experience. This coherence is never complete because there is always something more to learn that remains unconnected, but we might think of coherence, not as a goal reached once and for all but as an ideal worth pursuing continuously. Of course, cynicism and fragmentation are always options, too, and they require no special effort. One could easily live as though nothing and no one mattered, but in such a case, learning and living become exercises in futility. The New Humanities offer a better path.

Knowledge in Depth and Knowledge of the World

As everyone understands, formal education has been carefully designed to keep the disciplines separate. In economics classes, we typically read economics; in history classes, we typically read history. This approach allows information to be imparted in small, efficiently managed packages. We can divide, say, biology from chemistry, and then we can divide biology into vertebrate and invertebrate, and chemistry into organic and inorganic. We start with the general and move to the particular: ideally, we learn in depth, with increasing mastery of details that become more and more refined. At the end of the semester, if everything goes well, we can distinguish between an ecosystem and a niche, a polymer and a plastic, a neo-Kantian and a neo-Hegelian. We can contrast Hawthorne's treatment of the outsider with Salinger's, or we can explain the debate about whether slavery or states' rights actually caused the Civil War.

Knowledge in depth is indispensable. But it can also create a sense of disconnection, the impression that education is an empty ritual without real-world consequences beyond the receipt of a grade and the fulfillment of a requirement. In the classroom, we learn to calculate sine and cosine without ever discovering how these calculations might be used and why they were invented. Searching for symbols in a poem or a short story becomes a mental exercise on par with doing a crossword puzzle. Instead of reflecting on why events have happened and how they get remembered and recorded, we refine our ability to recapitulate strings of dates and names. At its worst, learning in depth can produce a strange disconnect: the purpose of learning becomes learning itself, while activity in the real world becomes incidental, even difficult to imagine. As students reach the final years of high school, they may understand vaguely that they ought to know *Hamlet,* and should be able to identify *The Declaration of Independence* and explain how photosynthesis has influenced the shape of leaves, but in response to an actual tragedy, an environmental disaster, or a real-life legal crisis, they might feel unqualified to speak and unprepared to act.

College-level learning can offer an escape from this predicament by giving students greater freedom to choose what they will study, and in many cases the subjects they choose are closely related to their real-world objectives. But even with this new-found freedom, the problem of disconnection crops up in other ways. After years of hard work, a student who has mastered electrical engineering may still leave college poorly informed about the globalized, commercial environment in which most engineers now do their work. Students well-versed in Renaissance drama or the history of World War I may find their own lives after graduation much more difficult to explain. For some people, this problem of disconnection may arise long before graduation. One who sets out to memorize facts from, say, a social psychology textbook may find that these facts grow increasingly stale. Easily memorized one day, they are quickly forgotten the next. The risk of knowledge in depth is that we lose our sense of the larger world and we forget that a field like psychology, for all its current sophistication, began with tentative and somewhat clumsy questions about the mind. Ironically, the more we treat an area of knowledge as a reality in itself, the less we may be able to understand and use what we have supposedly learned.

There is another kind of knowledge that we begin to create when we ask ourselves how our learning pertains to the world outside the classroom. This line of questioning is more complex than it might initially seem because the larger world is never simply out there waiting for us. All knowledge begins as a knowledge of parts and fragments, even our knowledge of the private lives we know in most detail. Each of our private lives may seem complete, in itself, just as a field like psychology can seem to explain everything once we are immersed in its methods and its facts. But this sense of completeness is an illusion produced by the limits of our perspective. Beyond the reach of what we know here and now, nothing seems to matter. We begin to get a glimpse of the larger world, however, only when we shift our focus from one reality to another: only then do we discover the deficiencies in our previous ways of thinking, and only then are we able to think in new and different ways. This movement from the known to the unknown is the essence of all learning; indeed, the most successful learners are generally those who have developed the highest tolerance for not knowing—those who continue to question and explore issues beyond their own areas of specialization, entertaining alternatives that others might find unimaginable.

Knowledge itself can be defined in many ways: as a quantity of information, as technical expertise, as cultivated taste, as a special kind of self-awareness. And as varied as these definitions may appear, they share an underlying principle. Whatever the form knowledge may take, it always emerges from a process we might call *connecting*. The eighteenth-century English scientist Sir Isaac Newton, who first understood the complex relations between force, mass, and acceleration, may have been inspired by connecting his scientific work with his deeply held religious convictions about the rational perfection of God and His Creation. Many other notable thinkers likewise found inspiration through connection. Roughly two hundred years after Newton's discoveries had sparked a technological revolution, a young lawyer born in India, Mohandas K. Gandhi, drew on Henry

David Thoreau's *Civil Disobedience,* written in support of abolitionists just before the Civil War, to launch a campaign of passive resistance against the racist government of South Africa. Two years before Gandhi spent his first term in jail as a political prisoner, a French artist and intellectual, Marcel Duchamps, shocked the art world with a painting—*Nude Descending a Staircase*—inspired by scientific photographs of athletes in motion. Whether we are talking about physics or political systems, epidemiology or aesthetics, knowledge by its very nature brings together disparate worlds of thought and action.

Creative Reading: From Explicit to Implicit

The selections in this book are intended for creative reading. The humanities should do more than convey information or give professors a chance to demonstrate their brilliance. After all, studies have consistently demonstrated that we retain little of what we have been taught unless we put that knowledge to use. At its best, education should offer beginners the chance to practice the same activities that more accomplished thinkers engage in: beyond receiving knowledge, beginners should participate in the making of knowledge. The articles and chapters collected in this book offer many opportunities for such participation. All of the selections are challenging, some because they are long and complex, some because they draw on specialized disciplines, and some because they open up unusual perspectives. These are not readings that lend themselves to simple summaries and multiple-choice answers. Instead, they require discussion—they were written to elicit activity and response.

It is important not to think of essays such as these as truths to be committed to memory or arguments to be weighed and then accepted or rejected. It might be more useful to see them in much the same way we now see Internet sites. Every site on the Internet is linked to countless others by the connections that Web authors and programmers have forged. As a result of their cumulative efforts, one site links us to another and then to the next, on and on for as long as we care to go. In some ways, even the most useful and informative written texts are less sophisticated than the simplest Web sites, and the Internet can transform the labor of many days—sifting through periodicals and rummaging through the library stacks—into the work of a few hours. Yet the Web also has limitations that the printed word does not. The Web, after all, can show us only those pathways that someone has already made semipermanent. By contrast, *all* connections to the printed text are *virtual* connections: any text can be linked to any other text in a web of inquiry and analysis potentially much vaster than the Internet itself. When we surf the Internet, we find only what others want us to find, but the connections we personally forge between one text and the next may truly be uncharted terrain.

Texts can be connected to other texts in any way a reader finds helpful and credible. But the ideas set forth in a text also offer a potential network of connections waiting to be made. Of course, every text has an explicit dimension: the words on the page in their most literal form and the order in which ideas are presented. Because of this explicit content, it is possible to memorize and repeat, more or less verbatim, the information that a text provides. We might try to remember, for example, all the major authors Karen Armstrong reviews in "Does God Have a Future?" Yet the meaning of a text is something more than what the words on the page explicitly state. A text becomes meaningful only through the implicit connections it motivates. To understand a text, as opposed to simply repeating it, is to move back and forth from the explicit to the implicit until an interpretation takes shape. In Armstrong's case what matters more than the particular figures she mentions is the overall direction of religious thought in the twentieth century—a direction Armstrong traces out but leaves for us to understand and assess.

Remember that these implicit dimensions are always virtual. An essay on the politics of AIDS, for example, may not be explicitly related to an article on bicycles in West Africa. But between them a connection could still be made, an important and original one. While some connections might seem potentially more fruitful and easily forged than others, improbable connections have sometimes revealed enormous vistas of knowledge. In practice this means that the most creative readers are also those most willing to take constructive risks, exploring connections that others have overlooked. At the same time, a connection must be credible, and the more sustained that connection becomes—the more deeply and widely it extends across the details of the texts at hand—the more persuasive the interpretation that arises from it.

The most basic form of interpretation starts when we connect one part of a text with other parts. Consider, for example, the first sentence of Jonathan Boyarin's "Waiting for a Jew." "My story begins in a community," he writes, "with an illusion of wholeness." Needless to say, this statement can stand alone, but it also serves as a point of departure. Practically every detail that follows in Boyarin's account can be connected in some way to this key phrase "the illusion of wholeness." Sometimes the experiences he recalls may appear to underscore the word *illusion,* confirming the irreparable loss of the community in which he had grown up. But other moments in his narrative might speak directly to *wholeness*—to the persistence of communities of shared belief in the midst of a larger, unbelieving world. Explicitly, of course, Boyarin's text makes no such point, but implicitly the point is waiting to be made, and by making it we become interpreters of the text.

When we read for content, we are reading to preserve the knowledge made by others. But when we read for implicit connections, we become cocreators with the authors themselves. To recapitulate some portion of Boyarin's narrative might help us pass a quiz or defend a point of view in the context of a debate, but when we use Boyarin's narrative as an opportunity to make connections of our own, we join in the same questioning that started him on his path. The purpose of such reading is not to get the "right answer" but to understand more fully the world in which we live, a process literally without end. In this sense, the best interpretations leave the texts behind as they move forward, toward other questions and other texts.

Connective Thinking: The Search for a Shared Horizon

Much of formal education promotes mimetic, or imitative, thinking: we learn to reproduce information already collected and organized by someone else. Mimetic thinking presupposes the adequacy of knowledge in its present state. But what happens when we discover that our knowledge leaves something out? Perhaps the lecture in English class this afternoon contradicted a point made yesterday in anthropology class. Or perhaps an assigned article has described an aspect of the social world in a manner that we find inaccurate or disconcerting. On occasions like these, when we encounter the limits or defects of knowledge, mimetic thinking cannot help us; instead, we are obliged to think connectively—to think *across* domains of knowledge rather than thinking from within them.

Sometimes connective thinking happens in response to crisis. The complex body of knowledge we call immunology, for example, has advanced rapidly in an effort to counter the spread of HIV and AIDS. So, too, a growing crisis in farming, caused by the overuse of pesticides, has spurred extensive research in plant genetics. But whether or not real-world crises bear down on us, the construction of knowledge of any kind necessarily produces contradictions. In his essay "Playing God in the Garden," Michael Pollan describes the reactions of Idaho farmers to the biotech industry. Even if we do not share Pollan's ambivalence about genetic engineering, few readers would doubt the truthfulness of the evidence he presents. And fewer still would question Pollan's abilities: his account is well written, carefully researched, and coherently organized. It is precisely the coherence of Pollan's case, however, that limits its value for readers. At best, because he is just one person, he can offer us only one perspective.

As soon as we have read more than a single text, we encounter discontinuous images and perspectives of the world that we must somehow reconcile. Precisely because most accounts are more or less true to the perspectives they adopt, the way out of this discontinuity seldom lies with a blanket rejection of one perspective or another, a simple "right" or "wrong." Instead, the most constructive and creative response is to search for a larger shared horizon, a new way of thinking that is broad enough in scope to do justice to both accounts. This search is not quite the same as "compare and contrast." After all, we can endlessly compare and contrast details that are relatively trivial and that do not bridge the gaps between texts. A shared horizon, on the other hand, is more inclusive than either text alone and often connects them on the level of implications, not explicit claims. And once a shared horizon presents itself, the connections we make gradually prompt us to explore questions we raise—and answer—for ourselves.

When an observer of world events like Amy Chua contemplates the rise of ethnic violence, she proposes that different societies may need to follow different routes to economic and political development. On the other hand, Martha Nussbaum, a philosopher, looks askance at any claim that cultures other than ours must be judged exclusively by their own standards. Confronting these two disparate positions, we are bound to be puzzled about their possible connections. Do the two arguments simply contradict one another? If they do, then perhaps you will find Chua's reasoning more persuasive, or perhaps you will favor Nussbaum's position. However, no two essays simply exist in a state of contradiction. To a greater or lesser extent they will also confirm and complement one another. We might assume, as Nussbaum does, that everyone stands to benefit from accepting Western values, yet imposing our values elsewhere in the world may increase social tensions to the breaking point. Conversely, we might prefer to believe, along with Chua, that differences of culture and history need to be respected. But what happens when respect for cultural differences leads us to ignore the suffering of women and minorities? The point of connective thinking is not to say "yes" to one writer and "no" to the other. Nor is it to declare blithely that we all have a right to our personal opinions. Instead, connective thinking allows us to explore the many ways in which the two discussions might fit together, forming a whole that is greater than the sum of its parts.

Connective thinking is creative and independent in a way that mimetic thinking can never be. No matter how ably we summarize the views of Chua and Nussbaum, this is not the same as connecting them within the context of a larger question or debate. Yet these connections are never waiting for us fully formed already: there is always the need for a leap of imagination. Chua's primary concern is the alleviation of global instability, the burden of which often falls most heavily on minorities and "outsiders." Nussbaum's goal may very well be to overturn established social orders everywhere if they violate universal norms of justice. At first, when we consider these differences, no shared horizon may present itself, but we can push our thinking farther. The best advice is not to stop at what the authors have said but to ask about the implications of their ideas—to ask how the issues they have raised might have an impact on us personally and how they might affect both our society and our world. Chua and Nussbaum may appear to be miles apart at first, but a shared horizon might begin to open up when we contemplate the possibility that universal standards of human conduct could obligate us to respect many cultural differences, or when we recognize that both authors share a basic commitment to social justice and human happiness.

Writing to Tell, Writing to See

Mimetic thinking goes hand in hand with writing to tell—writing for the purpose of demonstrating mastery over an existing body of information. In American schools, the classic example of writing to tell is the venerable book report. Like mimetic thinking, writing to tell has its appropriate place. Connective thinking calls, however, for writing of a different kind, which might be described as writing to see. In this case, the writer has to do something more than recount the knowledge of others; like connective thinking, it is an active pursuit in which the writer takes that knowledge somewhere new. In the act of writing to tell, people give answers. In the process of writing to see, we start with a question inspired by others and go on to explore what they have left unexplored; we engage in the kind of writing that higher education at its best can foster: exploratory writing, writing to see. A good example of such writing is "The Mind's Eye," by Oliver Sacks. Because Sacks is a neurologist—an Oxford-trained physician and a professor of medicine—we might have expected him to present some of the answers he has found in his four decades of research. Instead he begins with a question, one that seems startling in its simplicity: "to what extent are we . . . shaped, predetermined, by our brains, and to what extent do we shape our own brains?" In his attempt to think through the question he has posed, Sacks might have drawn on research by other specialists in fields like chemistry, genetics, and neuroanatomy. He might have taped electrodes to the heads of volunteers or studied their brains with an MRI machine. But instead, the sources Sacks decides to work with are books written by people who have adapted to blindness in a surprising variety of ways.

It may have been the case that the question Sacks poses—do our brains shape us, or do we shape our brains?—has followed him from the earliest years of his medical practice. But he may have formulated the question only after he had read the books he refers to in his essay. What seems certain, no matter how his project began, is that Sacks realized sooner or later that these books called into doubt much that he had once assumed about the development of the brain. On the one hand, his training led him to believe that the tasks handled by the different areas of the brain were essentially fixed after childhood. On the other hand, accounts by people who had lost their sight strongly suggest that brains can rebuild themselves—that brains are capable of significant change, even far into adulthood. We cannot know exactly what inspired Sacks to write, but surely one powerful motive was the discontinuity between his old assumptions and the new evidence.

Discontinuity is where the most valuable and valued writing starts. From time immemorial, teachers of English have told their students to begin the task of writing only after they know clearly what they want to say. These instructions have always expressed more fantasy than truth. Typically, a position—a thesis or argument—will remain fairly vague until we have done a great deal of preliminary writing. Discontinuities lead us to the search for a shared horizon, and from this shared horizon our own questions come. Then, provided we are willing to push far enough, a coherent position begins to emerge, not all at once in a grand vision but cumulatively, with one insight building on the next. At some point, as these insights begin to cohere, we recognize the direction of our thoughts, a direction that writing itself has revealed. We write and then we see where our writing has taken us. Only then are we in a position to convey our discoveries to others in a well-crafted presentation.

In order for Sacks to become a source for our own writing, we need to start with a question his work leaves unresolved. If human brains are inherently as flexible as he suggests, then why do people usually seem so similar in their outlooks and behavior? Could it be that education, and not nature or evolution, has made us all the same? If at some point in the future we abolish formal schooling, would our mental lives become far less uniform than they are now? Of course, each of us is free to conclude that human nature will never change, regardless of our brains, and in that case we might choose to brush aside the implications of Sacks's ideas. But these ideas might also prompt us to rethink a number of our presuppositions. If events in our lives are actually capable of changing the structure of our brains, then perhaps we are doing serious damage to ourselves when we spend countless hours glued to television shows that routinely push their viewers into emotions like envy, anger, and contempt. Could it be that we need to care for our mental health much as we care for our bodies through diet and exercise? As we set out to explore questions of this kind, we might also draw on Martha Stout's discussion of the way the brain responds to psychological trauma. Or we might make some fruitful connections to Robert Thurman's thoughts about the pursuit of wisdom. Ultimately, through our reading and thinking, we might start to develop a position of our own.

Developing a Position

A position is not exactly an argument in the ordinary sense of the word. In everyday speech, the term *argument* suggests an adversarial stance: we might argue for, or against, William Greider's ideas about worker-owned businesses. "Making an argument" tends to mean deciding ahead of time what you think about an issue and then finding "support" to back up your points. There is, however, another way. Instead of simply ratifying an existing belief, each of us can use the readings to formulate a position of our own. To do so is to imagine ourselves in a different way, not as combatants but as participants in an ongoing conversation. Even if we read a writer with distaste, what matters most are the questions raised, not the answers given. Precisely because the search for a position begins with some degree of uncertainty, it requires a willingness on our part to suspend judgment and to pursue ideas wherever they might lead. It is important to remember that this pursuit does not require complete assent or unwavering commitment. We can always explore ideas that we eventually reject. The proper spirit for writing to see might be described as exploratory and experimental.

An experiment involves a "dialogue" between projection and revision. First, we imagine or "project" an outcome based on our prior knowledge and experience. We make an educated guess about the conclusion we will probably draw from our reading of an author or authors. Perhaps we start with the claim that Chris McCandless, the young man whose travels and death Jon Krakauer retraces, was spoiled and self-deceiving. Yet when we turn to Alexander Stille's account of alternative attitudes toward the natural world, our opinion of McCandless may grow less clear. As we write, our thinking may appear to lose its way and we may realize, after three or four pages, that we have contradicted ourselves. Perhaps McCandless's actions now seem justified, even commendable. Instead of treating this change in our position as a failure or a lapse, we should appreciate its value as a discovery, which we could make only after a great deal of hard work. And rather than return to our original stance, we should revise what we have written in order to present a revised position. But revision, too, involves experiment and discovery. The point of a new draft is never simply to change a position: the point is also to explain how and why the position has changed.

The Spirit of the New Humanities

Because we can learn from everything, no one should fear making mistakes. We should never forget that the greatest thinkers of every age have often been refuted later, whereas ordinary people have sometimes lived more wisely than they were given credit for. Not so long ago, the best-educated Europeans believed that all celestial bodies beyond the moon were eternal and changeless. The learned taught that matter in every form could be reduced to the basic elements of earth, air, fire, and water. Medical experts sternly warned against the perils of regular bathing and eating whole grains. In sexual reproduction, men were supposed to contribute the blueprint, while women provided the raw material. One could spend a lifetime enumerating the follies that have passed for knowledge. And when we pause to consider such a checkered history, we might decide that education is itself a folly.

But maybe not. Instead of expecting knowledge to be true once and for all, we might try to see it as pragmatic and provisional, always subject to revision given further evidence or new circumstances. In our society today, the sciences may offer the best example of this experimentalist attitude, but some philosophers and artists of every generation have also refused the twin consolations of dogmatism and disillusionment. In the years ahead, our society will face many challenges—environmental, social, cultural, economic, and political—that are sure to seem overwhelming. Given the high level of uncertainty that has become a constant feature of our lives, people may be drawn to ideologies that promise truths exempt from all revision and insulated from the challenges of diversity. If this book does nothing else, we hope that it will offer an alternative more compatible with the values espoused by the readings we have chosen: trust in the world, and trust in ourselves.

Web Site

For details on the companion Web site www.newhum.com, please refer to the inside cover. This Web site provides many helpful materials for both students and instructors.

Acknowledgments

We would like to express our deep appreciation to the following colleagues for their support and suggestions:

Lynn Z. Bloom, University of Connecticut, Storrs; John C. Brereton; Susan E. Carlisle, Boston University; Melora Giardetti; Alfred E. Guy, Jr., Yale University; Susanmarie Harrington, Indiana University–Purdue University, Indianapolis; Deborah H. Holdstein, Governors State University; Thomas C. Laughner, University of Notre Dame; Jennifer Lee, University of Pittsburgh; Gina L. Maranto, University of Miami; Stephen M. North, SUNY Albany; Judith Gatton Prats, University of Kentucky; Thomas Recchio, University of Connecticut; Tony Spicer, Eastern Michigan University; Roberta J. Stagnaro, San Diego State University; Gordon P. Thomas, University of Idaho; and Anna Tripp, California State University, Northridge.

R.E.M.
K.S.

DAVID ABRAM

DAVID ABRAM IS an ecologist, anthropologist, and philosopher, but it is work with magic that has most shaped his research on the connections between the environment, human experience, and modes of perception. After the magic trick has been performed, Abram believes, we are left "without any framework of explanation. We are suddenly floating in that open space of direct sensory experience, actually encountering the world without preconceptions, even if just for a moment." How would our thinking about the earth and our place on it change if we could suspend our preconceptions about our own central importance? This is the question that Abram brings to the fields of ecopsychology and environmental philosophy.

"The Ecology of Magic" is drawn from Abram's book, *The Spell of the Sensuous: Perception and Language in a More-Than-Human World* (1997), which explores our perception of the natural world and the way we use language and symbols to process our experience. In "The Ecology of Magic," Abram describes his travels through Sri Lanka, Indonesia, and Nepal to study the lifeways of magicians and healers. During the course of his research, Abram came to see the role of traditional magicians and healers as bridging the gap between humankind and nature; "the shaman or sorcerer," he tells us, "is the exemplary voyager in the intermediate realm between the human and the more-than-human worlds."

Abram could be characterized as just such a voyager. After receiving his doctorate in philosophy from the State University of New York at Stony Brook, he and his wife founded the Alliance for Wild Ethics, an organization that focuses on raising ecological awareness. When asked to explain why he draws so heavily on academic discourse and continues to write for an academic audience when his thinking has taken him in such unconventional directions, Abram answered that his goal in writing *The Spell of the Sensuous* was "to bridge the gap between the world of the imagination—the kind of magical world of these

---

Abram, David. "The Ecology of Magic." *The Spell of the Sensuous: Perception and Language in a More-Than-Human World.* New York: First Vintage Books, 1997. 3–29.

Quotations come from Scott London's interview with David Abram for the National Public Radio series, *Insight & Outlook* <http://www.scottlondon.com/insight/scripts/abram.html>.

indigenous, traditional societies—and the world of academia, the intelligentsia, and the scientific elite. But I didn't want to do that just by writing a scholarly or scientific analysis of indigenous, animistic ways of thinking. I wanted to do the opposite. I wanted to do an animistic analysis of rationality and the Western intellect, and to show that our Western, civilized ways of thinking are themselves a form of magic."

www **To learn more about David Abram and the practice of shamanism, visit the Link-O-Mat at <www.newhum.com>.**

■ ■

The Ecology of Magic
A Personal Introduction to the Inquiry

Late one evening I stepped out of my little hut in the rice paddies of eastern Bali and found myself falling through space. Over my head the black sky was rippling with stars, densely clustered in some regions, almost blocking out the darkness between them, and more loosely scattered in other areas, pulsing and beckoning to each other. Behind them all streamed the great river of light with its several tributaries. Yet the Milky Way churned beneath me as well, for my hut was set in the middle of a large patchwork of rice paddies, separated from each other by narrow two-foot-high dikes, and these paddies were all filled with water. The surface of these pools, by day, reflected perfectly the blue sky, a reflection broken only by the thin, bright green tips of new rice. But by night the stars themselves glimmered from the surface of the paddies, and the river of light whirled through the darkness underfoot as well as above; there seemed no ground in front of my feet, only the abyss of star-studded space falling away forever.

I was no longer simply beneath the night sky, but also *above* it—the immediate impression was of weightlessness. I might have been able to reorient myself, to regain some sense of ground and gravity, were it not for a fact that confounded my senses entirely: between the constellations below and the constellations above drifted countless fireflies, their lights flickering like the stars, some drifting up to join the clusters of stars overhead, others, like graceful meteors, slipping down from above to join the constellations underfoot, and all these paths of light upward and downward were mirrored, as well, in the still surface of the paddies. I felt myself at times falling through space, at other moments floating and drifting. I simply could not dispel the profound vertigo and giddiness; the paths of the fireflies, and their reflections in the water's surface, held me in a sustained trance. Even after I crawled back to my hut and shut the door on this whirling world, I felt that now the little room in which I lay was itself floating free of the earth.

Fireflies! It was in Indonesia, you see, that I was first introduced to the world of insects, and there that I first learned of the great influence that insects—such diminutive entities—could have upon the human senses. I had traveled to Indonesia on a research grant to study magic—more precisely, to study the relation between magic and medicine, first among the traditional sorcerers, or *dukuns*, of the Indonesian archipelago, and later among the *dzankris*, the traditional shamans of Nepal. One aspect of the grant was somewhat unique: I was to journey into rural Asia not outwardly as an anthropologist or academic researcher, but as a magician in my own right, in hopes of gaining a more direct access to the local sorcerers. I had been a professional sleight-of-hand magician for five years back in the United States, helping to put myself through college by performing in clubs and restaurants throughout New England. I had, as well, taken a year off from my studies in the psychology of perception to travel as a street magician through Europe and, toward the end of that journey, had spent some months in London, England, exploring the use of sleight-of-hand magic in psychotherapy, as a means of engendering communication with distressed individuals largely unapproachable by clinical healers.[1] The success of this work suggested to me that sleight-of-hand might lend itself well to the curative arts, and I became, for the first time, interested in the relation, largely forgotten in the West, between folk medicine and magic.

It was this interest that led to the aforementioned grant, and to my sojourn as a magician in rural Asia. There, my sleight-of-hand skills proved invaluable as a means of stirring the curiosity of the local shamans. For magicians—whether modern entertainers or indigenous, tribal sorcerers—have in common the fact that they work with the malleable texture of perception. When the local sorcerers gleaned that I had at least some rudimentary skill in altering the common field of perception, I was invited into their homes, asked to share secrets with them, and eventually encouraged, even urged, to participate in various rituals and ceremonies.

But the focus of my research gradually shifted from questions regarding the application of magical techniques in medicine and ritual curing toward a deeper pondering of the relation between traditional magic and the animate natural world. This broader concern seemed to hold the keys to the earlier questions. For none of the several island sorcerers that I came to know in Indonesia, nor any of the *dzankris* with whom I lived in Nepal, considered their work as ritual healers to be their major role or function within their communities. Most of them, to be sure, *were* the primary healers or "doctors" for the villages in their vicinity, and they were often spoken of as such by the inhabitants of those villages. But the villagers also sometimes spoke of them, in low voices and in very private conversations, as witches (or "lejaks" in Bali), as dark magicians who at night might well be practicing their healing spells backward (or while turning to the left instead of to the right) in order to afflict people with the very diseases that they would later work to cure by day. Such suspicions seemed fairly common in Indonesia, and often were harbored with regard to the most effective and powerful healers, those who were most renowned for their skill in driving out illness. For it was assumed that a magician, in order to expel malevolent influences, must have a strong understanding of those influences and demons—even, in some areas, a close rapport with such powers. I myself never consciously saw any of those magicians or shamans with whom I became acquainted engage in magic for harmful purposes, nor any convincing evidence that they had ever done so. (Few of the magicians that I came to know even accepted money in return for their services, although they did accept gifts in the way of food, blankets, and the like.) Yet I was struck by the fact that none of them ever did or said anything to counter such disturbing rumors and speculations, which circulated quietly through the regions where they lived. Slowly, I came to recognize that it was through the agency of such rumors, and the ambiguous fears that such rumors engendered in the village people, that the sorcerers were able to maintain a basic level of privacy. If the villagers did not entertain certain fears about the local sorcerer, then they would likely come to obtain his or her magical help for every little malady and disturbance; and since a more potent practitioner must provide services for several large villages, the sorcerer would be swamped from morning to night with requests for ritual aid. By allowing the inevitable suspicions and fears to circulate unhindered in the region (and sometimes even encouraging and contributing to such rumors), the sorcerer ensured that *only* those who were in real and profound need of his skills would dare to approach him for help.

This privacy, in turn, left the magician free to attend to what he acknowledged to be his primary craft and function. A clue to this function may be found in the circumstance that such magicians rarely dwell at the heart of their village; rather, their dwellings are commonly at the spatial periphery of the community or, more often, out beyond the edges of the village—amid the rice fields, or in a forest, or a wild cluster of boulders. I could easily attribute this to the just-mentioned need for privacy, yet for the magician in a traditional culture it seems to serve another purpose as well, providing a spatial expression of his or her symbolic position with regard to the community. For the magician's intelligence is not encompassed *within* the society; its place is at the edge of the community, mediating *between* the human community and the larger community of beings upon which the village depends for its nourishment and sustenance. This larger community includes, along with the humans, the multiple nonhuman entities that constitute the local landscape, from the diverse plants and the myriad animals—birds, mammals, fish, reptiles, insects—that inhabit or migrate through the region, to the particular winds and weather patterns that inform the local geography, as well as the various landforms—forests, rivers, caves, mountains—that lend their specific character to the surrounding earth.

The traditional or tribal shaman, I came to discern, acts as an intermediary between the human community and the larger ecological field, ensuring that there is an appropriate flow of nourishment, not just from the landscape to the human inhabitants, but from the human community back to the local earth. By his constant rituals, trances, ecstasies, and "journeys," he ensures that the relation between human society and the larger society of beings is balanced and reciprocal, and that the village never takes more from the living land than it returns to it—not just materially but with prayers, propitiations, and praise. The scale of a harvest or the size of a hunt are always negotiated between the tribal community and the natural world that it inhabits. To some extent every adult in the community is engaged in this process of listening and attuning to the other presences that surround and influence daily life. But the shaman or sorcerer is the exemplary voyager in the intermediate realm between the human and the more-than-human worlds, the primary strategist and negotiator in any dealings with the Others.

And it is only as a result of her continual engagement with the animate powers that dwell beyond the human community that the traditional magician is able to alleviate many individual illnesses that arise *within* that community. The sorcerer derives her ability to cure ailments from her more continuous practice of "healing" or balancing the community's relation to the surrounding land. Disease, in such cultures, is often conceptualized as a kind of systemic imbalance within the sick person, or more vividly as the intrusion of a demonic or malevolent presence into his body. There are, at times, malevolent influences within the village or tribe itself that disrupt the health and emotional well-being of susceptible individuals within the community. Yet such destructive influences within the human community are commonly traceable to a disequilibrium between that community and the larger field of forces in which it is embedded. Only those persons who, by their everyday practice, are involved in monitoring and maintaining the relations *between* the human village and the animate landscape are able to appropriately diagnose, treat, and ultimately relieve personal ailments and illnesses arising *within* the village. Any healer who was not simultaneously attending to the intertwined relation between the human community and the larger, more-than-human field, would likely dispel an illness from one person only to have the same problem arise (perhaps in a new guise) somewhere else in the community. Hence, the traditional magician or medicine person functions primarily as an intermediary between human and nonhuman worlds, and only secondarily as a healer.[2] Without a continually adjusted awareness of the relative balance or imbalance between the human group and its nonhuman environ, along with the skills necessary to modulate that primary relation, any "healer" is worthless—indeed, not a healer at all. The medicine person's primary allegiance, then, is not to the human community, but to the earthly web of relations in which that community is embedded—it is from this that his or her power to alleviate human illness derives—and this sets the local magician apart from other persons.

The primacy for the magician of nonhuman nature—the centrality of his relation to other species and to the earth—is not always evident to Western researchers. Countless anthropologists have managed to overlook the ecological dimension of the shaman's craft, while writing at great length of the shaman's rapport with "supernatural" entities. We can attribute much of this oversight to the modern, civilized assumption that the natural world is largely determinate and mechanical, and that which is regarded as mysterious, powerful, and beyond human ken must therefore be of some other, nonphysical realm *above* nature, "supernatural."

The oversight becomes still more comprehensible when we realize that many of the earliest European interpreters of indigenous lifeways were Christian missionaries. For the Church had long assumed that only human beings have intelligent souls, and that the other animals, to say nothing of trees and rivers, were "created" for no other reason than to serve humankind. We can easily understand why European missionaries, steeped in the dogma of institutionalized Christianity, assumed a belief in supernatural, otherworldly powers among those tribal persons whom they saw awestruck and entranced by nonhuman (but nevertheless natural) forces. What is remarkable is the extent to which contemporary anthropology still preserves the ethnocentric bias of these early interpreters. We no longer describe the shamans' enigmatic spirit-helpers as the "superstitious claptrap of heathen primitives"—we have cleansed ourselves of at least *that* much ethnocentrism; yet we still refer to such enigmatic forces, respectfully now, as "supernaturals"—for we are unable to shed the sense, so endemic to scientific civilization, of nature as a rather prosaic and predictable realm, unsuited to such mysteries. Nevertheless, that which is regarded with the greatest awe and wonder by indigenous, oral cultures is, I suggest, none other than what we view as nature itself. The deeply mysterious powers and entities with whom the shaman enters into a rapport are ultimately the same forces—the same plants, animals, forests, and winds—that to literate, "civilized" Europeans are just so much scenery, the pleasant backdrop of our more pressing human concerns.

The most sophisticated definition of "magic" that now circulates through the American counterculture is "the ability or power to alter one's consciousness at will." No mention is made of any *reason* for altering one's consciousness. Yet in tribal cultures that which we call "magic" takes its meaning from the fact that humans, in an indigenous and oral context, experience their own consciousness as simply one form of awareness among many others. The traditional magician cultivates an ability to shift out of his or her common state of consciousness precisely in order to make contact with the other organic forms of sensitivity and awareness with which human existence is entwined. Only by temporarily shedding the accepted perceptual logic of his culture can the sorcerer hope to enter into relation with other species on their own terms; only by altering the common organization of his senses will he be able to enter into a rapport with the multiple nonhuman sensibilities that animate the local landscape. It is this, we might say, that defines a shaman: the ability to readily slip out of the perceptual boundaries that demarcate his or her particular culture—boundaries reinforced by social customs, taboos, and most importantly, the common speech or language—in order to make contact with, and learn from, the other powers in the land. His magic is precisely this heightened receptivity to the meaningful solicitations—songs, cries, gestures—of the larger, more-than-human field.

Magic, then, in its perhaps most primordial sense, is the experience of existing in a world made up of multiple intelligences, the intuition that every form one perceives—from the swallow swooping overhead to the fly on a blade of grass, and indeed the blade of grass itself—is an *experiencing* form, an entity with its own predilections and sensations, albeit sensations that are very different from our own.

To be sure, the shaman's ecological function, his or her role as intermediary between human society and the land, is not always obvious at first blush, even to a sensitive observer. We see the sorcerer being called upon to cure an ailing tribesman of his sleeplessness, or perhaps simply to locate some missing goods; we witness him entering into trance and sending his awareness into other dimensions in search of insight and aid. Yet we should not be so ready to interpret these dimensions as "supernatural," nor to view them as realms entirely "internal" to the personal psyche of the practitioner. For it is likely that the "inner world" of our Western psychological experience, like the supernatural heaven of Christian belief, originates in the loss of our ancestral reciprocity with the animate earth. When the animate powers that surround us are suddenly construed as having less significance than ourselves, when the generative earth is abruptly defined as a determinate object devoid of its own sensations and feelings, then the sense of a wild and multiplicitous otherness (in relation to which human existence has always oriented itself) must migrate, either into a supersensory heaven beyond the natural world, or else into the human skull itself—the only allowable refuge, in this world, for what is ineffable and unfathomable.

But in genuinely oral, indigenous cultures, the sensuous world itself remains the dwelling place of the gods, of the numinous powers that can either sustain or extinguish human life. It is not by sending his awareness out beyond the natural world that the shaman makes contact with the purveyors of life and health, nor by journeying into his personal psyche; rather, it is by propelling his awareness laterally, outward into the depths of a landscape at once both sensuous and psychological, the living dream that we share with the soaring hawk, the spider, and the stone silently sprouting lichens on its coarse surface.

The magician's intimate relationship with nonhuman nature becomes most evident when we attend to the easily overlooked background of his or her practice—not just to the more visible tasks of curing and ritual aid to which she is called by individual clients, or to the larger ceremonies at which she presides and dances, but to the content of the prayers by which she prepares for such ceremonies, and to the countless ritual gestures that she enacts when alone, the daily propitiations and praise that flow from her toward the land and *its* many voices.

All this attention to nonhuman nature was, as I have mentioned, very far from my intended focus when I embarked on my research into the uses of magic and medicine in Indonesia, and it was only gradually that I became aware of this more subtle dimension of the native magician's craft. The first shift in my preconceptions came rather quietly, when I was staying for some days in the home of a young "balian," or magic practitioner, in the interior of Bali. I had been provided with a simple bed in a separate, one-room building in the balian's family compound (most compound homes, in Bali, are comprised of several separate small buildings, for sleeping and for cooking, set on a single enclosed plot of land), and early each morning the balian's wife came to bring me a small but delicious bowl of fruit, which I ate by myself, sitting on the ground outside, leaning against the wall of my hut and watching the sun slowly climb through the rustling palm leaves. I noticed, when she delivered the fruit, that my hostess was also balancing a tray containing many little green plates: actually, they were little boat-shaped platters, each woven simply and neatly from a freshly cut section of palm frond. The platters were two or three inches long, and within each was a little mound of white rice. After handing me my breakfast, the woman and the tray disappeared from view behind the other buildings, and when she came by some minutes later to pick up my empty bowl, the tray in her hands was empty as well.

The second time that I saw the array of tiny rice platters, I asked my hostess what they were for. Patiently, she explained to me that they were offerings for the household spirits. When I inquired about the Balinese term that she used for "spirit," she repeated the same explanation, now in Indonesian, that these were gifts for the spirits of the family compound, and I saw that I had understood her correctly. She handed me a bowl of sliced papaya and mango, and disappeared around the corner. I pondered for a minute, then set down the bowl, stepped to the side of my hut, and peered through the trees. At first unable to see her, I soon caught sight of her crouched low beside the corner of one of the other buildings, carefully setting what I presumed was one of the offerings on the ground at that spot.

Then she stood up with the tray, walked to the other visible corner of the same building, and there slowly and carefully set another offering on the ground. I returned to my bowl of fruit and finished my breakfast. That afternoon, when the rest of the household was busy, I walked back behind the building where I had seen her set down the two offerings. There were the little green platters, resting neatly at the two rear corners of the building. But the mounds of rice that had been within them were gone.

The next morning I finished the sliced fruit, waited for my hostess to come by for the empty bowl, then quietly headed back behind the buildings. Two fresh palm-leaf offerings sat at the same spots where the others had been the day before. These were filled with rice. Yet as I gazed at one of these offerings, I abruptly realized, with a start, that one of the rice kernels was actually moving.

Only when I knelt down to look more closely did I notice a line of tiny black ants winding through the dirt to the offering. Peering still closer, I saw that two ants had already climbed onto the offering and were struggling with the uppermost kernel of rice; as I watched, one of them dragged the kernel down and off the leaf, then set off with it back along the line of ants advancing on the offering. The second ant took another kernel and climbed down with it, dragging and pushing, and fell over the edge of the leaf, then a third climbed onto the offering. The line of ants seemed to emerge from a thick clump of grass around a nearby palm tree. I walked over to the other offering and discovered another line of ants dragging away the white kernels. This line emerged from the top of a little mound of dirt, about fifteen feet away from the buildings. There was an offering on the ground by a corner of my building as well, and a nearly identical line of ants. I walked into my room chuckling to myself: the balian and his wife had gone to so much trouble to placate the household spirits with gifts, only to have their offerings stolen by little six-legged thieves. What a waste! But then a strange thought dawned on me: what if the ants were the very "household spirits" to whom the offerings were being made?

I soon began to discern the logic of this. The family compound, like most on this tropical island, had been constructed in the vicinity of several ant colonies. Since a great deal of cooking took place in the compound (which housed, along with the balian and his wife and children, various members of their extended family), and also much preparation of elaborate offerings of foodstuffs for various rituals and festivals in the surrounding villages, the grounds and the buildings at the compound were vulnerable to infestations by the sizable ant population. Such invasions could range from rare nuisances to a periodic or even constant siege. It became apparent that the daily palm-frond offerings served to preclude such an attack by the natural forces that surrounded (and underlay) the family's land. The daily gifts of rice kept the ant colonies occupied—and, presumably, satisfied. Placed in regular, repeated locations at the corners of various structures around the compound, the offerings seemed to establish certain boundaries between the human and ant communities; by honoring this boundary with gifts, the humans apparently hoped to persuade the insects to respect the boundary and not enter the buildings.

Yet I remained puzzled by my hostess's assertion that these were gifts "for the spirits." To be sure, there has always been some confusion between our Western notion of "spirit" (which so often is defined in contrast to matter or "flesh"), and the mysterious presences to which tribal and indigenous cultures pay so much respect. I have already alluded to the gross misunderstandings arising from the circumstance that many of the earliest Western students of these other customs were Christian missionaries all too ready to see occult ghosts and immaterial phantoms where the tribespeople were simply offering their respect to the local winds. While the notion of "spirit" has come to have, for us in the West, a primarily anthropomorphic or human association, my encounter with the ants was the first of many experiences suggesting to me that the "spirits" of an indigenous culture are primarily those modes of intelligence or awareness that do *not* possess a human form.

As humans, we are well acquainted with the needs and capacities of the human body—we *live* our own bodies and so know, from within, the possibilities of our form. We cannot know, with the same familiarity and intimacy, the lived experience of a grass snake or a snapping turtle; we cannot readily experience the precise sensations of a hummingbird sipping nectar from a flower or a rubber tree soaking up sunlight. And yet we do know how it feels to sip from a fresh pool of water or to bask and stretch in the sun. Our experience may indeed be a variant of these other modes of sensitivity; nevertheless, we cannot, as humans, precisely experience the living sensations of another form. We do not know, with full clarity, their desires or motivations; we cannot know, or can never be sure that we know, what they know. That the deer does experience sensations, that it carries knowledge of how to orient in the land, of where to find food and how to protect its young, that it knows well how to survive in the forest without the tools upon which we depend, is readily evident to our human senses. That the mango tree has the ability to create fruit, or the yarrow plant the power to reduce a child's fever, is also evident. To humankind, these Others are purveyors of secrets, carriers of intelligence that we ourselves often need: it is these Others who can inform us of unseasonable changes in the weather, or warn us of imminent eruptions and earthquakes, who show us, when foraging, where we may find the ripest berries or the best route to follow back home. By watching them build their nests and shelters, we glean clues regarding how to strengthen our own dwellings, and their deaths teach us of our own. We receive from them countless gifts of food, fuel, shelter, and clothing. Yet still they remain Other to us, inhabiting their own cultures and displaying their own rituals, never wholly fathomable.

Moreover, it is not only those entities acknowledged by Western civilization as "alive," not only the other animals and the plants that speak, as spirits, to the senses of an oral culture, but also the meandering river from which those animals drink, and the torrential monsoon rains, and the stone that fits neatly into the palm of the hand. The mountain, too, has its thoughts. The forest birds whirring and chattering as the sun slips below the horizon are vocal organs of the rain forest itself.[3]

Bali, of course, is hardly an aboriginal culture; the complexity of its temple architecture, the intricacy of its irrigation systems, the resplendence of its colorful festivals and crafts all bespeak the influence of various civilizations, most notably the Hindu complex of India. In Bali, nevertheless, these influences are thoroughly intertwined with the indigenous animism of the Indonesian archipelago; the Hindu gods and goddesses have been appropriated, as it were, by the more volcanic, eruptive spirits of the local terrain.

Yet the underlying animistic cultures of Indonesia, like those of many islands in the Pacific, are steeped as well in beliefs often referred to by ethnologists as "ancestor worship," and some may argue that the ritual reverence paid to one's long-dead human ancestors (and the assumption of their influence in present life), easily invalidates my assertion that the various "powers" or "spirits" that move through the discourse of indigenous, oral peoples are ultimately tied to nonhuman (but nonetheless sentient) forces in the enveloping landscape.

This objection rests upon certain assumptions implicit in Christian civilization, such as the assumption that the "spirits" of dead persons necessarily retain their human form, and that they reside in a domain outside of the physical world to which our senses give us access. However, most indigenous tribal peoples have no such ready recourse to an immaterial realm outside earthly nature. Our strictly human heavens and hells have only recently been abstracted from the sensuous world that surrounds us, from this more-than-human realm that abounds in its own winged intelligences and cloven-hoofed powers. For almost all oral cultures, the enveloping and sensuous earth remains the dwelling place of both the living *and* the dead. The "body"—whether human or otherwise—is not yet a mechanical object in such cultures, but is a magical entity, the mind's own sensuous aspect, and at death the body's decomposition into soil, worms, and dust can only signify the gradual reintegration of one's ancestors and elders into the living landscape, from which all, too, are born.

Each indigenous culture elaborates this recognition of metamorphosis in its own fashion, taking its clues from the particular terrain in which it is situated. Often the invisible atmosphere that animates the visible world—the subtle presence that circulates both within us and between all things—retains within itself the spirit or breath of the dead person until the time when that breath will enter and animate another visible body—a bird, or a deer, or a field of wild grain. Some cultures may burn, or "cremate," the body in order to more completely return the person, as smoke, to the swirling air, while that which departs as flame is offered to the sun and stars, and that which lingers as ash is fed to the dense earth. Still other cultures may dismember the body, leaving certain parts in precise locations where they will likely be found by condors, or where they will be consumed by mountain lions or by wolves, thus hastening the reincarnation of that person into a particular animal realm within the landscape. Such examples illustrate simply that death, in tribal cultures, initiates a metamorphosis wherein the person's presence does not "vanish" from the sensible world (where would it go?) but rather remains as an animating force within the vastness of the landscape, whether subtly, in the wind, or more visibly, in animal form, or even as the eruptive, ever to be appeased, wrath of the volcano. "Ancestor worship," in its myriad forms, then, is ultimately another mode of attentiveness to nonhuman nature; it signifies not so much an awe or reverence of human powers, but rather a reverence for those forms that awareness takes when it is *not* in human form, when the familiar human embodiment dies and decays to become part of the encompassing cosmos.

This cycling of the human back into the larger world ensures that the other forms of experience that we encounter—whether ants, or willow trees, or clouds—are never absolutely alien to ourselves. Despite the obvious differences in shape, and ability, and style of being, they remain at least distantly familiar, even familial. It is, paradoxically, this perceived kinship or consanguinity that renders the difference, or otherness, so eerily potent.[4]

Several months after my arrival in Bali, I left the village in which I was staying to visit one of the pre-Hindu sites on the island. I arrived on my bicycle early in the afternoon, after the bus carrying tourists from the coast had departed. A flight of steps took me down into a lush, emerald valley, lined by cliffs on either side, awash with the speech of the river and the sighing of the wind through high, unharvested grasses. On a small bridge crossing the river I met an old woman carrying a wide basket on her head and holding the hand of a little, shy child; the woman grinned at me with the red, toothless smile of a beetle nut chewer. On the far side of the river I stood in front of a great moss-covered complex of passageways, rooms, and courtyards carved by hand out of the black volcanic rock.

I noticed, at a bend in the canyon downstream, a further series of caves carved into the cliffs. These appeared more isolated and remote, unattended by any footpath I could discern. I set out through the grasses to explore them. This proved much more difficult than I anticipated, but after getting lost in the tall grasses, and fording the river three times, I at last found myself beneath the caves. A short scramble up the rock wall brought me to the mouth of one of them, and I entered on my hands and knees. It was a wide but low opening, perhaps only four feet high, and the interior receded only about five or six feet into the cliff. The floor and walls were covered with mosses, painting the cave with green patterns and softening the harshness of the rock; the place, despite its small size—or perhaps because of it—had an air of great friendliness. I climbed to two other caves, each about the same size, but then felt drawn back to the first one, to sit cross-legged on the cushioning moss and gaze out across the emerald canyon. It was quiet inside, a kind of intimate sanctuary hewn into the stone. I began to explore the rich resonance of the enclosure, first just humming, then intoning a simple chant taught to me by a balian some days before. I was delighted by the overtones that the cave added to my voice, and sat there singing for a long while. I did not notice the change in the wind outside, or the cloud shadows darkening the valley, until the rains broke—suddenly and with great force. The first storm of the monsoon!

I had experienced only slight rains on the island before then, and was startled by the torrential downpour now sending stones tumbling along the cliffs, building puddles and then ponds in the green landscape below, swelling the river. There was no question of returning home—I would be unable to make my way back through the flood to the valley's entrance. And so, thankful for the shelter, I recrossed my legs to wait out the storm. Before long the rivulets falling along the cliff above gathered themselves into streams, and two small waterfalls cascaded across the cave's mouth. Soon I was looking into a solid curtain of water, thin in some places, where the canyon's image flickered unsteadily, and thickly rushing in others. My senses were all but overcome by the wild beauty of the cascade and by the roar of sound, my body trembling inwardly at the weird sense of being sealed into my hiding place.

And then, in the midst of all this tumult, I noticed a small, delicate activity. Just in front of me, and only an inch or two to my side of the torrent, a spider was climbing a thin thread stretched across the mouth of the cave. As I watched, it anchored another thread to the top of the opening, then slipped back along the first thread and joined the two at a point about midway between the roof and the floor. I lost sight of the spider then, and for a while it seemed that it had vanished, thread and all, until my focus rediscovered it. Two more threads now radiated from the center to the floor, and then another; soon the spider began to swing between these as on a circular trellis, trailing an ever-lengthening thread which it affixed to each radiating rung as it moved from one to the next, spiraling outward. The spider seemed wholly undaunted by the tumult of waters spilling past it, although every now and then it broke off its spiral dance and climbed to the roof or the floor to tug on the radii there, assuring the tautness of the threads, then crawled back to where it left off. Whenever I lost the correct focus, I waited to catch sight of the spinning arachnid, and then let its dancing form gradually draw the lineaments of the web back into visibility, tying my focus into each new knot of silk as it moved, weaving my gaze into the ever-deepening pattern.

And then, abruptly, my vision snagged on a strange incongruity: another thread slanted across the web, neither radiating nor spiraling from the central juncture, violating the symmetry. As I followed it with my eyes, pondering its purpose in the overall pattern, I began to realize that it was on a different plane from the rest of the web, for the web slipped out of focus whenever this new line became clearer. I soon saw that it led to its own center, about twelve inches to the right of the first, another nexus of forces from which several threads stretched to the floor and the ceiling. And then I saw that there was a *different* spider spinning this web, testing its tautness by dancing around it like the first, now setting the silken cross weaves around the nodal point and winding outward. The two spiders spun independently of each other, but to my eyes they wove a single intersecting pattern. This widening of my gaze soon disclosed yet another spider spiraling in the cave's mouth, and suddenly I realized that there were *many* overlapping webs coming into being, radiating out at different rhythms from myriad centers poised—some higher, some lower, some minutely closer to my eyes and some farther—between the stone above and the stone below.

I sat stunned and mesmerized before this ever-complexifying expanse of living patterns upon patterns, my gaze drawn like a breath into one converging group of lines, then breathed out into open space, then drawn down into another convergence. The curtain of water had become utterly silent—I tried at one point to hear it, but could not. My senses were entranced.

I had the distinct impression that I was watching the universe being born, galaxy upon galaxy. . . .

Night filled the cave with darkness. The rain had not stopped. Yet, strangely, I felt neither cold nor hungry—only remarkably peaceful and at home. Stretching out upon the moist, mossy floor near the back of the cave, I slept.

When I awoke, the sun was staring into the canyon, the grasses below rippling with bright blues and greens. I could see no trace of the webs, nor their weavers. Thinking that they were invisible to my eyes without the curtain of water behind them, I felt carefully with my hands around and through the mouth of the cave. But the webs were gone. I climbed down to the river and washed, then hiked across and out of the canyon to where my cycle was drying in the sun, and headed back to my own valley.

I have never, since that time, been able to encounter a spider without feeling a great strangeness and awe. To be sure, insects and spiders are not the only powers, or even central presences, in the Indonesian universe. But they were *my* introduction to the spirits, to the magic afoot in the land. It was from them that I first learned of the intelligence that lurks in nonhuman nature, the ability that an alien form of sentience has to echo one's own, to instill a reverberation in oneself that temporarily shatters habitual ways of seeing and feeling, leaving one open to a world all alive, awake, and aware. It was from such small beings that my senses first learned of the countless worlds within worlds that spin in the depths of this world that we commonly inhabit, and from them that I learned that my body could, with practice, enter sensorially into these dimensions. The precise and minuscule craft of the spiders had so honed and focused my awareness that the very webwork of the universe, of which my own flesh was a part, seemed to be being spun by their arcane art. I have already spoken of the ants, and of the fireflies, whose sensory likeness to the lights in the night sky had taught me the fickleness of gravity. The long and cyclical trance that we call malaria was also brought to me by insects, in this case mosquitoes, and I lived for three weeks in a feverish state of shivers, sweat, and visions.

I had rarely before paid much attention to the natural world. But my exposure to traditional magicians and seers was shifting my senses; I became increasingly susceptible to the solicitations of nonhuman things. In the course of struggling to decipher the magicians' odd gestures or to fathom their constant spoken references to powers unseen and unheard, I began to *see* and to *hear* in a manner I never had before. When a magician spoke of a power or "presence" lingering in the corner of his house, I learned to notice the ray of sunlight that was then pouring through a chink in the roof, illuminating a column of drifting dust, and to realize that that column of light was indeed a power, influencing the air currents by its warmth, and indeed influencing the whole mood of the room; although I had not consciously seen it before, it had already been structuring my experience. My ears began to attend, in a new way, to the songs of birds—no longer just a melodic background to human speech, but meaningful speech in its own right, responding to and commenting on events in the surrounding earth. I became a student of subtle differences: the way a breeze may flutter a single leaf on a whole tree, leaving the other leaves silent and unmoved (had not that leaf, then, been brushed by a magic?); or the way the intensity of the sun's heat expresses itself in the precise rhythm of the crickets. Walking along the dirt paths, I learned to slow my pace in order to *feel* the difference between one nearby hill and the next, or to taste the presence of a particular field at a certain time of day when, as I had been told by a local *dukun,* the place had a special power and proffered unique gifts. It was a power communicated to my senses by the way the shadows of the trees fell at that hour, and by smells that only then lingered in the tops of the grasses without being wafted away by the wind, and other elements I could only isolate after many days of stopping and listening.

And gradually, then, other animals began to intercept me in my wanderings, as if some quality in my posture or the rhythm of my breathing had disarmed their wariness; I would find myself face-to-face with monkeys, and with large lizards that did not slither away when I spoke, but leaned forward in apparent curiosity. In rural Java, I often noticed monkeys accompanying me in the branches overhead, and ravens walked toward me on the road, croaking. While at Pangandaran, a nature preserve on a peninsula jutting out from the south coast of Java ("a place of many spirits," I was told by nearby fishermen), I stepped out from a clutch of trees and found myself looking into the face of one of the rare and beautiful bison that exist only on that island. Our eyes locked. When it snorted, I snorted back; when it shifted its shoulders, I shifted my stance; when I tossed my head, it tossed *its* head in reply. I found myself caught in a nonverbal conversation with this Other, a gestural duet with which my conscious awareness had very little to do. It was as if my body in its actions was suddenly being motivated by a wisdom older than my thinking mind, as though it was held and moved by a logos, deeper than words, spoken by the Other's body, the trees, and the stony ground on which we stood.

Anthropology's inability to discern the shaman's allegiance to nonhuman nature has led to a curious circumstance in the "developed world" today, where many persons in search of spiritual understanding are enrolling in workshops concerned with "shamanic" methods of personal discovery and revelation. Psychotherapists and some physicians have begun to specialize in "shamanic healing techniques." "Shamanism" has thus come to connote an alternative form of therapy; the emphasis, among these new practitioners of popular shamanism, is on personal insight and curing. These are noble aims, to be sure, yet they are secondary to, and derivative from, the primary role of the indigenous shaman, a role that cannot be fulfilled without long and sustained exposure to wild nature, to its patterns and vicissitudes. Mimicking the indigenous shaman's curative methods without his intimate knowledge of the wider natural community cannot, if I am correct, do anything more than trade certain symptoms for others, or shift the locus of disease from place to place within the human community. For the source of stress lies in the relation *between* the human community and the natural landscape.

Western industrial society, of course, with its massive scale and hugely centralized economy, can hardly be seen in relation to any particular landscape or ecosystem; the more-than-human ecology with which it is directly engaged is the biosphere itself. Sadly, our culture's relation to the earthly biosphere can in no way be considered a reciprocal or balanced one: with thousands of acres of nonregenerating forest disappearing every hour, and hundreds of our fellow species becoming extinct each month as a result of our civilization's excesses, we can hardly be surprised by the amount of epidemic illness in our culture, from increasingly severe immune dysfunctions and cancers, to widespread psychological distress, depression, and ever more frequent suicides, to the accelerating number of household killings and mass murders committed for no apparent reason by otherwise coherent individuals.

From an animistic perspective, the clearest source of all this distress, both physical and psychological, lies in the aforementioned violence needlessly perpetrated by our civilization on the ecology of the planet; only by alleviating the latter will we be able to heal the former. While this may sound at first like a simple statement of faith, it makes eminent and obvious sense as soon as we acknowledge our thorough dependence upon the countless other organisms with whom we have evolved. Caught up in a mass of abstractions, our attention hypnotized by a host of human-made technologies that only reflect us back to ourselves, it is all too easy for us to forget our carnal inherence in a more-than-human matrix of sensations and sensibilities. Our bodies have formed themselves in delicate reciprocity with the manifold textures, sounds, and shapes of an animate earth—our eyes have evolved in subtle interaction with *other* eyes, as our ears are attuned by their very structure to the howling of wolves and the honking of geese. To shut ourselves off from these other voices, to continue by our lifestyles to condemn these other sensibilities to the oblivion of extinction, is to rob our own senses of their integrity, and to rob our minds of their coherence. We are human only in contact, and conviviality, with what is not human.

Although the Indonesian islands are home to an astonishing diversity of birds, it was only when I went to study among the Sherpa people of the high Himalayas that I was truly initiated into the avian world. The Himalayas are young mountains, their peaks not yet rounded by the endless action of wind and ice, and so the primary dimension of the visible landscape is overwhelmingly vertical. Even in the high ridges one seldom attains a view of a distant horizon; instead one's vision is deflected upward by the steep face of the next mountain. The whole land has surged skyward in a manner still evident in the lines and furrows of the mountain walls, and this ancient dynamism readily communicates itself to the sensing body.

In such a world those who dwell and soar in the sky are the primary powers. They alone move easily in such a zone, swooping downward to become a speck near the valley floor, or spiraling into the heights on invisible currents. The wingeds, alone, carry the immediate knowledge of what is unfolding on the far side of the next ridge, and hence it is only by watching them that one can be kept apprised of climatic changes in the offing, as well as of subtle shifts in the flow and density of air currents in one's own valley. Several of the shamans that I met in Nepal had birds as their close familiars. Ravens are constant commentators on village affairs. The smaller, flocking birds perform aerobatics in unison over the village rooftops, twisting and swerving in a perfect sympathy of motion, the whole flock appearing like a magic banner that floats and flaps on air currents over the village, then descends in a heap, only to be carried aloft by the wind a moment later, rippling and swelling.

For some time I visited a Sherpa *dzankri* whose rock home was built into one of the steep mountainsides of the Khumbu region in Nepal. On one of our walks along the narrow cliff trails that wind around the mountain, the *dzankri* pointed out to me a certain boulder, jutting out from the cliff, on which he had "danced" before attempting some especially difficult cures. I recognized the boulder several days later when hiking back down toward the *dzankri*'s home from the upper yak pastures, and I climbed onto the rock, not to dance but to ponder the pale white and red lichens that gave life to its surface, and to rest. Across the dry valley, two lammergeier condors floated between gleaming, snow-covered peaks. It was a ringing blue Himalayan day, clear as a bell. After a few moments I took a silver coin out of my pocket and aimlessly began a simple sleight-of-hand exercise, rolling the coin over the knuckles of my right hand. I had taken to practicing this somewhat monotonous exercise in response to the endless flicking of prayer-beads by the older Sherpas, a practice usually accompanied by a repetitively chanted prayer: "*Om Mani Padme Hum*" (O the Jewel in the Lotus). But there was no prayer accompanying my revolving coin, aside from my quiet breathing and the dazzling sunlight. I noticed that one of the two condors in the distance had swerved away from its partner and was now floating over the valley, wings outstretched. As I watched it grow larger, I realized, with some delight, that it was heading in my general direction; I stopped rolling the coin and stared. Yet just then the lammergeier halted in its flight, motionless for a moment against the peaks, then swerved around and headed back toward its partner in the distance. Disappointed, I took up the coin and began rolling it along my knuckles once again, its silver surface catching the sunlight as it turned, reflecting the rays back into the sky. Instantly, the condor swung out from its path and began soaring back in a wide arc. Once again, I watched its shape grow larger. As the great size of the bird became apparent, I felt my skin begin to crawl and come alive, like a swarm of bees all in motion, and a humming grew loud in my ears. The coin continued rolling along my fingers. The creature loomed larger, and larger still, until suddenly, it was there—an immense silhouette hovering just above my head, huge wing feathers rustling ever so slightly as they mastered the breeze. My fingers were frozen, unable to move; the coin dropped out of my hand. And then I felt myself stripped naked by an alien gaze infinitely more lucid and precise than my own. I do not know for how long I was transfixed, only that I felt the air streaming past naked knees and heard the wind whispering in my feathers long after the Visitor had departed.

I returned to a North America whose only indigenous species of condor was on the brink of extinction, mostly as a result of lead poisoning from bullets in the carrion it consumes. But I did not think about this. I was excited by the new sensibilities that had stirred in me—my newfound awareness of a more-than-human world, of the great potency of the land, and particularly of the keen intelligence of other animals, large and small, whose lives and cultures interpenetrate our own. I startled neighbors by chattering with squirrels, who swiftly climbed down the trunks of their trees and across lawns to banter with me, or by gazing for hours on end at a heron fishing in a nearby estuary, or at gulls opening clams by dropping them from a height onto the rocks along the beach.

Yet, very gradually, I began to lose my sense of the animals' own awareness. The gulls' technique for breaking open the clams began to appear as a largely automatic behavior, and I could not easily feel the attention that they must bring to each new shell. Perhaps each shell was entirely the same as the last, and *no* spontaneous attention was really necessary. . . .

I found myself now observing the heron from outside its world, noting with interest its careful high-stepping walk and the sudden dart of its beak into the water, but no longer feeling its tensed yet poised alertness with my own muscles. And, strangely, the suburban squirrels no longer responded to my chittering calls. Although I wished to, I could no longer focus my awareness on engaging in their world as I had so easily done a few weeks earlier, for my attention was quickly deflected by internal, verbal deliberations of one sort or another—by a conversation I now seemed to carry on entirely within myself. The squirrels had no part in this conversation.

It became increasingly apparent, from books and articles and discussions with various people, that other animals were not as awake and aware as I had assumed, that they lacked any real language and hence the possibility of thought, and that even their seemingly spontaneous responses to the world around them were largely "programmed" behaviors, "coded" in the genetic material now being mapped by biologists. Indeed, the more I spoke *about* other animals, the less possible it became to speak *to* them. I gradually came to discern that there was no common ground between the unlimited human intellect and the limited sentience of other animals, no medium through which we and they might communicate with and reciprocate one another.

As the expressive and sentient landscape slowly faded behind my more exclusively human concerns, threatening to become little more than an illusion or fantasy, I began to feel—particularly in my chest and abdomen—as though I were being cut off from vital sources of nourishment. I was indeed reacclimating to my own culture, becoming more attuned to its styles of discourse and interaction, yet my bodily senses seemed to be losing their acuteness, becoming less awake to subtle changes and patterns. The thrumming of crickets, and even the songs of the local blackbirds, readily faded from my awareness after a few moments, and it was only by an effort of will that I could bring them back into the perceptual field. The flight of sparrows and of dragonflies no longer sustained my focus very long, if indeed they gained my attention at all. My skin quit registering the various changes in the breeze, and smells seemed to have faded from the world almost entirely, my nose waking up only once or twice a day, perhaps while cooking, or when taking out the garbage.

In Nepal, the air had been filled with smells—whether in the towns, where burning incense combined with the aromas of roasting meats and honeyed pastries and fruits for trade in the open market, and the stench of organic refuse rotting in the ravines, and sometimes of corpses being cremated by the river; or in the high mountains, where the wind carried the whiffs of countless wildflowers, and of the newly turned earth outside the villages where the fragrant dung of yaks was drying in round patties on the outer walls of the houses, to be used, when dry, as fuel for the household fires, and where smoke from those many home fires always mingled in the outside air. And sounds as well: the chants of aspiring monks and adepts blended with the ringing of prayer bells on near and distant slopes, accompanied by the raucous croaks of ravens, and the sigh of the wind pouring over the passes, and the flapping of prayer flags, and the distant hush of the river cascading through the far-below gorge.

There the air was a thick and richly textured presence, filled with invisible but nonetheless tactile, olfactory, and audible influences. In the United States, however, the air seemed thin and void of substance or influence. It was not, here, a sensuous medium—the felt matrix of our breath and the breath of the other animals and plants and soils—but was merely an absence, and indeed was constantly referred to in everyday discourse as mere empty space. Hence, in America I found myself lingering near wood fires and even garbage dumps—much to the dismay of my friends—for only such an intensity of smells served to remind my body of its immersion in an enveloping medium, and with this experience of being immersed in a world of influences came a host of body memories from my year among the shamans and village people of rural Asia.

I began to find other ways, as well, of tapping the very different sensations and perceptions that I had grown accustomed to in the "undeveloped world," by living for extended periods on native Indian reservations in the southwestern desert and along the northwestern coast, or by hiking off for weeks at a time into the North American wilderness. Intermittently, I began to wonder if my culture's assumptions regarding the lack of awareness in other animals and in the land itself was less a product of careful and judicious reasoning than of a strange inability to clearly perceive other animals—a real inability to clearly see, or focus upon, anything outside the realm of human technology, or to hear as meaningful anything other than human speech. The sad results of our interactions with the rest of nature were being reported in every newspaper—from the depletion of topsoil due to industrial farming techniques to the fouling of groundwater by industrial wastes, from the rapid destruction of ancient forests to, worst of all, the ever-accelerating extinction of our fellow species—and these remarkable and disturbing occurrences, all readily traceable to the ongoing activity of "civilized" humankind, did indeed suggest the possibility that there was a perceptual problem in my culture, that modern, "civilized" humanity simply did not perceive surrounding nature in a clear manner, if we have even been perceiving it at all.

The experiences that shifted the focus of my research in rural Indonesia and Nepal had shown me that nonhuman nature can be perceived and experienced with far more intensity and nuance than is generally acknowledged in the West. What was it that made possible the heightened sensitivity to extrahuman reality, the profound attentiveness to other species and to the Earth that is evidenced in so many of these cultures, and that had so altered my awareness that my senses now felt stifled and starved by the patterns of my own culture? Or, reversing the question, what had made possible the absence of this attentiveness in the modern West? For Western culture, too, has its indigenous origins. If the relative attunement to environing nature exhibited by native cultures is linked to a more primordial, participatory mode of perception, how had Western civilization come to be so exempt from this sensory reciprocity? How, that is, have we become so deaf and so blind to the vital existence of other species, and to the animate landscapes they inhabit, that we now so casually bring about their destruction?

To be sure, our obliviousness to nonhuman nature is today held in place by ways of speaking that simply deny intelligence to other species and to nature in general, as well as by the very structures of our civilized existence—by the incessant drone of motors that shut out the voices of birds and of the winds; by electric lights that eclipse not only the stars but the night itself; by air "conditioners" that hide the seasons; by offices, automobiles, and shopping malls that finally obviate any need to step outside the purely human world at all. We consciously encounter nonhuman nature only as it has been circumscribed by our civilization and its technologies: through our domesticated pets, on the television, or at the zoo (or, at best, in carefully managed "nature preserves"). The plants and animals we consume are neither gathered nor hunted—they are bred and harvested in huge, mechanized farms. "Nature," it would seem, has become simply a stock of "resources" for human civilization, and so we can hardly be surprised that our civilized eyes and ears are somewhat oblivious to the existence of perspectives that are not human at all, or that a person either entering into or returning to the West from a nonindustrial culture would feel startled and confused by the felt absence of nonhuman powers.

Still, the current commodification of "nature" by civilization tells us little or nothing of the perceptual shift that made possible this reduction of the animal (and the earth) to an object, little of the process whereby our senses first relinquished the power of the Other, the vision that for so long had motivated our most sacred rituals, our dances, and our prayers.

But can we even hope to catch a glimpse of this process, which has given rise to so many of the habits and linguistic prejudices that now structure our very thinking? Certainly not if we gaze toward that origin from within the midst of the very civilization it engendered. But perhaps we may make our stand along the *edge* of that civilization, like a magician, or like a person who, having lived among another tribe, can no longer wholly return to his own. He lingers half within and half outside of his community, open as well, then, to the shifting voices and flapping forms that crawl and hover beyond the mirrored walls of the city. And even there, moving along those walls, he may hope to find the precise clues to the mystery of how those walls were erected, and how a simple boundary became a barrier, only if the moment is timely—only, that is, if the margin he frequents is a temporal as well as a spatial edge, and the temporal structure that it bounds is about to dissolve, or metamorphose, into something else.   ■

NOTES

1. This work was done at the Philadelphia Association, a therapeutic community directed by Dr. R. D. Laing and his associates.

2. A simple illustration of this may be found among many of the indigenous peoples of North America, for whom the English term "medicine" commonly translates a word meaning "power"—specifically, the sacred power received by a human person from a particular animal or other nonhuman entity. Thus, a particular *medicine person* may be renowned for her "badger medicine" or "bear medicine," for his "eagle medicine," "elk medicine," or even "thunder medicine." It is from their direct engagement with these nonhuman powers that medicine persons derive their own abilities, including their ability to cure human ailments.

3. To the Western mind such views are likely to sound like reckless "projections" of human consciousness into inanimate and dumb materials, suitable for poetry perhaps, but having nothing, in fact, to do with those actual birds or that forest. Such is our common view. This text will examine the possibility that it is civilization that has been confused, and not indigenous peoples. It will suggest, and provide evidence, that one perceives a world at all only by projecting oneself into that world, that one makes contact with things and others only by actively participating in them, lending one's sensory imagination to things in order to discover how they alter and transform that imagination, how they reflect us back changed, how they are different from us. It will suggest that perception is *always* participatory, and hence that modern humanity's denial of awareness in nonhuman nature is borne not by any conceptual or scientific rigor, but rather by an inability, or a refusal, to fully perceive other organisms.

4. The similarity between such animistic world views and the emerging perspective of contemporary ecology is not trivial. Atmospheric geochemist James Lovelock, elucidating the well-known Gaia hypothesis—a theory stressing the major role played by organic life in the ceaseless modulation of the earth's atmospheric and climatic conditions—insists that the geological environment is itself constituted by organic life, and by the products or organic metabolism. In his words, we inhabit "a world that is the breath and bones of our ancestors." See, for instance, "Gaia: The World as Living Organism," in the *New Scientist*, December 18, 1986, as well as *Scientists on Gaia*, ed. Stephen Schneider and Penelope Boston (Cambridge: M.I.T. Press, 1991).

▪ *QUESTIONS FOR MAKING CONNECTIONS WITHIN THE READING* ▪

1. David Abram's essay begins with a description of his travels in eastern Bali and ends with his return to the United States. What happens to Abram during the course of his travels? When he says, "I began to *see* and to *hear* in a manner I never had before," what does he mean?

2. Abram tells us that one cannot become a shaman without "long and sustained exposure to wild nature, to its patterns and vicissitudes." What is "wild nature"? How does it differ from the kinds of nature one finds in a city, a suburb, or a state park? How does Abram's experience of "wild nature" differ from the experience one might have in each of these places?

3. As Abram reflects on the differences between how he felt when he was in Indonesia and how he felt on his return to the United States, he considers the possibility that Westerners might have "a real inability to clearly see, or focus upon, anything outside the realm of human technology, or to hear as meaningful anything other than human speech." What is it that Abram would like for us to focus on instead?

▪ *QUESTIONS FOR WRITING* ▪

1. In "The Ecology of Magic," Abram describes how his travels made him "a student of subtle differences." What does it mean to become such a student? What does one notice? And why is it important to notice such things?

2. As Abram sees it, there is a qualitative difference between the ways Westerners experience nature and the ways shamans experience nature. And yet, somehow, Abram himself was able to transcend the difference and access these other ways of feeling. What made it possible for Abram to do this? Could anyone have the experiences Abram describes?

▪ *QUESTIONS FOR MAKING CONNECTIONS BETWEEN READINGS* ▪

1. In "The Mind's Eye," Oliver Sacks asks, "to what extent are we—our experiences, our reactions—shaped, predetermined, by our brains, and to what extent do we shape our own brains?" By phrasing the question in this way, Sacks asks us to consider "to what extent" the brain shapes experience *and* experience shapes the brain. Drawing on Abram's discussion of sensuous experience and shamanism for your examples, respond to Sacks's question. Is the relationship between the shaping power of the brain and the power of personal experience one of relative equality?

Is the brain itself largely responsible for who we are and how we experience the world, or is sensuous experience more decisive?

2. Abram defines humanity in the following way: "We are human only in contact, and conviviality, with what is not human." In "Playing God in the Garden," Michael Pollan discusses biogenetic engineering as one way that the food industry redefines the relationship between humans, plants, and animals. Is it possible to have a "convivial" relationship with "what is not human" in the age of technology? What relationship should humans have to the natural world?

www **For additional suggestions about making connections between readings, visit the Link-O-Mat and More Sample Assignments at <www.newhum.com>.**

LILA ABU-LUGHOD

WHEN LILA ABU-LUGHOD was completing her graduate work in anthropology at Harvard University in the late 1970s, she designed a fieldwork project that took her to Egypt to study interpersonal relations between male and female members of a nomadic Bedouin community. Once there, Abu-Lughod noticed that the people she was living with frequently punctuated their talk, both in public and in private, by reciting short pieces of poetry. Although this wasn't what she had come to study, she became fascinated by the "radical difference between the sentiments expressed in [the oral poetry] and those expressed about the same situations in ordinary social interactions and conversations." Her first book, *Veiled Sentiments: Honor and Poetry in a Bedouin Society* (1986), grew out of her efforts to understand what produced these two very different ways of using language.

Currently a professor of anthropology at Columbia University, Abu-Lughod is internationally recognized for her contributions to feminist ethnography and to the study of gender politics in the Muslim world. What makes her work so distinctive and so unsettling is her insistence upon the importance of carefully examining both the actions and the assumptions that make up our everyday lives. Thus, while Abu-Lughod works hard to understand how women can gain power in traditional societies, she also encourages all who pursue such research to consider what women lose when they adopt the lifeways and the values of modern society. "Feminists, leftists, progressives, and other intellectuals still haven't questioned the idea of development, progress, modernity, as wholly a good thing," she has said. "No one has challenged this concept . . . that we have to follow a certain path, and as people get educated, they will get more enlightened."

In "Honor and Shame," which comes from her second book, *Writing Women's Worlds: Bedouin Stories* (1993), Abu-Lughod focuses on this question

Abu-Lughod, Lila. "Honor and Shame." *Writing Women's Worlds: Bedouin Stories.* Berkeley: Univ. of California Press, 1993. 205–242.

Initial quotation from *Veiled Sentiments: Honor and Poetry in a Bedouin Society* (Berkeley: Univ. of California Press, 1986); closing quotation from Sarwat Ahmad, "A Muddled Modernity," *Cairo Times,* Vol. 3, Issue 1, March, 1999, 14–17. <http://www.cairotimes.com/content/issues/Women/lughod.html>.

quite directly. What does Kamla, the subject of "Honor and Shame," stand to gain by breaking with her tradition and completing her education? What does she stand to lose? Under the circumstances, what outcome should one hope for? By telling Kamla's story in just this way, Abu-Lughod arouses the very kind of sentiments she most wants her readers to explore.

www To learn more about Lila Abu-Lughod and Bedouin culture, visit the Link-O-Mat at <www.newhum.com>.

Honor and Shame

Say to the believing men that they should lower their gaze and guard their modesty; that will make for greater purity for them. And God is well acquainted with all that they do.

And say to the believing women that they should lower their gaze and guard their modesty; that they should not display their beauty and ornaments except what (ordinarily) appear thereof; that they should draw their veils over their bosoms and not display their beauty except to their husbands, their fathers, their husbands' fathers, their sons, their husband's sons, their brothers or their brothers' sons, or their sisters' sons, or their women, or the slaves their right hands possess, or male attendants free of sexual desires, or small children who have no carnal knowledge of women.

Qur'an 24:30–31

In a letter dated July 30, 1989, Kamla, another daughter of Gateefa and Sagr, wrote to tell me her good news.

In the Name of God the All-Merciful and Compassionate. It gives me pleasure to send this letter to my dear sister, Dr. Lila, hoping from God on high, the All-Powerful, that it reaches you carrying love and greetings to you and your family while you are all in the best of health and in perfect happiness.

By name she mentioned my brother and sisters (none of whom she has met) and asked me to convey her greetings and those of her family to them and to my parents, as well as to the one American friend of mine they had met ten years ago—in short, to everyone they knew about in my life in America. I had confided during my last visit that I would be getting married soon. She asked if I had; if so, she wrote, she sent a thousand congratulations and hoped, God willing, that he was a good man who would understand me. She hoped also that their new in-law was a noble man, the best in all of America, and that they would meet him soon. After wishing me many children (six boys and six girls) and more greetings, she squeezed her piece of news onto the bottom of the page.

> Your sister Kamla has become engaged to Engineer Ibrahim Saleem, Aisha's brother.

I could hardly believe it. We had teased Kamla about him ever since his name had been floated four years before as a prospect. This was the match she scarcely dared hope her father would arrange. Not that she had ever met the young man. What mattered was that he was educated, came from a family that believed in educating girls, and lived in a town. She would be able to escape the kind of life her family lived, a life that annoyed her—the only one in her family, male or female, to have made it through high school—more and more.

Because she complained so much, I had asked her in the summer after she graduated to write me an essay on how young Bedouin women's lives were changing and what of the past she hoped the Awlad 'Ali would retain and what she wished they would abandon. She had proudly told me that her teacher had sent off for publication an essay on Awlad 'Ali weddings she had written in school. You can trace, in the stilted words of her essay and the candid comments (in parentheses) she made as she read it aloud to me, the outlines of the new world she hoped to gain by marrying the likes of Engineer Ibrahim Saleem.

The Education of Girls

An Essay on the Young Bedouin Woman of Egypt and the Changes in Her Life over 40 Years

If we are to speak of the Bedouin girl in Egypt we find that her life differs from one era to another. The circumstances of the home and family relations change from one age to another. If we go back to discuss the way she was around forty years ago, we find that the Bedouin girl was living a life in which she was of no value. When she came of age, or maturity (as the Egyptians say—I mean the years when she is ready for marriage), *she had to do housework at her family's home—for example, cooking, washing clothes, and preparing firewood.* (Her only value was in the housework she did—the sweeping and washing—and if she didn't do it they'd laugh at her and gossip about her laziness. She was forced to do it, even if she weren't capable. No matter what her health was like. I'm talking about those who were my age, from around the age of twelve on.)

Also, she used to spin and weave, even though it is very difficult, painful, and strenuous. (When she was around fifteen, her mother or any woman in the household, an aunt for instance, would teach her. It's supposed to be the mother, though. Her goal was to teach her daughter to spin and to make something, anything. The important thing was for her to weave something, if only a border for the tent.) *She had to learn this skill.* (This is what is important for the Bedouins, housework, weaving, and such things. Forty years ago this was what a girl had to put up with.)

Kamla had been resenting housework. Now that she had finished school she rarely left the house. With two sisters, she was responsible for the cooking and cleaning one day out of three. On another of those days she was in charge of baking bread with them. She was on call much of the rest of the time, seeing to it that her little brothers and sisters were bathed, dressed, and staying out of mischief. Piles of laundry collected in the back room to be done when there was time.

Where before she had worn clean clothes for school, studied with her brothers in a quiet room of her own, and been given few household duties, now she had no privileges. Her clothes were as caked with dough and soot as her sisters'. Kamla's only escape was listening to the radio. She carried my transistor with her wherever in the house or courtyard she was working. She kept an eye on the time so as not to miss the radio soap operas. When she was free, she stared into space as she listened to Egyptian music, talk shows, and the news. So attached was she to the radio that I called it her sweetheart. Her mother, irritable from fatigue herself, scolded her and threatened to lock up the radio. When Gateefa complained, "My daughters are becoming lazy sluts," Kamla, like her sisters, simply ignored her.

Kamla had scored high enough on her final exams to secure a place in the agricultural college for which her high school had prepared her. She had no special interest in agriculture and had gone to this secondary school only because the regular high school was on the far side of town. Her uncles had given her a choice: quit school or go to the nearby agriculture school. School was still much on her mind. Her essay continued:

Education for the Bedouin girl used not to exist. It was impossible for her to study. (Forty years ago she lived a life, as I said earlier, that had no value at all.) *She was governed by the customs and traditions that the Bedouin families followed. These customs and traditions forbade a girl to leave the house under any circumstances. So going to school* (this is an example) *would be the greatest shame. She couldn't say that she wished to study, no matter what. Even if, as they say, she was the daughter of a tribal leader.* (So for example, a girl's father would be a tribal leader and she'd want to study, but her relatives would say no you can't. She'd say, but I'm the daughter of the head of a lineage. I must learn. They'd forbid her.)

This hypothetical example was, of course, from her own experience. She had been allowed to continue her schooling against the wishes of her uncles. They wanted to pull her out when she was no longer little. Because she was so determined, she and her parents had put up with the uncles' general suspicion and occasional accusations. She was a fierce child who had early on decided she wanted to go to school. She was not allowed to enroll in the public school, though, because, as is often the case, her father had never registered her birth. Yet still she went each day, as a visitor, borrowing her brothers' books. After three years of this her teacher finally required her to register officially. Haj Sagr went and had her papers drawn up. From then on she came in at the top of her class, while her brothers and male cousins flunked out. I had recorded in my notes from 1979 her bashful reaction when her brother told their father she had been appointed school monitor. Sagr had been hugging his youngest son, then in his first year of school, proudly predicting that his son would come out above the rest.

The primary school had been within sight of the camp, and its students were mostly relatives and neighbors. The secondary school, though, was about three kilometers away. Kamla's class had only four Bedouin girls; the rest of the girls were Egyptians from town. To get to this school she had to walk along the road past houses of people who did not know her. She said she walked with her head down, looking neither right nor left, but she still had to endure catcalls from men driving by.

Her relatives' suspicions were harder to cope with. One aunt had come twice to Gateefa to accuse Kamla of taking her son's schoolbook to give to a boy from a neighboring tribe. Kamla's mother had defended her. True, she had given the boy a schoolbook, but it was in exchange for a book that he had given her the previous year. And the book was one that her father had bought her, not one she had taken from her cousin. Fortunately, when they questioned the aunt's son, he backed Gateefa.

Kamla and her mother were angrier when Kamla's uncle told Haj Sagr that he had seen his niece Kamla walking home with a boy. Gateefa felt she'd been hit in the stomach with a rock. She argued, to me, "If it were true, why didn't he stop for her and put her in the car? Why didn't he get out and beat her right there, if he really saw her? If he's so afraid for her, why doesn't he ever offer to drive her to school?"

Kamla told the story as she knew it. She believed the problem began during her second year of high school. Her uncle had not wanted her to continue, but Sagr had defended his daughter's right to stay in school. Furious, her uncle did everything he could to prevent her from studying. If, for example, guests came to the house, he would knock on her door to ask her to make the tea. She'd try to escape, sneaking off to study outdoors under the trees. Two days before her final exams (when, as we all know, she added, nerves are on edge), she was walking home from school. Across the road a boy she had known since she was small was going the same direction. Because she always walked with her head down, she noticed her uncle drive by only after he had passed. He went straight to her father and told him, "Your daughter was walking hand in hand with a boy." Her father had questioned him carefully, then called in Kamla's mother. Gateefa in turn had come to her ("And you know how upset she gets!" she said to me) to ask her about it. Kamla refused to say "yes, no, or maybe" unless her uncle came and accused her to her face.

Her father, she said lovingly, believed in her. He asked her why she didn't walk home from school with her cousin, and she explained that she was not about to go out of her way just to walk with him. If he wished to walk with her along her route before cutting off to his house, he was welcome to. Kamla's uncle had also told her father that this cousin had informed him that the boy waited for Kamla at the school gates to walk home with her every day. Fortunately for Kamla, her cousin happened to pass by the house that afternoon. Sagr called him over to question him— right in front of her uncle. The boy swore that he had never said such a thing. That ended it.

Arranged Marriage

The next paragraph of Kamla's essay took up the matter of marriage. Commenting on it, Kamla said, "This was a topic the Bedouin girl would hear nothing about and wasn't supposed to have anything to do with."

She had no right to an opinion in any matter, however much the matter might concern her personally. She had no say even in the choice of a husband. She had absolutely no say in this matter. (And to this day, no matter how educated she's become, very seldom does she have any opinion. The Bedouin girl has no say.) *In this matter what she had to do was carry out her family's orders even if she didn't want to. It was not right for her to refuse.* (Even if she didn't want him, she had to agree to it against her will. Even if he was older than she was, for example, or very different from her, she had to agree to what the family wanted. For example, if they said I had to marry someone and I didn't want him—I hated him—but if my kinsmen had agreed to the match and told me I had to marry him, what I would have to do, despite my wishes, was marry him.)

I was surprised that Kamla depicted women as powerless in decisions about marriage. She had heard the same stories I had—stories, like her grandmother Migdim's, of resistance to marriages arranged for them by their kinsmen. She knew plenty of young women like one who, in love with someone else, had married Kamla's cousin but then had gone home to her father's household at the slightest provocation, eventually forcing her husband to divorce her. The specter of forced marriage, especially to paternal cousins, may have loomed large for Kamla because she, like her sister Sabra, was waiting. As her mother joked with a friend, "Kamla's got her diploma. Now we're going to give her the other diploma!"

Her religious training at school had given Kamla moral ammunition against arranged marriage. The Prophet, she would explain, says that it is wrong to marry someone you have never seen. Moreover, the girl must give her consent: the bride's relatives are supposed to ask her opinion. Kamla is not sure her opinion will be sought. Already she has made it known throughout the women's community that she does not want to marry her cousin Salih, the young man closest to her in age who has been lined up with her, at least according to the calculations of his father and uncles about marriages between their children.

Kamla is fond of Salih, but he is "like a brother." She and her sisters boldly ask him to get them things they want from town; they reach into his pockets to grab the latest cassettes he has brought for himself. Kamla sometimes teases him, threatening to make him wash the dishes and sweep the floor if he marries her. Kamla even jokes with his mother. I had seen the woman grab Kamla and warn her to be good or else she'd exercise her prospective rights as a mother-in-law and make her quit school. Kamla broke free easily, laughing as she shouted defiantly, "Not until I come to live with you!"

Women in the camp mutter that Salih is not right for Kamla. Even her grandmother half supports her. Although Migdim tries to persuade her granddaughters of the virtues of marrying cousins, she is angry with her sons for wanting "what nothing good will come of"—this set of matches within the family between children who have grown up together and say they feel like siblings. She fumed, "Her father wants Kamla for Salih, and Kamla says she won't marry him. And Salih says he won't marry Kamla. She's older than he is!"

Her unmarried granddaughters enjoy provoking Migdim by maligning cousin marriage. They say they want out: they want to marry men who live far away so they can have new lives.

"They're good for nothing!" insisted one of Kamla's cousins once about her male cousins.

Migdim scolded her, "You slut! What is this outrage? You gypsy!"

She and her sister laughed wildly, "Damn them, our cousins! What do you see in them?"

A cousin agreed, "They're all ugly. Not a handsome one among them. No, we'll marry outsiders, Grandma, ugly or handsome."

Kamla shook her head. "I'm marrying an Egyptian! Someone educated."

Her grandmother retorted, "Your father won't agree to it!"

Kamla hugged her grandmother. "We're just talking with you to see what you'll say. Is there anything in our hands, Grandma? Or in my father's? Only God knows what will happen."

Generations

In the past, according to Kamla, a girl had no say in the matter of marriage because, as her essay continued,

> *They thought that girls shouldn't be concerned with anything but clothing and food and drink. In her kinsmen's eyes a girl had no value.* (Even now it's true. You might think conditions had changed and advanced a bit, but it's still true.) *They did not know that a girl had something she valued more than food and such things—and that was feelings.* (Feelings were forbidden to the girl.) *But she had feelings and sensitivity and affections just like any other person on this earth.* (This is true. There is no person God has created without feelings or sensitivity.) *Her kinsmen had feelings and sensitivities and affections.* (Take my father, for example. My father loved in the days of his youth; but then he thinks a girl doesn't have any such feelings.) *But they did not care if the girl had feelings. Her feelings and desires were not important.*

Kamla laughed conspiratorially as she read the next section.

> *So, for example, if she loved a person, she could not show this love, however precious and strong her love was. She would be very afraid that her relatives would hear about it, because they considered it a big scandal for a girl to love, even though they had. They say that only men have the right—a young woman does not have the right to know or speak with any man except her brothers and their relatives. All of this has governed the Bedouin girl for as long as she has lived on this earth.* (This is true. For example, if a boy meets a girl and talks with her, they say it doesn't matter—"He's a man." But you, the girl, if you do this? They don't say anything to him. If my father heard that my brother was in love with someone and talked with her, he wouldn't say anything. But if it was me? That would be dealt with very differently.)

This talk of love and vocabulary of feelings was new. Ever since I had known Kamla, from the age of twelve or so, she had been a tough little girl, the kind who would say to her uncle's new wife, "I don't even know what this 'love' is. I hear about it in songs and hear about this one giving her necklace and that one her ring, but I don't know what they are feeling." She used to amuse her great-aunts when they hugged her and teased her about which of her young cousins she would grow up to marry by proudly shouting, "I'm never going to marry."

Just a year before she wrote this essay she had demanded of her mother, "Does a woman have to marry? Does she have to have someone to tell her what to do, to boss her around?"

"Yes, a woman has to marry," Gateefa had answered. "If she doesn't, people will say, 'The poor thing!'"

But things had changed. Kamla now quoted from a book she had read at school: it was natural as one entered adolescence to begin thinking about members of the opposite sex. She admitted that such things had never even crossed her mind before. But then it had happened. It was at her cousin Selima's wedding that she had first revealed to me the new experiences she had begun to have at school. During a quiet period of the day before the wedding we had gone for a stroll on the hillside. Scattered on the ridge were groups of women in twos and threes, sisters who rarely saw each other, aunts and their nieces, old friends, also talking privately.

Looking into the distance—and, as it turned out, toward a certain house—Kamla had asked me, "What do you think, Lila? Is it wrong for two people to think about each other all the time?" I was puzzled. She told me about a young man at school—a well-behaved and good person, she added quickly—who had taken notice of her. He had asked her friends whether they could persuade her to agree to talk to him. She had refused at first. Finally she agreed to a brief meeting, with friends present. He wanted to know if she would be willing to marry him if he got his father to request her from Haj Sagr. She wondered if there was any hope that her father would accept. Knowing the family, I said I doubted it.

Usually she was more realistic. When I would ask whom she wanted to marry she would give various answers. She was adamant about her cousins: "If they think I'm going to take any of these, my cousins, or anyone from the camp, they're wrong." Then she would deny that she cared whether or not it was the boy she knew from school. The brother of their family friend Aisha would be just fine. As long as the man was educated. Backtracking she would say, "It's not even important that he's well educated. But he must be knowledgeable." The boys in her camp didn't know anything; they would not know how to get on in the world. Dependent on their fathers to feed, dress, and marry them off, they were incapable of taking care of themselves. "They're men in name only," she scoffed.

She blamed her elder kinsmen, especially her father, for her cousins' failures. Despite the double standard in matters of the heart, she acknowledged that her cousins and her brothers were having almost as hard a time dealing with their old-fashioned elders as she was. One time when I returned from a short trip to Cairo, Kamla greeted me with the news that her grandmother was distraught because her cousin Salih, the woman's favorite grandson, had run away from home after his father had hit him. No one knew where he had gone.

I would hear the story several times from Migdim, once as she told it to a visiting niece who began by asking, "Who hit Salih?"

"His father hit him."

"And why?"

"He went to a wedding at So-and-so's and they say he drank liquor."

"Liquor? What kind of liquor?"

Migdim didn't know much about it. "The stuff you drink that makes them drunk. They said he drank. Each of the men came and asked him. They'd told his father on him."

"Beer, must have been beer." Migdim's niece knew things. Her husband, now dead, was rumored to have been a womanizer and an alcoholic.

Migdim did not want her story interrupted. "His father came here and hit him."

"Beer. Liquor?—why a bottle costs twenty-five pounds! There is beer and white water. The beer costs two pounds fifty a bottle."

Migdim went on. "I said, 'Son, listen, sometimes he hits his sisters just to get half a pound from them. Another time he'll need a pound. By God, he doesn't have a piaster.' I said, 'Son, your boy didn't drink. He doesn't have any money.' Salih told him, 'Father, I didn't buy any. Dad, I didn't taste it. Dad, I didn't drink.' Every time he said something, his father would give him a slap. And in the end he looked for something big to hit him with, but we grabbed it away."

Her niece was shocked.

"The women stopped him. The boy cried and cried—and I was crying too—until his eyes were red. And he said, 'Swear to God, I'll go to Libya. I'm leaving.' I thought maybe he'd go stay with his maternal uncle. That would have been fine. In the end, though, they said he headed east."

Migdim went on about her own feelings. The night Salih left, she says, her head never touched the pillow. She and his sisters sat up crying all night. "It was hard on me. He really was so generous, he was generous. I swear to God, that time he got a job with his uncle out west and had some money, he'd give me five pounds, his sister five pounds, his aunt five pounds, and his nephews one pound each. So generous. And in the morning, he never left without coming to say, 'Good morning, Grandmother. How are you, Grandma?' And he'd kiss me from this side and that. He was always there around me."

Although they thought Salih was wrong to run away, the other women in the community were angrier with his father. One of them had tried to calm the man, saying, "It's something that's already happened. If the boy went astray it has passed, and if it didn't really happen, then people lied. He's your son." The man had refused to be calmed.

Migdim was upset that her son was now threatening to pursue the boy. She says she cursed him, "You've gone crazy, my son, and you've made him go crazy. If you got him angry, may God bring you no success! May God not grant you success!"

Her niece commiserated.

Migdim continued, "I told him, 'If you hit him, may God not favor you! You should just talk to him. How can you say you're going to make him go out to herd the camels, living for three or four months on unleavened bread? You drove him crazy! Why didn't you scold him gently and say, 'Son, this is wrong, this is shameful?'"

Migdim's niece gave an alternative. The man should have said to his son, "Okay, it was the first time. Now say it will be the last time." She added, "After all, someone invited him, rottenest of invitations. The boys figured it would pass, but they caught it."

Had Salih really bought the liquor? Who was with him? The women of the family disagreed. Migdim cursed the family that held the wedding. "May God ruin their houses, those who had a wedding and brought—I don't know what dog it was who brought a box and sold bottles from it— who was it?" Others knew that beer was often sold at these kinds of weddings, where professional performers entertained. They suspected that the drinking had gone on. All the women agreed that the boys were just kids who didn't know better; his father should have reprimanded the boy, "My son, this is wrong. This is the Devil's work."

Kamla, too, criticized her father and her uncles, but not just for the way they had reacted to this rumor of alcohol. She thought they were mistaken to be so strict with the boys. They wanted the boys to be straight, but all they would get from applying this pressure was stubbornness. The pressure, she warned, would produce the opposite of what they wanted. She gave examples. The men wouldn't let the boys play soccer. "What's wrong with soccer? It's exercise." They wouldn't let them have a television, go to cafés, or visit the local cafeteria where videos are shown. Needless to say, they wouldn't permit them to grow their hair long. The men wouldn't even let the boys get jobs, making them stay on the land and tend the new fig trees. Noting that her brothers and cousins had no money, Kamla added, "They treat them like girls. If only they would give them a bit of freedom."

The freedom she wants for them, and perhaps for herself, is the subject of a popular song, an early recording by 'Awadh al-Maalky, that includes a comical tale of woe. The singer is moved, he begins, by the suffering that customs of the past have caused a young man. Hundreds of others have come to him to complain. Assuming the voice of the aggrieved young man, the poet describes what happened in the three marriages his kin arranged for him: when he reached out on the wedding night to touch his first bride, he discovered she was completely bald; the second bride, though beautiful with long thick braids, could not speak; the third tried to strangle him in his sleep—she was insane. The young man declares he won't marry again unless he is allowed to choose his own bride. Resuming his own voice the singer comments on the young man's predicament with some advice to the elders:

My warnings are to the old man
who imprisons the freedom of the young,
who has forgotten a thing called love,
affection, desire, burning flames,
forgotten the strength of lovers' fire,
the fire of lovers who long for one another.
What's exquisite is that they're afraid,
they say, any minute my prying guard will turn up:
my father's about to catch us.

The Dangers of Schooling

Kamla thinks her elders are wrong to fear an abuse of freedom. Her essay described what happened when her generation began to go to school.

Life began to change for the Bedouins, a change of conditions and location. Those Bedouins who began living in town started sending their sons and also their daughters to school to learn right from wrong, prayer, and writing. (That was my father's single goal in educating us. He wanted us to know this. They don't put us in school to learn—who cared if I got educated? My own reason for being there was to learn right from wrong and the Qur'an. That's all.) *After that they would pull them out of school.* (Even if a girl was clever and came out first in her class, once she had learned right from wrong and had come to understand, they would say to her, "Come on, that's enough.") *Some might let her stay through secondary school.* (Like me. After I finished secondary school, that was it.) *The Bedouin girl could even gain such a mastery of learning and knowledge* (it would be great if every girl could go to high school) *that she could enter university.* (In Alexandria you'll find Bedouin girls who've gone to university.)

Kamla was grateful to have been allowed to continue so long in school. She had dreamt, when still in primary school, of going to college to study politics and economics. At the time, she says with amazement, she didn't understand the problem of being a girl. She had hope. Now they tease her younger sister for similar ambitions. Her father had proudly congratulated the younger girl for a good report card and said it was a pity her brothers had given her such a hard time when she announced that she wanted to be a doctor. Kamla was scornful. "They'll make her quit long before she becomes a doctor."

The problem with being a girl, as Kamla explained in her essay, was what other people would say and think about her family if they let her go to school.

What happened was that people began competing over the schooling of girls. (For example, my father sees Aisha's father, who has educated all his daughters;

so my father looks at him and says, "Why should he educate his daughters and not me? I have to educate my daughters." One looked at the next until all of them started educating their daughters. . . . But around here, they see that others' daughters aren't in school. No one here has daughters in university. In Marsa Matruh they all sent their girls to school, each imitating the other. My father looks over at Aisha's father and his daughters. If one of them did anything wrong—may God protect us!—*anything* wrong, my father and all of them would decide not to follow. But when I look, I see that the Bedouin girl does not give up her Bedouin values. The girls went to school and nothing bad happened.) *They put them in school, and the girls repaid their precious trust. The Bedouin girl made them see clearly that their daughter was as good as any girl from the biggest city—in intelligence and level of learning. She would get the highest grades in all fields of learning.* (This is true. If, for example, you compare someone from Marsa Matruh and someone from Cairo who've both graduated from the same school, you'll find them equally good. You'll even find that the Bedouin girl is better because she is also modest, pious, and respectful of her traditions and customs—better than the Egyptian girl who may have graduated from medical school but does not dress properly. Everything in her lifestyle is not right. Even if she gets educated, the Bedouin girl is better. You know, the Bedouins used to think that girls were a scandal. They used to think that if a Bedouin girl left the house she would have to do something wrong. They were sure of it. They'd say she can't go out—she's an idiot, she can't think. Like a beast of burden, she wouldn't know right from wrong. But when she got educated she showed them that what they had thought was wrong.)

Kamla still struggled against community opinion. Her relatives opposed sending her to college. An aunt put it bluntly: "What? Let her study in Alexandria? She's a kid. What does she know? Someone might take advantage of her. If it were here in our territory, it would be fine. But it's in Alexandria. She's gotten enough schooling."

Her father was more honest about their concerns. He had defied his brothers (with Aisha and perhaps even me in mind) to let her complete high school. The summer she graduated a school friend of Kamla's came to visit. She was dressed differently from the girls in our camp, having adopted the modern Islamic modest dress that included a severe headcovering. Haj Sagr knew her family; she spoke freely to Kamla's father, while his own daughter sat silent. The young woman told him how they wished they could go on to college. At first he tried to dismiss the idea by asking what use agricultural college (the only kind they were qualified to enter) would be for a girl. Then he got to the heart of the problem: "What would people say? 'His daughter's in college. I wonder if she's really studying or just going out a lot.'" Even if she were truly doing nothing wrong, he said, people would talk. The young woman argued with him, but he ended, as Kamla had predicted, by saying, "Listen, if your father agrees to it, tell him I'll agree too."

He inquired about her family situation, and she told him her father was refusing to marry any of his daughters to cousins. His excuse was that blindness ran in the family. Kamla was encouraged, momentarily, when her father agreed that a girl who is educated should be married to an educated man so there could be mutual understanding. But then Haj Sagr suddenly reversed his argument. He told Kamla's friend that he had been willing to send his daughters to school because he wanted them to know how to organize their lives, their home, and their children. An educated mother could help her children with their schoolwork. Therefore, he said, he would prefer to keep these girls in the family: even if their husbands were not educated, the next generation of the family would benefit. If you give women to outsiders, he noted, the benefits go to the other tribe.

His model was Aisha, the woman whose father had been an old friend, whose husband was Sagr's business partner, and whose brother he was eventually to accept as a son-in-law. Aisha was the only college-educated Bedouin woman they knew. Whenever she and her children accompanied her husband on a visit, Kamla assumed special charge. Although all the women were warm, it was Kamla who saw to it that Aisha got water for ablutions, a prayer mat when she wanted, and who kept the conversation going.

Aisha was tall, slender, and elegant. She wore nicely styled full-length, long-sleeved dresses. Instead of the usual black headcloth, she wore the fashionable modern headcovering that now marks Muslim modesty and piety. Unlike the Egyptian women who sometimes visited, she did not turn up her nose at the food that was offered her, and she was relaxed with the women of the household. She'd just laugh when old Migdim teased her about her husband. "After He created your husband's tribe, God created the donkey." Insults were expected between people from Aisha's tribe and that of her husband.

Aisha was and was not part of their world. A distant relative, she had people and interests in common with Migdim, Gateefa, and the others, but she was defensive about her family. Although they lived in the city, she was quick to tell stories that showed her brothers to be proper Bedouins. Describing her own wedding, she recalled how her husband—whose family were real desert Bedouins—came to her house the evening before the ceremony. He had brought along a Western-style suit, intending to have his photograph taken with her. Her brothers, she reported, had said, "If you're coming to have dinner with us, that's fine, you are very welcome. But if you're coming for anything else, don't bother."

Later she would try to cover for her sister, who made an unconventional marriage. We had met this young woman once, a student of pharmacology at Alexandria University who came to visit dressed in a long woolen suit, her hair covered with a turban and scarf, an alternative "Islamic" style. We heard later that her brothers had agreed to a marriage offer from an Egyptian doctor living in Marsa Matruh. Aisha insisted that even though the groom was Egyptian, her brothers had required a Bedouin engagement ceremony, where sheep are brought and eaten, first, before the Egyptian-style engagement party the groom's family wanted. She also claimed that they held a traditional henna party on the eve of the wedding—before the Egyptian-style wedding in a club. She denied that anyone except one brother had attended the wedding itself, but I didn't believe her: I knew she knew how scandalous it would be to admit that the bride's relatives had attended such a wedding.

Aisha switched easily between the Bedouin and Egyptian dialects. When she and her husband entertained Bedouins in their home, she served the men the customary lamb and rice but otherwise remained in a separate room from them. When they were with Egyptian friends, she served different foods and they all ate together. They even got different videos to entertain their guests. For Bedouins they always rented the same film about the Libyans' struggle against the Italian colonists. Their guests, Aisha explained, loved the early scenes showing a traditional Libyan Bedouin wedding and the scenes of men fighting on horseback. Egyptian films, she said, contained risqué scenes, so these were never shown to Bedouin guests. Aisha also owned two photo albums: one she showed to their more traditional Bedouin friends and family; the other one she kept hidden because it contained photographs, taken with a self-timer, of herself holding hands with her husband. Yet Aisha worried about trying to raise her two small children in an apartment on the outskirts of Alexandria. She did not want them to play with the neighbors. She feared they were learning bad language, and she apologized for their having picked up the Egyptian dialect. Her five-year-old daughter had just begun school and had started to deny that she was an Arab. "She says she's Egyptian," her mother reported. "You know," Aisha said earnestly to Kamla, "Egyptians aren't like us."

Egyptians

Could Bedouin identity be maintained after schooling? Kamla's essay took up this question.

> *The Bedouin girl preserves the traditions and customs she was raised by.* (People stay with what they have grown up with because they came of age with it. Me, for example, I grew up knowing this was shameful and that was not right, there are customs, there's respect and modesty. Even when I'm old and my hair is grey, I'll have to follow these.) *She has sense and preserves her family's reputation.* (Of course, she'd be afraid that if she did something wrong they'd pull her out of school.) *The Bedouin girl tries to overcome the special obstacles she must confront.* (For example, she doesn't let her customs and

traditions, or people's talk—saying this is wrong and that is shameful—make her fall behind other girls. The Bedouin girl follows her customs but in a way that doesn't tie her up or block the path before her.) *She attempts to live a life enlightened by learning, happiness, and contributions to her country and family.* (She gives to her country. The Bedouin girl feels for her country and understands the meaning of Egypt as much as any girl from Cairo. The girl living in the Western Desert has feelings for Egypt that may be even stronger than the Egyptian girl's. The educated Bedouin girl knows the meaning of her country. . . . Boy, if my father heard this!)

Kamla's comment about her father gives a clue as to the obstacles she faces as she moves between home and her state school run by Egyptian teachers. While Haj Sagr bemoans the Awlad 'Ali's lack of foresight in failing to request an independent state from the British and chafes against every government restriction on his activities, Kamla patriotically defends Egypt and speaks proudly of President Mubarak. Once, when her father confronted her for being a few hours late from a school trip, she argued back. He then scolded her for raising her voice and waving her hands as she spoke. "This is the work of Egyptians!" he yelled. Anger fighting fear, she answered, "I *am* an Egyptian. And they are the best people, and this is the best country!"

Kamla listened closely to the detailed reports of city life that Safiyya, her father's second wife, gave each time she returned from visits to her brothers' homes. These were brothers whose sons were becoming lawyers. Kamla was also riveted to broadcasts of Egyptian radio melodramas, with plots like that of "Bride by Computer," about a young man whose life is nearly ruined by computer matchmaking. Kamla can envision this world better than her sisters can, although she was as puzzled as they were about what a computer might be, and just as disapproving of the female characters in this conservative moral tale.

The plot of this serial, as the girls explained, followed the usual formula: A man loves someone but cannot marry her; in the end, though, he succeeds in getting her. The main character was a young Egyptian who worked in a company. When his mother objected to him marrying a co-worker whom he loved, a friend suggested he "talk to the computer to find a bride." The results, predictably, were disastrous. The first bride was a doctor. "She worked day and night," Kamla recalled. "Even the night of the wedding she was busy."

"You know what she was doing?" Kamla's neighbor intervened. "She was doing experiments with mosquitoes and rats."

"So he divorced her," Kamla went on. "He got engaged to another girl but didn't marry her. After he got engaged to her, she wanted him to go swimming with her and to dance with her, to act like foreigners."

The neighbor was excited. "The day he wanted to marry her she told him she wanted him to come over. He went there and found it wild. There was loud music."

Sabra explained. "She was at a nightclub. When he got there she said, 'Play that music,' and people started dancing. She asked him if he knew how to dance. He said no. She said, 'Look, see that man who's moving wildly on the floor?' The girl moved wildly as well, asking them to play a foreign tape."

The young women laughed as they described her. "She said to him, 'Get up, get up.' But he wouldn't go with her. He wouldn't dance with her."

When they paused I asked, "What was the problem with the third bride?"

The girls were confused. Sabra ventured, "I don't know, she had put . . . she had made a workshop in the house. They had a guest room, and she put her workshop in that room."

"No, she turned the bedroom into a factory."

"And she started fighting with her in-laws. She experimented on the old woman. She gave her something to try that made her almost die. When the man came home from work he asked his wife, 'Where is my mother?' She told him, 'I took her to the hospital.' He asked, 'Why, what's the matter?' He couldn't bear that any harm would come to his mother. When he went to see her she talked to him. She said, 'She was doing an experiment and I'm the one who drank the medicine.'"

They giggled as Kamla repeated, "The old woman almost died. He said, 'No, if she wants to kill my mother, I don't want her.'"

"He loved his mother," Sabra noted.

"And the fourth one, he brought her and then couldn't get any peace. She gave him a headache. She'd bring the onions and potatoes to peel. The man would be resting on the bed and she'd climb up next to him at night to peel potatoes. She'd say, 'Put down that newspaper and let's talk, me and you.'"

The girls found it hilarious to think of the woman peeling potatoes in bed. One of them explained, "She was a real peasant."

Kamla argued, "It's just lies. A peasant woman wouldn't do that."

Her neighbor was emphatic. "She was a peasant from Upper Egypt. They are like that."

Kamla will only go so far in her defense of Egyptians. She often criticized their neighbors, a poor family who had lived among Egyptians and had picked up different ways. As evidence of their immorality she disclosed that the men and women ate together. Another nearby household fared little better. They knew no modesty, she said: the son listened to cassettes in front of his father, and the young daughter-in-law neither covered her hair with a black headcloth nor avoided her father-in-law.

In her essay, and even more clearly in her commentary, Kamla underlined this distinction between Bedouin morality and Egyptian immorality. Still writing about the young Bedouin woman who had become educated, she said:

> *She doesn't forget her origins or her customs and traditions. She raises her children as well as the people of the city do.* (Now we're talking about what the Bedouin

woman does after she gets educated. Does she forget her duties as a mother? The difference between the Bedouins and the Egyptians is that when the Egyptian woman has a baby, she gives it to her mother to raise for her, and she takes it to day care. She doesn't do her duty to the child nor give it the required care. For example, she nurses only up to the fortieth day or at most for two months. And then she leaves it with her mother, her sister, or day care and goes out to work. But the Bedouin woman gives the child its due, even if she's educated and has an advanced degree. Not her mother, not anyone else—she herself does the work.

And she raises her child according to her customs. Let's say she's a Bedouin who marries an Egyptian or an educated Bedouin. She doesn't raise her child by the customs or traditions of the Egyptians. She raises her child with the customs and traditions of the Bedouin, except that she is slightly more informed. I mean, she tells her daughter, "This is shameful" and "That is right." Take an educated Bedouin girl like me, for example. If I were to marry an educated man and live the city life, I wouldn't let my daughter follow the ways of the Egyptians where a girl wears short dresses or goes out to clubs. No, of course that is wrong. We must be modest. It is wrong for us Bedouins, and we must respect our traditions. This is necessary. You wouldn't find an educated Bedouin woman allowing her daughter to do things that she could not do when she was with her family. Or maybe even if her parents permitted it, the girl herself would not do it. "No," she'd know, "that's wrong." Bedouin women are the ones who really know how to raise their daughters. They are better than Egyptians because the Egyptian woman won't hit her daughter. Very rarely do you find an Egyptian who can hit her daughter. But the Bedouin woman, if her daughter does something wrong, she must hit her. Even if she's not that young. She must hit her to teach her right and wrong. You don't learn right from wrong if you're not beaten. The Egyptians don't do it and their girls—well, you know . . .)

Poets have long reflected on the differences between Bedouins and their peasant neighbors. Only fragments are remembered, however, like the lines of a love story about a wealthy peasant and a beautiful Bedouin girl named Khawd. Drought had driven her family into his fields in search of pasture for their herds. He allowed them to stay and graze their animals when he saw Khawd. One day, though, his beloved announced that her family had decided to return to the desert; she asked him to migrate with them. In despair the young man answered:

> O Khawd, I have no camels that I might travel your distances
> I have nothing but buffalo and cows, who will find no pastures near you

Kamla's aunt Dhahab had once recited a short poem on a similar theme—it was her comment when I declined her polite suggestion that I marry her son so that I could come live with her. The song came, she said, from a story about a bull who fell in love with a camel and tried to follow her into the desert. She warned him that he would exhaust himself if he tried, since he had to eat and drink every day and she drank only every five days. He said that for her sake he'd drink only every other day, but she knew he couldn't keep up with her. She told him:

> You'll kill yourself bellowing
> O bull, if you try to follow . . .

Some women were tolerant of moral differences between themselves and Egyptians. I talked once about television with two poor women who had recently moved to the area from near the Libyan border. They said they found television entertaining to watch when they had no work to do. Their favorite shows, of course, were the Egyptian serialized dramas.

I was curious. "But the Egyptians on these programs are not like you, are they?"

One of them laughed. "The Egyptians are citified, not like the Bedouins, the poor things."

They explained that it didn't matter because they would never watch television with people they should respect and be modest in front of. Girls would never watch if their fathers were there; women would leave the room if their husbands had visitors.

"So you don't feel embarrassed by what you see on television?"

"No, if you're by yourself it doesn't matter," replied the older of the two.

"What if you see people in love?"

The younger of the two women laughed. "They're free to do that. We don't worry about them. The Egyptians have no modesty. They have no religion. They just do everything. It's their way."

The older one agreed. "Yes, let them do what they want. We just laugh at them."

Kamla and Sabra had a younger sister who loved television. She thought her father was wrong not to let them have a TV set. Although she conceded that foreign films were immoral, she argued that Egyptian films were different. Haj Sagr had taken away the television set when he heard that the girls were watching films in which people hugged and kissed each other. "He didn't want us watching. He said it was shameful." But these films and stories, she persisted, always showed the correct path in the end, even though they had people doing such things in early scenes. Egyptian films show how the girl who went off with a man later realized that he had tricked and used her. The importance of proper moral behavior always became clear ultimately.

Kamla's sister wondered anyway what her father could be thinking when he worried about his daughters' exposure to these things. Realistically she asked, "Where do we ever go? Nowhere but this house or the rest of the camp, where it's all family. Where does he think these things could happen?"

Kamla's father did fear the influence of Egyptians on the Bedouin community. In his opinion, the most serious problem the Bedouins faced was that of intermarriage between Bedouins and Egyptians. In the past, he maintained, no Arab, even the simplest shepherd, would give his daughter in marriage to "a peasant," as they used to call all Egyptians, even if the man were a company president. Things were more difficult now. Whereas before the area had been almost completely Bedouin, now, in regions like theirs that were close to large towns, Egyptians made up fifty percent of the population.

The trouble with the Egyptian presence, he went on, was that the Egyptian girls looked so pretty. They always dressed up, combed out their hair, and wore short dresses. A group of Bedouin elders had met recently to discuss what to do about these women who "walk around naked." Their concern was that the young men would find them attractive and want to marry them. And their fathers, wanting to make them happy, might agree. If the young men married Egyptian girls, there would no longer be any difference between Bedouin and Egyptian in the next generation. Sagr had warned the elders of this danger at the meeting. He admitted, though, that the process would be hard to stop now that the boys see these girls in school. Although he was afraid that Bedouin girls might pick up attitudes and habits from Egyptians—like having boyfriends, which the Egyptian girls don't think twice about—his real fear was intermarriage. That would bring about the end of tribal bonds.

Europeans

Sagr sensed the gradual shift in the boundaries of the moral community. Egyptians and Awlad 'Ali are being brought together by roads, newspapers, radio, television, schools, agricultural cooperatives, the army, and Parliament. With foreigners—Europeans—however, the divide remains absolute. Even Kamla, who sometimes pleaded with me, exasperated with her rambunctious little brothers and sisters, to take her away with me ("Put me in your suitcase and get me out of here!") and who proudly told me about several young Bedouin women with M.A.'s in veterinary medicine who had been sent, tattoos and all, to London for further training—even she did not approve of the Godless Europeans. Unlike Egyptian Christians, she argued, Europeans do not recognize God. "Every Muslim, even the most ignorant and uneducated, knows that there is a God and that He created all things." Worse, Europeans do not pray. When I contradicted her to say that many prayed in church, she challenged me. "What? What kind of person prays with his shoes on? May God protect us!"

The Westerner's lack of faith in God provides powerful imagery for inhumanity. Kamla's uncle's wife once lamented her lost brother with a poem that exploited this view:

The European, with all his lack of faith,
wept when I told him of my condition . . .

To show the magnitude of their compassion for girls, women sang a wedding rhyme that also mentioned Europeans:

God protect every girl
even the Christian woman's daughter

Kamla has not seen the new tourists who visit the Western Desert, but she has heard about them. In 1986 a favorite commercial cassette was the song called "The Japanese Woman" by the young Bedouin star Si'daawy al-Git'aany. The singer, identifying himself by tribe, says he lost his heart to a foreigner. (Although he calls her Japanese, the details of his song suggest a melding of many nationalities.)

Spanning many verses, the tale begins with his first sight of the woman. She had come to Egypt to relax, he sings, and in the gardens of a summer resort hotel in Marsa Matruh she was swinging on a swing. Her father, sitting on a chair ("like a boss") was grotesque and frightening: a European Christian with a long beard eating platefuls of pork and drinking quantities of beer. "We are Bedouins who like the desert," the singer goes on, "and they are Europeans. Fate brought us together." In her company he forgot his cares, and although they were accustomed to different ways, she made him lose interest in Bedouin women, who only cared about tying up goats and waiting for the sheep to come home in the evening.

She wore a cross and made him sit on chairs. Oh, he knew their ways were different, but he went astray, unable to stop himself from falling in love with a Christian. As she sat under an umbrella they talked. He had been to school and knew her language. She asked him to come home with her, but he first wanted to show her his home and the desert snail shells. Then she telephoned the governor and got permission for him to travel with her. So there he found himself, walking behind her, carrying her suitcases to board an airplane. Like a bird it took off, and he was scared. Everything is by God's will—that a man from the desert should end up with a Japanese woman.

Contrasting her country with his, he finds that the sea is to the south instead of the north. Her country is famous for its buses and trucks, he sings, whereas our women know only how to spin and to churn butter in goatskin bags. The moral contrasts are harsher. There, women's hair is uncovered and men wear straw baskets on their heads instead of skull caps. Women go wherever they wish and everyone says hello to them.

Accompanying his lover to a nightclub, he found people dancing like birds as someone howled while playing the piano. People got drunk and started fighting and throwing things around. His story would make a good soap opera, he sings. Things were different once they got to her country and she lost interest in him. The song ends with a refrain about the treachery of women, an ending that always got a rise out of Kamla and her sisters. "He got what he deserved," they insisted. "Who told him to go chasing after the foreigner, carrying her suitcases?"

Piety

Kamla reflected, in her essay, on what aspects of Bedouin life she would like to see preserved. Her father would have been proud of the list of positive features she drew up.

> *We all know that everything in life has its good qualities and its bad.* (Weren't you asking what was good about the Bedouins and what wasn't?) *The virtues of the Bedouins are:*
>
> 1. *Their piety and their total adherence to the traditions of the Prophet, despite their lack of education.* (This is the thing I hope will continue until Judgment Day. This is the best thing—that they are religious. Even though ninety percent of them aren't educated, they are pious. Long clothing, respect, and modesty. The woman is as pious as the man. No woman can talk with a man she doesn't know or have him visit her at home. And she doesn't show her face or talk with any older man. This is what I hope Bedouin women and girls will never abandon.)
> 2. *Their total respectfulness. The old respect the young, and the young respect the old, whether they are strangers or kin.*
> 3. *Their generosity.* (It's true. You won't find anything on this earth like the generosity of the Bedouins. Even someone they don't know—they must invite him to the house and bring him food. Maybe no one else has this quality. I hope the Bedouins will hold on to this.)
> 4. *Hospitality and respect for the guest.*
> 5. *The ties of kinship that link various parts of the family and the cooperation of relatives in all situations.* (The other thing I want them to hold onto is this mutual assistance—they help each other in all circumstances. For example, even someone from a family that is related distantly to another must help a person from that family. Even among the women. When a Bedouin woman sets up a loom, for instance, her neighbors come to help her. Others always come to help. I wish the whole world—never mind just families—the whole world would help each other and that Muslims would cooperate the way our religion tells us to. Ninety-nine percent of Bedouin women haven't been educated. But they are pious. They're ignorant and illiterate, but they dress the right way, they fear God, and they pray. Sometimes they don't even know how to pray properly, but they pray anyhow. They are totally respectable, and they follow the traditions of the Prophet. They say the Prophet used to do

this, the Prophet used to do that. They learn it from their husbands or
their educated sons.)

Interestingly, Kamla had little to say about any of the traditional virtues
except the first, piety. Although she was vehement in asserting their importance, perhaps she could not afford to think through their implications. She
was proud of her father's generosity and hospitality, for instance, but it was
also a source of tension, since the burden of feeding his many guests fell on
the overworked women of the household. And if she were to think about
how the extensive bonds between kin are to be maintained, she would have
to admit the virtues of marriages to paternal cousins, the kind of marriage
she wanted desperately to avoid.

Piety was a different matter. Like many, Kamla was becoming defensive
in the face of new pressure from those sympathetic to Islamic activists in
Egypt. She was correct to point out how tied up with their faith her kin
were. They reckoned the months by the Islamic lunar calendar, the years by
the annual religious feasts, age by the number of years a person has fasted
the month of Ramadan, and the hours of the day by the five times for prayer.
All the older women and many of the younger ones prayed regularly. Doing
without the accoutrements of city people, women simply prayed where they
were, facing southeast and laying a small kerchief on the ground before
them. The men like Kamla's father tended to know more. They would have
learned as children to recite the Qur'an, and they continued to learn from
the lectures at the mosque every Friday.

Their reactions to the sanctimonious Egyptians—and now to some
Bedouins from the cities, who were becoming, as they put it, "followers of the
model," meaning the life of the Prophet—have been mixed. The older women
are not cowed. They argue, as Kamla did, that they have always worn modest
clothing and covered their hair with a headcloth. They resent being told that
some of the ways they have demonstrated their devoutness are wrong.

Kamla is more unsure. Sometimes she defends these Muslim Sisters and
Brothers and sometimes she goes along with the old Bedouin women as
they make fun of them. One evening, having recited some poetry and told
some traditional tales for my benefit, Kamla's aunt Dhahab turned to her
niece and asked, "Hey Kamla, have you given Lila any songs?"

Kamla was coy. "I'm not a song person. I'm just a simple person minding my own business. I'm with God. I'm pious and know my Lord."

Her sister hooted, perhaps thinking of Kamla's love of the radio and
scandalous movie magazines. But Kamla went on, only half joking, "Auntie,
I've become pious. I don't have anything to do with songs."

Her aunt mocked her. "What's this? You've become pious?" Everyone
laughed as the old aunt continued, "God's blessings! God's blessings! So,
you're joining the 'Beard Family'?"

There was a commotion, with everyone talking at once about the topic that was so often in the air these days: the Islamists. Kamla spoke on their behalf. "They say, 'We are religious people, . . . following God's path, the path to heaven.'"

Her aunt was hardly convinced. "I swear to God, they've never seen heaven. God is the only judge. God is present."

Sabra thought they should be more respectful. But she admitted, "May God protect them, they do some things that aren't necessary. Do you know what our aunt who lives out west says? She says they say that the sugar dolls are wrong, even the food we make to celebrate the Prophet's birthday. Rotten life! The special food for the birthday that the whole world celebrates—they say it is forbidden!"

Her aunt concurred. "Have you ever heard of such a thing!"

Some women were even more irreverent. Once when an old friend from the nearby town was visiting, the evening conversation turned to the topic of these new religious types. She complained that they had forbidden celebrations of saints' birthdays, including the candy and meat eaten at them. They had said it was wrong to call any holyman "Saint So-and-so." She said, "They have forbidden everything. Why, the next thing you know they'll forbid the clothes we wear and make us go around naked."

She then described to the group gathered around her how these people dressed. She told them about the wife of a Muslim Brother called Mr. Muhammad who had moved to her town. The woman was offering lessons on religion every Tuesday afternoon for any woman who wished to learn. She wore a veil that covered her head and her face, "except for her eyes"; she wore gloves, a dress down to the ground, and shoes. As the old woman put it, "She looks like a ghost."

Kamla showed off her knowledge of religion. "It is wrong for a woman to veil her face. What is required is that your head be covered; it is fine to expose your hands, your feet, and your face."

The old woman then commented on the men. "They all run around with those beards. Why, Doctor Ahmed's sticks out like this! It looks like pubic hair."

Kamla had to raise her voice to be heard over the wild laughter. "But Auntie, the beard is a tradition of the Prophet."

Kamla's cousin Salih had tried briefly to grow a beard, but the teasing had been merciless. No matter how many times Kamla told them it was the tradition of the Prophet, Gateefa and his other aunts accused him of looking like a Coptic priest. He finally shaved it off.

Kamla had confided to me that she would have liked to replace her kerchief with the new Islamic headcovering but she was afraid her family would object. A photograph of her with her school friends revealed that she was the only one among them not wearing the new modest dress. Yet Kamla criticized some of her classmates who wore this type of clothing but added flowers and multicolored headbands to their veils. She said their religion teacher had given them a real talking to and had confiscated their flowers and headbands saying, "If you want to take on the veil, do it seriously." Kamla said she would adopt this kind of headcovering "if God opens the way for me and I get to marry someone educated."

A New Order

The final part of Kamla's essay was to have been about what she hoped would change in her community. All she had written, though, was this:

As for the bad things, I will talk about them.

She read this final sentence and looked at me. "What are the wrongs I wish the Bedouins would finish with? I've already discussed these. First, their ideas about girls. They are totally meaningless and wrong. I wish they would give her the opportunity to get educated. They see her as a worthless being. You know this, Lila. . . . This is what I hope the Bedouins will leave behind. They should see that a girl is a person, a noble person created just as God created men. She has feelings, sensitivities, and desires.

"Another thing I wish is that they wouldn't let their customs and traditions rule them to such an extent that they believe that the customs of the city people are wrong and theirs right. Whenever they see that a person is educated, they say he's wrong, we're right. I wish they would respect the educated. I wish they would preserve their customs and traditions but be a bit more advanced. A girl who goes to school doesn't forget her customs and traditions, no matter how educated she becomes. Even if she goes to Europe or America, the Bedouin girl will preserve her customs and traditions. They should give her more freedom.

"Another thing I wish is that they would get more organized. I wish they would put a little order in their lives. Among Bedouins, order is completely lacking. In every area of their lives—in terms of food, in having too many children, in the way they raise the children—there's no order. And in the house—anything goes!"

I was curious about what Kamla meant by "order." She gave examples from close to home. "Say you've got two brothers living in one house. If they organized their lives, they'd put each one in his own house. And the business of marrying more than one wife—I wish they'd change their views on this. It is the biggest sin. The Prophet—it is not forbidden, but the Prophet said only if you can treat them fairly. But a man can't, it can't be done. Even if he has money, he can't. As a person, in his thoughts and his actions, he can't be fair. He'll like one more than another.

"The generation that's coming now, after my father's and mother's, they wouldn't think of it or do it. Why? So they won't have a house with thirty or forty people living in it. A household with two women in it will have thirty or forty people in it. Their lives will be lousy. They won't have good food, good clothes, or good childrearing. They won't be clean. A woman alone in her own house can handle her children. When there are two women, one will say, 'Why should I hit my children when that one doesn't hit hers?' They watch each other. When one does something, the other is looking. If one cleans and washes and the other doesn't, she says, 'Why should I do this when she doesn't?' If she is alone, a woman won't be able to say that. Who's going to do it for her? She'll do it herself and she'll know what's what. When she's alone she doesn't have to depend on anyone. And even her daughter will turn out well, like her mother. The other way they're always getting into fights over any little thing. Even without my saying this, you know it, Lila. This is what I wish would change.

"Bedouins think that as long as they have a house and can eat, drink, and be clothed, that's enough. That's life. And they marry and have kids and marry again. But a man should live a more ordered and relaxed life. Should a man come home at the end of his day tired from working and find it filthy and the kids and women fighting? He comes wanting to relax, and finds this? This is what makes someone say, 'No, there should be order.'"

For years I had heard Kamla's call for order. Living in a household of twenty or more, half of whom are under ten years old, can be chaotic. Fed up, Kamla would sometimes say, "This isn't a house, it's a breeding station!" She and Sabra often teased their mother, calling her Shalabiyya, the name of a character they had seen in a family planning advertisement on television. Shalabiyya was a woman with too many children: in her lap, on her shoulders, on her head. When she tried to draw water or milk the cow, they climbed all over her and trailed behind her. Gateefa would apologize, "We can't change the way we are."

When Kamla was young, she would come home from school announcing that she was going to marry an Egyptian doctor and have only one child. Other times she'd say she was going to have only two children, both daughters. She was going to live alone in a house with her husband, just them, no relatives. Bedouin men, she would say, make women work hard and don't pay attention to them. Even if the woman is ill, the man won't lift a finger to help, not even to pick up a crying baby. Egyptian men help their wives, respect them, and treat them well. When Kamla's younger sister, echoing their father, accused Egyptians of being stingy and not offering food to their guests, Kamla defended them to support her favorite theme. She argued that they just did things in an organized manner; they had special meal times, unlike the Bedouins who brought out food whenever anyone stopped by.

Perhaps because tensions between her father's wives had recently intensified, Kamla was impassioned in her final commentary. "Even without becoming educated, the Bedouins could organize their lives. It is enough to marry just one. Or if a man wants to marry more than one, he should put each wife in her own house. They won't fight then. But if the two are together, you'll always find this one saying, 'That one did and said' and that one saying, 'This one said this and did that.' Even if they are friends, the people outside the household won't let them be. Someone will come and say, 'That one said this' and 'This one said that.' Women are famous for this kind of talk.

"Yes, Bedouin women are famous for their talk. The Prophet said, 'Women—if not for their tongues, women would go to heaven.' They asked him, 'Why should a woman go to heaven?' He said, 'Because she gives milk.' Praise be to God, milk flows from her. And beyond that, she works harder than a man. She's weaker—that's right, she's weak compared to the man, whom nothing bothers—but she has to work more. She has children and cares for them. They asked the Prophet, 'So what is it that keeps her from entering heaven?' He said, 'It is because of her tongue.' In a second she'll turn things around. She'll gossip about everyone. Women talk about people more than men do."

Kamla is critical of the older women in her community. She confessed, too, that she belonged to two worlds. With her sisters and cousins she talked about the things they knew, not letting on that she was different. But there were so many things she could talk to her school friends about that she could not talk about with the girls in her family—things like politics. Sometimes she seemed to accept her double life with equanimity. When I saw her spinning with her aunt one day, I asked, "Hey Kamla, so you know how to spin too?" She had laughed. "Yes, I can go either way. If it turns out I'm to be citified, I'll do that. And if it turns out I'll be a Bedouin, I'll know how."

When I suggested that she might be lonely if she moved into a house of her own, she was adamant: "No, I won't miss them at all." Yet this is someone who is fiercely proud of her father for being an important man who is also generous and pious. Despite occasional confrontations, she spends, like her sisters, nearly every evening sitting close to her mother and talking. Even her brood of little siblings only sometimes drives her really crazy. The youngest she can rarely resist grabbing to hug. Delighted by this two-year-old's every new accomplishment, she whispers new words in her ear and kisses her when she repeats them.

Most of the time, though, she says she wants to get out. I worry about Kamla's blithe confidence that life in the city will be so much better. I disagree with her assessment of Bedouin women's lives. I argue with Kamla that she deliberately ignores the richness of their relationships and the way they have always struggled back (and were expected to). Her own life is evidence. There was not a single woman in the camp who had not admired her for being a willful little girl. Even her father had been amused by her opinions and determination. As she had grown up, her strength of purpose had enabled her to withstand the social pressure against her going to school. The independence she displayed reminded me of her grandmother Migdim, with her stories of resistance to marriage and her struggles to have her way with her sons. It even reminded me of her mother, Gateefa, who had earned the respect of her husband.

Yet when her letter arrived I was happy for her—happy that it was her fate not to have to marry her cousin after all and glad that her father had been willing to take her wishes into consideration. Armed with romantic visions inspired by Egyptian radio melodramas, cloying love songs, and her tattered collection of hokey postcards showing blonde brides and grooms looking deeply into each other's eyes, she will go off to live with her Egyptianized, educated husband in a small and ordered household. She will never work outside the home. She will rarely even leave her apartment. She expects to clean house, cook meals, and serve her husband. If God brings children, she'll take care of them and raise them well.

Because she has none of his sister Aisha's feminine refinement, I was worried. What would her husband think when he first saw this sturdy young woman with her wide feet and callused hands? Because she is the daughter of a wealthy tribal leader, the fabric of her dresses would be expensive and she would bring many with her; but they would have been tailored by local seamstresses, whose renditions of city clothes are always awkward. And would she know how to dress for the wedding night, this girl who had to fight her mother's horrified accusations of immodesty when she wore a home-made bra? Would Engineer Ibrahim Saleem find charming her outspoken ways?

I wrote back to wish her all happiness and to apologize for not being able to attend the wedding. An older sister would sing at the henna party on the eve of the wedding, so I looked through my collection of Bedouin wedding songs to see if any seemed right. I ended my letter with three that I hoped would mean something to her. The first let her know how much I thought of her family:

> Her father has a good name
> and those who have come to marry will find happiness . . .

The second reminded her that I knew how much she wanted this:

> Her morning is blessed
> she got what she desired and was honored . . .

And the third expressed my best wishes for this young woman, vulnerable and beautiful as are all young brides heading off into the unknown:

> Neighbors, come say farewell
> a gazelle from our land is about to journey . . .   ∎

■ *QUESTIONS FOR MAKING CONNECTIONS WITHIN THE READING* ■

1. One of the challenges that readers of Abu-Lughod's "Honor and Shame" must tackle is keeping track of the relationships between all of the people mentioned in the essay. Who is Kamla? What is her relationship to Abu-Lughod, Gateefa, Haj Sagr, Migdim, Salih, Aisha, Sabra, and Dhahab? Draw a chart that shows the relationships between all of the central figures in "Honor and Shame."

2. Who are the Bedouin? What is their relationship to Egypt? To Islam? What does it mean, within the context of Abu-Lughod's "Honor and Shame," to be "Egyptianized"?

3. "Honor and Shame" ends with a confession: Kamla acknowledges that she has "belonged to two worlds" and that she lives a "double life." What are the two worlds that she inhabits? Which world does she wish to live in? Which world does Abu-Lughod want her to live in?

■ *QUESTIONS FOR WRITING* ■

1. At one point in her discussion of her essay on the education of Bedouin girls, Kamla stops midsentence and says, "Boy, if my father heard this!" This is one of many private moments that Abu-Lughod records and repeats for the readers of "Honor and Shame" to consider. What is gained by recording such moments? What is lost? Does the study of another culture require such violations of privacy?

2. In a sense, "Honor and Shame" is an essay about student writing: Kamla reads aloud and comments on an essay that she has written for school; Abu-Lughod listens, responds to, and comments on what Kamla has written and then provides additional background to illustrate, extend, and complicate the assertions Kamla has made. Is Abu-Lughod studying Kamla? Is she teaching her? Who benefits from the work Abu-Lughod has done with Kamla's essay?

■ *QUESTIONS FOR MAKING CONNECTIONS BETWEEN READINGS* ■

1. *"As for the bad things, I will talk about them."* In Abu-Lughod's "Honor and Shame," Kamla records her thoughts about how life has changed for Bedouin girls over the past forty years. How would James C. Scott interpret the stories that Kamla has told? How many different transcripts are present in "Honor and Shame"? Who is best positioned to read and interpret these transcripts?

2. Abu-Lughod confides, "I worry about Kamla's blithe confidence that life in the city will be so much better." Is Kamla's vision of city life a case of "miswanting" as Gilbert and Loewenstein define the term in Jon Gertner's "The Futile Pursuit of Happiness"? If so, where does the miswanting originate: Does it start with Kamla? With Kamla's parents? With Abu-Lughod? Does Gilbert and Loewenstein's research suggest that Kamla should do anything differently? Does this research suggest that it doesn't matter what anyone does, because happiness will always be elusive? Write an essay in which you explore the usefulness of Gilbert and Loewenstein's work for a better understanding of the Bedouin.

www   **For additional suggestions about making connections between readings, visit the Link-O-Mat and More Sample Assignments at <www.newhum.com>.**

KAREN ARMSTRONG

IN 1981, KAREN ARMSTRONG published *Through the Narrow Gate*, a controversial account of her experiences as a Sister of the Society of the Holy Child Jesus, a Roman Catholic order. Armstrong had left the convent and the Church in 1972, "wearied by religion" and "worn out by years of struggle" and then spent the intervening years pursuing a doctorate in literature and teaching at a girls' school. Although she was gratified by the success of her book, Armstrong has described the real turning point in her life as having occurred during a series of trips she made to Jerusalem beginning in 1982. Shocked both by the Israeli invasion of Lebanon and by the Palestinian intifada, Armstrong found herself questioning just how much Westerners—herself, included—knew or understood about the living conditions and the beliefs of Muslims living in the Middle East.

After realizing that Westerners "were posing as a tolerant and compassionate society and yet passing judgments from a position of extreme ignorance and irrationality," Armstrong committed herself to combating cross-cultural misperceptions and religious misunderstandings. She has written a number of books that explore relations between Judaism, Christianity, and Islam, including *Holy War: The Crusades and Their Impact on Today's World* (1991); *Mohammed: A Biography of the Prophet* (1992); and *Islam: A Short History* (2000). She has also written, more recently, a biography, *Buddha* (2001), and *The Battle for God* (2000), a study of the rise of fundamentalism.

The selection that follows comes from *A History of God: The 4,000-Year Quest of Judaism, Christianity and Islam*, where Armstrong sets out to catalog ways that Jews, Christians, and Muslims have named and understood the experience of the divine. While working on this book, Armstrong has said that she came to understand the difference between religion per se and neurological conditions that skeptics believe are at the root of mystical visions and insights: "the difference is

Armstrong, Karen. "Does God Have a Future?" *A History of God: The 4,000-Year Quest of Judaism, Christianity and Islam*. New York: Knopf, 1993. 377–399.

Biographical information and opening and closing quotations drawn from the Random House Web site <http://www.randomhouse.com/modernlibrary/karmstrong.html>. Middle quotation drawn from M. M. Ali's profile of Karen Armstrong in the *Washington Report on Middle East Affairs*, Feb. 1993, p. 38. <http://www.washington-report.org/backissues/0293/9302038.htm>.

compassion," Armstrong notes, "which in religion is ethically based." By asking, "Does God have a future?" Armstrong bids her readers to consider what roles organized religion and personal experiences of the divine will have in the years to come.

www   **To learn more about Karen Armstrong and the role of religion in contemporary society, visit the Link-O-Mat at <www.newhum.com>.**

■ ■

Does God Have a Future?

As we approach the end of the second millennium, it seems likely that the world we know is passing away. For decades we have lived with the knowledge that we have created weapons that could wipe out human life on the planet. The Cold War may have ended, but the new world order seems no less frightening than the old. We are facing the possibility of ecological disaster. The AIDS virus threatens to bring a plague of unmanageable proportions. Within two or three generations, the population will become too great for the planet to support. Thousands are dying of famine and drought. Generations before our own have felt that the end of the world is nigh, yet it does seem that we are facing a future that is unimaginable. How will the idea of God survive in the years to come? For 4000 years it has constantly adapted to meet the demands of the present, but in our own century, more and more people have found that it no longer works for them, and when religious ideas cease to be effective they fade away. Maybe God really is an idea of the past. The American scholar Peter Berger notes that we often have a double standard when we compare the past with our own time. Where the past is analyzed and made relative, the present is rendered immune to this process and our current position becomes an absolute: thus "the New Testament writers are seen as afflicted with a false consciousness rooted in *their* time, but the analyst takes the consciousness of *his* time as an unmixed intellectual blessing."[1] Secularists of the nineteenth and early twentieth centuries saw atheism as the irreversible condition of humanity in the scientific age.

There is much to support this view. In Europe, the churches are emptying; atheism is no longer the painfully acquired ideology of a few intellectual pioneers but a prevailing mood. In the past it was always produced by a particular idea of God, but now it seems to have lost its inbuilt relationship to theism and become an automatic response to the experience of living in a secularized society. Like the crowd of amused people surrounding Nietzsche's madman, many are unmoved by the prospect of life without God. Others find his absence a positive relief. Those of us who have had a difficult time with religion in the past find it liberating to be rid of the God who terrorized our childhood. It is wonderful not to have to cower before a vengeful deity, who threatens us with eternal damnation if we do not abide by his rules. We have a new intellectual freedom and can boldly follow up our own ideas without pussyfooting around difficult articles of faith, feeling all the while a sinking loss of integrity. We imagine that the hideous deity we have experienced is the authentic God of Jews, Christians and Muslims and do not always realize that it is merely an unfortunate aberration.

There is also desolation. Jean-Paul Sartre (1905–80) spoke of the God-shaped hole in the human consciousness, where God had always been. Nevertheless, he insisted that even if God existed, it was still necessary to reject him, since the idea of God negates our freedom. Traditional religion tells us that we must conform to God's idea of humanity to become fully human. Instead, we must see human beings as liberty incarnate. Sartre's atheism was not a consoling creed, but other existentialists saw the absence of God as a positive liberation. Maurice Merleau-Ponty (1908–61) argued that instead of increasing our sense of wonder, God actually negates it. Because God represents absolute perfection, there is nothing left for us to do or achieve. Albert Camus (1913–60) preached a heroic atheism. People should reject God defiantly in order to pour out all their loving solicitude upon mankind. As always, the atheists have a point. God had indeed been used in the past to stunt creativity; if he is made a blanket answer to every possible problem and contingency, he can indeed stifle our sense of wonder or achievement. A passionate and committed atheism can be more religious than a weary or inadequate theism.

During the 1950s, Logical Positivists such as A. J. Ayer (1910–91) asked whether it made sense to believe in God. The natural sciences provided the only reliable source of knowledge because it could be tested empirically. Ayer was not asking whether or not God existed but whether the idea of God had any meaning. He argued that a statement is meaningless if we cannot see how it can be verified or shown to be false. To say "There is intelligent life on Mars" is not meaningless since we can see how we could verify this once we had the necessary technology. Similarly a simple believer in traditional Old Man in the Sky is not making a meaningless statement when he says: "I believe in God," since after death we should be able to find out whether or not this is true. It is the more sophisticated believer who has problems, when he says: "God does not exist in any sense that we can understand" or "God is not good in the human sense of the word." These statements are too vague; it is impossible to see how they can be tested; therefore, they are meaningless. As Ayer said: "Theism is so confused and the sentences in which 'God' appears so incoherent and incapable of verifiability or falsifiability that to speak of belief or unbelief, faith or unfaith, is logically impossible."[2] Atheism is as unintelligible and meaningless as theism. There is nothing in the concept of "God" to deny or be skeptical about.

Like Freud, the Positivists believed that religious belief represented an immaturity which science would overcome. Since the 1950s, linguistic philosophers have criticized Logical Positivism, pointing out that what Ayer called the Verification Principle could not itself be verified. Today we are less likely to be as optimistic about science, which can only explain the world of physical nature. Wilfred Cantwell Smith pointed out that the Logical Positivists set themselves up as scientists during a period when, for the first time in history, science saw the natural world in explicit disjunction from humanity.[3] The kind of statements to which Ayer referred work very well for the objective facts of science but are not suitable for less clear-cut human experiences. Like poetry or music, religion is not amenable to this kind of discourse and verification. More recently linguistic philosophers such as Antony Flew have argued that it is more rational to find a natural explanation than a religious one. The old "proofs" do not work: the argument from design falls down because we would need to get outside the system to see whether natural phenomena are motivated by their own laws or by Something outside. The argument that we are "contingent" or "defective" beings proves nothing, since there could always be an explanation that is ultimate but not supernatural. Flew is less of an optimist than Feuerbach, Marx or the Existentialists. There is no agonizing, no heroic defiance but simply a matter-of-fact commitment to reason and science as the only way forward.

[. . .] However, [. . .] not all religious people have looked to "God" to provide them with an explanation for the universe. Many have seen the proofs as a red herring. Science has been felt to be threatening only by those Western Christians who got into the habit of reading the scriptures literally and interpreting doctrines as though they were matters of objective fact. Scientists and philosophers who find no room for God in their systems are usually referring to the idea of God as First Cause, a notion eventually abandoned by Jews, Muslims and Greek Orthodox Christians during the Middle Ages. The more subjective "God" that they were looking for could not be proved as though it were an objective fact that was the same for everybody. It could not be located within a physical system of the universe, any more than the Buddhist nirvana.

More dramatic than the linguistic philosophers were the radical theologians of the 1960s who enthusiastically followed Nietzsche and proclaimed the death of God. In *The Gospel of Christian Atheism* (1966), Thomas J. Altizer claimed that the "good news" of God's death had freed us from slavery to a tyrannical transcendent deity: "Only by accepting and even willing the death of God in our experience can we be liberated from a transcendent beyond, an alien beyond which has been emptied and darkened by God's self-alienation in Christ."[4] Altizer spoke in mystical terms of the dark night of the soul and the pain of abandonment. The death of God represented the silence that was necessary before God could become meaningful again. All our old conceptions of divinity had to die before theology could be reborn. We were waiting for a language and a style in which God could once more become a possibility. Altizer's theology was a passionate dialectic which attacked the dark God-less world in the hope that it would give up its secret. Paul Van Buren was more precise and logical. In *The Secular Meaning of the Gospel* (1963), he claimed that it was no longer possible to speak of God acting in the world. Science and technology had made the old mythology invalid. Simple faith in the Old Man in the Sky was clearly impossible, but so was the more sophisticated belief of the theologians. We must do without God and hold on to Jesus of Nazareth. The Gospel was "the good news of a free man who has set other men free." Jesus of Nazareth was the liberator, "the man who defines what it means to be a man."[5]

In *Radical Theology and the Death of God* (1966), William Hamilton noted that this kind of theology had its roots in the United States, which had always had a utopian bent and had no great theological tradition of its own. The imagery of the death of God represented the anomie and barbarism of the technical age, which made it impossible to believe in the biblical God in the old way. Hamilton himself saw this theological mood as a way of being Protestant in the twentieth century. Luther had left his cloister and gone out into the world. In the same way, he and the other Christian radicals were avowedly secular men. They had walked away from the sacred place where God used to be to find the man Jesus in their neighbor out in the world of technology, power, sex, money and the city. Modern secular man did not need God. There was no God-shaped hole within Hamilton: he would find his own solution in the world.

There is something rather poignant about this buoyant sixties optimism. Certainly, the radicals were right that the old ways of speaking about God had become impossible for many people, but in the 1990s it is sadly difficult to feel that liberation and a new dawn are at hand. Even at the time, the Death of God theologians were criticized, since their perspective was that of the affluent, middle-class, white American. Black theologians such as James H. Cone asked how white people felt they had the right to affirm freedom through the death of God when they had actually enslaved people in God's name. The Jewish theologian Richard Rubenstein found it impossible to understand how they could feel so positive about God-less humanity so soon after the Nazi Holocaust. He himself was convinced that the deity conceived as a God of History had died forever in Auschwitz. Yet Rubenstein did not feel that Jews could jettison religion. After the near-extinction of European Jewry, they must not cut themselves off from their past. The nice, moral God of liberal Judaism was no good, however. It was too antiseptic; it ignored the tragedy of life and assumed that the world would improve. Rubenstein himself preferred the God of the Jewish mystics. He was moved by Isaac Luria's doctrine of *tsimtsum*, God's voluntary act of self-estrangement which brought the created world into being. All mystics had seen God as a Nothingness from which we came and to which we will return. Rubenstein agreed with Sartre that life is empty; he saw the God of the mystics as an imaginative way of entering this human experience of nothingness.[6]

Other Jewish theologians have also found comfort in Lurianic Kabbalah. Hans Jonas believes that after Auschwitz we can no longer believe in the omnipotence of God. When God created the world, he voluntarily limited himself and shared the weakness of human beings. He could do no more now, and human beings must restore wholeness to the Godhead and the world by prayer and Torah. The British theologian Louis Jacobs, however, dislikes this idea, finding the image of *tsimtsum* coarse and anthropomorphic: it encourages us to ask *how* God created the world in too literal a manner. God does not limit himself, holding his breath, as it were, before exhaling. An impotent God is useless and cannot be the meaning of human existence. It is better to return to the classic explanation that God is greater than human beings and his thought and ways are not ours. God may be incomprehensible, but people have the option of trusting this ineffable God and affirming *a* meaning, even in the midst of meaninglessness. The Roman Catholic theologian Hans Kung agrees with Jacobs, preferring a more reasonable explanation for tragedy than the fanciful myth of *tsimtsum*. He notes that human beings cannot have faith in a weak God but in the living God who made people strong enough to pray in Auschwitz.

Some people still find it possible to find meaning in the idea of God. The Swiss theologian Karl Barth (1886–1968) set his face against the Liberal Protestantism of Schleiermacher, with its emphasis on religious experience. But he was also a leading opponent of natural theology. It was, he thought, a radical error to seek to explain God in rational terms not simply because of the limitations of the human mind but also because humanity has been corrupted by the Fall. Any natural idea we form about God is bound to be flawed, therefore, and to worship such a God was idolatry. The only valid source of God-knowledge was the Bible. This seems to have the worst of all worlds: experience is out; natural reason is out; the human mind is corrupt and untrustworthy; and there is no possibility of learning from other faiths, since the Bible is the only valid revelation. It seems unhealthy to combine such radical skepticism in the powers of the intellect with such an uncritical acceptance of the truths of scripture.

Paul Tillich (1868–1965) was convinced that the personal God of traditional Western theism must go, but he also believed that religion was necessary for humankind. A deep-rooted anxiety is part of the human condition: this is not neurotic, because it is ineradicable and no therapy can take it away. We constantly fear loss and the terror of extinction, as we watch our bodies gradually but inexorably decay. Tillich agreed with Nietzsche that the personal God was a harmful idea and deserved to die:

> The concept of a "Personal God" interfering with natural events, or being "an independent cause of natural events," makes God a natural object beside others, an object among others, a being among beings, maybe the highest, but nevertheless *a* being. This indeed is not only the destruction of the physical system but even more the destruction of any meaningful idea of God.[7]

A God who kept tinkering with the universe was absurd; a God who inter-fered with human freedom and creativity was a tyrant. If God is seen as a self in a world of his own, an ego that relates to a thou, a cause separate from its effect, "he" becomes *a* being, not Being itself. An omnipotent, all-knowing tyrant is not so different from earthly dictators who made every-thing and everybody mere cogs in the machine which they controlled. An atheism that rejects such a God is amply justified.

Instead we should seek to find a "God" above this personal God. There is nothing new about this. Ever since biblical times, theists had been aware of the paradoxical nature of the God to which they prayed, aware that the personalized God was balanced by the essentially transpersonal divinity. Each prayer was a contradiction, since it attempted to speak to somebody to whom speech was impossible; it asked favors of somebody who had either bestowed them or not before he was asked; it said "thou" to a God who, as Being itself, was nearer to the "I" than our own ego. Tillich preferred the def-inition of God as the Ground of being. Participation in such a God above "God" does not alienate us from the world but immerses us in reality. It re-turns us to ourselves. Human beings have to use symbols when they talk about Being-itself: to speak literally or realistically about it is inaccurate and untrue. For centuries the symbols "God," "providence" and "immortality" have enabled people to bear the terror of life and the horror of death, but when these symbols lose their power there is fear and doubt. People who ex-perience this dread and anxiety should seek the God above the discredited "God" of a theism which has lost its symbolic force.

When Tillich was speaking to laypeople, he preferred to replace the rather technical term "Ground of being" with "ultimate concern." He em-phasized that the human experience of faith in this "God above God" was not a peculiar state distinguishable from others in our emotional or intellec-tual experience. You could not say: "I am now having a special 'religious' ex-perience," since the God which is Being precedes and is fundamental to all our emotions of courage, hope and despair. It was not a distinct state with a name of its own but pervaded each one of our normal human experiences. A century earlier Feuerbach had made a similar claim when he had said that God was inseparable from normal human psychology. Now this atheism had been transformed into a new theism.

Liberal theologians were trying to discover whether it was possible to be-lieve and to belong to the modern intellectual world. In forming their new conception of God, they turned to other disciplines: science, psychology, so-ciology and other religions. Again, there was nothing new in this attempt. Origen and Clement of Alexandria had been Liberal Christians in this sense in the third century when they had introduced Platonism into the Semitic re-ligion of Yahweh. Now the Jesuit Pierre Teilhard de Chardin (1881–1955) combined his belief in God with modern science. He was a paleontologist with a special interest in prehistoric life and drew upon his understanding of evolution to write a new theology. He saw the whole evolutionary struggle as a divine force which propelled the universe from matter to spirit to personality and, finally, beyond personality to God. God was immanent and incarnate in the world, which had become a sacrament of his presence. De Chardin suggested that instead of concentrating on Jesus the man, Christians should cultivate the cosmic portrait of Christ in Paul's epistles to the Colossians and Ephesians: Christ in this view was the "omega point" of the universe, the climax of the evolutionary process when God becomes all in all. Scripture tells us that God is love, and science shows that the natural world progresses towards ever-greater complexity *and* to greater unity in this variety. This unity-in-differentiation was another way of regarding the love that animates the whole of creation. De Chardin has been criticized for identifying God so thoroughly with the world that all sense of his transcendence was lost, but his this-worldly theology was a welcome change from the *contemptus mundi* which had so often characterized Catholic spirituality.

In the United States during the 1960s, Daniel Day Williams (b. 1910) evolved what is known as Process theology, which also stressed God's unity with the world. He had been greatly influenced by the British philosopher A. N. Whitehead (1861–1947), who had seen God as inextricably bound up with the world process. Whitehead had been able to make no sense of God as an-other Being, self-contained and impassible, but had formulated a twentieth-century version of the prophetic idea of God's pathos:

> I affirm that God does suffer as he participates in the ongoing life of the society of being. His sharing in the world's suffering is the supreme instance of knowing, accepting, and transforming in love the suffering which arises in the world. I am affirming the divine sensitivity. Without it, I can make no sense of the being of God.[8]

He described God as "the great companion, the fellow-sufferer, who understands." Williams liked Whitehead's definition; he liked to speak of God as the "behavior" of the world or an "event."[9] It was wrong to set the supernatural order over against the natural world of our experience. There was only one order of being. This was not reductionist, however. In our concept of the natural we should include *all* the aspirations, capacities and potential that had once seemed miraculous. It would also include our "religious experiences," as Buddhists had always affirmed. When asked whether he thought God was separate from nature, Williams would reply that he was not sure. He hated the old Greek idea of *apatheia*, which he found almost blasphemous: it presented God as remote, uncaring and selfish. He denied that he was advocating pantheism. His theology was simply trying to correct an imbalance, which had resulted in an alienating God which was impossible to accept after Auschwitz and Hiroshima.

Others were less optimistic about the achievements of the modern world and wanted to retain the transcendence of God as a challenge to men and women. The Jesuit Karl Rahner has developed a more transcendental theology, which sees God as the supreme mystery and Jesus as the decisive manifestation of what humanity can become. Bernard Lonergan also emphasized the importance of transcendence and of thought as opposed to experience. The unaided intellect cannot reach the vision it seeks: it is continually coming up against barriers to understanding that demand that we change our attitudes. In all cultures, human beings have been driven by the same imperatives: to be intelligent, responsible, reasonable, loving and, if necessary, to change. The very nature of humanity, therefore, demands that we transcend ourselves and our current perceptions, and this principle indicates the presence of what has been called the divine in the very nature of serious human inquiry. Yet the Swiss theologian Hans Urs von Balthasar believes that instead of seeking God in logic and abstractions, we should look to art: Catholic revelation has been essentially Incarnational. In brilliant studies of Dante and Bonaventure, Balthasar shows that Catholics have "seen" God in human form. Their emphasis on beauty in the gestures of ritual, drama and in the great Catholic artists indicates that God is to be found by the senses and not simply by the more cerebral and abstracted parts of the human person.

Muslims and Jews have also attempted to look back to the past to find ideas of God that will suit the present. Abu al-Kalam Azad (d. 1959), a notable Pakistani theologian, turned to the Koran to find a way of seeing God that was not so transcendent that he became a nullity and not so personal that he became an idol. He pointed to the symbolic nature of the Koranic discourse, noting the balance between metaphorical, figurative and anthropomorphic descriptions, on the one hand, and the constant reminders that God is incomparable on the other. Others have looked back to the Sufis for insight into God's relationship with the world. The Swiss Sufi Frithjof Schuon revived the doctrine of the Oneness of Being *(Wahdat al-Wujud)* later attributed to Ibn al-Arabi, which asserted that since God is the *only* reality, nothing exists but him, and the world itself is properly divine. He qualifies this with the reminder that this is an esoteric truth and can only be understood in the context of the mystical disciplines of Sufism.

Others have made God more accessible to the people and relevant to the political challenge of the time. In the years leading up to the Iranian revolution, the young lay philosopher Dr. Ali Shariati drew enormous crowds from among the educated middle classes. He was largely responsible for recruiting them against the shah, even though the mullahs disapproved of a good deal of his religious message. During demonstrations, the crowds used to carry his portrait alongside those of the Ayatollah Khomeini, even though it is not clear how he would have fared in Khomeini's Iran. Shariati was convinced that Westernization had alienated Muslims from their cultural roots and that to heal this disorder they must reinterpret the old symbols of their faith. Muhammad had done the same when he had given the ancient pagan rites of the *hajj* a monotheistic relevance. In his own book *Hajj*, Shariati took his readers through the pilgrimage to Mecca, gradually articulating a dynamic conception of God which each pilgrim had to create imaginatively for him- or herself. Thus, on reaching the Kabah, pilgrims would realize how suitable it was that the shrine is empty: "This is not your final destination; the Kabah is a sign so that the way is not lost; it only shows you the direction."[10] The Kabah witnessed to the importance of transcending all human expressions of the divine, which must not become ends in themselves. Why is the Kabah a simple cube, without decoration or ornament? Because it represents "the secret of God in the universe: God is shapeless, colorless, without simularity, whatever form or condition mankind selects, sees or imagines, it is not God."[11] The *hajj* itself was the antithesis of the alienation experienced by so many Iranians in the postcolonial period. It represents the existential course of each human being who turns his or her life around and directs it toward the ineffable God. Shariati's activist faith was dangerous: the Shah's secret police tortured and deported him and may even have been responsible for his death in London in 1977.

Martin Buber (1878–1965) had an equally dynamic vision of Judaism as a spiritual process and a striving for elemental unity. Religion consisted entirely of an encounter with a personal God, which nearly always took place in our meetings with other human beings. There were two spheres: one the realm of space and time where we relate to other beings as subject and object, as I-It. In the second realm, we relate to others as they truly are, seeing them as ends in themselves. This is the I-Thou realm, which reveals the presence of God. Life was an endless dialogue with God, which does not endanger our freedom or creativity, since God never tells us *what* he is asking of us. We experience him simply as a presence and an imperative and have to work out the meaning for ourselves. This meant a break with much Jewish tradition, and Buber's exegesis of traditional texts is sometimes strained. As a Kantian, Buber had no time for Torah, which he found alienating: God was not a lawgiver! The I-Thou encounter meant freedom and spontaneity, not the weight of a past tradition. Yet the *mitzvot* are central to much Jewish spirituality, and this may explain why Buber has been more popular with Christians than with Jews.

Buber realized that the term "God" had been soiled and degraded, but he refused to relinquish it. "Where would I find a word to equal it, to describe the same reality?" It bears too great and complex a meaning, has too many sacred associations. Those who do reject the word "God" must be respected, since so many appalling things have been done in its name.

> It is easy to understand why there are some who propose a period of silence about "the last things" so that the misused words may be redeemed. But this is not the way to redeem them. We cannot clean up the term "God" and we cannot make it whole; but, stained and mauled as it is, we can raise it from the ground and set it above an hour of great sorrow.[12]

Unlike the other rationalists, Buber was not opposed to myth: he found Lurianic myth of the divine sparks trapped in the world to be of crucial symbolic significance. The separation of the sparks from the Godhead represent the human experience of alienation. When we relate to others, we will restore the primal unity and reduce the alienation in the world.

Where Buber looked back to the Bible and Hasidism, Abraham Joshua Heschel (1907–72) returned to the spirit of the Rabbis and the Talmud. Unlike Buber, he believed that the *mitzvot* would help Jews to counter the dehumanizing aspects of modernity. They were actions that fulfilled God's need rather than our own. Modern life was characterized by depersonalization and exploitation: even God was reduced to a thing to be manipulated and made to serve our purposes. Consequently religion became dull and insipid; we needed a "depth theology" to delve below the structures and recover the original awe, mystery and wonder. It was no use trying to prove God's existence logically. Faith in God sprang from an immediate apprehension that had nothing to do with concepts and rationality. The Bible must be read metaphorically like poetry if it is to yield that sense of the sacred. The *mitzvot* should also be seen as symbolic gestures that train us to live in God's presence. Each *mitzvah* is a place of encounter in the tiny details of mundane life and, like a work of art, the world of the *mitzvot* has its own logic and rhythm. Above all, we should be aware that God needs human beings. He is not the remote God of the philosophers but the God of pathos described by the prophets.

Atheistic philosophers have also been attracted by the idea of God during the second half of the twentieth century. In *Being and Time* (1927) Martin Heidegger (1899–1976) saw Being in rather the same way as Tillich, though he would have denied that it was "God" in the Christian sense: it was distinct from particular beings and quite separate from the normal categories of thought. Some Christians have been inspired by Heidegger's work, even though its moral value is called into question by his association with the Nazi regime. In *What Is Metaphysics?*, his inaugural lecture at Freiburg, Heidegger developed a number of ideas that had already surfaced in the work of Plotinus, Denys and Erigena. Since Being is "Wholly Other," it is in fact Nothing—no thing, neither an object nor a particular being. Yet it is what makes all other existence possible. The ancients had believed that nothing came from nothing, but Heidegger reversed this maxim: *ex nihilo omne qua ens fit*. He ended his lecture by posing a question asked by Leibniz: "Why are there beings at all, rather than just nothing?" It is a question that evokes the shock of surprise and wonder that has been a constant in the human response to the world: why should anything exist at all? In his *Introduction to Metaphysics* (1953), Heidegger began by asking the same question. Theology believed that it had the answer and traced everything back to Something Else, to God. But this God was just another being rather than something that was wholly other. Heidegger had a somewhat reductive idea of the God of religion—though one shared by many religious people—but he often spoke in mystical terms about Being. He speaks of it as a great paradox; describes the thinking process as a waiting or listening to Being and seems to experience a return and withdrawal of Being, rather as mystics feel the absence of God. There is nothing that human beings can do to think Being into existence. Since the Greeks, people in the Western world have tended to forget Being and have concentrated on beings instead, a process that has resulted in its modern technological success. In the article written toward the end of his life titled "Only a God Can Save Us," Heidegger suggested that the experience of God's absence in our time could liberate us from preoccupation with beings. But there was nothing we could do to bring Being back into the present. We could only hope for a new advent in the future.

The Marxist philosopher Ernst Bloch (1885–1977) saw the idea of God as natural to humanity. The whole of human life was directed toward the future: we experience our lives as incomplete and unfinished. Unlike animals, we are never satisfied but always want more. It is this which has forced us to think and develop, since at each point of our lives we must transcend ourselves and go on to the next stage: the baby must become a toddler, the toddler must overcome its disabilities and become a child, and so forth. All our dreams and aspirations look ahead to what is to come. Even philosophy begins with wonder, which is the experience of the not-knowing, the not-yet. Socialism also looks forward to a utopia, but, despite the Marxist rejection of faith, where there is hope there is also religion. Like Feuerbach, Bloch saw God as the human ideal that has not yet come to be, but instead of seeing this as alienating he found it essential to the human condition.

Max Horkheimer (1895–1973), the German social theorist of the Frankfurt school, also saw "God" as an important ideal in a way that was reminiscent of the prophets. Whether he existed or not or whether we "believe in him" is superfluous. Without the idea of God there is no absolute meaning, truth or morality: ethics becomes simply a question of taste, a mood or a whim. Unless politics and morality somehow include the idea of "God," they will remain pragmatic and shrewd rather than wise. If there is no absolute, there is no reason that we should not hate or that war is worse than peace. Religion is essentially an inner feeling that there *is* a God. One of our earliest dreams is a longing for justice (how frequently we hear children complain: "It's not fair!"). Religion records the aspirations and accusations of innumerable human beings in the face of suffering and wrong. It makes us aware of our finite nature; we all hope that the injustice of the world will not be the last word.

The fact that people who have no conventional religious beliefs should keep returning to central themes that we have discovered in the history of God indicates that the idea is not as alien as many of us assume. Yet during the second half of the twentieth century, there has been a move away from the idea of a personal God who behaves like a larger version of us. There is nothing new about this. As we have seen, the Jewish scriptures, which

Christians call their "Old" Testament, show a similar process; the Koran saw al-Lah in less personal terms than the Judeo-Christian tradition from the very beginning. Doctrines such as the Trinity and the mythology and symbolism of the mystical systems all strove to suggest that God was beyond personality. Yet this does not seem to have been made clear to many of the faithful. When John Robinson, Bishop of Woolwich, published *Honest to God* in 1963, stating that he could no longer subscribe to the old personal God "out there," there was uproar in Britain. A similar furor has greeted various remarks by David Jenkins, Bishop of Durham, even though these ideas are commonplace in academic circles. Don Cupitt, Dean of Emmanuel College, Cambridge, has also been dubbed "the atheist priest": he finds the traditional realistic God of theism unacceptable and proposes a form of Christian Buddhism, which puts religious experience before theology. Like Robinson, Cupitt has arrived intellectually at an insight that mystics in all three faiths have reached by a more intuitive route. Yet the idea that God does not really exist and that there is Nothing out there is far from new.

There is a growing intolerance of inadequate images of the Absolute. This is a healthy iconoclasm, since the idea of God has been used in the past to disastrous effect. One of the most characteristic new developments since the 1970s has been the rise of a type of religiosity that we usually call "fundamentalism" in most of the major world religions, including the three religions of God. A highly political spirituality, it is literal and intolerant in its vision. In the United States, which has always been prone to extremist and apocalyptic enthusiasm, Christian fundamentalism has attached itself to the New Right. Fundamentalists campaign for the abolition of legal abortion and for a hard line on moral and social decency. Jerry Falwell's Moral Majority achieved astonishing political power during the Reagan years. Other evangelists such as Maurice Cerullo, taking Jesus' remarks literally, believe that miracles are an essential hallmark of true faith. God will give the believer anything that he asks for in prayer. In Britain, fundamentalists such as Colin Urquhart have made the same claim. Christian fundamentalists seem to have little regard for the loving compassion of Christ. They are swift to condemn the people they see as the "enemies of God." Most would consider Jews and Muslims destined for hellfire, and Urquhart has argued that all oriental religions are inspired by the devil.

There have been similar developments in the Muslim world, which have been much publicized in the West. Muslim fundamentalists have toppled governments and either assassinated or threatened the enemies of Islam with the death penalty. Similarly, Jewish fundamentalists have settled in the Occupied Territories of the West Bank and the Gaza Strip with the avowed intention of driving out the Arab inhabitants, using force if necessary. Thus they believe that they are paving a way for the advent of the Messiah, which is at hand. In all its forms, fundamentalism is a fiercely reductive faith. Thus Rabbi Meir Kahane, the most extreme member of Israel's Far Right until his assassination in New York in 1990:

> There are not several messages in Judaism. There is only one. And this message is to do what God wants. Sometimes God wants us to go to war, sometimes he wants us to live in peace. . . . But there is only one message: God wanted us to come to this country to create a Jewish state.[13]

This wipes out centuries of Jewish development, returning to the Deuteronomist perspective of the Book of Joshua. It is not surprising that people who hear this kind of profanity, which makes "God" deny other people's human rights, think that the sooner we relinquish him the better.

Yet [. . .], this type of religiosity is actually a retreat from God. To make such human, historical phenomena as Christian "Family Values," "Islam" or "the Holy Land" the focus of religious devotion is a new form of idolatry. This type of belligerent righteousness has been a constant temptation to monotheists throughout the long history of God. It must be rejected as inauthentic. The God of Jews, Christians and Muslims got off to an unfortunate start, since the tribal deity Yahweh was murderously partial to his own people. Latter-day crusaders who return to this primitive ethos are elevating the values of the tribe to an unacceptably high status and substituting manmade ideals for the transcendent reality which should challenge our prejudices. They are also denying a crucial monotheistic theme. Ever since the prophets of Israel reformed the old pagan cult of Yahweh, the God of monotheists has promoted the ideal of compassion.

[. . .] Compassion was a characteristic of most of the ideologies that were created during the Axial Age. The compassionate ideal even impelled Buddhists to make a major change in their religious orientation when they introduced devotion (*bhakti*) to the Buddha and *bodhisattvas*. The prophets insisted that cult and worship were useless unless society as a whole adopted a more just and compassionate ethos. These insights were developed by Jesus, Paul and the Rabbis, who all shared the same Jewish ideals and suggested major changes in Judaism in order to implement them. The Koran made the creation of a compassionate and just society the essence of the reformed religion of al-Lah. Compassion is a particularly difficult virtue. It demands that we go beyond the limitations of our egotism, insecurity and inherited prejudice. Not surprisingly, there have been times when all three of the God-religions have failed to achieve these high standards. During the eighteenth century, deists rejected traditional Western Christianity largely because it had become so conspicuously cruel and intolerant. The same will hold good today. All too often, conventional believers, who are not fundamentalists, share their aggressive righteousness. They use "God" to prop up their own loves and hates, which they attribute to God himself. But Jews, Christians and Muslims who punctiliously attend divine services yet denigrate people who belong to different ethnic and ideological camps deny one of the basic truths of their religion. It is equally inappropriate for people who call themselves Jews, Christians and Muslims to condone an inequitable social system. The God of historical monotheism demands mercy not sacrifice, compassion rather than decorous liturgy.

There has often been a distinction between people who practice a cultic form of religion and those who have cultivated a sense of the God of compassion. The prophets fulminated against their contemporaries who thought that temple worship was sufficient. Jesus and St. Paul both made it clear that external observance was useless if it was not accompanied by charity: it was little better than sounding brass or a tinkling cymbal. Muhammad came into conflict with those Arabs who wanted to worship the pagan goddesses alongside al-Lah in the ancient rites, without implementing the compassionate ethos that God demanded as a condition of all true religion. There had been a similar divide in the pagan world of Rome: the old cultic religion celebrated the status quo, while the philosophers preached a message that they believed would change the world. It may be that the compassionate religion of the One God has only been observed by a minority; most have found it difficult to face the extremity of the God-experience with its uncompromising ethical demands. Ever since Moses brought the tablets of the Law from Mount Sinai, the majority have preferred the worship of a Golden Calf, a traditional, unthreatening image of a deity they have constructed for themselves, with its consoling, time-honored rituals. Aaron, the high priest, presided over the manufacture of the golden effigy. The religious establishment itself is often deaf to the inspiration of prophets and mystics who bring news of a much more demanding God.

God can also be used as an unworthy panacea, as an alternative to mundane life and as the object of indulgent fantasy. The idea of God has frequently been used as the opium of the people. This is a particular danger when he is conceived as an-other Being—just like us, only bigger and better—in his own heaven, which is itself conceived as a paradise of earthly delights. Yet originally, "God" was used to help people to concentrate on this world and to face up to unpleasant reality. Even the pagan cult of Yahweh, for all its manifest faults, stressed his involvement in current events in profane time, as opposed to the sacred time of rite and myth. The prophets of Israel forced their people to confront their own social culpability and impending political catastrophe in the name of the God who revealed himself in these historical occurrences. The Christian doctrine of Incarnation stressed the divine immanence in the world of flesh and blood. Concern for the here and now was especially marked in Islam: nobody could have been more of a realist than Muhammad, who was a political as well as a spiritual genius. As we have seen, later generations of Muslims have shared his concern to incarnate the divine will in human history by establishing a just and decent society. From the very beginning, God was experienced as an imperative to action. From the moment when—as either El or Yahweh—God called Abraham away from his family in Haran, the cult entailed concrete action in this world and often a painful abandonment of the old sanctities.

This dislocation also involved great strain. The Holy God, who was wholly other, was experienced as a profound shock by the prophets. He demanded a similar holiness and separation on the part of his people. When he spoke to Moses on Sinai, the Israelites were not allowed to approach the foot of the mountain. An entirely new gulf suddenly yawned between humanity and the divine, rupturing the holistic vision of paganism. There was, therefore, a potential for alienation from the world, which reflected a dawning consciousness of the inalienable autonomy of the individual. It is no accident that monotheism finally took root during the exile to Babylon, when the Israelites also developed the ideal of personal responsibility, which has been crucial in both Judaism and Islam.[14] [. . .] The Rabbis used the idea of an immanent God to help Jews to cultivate a sense of the sacred rights of the human personality. Yet alienation has continued to be a danger in all three faiths: in the West the experience of God was continually accompanied by guilt and by a pessimistic anthropology. In Judaism and Islam there is no doubt that the observance of Torah and Shariah has sometimes been seen as a heteronymous compliance with an external law, even though we have seen that nothing could have been further from the intention of the men who compiled these legal codes.

Those atheists who preached emancipation from a God who demands such servile obedience were protesting against an inadequate but unfortunately familiar image of God. Again, this was based on a conception of the divine that was too personalistic. It interpreted the scriptural image of God's judgment too literally and assumed that God was a sort of Big Brother in the sky. This image of the divine Tyrant imposing an alien law on his unwilling human servants has to go. Terrorizing the populace into civic obedience with threats is no longer acceptable or even practicable, as the downfall of communist regimes demonstrated so dramatically in the autumn of 1989. The anthropomorphic idea of God as Lawgiver and Ruler is not adequate to the temper of post-modernity. Yet the atheists who complained that the idea of God was unnatural were not entirely correct. [. . .] Jews, Christians and Muslims have developed remarkably similar ideas of God, which also resemble other conceptions of the Absolute. When people try to find an ultimate meaning and value in human life, their minds seem to go in a certain direction. They have not been coerced to do this; it is something that seems natural to humanity.

Yet if feelings are not to degenerate into indulgent, aggressive or unhealthy emotionalism, they need to be informed by the critical intelligence. The experience of God must keep abreast of other current enthusiasms, including those of the mind. The experiment of Falsafah was an attempt to relate faith in God with the new cult of rationalism among Muslims, Jews and, later, Western Christians. Eventually Muslims and Jews retreated from philosophy. Rationalism, they decided, had its uses, especially in such empirical studies as science, medicine and mathematics, but it was not entirely appropriate in the discussion of a God who lay beyond concepts. The Greeks had already sensed this and developed an early distrust of their native metaphysics. One of the drawbacks of the philosophic method of discussing God was that it could make it sound as though the Supreme Deity were simply an-other Being, the highest of all the things that exist, instead of a reality of an entirely different order. Yet the venture of Falsafah was important, since it showed an appreciation of the necessity of relating God to other experiences—if only to define the extent to which this was possible. To push God into intellectual isolation in a holy ghetto of his own is unhealthy and unnatural. It can encourage people to think that it is not necessary to apply normal standards of decency and rationality to behavior supposedly inspired by "God."

From the first, Falsafah had been associated with science. It was their initial enthusiasm for medicine, astronomy and mathematics which had led the first Muslim Faylasufs to discuss al-Lah in metaphysical terms. Science had effected a major change in their outlook, and they found that they could not think of God in the same way as their fellow Muslims. The philosophic conception of God was markedly different from the Koranic vision, but Faylasufs did recover some insights that were in danger of being lost in the *ummah* at that time. Thus the Koran had an extremely positive attitude to other religious traditions: Muhammad had not believed that he was founding a new, exclusive religion and considered that all rightly guided faith came from the One God. By the ninth century, however, the *ulema* were beginning to lose sight of this and were promoting the cult of Islam as the one true religion. The Faylasufs reverted to the older universalist approach, even though they reached it by a different route. We have a similar opportunity today. In our scientific age, we cannot think about God in the same way as our forebears, but the challenge of science could help us to appreciate some old truths.

[. . .] Albert Einstein had an appreciation of mystical religion. Despite his famous remarks about God not playing dice, he did not believe that his theory of relativity should affect the conception of God. During a visit to England in 1921, Einstein was asked by the Archbishop of Canterbury what were its implications for theology. He replied: "None. Relativity is a purely scientific matter and has nothing to do with religion."[15] When Christians are dismayed by such scientists as Stephen Hawking, who can find no room for God in his cosmology, they are perhaps still thinking of God in anthropomorphic terms as a Being who created the world in the same way as we would. Yet creation was not originally conceived in such a literal manner. Interest in Yahweh as Creator did not enter Judaism until the exile to Babylon. It was a conception that was alien to the Greek world: creation *ex nihilo* was not an official doctrine of Christianity until the Council of Nicaea in 341. Creation is a central teaching of the Koran, but, like all its utterances about God, this is said to be a "parable" or a "sign" *(aya)* of an ineffable truth. Jewish and Muslim rationalists found it a difficult and problematic doctrine, and many rejected it. Sufis and Kabbalists all preferred the Greek metaphor of emanation. In any case, cosmology was not a scientific description of the origins of the world but was originally a symbolic expression of a spiritual and psychological truth. There is consequently little agitation about the new science in the Muslim world: [. . .] the events of recent history have been more of a threat than has science to the traditional conception of God. In the West, however, a more literal understanding of scripture has long prevailed. When some Western Christians feel their faith in God undermined by the new science, they are probably imagining God as Newton's great Mechanick, a personalistic notion of God which should, perhaps, be rejected on religious as well as on scientific grounds. The challenge of science might shock the churches into a fresh appreciation of the symbolic nature of scriptural narrative.

The idea of a personal God seems increasingly unacceptable at the present time for all kinds of reasons: moral, intellectual, scientific and spiritual. Feminists are also repelled by a personal deity who, because of "his" gender, has been male since his tribal, pagan days. Yet to talk about "she"—other than in a dialectical way—can be just as limiting, since it confines the illimitable God to a purely human category. The old metaphysical notion of God as the Supreme Being, which has long been popular in the West, is also felt to be unsatisfactory. The God of the philosophers is the product of a now outdated rationalism, so the traditional "proofs" of his existence no longer work. The widespread acceptance of the God of the philosophers by the deists of the Enlightenment can be seen as the first step to the current atheism. Like the old Sky God, this deity is so remote from humanity and the mundane world that he easily becomes *Deus Otiosus* and fades from our consciousness.

The God of the mystics might seem to present a possible alternative. The mystics have long insisted that God is not an-Other Being; they have claimed that he does not really exist and that it is better to call him Nothing. This God is in tune with the atheistic mood of our secular society, with its distrust of inadequate images of the Absolute. Instead of seeing God as an objective Fact, which can be demonstrated by means of scientific proof, mystics have claimed that he is a subjective experience, mysteriously experienced in the ground of being. This God is to be approached through the imagination and can be seen as a kind of art form, akin to the other great artistic symbols that have expressed the ineffable mystery, beauty and value of life. Mystics have used music, dancing, poetry, fiction, stories, painting, sculpture and architecture to express this Reality that goes beyond concepts. Like all art, however, mysticism requires intelligence, discipline and self-criticism as a safeguard against indulgent emotionalism and projection. The God of the mystics could even satisfy the feminists, since both Sufis and Kabbalists have long tried to introduce a female element into the divine.

There are drawbacks, however. Mysticism has been regarded with some suspicion by many Jews and Muslims since the Shabbetai Zevi fiasco and the decline of latter-day Sufism. In the West, mysticism has never been a mainstream religious enthusiasm. The Protestant and Catholic Reformers either outlawed or marginalized it, and the scientific Age of Reason did not encourage this mode of perception. Since the 1960s, there has been a fresh interest in mysticism, expressed in the enthusiasm for Yoga, meditation and Buddhism, but it is not an approach that easily consorts with our objective, empirical mentality. The God of the mystics is not easy to apprehend. It requires long training with an expert and a considerable investment of time. The mystic has to work hard to acquire this sense of the reality known as God (which many have refused to name). Mystics often insist that human beings must deliberately create this sense of God for themselves, with the same degree of care and attention that others devote to artistic creation. It is not something that is likely to appeal to people in a society which has become used to speedy gratification, fast food and instant communication. The God of the mystics does not arrive readymade and prepackaged. He cannot be experienced as quickly as the instant ecstasy created by a revivalist preacher, who quickly has a whole congregation clapping its hands and speaking in tongues.

It is possible to acquire some of the mystical attitudes. Even if we are incapable of the higher states of consciousness achieved by a mystic, we can learn that God does not exist in any simplistic sense, for example, or that the very word "God" is only a symbol of a reality that ineffably transcends it. The mystical agnosticism could help us to acquire a restraint that stops us rushing into these complex matters with dogmatic assurance. But if these notions are not felt upon the pulse and personally appropriated, they are likely to seem meaningless abstractions. Secondhand mysticism could prove to be as unsatisfactory as reading the explanation of a poem by a literary critic instead of the original. [. . .] Mysticism was often seen as an esoteric discipline, not because the mystics wanted to exclude the vulgar herd but because these truths could only be perceived by the intuitive part of the mind after special training. They mean something different when they are approached by this particular route, which is not accessible to the logical, rationalist faculty.

Ever since the prophets of Israel started to ascribe their own feelings and experiences to God, monotheists have in some sense created a God for themselves. God has rarely been seen as a self-evident fact that can be encountered like any other objective existent. Today many people seem to have lost the will to make this imaginative effort. This need not be a catastrophe. When religious ideas have lost their validity, they have usually faded away painlessly: if the human idea of God no longer works for us in the empirical age, it will be discarded. Yet in the past people have always created new symbols to act as a focus for spirituality. Human beings have always created a faith for themselves, to cultivate their sense of the wonder and ineffable significance of life. The aimlessness, alienation, anomie and violence that characterize so much of modern life seem to indicate that now that they are not deliberately creating a faith in "God" or anything else—it matters little what—many people are falling into despair.

In the United States, [. . .] ninety-nine percent of the population claim to believe in God, yet the prevalence of fundamentalism, apocalypticism and "instant" charismatic forms of religiosity in America is not reassuring. The escalating crime rate, drug addiction and the revival of the death penalty are not signs of a spiritually healthy society. In Europe there is a growing blankness where God once existed in the human consciousness. One of the first people to express this dry desolation—quite different from the heroic atheism of Nietzsche—was Thomas Hardy. In "The Darkling Thrush," written on December 30, 1900, at the turn of the twentieth century, he expressed the death of spirit that was no longer able to create a faith in life's meaning:

I leant upon a coppice gate
    When Frost was spectre-grey
And Winter's dregs made desolate
    The weakening eye of day.
The tangled bine-stems scored the sky
    Like strings of broken lyres,
And all mankind that haunted nigh
    Had sought their household fires.

The land's sharp features seemed to be
    The Century's corpse outleant,
His crypt the cloudy canopy,
    The wind his death-lament.
The ancient pulse of germ and birth
    Was shrunken hard and dry,
And every spirit upon earth
    Seemed fervourless as I.

At once a voice arose among
    The bleak twigs overhead
In a full-hearted evensong
    Of joy illimited;
An aged thrush, frail, gaunt, and small,
    In blast-beruffled plume,
Had chosen thus to fling his soul
    Upon the growing gloom.

So little cause for carolings
    Of such ecstatic sound
Was written on terrestrial things
    Afar or nigh around,
That I could think there trembled through
    His happy good-night air
Some blessed Hope, whereof he knew
    And I was unaware.

Human beings cannot endure emptiness and desolation; they will fill the vacuum by creating a new focus of meaning. The idols of fundamentalism are not good substitutes for God; if we are to create a vibrant new faith for the twenty-first century, we should, perhaps, ponder the history of God for some lessons and warnings. ■

NOTES

1. Peter Berger, *A Rumour of Angels* (London, 1970), p. 58.
2. A. J. Ayer, *Language, Truth and Logic* (Harmondsworth, 1974), p. 152.
3. Wilfred Cantwell Smith, *Belief and History* (Charlottesville, 1985), p. 10.
4. Thomas J. J. Altizer, *The Gospel of Christian Atheism* (London, 1966), p. 136.
5. Paul Van Buren, *The Secular Meaning of the Gospel* (London, 1963), p. 138.
6. Richard L. Rubenstein, *After Auschwitz, Radical Theology and Contemporary Judaism* (Indianapolis, 1966), passim.
7. Paul Tillich, *Theology and Culture* (New York and Oxford, 1964), p. 129.
8. Alfred North Whitehead, "Suffering and Being," in *Adventures of Ideas* (Harmondsworth, 1942), pp. 191–92.
9. *Process and Reality* (Cambridge, 1929), p. 497.
10. Ali Shariati, *Hajj,* trans. Laleh Bakhtiar (Teheran, 1988), p. 46.
11. Ibid., p. 48.
12. Martin Buber, "Gottesfinsternis, Betrachtungen zur Beziehung zwischen Religion und Philosophie," quoted in Hans Kung, *Does God Exist? An Answer for Today,* trans. Edward Quinn (London, 1978), p. 508.
13. Quoted in Raphael Mergui and Philippa Simmonot, *Israel's Ayatollahs; Meir Kahane and the Far Right in Israel* (London, 1987), p. 43.
14. Personal responsibility is also important in Christianity, of course, but Judaism and Islam have stressed it by their lack of a mediating priesthood, a perspective that was recovered by the Protestant Reformers.
15. Philipp Frank, *Einstein: His Life and Times* (New York, 1947), pp. 189–90.

■ *QUESTIONS FOR MAKING CONNECTIONS WITHIN THE READING* ■

1. Armstrong's title poses a question: Does God have a future? A more conventional writer might answer that question with a "Yes" or a "No," supported by a series of arguments. But Armstrong does something else, demonstrating an approach some readers might find unexpected in the context of a "philosophical" issue. How would you characterize this approach? Is the absence of a final answer consistent with Armstrong's approach, or does it call that approach into doubt?

2. By means of direct quotation and paraphrase, many thinkers make their voices heard through Armstrong's own words. At times, this chorus of voices may become so closely fused that readers might have trouble

distinguishing Armstrong's own views from the views of the thinkers she draws on. At what moments in the argument does Armstrong speak for herself, and at what moments do other writers speak through her words? Would you say that her accounts of other writers' views are uniformly neutral, or are there places where Armstrong's descriptions become more openly evaluative?

3. How has Armstrong organized this chapter? Why does she start where she does? What are her criteria for choosing examples? Why does she end where she does? Is she making an argument or offering a neutral description of the way things are?

▪ QUESTIONS FOR WRITING ▪

1. Would you say that Armstrong herself believes in God? What does "belief" mean to her? What does "God" mean? In what ways does her understanding of religion differ from those you have held or may now hold? Does the word *God* become nonsensical if people from different times and places have understood it in different ways?

2. Armstrong concludes her argument by citing Thomas Hardy's poem, "The Darkling Thrush," in its entirety. In what sense does Hardy's poem provide a conclusion to Armstrong's discussion? What does the poem have to say that Armstrong couldn't say for herself? Why has she given a poet the final word on the future of God?

▪ QUESTIONS FOR MAKING CONNECTIONS BETWEEN READINGS ▪

1. We might say that in "Waiting for a Jew: Marginal Redemption at the Eighth Street Shul," Jonathan Boyarin also takes on Armstrong's question, "Does God have a future?" But Boyarin poses the question in a rather different way, concerned less with the disappearance of God than with the disappearance of a community of believers. As he recalls, the religious community of his childhood is today "as obliterated as any *shtetl* in Eastern Europe." If the survival of God depends on the reinvention of such communities in the ways that Boyarin describes, then what are we to make of Armstrong's call for a turn away from a "personal God" and toward a more mystical religion? Will this turn renew waning communities of faith or will it only hasten their disappearance?

2. When Armstrong refers to the future of God, she has in mind primarily the notions of God embraced by theologians and philosophers in Western Europe and the United States. In "The Ganges' Next Life," however, Alexander Stille offers a portrait of religious life among Hindus in South

Asia. After reading both Armstrong and Stille, would you say that the "death of God" is a problem only for the West? What forces does Armstrong identify with the gradual decline of religious conviction? Given what Stille tells us about India, are those same forces at work in Veer Bhadra Mishra's world, or does his society face challenges very different from the ones that Armstrong describes?

www   For additional suggestions about making connections between readings, visit the Link-O-Mat and More Sample Assignments at <www.newhum.com>.

JONATHAN BOYARIN

JONATHAN BOYARIN IS an anthropologist and an ethnographer who has studied the lifestyle and culture of Jews the world over. Although anthropology originally emerged as a way for outsiders to study and understand foreign cultures, the anthropology that Boyarin practices is of a different sort: he provides an insider's view of cultures and traditions that are, in some ways, his own.

Thus, in pursuing his fieldwork, Boyarin has been concerned not only with describing Jewish identity in Paris, New York, and Jerusalem, but also with contributing to the broader project of preserving Jewish culture. This approach to anthropology has helped Boyarin invent for himself a "funky Orthodox" Jewish identity, as "Waiting for a Jew" chronicles.

Currently the Beren Professor of Modern Jewish Studies at Kansas University, Boyarin is considered one of America's most original thinkers about Jewish culture. Boyarin has written extensively about the roles that history, memory, and geography have played in the formation of Jewish identity. In *A Storm from Paradise: The Politics of Jewish Memory* (1992), *Palestine and Jewish History: Criticism at the Borders of Ethnography* (1996), and *Thinking in Jewish* (1996), Boyarin asks his readers to consider whether there is such a thing as an "essential" Jewish identity. While the notion that there is an essential, unchanging self at the core of every human being has fallen out of favor in academic circles, Boyarin bids his readers to recognize that identity does not serve the same function for marginalized groups that it serves for dominant groups. As Boyarin puts it in *Remapping Memory: The Politics of TimeSpace* (1994), "For people who are somehow part of a dominant group, any assertions of essence are ipso facto products and reproducers of the system of domination. For subaltern groups, however, essentialism is resistance, the insistence on the 'right' of the group actually to exist." As "Waiting for a Jew" documents, answering the question "Who are you?" is not as simple as it might seem, for the answer requires that one first consider the histories, traditions, and communal life experiences that have made the notions of "an identity" and "one's own identity" possible.

www To learn more about Jonathan Boyarin and the construction of Jewish identity, visit the Link-O-Mat at <www.newhum.com>.

Boyarin, Jonathan. "Waiting for a Jew." *Thinking in Jewish*. Chicago: The University of Chicago Press, 1996. 8–34.

Waiting for a Jew
Marginal Redemption at the Eighth Street Shul

My story begins in a community, with an illusion of wholeness. I am between the age when consciousness begins and the age of ten, when my family leaves the community and my illusion is shattered. Our family lives on the edge of the Pine Barrens in Farmingdale, New Jersey, along with hundreds of other families of Jewish chicken farmers who have come from Europe and New York City in several waves, beginning just after World War I.

Among the farmers are present and former Communists, Bundists, Labor Zionists, German refugees who arrived in the 1930s, and Polish survivors of concentration camps. These, however, are not the distinctions I make among them as a child. Johannes Fabian has shown us that when we write ethnography we inevitably trap those about whom we write into a hypostatic, categorical, grammatical "present" (Fabian 1983). An autobiographer has the same power over the memory of himself and those he knew in prior times as the fieldworker who later obliterates the narrative aspect of his encounter with his subjects—the power to deny their autonomy in hindsight.[1] Those of the farming community whom I will later remember, I know therefore by their own names and places: my grandparents closer to Farmingdale proper; the Silbers off on Yellowbrook Road, with a tree nursery now instead of chickens; the Lindauers, stubbornly maintaining an egg-packing and -distribution business, while others find different ways to earn a living.

My child's world is not exclusively Jewish, nor am I brought up to regard it as such. Across our road and down a few hundred yards is a tiny house built by Jewish farmers when they first came to settle here. It is now, incredibly, occupied by a black family of ten. Next to them lives an equally poor and large white family. Shortly before we leave Farmingdale, the old Jew in the farm next to ours passes away, and the property passes to a Japanese businessman. The young men he hires live in the farmhouse, growing oriental vegetables on the open field and bonsai in a converted chicken coop, and they introduce me to the game of Go. The nearest Jewish household is that of my great-uncle Yisroel and his wife Helen, the third house to the right of ours.

Yet we are near the heart of Jewish life in Farmingdale. Half a mile—but no, it must be less—down Peskin's Lane (the name my grandfather Israel Boyarin gave to what was a dirt road in the 1930s) is the Farmingdale Jewish Community Center, on the next plot of land after Uncle Yisroel's house.

Just past the community center is the farm that once belonged to my father's uncle Peskin, the first Jew in Farmingdale. Fifteen years after Peskin's death, the bodies of two gangsters were found buried on the farm. The local papers noted: "Mr. Peskin was not available for comment."

Our own farm consists of eleven acres. Facing the road is the house my grandfather built, with a large front lawn and an apple tree in back. Farther back, four large chicken coops mark the slope of a hill ending in our field, behind which woods conceal the tiny Manasquan River. The field, well fertilized by chickens allowed to scratch freely on it during the day, is leased each summer by a dirt farmer who grows corn. My father has joined the insurance agency begun by my mother, and they have gotten rid of the birds. The coops stand empty by my fourth birthday. One day, though, while a friend and I chase each other through the coops in play, we are startled by a pair of chickens. Their presence in the stillness and the faint smell of ancient manure is inexplicable and unforgettable. Thus, on the abandoned farm, my first memories are tinged with a sense of traces, of mystery, of loss. Do all who eventually become anthropologists have this experience in some form, at some time in their early lives?

My mother's turn to business is wise: chicken farming as the basis for the community's livelihood is quickly becoming untenable. Nor is it surprising, as she had given up a career as a chemist to come live with my father on the farm—thus taking part in the process of Jewish dispersal from the immigrants' urban centers, which in the last quarter of the century would be mirrored by a shrinking of Jewish communities in small towns and a reconsolidation of the Orthodox centers. My mother's father, an Orthodox Jew from a leading Lithuanian rabbinical family, has struggled to learn English well and has gone into the insurance business himself. After his death, my mother tells me that he had originally resisted her desire to marry the son of a Jewish socialist, but he consented when he met my father's father's father, a Lubavitcher Hasid named Mordechai.

My grandfather's concern for his daughter's future as an observant Jew was well founded. The Sabbath is marked in our family only on Friday nights: by my mother's candle-lighting, and her chicken soup in winter; by the challah; by the presence of my grandfather. We do not keep kosher, nor do we go to shul on *shabbes*.

The Jewish Community Center—with its various functions as social and meeting hall, synagogue, and school—is nevertheless a focus of our family's life. Most of the ten or so other children in these classes I see at other times during the week as well, either in public school or playing at one another's homes. I am there three times each week, first for Sunday school, and then for Hebrew school on Tuesday and Thursday afternoons. This odd distinction is no doubt a practical one, since some parents do not choose to send their children three times a week. But since Sunday school was first a Christian institution, it also reflects an accommodation to Christian church patterns, as evidenced by the fact that Sundays are devoted to teaching stories of the Bible. One Sunday school teacher we have in our kindergarten year captivates me with his skill in making these stories come to life, as when he imitates the distress of an Egyptian waking up to find his bed covered with frogs.

Another teacher, a young woman with a severe manner and a heavy black wig, the wife of a member of the Orthodox yeshiva in Lakewood, later causes general misery because of her inability to understand children, although I will eventually appreciate the prayers she teaches us to read. One time I come in to Hebrew school immediately after yet another in a series of martyred family dogs has been run over in front of our house. Her attempt to comfort me is like some malicious parody of Talmudic reasoning: "You shouldn't be so upset about an animal. If a chicken and a person both fell down a well, which one would you save first?"

In addition to this somewhat haphazard religious training, there is the local chapter of Habonim, the Labor Zionist Youth Organization, to which my older brother and sister belong. I tag along and am tolerated by their peers. Once I am given a minor role in a stage performance by the chapter. Though I am too young to remember quite what it is about, the phrase *komets-aleph:aw* stands in my memory.

Later I will learn that this phrase occurs in a famous and sentimental Yiddish folksong. It is the first letter of the Hebrew alphabet, the first thing countless generations of Jewish children have been taught. Here is an unusual case in which a traditional lesson—how to pronounce the alphabet—is successfully inculcated in the secularized framework of a dramatic performance about the traditional setting. Perhaps this is because of the necessary rehearsals, in which I must have heard, as the song puts it, "once more, over and over again, *komets-aleph:aw*." The memory reinforces my later preference for this older, European pronunciation of the Hebrew vowels, my sense of the Israeli *kamets-aleph:ah* as inauthentic.

Also memorable at the Jewish Community Center is the annual barbecue run by the Young Couples' Club. Though my father will assure me in an interview years later that its association with the Fourth of July was purely a matter of convenience, the atmosphere is certainly one of festival, even including "sacrifices" and "altars": My father and his friends set up huge charcoal pits with cement blocks, and broil vast amounts of chicken; corn is boiled in aluminum garbage cans to go with it.[2] For the children, a Purim-like element of riotous excess is added: This one time each year, we are allowed to drink as much soda as we want. One year "wild," blond-haired Richie L., whose parents have a luncheonette booth for a kitchen table and an attic filled with antiques, claims to drink fourteen bottles, thus adding to the mystique he holds for me.

But it is the days when the Community Center becomes a synagogue that leave the strongest impression on my memory. There must be services every Saturday morning, but I am completely unaware of them. What I will remember are the holidays: Purim, Rosh Hashanah, Yom Kippur, Simchas

Torah, and a crowd of people who just a few years later will never be there again. On the fall holidays, the shul is full of movement, impatience, noise, and warmth. Except for a few moments such as the shofar blowing, we children are free to come and go: By the steps in front, tossing the juicy, poisonous red berries of a yew that was planted, I am told, in memory of my brother Aaron, whom I never knew; inside the main doors, to look left at Walter Tenenbaum wrapped in a *tallis* that covers his head, standing at a lectern by the Ark of the Torah as he leads the service, or to look right, along the first long row of folding chairs for our fathers; thence a few rows back to where our mothers sit separately from the men, although unlike most synagogues that look and sound as traditional as this one, there is no *mekhitse*, no barrier between women and men; and finally out through the side door and down a flight of wooden steps to the monkey bars, into the ditch where one miraculous day we found and drank an intact bottle of orange soda, or into the kitchen, social room, and classroom in the basement. Once each year we children are the center of attention, as we huddle under a huge tallis in front of the Ark on Simchas Torah to be blessed.

In classic ethnographies of hunting-and-gathering groups, landscapes are described as personalized, integral elements of culture. This was true of the landscape of my childhood friendships, which today is as obliterated as any *shtetl* in Eastern Europe. Any marginal group in mass society may be subject without warning to the loss of its cultural landscape, and therefore those who are able to create portable landscapes for themselves are the most likely to endure.

The Jews have been doing so for thousands of years; the Simchas Torah tallis can stand in front of any Ark, and the original Ark, in the biblical account, was itself transported from station to station in the desert. Yet the members of a community are orphaned when the naïve intimacy of a living environment is torn away from them. Such a break appears often in Jewish literature—significantly with the emphasis not forward on the beginning of adulthood, as in the European *Bildungsroman*, but rather on the end of childhood.[3]

I suddenly discover the distance between the world and myself at the end of August in 1966. When my parents pick me up from camp, they take me to a new house. For the last time, we attend high holiday services in Farmingdale. It is the only time we will ever drive there, and our family's friends no longer join us during the afternoon break on Yom Kippur for a surreptitious glass of tea and a slice of challah. Farmingdale is no longer home, and though our new house is only ten miles away, it is another world.

We live now in an almost exclusively white, middle-class suburb with many Jews, but our older, brick house is isolated on a block of working-class cubes. While neighbors my age play football in our yard, I often retreat to my room and console myself with sports books for preadolescents. My new and bewildering sense of marginality leads me to develop an exquisite self-consciousness. It is manifested in an almost constant internal dialogue, which keeps me company and will interfere with my adolescent sexuality.

Ostracism is often the fate of a new kid on the block, and it may last longer when his family is Jewish and his home better than those on either side. There is a custom in this part of New Jersey of tolerating petty vandalism on "mischief night," the night before Halloween. Pumpkins are smashed, and we, along with other unpopular families on the block, have the windows of our cars and house smeared with soap. One Halloween I wake up to see graffiti chalked in bold letters on the sidewalk in front of our house: "Jon the Jew, a real one too." My father summons the kids next door—whom we suspect of being the authors—to scrape the words off the sidewalk, as I burn with shame.

He and I never discuss the incident, but later I will compare it with a memory of Freud's: As a child, he was walking with his father, when a gentile knocked his father's hat off. Rather than confronting the man, Freud's father meekly bent over to pick up the hat, and his son's humiliation persisted into adulthood (Bakan 1958; D. Boyarin 1997). The moral is that a victim is likely to view any response as adding insult to injury. In my case, as my father asserts the American principle of equality and "teaches a lesson" to my occasional and vindictive playmates by forcing them to erase what they have written, I feel as though he is inviting them to write the words again, this time making me watch my own degradation.

The new synagogue my parents join is only a partial refuge. It exemplifies the difference between a shul and a temple. Everything in Farmingdale had faced inward: little concern was paid for praying in unison, and though the *shammes* would bang his hand on the table for silence, he was seldom heeded; even the cantor was alone with God, facing away from everyone else, rather than performing for the congregation. Calling a synagogue a temple, by contrast, is doubly revealing. On the one hand, it indicates a striving for the majesty of the ancient House in Jerusalem. On the other hand, just like the English term used to designate it, its trappings are borrowed from the Christian world, down to the black robes worn by the rabbi and cantor.

These robes lack the warm mystery of Walter Tenenbaum's tallis. The responsive readings of Psalms in English seem ridiculously artificial to me from the first. And my mother, who still comes only on the holidays though I sometimes drag my father to temple on Friday nights, complains of the rabbi's long-winded sermons and yearns aloud for the intimate conversations along the back wall of the Farmingdale Jewish Community Center.

Unlike some, I do not leave the synagogue immediately after my bar mitzvah. I teach the blessings of the Haftorah to two reluctant boys a year younger than me. I briefly experience religious inspiration, and for perhaps two weeks put on *tefillin* every morning. But the atmosphere is hollow, and the emptiness breeds cynicism in me in my teens.

The coldness of the building itself is symptomatic of the lack of sustenance I sense there. The pretense and bad taste of modern American synagogues are well-known yet puzzling phenomena that deserve a sociological explanation of their own. Even the walls of the temple are dead concrete blocks, in contrast to the wood of the Farmingdale Jewish Community Center. Services are held in a "sanctuary," unlike the room at the Community Center where activities as varied as dances and political meetings were conducted when services were not being held. Aside from any question of Jewish law, there is a loss of community marked by the fact that everyone drives to the temple rather than walking. It is a place separated from the home, without the strong and patient webs spun by leisurely strolling conversations to and from a shul.

Most generally, the temple is victim to the general alienation of the suburbs. What happens or fails to happen there is dependent on what the people who come there expect from each other. Those who belong (there are vastly more "members" than regular attendees) seem bound primarily by a vague desire to have Jewish grandchildren. The poor rabbi, typical of Conservative congregations, seems hired to be a stand-in Jew, to observe all the laws and contain all the knowledge they don't have the time for. They are not bound to each other by Jewish religious ways, nor do they share the common interests of everyday life—the same livelihood or language—that helped to make a complete community in Farmingdale.

I go off to college and slowly discover that my dismissal of Judaism leaves me isolated, with few resources. I had realized my individual difference on leaving Farmingdale. Now, much more removed from a Jewish environment than ever before, I become aware of my inescapable Jewishness. In the small northwestern college of my dreams, everyone around me seems "American" and different, though I have never thought of myself as anything but American. Even in the humanities curriculum on which the school prides itself, Jewish civilization is absent. It is as though Western cultural history were just a triumphant straight line from the Greeks to Augustine and Michelangelo (with his horned Moses and uncircumcised David), confusion setting in at last only with Marx and Freud.

Five years too late to benefit me, a Jewish Studies position will in fact be established at the college. Such positions are usually funded by Jewish individuals or organizations, and hence they represent the growing acculturation (not assimilation) of Jews into American academic life. The fact that they are regarded as legitimate by the academic community, however, is part of a reintegration of Jewish thought into the concept of Western humanities. Jewish ethnographers can contribute to this movement—for example, by elucidating the dialectic of tradition and change as worked out in communities facing vastly different historical challenges. We may then move beyond efforts to explain the explosive presence of Jews in post-Enlightenment intellectual life as a result of their "primitive" encounter with "civility" (Cuddihy 1974) to explore how the Jewish belief that "Creation as the (active) speech or writing of God posits first of all that the Universe is essentially intelligible" (Faur 1986: 7) provided a pathway from Torah to a restless, unifying modern impulse in the natural and social sciences.

Such notions are far beyond me as an undergraduate. At my college in the 1970s, the social scientists in their separate departments strive to separate themselves from their "objects of study"; the humanists treasure the peace of their cloisters; the artists, knowing they are intellectually suspect, cultivate a cliquish sense of superiority; and there is none of the give-and-take between learning and everyday experience that I have come to associate with the best of Jewish scholarship.

I find a friend, a Jew from Long Island, and we begin to teach each other that we need to cultivate our Jewishness. We discuss the "Jewish mentality" of modern thinkers, and paraphrasing Lenny Bruce's category of the *goyish*, sarcastically reject all that is "white." "I am not 'white,' " my friend Martin proudly postures, "I am a Semite." Meanwhile, reflecting on my own dismissal of suburban Judaism, I decide not to end willingly an almost endless chain of Jewish cultural transmission. I stake my future on the assumption that a tradition so old and varied must contain the seeds of a worthwhile life for me, and decide to begin to acquire them through study.

Besides, my reading as a student of anthropology leads me to reason that if I concentrate on Jewish culture, no one will accuse me of cultural imperialism (see Gough 1968). No doubt others in my generation who choose to do fieldwork with Jews are motivated by similar considerations. Jewish anthropologists as a class are privileged to belong to the world of academic discourse, and to have an entrée into a variety of unique communities that maintain cultural frameworks in opposition to mass society.

Something deeper than Marxist critiques of anthropology draws me to Yiddish in particular. Before I left Farmingdale, my best friend had been a child of survivors from Lemberg. I remember being at his house once, and asking with a sense of wonder: "Ralph, do you really know Yiddish?"

Ralph told me that although he understood the language—which his parents still spoke to him—he had never learned to speak it. Still, I was impressed that he knew this secret code. And now that I am finished with college and looking to find my own way home, Yiddish seems to be the nearest link to which I can attach myself. It is the key to a sense of the life of the *shtetl*, that Jewish dreamtime that I inevitably associate with my lost Farmingdale.

The Farmingdale community has, by this point, completely disintegrated: Virtually no Jews in that part of New Jersey earn their living as chicken farmers anymore. Many of those who have gone into business have moved to nearby towns like Lakewood. The Torah scrolls of the Community Center have been ceremoniously transferred to a new synagogue near housing developments on the highway between Farmingdale and Lakewood. I have never considered becoming a chicken farmer myself.

So, when I finish my college courses, without waiting for graduation, I flee back to New York. "Flee": No one chases me out of Portland, Oregon,

God forbid! "Back": The city, though a magnet and a refuge, has never been my home before. Yet for three years I have shaped my identity in opposition to the "American" world around me, and I have reverted, along with my close friends, to what we imagine is an authentic New York accent—the "deses" and "doses" that were drilled out of my parents' repertoire in the days when New York public school teachers had to pass elocution exams.

Rejecting suburban Judaism, belatedly pursuing the image of the sixties' counterculture to the Pacific Northwest, and self-consciously affecting a "New York Jew" style were all successive attempts to shape a personal identity. In each case, the identity strategy was in opposition to the prevailing conventions of the immediate social order. Similarly, opposition to their parents' perceived bourgeois complacency may underlie the involvement of young people with Judaism. Yet as Dominique Schnapper has noted (1983), for young, intellectual Jews becoming involved in Jewish religion, politics, or culture, there can be no question of canceling out prior experience and "becoming traditional." In fact, this is true even of the most seemingly Orthodox and insular Jewish communities. There is a difference between learning about great rabbis of the past through meetings with Jewish gray-beards who knew them, and through reading about their merits in the Williamsburg newspaper *Der Yid*.

Of course, not only Jews are in the position of reconstituting interrupted tradition (cf. Clifford 1986: 116 ff.). But since they have been in the business of reshaping tradition in a dialogue with written texts for thousands of years, Jews may benefit more directly than others from learning about what other Jews are doing with their common tradition. It is conceivable that individuals may choose to adopt traits from other communities or even join those communities based on what they read in ethnographies. Whether such cultural borrowings and recombinations are effected in an "authentic" manner will depend less on precedent than on the degree of self-confident cultural generosity that results.

Arriving in New York, I adopt a knitted yarmulke, although my hair still falls below my shoulders. I immediately begin a nine-week summer course in Yiddish at Columbia, and it seems as though the language were being brought out from deep inside me. When I go to visit my parents on weekends, my father remembers words he'd never noticed forgetting. When I take the IRT after class back down to the Village, it seems as if everybody on the train is speaking Yiddish. Most important for my sense of identity, phrases here and there in my own internal dialogue are now in Yiddish, and I find I can reflect on myself with a gentle irony that was never available to me in English.

Then, after my first year in graduate school, I am off to Europe the following summer, courtesy of my parents. I arrive at the Gare du Nord in Paris with the address of a friend and without a word of French. I am spotted wearing my yarmulke by a young North African Jew who makes me understand, in broken English, that he studies at the Lubavitch yeshiva in

Paris. He buys me a Paris guidebook and sets me on my way in the Metro. At the end of the summer, this meeting will stand as the first in a set of Parisian reactions to my yarmulke which crystallize in my memory:

—The reaction of the generous young Trotskyist with whom my friend had grown close and with whom I stayed for two weeks: She could see the yarmulke only as a symbol of Jewish nationalism and argued bitterly that it was inherently reactionary;

—Of a young North African Jew, selling carpets at the flea market at Clignoncourt, who grabbed my arm and cried, "*Haver! Haver!* Brother Jew!";

—Of another young man, minding a booth outside one of the great department stores, who asked me if I were Orthodox, and interrupted my complicated response to explain that, although he was Orthodox himself, he was afraid to wear a yarmulke in the street;

—Of an old man at the American Express office who spoke to me in Yiddish and complained that the recent North African migrants dominated the Jewish communal organizations, and that there was no place for a Polish Jew to go.

Those first, fragmentary encounters are my fieldwork juvenilia. In assuming the yarmulke, I perhaps do not stop to consider that neither my actions nor my knowledge match the standards that it symbolically represents. But it works effectively, almost dangerously, as a two-way sensor, inducing Jews to present themselves to me and forcing me to try to understand how I am reflected in their eyes.

Externally, I learn many things about the situation of French Jewry. From the patent discomfort my non-Jewish Trotskyist friend feels at my display of Jewish specificity, I gain some sense of the conflicts young French Jews—coming out of the universalist, antihistorical revolutionary apogee of May 1968—must have felt years later when they first began to distinguish themselves from their comrades and view the world from the vantage point of their specific history. From the young street peddlers, I learn about how much riskier public proclamation of oneself as a Jew is perceived as being in Paris than in New York, and a concomitant depth of instant identification of one Jew with another. My meeting with the old Polish Jew at the American Express office hints at the dynamics of dominant and declining ethnic groups within the Jewish community, so vastly different from those dynamics in the United States.

Internally, I begin to understand that an identifiably Jewish headcovering places its own claims on the one who wears it. The longer it stays put, the more its power to keep him out of non-kosher restaurants grows. More important, people want to know who he is as a Jew. And if he does not know, the desire for peace of mind will spur further his effort to shape an identity.

Returning from Paris, I find an apartment at Second Avenue and Fifth Street in Manhattan. I tell people, "After three generations, my family has finally made it back to the Lower East Side." In fact, none of my grandparents lived on the East Side for a long time after immigrating, even though my mother tells me she regrets having missed the Yiddish theater on Second Avenue during her girlhood. By the time I move in, there is no Yiddish theater left. The former Ratner's dairy restaurant on Second Avenue, where, I'm told, Trotsky was a lousy tipper, is now a supermarket. Though sometimes one still sees a white newspaper truck with the word *Forverts* in lovely blue Hebrew letters on its side drive by late at night, this neighborhood has been the East Village since the sixties, and I think of it as such.

A new friend, who devotes his time to a frustrating effort to rescue Lower East Side synagogues, tells me of a shul still in use on an otherwise abandoned block east of Tompkins Square Park. Though my friend has never been inside, he is sure that I will be welcomed, since such an isolated congregation must be looking for new blood.

The place is called the Eighth Street Shul, but its full name is Kehilas Bnei Moshe Yakov Anshei Zavichost veZosmer—Congregation Children of Moses and Jacob, People of Zavichost and Zosmer. It is owned by a *landsmanshaft* (hometown society) founded by émigrés and refugees from two towns in south central Poland. No one born in either town prays regularly at the shul now, and only one or two of the congregants are actually members of the society.

The shul is located in the center of what New York Latinos call "Loisaida"—an area bounded by Avenue A on the east, Avenue D on the west, Houston Street on the south, and Fourteenth Street on the north. Once the blocks up to Tenth Street were almost exclusively Jewish, and on nearly every one stood a synagogue or a religious school. Now two of those former synagogues stand abandoned, several more have become churches, and the rest have disappeared.

Eighth Street is a typical and not especially distinguished example of turn-of-the-century Lower East Side synagogue architecture.[4] It consists of five levels. The lowest contains a cranky and inadequate boiler. The second is the *besmedresh* or study room, which was destroyed by a suspicious fire in August 1982. The third level is the main sanctuary, long and narrow like the tenements among which it was tucked when it was built. Two rows of simple pews are separated by an aisle, which is interrupted in the center of the room by the raised table from which the weekly Torah portion is read. At the very front is the Ark, surrounded by partially destroyed wooden carvings that are the most artistic aspect of the shul. The walls are decorated with representations of the traditional Jewish signs for the zodiac; the two in front on the left have been obliterated by water damage from the leaky roof. Covering most of this level, with roughly an eight-foot opening extending toward the back, is the women's gallery. The gallery is constructed in such a way that it is easier for women sitting on opposite sides of the opening to converse with one another than to see what the men are doing downstairs. Finally, upstairs from the women's gallery is an unused and cramped apartment that was once occupied by the shul's caretaker. In the roof behind it, an opening that was a skylight until there was a break-in is now covered with a solid wooden framework, allowing neither light nor vandals to enter.

Avenues B and C, which mark off the block, were once lively commercial streets with mostly Jewish storekeepers. There were also several smaller streets lined with tenements, right up to the edge of the East River. When the FDR Drive was built along the river, all the streets east of Avenue D disappeared, the tenements on the remaining available land were replaced by municipal housing, and the stores declined rapidly. During the same years, a massive middle-class housing cooperative, funded by a government mortgage, was built along Grand Street one mile to the south. Many of the remaining Jewish families moved into those houses, leaving virtually no Jews in the immediate area of the Eighth Street Shul.

Yet a minyan has continued to meet there every Saturday morning, with virtually no interruptions, throughout the years of the neighborhood's decline, while the block served as the Lower East Side's heaviest "shopping street" for hard drugs. It has lasted into the present, when buildings all around it are being speculated upon and renovated by both squatters and powerful real estate interests. It appears that until recently the main reason for this continuity was a felicitous rivalry between two men who were unwilling to abandon the synagogue because their fathers had both been presidents of it at one time. Perhaps if there had been only one, he would have given up and made peace with his conscience. Perhaps if the two men had naturally been friends they could have agreed to sell the building and officially merge their society with another still functioning further south in the neighborhood. If they had been able to agree on anything besides continuing to come to the shul, the shul might not have survived this long.

The first time I walk in, a clean-shaven, compact man in his sixties—younger than several of the congregants, who number perhaps seventeen in all—hurries forward to greet me. What's my name? Where do I live? Where am I from originally? And where do I usually go to pray on shabbes? His name is Moshe Fogel, and he sees to it that I am called to the Torah, the honor accorded any guest who comes for the first time, without asking any questions as to his level of religious observance. Later, an older member explains to me: "Once upon a time, you wouldn't get called to the Torah unless you kept kosher and observed shabbes." Now, Moish prefers simply to leave those matters undiscussed.

The history of the East Side as a place where all types of Jews have lived together reinforces his discretion. Externalities such as proper or improper clothing are not essential criteria for participation. This is true of the entire Orthodox community on the East Side and has even become part of its mystique. Rabbi Reuven Feinstein, head of the Staten Island branch of the East Broadway-based yeshiva, Tifereth Jerusalem, noted in a recent speech the common reaction in Boro Park and other thriving Orthodox centers to the nonconformist dress of East Side visitors: "It's okay, you're from the East Side." The president at Eighth Street still wears a traditional *gartl* when he prays, a belt worn over his jacket to separate the pure from the base parts of his body, and no one has suggested that such old customs are out of place today. But partly because the older members at the Eighth Street Shul walked through the East Village in the 1960s and knew there were many young Jews among the longhairs—even if they were horrified at the thought—they were willing to include in the minyan a young man in the neighborhood who, when he first came, wore dreadlocks under a Rastafarian-style knitted cap. It is also doubtless true that at that time there was no other Orthodox synagogue anywhere that he would have contemplated entering.

By contrast, it is impossible for any Jew raised in the middle of secular society (including a Jewish anthropologist) to join a traditionalist community without giving up major parts of his or her identity. The ways in which a researcher of contemporary Hasidic life "becomes a Hasid" are much more dramatic than the way in which one becomes a regular at Eighth Street—but they are probably more transient as well. In order to gain the confidence of the traditionalist communities, the fieldworker has to give the impression, whether implicitly or explicitly, that he or she is likely eventually to accept their standards in all areas of life (Belcove-Shalin 1988). All one has to do at Eighth Street is agree to come back—"a little earlier next time, if possible."

Two things will draw me back to join this congregation, occasionally referred to as "those holy souls who *daven* in the middle of the jungle." The first pull is the memory of Farmingdale: the Ashkenazic accents and melodies (though here they are Polish, whereas Walter Tenenbaum had prayed in his native Lithuanian accent); the smell of herring on the old men's breath and hands; the burning sensation of whiskey, which I must have tasted surreptitiously at the conclusion of Yom Kippur one year in Farmingdale.

The second thing that draws me, though I do not come every week, is a feeling that I am needed and missed when I am absent. It's hard for me to get up early on Saturday mornings, after being out late Friday nights. It still seems like a sacrifice, as though I were stealing part of my weekend from myself. If I arrive in time for the *Shema*, about half an hour into the service, I congratulate myself on my devotion. The summer before I marry, in 1981, I hardly come at all. When I go with my brother to meet Moshe Fogel at the shul and give him the provisions for the kiddush I am giving to celebrate my upcoming wedding, I tell Dan that I usually arrive "around nine-thirty," to which Moish retorts: "Even when you used to come, you didn't show up at nine-thirty!" Though he says it with a smile, a message comes through clearly: If I want to claim to belong, I should attend regularly and arrive on time. Although I am always welcome, only if I can be counted on am I part of the minyan. The dependence of Jews on each other—a theme running through biblical and rabbinic literature—is pressingly literal at Eighth Street.

Meanwhile, my feelings about Paris coalesce into a plan. I know I want to live there for a time, but only if I will be among Jews. Since I am at the point in my graduate school career when I must find a dissertation topic, I decide to look for fieldwork situations with Jews in Paris. I make an exploratory visit with my fiancée, Elissa. Will she agree to a pause in her own career to follow me on this project? Will the organizations of Polish Jewish immigrants whom I have chosen to study be willing to have me study them?

The answer is yes to both questions. Speaking Yiddish and appearing as a nice young Jewish couple seem to be the critical elements in our success. We are invited to sit in on board meetings, negotiations aimed at the reunification of societies split by political differences for over half a century. I am struck by the fact that these immigrants seem so much more marked by their political identification than the East European Jews I've met in New York. Also, I am impressed at the number of societies remaining in a country that has suffered Nazi occupation and that historically has shown little tolerance for immigrant cultural identifications.

But I am drawn not so much by the differences between these Yiddish speakers and those I know in New York as by encountering them in an environment that is otherwise so foreign. Speaking Yiddish to people with whom I have no other common language confirms its legitimacy and reinforces the sense of a distinctive Jewish identity that is shared between generations. I go for a trial interview of one activist, who is disappointed that I didn't bring "the girl," Elissa, along with me. When he discovers to my embarrassment that I have been secretly taping the interview, he is flattered.

Just before leaving Paris, Elissa and I climb the steps of Sacré Coeur. The cathedral itself is an ungracious mass, and the city looks gray and undifferentiated below us. I experience a moment of vertigo, as if I could tumble off Montmartre and drown. Part of my dream of Paris, "capital of the nineteenth century," is an infantile fantasy of becoming a universal intellectual— to be free both of the special knowledge and of the limitations of my knowledge that follow on my personal history. Yet I know I cannot come to Paris and immediately move among its confident, cliquish intellectual elite. Even less will I ever have contact with that "quintessentially French" petite bourgeoisie typified by the stolid Inspector Maigret. My first place will be with the immigrants, whose appearance, strange language, and crowded quarters provided material for unkind portraits by Maigret's creator, Simenon, in the 1930s.[5] If I am unable to come to see Paris as they have seen it, if I cannot make out of a shared marginality a niche in the city for myself, I will be lost, as much as the "lost generation," and in a most unromantic way.

During the two years between our decision to spend a year in Paris and the beginning of that year, I attend the Eighth Street Shul more and more regularly, and Elissa occasionally joins me. Gradually, my feelings when I miss a week shift from guilt to regret. One shabbes, waking up late but not wanting to miss attending altogether, I arrive just in time for the kiddush, to the general amusement of the entire minyan. One February morning I wake up to see snow falling and force myself to go outside against my will, knowing that on a day like this I am truly needed.

Other incidents illustrate the gap in assumptions between myself and the other congregants. I try to bring friends into the shul, partly because it makes me more comfortable, and partly to build up the congregation. A friend whose hair and demeanor reflect his love of reggae music and his connections with Jamaican Rastafarians comes along one Yom Kippur. We reach the point in the service when pious men, remembering the priests in the days of the Temple, descend to their knees and touch their foreheads to the floor. Since no one wants to soil his good pants on the dirty floor, sheets of newspaper are provided as protection. Reb Simcha Taubenfeld, the senior member of the congregation, approaches my friend with newspaper in hand and asks in his heavy Yiddish accent: "Do you fall down?" The look of bewilderment on my friend's face graphically illustrates the term "frame of reference."

Another week, the same friend, failing to observe the discretion with regard to the expression of political opinions that I have learned to adopt at shul, gets into a bitter argument over the Palestinian question. Fishel Mandel, a social worker and one of the younger members of the congregation, calls me during the week to convey the message that "despite our political differences, your friend is still welcome."

After our wedding, I attend virtually every week. When Elissa comes, she is doubly welcome, since the only other woman who attends regularly is Goldie Brown, Moish Fogel's sister. Though Goldie doesn't complain about being isolated in the women's gallery one flight above the men, she seconds Elissa's suggestion that a mekhitse be set up downstairs. The suggestion gets nowhere, however: It would entail displacing one of the regular members of the congregation from his usual seat, and though there is no lack of available places (I myself usually wander from front to back during the course of the service), he refuses to consider moving.

I reason that I will have more of a voice concerning questions such as the seating of women if I formalize my relationship to the shul by becoming a member. My timid announcement that I would like to do so meets with initial confusion on the part of the older members of the society present. Then Fishel, ever the mediator and interpreter, explains to me that the shul is not organized like a suburban synagogue: "There's a *chevra*, a society, that owns the shul. In order to join, you have to be *shomer mitzves*, you have to keep kosher and strictly observe the Sabbath."

I drop my request. Shiye the president reassures me with a speech in his usual roundabout style to the effect that belonging to the chevra is a separate question from being a member of the minyan: "They send their money in from New Jersey and Long Island, but the shul couldn't exist without the people that actually come to pray here."

Meanwhile, our plans to go to Paris proceed. Our travel plans become a topic for discussion over kiddush at shul. One of the older, Polish-born members tells us for the first time that he lived in Paris for nine years after the war. We ask him why he came to America, and he answers, "*Vern a frantsoyz iz shver* [It's hard to become a Frenchman]," both to obtain citizenship and to be accepted by neighbors.

At the end of the summer, we expect to give a farewell kiddush at the shul. A few days before shabbes, I get a phone call from Moish Fogel: "Don't get things for kiddush. We won't be able to daven at Eighth Street for a while. There's been a fire. Thank God, the Torah scrolls were rescued, but it's going to take a while to repair the damage." It is two weeks after Tisha B'Av, the fast commemorating the destruction of the Temple in Jerusalem.

Leaving New York without saying goodbye to the shul and its congregation, we fly overnight to Brussels and immediately *shlep* (the word "drag" would not do the burden justice) our seven heavy suitcases onto a Paris train. Arriving again at the Gare du Nord, I think of the thousands of Polish Jews who were greeted at the station in the twenties and thirties by fellow immigrants eager to hire workers. As soon as we get off the train, Elissa immediately "gets involved," demanding the credentials of two men who claim to be policemen and attempt to "confiscate" a carpet two Moroccan immigrants are carrying. Upon Elissa's challenge, the "policemen" demur.

We practice our French on the cab driver: I explain to him why we've come to Paris. He warns us that we shouldn't tell strangers we're Jewish. It is only a few weeks since the terrorist attack on Goldenberg's restaurant, and no one knows when the next anti-Semitic attack may come. I reply that if I hadn't said we were Jewish, we wouldn't have found out he was a Jew as well, adding that in New York the names of taxi drivers are posted inside the cabs. He says he wouldn't like that at all.

So we receive an early warning that ethnicity in Paris is not celebrated publicly as it is in New York, nor are ethnic mannerisms and phrases so prevalent as a deliberate element of personal style. This is the repressive underside of marginality. It appears wherever the individual or community think it is better not to flaunt their distinctiveness, even if they cannot fully participate in the host culture. It leads to suspicion and silence, to the taxi driver's desire for anonymity.

Arriving at our rented apartment, we meet our neighbor Isabel, who will be our only non-Jewish friend during the year in Paris, and who later explains that meeting us has helped dispel her prejudices about Jews. Over the next few days, we introduce ourselves to Jewish storekeepers in the neighborhood: Guy, the Tunisian kosher butcher; Chanah, the Polish baker's wife; Leon, the deli man from Lublin, who insists he didn't learn Yiddish until he came to Paris.

We have a harder time finding a synagogue where we feel at home. For Rosh Hashanah and Yom Kippur, we have purchased tickets at one of the "official" synagogues run by the Consistoire, the recognized religious body of French Jewry set up under Napoleon. Most synagogues run by the Consistoire are named after the streets on which they're located. Meeting a Hasid on the street, I ask him whether he happens to know when Rosh

Hashanah services begin at "Notre Dame de Nazareth." He grimaces and makes as if spitting: "Don't say that name, *ptu ptu ptu!*"

The synagogue is strange to us as well. Most of the crowd seems if anything more secular than most American Jews, who go to the synagogue only on the high holidays. Many teenagers wear jeans or miniskirts. Because of the fear of terrorism, everyone is frisked on entering. Inside, the synagogue is picturesque with its nineteenth-century pseudo-Moorish motifs; when it was built, Offenbach was the choirmaster. Yet it is as religiously dissatisfying as the suburban American temple I used to attend. The services seem to be conducted in a traditional manner, but it is hard to tell from among the noisy throng in back. The shammes, as a representative of the government, wears a Napoleonic hat, and the rabbi delivers his sermon from a high pulpit.

After Yom Kippur, I think idly about the need to find a more comfortable shul, and when I hear about an East European-style minyan within walking distance, I consider going on Simchas Torah. Watching television reports of terrorist attacks on Simchas Torah in other European capitals, I am consumed with shame at my own apathy, and thus I walk a kilometer or two to find the synagogue on the rue Basfroi the following shabbes.

Going in, I am first shown into a side room, where men are reciting incomprehensible prayers with strange and beautiful melodies. Eventually I realize that they are North African Jews, and I venture into the main room to ask, "Is there an Ashkenazic minyan here?"

The man I ask replies in French, "We're not racists here! We're all Jews!" at which his friend points out:

"The young man spoke to you in Yiddish!" Continuing in Yiddish, he explains that while everyone is welcome in the main synagogue, the services there are in fact Ashkenazic, and so some of the North African men prefer to pray in their own style in the smaller room.

Gradually I settle in, though I have trouble following the prayers in the beginning. Remembering a particular turn in the melody for the reader's repetition of the Amidah that the president at Eighth Street uses, I listen for it from the cantor here at the rue Basfroi, and hear a satisfying similarity in his voice. I feel like a new immigrant coming to his landsmanshaft's shul to hear the melodies from his town.

Throughout our year in Paris, I attend this synagogue about as frequently as I had gone to Eighth Street at first. Although the congregation is not unfriendly, no one invites me home for lunch, partly out of French reserve, and perhaps also because it is clear that I'm not very observant. I feel "unobservant" here in another sense: I do not register the vast store of information obviously available here about the interaction of religious Jews from different ethnic backgrounds. It escapes me, as though I were "off duty." In contrast to my feelings at Eighth Street, I am not motivated by the desire to make myself a regular here. And this is not my fieldwork situation: Nothing external moves me to push my way through socially, to find out who these people really are and let them see me as well.

The Jews I encounter in the course of my research belong to an entirely different crowd. The landsmanshaftn to which they belong are secular organizations. If I wanted to observe the Sabbath closely, it would be difficult for me to do my fieldwork. The immigrants hold many meetings on Saturdays, including a series of *shabbes-shmuesn*, afternoon discussions at which the main focus this year is the war in Lebanon.

I mention to one of my informants that I sometimes go to the synagogue. "I admire that," he responds. "I can't go back to the synagogue now. I've been away too long; it's too late for me." Toward the end of the year, we invite an autodidact historian of the immigrant community to dinner on Friday night and ask him to say the blessing over the challah. "I can't," he refuses, and will not explain further. Though his intellectual curiosity has led him to become friendly with us, and he is considering doing research on the resurgence of Orthodoxy among French Jews, his critical stance vis-à-vis his own secularist movement is insufficient to allow him to accept this religious honor. Enjoying the possibilities offered by marginality is sometimes impossible for those who are neither young nor well educated and who have often been deceived in their wholehearted commitments.

Throughout the year, Elissa has been growing stricter regarding *kashres*. She refuses to eat nonkosher meat and will order only fish in restaurants. She articulates our shared impression that Jewish secularism has failed to create everyday lifeways that can be transmitted from generation to generation, and that any lasting Judaism must be grounded in Jewish law and learning. Before parting for the summer—she to study Yiddish at Oxford, I to Jerusalem, to acquire the Hebrew that I will need to learn about Jewish law—we discuss the level of observance we want to adopt on our return to New York, but we come to no decision.

Elissa and I meet at the end of the summer in Los Angeles, for the bar mitzvah of her twin cousins. I am uncomfortable riding on shabbes; after spending an entire summer in Jerusalem, for the first time, it seems like a violation of myself. The roast beef sandwich I eat at the reception is the first nonkosher food I've eaten since leaving Paris.

Thus, without having made a formal declaration, I join Elissa in observing kashres (save for occasional lapses that I call my "*treyf* of the month club" and that become less and less frequent), and she joins me in keeping shabbes, albeit with some reluctance. Preparing to fulfill a promise made in a dream I had while in Paris, I take a further step: At the beginning of November, I begin attending daily services at another East Side shul and thus putting on tefillin again. One of my mother's cousins at the Telshe Yeshiva in Cleveland—whom I have never met—told me in the dream that I would always be welcome there, and I responded that if I got there, I would put on tefillin every day from then on. Later in November, Elissa and I fly to Cleveland for the weekend. Though we are welcomed warmly, it is clear that the rabbis and *rebetsins* at the yeshiva hoped for something more Jewish from me, the great-grandson of the Rosh Yeshiva's second wife, Miriam.

We return to the Eighth Street Shul as well, which has been secured and repaired sufficiently to make it usable once again. There are changes. Old Mr. Klapholz, with whom I hardly had exchanged a word, has passed away. Fishel's uncle Mr. Hochbaum, a congregant for half a century, no longer attends, since he is unable to walk all the way from Grand Street. On the other hand, my long-haired friend has moved into the neighborhood and attends regularly. Two of the younger members of the congregation have small children now, and they must go to a shul where there are other children for their son and daughter to play with. In February, our oldest member passes away, and after Shavuot, another member moves to Jerusalem. Two more young men eventually begin coming regularly and bring along their infant children. Now, in June 1986, the shul has thirteen regular male attendees. I am no longer free to sleep late on Saturday mornings, and fortunately I no longer want to.

All of this, to the extent it is of my own making, is the result of a search to realize that fragile illusion of wholeness which was destroyed when my family and almost all the others left Farmingdale. I will hazard a guess that Jewish anthropologists—perhaps anthropologists in general—are motivated by a sense of loss. Yet the seamless image of community is inevitably a child's image. We cannot regain what is lost, if only because it never existed as we remember it. Nothing in society is quite as harmonious as it seemed to me then, and I later learned about bitter political struggles that had taken place in Farmingdale, just as they had among the immigrants in Paris.

Our strategy, rather, should be to attempt to understand what it is we miss and need, which is available in still-living communities in another form. The image of wholeness which we share is foreshadowed by communities all of us stem from, however many generations back, and it can serve as a guide in the search for the reciprocal relationships of autonomous adulthood.

Anthropology is a tool for mediating between the self and the community. It has helped me to come to belong at the Eighth Street Shul: to withhold my opinions when it seems necessary, without feeling the guilt of self-compromise; to accept instruction and gentle reprimands with good humor; to believe it is worthwhile preserving something that might otherwise disappear. But belonging at Eighth Street does not mean that I have dissolved myself into an ideal Orthodox Jew. If I attempted to do so, I would be unable to continue being an anthropologist. If I fit into any category, it may be what my friend Kugelmass calls the "funky Orthodox": that is, those who participate in the community but whose interests and values are not confined to the Orthodox world. In fact, there are no ideal Orthodox Jews at Eighth Street; it is our respective quirks that provide the *raison d'être* of this haphazard but now intentional once-a-week community.

The fact that I have found a religious community that needs me because of its marginality and will tolerate me because of a generosity born of tradition is what I mean by the marginal redemption of one Jew. Likewise, if the shul survives, it will be because of its very marginality, because of the many individuals who have recognized the creative possibilities of a situation that demands that they create a new unity, while allowing each of them to retain their otherness. Isn't this the dream of anthropologists? Whether attempting to communicate knowledge between different Jewish communities, or between communities much more distant in tradition and empathy, we are messengers. We spend our own lives in moving back and forth among the worlds of others. As we do so, in order to avoid getting lost along the way we must become cultural pioneers, learning to "get hold of our *trans*cultural selves" (Wolff 1970: 40). Communities on the edge of mass society, or even on the fringes of ethnic enclaves, seem to be among the most congenial fields in which to do so.

Let me finish with a parable:

Two Jews can afford to be fastidious about the dress, comportment, and erudition of a third. It gives them something to gossip about and identify against. Ten healthy Jews can have a similar luxury; an eleventh means competition for the ritual honors. It's nine Jews who are the most tolerant, as I learned one forlorn shabbes at Eighth Street. It was almost ten o'clock, and there was no minyan. Since everyone seemed content to wait patiently, I assumed that someone else had promised to come, and asked, "Who are we waiting for?"

"A *yid*," our oldest member replied without hesitation.

Eventually a Jew came along.   ∎

NOTES

1. Compare Pierre Bourdieu's critique of the structuralist theory of "reciprocal" gift exchange: "Even if reversibility [i.e., the assumption that gifts entail counter-gifts of equivalent value] is the objective truth of the discrete acts which ordinary experience knows in discrete form and calls gift exchanges, it is not the whole truth of a practice which could not exist if it were consciously perceived in accordance with the model. The temporal structure of gift exchange, which objectivism ignores, is what makes possible the coexistence of two opposing truths, which defines the full truth of the gift" (1977:6).

   Similarly, in a narrative such as this one, because I, as author, already know the ending, it may seem as though each successive element fits into those that precede and follow it in such a way that their necessity is perfectly known. Actually my aim is to show how the background that nurtured me shaped in part my unpredictable responses to situations that in themselves were historically rather than culturally determined. See my conclusion, where I refer to one of the communities I now participate in as "haphazard but intentional."

2. Even if it was no more than a matter of convenience, this annual event demonstrates Jonathan Woocher's point that American Jewish "civil religion expects Jews to take advantage of the opportunities which America provides, and to use them to help fulfill their Jewish responsibilities" (1985:161).

3. This may seem an outrageously loose claim, and I am quite willing to be proven wrong by literary scholars. But compare the conclusion of James Joyce's *Portrait of the Artist as a Young Man:*

> Mother is putting my new secondhand clothes in order. She prays now, she says, that I may learn in my own life and away from home and friends what the heart is and what it feels. Amen. So be it. Welcome, O life! I go to encounter for the millionth time the reality of experience and to forge in the smithy of my soul the uncreated conscience of my race. (1968:252–53)

with the end of Moshe Szulsztein's memoir of a Polish Jewish childhood:

> When the truck was already fairly far along Warsaw Street and Kurow was barely visible, two more relatives appeared in a great rush, wanting to take their leave. These were my grandfather's pair of pigeons. The pigeons knew me, and I knew them. I loved them, and perhaps they loved me as well . . . But the truck is stronger than they are, it drives and drives further and further away from Kurow. My poor pigeons can't keep up, they remain behind . . . Before they disappear altogether from my view I still discern them within the distant evening cloud, two small flying silver dots, one a bit behind the other. That, I know, is the male, and the second, a bit in front, is the female. (1982:352)

4. For photographs of Eighth Street and other Lower East Side shuls, both surviving and abandoned, see Fine and Wolfe (1978).

5. "In every corner, in every little patch of darkness, up the blind alleys and the corridors, one could sense the presence of a swarming mass of humanity, a sly, shameful life. Shadows slunk along the walls. The stores were selling goods unknown to French people even by name" (Simenon 1963: 45).

REFERENCES

Bakan, David. 1958. *Sigmund Freud and the Jewish Mystical Tradition.* Princeton, N.J.: Van Nostrand.

Belcove-Shalin, Janet. 1988. "Becoming More of an Eskimo." In *Between Two Worlds: Ethnographic Essays on American Jews.* Pp. 77–98. Ithaca, N.Y.: Cornell University Press.

Bourdieu, Pierre. 1977. *Outline of a Theory of Practice.* Cambridge: Cambridge University Press.

Boyarin, Daniel. 1997. *Judaism as a Gender.* Berkeley and Los Angeles: University of California Press.

Clifford, James. 1986. "On Ethnographic Allegory." In *Writing Culture: The Poetics and Politics of Ethnography,* edited by James Clifford and George Marcus. Pp. 98–121. Berkeley and Los Angeles: University of California Press.

Cuddihy, John. 1974. *The Ordeal of Civility: Freud, Marx, Lévi-Strauss and the Jewish Struggle with Modernity.* New York: Basic Books.

Fabian, Johannes. 1983. *Time and the Other.* New York: Columbia University Press.

Faur, José. 1986. *Golden Doves with Silver Dots.* Bloomington: Indiana University Press.

Fine, Jo Renée, and Gerard Wolfe. 1978. *The Synagogues of New York's Lower East Side.* New York: Washington Mews Books.

Gough, Kathleen. 1968. "Anthropology and Imperialism." *Monthly Review* 19: 12–27.

Joyce, James. 1968 (1916). *Portrait of the Artist as a Young Man.* New York: Viking Press.

Schnapper, Dominique. 1983. *Jewish Identities in France: An Analysis of Contemporary French Jewry,* translated by Arthur Goldhammer. Chicago: University of Chicago Press.

Simenon, Georges. 1963. *Maigret and the Enigmatic Lett,* edited by Daphne Woodward. New York: Penguin Books.

Szulsztein, Moshe. 1982. *Dort vu mayn vig iz geshtanen.* Paris: Published by a Committee.

Wolff, Kurt. 1970. "The Sociology of Knowledge and Sociological Theory." In *The Sociology of Sociology,* edited by Larry T. Reynolds and Janice M. Reynolds. Pp. 31–67. New York: David McKay.

Woocher, Jonathan. 1985. "Sacred Survival." *Judaism* 34 (2):151–62.

▪ QUESTIONS FOR MAKING CONNECTIONS WITHIN THE READING ▪

1. When Jonathan Boyarin describes his childhood in Farmingdale, New Jersey, he takes us into a world of Jewish traditions and references that may be unfamiliar to some readers: indeed, Boyarin's essay is concerned, in part, with tracing the author's efforts to grow more familiar with and gain a greater understanding of his own traditions. In the process, he describes many different kinds of Jews: an Orthodox Jew, a Jewish socialist, a Lubavitcher Hasid, an observant Jew, Zionists, and Jews who have been acculturated into American academic life, to name a few. What is the difference between the groups that Boyarin identifies? Why is he drawn to one group more than another?

2. "Waiting for a Jew" opens with the statement, "My story begins in a community . . . ." What is the difference between an essay and a story? Why has Boyarin elected to tell his fellow anthropologists a story? What are the major events or pieces of this story? Is this a story that has a point? A moral? An argument?

3. The subtitle Boyarin has selected for his essay is "Marginal Redemption at the Eighth Street Shul." What is "marginal redemption"? What is it that gets redeemed in "Waiting for a Jew"?

▪ QUESTIONS FOR WRITING ▪

1. "[O]n the abandoned farm," Boyarin writes, "my first memories are tinged with a sense of traces, of mystery, of loss. Do all who eventually become anthropologists have this experience in some form, at some time in their early lives?" In posing this question, Boyarin suggests that there might be a connection between anthropology and a sense of loss. What might this connection be? In what ways has Boyarin's own research been shaped by this sense of loss?

2. Boyarin believes that "[a]ny marginal group in mass society may be subject without warning to the loss of its cultural landscape, and therefore those who are able to create portable landscapes for themselves are the most likely to endure." What is the difference between a "cultural landscape" and a "portable landscape"? At the end of Boyarin's story, what kind of landscape does he inhabit?

■ *QUESTIONS FOR MAKING CONNECTIONS BETWEEN READINGS* ■

1. Lila Abu-Lughod, an anthropologist of Arab descent, and Jonathan Boyarin, a Jewish anthropologist, can be considered "insiders," part of the very cultures they are studying. What difference does it make whether a culture is studied by insiders or outsiders? Who benefits from such work? And how does one determine whether such work has been successful or not?

2. In "The Myth of the Ant Queen," Steven Johnson argues that complex systems have an intelligence of their own. And he suggests that as such systems develop, the individuals involved—whether humans or ants— may remain largely oblivious to the larger patterns of change. Individuals may assume they are doing one sort of thing, but the system as a whole is doing something else. Does Boyarin appear to share this way of thinking? Is culture also a complex system that unfolds in directions the individual actors might not always control or even understand fully? When we look at cultural change as exemplified by Boyarin's religious odyssey, does that change appear to be directed by a "unified, top-down" intelligence, or does it take place from the bottom-up, as a result of individual choices made by many different people? Are some cultures, institutions, and religions organized differently—that is, in a more top-down way?

www   **For additional suggestions about making connections between readings, visit the Link-O-Mat and More Sample Assignments at <www.newhum.com>.**

AMY CHUA

WILL DEMOCRACY AND the free market succeed in all parts of the world? Should they always be pursued? Do they always go together? Amy Chua poses these provocative questions in "A World on the Edge," an investigation into the relations, in many different countries, between economics, politics, and ethnic identity. A law professor who spent the early part of her career working in international business, Chua sees patterns of poverty, resentment, and violence emerging everywhere in the wake of globalization. Most observers hail the spread of democracy and capitalism as the start of a "new world order," but Chua offers a darker and more guarded view of such changes. Rather than usher in an era of greater wealth, opportunity, and freedom, the shift to open markets and popular elections has deepened long-standing conflicts among ethnic groups and nations. The results, Chua argues, are less stable and more volatile societies.

When Chua's aunt, a wealthy Chinese businesswoman living in the Philippines, was murdered by her Filipino chauffeur, the only motive listed on the police report was "revenge." In an effort to learn why her aunt was murdered and why "revenge" was identified as the official cause, Chua forced herself to look beyond her personal feelings about the brutal event. Her research led her to see the Philippines in a new light as a nation with a destitute majority of native Filipinos and a small minority of economically privileged ethnic Chinese. Then Chua began to recognize the parallels between the Philippines and other developing countries, where poor majorities live apart from the "market-dominant minorities."

Ultimately Chua's investigation led her to conclude that globalization creates an economic system that may actually make things worse for almost everyone outside the prosperous, developed First World. In the face of this possibility, she has called for the market-dominant minorities—including the United States—to play a more active role in assisting those who have been left behind by the march of progress.

Chua, Amy. "A World on the Edge." *Wilson Quarterly* 26(4) (Autumn 2002): 62–78.

Biographical information is drawn from Chua's home page <http://globetrotter.berkeley.edu/people4/Chua/chua-con0.html> and from <http://www.sjc.edu/content.cfm/pageid/4841>.

In a revised form, the essay reprinted here was incorporated into Chua's book *World on Fire: How Exporting Free Market Democracy Breeds Ethnic Hatred and Global Instability* (2003), which was a *New York Times* bestseller and was also named a Best Book of 2003 by *The Economist*. She is currently a professor at the Yale Law School.

www To learn more about Amy Chua and the history of the Philippines, please visit the Link-O-Mat at <www.newhum.com>.

A World on the Edge

One beautiful blue morning in September 1994, I received a call from my mother in California. In a hushed voice, she told me that my Aunt Leona, my father's twin sister, had been murdered in her home in the Philippines, her throat slit by her chauffeur. My mother broke the news to me in our native Hokkien Chinese dialect. But "murder" she said in English, as if to wall off the act from the family through language.

The murder of a relative is horrible for anyone, anywhere. My father's grief was impenetrable; to this day, he has not broken his silence on the subject. For the rest of the family, though, there was an added element of disgrace. For the Chinese, luck is a moral attribute, and a lucky person would never be murdered. Like having a birth defect, or marrying a Filipino, being murdered is shameful.

My three younger sisters and I were very fond of my Aunt Leona, who was petite and quirky and had never married. Like many wealthy Filipino Chinese, she had all kinds of bank accounts in Honolulu, San Francisco, and Chicago. She visited us in the United States regularly. She and my father— Leona and Leon—were close, as only twins can be. Having no children of her own, she doted on her nieces and showered us with trinkets. As we grew older, the trinkets became treasures. On my 10th birthday she gave me 10 small diamonds, wrapped up in toilet paper. My aunt loved diamonds and bought them up by the dozen, concealing them in empty Elizabeth Arden face moisturizer jars, some right on her bathroom shelf. She liked accumulating things. When we ate at McDonald's, she stuffed her Gucci purse with free ketchups.

According to the police report, my Aunt Leona, "a 58-year-old single woman," was killed in her living room with "a butcher's knife" at approximately 8 P.M. on September 12, 1994. Two of her maids were questioned, and they confessed that Nilo Abique, my aunt's chauffeur, had planned and executed the murder with their knowledge and assistance. "A few hours before the actual killing, respondent [Abique] was seen sharpening the knife allegedly used in the crime." After the killing, "respondent joined the two witnesses and told them that their employer was dead. At that time, he was wearing a pair of bloodied white gloves and was still holding a knife, also with traces of blood." But Abique, the report went on to say, had "disappeared," with the warrant for his arrest outstanding. The two maids were released.

Meanwhile, my relatives arranged a private funeral for my aunt in the prestigious Chinese cemetery in Manila where many of my ancestors are buried in a great, white-marble family tomb. According to the feng shui monks who were consulted, my aunt could not be buried with the rest of the family because of the violent nature of her death, lest more bad luck strike her surviving kin. So she was placed in her own smaller vault, next to—but not touching—the main family tomb.

After the funeral, I asked one of my uncles whether there had been any further developments in the murder investigation. He replied tersely that the killer had not been found. His wife explained that the Manila police had essentially closed the case.

I could not understand my relatives' almost indifferent attitude. Why were they not more shocked that my aunt had been killed in cold blood, by people who worked for her, lived with her, saw her every day? Why were they not outraged that the maids had been released? When I pressed my uncle, he was short with me. "That's the way things are here," he said. "This is the Philippines—not America."

My uncle was not simply being callous. As it turns out, my aunt's death was part of a common pattern. Hundreds of Chinese in the Philippines are kidnapped every year, almost invariably by ethnic Filipinos. Many victims, often children, are brutally murdered, even after ransom is paid. Other Chinese, like my aunt, are killed without a kidnapping, usually in connection with a robbery. Nor is it unusual that my aunt's killer was never apprehended. The police in the Philippines, all poor ethnic Filipinos themselves, are notoriously unmotivated in these cases. When asked by a Western journalist why it is so frequently the Chinese who are targeted, one grinning Filipino policeman explained that it was because "they have more money."

My family is part of the Philippines' tiny but entrepreneurial and economically powerful Chinese minority. Although they constitute just one percent of the population, Chinese Filipinos control as much as 60 percent of the private economy, including the country's four major airlines and almost all of the country's banks, hotels, shopping malls, and big conglomerates. My own family in Manila runs a plastics conglomerate. Unlike taipans Lucio Tan, Henry Sy, or John Gokongwei, my relatives are only "third-tier" Chinese tycoons. Still, they own swaths of prime real estate and several vacation homes. They also have safe deposit boxes full of gold bars, each one roughly the size of a Snickers bar, but strangely heavy. I myself have such a gold bar. My Aunt Leona express-mailed it to me as a law school graduation present a few years before she died.

Since my aunt's murder, one childhood memory keeps haunting me. I was eight, staying at my family's splendid hacienda-style house in Manila. It was before dawn, still dark. Wide awake, I decided to get a drink from the kitchen. I must have gone down an extra flight of stairs, because I literally stumbled onto six male bodies. I had found the male servants' quarters, where my family's houseboys, gardeners, and chauffeurs—I sometimes imagine that Nilo Abique was among them—were sleeping on mats on a dirt floor. The place stank of sweat and urine. I was horrified.

Later that day I mentioned the incident to my Aunt Leona, who laughed affectionately and explained that the servants—there were perhaps 20 living on the premises, all ethnic Filipinos—were fortunate to be working for our family. If not for their positions, they would be living among rats and open sewers, without a roof over their heads. A Filipino maid then walked in; I remember that she had a bowl of food for my aunt's Pekingese. My aunt took the bowl but kept talking as if the maid were not there. The Filipinos, she continued—in Chinese, but plainly not caring whether the maid understood or not—were lazy and unintelligent and didn't really want to do much. If they didn't like working for us, they were free to leave at any time. After all, my aunt said, they were employees, not slaves.

Nearly two-thirds of the roughly 80 million ethnic Filipinos in the Philippines live on less than $2 a day. Forty percent spend their entire lives in temporary shelters. Seventy percent of all rural Filipinos own no land. Almost a third have no access to sanitation. But that's not the worst of it. Poverty alone never is. Poverty by itself does not make people kill. To poverty must be added indignity, hopelessness, and grievance. In the Philippines, millions of Filipinos work for Chinese; almost no Chinese work for Filipinos. The Chinese dominate industry and commerce at every level of society. Global markets intensify this dominance: When foreign investors do business in the Philippines, they deal almost exclusively with Chinese. Apart from a handful of corrupt politicians and a few aristocratic Spanish mestizo families, all of the Philippines' billionaires are of Chinese descent. By contrast, all menial jobs in the Philippines are filled by Filipinos. All peasants are Filipinos. All domestic servants and squatters are Filipinos. My relatives live literally walled off from the Filipino masses, in a posh, all-Chinese residential enclave, on streets named Harvard, Yale, Stanford, and Princeton. The entry points are guarded by armed private-security forces.

Each time I think of Nilo Abique—he was six-feet-two and my aunt was four-feet-eleven—I find myself welling up with a hatred and revulsion so intense it is actually consoling. But over time I have also had glimpses of how the vast majority of Filipinos, especially someone like Abique, must see the

Chinese: as exploiters, foreign intruders, their wealth inexplicable, their superiority intolerable. I will never forget the entry in the police report for Abique's "motive for murder." The motive given was not robbery, despite the jewels and money the chauffeur was said to have taken. Instead, for motive, there was just one word—"revenge."

My aunt's killing was just a pinprick in a world more violent than most of us have ever imagined. In America, we read about acts of mass slaughter and savagery—at first in faraway places, now coming closer home. We do not understand what connects these acts. Nor do we understand the role we have played in bringing them about.

In the Serbian concentration camps of the early 1990s, the women prisoners were raped over and over, many times a day, often with broken bottles, often together with their daughters. The men, if they were lucky, were beaten to death as their Serbian guards sang national anthems; if they were not so fortunate, they were castrated or, at gunpoint, forced to castrate their fellow prisoners, sometimes with their own teeth. In all, thousands were tortured and executed.

In Rwanda in 1994, ordinary Hutus killed 800,000 Tutsis over a period of three months, typically hacking them to death with machetes. Bill Berkeley writes in *The Graves Are Not Yet Full* (2001) that young children would come home to find their mothers, fathers, sisters, and brothers on the living room floor, in piles of severed heads and limbs.

In Jakarta in 1998, screaming Indonesian mobs torched, smashed, and looted hundreds of Chinese shops and homes, leaving more than 2,000 dead. One who survived—a 14-year-old Chinese girl—later committed suicide by taking rat poison. She had been gang-raped and genitally mutilated in front of her parents.

In Israel in 1998, a suicide bomber driving a car packed with explosives rammed into a school bus filled with 34 Jewish children between the ages of six and eight. Over the next few years such incidents intensified, becoming daily occurrences and a powerful collective expression of Palestinian hatred. "We hate you," a senior aide to Yasir Arafat elaborated in April 2002. "The air hates you, the land hates you, the trees hate you, there is no purpose in your staying on this land."

On September 11, 2001, Middle Eastern terrorists hijacked four American airliners, intent on using them as piloted missiles. They destroyed the World Trade Center and the southwest side of the Pentagon, crushing or incinerating more than 3,000 people. "Americans, think! Why you are hated all over the world," proclaimed a banner held by Arab demonstrators.

There is a connection among these episodes apart from their violence. It lies in the relationship—increasingly, the explosive collision—among the three most powerful forces operating in the world today: markets, democracy, and ethnic hatred. There exists today a phenomenon—pervasive outside the West yet rarely acknowledged, indeed often viewed as taboo—that turns free-market democracy into an engine of ethnic conflagration. I'm speaking of the phenomenon of market-dominant minorities: ethnic minorities who, for widely varying reasons, tend under market conditions to dominate economically, often to a startling extent, the "indigenous" majorities around them.

Market-dominant minorities can be found in every corner of the world. The Chinese are a market-dominant minority not just in the Philippines but throughout Southeast Asia. In 1998 Chinese Indonesians, only three percent of the population, controlled roughly 70 percent of Indonesia's private economy, including all of the country's largest conglomerates. In Myanmar (formerly Burma), entrepreneurial Chinese recently have taken over the economies of Mandalay and Yangon. Whites are a market-dominant minority in South Africa—and, in a more complicated sense, in Brazil, Ecuador, Guatemala, and much of Latin America. Lebanese are a market-dominant minority in West Africa, as are the Ibo in Nigeria. Croats were a market-dominant minority in the former Yugoslavia, as Jews almost certainly are in postcommunist Russia.

Market-dominant minorities are the Achilles' heel of free-market democracy. In societies with such a minority, markets and democracy favor not just different people or different classes but different ethnic groups. Markets concentrate wealth, often spectacular wealth, in the hands of the market-dominant minority, while democracy increases the political power of the impoverished majority. In these circumstances, the pursuit of free-market democracy becomes an engine of potentially catastrophic ethnonationalism, pitting a frustrated "indigenous" majority, easily aroused by opportunistic, vote-seeking politicians, against a resented, wealthy ethnic minority. This conflict is playing out in country after country today, from Indonesia to Sierra Leone, from Zimbabwe to Venezuela, from Russia to the Middle East.

Since September 11, the conflict has been brought home to the United States. Americans are not an ethnic minority (although we are a national-origin minority, a close cousin). Nor is there democracy at the global level. Nevertheless, Americans today are everywhere perceived as the world's market-dominant minority, wielding outrageously disproportionate economic power relative to our numbers. As a result, we have become the object of the same kind of mass popular resentment that afflicts the Chinese of Southeast Asia, the whites of Zimbabwe, and other groups.

Global anti-Americanism has many causes. One of them, ironically, is the global spread of free markets and democracy. Throughout the world, global markets are bitterly perceived as reinforcing American wealth and dominance. At the same time, global populist and democratic movements give strength, legitimacy, and voice to the impoverished, frustrated, excluded masses of the world—in other words, precisely the people most susceptible to anti-American demagoguery. In more non-Western countries than Americans would care to admit, free and fair elections would bring to power antimarket, anti-American leaders. For the past 20 years, Americans have been grandly promoting both marketization and democratization throughout the world. In the process, we have directed at ourselves what the Turkish writer Orhan Pamuk calls "the anger of the damned."

The relationship between free-market democracy and ethnic violence around the world is inextricably bound up with globalization. But the phenomenon of market-dominant minorities introduces complications that have escaped the view of both globalization's enthusiasts and its critics.

To a great extent, globalization consists of, and is fueled by, the unprecedented worldwide spread of markets and democracy. For more than two decades now, the American government, along with American consultants and business interests, has been vigorously promoting free-market democracy throughout the developing and postcommunist worlds. Both directly and through powerful international institutions such as the World Bank, International Monetary Fund, and World Trade Organization (WTO), it has helped bring capitalism and democratic elections to literally billions of people. At the same time, American multinationals, foundations, and non-governmental organizations (NGOs) have touched every corner of the world, bringing with them ballot boxes and Burger Kings, hip-hop and Hollywood, banking codes and American-drafted constitutions.

The prevailing view among globalization's supporters is that markets and democracy are a kind of universal elixir for the multiple ills of underdevelopment. Market capitalism is the most efficient economic system the world has ever known. Democracy is the fairest political system the world has ever known, and the one most respectful of individual liberty. Together, markets and democracy will gradually transform the world into a community of prosperous, war-shunning nations, and individuals into liberal, civic-minded citizens and consumers. Ethnic hatred, religious zealotry, and other "backward" aspects of underdevelopment will be swept away.

Thomas Friedman of the *New York Times* has been a brilliant proponent of this dominant view. In his best-selling book *The Lexus and the Olive Tree* (1999), he reproduced a Merrill Lynch ad that said "the spread of free markets and democracy around the world is permitting more people everywhere to turn their aspirations into achievements," erasing "not just geographical borders but also human ones." Globalization, Friedman elaborated, "tends to turn all friends and enemies into 'competitors.'" Friedman also proposed his "Golden Arches Theory of Conflict Prevention," which claims that "no two countries that both have McDonald's have ever fought a war against each other." (Unfortunately, notes Yale University historian John Lewis Gaddis, "the United States and its NATO allies chose just that inauspicious moment to begin bombing Belgrade, where there was an embarrassing number of golden arches.")

For globalization's enthusiasts, the cure for group hatred and ethnic violence around the world is straightforward: more markets and more democracy. Thus, after the September 11 attacks, Friedman published an op-ed piece pointing to India and Bangladesh as good "role models" for the Middle East and citing their experience as a solution to the challenges of terrorism and militant Islam: "Hello? Hello? There's a message here. It's democracy, stupid!"—". . . multiethnic, pluralistic, free-market democracy."

I believe, rather, that the global spread of markets and democracy is a principal aggravating cause of group hatred and ethnic violence throughout the non-Western world. In the numerous societies around the world that have a market-dominant minority, markets and democracy are not mutually reinforcing. Because markets and democracy benefit different ethnic groups in such societies, the pursuit of free-market democracy produces highly unstable and combustible conditions. Markets concentrate enormous wealth in the hands of an "outsider" minority, thereby fomenting ethnic envy and hatred among often chronically poor majorities. In absolute terms, the majority may or may not be better off—a dispute that much of the globalization debate revolves around—but any sense of improvement is overwhelmed by its continuing poverty and the hated minority's extraordinary economic success. More humiliating still, market-dominant minorities, along with their foreign-investor partners, invariably come to control the crown jewels of the economy, often symbolic of the nation's patrimony and identity—oil in Russia and Venezuela, diamonds in South Africa, silver and tin in Bolivia, jade, teak, and rubies in Myanmar.

Introducing democracy under such circumstances does not transform voters into open-minded co-citizens in a national community. Rather, the competition for votes fosters the emergence of demagogues who scapegoat the resented minority and foment active ethnonationalist movements demanding that the country's wealth and identity be reclaimed by the "true owners of the nation." Even as America celebrated the global spread of democracy in the 1990s, the world's new political slogans told of more ominous developments: "Georgia for the Georgians," "Eritreans out of Ethiopia," "Kenya for Kenyans," "Venezuela for Pardos," "Kazakhstan for Kazakhs," "Serbia for Serbs," "Hutu Power," "Jews out of Russia." Vadim Tudor, a candidate in Romania's 2001 presidential election, was not quite so pithy. "I'm Vlad the Impaler," he declared, and referring to the historically dominant Hungarian minority, he promised, "We will hang them directly by their Hungarian tongue!"

When free-market democracy is pursued in the presence of a market-dominant minority, the result, almost invariably, is backlash. Typically, it takes one of three forms. The first is a backlash against markets that targets the market-dominant minority's wealth. The second is an attack against democracy by forces favorable to the market-dominant minority. And the third is violence, sometimes genocidal, directed against the market-dominant minority itself.

Zimbabwe today is a vivid illustration of the first kind of backlash—an ethnically targeted antimarket reaction. For several years now, President Robert Mugabe has encouraged the violent seizure of 10 million acres of white-owned commercial farmland. As one Zimbabwean explained, "The land belongs to us. The foreigners should not own land here. There is no black Zimbabwean who owns land in England. Why should any European own land here?" Mugabe has been more explicit: "Strike fear in the heart of the white man, our real enemy." Most of the country's white "foreigners" are third-generation Zimbabweans. They are just one percent of the population, but they have for generations controlled 70 percent of the country's best land, largely in the form of highly productive 3,000-acre tobacco and sugar farms.

Watching Zimbabwe's economy take a free fall as a result of the mass land grab, the United States and United Kingdom, together with dozens of human rights groups, urged President Mugabe to step down and called resoundingly for "free and fair elections." But the idea that democracy is the answer to Zimbabwe's problems is breathtakingly naive. Perhaps Mugabe would have lost the 2002 elections in the absence of foul play. But even if that's so, it's important to remember that Mugabe himself is a product of democracy. The hero of Zimbabwe's black liberation movement and a master manipulator of the masses, he swept to victory in the closely monitored elections of 1980 by promising to expropriate "stolen" white land. Repeating that promise has helped him win every election since. Moreover, Mugabe's land-seizure campaign was another product of the democratic process. It was deftly timed in anticipation of the 2000 and 2002 elections, and deliberately calculated to mobilize popular support for Mugabe's teetering regime. According to *The Economist,* 95 percent of Zimbabwe's largely white-owned commercial farms are now earmarked for confiscation without compensation, and many farmers have been ordered off the land.

In the contest between an economically powerful ethnic minority and a numerically powerful impoverished majority, the majority does not always prevail. Rather than a backlash against the market, another possible outcome is a backlash against democracy that favors the market-dominant minority. Examples of this dynamic are extremely common. The world's most notorious cases of "crony capitalism" have all involved partnerships between a market-dominant ethnic minority and a cooperative autocrat. Ferdinand Marcos's dictatorship in the Philippines, for example, sheltered and profited from the country's wealthy Chinese before he was driven from office in 1986. In Kenya, President Daniel arap Moi, who had once warned Africans to "beware of bad Asians," is sustained by a series of "business arrangements" with a handful of local Indian tycoons. And the bloody tragedy of Sierra Leone's recent history can be traced in significant part to the regime of President Siaka Stevens, who converted his elective office into a dictatorship during the early 1970s and promptly formed a shadow alliance with five of the country's Lebanese diamond dealers.

In Sierra Leone, as in many other countries, independence (which came in 1961) had been followed by a series of antimarket measures and policies that took direct aim at market-dominant minorities. People of "European or Asiatic origin," including the Lebanese, were denied citizenship. Stevens's approach thus represented a complete about-face—a pattern that's been repeated in country after country. Stevens protected the economically powerful Lebanese, and in exchange, they—with their business networks in Europe, the Soviet Union, and the United States—worked economic wonders, generating enormous profits and kicking back handsome portions to Stevens and other officials. (It is just such webs of preexisting relationships with the outside world that have given economically dominant minorities their extraordinary advantages in the current era of globalization.) Stevens was succeeded by other autocrats, who struck essentially the same deal while also successfully courting foreign investment and aid. In 1989 and 1990, the International Monetary Fund championed a "bold and decisive" free-market reform package that included a phase-out of public subsidies for rice and other commodities. Already living in indescribable poverty, Sierra Leoneans watched the cost of rice nearly double, and many blamed the Lebanese. In any event, the rebel leader Foday Sankoh had little trouble finding recruits for his insurgency. Some 75,000 died in the ensuing chaos.

The third and most ferocious kind of backlash is majority-supported violence aimed at eliminating a market-dominant minority. Two recent examples are the "ethnic cleansing" of Croats in the former Yugoslavia and the mass slaughter of Tutsi in Rwanda. In both cases, sudden, unmediated democratization encouraged the rise of megalomaniacal ethnic demagogues and released long-suppressed hatreds against a disproportionately prosperous ethnic minority.

Of course, markets and democracy were not the only causes of these acts of genocide, but they were neglected factors. In the former Yugoslavia, for example, the Croats, along with the Slovenes, have long enjoyed a strikingly higher standard of living than the Serbs and other ethnic groups. Croatia and Slovenia are largely Catholic, with geographical proximity and historical links to Western Europe, while the Eastern Orthodox Serbs inhabit the rugged south and lived for centuries under the thumb of the Ottoman Empire. By the 1990s, per capita income in northern Yugoslavia had risen to three times that in the south. The sudden coming of Balkan electoral democracy helped stir ancient enmities and resentments. In Serbia, the demagogue and future "ethnic cleanser" Slobodan Milosevic swept to power in 1990 as supporters declared to hysterical crowds, "We will kill Croats with rusty spoons because it will hurt more!" (In the same year, Franjo Tudjman won a landslide victory in Croatia preaching anti-Serb hatred; the subsequent mass killing of Croatia's Serbs shows that market-dominant minorities aren't always the victims of persecution.) In a now-famous speech delivered in March 1991—which contains a telling allusion to Croat and Slovene market dominance—Milosevic declared: "If we must fight, then my God we will fight. And I hope they will not be so crazy as to fight against us. Because if we don't know how to work well or to do business, at least we know how to fight well!"

To their credit, critics of globalization have called attention to the grotesque imbalances that free markets produce. In the 1990s, writes Thomas Frank in *One Market under God* (2000), global markets made "the corporation the most powerful institution on earth," transformed "CEOs as a class into one of the wealthiest elites of all time," and, from America to Indonesia, "forgot about the poor with a decisiveness we hadn't seen since the 1920s." A host of strange bedfellows have joined Frank in his criticism of "the almighty market": American farmers and factory workers opposed to the North American Free Trade Agreement, environmentalists, the American Federation of Labor—Congress of Industrial Organizations, human rights activists, Third World advocates, and sundry other groups that protested in Seattle, Davos, Genoa, and New York City. Defenders of globalization respond, with some justification, that the world's poor would be even worse off without global marketization, and recent World Bank studies show that, with some important exceptions, including most of Africa, globalization's "trickle down" has benefited the poor as well as the rich in developing countries.

More fundamentally, however, Western critics of globalization, like their pro-globalization counterparts, have overlooked the ethnic dimension of market disparities. They tend to see wealth and poverty in terms of class conflict, not ethnic conflict. This perspective might make sense in the advanced Western societies, but the ethnic realities of the developing world are completely different from those of the West. Essentially, the anti-globalization movement asks for one thing: more democracy. At the 2002 World Social Forum in Brazil, Lori Wallach of Public Citizen rejected the label "anti-globalization" and explained that "our movement, really, is globally for democracy, equality, diversity, justice and quality of life." Wallach has also warned that the WTO must "either bend to the will of the people worldwide or it will break." Echoing these voices are literally dozens of NGOs that call for "democratically empowering the poor majorities of the world." But unless democratization means something more than unrestrained majority rule, calling for democracy in the developing world can be shortsighted and even dangerous. Empowering the Hutu majority in Rwanda did not produce desirable consequences. Nor did empowering the Serbian majority in Serbia.

Critics of globalization are right to demand that more attention be paid to the enormous disparities of wealth created by global markets. But just as it is dangerous to view markets as the panacea for the world's poverty and strife, so too it is dangerous to see democracy as a panacea. Markets and democracy may well offer the best long-run economic and political hope for developing and postcommunist societies. In the short run, however, they're part of the problem.

In the West, terms such as "market economy" and "market system" refer to a broad spectrum of economic systems based primarily on private property and competition, with government regulation and redistribution ranging from substantial (as in the United States) to extensive (as in the Scandinavian countries). Yet for the past 20 years the United States has been promoting throughout the non-Western world raw, laissez-faire capitalism—a form of markets that the West abandoned long ago. The procapitalism measures being implemented today outside the West include privatization, the elimination of state subsidies and controls, and free-trade and foreign investment initiatives. As a practical matter they rarely, if ever, include any substantial redistribution measures.

"Democracy," too, can take many forms. I use the term "democratization" to refer to the political reforms that are actually being promoted in the non-Western world today—the concerted efforts, for example, largely driven by the United States, to implement immediate elections with universal suffrage. It's striking to note that at no point in history did any Western nation ever implement laissez-faire capitalism and overnight universal suffrage simultaneously—though that's the precise formula for free-market democracy currently being pressed on developing countries around the world. In the United States, the poor were totally disenfranchised by formal property qualifications in virtually every state for many decades after the Constitution was ratified, and economic barriers to participation remained well into the 20th century.

It is ethnicity, however, that gives the combination of markets and democracy its special combustibility. Ethnic identity is not a static, scientifically determinable status but shifting and highly malleable. In Rwanda, for example, the 14 percent Tutsi minority dominated the Hutu majority economically and politically for four centuries, as a kind of cattle-owning aristocracy. But for most of this period, the lines between Hutus and Tutsi were permeable. The two groups spoke the same language, intermarriage occurred, and successful Hutus could "become Tutsi." That was no longer true after the Belgians arrived and, steeped in specious theories of racial superiority, issued ethnic identity cards on the basis of nose length and cranial circumference. The resulting sharp ethnic divisions were later exploited by the leaders of Hutu Power. Along similar lines, all over Latin America today— where it is often said that there are no "ethnic divisions" because everyone has "mixed" blood—large numbers of impoverished Bolivians, Chileans, and Peruvians are suddenly being told that they are Aymaras, Incas, or just indios, whatever identity best resonates and mobilizes. These indigenization movements are not necessarily good or bad, but they are potent and contagious.

At the same time, ethnic identity is rarely constructed out of thin air. Subjective perceptions of identity often depend on more "objective" traits assigned to individuals based on, for example, perceived morphological characteristics, language differences, or ancestry. Try telling black and white Zimbabweans that they are only imagining their ethnic differences—that "ethnicity is a social construct"—and they'll at least agree on one thing: You're not being helpful. Much more concretely relevant is the reality that there is roughly zero intermarriage between blacks and whites in Zimbabwe, just as there is virtually no intermarriage between Chinese and Malays in Malaysia or between Arabs and Israelis in the Middle East. That ethnicity can be at once an artifact of human imagination and rooted in the darkest recesses of history—fluid and manipulable, yet important enough to kill for—is what makes ethnic conflict so terrifyingly difficult to understand and contain.

The argument I am making is frequently misunderstood. I do not propose a universal theory applicable to every developing country. There are certainly developing countries without market-dominant minorities: China and Argentina are two major examples. Nor do I argue that ethnic conflict arises only in the presence of a market-dominant minority. There are countless instances of ethnic hatred directed at economically oppressed groups. And, last, I emphatically do not mean to pin the blame for any particular case of ethnic violence—whether the mass killings perpetrated by all sides in the former Yugoslavia or the attack on America—on economic resentment, on markets, on democracy, on globalization, or on any other single cause. Many overlapping factors and complex dynamics—religion, historical enmities, territorial disputes, or a particular nation's foreign policy—are always in play.

The point, rather, is this: In the numerous countries around the world that have pervasive poverty and a market-dominant minority, democracy and markets—at least in the raw, unrestrained forms in which they are currently being promoted—can proceed only in deep tension with each other. In such conditions, the combined pursuit of free markets and democratization has repeatedly catalyzed ethnic conflict in highly predictable ways, with catastrophic consequences, including genocidal violence and the subversion of markets and democracy themselves. That has been the sobering lesson of globalization over the past 20 years.

Where does this leave us? What are the implications of market-dominant minorities for national and international policymaking? Influential commentator Robert D. Kaplan offers one answer: Hold off on democracy until free markets produce enough economic and social development to make democracy sustainable. In *The Coming Anarchy* (2000), Kaplan argues that a middle class and civil institutions—both of which he implicitly assumes would be generated by market capitalism—are preconditions for democracy. Contrasting Lee Kuan Yew's prosperous authoritarian Singapore with the murderous, "bloodletting" democratic states of Colombia, Rwanda, and South Africa, Kaplan roundly condemns America's post–Cold War campaign to export democracy to "places where it can't succeed."

This is a refreshingly unromantic view, but ultimately unsatisfactory. As one writer has observed, "If authoritarianism were the key to prosperity, then Africa would be the richest continent in the world." Ask (as some do) for an Augusto Pinochet or an Alberto Fujimori, and you may get an Idi Amin or a Papa Doc Duvalier. More fundamentally, Kaplan overlooks the global problem of market-dominant minorities. He stresses the ethnic biases of elections but neglects the ethnic biases of capitalism. He is overly optimistic about the ability of markets alone to lift the great indigenous masses out of poverty, and he fails to see that markets favor not just some people over others but, often, hated ethnic minorities over indigenous majorities. Overlooking this reality, Kaplan blames too much of the world's violence and anarchy on democracy.

The best economic hope for developing and postcommunist countries does lie in some form of market-generated growth. Their best political hope lies in some form of democracy, with constitutional constraints, tailored to local realities. But if global free-market democracy is to succeed, the problem of market-dominant minorities must be confronted head-on. If we stop peddling unrestrained markets and overnight elections as cure-alls—both to ourselves and others—and instead candidly address the perils inherent in both markets and democracy, there is in many cases room for optimism.

The first and most obvious step is to isolate, where possible, and address, where appropriate, the causes of the market dominance of certain groups. In South Africa, expanding educational opportunities for the black majority—restricted for more than 70 years to inferior Bantu schooling—is properly a national priority and should be vigorously supported by the international community. Throughout Latin America, educational reform and equalization of opportunities for the region's poor indigenous-blooded majorities are imperative if global markets are to benefit more than just a handful of cosmopolitan elites.

Yet we must be realistic. The underlying causes of market dominance are poorly understood, difficult to reduce to tangible factors, and in any event highly intractable. Research suggests, for example, that additional spending on education, if not accompanied by major socioeconomic reforms, produces depressingly few benefits. Political favoritism, though often a sore point with the majority in many societies with a market-dominant minority, tends to be more the consequence than the cause of market dominance. Most market-dominant minorities, whether the Bamiléké in Cameroon or Indians in Fiji, enjoy disproportionate economic success at every level of society down to the smallest shopkeepers, who can rarely boast of useful political connections. Indeed, many of these minorities succeed despite official discrimination against them. Any explanation of their success will likely include a host of intangibles such as the influence of religion and culture.

To "level the playing field" in developing societies will thus be a painfully slow process, taking generations if it is possible at all. More immediate measures will be needed to address the potentially explosive problems of ethnic resentment and ethnonationalist hatred that threaten these countries.

A crucial challenge is to find ways to spread the benefits of global markets beyond a handful of market-dominant minorities and their foreign investor partners. Western-style redistributive programs—progressive taxation, social security, unemployment insurance—should be encouraged, but, at least in the short run, they have limited potential. There simply is not enough to tax, and nearly no one who can be trusted to transfer revenues. Other possibilities are somewhat more encouraging. The Peruvian economist Hernando de Soto makes a powerful case in *The Mystery of Capital* (2000) for the benefits of giving the poor in the developing world formal, legally defensible property rights to the land they occupy but to which, because of underdeveloped legal systems and the tangles of history, they very often lack legal title.

A more controversial strategy consists of direct government intervention in the market designed to "correct" ethnic wealth imbalances. The leading example of such an effort is Malaysia's New Economic Policy (NEP), a program established after violent riots in 1969 by indigenous Malays angry over the economic dominance of foreign investors and the country's ethnic Chinese minority. The Malaysian government adopted sweeping ethnic quotas on corporate equity ownership, university admissions, government licensing, and commercial employment. It also initiated large-scale purchases of corporate assets on behalf of the bumiputra (Malay) majority.

In many respects, the results have been impressive. While the NEP has not lifted the great majority of Malays (particularly in the rural areas) out of poverty, it has helped to create a substantial Malay middle class. Prime minister Mahathir Mohamad, who frankly concedes that the NEP has tended to favor elite, well-connected Malays, nevertheless contends that it serves an important symbolic function: "With the existence of the few rich Malays at least the poor can say their fate is not entirely to serve rich non-Malays. From the point of view of racial ego, and this ego is still strong, the unseemly existence of Malay tycoons is essential."

Efforts like the NEP, however, are far from a universal solution. Few countries enjoy the degree of prosperity that makes them feasible, and even Malaysia has not achieved its goal of eradicating poverty. Moreover, such programs may well exacerbate ethnic tensions rather than relieve them, especially when government leaders are themselves ethnic partisans. . . .

Open ethnic conflict is rare in "mixed blood" Latin America. But light-skinned minorities dominate many economies, and new leaders are rallying the discontented around their Indian roots. Serbia's Slobodan Milosevic was conducting a form of affirmative action on behalf of long-exploited majorities, as Zimbabwe's Robert Mugabe doubtless feels he is doing now.

For better or worse, the best hope for global free-market democracy lies with market-dominant minorities themselves. This is adamantly not to blame these groups for the ethnonationalist eruptions against them. But it is to suggest that they may be in the best position to address today's most pressing challenges. To begin with, it must be recognized that market-dominant minorities often engage in objectionable practices—bribery, discriminatory lending, labor exploitation—that reinforce ethnic stereotypes and besmirch the image of free-market democracy. In Indonesia, the notorious "crony capitalism" of President Suharto depended on a handful of Chinese magnates and fueled massive resentment of the Chinese community generally.

More affirmatively, if free-market democracy is to prosper, the world's market-dominant minorities must begin making significant and visible contributions to the local economies in which they are thriving. Although such efforts have been relatively few and by no means always successful in promoting goodwill, some valuable models can be found. The University of Nairobi, for example, owes its existence to wealthy Indians in Kenya. The Madhvani family, owners of the largest industrial, commercial, and agricultural complex in East Africa, not only provide educational, health, housing, and recreational opportunities for their African employees, but also employ Africans in top management and offer a number of wealth-sharing schemes. In Russia, there is the unusual case of the Jewish billionaire Roman Abramovich, whose generous philanthropy and ambitious proposals won him election as governor of the poverty-stricken Chukotka region in the Russian Far East. More typically, however, building ethnic goodwill would require collective action. Fortunately, most economically successful minorities do have the resources for such action, in the form of local ethnic chambers of commerce, clan associations, and other organizations.

What of the world's largest economically dominant minority? What are Americans to do? It's obviously true that anti-Americanism, including the virulent Islamicist strain, doesn't stem from economic deprivation alone. As others have pointed out, the Islamicists themselves rarely even speak of a desire for prosperity. And it is fantasy to think that U.S. economic aid can do anything more than make a small dent in world poverty, at least in the near future. Yet those who call for increases in U.S. aid to the world's poor do seem to have wisdom on their side. The United States now devotes only 0.1 percent of its gross domestic product to foreign aid, a smaller share than any other advanced country. Rightly or wrongly, for millions around the world the World Trade Center symbolized greed, exploitation, indifference, and cultural humiliation. By extending themselves to the world's poor, Americans could begin to send a different sort of message. Retreating into isolationism or glorifying American chauvinism holds no long-term promise. It is difficult to see, in any event, how a little generosity and humility could possibly hurt.

■ *QUESTIONS FOR MAKING CONNECTIONS*
WITHIN THE READINGS ■

1. Chua opens her essay with a story that engages the reader, but also complicates easy moral judgments by presenting multiple perspectives. Chua tells the story from her own perspective as an American niece of her murdered aunt, but we also glimpse events through other eyes as well. How does the Chinese community in the Philippines look at events of this sort and respond to them? How do the Filipino authorities view such matters? What about ordinary Filipinos—how might they regard the Chinese in their country? Should we understand the murder as one person's response to injustice, or do you regard "injustice" as an inappropriate choice of words? Would it be accurate to describe the Chinese as "oppressing" or "exploiting" the Filipinos, or is the situation more complex than these terms suggest? After all, Americans also qualify as a "market-dominant minority."

2. According to Chua, all peasants in the Philippines are Filipinos, whereas most members of the merchant class are Chinese. How has this situation developed in the Philippines, and why have similar imbalances arisen in other countries across the globe? Why might peasant-farmers be ill-suited to enter the world of international finance? What contributions to a society are made by "market-dominant minorities"? In what ways does the economic division in societies like the Philippines—with a majority of the native-born living in poverty while immigrants and their descendants dominate high finance—create a vicious circle in which the rich stay rich and the poor stay poor?

3. Chua identifies three causes of the "explosive violence" we are witnessing around the world: markets, democracy, and ethnic hatred. How exactly do these three causes reinforce one another? To a certain extent, everyone on earth wants the wealth and security that markets bring, and nearly everyone wants democracy. And yet, if Chua is correct in her claim that these two aspirations are unleashing ethnic hatred, then democracy and free markets by themselves cannot be the solution. Do you agree with Robert Kaplan's argument that poor countries need to begin their long march to development with authoritarian governments? Or do you find Chua's own proposals more compelling?

■ *QUESTIONS FOR WRITING* ■

1. Are democracy and globalization inherently compatible? Ordinarily, we associate free markets with democracy, and we assume that political democracy will foster greater economic opportunity. On the basis of Chua's evidence, however, would you say that these assumptions will hold true in most cases around the world? Could the rise of markets on a global scale actually strengthen the undemocratic power of local elites, or could it create a new global elite for whom genuine democracy holds very little appeal? Should democracy become the world's top priority, or should democracy take a back seat to the broadening of prosperity? Consider in particular a success story like Mahathir Mohamad's policies in Malaysia.

2. Americans have tried to solve the problem of ethnic hatred by relying on the influence of education and by asking for support from prominent public figures. The schools teach the value of diversity, while opinion makers in the public eye are asked to speak out against prejudice. Do you believe that such strategies are likely to work if we attempt to apply them on a global scale? Have they worked here in the United States? Are social problems like racism really unsolved economic problems? With the broadening of opportunity, is the problem of ethnic hatred likely to diminish or even disappear?

■ *QUESTIONS FOR MAKING CONNECTIONS BETWEEN READINGS* ■

1. In "Second Proms and Second Primaries: The Limits of Majority Rule," Lani Guinier writes about disadvantaged minorities in the United States, whereas Chua's focus in "A World on the Edge" is on minorities across the globe who enjoy enormous power and privilege. In spite of these differences, however, Guinier's critique of majority rule might help Chua to imagine another way to break the cycle of violence she describes in "A World on the Edge." Would the legislative changes of the kind Guinier proposes contribute to the protection of groups like the Chinese in the Philippines and Malaysia? How might these changes also benefit the native majorities?

2. Chua's "A World on the Edge" and Beth Loffreda's "Losing Matt Shepard" both begin with the aftermath of a murder that expresses tensions in the larger culture. What are some of those tensions? Matt Shepard's murderers kill him because he is gay, whereas Aunt Leona is targeted because of her Chinese ethnicity, but the commonalities of these victims may extend beyond their shared identity as outsiders or people who are different. In a certain sense, the gay subculture in America is a national, and

even global, phenomenon that cannot readily be contained by county lines or national boundaries. Similarly, the Chinese in Southeast Asia belong to an international community. To what degree do both murders and their aftermaths bear witness to a conflict between a local way of life and an intrusive, cosmopolitan culture?

www **For additional suggestions about making connections between readings, visit the Link-O-Mat and More Sample Assignments at <www.newhum.com>.**

Annie Dillard

In August and September 2004, hurricanes that swept through Central Florida destroyed billions of dollars of property and displaced tens of thousands of residents. Fortunately, few people died as a consequence. But three months later, in the very last week of the year, a tsunami—a massive tidal wave—triggered by an earthquake on the floor of the Indian Ocean, left more than two hundred and fifty thousand people dead while destroying the homes and livelihoods of millions throughout South and Southeast Asia. How can humanity ever come to terms with the colossal natural forces that unleash such destruction routinely? Is it true, as Annie Dillard speculates, that "the might of the universe is arrayed against us"?

Dillard, a poet, essayist, novelist, and writing teacher, won a Pulitzer Prize for her book of naturalist reflections, *Pilgrim at Tinker Creek* (1973), when she was just twenty-nine years old. In this, her first book, Dillard describes the life she elected to live in a remote part of the Blue Ridge Mountains after she had survived a near-fatal bout of pneumonia. Weaving together observations of her surroundings with mystical longings and theological reflections on the violence and the beauty that coexist in the natural world, Dillard set out, in her own words, "to learn, or remember, how to live. . . . I don't think I can learn from a wild animal how to live in particular . . . but I might learn something of mindlessness, something of the purity of living in the physical senses and the dignity of living without bias or motive."

In the many books that have followed, including *Teaching a Stone to Talk* (1982), her autobiographical musings in *An American Childhood* (1987), and her novel, *The Living* (1992), Dillard has continued to ruminate on the power of nature and to wonder about the place of humanity in the cosmos. For Dillard, the enduring appeal and importance of such a spiritual project is self-evident: "In nature I find grace tangled in a rapture with violence; I find an intricate land-

Dillard, Annie. "The Wreck of Time." *Harper's*, vol. 296, no. 1772 (January 1998): 51–56.

Quotations from Annie Dillard, *Pilgrim at Tinker Creek*, HarperPerennial, 1973; Annie Dillard, interview by Grace Suh, *The Yale Herald*, 4 October 1996, <http://www.yaleherald.com/archive/xxii/10.4.96/ae/dillard.html>; Annie Dillard, *For the Time Being*, Vintage Books, 2000.

scape whose forms are fringed in death; I find mystery, newness, and a kind of exuberant, spendthrift energy."

"The Wreck of Time" includes passages that appear in *For the Time Being* (2000), Dillard's most recent effort to define a spiritual vision that embraces a cosmos where grace "is tangled in a rapture with violence."Although Dillard was raised a Presbyterian, she converted to Catholicism in her twenties and now describes herself as a "Hasidic Christian," her meditations on the natural world having led her to unite Jewish mysticism with Christian spirituality. "The world is as glorious as ever, and exalting," Dillard announces at the beginning of *For the Time Being*, "but for credibility's sake let's start with the bad news." If one starts with the bad news, as Dillard does in "The Wreck of Time," is it possible to recover a sense that "the world is as glorious as ever"? That the future is bright? These are the questions that Dillard wrestles with—and asks her readers to wrestle with, as well.

www   **To learn more about Annie Dillard and the study of time, visit the Link-O-Mat at <www.newhum.com>.**

The Wreck of Time
Taking Our Century's Measure

Ted Bundy, the serial killer, after his arrest, could not fathom the fuss. What was the big deal? David Von Drehle quotes an exasperated Bundy in *Among the Lowest of the Dead*: "I mean, there are *so* many people."

One R. Houwink, of Amsterdam, uncovered this unnerving fact: The human population of earth, arranged tidily, would just fit into Lake Windermere, in England's Lake District.

Recently in the Peruvian Amazon a man asked the writer Alex Shoumatoff, "Isn't it true that the whole population of the United States can be fitted into their cars?"

How are we doing in numbers, we who have been alive for this most recent installment of human life? How many people have lived and died?

"The dead outnumber the living, in a ratio that could be as high as 20 to 1," a demographer, Nathan Keyfitz, wrote in a 1991 letter to the historian Justin Kaplan. "Credible estimates of the number of people who have ever lived on the earth run from 70 billion to over 100 billion." Averaging those figures puts the total persons ever born at about 85 billion. We living people now number 5.8 billion. By these moderate figures, the dead outnumber us about fourteen to one. The dead will always outnumber the living.

Dead Americans, however, if all proceeds, will not outnumber living Americans until the year 2030, because the nation is young. Some of us will be among the dead then. Will we know or care, we who once owned the still bones under the quick ones, we who spin inside the planet with our heels in the air? The living might well seem foolishly self-important to us, and overexcited.

We who are here now make up about 6.8 percent of all people who have appeared to date. This is not a meaningful figure. These our times are, one might say, ordinary times, a slice of life like any other. Who can bear to hear this, or who will consider it? Are we not especially significant because our century is—our century and its nuclear bombs, its unique and unprecedented Holocaust, its serial exterminations and refugee populations, our century and its warming, its silicon chips, men on the moon, and spliced genes? No, we are not and it is not.

Since about half of all the dead are babies and children, we will be among the longest-boned dead and among the dead who grew the most teeth—for what those distinctions might be worth among beings notoriously indifferent to appearance and all else.

In Juan Rulfo's novel *Pedro Páramo*, a dead woman says to her dead son, "Just think about pleasant things, because we're going to be buried for a long time."

II

On April 30, 1991—on that one day—138,000 people drowned in Bangladesh. At dinner I mentioned to my daughter, who was then seven years old, that it was hard to imagine 138,000 people drowning.

"No, it's easy," she said. "Lots and lots of dots, in blue water."

The paleontologist Pierre Teilhard de Chardin, now dead, sent a dispatch from a dig. "In the middle of the tamarisk bush you find a red-brick town, partially exposed. . . . More than 3,000 years before our era, people were living there who played with dice like our own, fished with hooks like ours, and wrote in characters we can't yet read."

Who were these individuals who lived under the tamarisk bush? Who were the people Ted Bundy killed? Who was the statistician who reckoned that everybody would fit into Lake Windermere? The Trojans likely thought well of themselves, one by one; their last settlement died out by 1,100 B.C.E. Who were the people Stalin killed, or any of the 79.2 billion of us now dead, and who are the 5.8 billion of us now alive?

"God speaks succinctly," said the rabbis.

Is it important if you have yet died your death, or I? Your father? Your child? It is only a matter of time, after all. Why do we find it supremely pertinent, during any moment of any century on earth, which among us is topsides? Why do we concern ourselves over which side of the membrane of topsoil our feet poke?

"A single death is a tragedy, a million deaths is a statistic." Joseph Stalin, that connoisseur, gave words to this disquieting and possibly universal sentiment.

How can an individual count? Do we individuals count only to us other suckers, who love and grieve like elephants, bless their hearts? Of Allah, the Koran says, "Not so much as the weight of an ant in earth or heaven escapes from the Lord." That is touching, that Allah, God, and their ilk care when one ant dismembers another, or note when a sparrow falls, but I strain to see the use of it.

Ten years ago we thought there were two galaxies for each of us alive. Lately, since we loosed the Hubble Space Telescope, we have revised our figures. There are nine galaxies for each of us. Each galaxy harbors an average of 100 billion suns. In our galaxy, the Milky Way, there are sixty-nine suns for each person alive. The Hubble shows, says a report, that the universe "is at least 15 billion years old." Two galaxies, nine galaxies . . . sixty-nine suns, 100 billion suns—
These astronomers are nickel-and-diming us to death.

III

What were you doing on April 30, 1991, when a series of waves drowned 138,000 people? Where were you when you first heard the astounding, heartbreaking news? Who told you? What, seriatim, were your sensations? Who did you tell? Did you weep? Did your anguish last days or weeks?

All my life I have loved this sight: a standing wave in a boat's wake, shaped like a thorn. I have seen it rise from many oceans, and I saw it rise from the Sea of Galilee. It was a peak about a foot high. The standing wave broke at its peak, and foam slid down its glossy hollow. I watched the foaming wave on the port side. At every instant we were bringing this boat's motor, this motion, into new water. The stir, as if of life, impelled each patch of water to pinch and inhabit this same crest. Each crest tumbled upon itself and released a slide of white foam. The foam's bubbles popped and dropped into the general sea while they were still sliding down the dark wave. They trailed away always, and always new waters peaked, broke, foamed, and replenished.
What I saw was the constant intersection of two wave systems. Lord Kelvin first described them. Transverse waves rise abaft the stern and stream away perpendicular to the boat's direction of travel. Diverging

waves course out in a V shape behind the boat. Where the waves converge, two lines of standing crests persist at an unchanging angle to the direction of the boat's motion. We think of these as the boat's wake. I was studying the highest standing wave, the one nearest the boat. It rose from the trough behind the stern and spilled foam. The curled wave crested over clear water and tumbled down. All its bubbles broke, thousands a second, unendingly. I could watch the present; I could see time and how it works.

On a shore, 8,000 waves break a day. James Trefil, a professor of physics, provides these facts. At any one time, the foam from breaking waves covers between 3 and 4 percent of the earth's surface. This acreage of foam is equal to the entire continent of North America. By coincidence, the U.S. population bears nearly the same relation to the world population: 4.6 percent. The U.S. population, in other words, although it is the third largest population among nations, is as small a portion of the earth's people as breaking waves' white foam is of the sea.

"God rises up out of the sea like a treasure in the waves," wrote Thomas Merton.

We see generations of waves rise from the sea that made them, billions of individuals at a time; we see them dwindle and vanish. If this does not astound you, what will? Or what will move you to pity?

IV

One tenth of the land on earth is tundra. At any time, it is raining on only 5 percent of the planet's surface. Lightning strikes the planet about a hundred times every second. The insects outweigh us. Our chickens outnumber us four to one.

One fifth of us are Muslims. One fifth of us live in China. And every seventh person is a Chinese peasant. Almost one tenth of us live within range of an active volcano. More than 2 percent of us are mentally retarded. We humans drink tea—over a billion cups a day. Among us we speak 10,000 languages.

We are civilized generation number 500 or so, counting from 10,000 years ago, when we settled down. We are *Homo sapiens* generation number 7,500, counting from 150,000 years ago, when our species presumably arose; and we are human generation number 125,000, counting from the earliest forms of *Homo*.

Every 110 hours a million more humans arrive on the planet than die into the planet. A hundred million of us are children who live on the streets. Over a hundred million of us live in countries where we hold no citizenship.

Twenty-three million of us are refugees. Sixteen million of us live in Cairo. Twelve million fish for a living from small boats. Seven and a half million of us are Uygurs. One million of us crew on freezer trawlers. Nearly a thousand of us a day commit suicide.

HEAD-SPINNING NUMBERS CAUSE MIND TO GO SLACK, the *Hartford Courant* says. But our minds must not go slack. How can we think straight if our minds go slack? We agree that we want to think straight.

Anyone's close world of family and friends composes a group smaller than almost all sampling errors, smaller than almost all rounding errors, a group invisible, at whose loss the world will not blink. Two million children die a year from diarrhea, and 800,000 from measles. Do we blink? Stalin starved 7 million Ukrainians in one year, Pol Pot killed 1 million Cambodians, the flu epidemic of 1918 killed 21 or 22 million people . . . shall this go on? Or do you suffer, as Teilhard de Chardin did, the sense of being "an atom lost in the universe"? Or do you not suffer this sense? How about what journalists call "compassion fatigue"? Reality fatigue? At what limit for you do other individuals blur? Vanish? How old are you?

V

Los Angeles airport has 25,000 parking spaces. This is about one space for every person who died in 1985 in Colombia when a volcano erupted. This is one space for each of the corpses of more than two years' worth of accidental killings from leftover land mines of recent wars. At five to a car, almost all the Inuit in the world could park at LAX. Similarly, if you propped up or stacked four bodies to a car, you could fit into the airport parking lot all the corpses from the firestorm bombing of Tokyo in March 1945, or the corpses of Londoners who died in the plague, or the corpses of Burundians killed in civil war since 1993. But you could not fit America's homeless there, not even at twenty to a car.

Since sand and dirt pile up on everything, why does the world look fresh for each new crowd? As natural and human debris raises the continents, vegetation grows on the piles. It is all a stage—we know this—a temporary stage on top of many layers of stages, but every year a new crop of sand, grass, and tree leaves freshens the set and perfects the illusion that ours is the new and urgent world now. When Keats was in Rome, I read once, he saw pomegranate trees overhead; they bloomed in dirt blown onto the Colosseum's broken walls. How can we doubt our own time, in which each bright instant probes the future? In every arable soil in the world we grow grain over tombs—sure, we know this. But do not the dead generations seem to us dark and still as mummies, and their times always faded like scenes painted on walls at Pompeii?

How can we see ourselves as only a new, temporary cast for a long-running show when a new batch of birds flies around singing and new clouds move? Living things from hyenas to bacteria whisk the dead away like stagehands hustling between scenes. To help a living space last while we live on it, we brush or haul away the blowing sand and hack or burn the greenery. We are mowing the grass at the cutting edge.

VI

In northeast Japan, a seismic sea wave killed 27,000 people on June 15, 1896. Do not fail to distinguish this infamous wave from the April 30, 1991, waves that drowned 138,000 Bangladeshi. You were not tempted to confuse, conflate, forget, or ignore these deaths, were you?

On the dry Laetoli plain of northern Tanzania, Mary Leakey found a trail of hominid footprints. The three barefoot people—likely a short man and woman and child *Australopithecus afarensis*—walked closely together. They walked on moist volcanic tuff and ash. We have a record of those few seconds from a day about 3.6 million years ago—before hominids even chipped stone tools. More ash covered their footprints and hardened. Ash also preserved the pockmarks of the raindrops that fell beside the three who walked; it was a rainy day. We have almost ninety feet of the three's steady footprints intact. We do not know where they were going or why. We do not know why the woman paused and turned left, briefly, before continuing. "A remote ancestor," Leakey said, "experienced a moment of doubt." Possibly they watched the Sadiman volcano erupt, or they took a last look back before they left. We do know we cannot make anything so lasting as these three barefoot ones did.

After archeologists studied this long strip of record for several years, they buried it again to save it. Along one preserved portion, however, new tree roots are already cracking the footprints, and in another place winds threaten to sand them flat; the preservers did not cover them deeply enough. Now they are burying them again.

Jeremiah, walking toward Jerusalem, saw the smoke from the Temple's blaze. He wept; he saw the blood of the slain. "He put his face close to the ground and saw the footprints of sucklings and infants who were walking into captivity" in Babylon. He kissed the footprints.

Who were these individuals? Who were the three who walked together and left footprints in the rain? Who was that eighteenth-century Ukrainian peasant the Baal Shem Tov, the founder of modern Hasidism, who taught, danced, and dug clay? He was among the generations of children of Babylonian exiles whose footprints on the bare earth Jeremiah kissed. Centuries later the Emperor Hadrian destroyed another such son of exile in Rome, Rabbi Akiba. Russian Christians and European Christians tried, and Hitler tried, to wipe all those survivors of children of exile from the ground of the earth as a man wipes a plate—survivors of exiles whose footprints on the ground I kiss, and whose feet.

Who and of what import were the men whose bones bulk the Great Wall, the 30 million Mao starved, or the 11 million children under five who die each year now? Why, they are the insignificant others, of course; living or dead, they are just some of the plentiful others. And you?

Is it not late? A late time to be living? Are not our current generations the important ones? We have changed the world. Are not our heightened times the important ones, the ones since Hiroshima? Perhaps we are the last generation—there is a comfort. Take the bomb threat away and what are we? We are ordinary beads on a never-ending string. Our time is a routine twist of an improbable yarn.

We have no chance of being here when the sun burns out. There must be something ultimately heroic about our time, something that sets it above all those other times. Hitler, Stalin, Mao, and Pol Pot made strides in obliterating whole peoples, but this has been the human effort all along, and we have only enlarged the means, as have people in every century in history. (That genocides recur does not mean that they are similar. Each instance of human evil and each victim's death possesses its unique history and form. To generalize, as Cynthia Ozick points out, is to "befog" evil's specificity.)

Dire things are happening. Plague? Funny weather? Why are we watching the news, reading the news, keeping up with the news? Only to enforce our fancy—probably a necessary lie—that these are crucial times, and we are in on them. Newly revealed, and I am in the know: crazy people, bunches of them! New diseases, sways in power, floods! Can the news from dynastic Egypt have been any different?

As I write this, I am still alive, but of course I might well have died before you read it. Most of the archeologists who reburied hominid footprints have likely not yet died their deaths; the paleontologist Teilhard is pushing up daisies.

Chinese soldiers who breathed air posing for 7,000 individual clay portraits—twenty-two centuries ago—must have thought it a wonderful difference that workers buried only their simulacra then so that their sons could bury their flesh a bit later. One wonders what they did in the months or years they gained. One wonders what one is, oneself, up to these days.

VII

Was it wisdom Mao Tse-tung attained when—like Ted Bundy—he awakened to the long view?

"The atom bomb is nothing to be afraid of," Mao told Nehru. "China has many people. . . . The deaths of ten or twenty million people is nothing to be afraid of." A witness said Nehru showed shock. Later, speaking in Moscow, Mao displayed yet more generosity: he boasted that he was willing to lose 300 million people, half of China's population.

Does Mao's reckoning shock me really? If sanctioning the death of strangers could save my daughter's life, would I do it? Probably. How many others' lives would I be willing to sacrifice? Three? Three hundred million?

An English journalist, observing the Sisters of Charity in Calcutta, reasoned: "Either life is always and in all circumstances sacred, or intrinsically of no account; it is inconceivable that it should be in some cases the one, and in some the other."

One small town's soup kitchen, St. Mary's, serves 115 men a night. Why feed 115 individuals? Surely so few people elude most demographics and achieve statistical insignificance. After all, there are 265 million Americans, 15 million people who live in Mexico City, 16 million in greater New York, 26 million in greater Tokyo. Every day 1.5 million people walk through Times Square in New York; every day almost as many people—1.4 million—board a U.S. passenger plane. And so forth. We who breathe air now will join the already dead layers of us who breathed air once. We arise from dirt and dwindle to dirt, and the might of the universe is arrayed against us. ∎

■ *QUESTIONS FOR MAKING CONNECTIONS WITHIN THE READING* ■

1. "The Wreck of Time" is divided into seven sections. What is each section about? How are the sections connected? Is there an argument that develops over the course of the seven sections? Are there themes that are repeated across the sections? What is it that Dillard would like her readers to see or understand when they've completed her essay?

2. In the third section of "The Wreck of Time," Dillard describes how a boat creates a standing wave. At the end of her description, she writes that watching such waves allowed her to "see time and how it works." How does time work? What does her vision of the standing wave have to do with the other images she details in her essay?

3. When Dillard's essay first appeared in *Harper's,* a series of images were interspersed throughout the text. What images do you think would be appropriate for this essay? Bring to class an image or series of images that you feel illustrates or comments on the argument Dillard is making in "The Wreck of Time." Be prepared to discuss why the image you've selected is appropriate.

■ *QUESTIONS FOR WRITING* ■

1. In many ways, Annie Dillard's "The Wreck of Time" defies our common expectations about what a piece of writing *should* do: the essay has no clear thesis statement; it has no marked transitions between the paragraphs; it provides no obvious connection between its various subsections. Indeed, on first reading Dillard's piece, one might be tempted to conclude that it's little more than the recitation of a series of unrelated statistics and the posing of a series of unanswered questions. What is the relationship between the way that Dillard has written this piece and what she has to say in the piece? What is it that Dillard wants us to think about while reading her essay?

2. "We who are here now make up about 6.8 percent of all people who have appeared to date," Dillard writes; "This is not a meaningful figure." "The Wreck of Time" is filled with statistics about world population, the size of the universe, natural and man-made disasters. Are any of these figures "meaningful"? Can such figures be invested with meaning?

■ *QUESTIONS FOR MAKING CONNECTIONS BETWEEN READINGS* ■

1. At the end of "Does God Have a Future?" Karen Armstrong asserts, "Human beings cannot endure emptiness and desolation; they will fill the vacuum by creating a new focus of meaning." Does Annie Dillard do this? What philosophical, religious, or moral system emerges from the vision Dillard has provided in "The Wreck of Time"?

2. Given the argument that Dillard develops in "The Wreck of Time," does it make sense to pursue a project like cleaning up the Ganges River that Alexander Stille describes? Is Dillard's view of the natural world consonant with Mishra's? Will the notion of "the sacred" last into the next century, or will it be replaced by science and information?

www For additional suggestions about making connections between readings, visit the Link-O-Mat and More Sample Assignments at <www.newhum.com>.

SUSAN FALUDI

PULITZER PRIZE–WINNING journalist Susan Faludi first became interested in writing about feminism in the fifth grade, when she polled her classmates to determine their feelings about the Vietnam War and legalized abortion. In the furor that followed Faludi's release of her data showing her peers' liberal attitudes, Faludi came to realize, as she put it in a recent interview, "the power that you could have as a feminist writer. Not being the loudest person on the block, not being one who regularly interrupted in class or caused a scene, I discovered that through writing I could make my views heard, and I could actually create change."

The daughter of a homemaker and a Hungarian holocaust survivor, Faludi was raised in Queens and attended Harvard, where she studied literature and American history. After graduating in 1981, Faludi worked for a number of newspapers, including the *New York Times* and the *Wall Street Journal,* before devoting her time to writing *Backlash: The Undeclared War Against American Women* (1991), a study of the media's assault on feminism. *Backlash* won the National Book Critics Circle Award for general nonfiction in 1991 and made Faludi a household name. She appeared on the cover of *Time* magazine alongside Gloria Steinem and, almost overnight, became a national spokesperson on women's rights and the future of feminism.

While doing research for *Backlash,* Faludi began to wonder why the men who opposed women's progress were so angry. In setting out to understand this anger, Faludi interviewed a religious brotherhood, the Promise Keepers, sex workers in the pornography industry, union members, the unemployed, and other males who felt disempowered or disenfranchised. "The Citadel," which presents Faludi's investigation into why male cadets were so enraged by the admission of women into the military academy, is one part of this project and has since been incorporated into Faludi's second book, *Stiffed: The Betrayal of the American Man* (1999). The surprising thesis of *Stiffed* is that

Faludi, Susan. "The Naked Citadel." *The New Yorker.* September 5, 1994. 62–81.

Initial quotation drawn from Brian Lamb's interview with Susan Faludi on Booknotes, October 25, 1992 <http://www.booknotes.org/transcripts/10096.htm>; closing quotation drawn from Kate Melloy's interview with Susan Faludi, "Feminist Author Susan Faludi Preaches Male Inclusion" <http://www.kollegeville.com/kampus/faludi.htm>.

men, too, have suffered during the recent social upheavals because "working with others anonymously and loyally to build something larger than yourself is no longer seen as glorious." Although Faludi holds out the hope for a society in which men and women can work together cooperatively, she also believes that "[t]o revive a genuine feminism, we must disconnect feminism from the individual pursuit of happiness and reconnect it with the individual desire for social responsibility: the basic human need and joy to be part of a larger, meaningful struggle, which engages the entire society."

WWW **To learn more about Susan Faludi and The Citadel, please visit the Link-O-Mat at <www.newhum.com>.**

The Naked Citadel

Along the edges of the quad, in the gutters, the freshman cadets were squaring their corners. The "knobs," as they are called for their nearly hairless doorknob pates, aren't allowed to step on the lawn of the broad parade ground, which is trimmed close, as if to match their shorn heads. Keeping off the grass is one of many prohibitions that obtain at The Citadel, a public military college on Charleston's Ashley River. Another is the rule that so many of the cadets say brought them to this Moorish-style, gated campus: Girls keep out.

The campus has a dreamy, flattened quality, with its primary colors, checkerboard courtyards, and storybook-castle barracks. It feels more like an architect's rendering of a campus—almost preternaturally clean, orderly, antiseptic—than the messy real thing. I stood at the far end of the quad, at the academic hall's front steps, and watched the cadets make their herky-jerky perpendicular turns as they drew closer for the first day of class. They walked by stiffly, their faces heat-blotched and vulnerable, and as they passed each in turn shifted his eyes downward. I followed one line of boys into a classroom, a Western Civ class—except, of course, they weren't really boys at all. These were college men, manly recruits to an élite military college whose virile exploits were mythicized in best-selling novels by Calder Willingham and Pat Conroy, both Citadel alumni. So why did I expect their voices to crack when they spoke for the first time? Partly, it was the grammar-schoolish taking of attendance, compulsory at The Citadel. Multiple absences can lead to "tours," hours of marching back and forth in the courtyard with a pinless rifle over one shoulder; or to "cons," confinement to one's room.

But mostly it was the young men themselves, with their doughy faces and twitching limbs, who gave me the urge to babysit. Despite their enrollment in a college long considered "the big bad macho school" (as a former R.O.T.C. commander, Major General Robert E. Wagner, once put it), the cadets lacked the swagger and knowingness of big men on campus. They perched tentatively on their chairs, their hands arranged in a dutiful clasp on their desktops, as if they were expecting a ruler slap to the knuckles. A few dared to glance over at the female visitor, but whenever they made eye contact they averted their gaze and color stained their cheeks.

"As many of you probably know," their teacher said, "this was almost the day the first woman joined The Citadel." The cadets continued to study their polished shoes. "How do you, in fact, feel about whether women should be allowed to attend?"

Silence reigned. Maybe the cadets felt the question put them in an awkward spot. Not only was their teacher in favor of admitting women to The Citadel's Corps of Cadets, the teacher *was* a woman. Indeed, Professor Jane Bishop seemed to be in the strange situation of calling in an air strike on her own position. It was the first day of fall classes in the 1993–94 academic year at The Citadel, and she was broaching the question of the hour. But this incongruity wasn't limited to her classroom. From the moment I stepped onto the school's campus, I had been struck by an unexpected circumstance: though an all-male institution—an institution, moreover, whose singular mission was "making men"—The Citadel was by no means free of women. Female teachers were improving cadets' minds, female administrators were keeping their records, and an all-female (and all-black) staff served the meals in the mess hall. There was also the fact that female students made up seventy-seven percent of the enrollment of the evening school, and many other female students attended summer school with the cadets. What about them? Of course, summer school and evening school aren't part of the military college proper. Cadets don't attend the evening school; and as Major Rick Mill, The Citadel's public-relations director, notes, those cadets who attend the summer school "aren't wearing their uniforms."

Today they were, and so was their teacher. All permanent instructors, regardless of their sex (about fifteen percent are women), wear uniforms as part of their required affiliation with a largely ceremonial outfit once known as the South Carolina Unorganized Militia, and still called by the unfortunate acronym SCUM. Bishop wore hers with what seemed like a deliberate air of disarray.

The cadets' uniforms were considerably tidier—testament to the efficacy of the famous cadet shirt tuck, a maneuver akin to hospital-corners bedmaking and so exacting a cadet cannot perform it without assistance. Even so, the gray cadet uniform, with the big black stripe down the side of the pants

Freshmen are in the "fourth-class system," a regimen to "strip" each recruit of his identity and remold him into the "Whole Man." Illustration by Mark Zingarelli, originally published in *The New Yorker*.

and the nametag above the left breast, is the sort more often seen on high-school band members than on fighting soldiers.

"Remember," Bishop prodded them, "speech is free in the classroom."

At last, a cadet unclasped and raised a hand. "Well, I'd have no problem with her in the day program, but she can't join the Corps."

"She," as everyone there knew, was Shannon Faulkner, the woman who had challenged the school's hundred-and-fifty-year-old all-male policy by omitting reference to her sex from her application and winning acceptance to the Corps of Cadets earlier that year—acceptance that was rescinded once the administrators discovered their error. Faulkner's attempt to gain entrance then shifted from the admissions office to the courts. She was allowed under court order to attend day classes during the spring semester of 1994, the first woman to do so. On July 22nd, a United States District Court ruled that The Citadel must admit Faulkner into the Corps of Cadets proper; three weeks later, the Fourth United States Circuit Court of Appeals granted The Citadel a stay pending appeal.

Yet why shouldn't she be permitted into the Corps, Bishop pressed. One of her students recited the fitness requirement—forty-five pushups and fifty-five sit-ups in two-minute sets, and a two-mile run in sixteen minutes. But the administration made passing the fitness test a requirement for graduation only *after* Shannon Faulkner filed suit. An alumnus recounted in court that many upperclassmen he knew who had failed the test skipped the punitive morning run and "sat around and ate doughnuts." Another of Bishop's students cited the shaved-head rule. But this, too, seemed a minor point. A woman cadet could conceivably get a buzz cut. Sinéad O'Connor had done it, Bishop pointed out, without undue injury to her career. And, anyway, after freshman year the men no longer get their heads shaved. Other deprivations of freshman year were invoked: having to "brace" on demand—that is, assume a stance in which a knob stands very erect and tucks in his chin until it puckers up like a rooster's wattle—and having to greet every upperclassman's bellowed command and rebuke with "Sir, yes sir!" or "Sir, no sir!" or "Sir, no excuse sir!" But women, obviously, aren't incapable of obeisance; one might even say they have a long history of it.

Weighing heaviest on the cadets' minds, it turned out, was the preservation of the all-male communal bathroom. The sharing of the stall-less showers and stall-less toilets is "at the heart of the Citadel experience," according to more than one cadet. The men bathe as a group; they walk to the shower down the open galleries, in full view of the courtyard below, and do so, one cadet said, in "nothing but our bathrobes" or "even without any clothes." Another cadet said, "I know it sounds trivial, but all of us in one shower, it's like we're all one, we're all the same, and—I don't know—you feel like you're exposed, but you feel safe. You know these guys are going to be your friends for life." His voice trailed off. "I just can't explain it but when they take that away, it's over. This place will be ruined."

"If women come here, they'll have to put up window shades in all the rooms," a cadet said. "Think of all the windows in the barracks. That could be eight thousand, nine thousand dollars. You've got to look at the costs."

At the end of the hour, the cadets filed out and resumed their double-time jog along the gutters—and their place in the "fourth-class system." This "system" is a nine-month regimen of small and large indignities intended to "strip" each young recruit of his original identity and remold him into the "Whole Man," a vaguely defined ideal, half Christian soldier, half Dale Carnegie junior executive. As a knob explained it to me, "We're all suffering together. It's how we bond." Another knob said, "It's a strange analogy, but it's almost like a P.O.W. camp."

One cadet dawdled, glancing nervously around, then sidled up to me. He spoke in a near whisper, and what he had to say had nothing to do with lavatory etiquette or military tradition. "The great majority of the guys here are very misogynistic," he said. "All they talk about is how girls are pigs and sluts."

I asked him to explain at greater length. He agonized. "I have to keep quiet," he said, but he finally agreed to meet me later, in an out-of-the-way spot on the upper floor of the student-activities center. He rejoined his class-mates with that distinctive knob march, "the march of the puppets," as a professor described it to me later. It was a gait caused in some cases, I was told, by the most conscientious cadets' efforts to keep their shirts perfectly straight with the help of garters—one end of the garter clipped to the shirt-tail, the other end to the socks.

As I waited for my cadet informant, I decided to kill an hour on the vast pa-rade ground, where the Corps of Cadets marches every Friday afternoon in full dress uniforms, and where, according to an old school brochure, "man-hood meets mastery." This is a paramilitary display, not a military one. De-spite the regalia and officer ranks, and despite its notoriously fierce military discipline ("To discipline is to teach" is the motto emblazoned on one of the school's books of regulations), this is a military academy by self-designation only. Unlike the federal service academies—West Point, An-napolis, the Air Force Academy—The Citadel has no connection with the United States Armed Forces (other than its R.O.T.C. program and its em-ployment of some active and retired officers). Its grounds are adorned with dusty and decommissioned military hardware—a Sherman tank, a subma-rine's torpedo-loading hatch, a Phantom jet named Annette, two cannons named Betsy and Lizzie. In most cases, the weapons, including the pinless M-14s the cadets carry, are inoperative. The mouths of the various cannons are stuffed with cement—all except those of Betsy and Lizzie, which are fired during parades, but carefully aimed high enough so that their powder does not dust the crenellated barracks. The over-all effect is that of a theme park for post–Cold War kids.

The hokeyness and childlike innocence of the scene—the stage-prop artillery, the toy-soldier clip-clop of the cadets as they squared their corners—were endearing, in a Lost Boys sort of way, and I strolled over to the student-activities center for my rendezvous with my cadet informant thinking that The Citadel's version of martial culture was not so menacing after all. The cadet was not in evidence. I spent the next thirty minutes prowling the halls, which were lined with portraits of stern-faced "generals" (I couldn't tell which were United States military and which were SCUM), and examining ads on the student bulletin board for items like "Save the Males" bumper stickers. I tried to reach the cadet's room by phone—women aren't admitted into the barracks—but he was not there. A bit thoughtlessly, I left a message with an upper-classman and headed toward town.

At my hotel, the receptionist handed me a message from my vanished cadet. "Please, don't ever call here again!" it read. The phone clerk peered at me curiously. "Sorry about that exclamation mark, but he seemed quite distraught," she said. "His voice was shaking."

What brought a young man to an all-male preserve in the last decade of the twentieth century, anyway? What was going on outside the academy gates that impelled thousands of boys, Southern and Northern alike (about a fifth of its student body of about two thousand are Yankees), to seek refuge behind a pair of corroding cannons?

"The forces arrayed against us," an attorney named Robert Patterson declared in a February, 1994, court hearing, consider his military academy to be "some big-game animal to be hunted down, tracked, caught, badgered, and killed so that some lawyer or some organization can go back up and hang a trophy on a wall in an office." Patterson was defending not The Citadel but the Virginia Military Institute, which is the only other public military academy in the United States that does not admit women, and which was involved in a similar sex-discrimination suit. (Three months later, Patterson, a V.M.I. alumnus, returned to court to defend The Citadel.) "I will say this, Your Honor," he went on. "This quest by these people constitutes the longest and most expensive publicly financed safari in the annals of big-game hunting."

The Citadel's administration has fought the female hunters with a legal arsenal of nearly a million dollars and with dour, tight-lipped determination, which has only increased with time. The Citadel's president, Claudius Elmer (Bud) Watts III, who is a retired Air Force lieutenant general and a second-generation Citadel alumnus, views Shannon Faulkner's legal efforts as an enemy invasion, placing his young troops "under attack." "The Citadel is in this to the end," he pronounced at a press conference held in the spring of 1994 on the parade ground, his feet planted between Betsy and Lizzie, his uniform decked with ribbons, and his chin tucked in, as is his custom, as if in a permanent brace position.

Later, in his living room, surrounded by coffee-table books on football, Watts told me firmly, "You cannot put a male and a female on that same playing field," though he couldn't say exactly why. Of his own Citadel years he conceded, "I've not the foggiest notion if it would have been different" had women attended. He was just glad there were no female cadets then; otherwise, he said, the cadets would have faced "a different form of intimidation—not wanting to be embarrassed in front of a girl."

Faulkner has been opposed not only by many Citadel staff and alumni but—at least, publicly—by almost all the current cadets. They say that her presence in the Corps would absolutely destroy a basic quality of their experience as Citadel men. She would be what one Citadel defender called in his court deposition "a toxic kind of virus." Tellingly, even before the United States District Court judge enjoined The Citadel to admit Faulkner to the Corps of Cadets for the fall of 1994, and before the injunction was set aside, the administration announced its selection of her living quarters: the infirmary.

Cadets cite a number of reasons that women would have a deleterious effect on the Corps of Cadets, and the reasons are repeated so often as to be easily predictable, though their expression can be novel. "Studies show—I can't cite them, but studies show that males learn better when females aren't there," one cadet explained to me (a curious sentiment at a school where a knob motto about grades is "2.0 and Go"). "If a girl was here, I'd be concerned not to look foolish. If you're a shy student, you won't be as inhibited." Another cadet said, "See, you don't have to impress them here. You're free." From a third: "Where does it end? Will we have unisex bathrooms?" But among the reasons most frequently heard for repelling Faulkner at the gate is this: "She would be destroying a long and proud tradition."

The masculine traditions of West Point and Annapolis were also closely guarded by their male denizens, but the resistance to women joining their ranks was nowhere near as fierce and filled with doomsday rhetoric as The Citadel's efforts to repel feminine interlopers. At Norwich University, a private military college in Northfield, Vermont, that voluntarily opened its barracks to women in 1974, two years before the federal service academies, the administration actually made an effort to recruit and accommodate women. "There was no storm of protest," said a Norwich spokeswoman, Judy Clauson. But then, "it was a time when there were so many rules that were being loosened." The Air Force veteran Linnea Westberg, who was one of the eight women in Norwich's first coed class, recalled, of her integration into its corps, that "ninety-five percent of the male cadets were fine, especially the freshmen, who didn't know any different." Westberg said she was baffled by the intensity of The Citadel's opposition to women in its corps. "It's hard for me to believe it's still an issue."

"The Citadel is a living museum to the way things used to be," John Drennan, a Citadel graduate and a public defender in Charleston, told me one day during The Citadel's legal proceedings. But how, exactly, did things use to be? The cadets and the alumni of the school, along with those protesting against its exclusionary policies, envision its military tradition above all.

And The Citadel once did have a strong military aspect: it was formed as an arsenal in 1822 in response to a slave revolt purportedly planned by the freed Charleston slave Denmark Vesey, which, though it was foiled, aroused widespread alarm in the region. Yet twenty years later the guns and the gold braid became mere adornment as The Citadel turned into an industrial school of domestic and practical skills. Union troops shut down The Citadel at the end of the Civil War, but it was reinvented and reopened in 1882, after the Union's Reconstruction officials had thoroughly stripped the school of all military muscle. Its new mission was to reinvigorate the masculinity of the South by showing its men how to compete with the business and industrial skills of the Yankee carpetbaggers, who were believed to be much better prepared than the sons of Dixie to enter the Darwinian fray of modern commerce. John Peyre Thomas, who ran The Citadel from 1882 to 1885, wrote of the need to teach spoiled plantation boys the rudiments of self-reliance. "It must be admitted that the institution of African slavery, in many respects, affected injuriously the white youth of the South," he wrote. "Reared from infancy to manhood with servants at his command to bring his water, brush his shoes, saddle his horse, and, in fine, to minister to his personal wants, the average Southern boy grew up in some points of character dependent, and lazy, and inefficient. He was found, too, wanting in those habits of order and system that come from the necessity, in man, to economize time and labor."

What makes the school's Reconstruction-era mission important is that in so many ways it remains current; the masculine and industrial culture of our age and that of the conquered South may have more in common than we care to imagine. Again, we are at a psychic and economic crisis point for manhood. And, again, the gun issues hide the butter issues: the bombast masks a deep insecurity about employment and usefulness in a world where gentleman soldiers are an anachronism and a graduate with gentleman's C's may find himself busing tables at Wendy's.

The uncertain prospects of Citadel graduates are worsened by military downsizing. Only about a third of recent graduates entered the military—a figure that has fallen steeply since the mid-seventies, when half of The Citadel's graduating class routinely took a service commission. News of Shannon Faulkner's court case competed in the Charleston *Post & Courier* with news of the shutting down of the local shipyards and decommissionings from the local military installations.

The night before the closing arguments in Faulkner's suit, I had dinner at the on-campus home of Philippe and Linda Ross, who have both taught at The Citadel. Philippe, the head of the Biology Department, had just completed his first round of moonlighting as a "retraining" instructor at the Charleston Naval Shipyard. He had been prepping laid-off nuclear engineers to enter one of the few growth industries in the area—toxic-waste management. Facing a room filled with desperate men each day had been a dispiriting experience, he said. He recalled the plea of a middle-aged engineer, thrust out of the service after twenty-six years: "All I want to do is work." Linda Ross, who was then teaching psychology at The Citadel, looked across the table with a pained expression. "That whole idea that if a young man went to college he could make a decent living and buy a house, and maybe even a boat, just does not hold anymore," she said softly. "There's a Citadel graduate working as a cashier at the grocery store. And the one thing these young men felt they could count on was that if things got hard they could always go into the military. No more. And they are bitter and angry."

In the fall of 1991, Michael Lake, a freshman, decided to leave The Citadel. He had undergone weeks of bruising encounters with upperclassmen—encounters that included being knocked down with a rifle butt and beaten in the dark by a pack of cadets. Incidents of hazing became so violent that, in a school where publicly criticizing the alma mater is virtually an act of treason, several athletes told their stories to *Sports Illustrated*. Much of the violence was aimed at star freshman athletes: a member of the cycling team was forced to hang by his fingers over a sword poised two inches below his testicles; a placekicker had his head dunked in water twenty times until he was unconscious; a linebacker was forced to swallow his chewing tobacco and tormented until, he said later, "I was unable even to speak clearly in my classes." It was a time when the Churchill Society, a literary club reportedly containing a white-supremacist faction, was organized on campus. It was a time when the local chapter of the National Association for the Advancement of Colored People urged a federal investigation into a pair of racial incidents on the school's campus: the appearance of a noose over the bed of a black freshman who had earlier refused to sing "Dixie," and the shooting and wounding of a black cadet by a sniper who was never identified. (A few years earlier, upperclassmen wearing Klan-like costumes left a charred paper cross in the room of a black cadet.) And it was a time when a leader of the Junior Sword Drill, a unit of cadet sword-bearers, leaped off a five-foot dresser onto the head of a prostrate cadet, then left him in a pool of blood in a barracks hall. According to one cadet, a lacrosse-team member returning from an away game at three in the morning stumbled upon the victim's unconscious body, his face split open, jaw and nose broken, mouth a jack-o'-lantern of missing teeth.

One night, at about 2 A.M., high-ranking cadets trapped a raccoon in the barracks and began to stab it with a knife. Beau Turner, a student at the school, was awakened by the young men's yelling. "My roommate and I went out there to try and stop it," Turner recalled, "but we were too late." Accounts of the episode vary. In a widely circulated version (which was referred to in a faculty member's testimony), the cadets chanted, "Kill the bitch! Kill the bitch!" as they tortured the raccoon to death.

In October, 1993, two upperclassmen burst into the room of two fresh-men and reportedly kneed them in the genitals, pulled out some of their chest hair, and beat them up. They were arrested on charges of assault and battery, and agreed to a program of counselling and community service, which would wipe clean their records. They withdrew from The Citadel, in lieu of expulsion, the spokesman Major Rick Mill said.

One of the offending cadets, Adrian Baer, told me that he and the other accused sophomore, Jeremy Leckie, did indeed come back from drinking, burst into the knobs' room after 10 P.M., and "repeatedly struck them in the chest and stomach" and bruised one of them in the face, but he denied hav-ing kicked them in the groin and yanked out chest hair. He said that what he did was common procedure—and no different from the "motivational" treatment he had received as a knob at the hands of a senior who came into *his* room. They entered the freshmen's room, Baer explained, because they viewed one of the occupants as "a problem" knob who "needed some extra motivation." Baer elaborated: "His pinkie on his right hand wouldn't com-pletely close when he went to salute. He caught a lot of heat for that, of course, because it's a military school; it's important to salute properly." The strict rule that upperclassmen not fraternize with knobs, he said, meant that they couldn't simply counsel the freshman kindly. "If we just sat down and said, 'Listen, guy, we have a little problem,' that would be fraternization. And more important, knobs would lose respect for upperclassmen. It's a lot of denial on the part of officials at The Citadel about hazing," Baer said. "They don't want to believe it goes on." Leckie's father, Timothy Rinaldi, said that while he believed his son "was definitely in the wrong," he felt The Citadel's fourth-class system bred such behavior. "They help build this monster," he said of The Citadel, "the monster gets up off the table and starts walking through town—and now Dr. Frankenstein wants to shoot it."

Needless to say, not every cadet embraces the climate of cruelty; the noc-turnal maulings likely frighten as many cadets as they enthrall. But the group mentality that pervades The Citadel assures that any desire on the part of a cadet to speak out about the mounting violence will usually be squelched by the threat of ostracism and shame. While group rule typifies many institutions, military and civilian, that place a premium on conformity, the power and authoritarianism of the peer group at The Citadel is excep-tional, because the college gives a handful of older students leave to "gov-ern" the others as they see fit. (A lone officer provided by the military, who sleeps in a wing off one of the dorms, seldom interferes.) This is a situation that, over the years, an occasional school official has challenged, without success. A former assistant commandant for discipline, Army Lieutenant Colonel T. Nugent Courvoisie, recalled that he "begged" the school's presi-dent back in the sixties to place more military officers—and ones who were more mature—in the barracks, but his appeals went unheeded. Discipline and punishment in the dorms is in the hands of the student-run regimental command, and ascendancy in this hierarchy is not always predicated on compassion for one's fellow-man. In consequence, the tyranny of the few buys the silence of the many.

This unofficial pact of silence could, of course, be challenged by the Citadel officialdom. On a number of occasions over the past three decades—most recently when some particularly brutal incidents found their way into the media—The Citadel has commissioned "studies." But when the administration does go on the offensive, its animus is primarily directed not at miscreant cadets but at the "unfair" media, which are "victimizing" the institution by publicizing the bad behavior of its boys.

In recent years, enough bad news leaked out locally to become a public-relations nightmare, and the school appointed a committee of Citadel loyalists to assess the situation. Even the loyalists concluded, in a January, 1992, report, that the practice of physical abuse of freshmen, along with food and sleep deprivation, had got out of hand. As a result, Major Mill told me, The Citadel ordered upperclassmen to stop using pushups as a "disciplinary tool" on individual cadets. "That was the most important one" of the reforms prompted by the report, Mill said. Other reforms were adopted: for example, freshmen would no longer be compelled to deliver mail to upperclassmen after their evening study hours, thus reducing opportunities for hazing; freshmen would—at least officially—no longer be compelled to "brace" in the mess hall. At the same time, the report declared that it "wholeheartedly endorses the concept of the fourth-class system," which it called "essential to the attainment of college objectives and the development of the Citadel man."

Institutions that boast of their insularity, whether convents or military academies, are commonly pictured in the public imagination as static, unchanging abstractions, isolated from the ebb and flow of current events. But these edifices are rarely as otherworldly as their guardians might wish; indeed, in the case of The Citadel, its bricked-off culture has functioned more as a barometer of national anxieties than as a garrison against them. The militaristic tendencies within the Corps seem to vary inversely with the esteem in which the American soldier is held in the larger society. In times when the nation has been caught up in a socially acceptable conflict, one in which its soldiers return as heroes greeted by tickertape parades, The Citadel has loosened its militaristic harness, or even removed it altogether. Thus, during perhaps the most acceptable war in American history, the Second World War, the fourth-class system of knob humiliation was all but discontinued. Upperclassmen couldn't even order a knob to brace. The changes began largely in response to the demands of the real military for soldiers they could use in a modern war. "The War Department and the Navy Department were asking R.O.T.C. to do less drilling, more calculus," Jamie Moore, a professor of history at The Citadel and a former member of the United

States Army's Historical Advisory Committee, told me. "The Citadel dismantled its fourth-class system because it was getting in the way of their military training." The changes didn't seem to interfere with the school's production of Whole Men; on the contrary, an extraordinary percentage of The Citadel's most distinguished graduates come from these years, among them United States Senator Ernest (Fritz) Hollings; Alvah Chapman, Jr., the former chief executive of Knight-Ridder; and South Carolina's former governor John C. West.

The kinder, gentler culture of the Second World War–era Citadel survived well into the next decade. Although a new fourth-class system was soon established, it remained relatively benign. "We didn't have the yelling we have today," Colonel Harvey Dick, class of '53 and now a member of The Citadel's governing body, recalled. "They didn't even shave the freshmen's heads."

The postwar years also brought the admission of women to the summer program, and without the hand-wringing provoked by Shannon Faulkner's application. "WOMEN INVADE CITADEL CLASSES FIRST TIME IN SCHOOL'S HISTORY," the Charleston daily noted back on page 16 of its June 21, 1949, edition. "Most male students took the advent of the 'amazons' in their stride," the paper reported cheerfully. "Only the younger ones seemed at all uneasy. Professors and instructors were downright glad to see women in their classes."

The Vietnam War, needless to say, did not inspire the same mood of relaxation on campus. "The fourth-class system was very physical," Wallace West, the admissions director, who was an undergraduate at The Citadel during the Vietnam War years, said. "When I was there, there was no true emphasis on academics, or on positive leadership. It was who could be worked to physical exhaustion." Alumni from those years recounted being beaten with sticks, coat hangers, and rifle butts. That was, of course, the era that inspired Pat Conroy's novel "The Lords of Discipline," a tale of horrific hazing, directed with special virulence against the school's first African-American cadet. "They just tortured us," Conroy recalled from his home, in Beaufort, South Carolina. "It taught me the exact kind of man I didn't want to be," he added.

In 1968, the administration appointed a committee to investigate the violence. The committee issued a report that, like its 1992 successor, concluded "there have been significant and extensive abuses to the [fourth-class] system." And, with its strong recommendation that hazing result in expulsion, the report seemed to promise a more pacific future on campus.

In the past decade and a half, however, the record of violence and cruelty at The Citadel has attracted increasing notice, even as the armed forces have been racked by downsizing and scandal. The Citadel president during much of this era, Major General James A. Grimsley, Jr., declined to discuss this or any other aspect of campus life during his tenure. "I don't do interviews," he said. "Thank you for calling, young lady." He then hung up. Others have been less reticent.

Thirteen years before Vice-Admiral James B. Stockdale consented to be Ross Perot's running mate, he took on what turned out to be an even more thankless task: fighting brutal forms of hazing at The Citadel. In 1979, Stockdale, who had graduated from Annapolis, was chosen to be The Citadel's president because of his status as a genuine military hero: he had survived eight years as a P.O.W. in Vietnam. This hero failed to see the point of manufactured adversity. In an afterword to the book "In Love and War," a collaboration between Stockdale and his wife, Sybil, he wrote that there was "something mean and out of control about the regime I had just inherited."

On his first day in the president's office, Stockdale opened a desk drawer and discovered "what turned out to be Pandora's box," he wrote. "From the top down, what was written on the papers I took out of the desk drawers—and conversations with some of their authors—was enough to break anybody's heart." Among them was a letter from an infuriated father who wanted to know what had happened to his son "to change him from a levelheaded, optimistic, aggressive individual to a fatigued, irrational, confused and bitter one." He also found copies of memos from The Citadel's staff physician complaining repeatedly of (as Stockdale recalled) "excessive hospitalization"—such as the case of a knob who had suffered intestinal bleeding and was later brought back to the infirmary, having been exercised to unconsciousness. Stockdale sought to reform the system, but he was stymied at every turn. He clashed with The Citadel's powerful Board of Visitors, an eleven-member committee of alumni that sets school policy. The Board of Visitors overruled his expulsion of a senior cadet who had reportedly been threatening freshmen with a pistol. A year into his presidency, Stockdale submitted his resignation. After he left, the board reinstated an avenging friend of the senior cadet who, according to Stockdale, had attempted to break into his house one evening. (The then chairman of the Board of Visitors maintains that the cadet was drunk and looking for the barracks.)

"They thought they were helping people into manhood," Stockdale recalled, from a more serene post, in Palo Alto, California, where he is a scholar at Stanford's Hoover Institution on War, Revolution, and Peace. "But they had no idea what that meant—or who they were."

After Watts became president, in 1989, some faculty members began to observe a creeping militarization imposed by the administration upon the Corps's already drill-heavy regimen. Four special military days were added to the academic year. At the beginning of one semester, President Watts held a faculty meeting in a room above the mess hall."Watts had these soldiers standing around the room with their hands behind them," Gardel Feurtado, a political-science professor and one of only two African-American professors, recalled. Watts, he said, lectured the faculty for about three hours. "He didn't talk about academics or educational goals. He just talked about cadets' training, and he showed us a film of it," Feurtado told me. According to Feurtado, Watts told the faculty to line up in groups behind the soldiers for a tour of the barracks. "I said, 'Enough of this,' and I started to walk out. And this soldier stopped me and said, 'Where do you think you're going, sir?' and I said, 'You do realize that I am not in the military?'" Feurtado had to push by him to leave.

Illustration by Mark Zingarelli, originally published in *The New Yorker*.

When Michael Lake looked back on the abuse he suffered during his abbreviated knob year of '91, he could now see before him, like the emergence of invisible ink on what appeared to be a blank piece of paper, the faint outlines of another struggle. What he saw was a submerged gender battle, a bitter but definitely fixed contest between the sexes, concealed from view by the fact that men played both parts. The beaten knobs were the women, "stripped" and humiliated, and the predatory upperclassmen were the men, who bullied and pillaged. If they couldn't re-create a male-dominant society in the real world, they could restage the drama by casting male knobs in all the subservient feminine roles.

"They called you a 'pussy' all the time," Lake recalled. "Or a 'fucking little girl.'" It started the very first day they had their heads shaved, when the upperclassmen stood around and taunted. "Oh, you going to get your little girlie locks cut off?" When they learned that Lake would be playing soccer that fall, their first response was "What is that, a girl's sport?" Another former cadet said that he had withstood "continual abuse," until he found himself thinking about jumping out the fourth-story window of the barracks—and quit. He reported an experience similar to Lake's. Virtually every taunt equated him with a woman: whenever he showed fear, they would say, "You look like you're having an abortion," or "Are you menstruating?" The knobs even experienced a version of domestic violence. The upperclassmen, this cadet recalled, "would go out and get drunk and they would come home and haze, and you just hoped they didn't come into your room."

"According to the Citadel creed of the cadet," Lake said, "women are objects, they're things that you can do with whatever you want to." In order to maintain this world view, the campus has to be free of women whose status might challenge it—a policy that, of course, is rarely enunciated. The acknowledged policy is that women are to be kept at a distance so they can be "respected" as ladies. Several months before Faulkner's lawsuit came to trial, I was sitting in the less than Spartan air-conditioned quarters of the senior regimental commander, Norman Doucet, the highest-ranking cadet, who commanded the barracks. Doucet, who was to be The Citadel's star witness at the Faulkner trial, was explaining to me how excluding women had enhanced his gentlemanly perception of the opposite sex. "The absence of women makes us understand them better," Doucet said. "In an aesthetic kind of way, we appreciate them more—because they are not there."

Women at less of a remove fare less well. In The Citadel's great chain of being, the "waitees"—as many students call that all-black, all-female mess-hall staff—rate as the bottom link. Some upperclassmen have patted them on their rear ends, tried to trip them as they pass the tables, or hurled food at their retreating backs. Cadets have summoned them with "Come here, bitch," or addressed one who dropped a plate or forgot an order as "you stupid whore." The pages of the *Brigadier,* the school's newspaper, bear witness to the cadets' contempt for these women. Gary Brown, now the editor-in-chief of the *Brigadier,* once advised fellow-cadets to beware of "waitee" food contamination—"the germ filled hands, the hair follicles, and other unknown horrors." Not only was he dismayed by "wavy little follicles in my food" but he found the women insufficiently obedient. "Duty is certainly not the sublimest word in the Waitee language," he wrote. In a letter to the editor, Jason S. Pausman, class of '94, urged fellow-cadets to demand "waitees without chronic diseases that involve sneezing, coughing or wiping of body parts. . . . The reality is simple, we CANNOT sit by and let the waitees of this school control us."

Some women faculty members report similarly resentful responses to their presence, despite—or because of—their positions of authority. Angry messages on a professor's door are one tactic. When Jane Bishop recently posted on her office door a photocopy of a *New York Times* editorial supporting women's admission to the Corps of Cadets, she found it annotated with heated rejoinders in a matter of days. "Dr. Bishop, you are a prime example of why women should not be allowed here," one scribble read. Another comment: "Women will destroy the world."

The Citadel men's approach to women seems to toggle between extremes of gentility and fury. "First, they will be charming to the women to get their way," Linda Ross said. "But if that doesn't work they don't know any other way. So then they will get angry." It's a pattern that is particularly evident in some cadets' reaction to younger faculty women.

December Green joined The Citadel's Political Science Department in 1988, the first woman that the department had ever hired for a tenure-track position. She was twenty-six and attractive—"someone the cadets might fantasize about," a colleague recalled. They were less enchanted, however, by her left-leaning politics. She soon found herself getting obscene phone calls in the middle of the night. Then obscenities began appearing on her office door. "Pussy" is the one that sticks in her mind.

Though Green's work at The Citadel was highly praised—she received an award for teaching, research, and service—she said that no one in the administration tried to stop her when she left in 1992, in despair over her inability to contain the cadets' fury. Nor, apparently, had anyone responded to her appeals to correct the situation. "A lot of terrible things happened to me

The legendary Citadel elder known as the Boo, who oversaw racial integration at The Citadel in the sixties, says, "With women, there's going to be sexual harassment." His wife, Margaret, counters, "Oh, honey, those cadets are harassing each other right now." "That's different," he says. "That's standard operating procedure."
Illustration by Mark Zingarelli, originally published in *The New Yorker*.

there," Green, who is now teaching in Ohio, said, reluctant to revisit them. The hostility ranged from glowering group stares in the hallway to death threats—some of which appeared on the cadets' teacher-evaluation forms. The male faculty offered little support. Green recalls the department chairman instructing her to "be more maternal toward the students" when a cadet lodged a complaint about her (she had challenged his essay in which he praised apartheid). And a professor who stood by one day while his students harassed her and another woman informed her, "You get what you provoke."

Green said she eventually had to get an unlisted number to stop the obscene calls, and also moved, in part out of fear of the cadets' vengeance. The last straw, however, came when she submitted the written threats she had received to her chairman, who passed them on to the dean of undergraduate studies, in hopes of remedial action. The dean, she said, did nothing for some months, then, after she inquired, said he had "misplaced" the offending documents.

The dean, Colonel Isaac (Spike) Metts, Jr., told me he didn't recall saying he misplaced the documents but "I might have said it's not on my desk at that time and I don't know where it is." He added that Green was a "very valuable" professor. "I don't know what else we could've done," Metts said. In any event, soon after submitting the threatening notes to the dean Green gave up. At her exit interview, she recalled, President Watts told her he didn't understand why she had been upset by the cadet harassment. "It's just a bunch of kid stuff," another male colleague said. (Lewis Spearman, the assistant to the president, said that, because of federal privacy law, Watts would have no response to Green's version of events.)

The remaining category of women that cadets have to deal with is "the dates," as the young women they socialize with are generally called. (There are no wives; Citadel policy forbids cadets to marry, and violators are expelled.) In some respects, these young women are the greatest challenge to the cadet's sense of gender hierarchy. While the "waitees" can be cast as household servants and the female teachers as surrogate mothers, the dates are more difficult to place. Young women their age are often college students, with the same aspirations as the cadets, or even greater ones. The cadets deal with young women's rising ambitions in a number of ways. One is simply to date high-school girls, an option selected by a number of cadets. Another strategy, facilitated by The Citadel, is to cast the young women who are invited on campus into the homecoming-queen mold. The college holds a Miss Citadel contest each year, and Anne Poole, whose husband, Roger, is the vice-president of academic affairs and the dean of the college, has sat on the judging panel. Each cadet company elects a young woman mascot from a photograph competition, and their faces appear in the yearbook.

The school also sends its young men to an in-house etiquette-training seminar, in which the Citadel "hostess," a pleasant woman in her forties named Susan Bowers, gives them a lecture on how "to act gentlemanly with the girls." She arms cadets with "The Art of Good Taste," a do's-and-don'ts manual with a chapter entitled "Helping the Ladies." The guidebook outlines the "correct way of offering an arm to a lady . . . to help her down the steps," and the best method for assisting "a lady in distress." (The example of distress provided involves an elderly woman trying to open a door when her arms are full of shopping bags.) Such pointers are illustrated with pictures of fifties-style coeds sporting Barbie-doll hair flips and clinging to the arms of their cadets, who are escorting them to "the Hop." The manual's preface states emphatically, "At all times [ladies] must be sheltered and protected not only from the elements and physical harm but also from embarrassment, crudity, or coarseness of any sort."

Susan Bowers explained the duties of her office: "At the beginning of the year, we do 'situation cards' for the freshmen. And we'll bring in cheerleaders and use them as props. . . . We show cadets how to go through the receiving line, how to introduce your date, and what to say to them. In the past, we didn't have the cheerleaders to use, so they dressed up some of the guys as girls." Bowers said she felt bad for the cadets, who often come to her seeking maternal consolation. "They are very timid—afraid, almost," she said. "They are so lost, and they need a shoulder."

"The Art of Good Taste" is silent on the subject of proper etiquette toward women who require neither deference nor rescue. And, as Linda Ross observed, when the gentlemanly approach fails them cadets seem to have only one fallback—aggression. Numerous cadets spoke to me of classmates who claimed to have "knocked around" uncompliant girlfriends. Some of those classmates, no doubt, were embellishing to impress a male audience, but not always. "I know lots of stories where cadets are violent toward women," a 1991 Citadel graduate named Ron Vergnolle said. He had witnessed cadets hitting their girlfriends at a number of Citadel parties—and observed one party incident in which two cadets held down a young woman while a third drunken cadet leaned over and vomited on her. Vergnolle, a magna-cum-laude graduate of the Citadel class of '91, recounted several such stories to me, and added that bragging about humiliating an ex-girlfriend is a common practice—and the more outrageous the humiliation, the better the story, as far as many cadets are concerned. Two such cadet storytellers, for example, proudly spread the word of their exploits on Dog Day, a big outdoor party sponsored by The Citadel's senior class. The two cadets told about the time they became enraged with their dates, followed them to the Portosans, and, after the women had entered, pushed the latrines over so they landed on the doors, trapping the occupants. The cadets left them there. Another cadet told Vergnolle that he had tacked a live hamster to a young woman's door. There was also the cadet who boasted widely that, as vengeance against an uncooperative young woman, he smashed the head of her cat against a window as she watched in horror. "The cat story," Vergnolle noted, "that was this guy's calling card."

Something of these attitudes shows up even in the ditties the cadets chant during their daily runs. Many of the chants are the usual military "jodies," well known for their misogynistic lyrics. But some are vintage Citadel, and include lyrics about gouging out a woman's eyes, lopping off body parts, and evisceration. A cadence remembered by one Citadel cadet, sung to the tune of "The Candy Man," begins, "Who can take two jumper cables / Clip 'em to her tit / Turn on the battery and watch the bitch twitch." Another verse starts with "Who can take an ice pick . . ." and so on.

The day after last Thanksgiving, the phone rang at one-thirty in the morning in the home of Sandy and Ed Faulkner, in Powdersville, South Carolina, a tiny community on the outskirts of Greenville. The caller was a neighbor. They had better come outside, he said—a car had been circling their block.

Sandy and Ed, the parents of Shannon Faulkner, went out on their front lawn and looked around. At first, they saw nothing. Then, as they turned back to the house, they saw that across the white porch columns and along the siding of the house, painted in gigantic and what Sandy later recalled as "blood-red" letters, were the words, "Bitch," "Dyke," "Whore," and "Lesbo." Ed got up again at 6 A.M. and, armed with a bucket of white paint, hurried to conceal the message from his daughter.

A few days after the judge ordered The Citadel to admit Faulkner to the Corps of Cadets, morning rush-hour drivers in Charleston passed by a huge portable sign that read "Die Shannon." At least this threat wasn't home delivered. In the past year, instances of vandalism and harassment have mounted at the Faulkner home. Someone crawled under the house and opened the emergency exhaust valve on the water heater. The gas tank on Sandy's car was pried open. Someone driving a Ford Bronco mowed down the mailbox. Another motorist "did figure-eights through my flower bed," Sandy said. "This year, I didn't even plant flowers, because I knew they would just tear them up." And someone with access to Southern Bell's voice-mail system managed, twice, to tap into their voice mail and change their greeting, both times to a recording featuring rap lyrics about a "bitch" with a "big butt." Callers phoned in the middle of the night with threatening messages. Sandy called the county sheriff's department about the vandalism, but in Anderson county, which has been home to many Citadel's graduates, the deputy who arrived was not particularly helpful. He told them, Sandy recalled, "Well, if you're going to mess with The Citadel, you're just going to have to expect that."

Every trial has its rare moments of clarity, when the bramble of admissibility arguments and technicalities is cut away and we see the actual issue in dispute. One such moment came toward the end of the Faulkner-Citadel trial, when Alexander Astin, the director of the Higher Education Research Institute at the University of California at Los Angeles, took the stand. Astin, who is widely viewed as a leading surveyor of college-student performance and attitudes, found no negative effects on male students in nineteen all-male colleges he had studied which had gone coeducational.

"Can you tell me what kind of woman you would think would want to attend a coeducational Citadel?" Robert Patterson, the Citadel attorney who had previously represented V.M.I., asked Astin, his voice full of unflattering insinuation about the kind of woman he imagined her to be.

ASTIN: I suppose the same as the kind of men who want to go there.

PATTERSON: Would it be a woman that would not be all that different from men?

ASTIN: Yes.

To Patterson, this was a triumphant moment, and he closed on it: he had forced the government's witness to admit that a woman like Shannon Faulkner would have to be a mannish aberration from her gender. But in fact

Astin's testimony expressed the precise point that the plaintiff's side had been trying to make all along, and that The Citadel strenuously resisted: that the sexes were, in the end, not all that different.

"I was considered the bitch of the band," Shannon Faulkner said, without embarrassment, of her four years in her high school's marching band—just stating a fact. She was lounging on the couch in her parents' living room, comfortable in an old T-shirt and shorts, one leg swung over an arm of the couch. "That's because I was the one who was mean and got it done." The phone rang, for the millionth time—another media call. "I'm not giving statements to the press right now," she said efficiently into the phone, and hung up. She did not apologize for her brusqueness, as I was half expecting her to do, after she put down the receiver. There is nothing of the good girl about her. Not that she is disagreeable; Shannon Faulkner just doesn't see the point in false deference. "I never let anyone push me around, male or female," Faulkner said, and that fact had been exasperatingly obvious to reporters who covered the trial: they found that all the wheedling and cheap flatteries that usually prompt subjects to say more than they should didn't work with Faulkner.

One could scrounge around in Faulkner's childhood for the key to what made her take on The Citadel. You could say that it was because she was born six weeks premature, and her fierce struggle to live forged a "survivor." You could cite her memory that as a small child she preferred playing outside with the boys to playing with certain girls whom she deemed "too prissy." You could point to her sports career in high school and junior high: she lettered in softball for four years and kept stats for three of the schools' four basketball teams. You could note her ability to juggle tasks: she edited the yearbook, wrote for the school paper, and graduated with a 3.48 grade-point average. And you could certainly credit the sturdy backbone and outspokenness of both her mother and her maternal grandmother; this is a family where the women talk and the men keep a low profile. Her father, Ed, owns a small fence-building business. At thirty, a few years after Shannon's birth, Sandy returned to college to get her degree, a double major in psychology and education, and became a high-school teacher of psychology, sociology, United States history, and minority cultures. When a male professor had complained about certain "older women" in his class who asked "too many questions," Sandy hurled one of her wedge-heeled sandals at him. "I said, 'I'm paying for this class, and don't you ever tell me what I can ask.'" Shannon's maternal grandmother, sixty-seven-year-old Evelyn Richey, was orphaned at six and worked most of her life in textile factories, where, she noted, "women could do the job and men got the pay." Of her granddaughter's suit she said, "Women have got to come ahead. I say, let's get on with the show."

But there's little point in a detailed inspection of family history, because there's no real mystery here. What is most striking about Shannon herself is that she's not particularly unusual. She reads novels by Tom Clancy and John Grisham, has worked in a local day-care center, is partial to places like Bennigan's. She wants a college education so she can support herself and have a career as a teacher or a journalist—she hasn't yet decided which. She might do a stint in the military, she might not. She is in many ways representative of the average striving lower-middle-class teenage girl, circa 1994, who intends to better herself and does not intend to achieve that betterment through a man—in fact, she has not for a moment entertained such a possibility.

Throughout the trial, cadets and Citadel alumni spoke of a feminist plot: she is "a pawn" of the National Organization for Women, or—a theory repeatedly posited to me by cadets—"Her mother put her up to it." Two Citadel alumni asked me in all seriousness if feminist organizations were paying Shannon Faulkner to take the stand. In truth, Shannon makes an unlikely feminist poster girl. She prefers to call herself "an individualist" and seems almost indifferent to feminist affairs; when I mentioned Gloria Steinem's name once in conversation, Shannon asked me, "Who's that?" After the judge issued his decision to admit her to the Corps, she told the *New York Times* that she didn't consider the ruling a victory "just for women"—only a confirmation of her belief that if you want something, "go for it." Shannon Faulkner's determination to enter The Citadel's Corps of Cadets was fuelled not so much by a desire to trailblaze as by a sense of amazement and indignation that this trail was barricaded in the first place. She had never, she told the court, encountered such a roadblock in all her nineteen years—a remark that perhaps only a young woman of her fortunate generation could make without perjuring herself.

Shannon Faulkner got the idea of attending The Citadel back in December of 1992. She was taking a preparatory education course at Wren High School, the local public school. Mike Hazel, the teacher, passed out articles for them to read and discuss, and Faulkner picked the article in *Sports Illustrated* about hazing at The Citadel. "It was almost as accidental as Rosa Parks," Hazel recalled. "I just held up *Sports Illustrated* and asked, 'Who wants to do this?'"

Faulkner told me she'd selected the article because "I had missed that issue." During the ensuing discussion, the class wandered off the subject of hazing and onto the question of what, exactly, a public state institution was doing barring women from its classrooms. After a while, Faulkner got up and went down to the counselor's office, and returned with an application form from The Citadel. "I said, 'Hey, it doesn't even say 'Male/Female,''" she recalled. While she was sitting in class, she filled it out. "I didn't really make a big to-do about it."

Two weeks after Faulkner received her acceptance letter, The Citadel got word she was a woman and revoked her admission, and in August of 1993 she went off to spend a semester at the University of South Carolina at Spartanburg while the courts thrashed out the next move. As the lawyers filed papers, The Citadel's defenders delivered their own increasingly agitated personal beliefs to the plaintiff herself. Faulkner worked evenings as a waitress in a local bar called Chiefs Wings and Firewater until the nightly tirades from the many drunk Citadel-graduate customers got to be too much. Actually, Faulkner said, she wouldn't have quit if some of her male college friends hadn't felt the need to defend her honor. "I didn't want them getting hurt," she said. Her manner of dealing with the Citadel crowd was more good-humored. One day at the bar, she recalled, "a guy came up to me. 'Are you Shannon Faulkner?' he asked, and I said, 'Why?'—very casual. Then he got real huffy-puffy, madder and madder." Finally, she said, he stuck his ring in her face, then slammed his hand down on the table. "You will never wear *that!*" he yelled. Shannon saw him a few times in the bar after that, scowling at her from a far table. To lighten the mood, she once had the bartender send him a beer. He wouldn't drink it.

"I never show my true emotions in public," Shannon said. "I consider that weak." She can laugh at the cadets' threats, even when they turn ugly, because she doesn't see the reason for all the fuss. Whenever she is asked to sign the latest T-shirt inspired by the controversy, which depicts a group of male bulldogs (The Citadel's mascot) in cadet uniforms and one female bulldog in a red dress, above the caption "1,952 Bulldogs and 1 Bitch," Faulkner told me, "I always sign under the 'Bitch' part."

The first day that Shannon Faulkner attended classes, in January, 1994, the cadets who had lined up by the academic building told the media the same thing over and over. "We were trained to be gentlemen, and that's what we'll be." But in Shannon's first class, biology, all three cadets assigned to sit in her row changed their seats. The teacher, Philippe Ross, had to threaten to mark them absent to get them to return to their places. (More than twenty unexcused absences a semester is grounds for failure.) Shortly thereafter, a rumor began to circulate that Faulkner was using a fake I.D. in the local bars. This summer, talk of a plot against Faulkner surfaced—to frame her, perhaps by planting drugs in her belongings. The threat seemed real enough for Faulkner to quit her summer job, in the Charleston area, and return home.

The *Brigadier*'s column "Scarlet Pimpernel" took up the anti-Shannon cause with a vengeance. The columnist dubbed her "the divine bovine," likening her to a plastic revolving cow at a nearby mall (the mounting of which is a cadet tradition). The "Pimpernel" comments on an incident that occurred on Faulkner's first day were particularly memorable. An African-American cadet named Von Mickle dared to shake her hand in front of the media and say, "It's time for women," and compared the exclusion of women to that of blacks. For this lone act, he was not only physically threatened by classmates but derided in the "Pimpernel." "The PIMP doth long to tame the PLASTIC COW on this most wondrous of nights," the anonymous author wrote, with the column's usual antique-English flourishes and coded references. "But it seems that we will have a live specimen, a home grown DAIRY QUEEN from the stables of Powdersville. Perhaps NON DICKLE will be the first to saddle up. He is DIVINE BOVINE's best friend after all."

More disturbing were cadet writings on Faulkner that were not for public consumption. Tom Lucas, a graduate student in The Citadel's evening program, told me about some "very harsh" graffiti that he'd found all over one of the men's rooms in The Citadel's academic building. The inscription that most stuck in his mind: "Let her in—then fuck her to death."

On the whole, The Citadel administrators to whom I spoke were defensive, evasive, or dismissive of the cadets' hostile words and deeds toward Faulkner. When I asked Citadel officials to respond to reports of barracks violence, harassment of women on staff, or verbal abuse of Faulkner, the responses were dismaying. Cases of violence and abuse were "aberrations"; cadets who spoke up were either "troublemakers" or "mama's boys"; and each complaint by a female faculty member was deemed a "private personnel matter" that could not be discussed further.

Certainly the administrators and trustees themselves are less than enthusiastic about Faulkner's arrival. William F. Prioleau, Jr., until recently a member of the Board of Visitors, implied on a radio talk show that abortions would go up as a result of the female invasion, as he claimed had happened at West Point. Meanwhile, in The Citadel's Math Department, all that was going up as a result of Shannon Faulkner's presence was the grade-point average. Faulkner's highest mark at the semester's end was in calculus, where she earned an A (prompting a surprised Dean Poole to comment to her that she was "certainly not the stereotypical woman"). The Math Department has in recent years invited A students to an annual party. But rather than include Faulkner, the department limited the guest list to math majors. Math professor David Trautman, who was in charge of invitations to the party, explained in an E-mail message to colleagues, "Her presence would put a damper on the evening."

Linda Ross, then a professor at The Citadel, was speaking one day with a seventy-six-year-old alumnus, and the talk turned to Faulkner's lawsuit. He asked her if she thought it possible that this young woman might prevail. "Well, it's probably an inevitable turning of the tide," Ross said, shrugging. To her amazement, the alumnus began to cry.

"I have the worst chance in society of getting a job, because I'm a white male," William H. Barnes, the senior platoon leader, shouted at me over the din in The Citadel's mess hall, a din created by the upperclassmen's tradition of berating knobs at mealtime. "And that's the major difference between me and my father." In a society where, at least since the Second World War, surpassing one's father has been an expected benchmark of American manhood, Barnes's point is a plangent one. But it's hard to say which Citadel generation is more undone by the loss of white male privilege—the young men who will never partake of a dreamed world of masculine advantage or the older men who are seeing that lived world split apart, shattered.

"I was in Vietnam in '63, and I'll defy you or Shannon or anyone else to hike through the rice paddies," the usually genial Colonel Harvey Dick, sixty-seven, a Board of Visitors member, an ex-marine, and an Army lieutenant colonel, was practically shouting from his recliner armchair in his Charleston home. He popped a Tums in his mouth. "There's just no way you can do that. . . . You can't pick up a ninety-five-pound projectile. There are certain things out there that are differences." On the wall above his head were seven bayonets. He was wearing his blue Citadel T-shirt, which matched the Citadel mementos that overwhelmed his den—Citadel mugs, hats, footballs, ceramic bulldogs. It was a room known in the Dick household as "Harvey's 'I Love Me' Room." Dick treated it as his command post—whenever the phone rang, he whipped it off the cradle and barked "Colonel Dick!"—but what he was commanding was unclear; he retired in 1993 from a sixteen-year stint as The Citadel's assistant commandant. Still, he at least knew that he was once in charge, that he once enjoyed lifetime job security as a career military man. This was something his son couldn't say: Harvey Dick II, a nuclear pipe fitter, had recently been laid off at the Charleston Naval Shipyard.

Colonel Dick wanted it known that he wasn't "one of those male-chauvinist pigs"; in fact, he believes that women are smarter than men. "Women used to let the men dominate," he said. "Maybe we need a male movement, since evidently we're coming out second on everything." He slipped another Tums from an almost empty roll. The sun was dropping as we spoke, and shadows fell across the Citadel hats and figurines in his room. "Go back and look at your Greek and Roman empires and why they fell," he said.

His wife cleared her throat. "This doesn't have anything to do with male-female," she said.

"I see a decline in this great nation of ours," Dick said. He crossed his arms and stared into the gathering darkness of the late summer afternoon. After a while, he said, "I guess I sound like a buffoon."

Unlike the cadets, the older male Citadel officials often have to face dissent from wives or daughters whose views and professional aspirations or accomplishments challenge their stand on women's proper place. Lewis Spearman, the assistant to the president, recently remarried, and his wife is a feminist paralegal who is now getting her master's degree in psychology. She says she engaged for more than a year in "shriekfests" with him over the Shannon Faulkner question before she halfheartedly came around to The Citadel party line on barring women. And, while the wife of Dean Poole may have sat on the Miss Citadel judging panel, their daughter, Mindy, had loftier ambitions. Despite the fact that she suffered from cystic fibrosis, she was an ardent skier, horseback rider, and college athlete, rising at 5 A.M. daily with her crew-team members at the University of Virginia. And, despite a double lung transplant during her junior year, she graduated in 1991 with honors and won a graduate fellowship. "She was an outstanding young lady," Poole said. "I was very proud of her." His eyes clouding over at the memory, he recalled that she had made him promise to take her to the big Corps Day parade on The Citadel's sesquicentennial. The day the father and daughter were to attend the parade was the day she died. "Sort of an interesting footnote," he said, wiping at his moist eyes. What if she had wanted to go to The Citadel? Well, actually, Poole said, she *had* talked about it. If she had persisted he would have tried to change her mind, he said, but he added, "I would never have stopped her from doing something she wanted to do."

One of the biggest spousal battles over Shannon Faulkner is waged nightly at the home of a man who might seem the least likely figure at The Citadel to wind up with a feminist wife. Probably The Citadel's most legendary elder, thanks to Pat Conroy's thinly veiled and admiring portrait of him in "The Lords of Discipline," is Lieutenant Colonel T. Nugent Courvoisie, who, as an assistant commandant in the sixties, oversaw the admission of the first African-American cadet to The Citadel. A gravelly-voiced and cigar-chomping tender tyrant, Courvoisie—or the Boo, as he is known, for obscure reasons—was a fixture at the school for more than two decades. There are two Citadel scholarships in his family name, and his visage peers down from two portraits on campus.

A courtly man, and still dapper at seventy-seven, the Boo, who has since given up cigars, insisted on picking me up at my hotel and driving me to his home, though I had a rental car sitting in the parking lot. On the drive over, he ticked off the differences between the sexes which he believed made it impossible for The Citadel to admit women—differences such as that "the average female is not as proficient athletically as the average male." When we were settled in the living room, the Boo on his recliner and his second wife, Margaret, who is also seventy-seven, in a straight-back chair, the subject of Shannon Faulkner was revisited. The first words out of Margaret's mouth were "The Citadel wants to chop the head off women." A low growl emanated from the Boo's corner. He lowered the recliner a notch. "We don't talk about it here," Margaret said—an obvious untruth. "We haven't come to blows yet, but—"

The Boo interrupted, "I have the correct view."

She retorted, "No one has the *correct* view." She turned and addressed me. "You have to understand him," she said of her husband of nine years.

"This is a man who went to military prep schools and a church that was male-dominated, naturally."

The Boo interrupted. "J.C. picked twelve *men* as his disciples," he said.

Margaret rolled her eyes. "See? He even takes it into the church—and he's on such familiar ground with Christ he calls him J.C."

The Boo said, "J.C. never picked a woman, except his mother."

Margaret said, "Oh God, see, this is why we don't go into it."

But, as usual, go into it they did. As the words got batted back and forth, with Margaret doing most of the batting, the Boo levered his recliner progressively lower, until all I could see of him were the soles of his shoes.

MARGARET: You had plenty of good women soldiers in Saudi Arabia.

BOO: Plenty of pregnant ones . . .

MARGARET: What, do you think [the cadets] didn't get girls pregnant before? There've been plenty of abortions. And I know of a number of cases that, by the time [a cadet] graduated, there were four or five kids.

BOO: That's an exaggeration. Maybe two or three . . . With women, there's going to be sexual harassment.

MARGARET: Oh, honey, those cadets are harassing each other right now, all the time.

BOO: That's different. That's standard operating procedure.

In the nineteen-sixties, Margaret worked in the library at The Citadel, where she would often see Charles Foster, the first African-American cadet (who died a few years ago) alone at one of the library desks. "He would just come to the library and sit there a lot. It's hard to be the only one, to be the groundbreaker. That's why I admire this girl."

Boo's voice boomed from the depths of his recliner: "But there's no need for her. She's ruining a good thing."

Margaret gave a mock groan. "This is the last vestige of male bastionship," she said, "and it's going to kill 'em when it crumbles." Boo raised his chair halfway back up and considered Margaret. "She has a good mind," he told me after a while.

Margaret smiled. "I'm a new experience for him. He's always been military. People didn't disagree with him."

The Boo showed the way upstairs, to the attic, where he has his own "Citadel room"—a collection of Citadel memorabilia vaster than but almost identical to Dick's. Around the house, there were sketches of Boo at various points in his Citadel career. He told me that, before he retired, the cadets commissioned a portrait of him that hangs in Jenkins Hall. "Man, I looked good in that," he said. "Like a man. A leader."

Margaret didn't think so. "No, it was horrible," she said. "It didn't look like you."

"If Shannon were in my class, I'd be fired by March for sexual harassment," Colonel James Rembert, an English professor, was saying as we headed to-

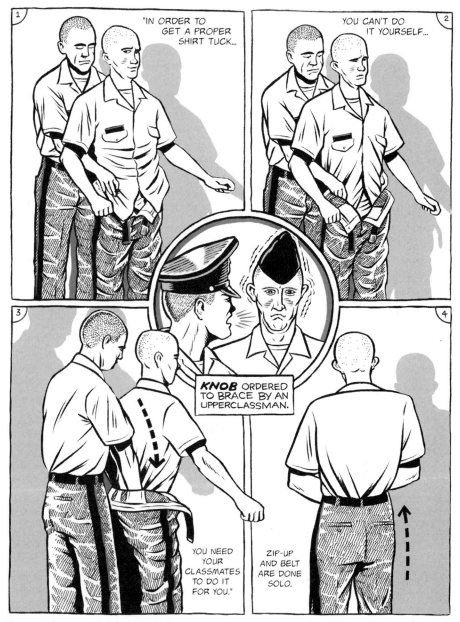

Dependency is a main theme in cadet relationships. Colonel James Rembert says that the cadets' intimate bond is "like a true marriage."
Illustration by Mark Zingarelli, originally published in *The New Yorker*.

ward his classroom. He had a ramrod bearing and a certain resemblance to Ted Turner (who, it happens, sent all three of his sons to The Citadel—Beau Turner among them—and donated twenty-five million dollars to the school earlier this year). The Colonel identifies himself as one of "the last white Remberts" in South Carolina, the Remberts being a Huguenot family of sufficiently ancient lineage to gain him admission to the St. John's Hunting Club, of South Carolina—an all-male society chaired by a Citadel alumnus. Rembert, who has a Cambridge University doctorate and wrote a book on Jonathan Swift, said he preferred the company of men, in leisure and in learning. "I've dealt with young men all my life," he went on. "I know how to play with them. I have the freedom here to imply things I couldn't with women. I don't want to have to watch what I say."

The literary work under discussion that day was "Beowulf," and the cadets agreed that it was all about "brotherhood loyalty" and, in the words of one student, "the most important characteristics of a man—glory and eternal fame." Then they turned to their papers on the topic.

"Mr. Rice," Rembert said in mock horror. "You turned in a single-spaced paper." This was a no-no. Rembert instructed him to take a pencil and "pen-e-trate"—Rembert drew the syllables out—the paper with the point. He shook his head. "What a pansy!" Rembert said. "Can't catch, can't throw, can't write." Another student was chastised for the use of the passive voice. "Never use the passive voice—it leads to effeminacy and homosexuality," Rembert told the class. "So next time you use the passive voice I'm going to make you lift up your limp wrist." Literary pointers concluded, Rembert floated the subject of Shannon Faulkner. The usual objections were raised. But then the class wandered into more interesting territory, provoked by a cadet's comment that "she would change the relationship between the men here." Just what is the nature of that relationship?

"When we are in the showers, it's very intimate," a senior cadet said. "We're one mass, naked together, and it makes us closer. . . . You're shaved, you're naked, you're afraid together. You can cry." Robert Butcher, another senior, said that the men take care of each classmate. "They'll help dress him, tuck in his shirt, shine his shoes." "You mean like a mother-child relationship?" I asked.

"That *is* what it is," another cadet said. "It's a family, even the way we eat—family style." A fourth cadet said, "Maybe it's a Freudian thing, but males feel more affection with each other when women are not around. Maybe we're all homosexuals."

The class groaned. "Speak for yourself, buddy," a number of cadets said, almost in a chorus.

Rembert said, "With no women, we can hug each other. There's nothing so nurturing as an infantry platoon."

The hooted-down cadet weighted in again: "When I used to wrestle in high school, we had this great tradition. Right before the game, the coach, he'd slap us really hard on the butt."

Rembert, a onetime paratrooper, said he and his skydiving buddies did that, too, right before they jumped. "First man out gets a pat right there."

Over lunch, Rembert returned to the theme of manly nurturance among Citadel men. "We hug each other," he said. One of his colleagues, "always kisses me on the cheek," he went on. "It's like a true marriage. There's an affectionate intimacy that you will find between cadets. With this security they can, without being defensive, project tenderness to each other."

Months later, I was sitting in court watching Norman Doucet, the cadet regimental commander, testify. He was showing the judge a video of the Citadel experience and explaining the various scenes. First we were shown "one of the great parts" of a knob's first day—the mothers looking weepy at the gate as their sons were led away. Doucet lingered over the head-shaving science. "This is what does it, right here," he said. "Mothers can't even tell their sons apart after this." Thus shielded from the prying maternal eye, the cadets began their new life, and the video action shifted to a typical day in the life of the Corps. But the editing made it a day as heavy on early-morning domestic chores as it was on martial activity. Much of the film was devoted to housekeeping: scenes of cadets making beds, dressing each other, sweeping, taking out the trash, all of which Doucet described as "like some kind of a ballet or a dance that's going on." This is a dance where the most important moves took place before the show, in the dressing room. "What they are doing here is the Citadel shirt tuck," Doucet said. The tuck requires that a cadet unzip his pant halfway and fold down his waistband, then stand still while his helper approaches him from the back, puts his arms around the cadet's waist, pulls the loose shirt material firmly to the back, jams it as far down in the pants as he can, and then pulls the cadet's pants up. "If you watch closely right here, this is what the fourth-class system is all about," Doucet continued. "In order to get a proper shirt tuck, you can't do it yourself—you need your classmates to do it for you. There's really a lot of dependence upon your classmates." But, as Doucet's account suggested, cadets can experience that dependence only in concealment, away from mothers, away from all women.

When a Citadel attorney asked Doucet why female cadets would pose a problem on the campus, the only issue he raised was the humiliation that cadets feel if women observed the cadets' on-campus interactions. He spoke of the shame that knobs feel when, on occasion, a woman happened to be on the parade ground while upperclassmen were disciplining them. The cadets observing in the courtroom nodded in agreement.

It may seem almost paradoxical that the fourth-class system should be so solicitous of the emotional vulnerability of its wards—the same wards it subjects to such rigors. And yet the making of Whole Men evidently requires an initial stage of infantilization. Indeed, the objective of recapitulating childhood development is plainly spelled out in The Citadel's yearbook, known as "the Sphinx." The 1990 "Sphinx" explained, "As a freshman enters, he begins to release his childhood and takes the first steps to becoming a 'Citadel Man.' . . . As a 'knob,' every aspect of life is taught, a new way to walk. . . . Knobs are told how, where, and when to walk." Reentrance into manhood for the toddling knobs occurs on Recognition Day, when the upperclassmen force the knobs to do calisthenics until they drop, then gently lift up their charges and nurse them with cups of water. At that moment, for the first time in nine months, the older cadets call the knobs by their first names and embrace them.

The relationship between knobs and upperclassmen following Recognition Day, as they are integrated into the Corps, shifts from maternal to matrimonial. The yearbooks of the last several years picture Citadel men spending a lot of time embracing and kissing. Of course, this impulse, when it is captured on film, is always carefully disarmed with a jokey caption.

One afternoon, a group of cadets recounted for me the campus's many "nudity rituals," as they jokingly called them. There's "Senior Rip-Off Day," a spring rite in which three hundred seniors literally rip each other's clothes off, burn them in a bonfire, and hug and wrestle on the ground. There's "Nude Platoon," in which a group of juniors, unclad except for their cross-webbing, run around the quad yelling, "We love the Nude Platoon!" And there's the birthday ritual, in which the birthday boy is stripped, tied to a chair, and covered with shaving cream, while his groin is coated in liquid shoe polish.

During the fall semester before graduation, the seniors receive their "band of gold" (as it is called) in the Ring Ceremony. The chaplain blesses each class ring. (Receiving the ring, which I was constantly reminded is "the biggest class ring of any college," is a near-sacrament, and the yearbooks are filled with pictures of young men holding up their rings in fervor, as if clutching a crucifix before a vampire.) Then each senior walks through a ten-foot replica of the class ring with his mother on one arm and his "date" on the other. In a sort of reverse marriage ceremony, the mother gives the cadet away. Mother and date accompany him through the towering ring; then he kisses Mother farewell and marches under the arched swords of the Junior Sword Drill, a new bride of the Corps. Several cadets and alumni told me that when a Citadel graduate marries, it is a tradition to slide the class ring over the wedding band. Indeed, I saw such an ordering of priorities on the fingers of a number of Citadel men in the courtroom.

In the late-twentieth-century setting of The Citadel, in a time when extreme insecurity and confusion about masculinity's standing run rampant, the Corps of Cadets once again seeks to obscure a domestic male paradise with an intensifying of virile showmanship and violence. The result is a ruthless intimacy, in which physical abuse stands in for physical affection, and every display of affection must be counterbalanced by a display of sadism. Knobs told me that they were forced to run through the showers while the upperclassmen "guards" knocked the soap out of their hands and, when the knobs leaned over to retrieve it the upperclassmen would unzip their pants and yell, "Don't pick it up, don't pick it up! We'll use you like we used those girls!" A former Citadel Halloween tradition, of upperclassmen dressing up—mostly in diapers and women's clothes—and collecting candy treats from knobs, has given way to "tricks" of considerable violence. (One upperclassman told me of cadets who knocked dressers over on candy-dispensing cadets and then walked on top of them.) The administration tried, unsuccessfully, to put a stop to the whole affair; too many freshmen were getting injured. And the playful pat on the butt that served to usher cadets into the brotherhood has degenerated into more invasive acts. According to a recent graduate one company of cadets recently devised a regimen in which the older cadets tested sophomores nightly with increasingly painful treatments—beatings and stompings and so forth. The process, which they dubbed "Bananarama," culminated on a night in which an unpeeled banana was produced—and shoved into a cadet's anus.

Given this precarious dynamic, it is not surprising that in the past few years at The Citadel social rage has been directed toward any men who were perceived to be gay. Several young men who were suspected of homosexual inclinations were hounded out of the school. One cadet, Herbert Parker, who said that he was falsely accused of having a sexual encounter with a male janitor, recalled a year of total isolation—cadets refused to sit near him in the mess hall or in classes—and terror: incessant threatening phone calls and death threats. The cadets and the administration—which had responded to the report of his encounter by sending out a campus-security police car with lights flashing to question him—acted "like I had murdered someone."

The scapegoating reached such brutal proportions that the counselling center recently set up a sort of group-therapy session for the targeted young men, who are known as It, as in the game of tag.

One evening after the trial, I went over to the Treehouse, a "mixed" bar in Charleston, with an upstairs gay bar and nightly drag shows on the weekends. My intention was to ask about cadet violence against gay men. I presumed that on a campus where every second epithet was "faggot" such hate crimes were all but inevitable. There were indeed a few such cases, I learned, but the circumstances were different from what I had imagined. Nor were those cases the essence of my findings that evening.

"The proper terminology for The Citadel," a customer at the bar named Chris said, "is The Closet." Up and down the bar, heads bobbed in agreement. "They love faggots like me." What he meant by "like me," however, was not that he was gay. That night, he looked like a male model—sleek black hair and a handsome, chiselled face. But on the nights he was dressed for a performance he could pass for a woman. Arching an eyebrow, Chris said, "The cadets go for the drag queens."

Chris's observation was echoed in ensuing conversations in the bar. There are thousands of cadets, presumably, who have not dated drag queens, but in two visits to the Treehouse I could find only two drag queens, out of maybe a dozen, who did not tell me of dating a cadet—and that was only because these two found Citadel men "too emotional." Cadets can also occasionally be dangerous, Chris told me. "You can get the ones who are violent. They think they want it, then afterwards they turn on you, like you made them do it." Nonetheless, a drag queen who called himself Holly had been happily involved with a cadet for three years now. Marissa, another drag queen, the reigning "Miss Treehouse, 1993–94," had gone out with one cadet, broken up, and was now in the throes of a budding romance with another. A third drag queen, who asked to be identified as Tiffany, was known to be a favorite of cadets.

As Chris and I were talking that first night, a drag queen called Lownie wandered in and settled on a bar stool. Lownie delighted in the Corps of Cadets pageantry—especially the Friday dress parades. "The parades are a big thing with the queers in Charleston," he said. "We'll have a cocktail party and go over and watch the boys. It's a very Southern-'lady' thing to do." Years ago, Lownie had been a student at the College of Charleston when he met *his* Citadel lover, and they had begun covert assignations—communicating through notes slipped in little-used books in the Citadel library. The only drawback, Lownie said, was dealing with his lover's constant emotional anxiety over making the grade at The Citadel. He was, in fact, a model macho cadet: a Junior Sword Drill member, a regimental officer, and a "hang king," who could dangle interminably from a closet rack by his fingertips. Lownie, who found such records more amusing than impressive, grinned, and said, "I used to make him wear his shako"—The Citadel's military cap—"when we were having sex. It's manhood at its most."

Lownie said he could begin to fathom his cadet's intense attachment to The Citadel—an emotion that he likened to a love affair—because he himself had spent four years in the Air Force. "The day-to-day aspect of being in a military environment is that you run around in a little bit of clothing and you are being judged as to how good a man you are by doing women's work—pressing pants, sewing, polishing shoes. You are a *better* man if you have mastery of womanly arts. . . . The camaraderie doesn't get any stronger than when you are in the barracks, sitting around at the end of the day in your briefs and T's and dogtags—like a bunch of hausfraus, talking and gossiping." The military stage set offers a false front and a welcome trapdoor—an escape hatch from the social burdens of traditional masculinity. Behind the martial backdrop, Lownie said, "you don't have to be a breadwinner. You don't have to be a leader. You can play back seat. It's a great relief. You can act like a human being and not have to act like a man."

"You know what the [cadet] I'm seeing now said to me?" Tiffany said. We were sitting in the dressing room a couple of hours before the night's performance, and as Tiffany spoke he peered into an elaborate mirror set illuminated with miniature movie-star lights, applying layer after layer of mascara and eyeliner with expert precision. "He said, 'You're more of a woman than a woman is.' And that's an exact quote." Tiffany stood up and struck a Southern belle pose by way of illustration. "I overexemplify everything a female is—my breasts, my hair, the way I hold myself." And who could better complete the hoopskirts picture than a fantasy gentleman in uniform?

Marissa, Miss Treehouse, looked up from his labors, painting row after row of fake nails with pink polish. "I love how they wear their caps slung low so you can't quite see their eyes," he said. "It's like all of us are female illusionists and they are male illusionists. A man in a uniform is a kind of dream."

Tiffany said, "For Halloween, you know what my cadet boyfriend wanted to dress as? A cadet."

The dressing-room scene before me, of a group of men tenderly helping each other get ready for the evening—an elaborate process of pinning and binding and stuffing—was not very different, in its way, from the footage in Norman Doucet's video of the cadets tucking in each other's shirts. As the drag queens conversed, they tossed stockings and Ace bandages and cosmetic bags back and forth. "Has anyone seen my mascara wand?" "O.K., who has the blush?" There was a homey comfort that reminded me of slumber parties when I was a girl, where we would put big pink spongy rollers in each other's hair and screech with laughter at the results. And suddenly it became obvious to me what was generating that void, that yearning, in the cadets' lives—and maybe in the lives of many American men. What was going on here was play—a kind of freedom and spontaneity that, in this culture, only women are permitted.

No wonder men found their Citadels, their Treehouses, where the rules of gender could be bent or escaped. For the drag queens of the Treehouse, the distinctions between the sexes are a goof, to be endlessly manipulated with fun-house-mirror glee. For cadets, despite the play set of The Citadel and the dress-up braids and ribbons, the guarding of their treehouse is a dead-serious business. Still, undercover at The Citadel, the cadets have managed to create for themselves a world in which they get half the equation that Lownie described: they can "act like human beings" in the safety of the daily domestic life of the barracks. But, in return, the institution demands that they never cease to "act like a man"—a man of cold and rigid bearing, a man no more male than Tiffany's Southern belle is female, a man that no one, humanly, can be. That they must defend their inner humanity with outer brutality may say as much about the world outside The Citadel walls as about the world within them. The cadets feel called to defend those walls. Never mind that their true ideal may not be the vaunted one of martial masculinity, just as their true enemy is not Shannon Faulkner. The cadets at The

Citadel feel that something about their life and routine is worthy on its merits and is endangered from without. And in that they may be right.   ■

■ *QUESTIONS FOR MAKING CONNECTIONS WITHIN THE READING* ■

1. In "The Naked Citadel," Susan Faludi provides a series of vignettes that describe life at the military school. Why does she present the vignettes in the order she does? Why does she start her article in Jane Bishop's classroom? Why does she then move to the courtroom? Make a chart that tracks the organization of Faludi's essay. What is the argument that Faludi is making by telling these vignettes in this order?

2. The sociologist Erving Goffman coined the term "total institutions" to describe places that become almost entirely self-enclosed and self-referential in their values and behaviors. Goffman's principal example was the mental asylum. Can we describe The Citadel accurately as a "total institution"? Are its values the product of its isolation, or does Faludi's account furnish evidence that the attitudes holding sway in The Citadel also persist outside the institution as well? Is The Citadel just an aberration, or does it tell us certain truths about our own society?

3. Faludi offers this overview of The Citadel:

   > In the late-twentieth-century setting of The Citadel, in a time when extreme insecurity and confusion about masculinity's standing run rampant, the Corps of Cadets once again seeks to obscure a domestic male paradise with an intensifying of virile showmanship and violence. The result is a ruthless intimacy, in which physical abuse stands in for physical affection, and every display of affection must be counterbalanced by a display of sadism.

   On the basis of the evidence Faludi provides, is this a fair assessment of the culture of The Citadel? What evidence confirms this assessment? What evidence might be said to complicate or even contradict it? What other explanations might we offer for events at The Citadel? Does masculinity have to occupy the central place in our analysis, or might other factors be more important?

■ *QUESTIONS FOR WRITING* ■

1. In what sense is Susan Faludi a feminist? If we define a feminist as someone who is specifically concerned with defending the rights of women, does she qualify? Does she regard the rights of women as practically or theoretically distinct from the rights of men? How about the needs and as-

pirations of women? Are these fundamentally different from the needs and aspirations of men? Does Faludi see men as "oppressors of women"? Does she imply that our society systematically empowers men while systematically disempowering women, or does disempowerment cross gender lines?

2. "The Naked Citadel" might be described as a case study of the relations between sexuality and social structures. In what ways do social structures shape sexuality at The Citadel? Does Faludi's account call into question the belief in a single, natural form of male sexual expression? Is the problem with The Citadel that natural sexuality has been perverted by linking it to relations of power? Can sexuality and power ever be separated?

■ *QUESTIONS FOR MAKING CONNECTIONS BETWEEN READINGS* ■

1. Faludi and Martha Nussbaum are both considered feminists, but are they feminists of the same kind? Do they share the same understanding of women, of women's dilemmas, and of the solutions to those dilemmas? In what ways do their feminisms intersect with other more general issues, such as the struggle for human rights? Is it possible that the degradation of different women in different contexts requires different approaches? Should we discuss *women's* rights at all, or should we concern ourselves primarily with *human* rights?

2. In "Selections from *The Myth of Sanity*," Martha Stout explores the psychological dynamics of dissociation. According to Stout, the experience of trauma "changes the brain itself." Under conditions of extreme pain or distress, the brain becomes unable to organize experience "usefully" or to integrate new experience with other, prior memories. Does it seem possible that dissociation plays a role in the training of cadets at The Citadel? What circumstantial evidence can you find to support this claim, or to dispute it? Does Stout's account of dissociation help to explain why so few cadets rebel against the treatment they receive? Is it possible that certain institutions use dissociation intentionally to weaken bonds sustained by affection and shared values? How might our society protect itself against the use of dissociation as a political instrument?

www For additional suggestions about making connections between readings, visit the Link-O-Mat and More Sample Assignments at <www.newhum.com>.

JON GERTNER

SINCE ITS PUBLICATION in September 2003, "The Futile Pursuit of Happiness" has been reproduced hundreds of times on the Internet and has become the subject of numerous blogs and college course syllabi. It was the most frequently e-mailed article of 2003, according to the *New York Times* Web site. "Futile Pursuit" has also catapulted "miswanting," the idea at the center of Gertner's piece, from academic seminars into popular conversation. If the claims of the article are startling, its implications are far-reaching as well: current research suggests that most people consistently overestimate how happy an imagined outcome will make them. In fact, the things we want seldom bring us happiness, and the things that bring us happiness are seldom what we wanted. To some readers, Gertner's essay may seem disenchanting. Not only does the research appear to support the old adage, dear to the hearts of many pessimists, that wanting is better than having, but it may even call into doubt the value of the quest for self-knowledge. Other readers, however, have found Gertner's article profoundly liberating. If happiness is not the sort of thing we can achieve if we just try hard enough, then it might turn up at any moment by sheer serendipity, regardless of whether we "win" or "lose" in one of life's little competitions.

Gertner profiles two professors who seek to measure human happiness: Daniel Gilbert, a psychologist at Harvard, and George Loewenstein, an economist at Carnegie-Mellon. According to Gilbert, his research essentially involves "how people think about the future." He says, "One of the worst ways to decide whether you'll be happy in the future is to close your eyes and imagine it." George Loewenstein's research addresses what he calls "the cold-to-hot empathy gap." A cold emotional state is one of relative satisfaction, without hunger, pain, or upset, whereas a hot emotional state is the opposite, marked by physical or emotional crisis. Loewenstein claims that we become virtually different

Gertner, Jon. "The Futile Pursuit of Happiness." *The New York Times Magazine*. September 7, 2003, pp. 45ff.

Biographical information on Gertner drawn from <http://www.inc.com/magazine/20031201/edlet.html>; on Gilbert from <http://www.thecrimson.com/article.aspx?ref=503961>; and on Loewenstein from <http://www.hss.cmu.edu/departments/sds/faculty/loewenstein.html>.

people as we move from one kind of state to another, and he po
more strikingly, that actions done in one state can make very little s
cool down or heat up. Considered together, Loewenstein's and Gilb
raises questions about the reliability of our own judgments about ou
about whether it is even possible to predict our future feelings and ac

www **To learn more about Daniel Gilbert's and George Loewenstein's research on happiness, please visit the Link-O-Mat at <www.newhum.com>.**

■ ■

The Futile Pursuit of Happiness

If Daniel Gilbert is right, then you are wrong. That is to say, if Daniel Gilbert is right, then you are wrong to believe that a new car will make you as happy as you imagine. You are wrong to believe that a new kitchen will make you happy for as long as you imagine. You are wrong to think that you will be more unhappy with a big single setback (a broken wrist, a broken heart) than with a lesser chronic one (a trick knee, a tense marriage). You are wrong to assume that job failure will be crushing. You are wrong to expect that a death in the family will leave you bereft for year upon year, forever and ever. You are even wrong to reckon that a cheeseburger you order in a restaurant—this week, next week, a year from now, it doesn't really matter when—will definitely hit the spot. That's because when it comes to predicting exactly how you will feel in the future, you are most likely wrong.

A professor in Harvard's department of psychology, Gilbert likes to tell people that he studies happiness. But it would be more precise to say that Gilbert—along with the psychologist Tim Wilson of the University of Virginia, the economist George Loewenstein of Carnegie-Mellon and the psychologist (and Nobel laureate in economics) Daniel Kahneman of Princeton—has taken the lead in studying a specific type of emotional and behavioral prediction. In the past few years, these four men have begun to question the decision-making process that shapes our sense of well-being: how do we predict what will make us happy or unhappy—and then how do we feel after the actual experience? For example, how do we suppose we'll feel if our favorite college football team wins or loses, and then how do we really feel a few days after the game? How do we predict we'll feel about purchasing jewelry, having children, buying a big house or being rich? And then how do we regard the outcomes? According to this small corps of

.cademics, almost all actions—the decision to buy jewelry, have kids, buy the big house or work exhaustively for a fatter paycheck—are based on our predictions of the emotional consequences of these events.

Until recently, this was uncharted territory. How we forecast our feelings, and whether those predictions match our future emotional states, had never been the stuff of laboratory research. But in scores of experiments, Gilbert, Wilson, Kahneman and Loewenstein have made a slew of observations and conclusions that undermine a number of fundamental assumptions: namely, that we humans understand what we want and are adept at improving our well-being—that we are good at maximizing our utility, in the jargon of traditional economics. Further, their work on prediction raises some unsettling and somewhat more personal questions. To understand affective forecasting, as Gilbert has termed these studies, is to wonder if everything you have ever thought about life choices, and about happiness, has been at the least somewhat naive and, at worst, greatly mistaken.

The problem, as Gilbert and company have come to discover, is that we falter when it comes to imagining how we will feel about something in the future. It isn't that we get the big things wrong. We know we will experience visits to Le Cirque and to the periodontist differently; we can accurately predict that we'd rather be stuck in Montauk than in a Midtown elevator. What Gilbert has found, however, is that we overestimate the intensity and the duration of our emotional reactions—our "affect"—to future events. In other words, we might believe that a new BMW will make life perfect. But it will almost certainly be less exciting than we anticipated; nor will it excite us for as long as predicted. The vast majority of Gilbert's test participants through the years have consistently made just these sorts of errors both in the laboratory and in real-life situations. And whether Gilbert's subjects were trying to predict how they would feel in the future about a plate of spaghetti with meat sauce, the defeat of a preferred political candidate or romantic rejection seemed not to matter. On average, bad events proved less intense and more transient than test participants predicted. Good events proved less intense and briefer as well.

Gilbert and his collaborator Tim Wilson call the gap between what we predict and what we ultimately experience the "impact bias"—"impact" meaning the errors we make in estimating both the intensity and duration of our emotions and "bias" our tendency to err. The phrase characterizes how we experience the dimming excitement over not just a BMW but also over any object or event that we presume will make us happy. Would a 20 percent raise or winning the lottery result in a contented life? You may predict it will, but almost surely it won't turn out that way. And a new plasma television? You may have high hopes, but the impact bias suggests that it will almost certainly be less cool, and in a shorter time, than you imagine. Worse, Gilbert has noted that these mistakes of expectation can lead directly to mistakes in choosing what we think will give us pleasure. He calls this "miswanting."

"The average person says, 'I know I'll be happier with a Porsche than a Chevy,'" Gilbert explains. "'Or with Linda rather than Rosalyn. Or as a doctor rather than as a plumber.' That seems very clear to people. The problem is, I can't get into medical school or afford the Porsche. So for the average person, the obstacle between them and happiness is actually getting the futures that they desire. But what our research shows—not just ours, but Loewenstein's and Kahneman's—is that the real problem is figuring out which of those futures is going to have the high payoff and is really going to make you happy.

"You know, the Stones said, 'You can't always get what you want,'" Gilbert adds. "I don't think that's the problem. The problem is you can't always know what you want."

Gilbert's papers on affective forecasting began to appear in the late 1990's, but the idea to study happiness and emotional prediction actually came to him on a sunny afternoon in October 1992, just as he and his friend Jonathan Jay Koehler sat down for lunch outside the psychology building at the University of Texas at Austin, where both men were teaching at the time. Gilbert was uninspired about his studies and says he felt despair about his failing marriage. And as he launched into a discussion of his personal life, he swerved to ask why economists focus on the financial aspects of decision making rather than the emotional ones. Koehler recalls, "Gilbert said something like: 'It all seems so small. It isn't really about money; it's about happiness. Isn't that what everybody wants to know when we make a decision?'" For a moment, Gilbert forgot his troubles, and two more questions came to him. Do we even know what makes us happy? And if it's difficult to figure out what makes us happy in the moment, how can we predict what will make us happy in the future?

In the early 1990's, for an up-and-coming psychology professor like Gilbert to switch his field of inquiry from how we perceive one another to happiness, as he did that day, was just a hairsbreadth short of bizarre. But Gilbert has always liked questions that lead him somewhere new. Now 45, Gilbert dropped out of high school at 15, hooking into what he calls "the tail end of the hippie movement" and hitchhiking aimlessly from town to town with his guitar. He met his wife on the road; she was hitching in the other direction. They married at 17, had a son at 18 and settled down in Denver. "I pulled weeds, I sold rebar, I sold carpet, I installed carpet, I spent a lot of time as a phone solicitor," he recalls. During this period he spent several years turning out science-fiction stories for magazines like *Amazing Stories*. Thus, in addition to being "one of the most gifted social psychologists of our age," as the psychology writer and professor David G. Myers describes him to me, Gilbert is the author of "The Essence of Grunk," a story about an encounter with a creature made of egg salad that jets around the galaxy in a rocket-powered refrigerator.

Psychology was a matter of happenstance. In the midst of his sci-fi career, Gilbert tried to sign up for a writing course at the local community

college, but the class was full; he figured that psych, still accepting regis-
trants, would help him with character development in his fiction. It led instead to an undergraduate degree at the University of Colorado at Denver,
then a Ph.D. at Princeton, then an appointment at the University of Texas,
then the appointment at Harvard. "People ask why I study happiness,"
Gilbert says, "and I say, 'Why study anything else?' It's the holy grail. We're
studying the thing that all human action is directed toward."

One experiment of Gilbert's had students in a photography class at
Harvard choose two favorite pictures from among those they had just taken
and then relinquish one to the teacher. Some students were told their
choices were permanent; others were told they could exchange their prints
after several days. As it turned out, those who had time to change their
minds were less pleased with their decisions than those whose choices were
irrevocable.

Much of Gilbert's research is in this vein. Another recent study asked
whether transit riders in Boston who narrowly missed their trains experienced the self-blame that people tend to predict they'll feel in this situation.
(They did not.) And a paper waiting to be published, "The Peculiar
Longevity of Things Not So Bad," examines why we expect that bigger
problems will always dwarf minor annoyances. "When really bad things
happen to us, we defend against them," Gilbert explains. "People, of course,
predict the exact opposite. If you ask, 'What would you rather have, a broken leg or a trick knee?' they'd probably say, 'Trick knee.' And yet, if your
goal is to accumulate maximum happiness over your lifetime, you just made
the wrong choice. A trick knee is a bad thing to have."

All of these studies establish the links between prediction, decision making and well-being. The photography experiment challenges our common
assumption that we would be happier with the option to change our minds
when in fact we're happier with closure. The transit experiment demonstrates that we tend to err in estimating our regret over missed opportunities. The "things not so bad" work shows our failure to imagine how grievously irritations compromise our satisfaction. Our emotional defenses snap
into action when it comes to a divorce or a disease but not for lesser problems. We fix the leaky roof on our house, but over the long haul, the broken
screen door we never mend adds up to more frustration.

Gilbert does not believe all forecasting mistakes lead to similar results; a
death in the family, a new gym membership and a new husband are not the
same, but in how they affect our well-being they are similar. "Our research
simply says that whether it's the thing that matters or the thing that doesn't,
both of them matter less than you think they will," he says. "Things that
happen to you or that you buy or own—as much as you think they make a
difference to your happiness, you're wrong by a certain amount. You're
overestimating how much of a difference they make. None of them make the
difference you think. And that's true of positive and negative events."

Much of the work of Kahneman, Loewenstein, Gilbert and Wilson takes its cue from the concept of adaptation, a term psychologists have used since at least the 1950's to refer to how we acclimate to changing circumstances. George Loewenstein sums up this human capacity as follows: "Happiness is a signal that our brains use to motivate us to do certain things. And in the same way that our eye adapts to different levels of illumination, we're designed to kind of go back to the happiness set point. Our brains are not trying to be happy. Our brains are trying to regulate us." In this respect, the tendency toward adaptation suggests why the impact bias is so pervasive. As Tim Wilson says: "We don't realize how quickly we will adapt to a pleasurable event and make it the backdrop of our lives. When any event occurs to us, we make it ordinary. And through becoming ordinary, we lose our pleasure."

It is easy to overlook something new and crucial in what Wilson is saying. Not that we invariably lose interest in bright and shiny things over time—this is a long-known trait—but that we're generally unable to recognize that we adapt to new circumstances and therefore fail to incorporate this fact into our decisions. So, yes, we will adapt to the BMW and the plasma TV, since we adapt to virtually everything. But Wilson and Gilbert and others have shown that we seem unable to predict that we will adapt. Thus, when we find the pleasure derived from a thing diminishing, we move on to the next thing or event and almost certainly make another error of prediction, and then another, ad infinitum.

As Gilbert points out, this glitch is also significant when it comes to negative events like losing a job or the death of someone we love, in response to which we project a permanently inconsolable future. "The thing I'm most interested in, that I've spent the most time studying, is our failure to recognize how powerful psychological defenses are once they're activated," Gilbert says. "We've used the metaphor of the 'psychological immune system'—it's just a metaphor, but not a bad one for that system of defenses that helps you feel better when bad things happen. Observers of the human condition since Aristotle have known that people have these defenses. Freud spent his life, and his daughter Anna spent her life, worrying about these defenses. What's surprising is that people don't seem to recognize that they have these defenses, and that these defenses will be triggered by negative events." During the course of my interviews with Gilbert, a close friend of his died. "I am like everyone in thinking, I'll never get over this and life will never be good again," he wrote to me in an e-mail message as he planned a trip to Texas for the funeral. "But because of my work, there is always a voice in the back of my head—a voice that wears a lab coat and has a lot of data tucked under its arm—that says, 'Yes, you will, and yes, it will.' And I know that voice is right."

Still, the argument that we imperfectly imagine what we want and how we will cope is nevertheless disorienting. On the one hand, it can cast a shadow of regret on some life decisions. Why did I decide that working 100 hours a week to earn more would make me happy? Why did I think retiring to Sun City, Ariz., would please me? On the other hand, it can be enlightening. No wonder this teak patio set hasn't made me as happy as I expected. Even if she dumps me, I'll be O.K. Either way, predicting how things will feel to us over the long term is mystifying. A large body of research on well-being seems to suggest that wealth above middle-class comfort makes little difference to our happiness, for example, or that having children does nothing to improve well-being—even as it drives marital satisfaction dramatically down. We often yearn for a roomy, isolated home (a thing we easily adapt to), when, in fact, it will probably compromise our happiness by distancing us from neighbors. (Social interaction and friendships have been shown to give lasting pleasure.) The big isolated home is what Loewenstein, 48, himself bought. "I fell into a trap I never should have fallen into," he told me.

Loewenstein's office is up a narrow stairway in a hidden corner of an enormous, worn brick building on the edge of the Carnegie-Mellon campus in Pittsburgh. He and Gilbert make for an interesting contrast. Gilbert is garrulous, theatrical, dazzling in his speech and writing; he fills a room. Loewenstein is soft-spoken, given to abstraction and lithe in the way of a hard-core athlete; he seems to float around a room. Both men profess tremendous admiration for the other, and their different disciplines—psychology and economics—have made their overlapping interests in affective forecasting more complementary than fraught. While Gilbert's most notable contribution to affective forecasting is the impact bias, Loewenstein's is something called the "empathy gap."

Here's how it expresses itself. In a recent experiment, Loewenstein tried to find out how likely people might be to dance alone to Rick James's "Super Freak" in front of a large audience. Many agreed to do so for a certain amount of money a week in advance, only to renege when the day came to take the stage. This sounds like a goof, but it gets at the fundamental difference between how we behave in "hot" states (those of anxiety, courage, fear, drug craving, sexual excitation and the like) and "cold" states of rational calm. This empathy gap in thought and behavior—we cannot seem to predict how we will behave in a hot state when we are in a cold state—affects happiness in an important but somewhat less consistent way than the impact bias. "So much of our lives involves making decisions that have consequences for the future," Loewenstein says. "And if our decision making is influenced by these transient emotional and psychological states, then we know we're not making decisions with an eye toward future consequences." This may be as simple as an unfortunate proclamation of love in a moment of lust, Loewenstein explains, or something darker, like an act of road rage or of suicide.

Among other things, this line of inquiry has led Loewenstein to collaborate with health experts looking into why people engage in unprotected sex when they would never agree to do so in moments of cool calculation. Data from tests in which volunteers are asked how they would behave in various "heat of the moment" situations—whether they would have sex with a minor, for instance, or act forcefully with a partner who asks them to stop—have consistently shown that different states of arousal can alter answers by astonishing margins. "These kinds of states have the ability to change us so profoundly that we're more different from ourselves in different states than we are from another person," Loewenstein says.

Part of Loewenstein's curiosity about hot and cold states comes from situations in which his emotions have been pitted against his intellect. When he's not teaching, he treks around the world, making sure to get to Alaska to hike or kayak at least once a year. A scholar of mountaineering literature, he once wrote a paper that examined why climbers have a poor memory for pain and usually ignore turn-back times at great peril. But he has done the same thing himself many times. He almost died in a whitewater canoeing accident and vowed afterward that he never wanted to see his runaway canoe again. (A couple of hours later, he went looking for it.) The same goes for his climbing pursuits. "You establish your turn-back time, and then you find yourself still far from the peak," he says. "So you push on. You haven't brought enough food or clothes, and then as a result, you're stuck at 13,000 feet, and you have to just sit there and shiver all night without a sleeping bag or warm clothes. When the sun comes up, you're half-frozen, and you say, 'Never again.' Then you get back and immediately start craving getting out again." He pushes the point: "I have tried to train my emotions." But he admits that he may make the same mistakes on his next trip.

Would a world without forecasting errors be a better world? Would a life lived without forecasting errors be a richer life? Among the academics who study affective forecasting, there seems little doubt that these sorts of questions will ultimately jump from the academy to the real world. "If people do not know what is going to make them better off or give them pleasure," Daniel Kahneman says, "then the idea that you can trust people to do what will give them pleasure becomes questionable." To Kahneman, who did some of the first experiments in the area in the early 1990's, affective forecasting could greatly influence retirement planning, for example, where mistakes in prediction (how much we save, how much we spend, how we choose a community we think we'll enjoy) can prove irreversible. He sees a role for affective forecasting in consumer spending, where a "cooling off" period might remedy buyer's remorse. Most important, he sees vital applications in health care, especially when it comes to informed consent. "We consider people capable of giving informed consent once they are told of the objective effects of a treatment," Kahneman says. "But can people anticipate how they and other people will react to a colostomy or to the removal of their vocal cords? The research on affective forecasting suggests that people may have little ability to anticipate their adaptation beyond the early stages." Loewenstein, along with his collaborator Dr. Peter Ubel, has done a great deal of work showing that nonpatients overestimate the displeasure of living with the loss of a limb, for instance, or paraplegia. To use affective forecasting to prove that people adapt to serious physical challenges far better and will be happier than they imagine, Loewenstein says, could prove invaluable.

There are downsides to making public policy in light of this research, too. While walking in Pittsburgh one afternoon, Loewenstein tells me that he doesn't see how anybody could study happiness and not find himself leaning left politically; the data make it all too clear that boosting the living standards of those already comfortable, such as through lower taxes, does little to improve their levels of well-being, whereas raising the living standards of the impoverished makes an enormous difference. Nevertheless, he and Gilbert (who once declared in an academic paper, "Windfalls are better than pratfalls, A's are better than C's, December 25 is better than April 15, and everything is better than a Republican administration") seem to lean libertarian in regard to pushing any kind of prescriptive agenda. "We're very, very nervous about overapplying the research," Loewenstein says. "Just because we figure out that X makes people happy and they're choosing Y, we don't want to impose X on them. I have a discomfort with paternalism and with using the results coming out of our field to impose decisions on people."

Still, Gilbert and Loewenstein can't contain the personal and philosophical questions raised by their work. After talking with both men, I found it hard not to wonder about my own predictions at every turn. At times it seemed like knowing the secret to some parlor trick that was nonetheless very difficult to pull off—when I ogled a new car at the Honda dealership as I waited for a new muffler on my '92 Accord, for instance, or as my daughter's fever spiked one evening and I imagined something terrible, and then something more terrible thereafter. With some difficulty, I could observe my mind overshooting the mark, zooming past accuracy toward the sublime or the tragic. It was tempting to want to try to think about the future more moderately. But it seemed nearly impossible as well.

To Loewenstein, who is especially attendant to the friction between his emotional and deliberative processes, a life without forecasting errors would most likely be a better, happier life. "If you had a deep understanding of the impact bias and you acted on it, which is not always that easy to do, you would tend to invest your resources in the things that would make you happy," he says. This might mean taking more time with friends instead of more time for making money. He also adds that a better understanding of the empathy gap—those hot and cold states we all find ourselves in on frequent occasions—could save people from making regrettable decisions in moments of courage or craving.

Gilbert seems optimistic about using the work in terms of improving "institutional judgment"—how we spend health care dollars, for example—

but less sanguine about using it to improve our personal judgment. He admits that he has taken some of his research to heart; for instance, his work on what he calls the psychological immune system has led him to believe that he would be able to adapt to even the worst turn of events. In addition, he says that he now takes more chances in life, a fact corroborated in at least one aspect by his research partner Tim Wilson, who says that driving with Gilbert in Boston is a terrifying, white-knuckle experience. "But I should have learned many more lessons from my research than I actually have," Gilbert admits. "I'm getting married in the spring because this woman is going to make me happy forever, and I know it." At this, Gilbert laughs, a sudden, booming laugh that fills his Cambridge office. He seems to find it funny not because it's untrue, but because nothing could be more true. This is how he feels. "I don't think I want to give up all these motivations," he says, "that belief that there's the good and there's the bad and that this is a contest to try to get one and avoid the other. I don't think I want to learn too much from my research in that sense."

Even so, Gilbert is currently working on a complex experiment in which he has made affective forecasting errors "go away." In this test, Gilbert's team asks members of Group A to estimate how they'll feel if they receive negative personality feedback. The impact bias kicks in, of course, and they mostly predict they'll feel terrible, when in fact they end up feeling O.K. But if Gilbert shows Group B that others have gotten the same feedback and felt O.K. afterward, then its members predict they'll feel O.K. as well. The impact bias disappears, and the participants in Group B make accurate predictions.

This is exciting to Gilbert. But at the same time, it's not a technique he wants to shape into a self-help book, or one that he even imagines could be practically implemented. "Hope and fear are enduring features of the human experience," he says, "and it is unlikely that people are going to abandon them anytime soon just because some psychologist told them they should." In fact, in his recent writings, he has wondered whether forecasting errors might somehow serve a larger functional purpose he doesn't yet understand. If he could wave a wand tomorrow and eliminate all affective-forecasting errors, I ask, would he? "The benefits of not making this error would seem to be that you get a little more happiness," he says. "When choosing between two jobs, you wouldn't sweat as much because you'd say: 'You know, I'll be happy in both. I'll adapt to either circumstance pretty well, so there's no use in killing myself for the next week.' But maybe our caricatures of the future—these overinflated assessments of how good or bad things will be—maybe it's these illusory assessments that keep us moving in one direction over the other. Maybe we don't want a society of people who shrug and say, 'It won't really make a difference.'

"Maybe it's important for there to be carrots and sticks in the world, even if they are illusions," he adds. "They keep us moving towards carrots and away from sticks." ∎

■ *QUESTIONS FOR MAKING CONNECTIONS WITHIN THE READING* ■

1. By choosing the title "The Futile Pursuit of Happiness" has Jon Gertner misunderstood or misrepresented the views of the psychologists whose work he describes? On the basis of the evidence and analysis presented by these psychologists, would you say that happiness is fundamentally an illusion? Or is it the *pursuit* of happiness that deserves to be reconsidered? If happiness is not something that we can pursue actively, then how might it be achieved? Would you conclude from Gertner's article that people should pursue something other than happiness?

2. In the course of his article, Gertner introduces a number of terms of art— that is, terms used by specialists in a particular branch of learning. These terms include "maximizing utility," "affective forecasting," "impact bias," "miswanting," "adaptation," "psychological immune system," "hot state," "cold state," and "informed consent." Explain in your own words the meaning of one of these terms, and discuss its connection to the other key terms. In what ways do these terms help to challenge our commonsense ideas about freedom, choice, and the good life? In what ways do the terms help to support common sense?

3. When Gertner describes the research of Gilbert and Loewenstein, he also tells us something about their lives. Gilbert, for example, once intended to be a writer and registered for a class in psychology only after he was closed out of the creative writing class he really wanted. Loewenstein is an avid outdoorsman who runs rapids and climbs mountains. Do you see any connections between the lives of these two men and the research they have done? If you regard these connections as significant, what conclusions might we reach about the linkages between ideas and life experience? Would you say, on the basis of Gertner's report, that psychological research is less creative than the writing of fiction?

■ *QUESTIONS FOR WRITING* ■

1. The Declaration of Independence proclaims that "all men" are "endowed by their Creator with certain unalienable rights," among them "Life, Liberty, and the pursuit of Happiness." What are the *political* implications of the research indicating that the pursuit of happiness is often misdirected because people typically fail to recognize the conditions that will really make them happy? Does the work of Gilbert and the other psychologists suggest that Thomas Jefferson's claim, when he drafted the Declaration, was based on a false assumption? Do you believe that the pursuit of happiness deserves to be recognized as an "unalienable" right along with the rights guaranteed by the U.S. Constitution—the right of free speech and assembly, trial by jury, and so on? Were the drafters of the Constitution mistaken in omitting any references to happiness?

2. According to Gertner, traditional economists assume that people are "good at maximizing [their] utility—are good, that is, at recognizing what they want and increasing their sense of well-being." But if we are, as the psychologists suggest, strongly prone to "miswanting," then what conclusions might we reach about our market-driven system? If people were better at "affective forecasting," would the consumer economy survive? Would it be fair to say that the consumer society traps modern people in a cycle of craving and disappointment? Given the research of Gilbert and the others, is it possible for us to make a sharper distinction between what we want and what we really need? Should people try harder to like what they already have? Is contentment a better life strategy than perpetual craving, or might it be the case, as Gilbert suspects, that our "forecasting errors" might serve "a larger functional purpose?" What purpose might that be?

■ *QUESTIONS FOR MAKING CONNECTIONS*
BETWEEN READINGS ■

1. In "The Enhanced and the Unenhanced," Gregory Stock argues for a free market in what he calls "advanced germinal choice." Essentially, Stock means that people in the near future should have the freedom to provide their children with the genetic enhancements they deem to be most desirable. When we stop to consider Gertner's argument, however, it may influence our response to Stock. Even if genetic technology can deliver on its bright promises, are the results likely to be as rewarding as Stock seems to believe? Is the idea of progress in general a collective expression of the same miswanting that psychologists find in single individuals? Or, conversely, does the potential of genetic technology show that the quest for happiness is not futile at all but at last within our reach?

2. What are the connections between the quest for happiness as psychologists and economists represent it and the cultivation of "wisdom" described in the chapter by that name from Robert Thurman's book *Infinite Life*. Do you see any connection, for example, between what Thurman calls the "pseudo-self" and the errors in "affective forecasting" that human beings typically make? Does the state of "alienation" that Thurman describes have anything to do with "impact bias"? Is the Buddhist experience of "nothingness" a way of freeing people from the hot states in which they overestimate their own capacity to find satisfaction by changing their external circumstances? What might the psychologists say about Thurman's description of consciousness as a "system"?

www   **For additional suggestions about making connections between readings, visit the Link-O-Mat and More Sample Assignments at <www.newhum.com>.**

MALCOLM GLADWELL

HOW DO CULTURES CHANGE? Is it possible to control and direct cultural change? These are the questions that most interest Malcolm Gladwell, author of the best-selling book, *The Tipping Point: How Little Things Can Make a Big Difference* (2000). Gladwell first became interested in the notion that ideas might spread through culture like an epidemic while he was covering the AIDS epidemic for the *Washington Post*. In epidemiology the phrase "the tipping point" is used to describe that moment when a virus reaches critical mass, and, as Gladwell learned while doing his research, AIDS reached its tipping point in 1982, "when it went from a rare disease affecting a few gay men to a worldwide epidemic." Fascinated by this medical fact, Gladwell found himself wondering whether it also applied to the social world. That is, is there some specific point at which a fad becomes a fashion frenzy? When delinquency and mischief turn into a crime wave? When repetition leads to understanding?

The Tipping Point is the result of Gladwell's effort to understand why some ideas catch on and spread like wildfire, while others fail to attract widespread attention and wither on the vine. Drawing on work in psychology, sociology, and epidemiology, Gladwell examines events as diverse as Paul Revere's ride, the success of *Sesame Street* and *Blue's Clues*, and the precipitous decline of the crime rate in New York City, which is discussed in "The Power of Context," the chapter included here. Working across these wide-ranging examples, Gladwell develops an all-encompassing model for how cultural change occurs, a model that highlights the influential role that context plays in shaping and guiding human acts and intentions.

Gladwell was born in 1963 in England and grew up in Canada. He graduated from the University of Toronto with a degree in history in 1984. Currently the Critic at Large for the *New Yorker*, Gladwell sees himself as "a kind of translator between the academic and non-academic worlds. There's just all sorts of

Gladwell, Malcolm. "The Power of Context: Bernie Goetz and the Rise and Fall of New York City Crime," *The Tipping Point: How Little Things Can Make a Big Difference*. Boston: Little, Brown, 2000. 133–168.

Quotations and biographical information from Author Q&A <http://www.gladwell .com/books2.html> and Malcolm Gladwell, interview by Toby Lester, *The Atlantic Unbound* <http://www.theatlantic.com/unbound/interviews/ba2000-03-29.htm>.

fantastic stuff out there, but there's not nearly enough time and attention paid to that act of translation. Most people leave college in their early twenties, and that ends their exposure to the academic world. To me that's a tragedy."

www **To learn more about Malcolm Gladwell and the role that context plays in cultural change, visit the Link-O-Mat at <www.newhum.com>.**

The Power of Context

Bernie Goetz and the Rise and Fall of New York City Crime

On December 22, 1984, the Saturday before Christmas, Bernhard Goetz left his apartment in Manhattan's Greenwich Village and walked to the IRT subway station at Fourteenth Street and Seventh Avenue. He was a slender man in his late thirties, with sandy-colored hair and glasses, dressed that day in jeans and a windbreaker. At the station, he boarded the number two downtown express train and sat down next to four young black men. There were about twenty people in the car, but most sat at the other end, avoiding the four teenagers, because they were, as eyewitnesses would say later, "horsing around" and "acting rowdy." Goetz seemed oblivious. "How are ya?" one of the four, Troy Canty, said to Goetz, as he walked in. Canty was lying almost prone on one of the subway benches. Canty and another of the teenagers, Barry Allen, walked up to Goetz and asked him for five dollars. A third youth, James Ramseur, gestured toward a suspicious-looking bulge in his pocket, as if he had a gun in there.

"What do you want?" Goetz asked.

"Give me five dollars," Canty repeated.

Goetz looked up and, as he would say later, saw that Canty's "eyes were shiny, and he was enjoying himself. . . . He had a big smile on his face," and somehow that smile and those eyes set him off. Goetz reached into his pocket and pulled out a chrome-plated five-shot Smith and Wesson .38, firing at each of the four youths in turn. As the fourth member of the group, Darrell Cabey, lay screaming on the ground, Goetz walked over to him and said, "You seem all right. Here's another," before firing a fifth bullet into Cabey's spinal cord and paralyzing him for life.

In the tumult, someone pulled the emergency brake. The other passengers ran into the next car, except for two women who remained riveted in panic. "Are you all right?" Goetz asked the first, politely. Yes, she said. The second woman was lying on the floor. She wanted Goetz to think she was dead. "Are you all right?" Goetz asked her, twice. She nodded yes. The conductor, now on the scene, asked Goetz if he was a police officer.

"No," said Goetz. "I don't know why I did it." Pause. "They tried to rip me off."

The conductor asked Goetz for his gun. Goetz declined. He walked through the doorway at the front of the car, unhooked the safety chain, and jumped down onto the tracks, disappearing into the dark of the tunnel.

In the days that followed, the shooting on the IRT caused a national sensation. The four youths all turned out to have criminal records. Cabey had been arrested previously for armed robbery, Canty for theft. Three of them had screwdrivers in their pockets. They seemed the embodiment of the kind of young thug feared by nearly all urban-dwellers, and the mysterious gunman who shot them down seemed like an avenging angel. The tabloids dubbed Goetz the "Subway Vigilante" and the "Death Wish Shooter." On radio call-in shows and in the streets, he was treated as a hero, a man who had fulfilled the secret fantasy of every New Yorker who had ever been mugged or intimidated or assaulted on the subway. On New Year's Eve, a week after the shooting, Goetz turned himself in to a police station in New Hampshire. Upon his extradition to New York City, the *New York Post* ran two pictures on its front page: one of Goetz, handcuffed and head bowed, being led into custody, and one of Troy Canty—black, defiant, eyes hooded, arms folded—being released from the hospital. The headline read, "Led Away in Cuffs While Wounded Mugger Walks to Freedom." When the case came to trial, Goetz was easily acquitted on charges of assault and attempted murder. Outside Goetz's apartment building, on the evening of the verdict, there was a raucous, impromptu street party.

1.

The Goetz case has become a symbol of a particular, dark moment in New York City history, the moment when the city's crime problem reached epidemic proportions. During the 1980s, New York City averaged well over 2,000 murders and 600,000 serious felonies a year. Underground, on the subways, conditions could only be described as chaotic. Before Bernie Goetz boarded the number two train that day, he would have waited on a dimly lit platform, surrounded on all sides by dark, damp, graffiti-covered walls. Chances are his train was late, because in 1984 there was a fire somewhere on the New York system every day and a derailment every other week. Pictures of the crime scene, taken by police, show that the car Goetz sat in was filthy, its floor littered with trash and the walls and ceiling thick with graffiti, but that wasn't unusual because in 1984 every one of the 6,000 cars in the Transit Authority fleet, with the exception of the midtown shuttle, was covered with graffiti—top to bottom, inside and out. In the winter, the cars were cold because few were adequately heated. In the summer, the cars were stiflingly hot because none were air-conditioned. Today, the number two train accelerates to over 40 miles an hour as it rumbles toward the Chambers Street express stop. But it's doubtful Goetz's train went that fast. In 1984, there were 500 "red tape" areas on the system—places where track damage had made it unsafe for trains to go more than 15 miles per hour. Fare-beating was so commonplace that it was costing the Transit Authority as much as $150 million in lost revenue annually. There were about 15,000 felonies on the system a year—a number that would hit 20,000 a year by the end of the decade—and harassment of riders by panhandlers and petty criminals was so pervasive that ridership of the trains had sunk to its lowest level in the history of the subway system. William Bratton, who was later to be a key figure in New York's successful fight against violent crime, writes in his autobiography of riding the New York subways in the 1980s after living in Boston for years, and being stunned at what he saw:

> After waiting in a seemingly endless line to buy a token, I tried to put a coin into a turnstile, and found it had been purposely jammed. Unable to pay the fare to get into the system, we had to enter through a slam gate being held open by a scruffy-looking character with his hand out; having disabled the turnstiles, he was now demanding that riders give him their tokens. Meanwhile, one of his cohorts had his mouth on the coin slots, sucking out the jammed coins and leaving his slobber. Most people were too intimidated to take these guys on: Here, take the damned token, what do I care? Other citizens were going over, under, around, or through the stiles for free. It was like going into the transit version of Dante's *Inferno.*

This was New York City in the 1980s, a city in the grip of one of the worst crime epidemics in its history. But then, suddenly and without warning, the epidemic tipped. From a high in 1990, the crime rate went into precipitous decline. Murders dropped by two-thirds. Felonies were cut in half. Other cities saw their crime drop in the same period. But in no place did the level of violence fall farther or faster. On the subways, by the end of the decade, there were 75 percent fewer felonies than there had been at the decade's start. In 1996, when Goetz went to trial a second time, as the defendant in a civil suit brought by Darrell Cabey, the case was all but ignored by the press, and Goetz himself seemed almost an anachronism. At a time when New York had become the safest big city in the country, it seemed hard to remember precisely what it was that Goetz had once symbolized. It was simply inconceivable that someone could pull a gun on someone else on the subway and be called a hero for it. . . .

3.

During the 1990s violent crime declined across the United States for a number of fairly straightforward reasons. The illegal trade in crack cocaine, which had spawned a great deal of violence among gangs and drug dealers, began to decline. The economy's dramatic recovery meant that many people who might have been lured into crime got legitimate jobs instead, and the general aging of the population meant that there were fewer people in the age range—males between eighteen and twenty-four—that is responsible for the majority of all violence. The question of why crime declined in New York City, however, is a little more complicated. In the period when the New York epidemic tipped down, the city's economy hadn't improved. It was still stagnant. In fact, the city's poorest neighborhoods had just been hit hard by the welfare cuts of the early 1990s. The waning of the crack cocaine epidemic in New York was clearly a factor, but then again, it had been in steady decline well before crime dipped. As for the aging of the population, because of heavy immigration to New York in the 1980s, the city was getting younger in the 1990s, not older. In any case, all of these trends are long-term changes that one would expect to have gradual effects. In New York the decline was anything but gradual. Something else clearly played a role in reversing New York's crime epidemic.

The most intriguing candidate for that "something else" is called the Broken Windows theory. Broken Windows was the brainchild of the criminologists James Q. Wilson and George Kelling. Wilson and Kelling argued that crime is the inevitable result of disorder. If a window is broken and left unrepaired, people walking by will conclude that no one cares and no one is in charge. Soon, more windows will be broken, and the sense of anarchy will spread from the building to the street on which it faces, sending a signal that anything goes. In a city, relatively minor problems like graffiti, public disorder, and aggressive panhandling, they write, are all the equivalent of broken windows, invitations to more serious crimes:

> Muggers and robbers, whether opportunistic or professional, believe they reduce their chances of being caught or even identified if they operate on streets where potential victims are already intimidated by prevailing conditions. If the neighborhood cannot keep a bothersome panhandler from annoying passersby, the thief may reason, it is even less likely to call the police to identify a potential mugger or to interfere if the mugging actually takes place.

This is an epidemic theory of crime. It says that crime is contagious—just as a fashion trend is contagious—that it can start with a broken window and spread to an entire community. The Tipping Point in this epidemic, though, isn't a particular kind of person. . . . It's something physical like graffiti. The impetus to engage in a certain kind of behavior is not coming from a certain kind of person but from a feature of the environment.

In the mid-1980s Kelling was hired by the New York Transit Authority as a consultant, and he urged them to put the Broken Windows theory into practice. They obliged, bringing in a new subway director by the name of David Gunn to oversee a multibillion-dollar rebuilding of the subway system. Many subway advocates, at the time, told Gunn not to worry about graffiti, to focus on the larger questions of crime and subway reliability, and it seemed like reasonable advice. Worrying about graffiti at a time when the entire system was close to collapse seems as pointless as scrubbing the decks of the *Titanic* as it headed toward the icebergs. But Gunn insisted. "The graffiti was symbolic of the collapse of the system," he says. "When you looked at the process of rebuilding the organization and morale, you had to win the battle against graffiti. Without winning that battle, all the management reforms and physical changes just weren't going to happen. We were about to put out new trains that were worth about ten million bucks apiece, and unless we did something to protect them, we knew just what would happen. They would last one day and then they would be vandalized."

Gunn drew up a new management structure and a precise set of goals and timetables aimed at cleaning the system line by line, train by train. He started with the number seven train that connects Queens to midtown Manhattan, and began experimenting with new techniques to clean off the paint. On stainless-steel cars, solvents were used. On the painted cars, the graffiti were simply painted over. Gunn made it a rule that there should be no retreat, that once a car was "reclaimed" it should never be allowed to be vandalized again. "We were religious about it," Gunn said. At the end of the number one line in the Bronx, where the trains stop before turning around and going back to Manhattan, Gunn set up a cleaning station. If a car came in with graffiti, the graffiti had to be removed during the changeover, or the car was removed from service. "Dirty" cars, which hadn't yet been cleansed of graffiti, were never to be mixed with "clean" cars. The idea was to send an unambiguous message to the vandals themselves.

"We had a yard up in Harlem on one hundred thirty-fifth Street where the trains would lay up over night," Gunn said. "The kids would come the first night and paint the side of the train white. Then they would come the next night, after it was dry, and draw the outline. Then they would come the third night and color it in. It was a three-day job. We knew the kids would be working on one of the dirty trains, and what we would do is wait for them to finish their mural. Then we'd walk over with rollers and paint it over. The kids would be in tears, but we'd just be going up and down, up and down. It was a message to them. If you want to spend three nights of your time vandalizing a train, fine. But it's never going to see the light of day."

Gunn's graffiti cleanup took from 1984 to 1990. At that point, the Transit Authority hired William Bratton to head the transit police, and the second stage of the reclamation of the subway system began. Bratton was, like Gunn, a disciple of Broken Windows. He describes Kelling, in fact, as his intellectual mentor, and so his first step as police chief was as seemingly quixotic as Gunn's. With felonies—serious crimes—on the subway system at an all-time high, Bratton decided to crack down on fare-beating. Why? Because he believed that, like graffiti, fare-beating could be a signal, a small expression of disorder that invited much more serious crimes. An estimated 170,000 people a day were entering the system, by one route or another, without paying a token. Some were kids, who simply jumped over the turnstiles. Others would lean backward on the turnstiles and force their way through. And once one or two or three people began cheating the system, other people—who might never otherwise have considered evading the law—would join in, reasoning that if some people weren't going to pay, they shouldn't either, and the problem would snowball. The problem was exacerbated by the fact fare-beating was not easy to fight. Because there was only $1.25 at stake, the transit police didn't feel it was worth their time to pursue it, particularly when there were plenty of more serious crimes happening down on the platform and in the trains.

Bratton is a colorful, charismatic man, a born leader, and he quickly made his presence felt. His wife stayed behind in Boston, so he was free to work long hours, and he would roam the city on the subway at night, getting a sense of what the problems were and how best to fight them. First, he picked stations where fare-beating was the biggest problem, and put as many as ten policemen in plainclothes at the turnstiles. The team would nab fare-beaters one by one, handcuff them, and leave them standing, in a daisy chain, on the platform until they had a "full catch." The idea was to signal, as publicly as possible, that the transit police were now serious about cracking down on fare-beaters. Previously, police officers had been wary of pursuing fare-beaters because the arrest, the trip to the station house, the filling out of necessary forms, and the waiting for those forms to be processed took an entire day—all for a crime that usually merited no more than a slap on the wrist. Bratton retrofitted a city bus and turned it into a rolling station house, with its own fax machines, phones, holding pen, and fingerprinting facilities. Soon the turnaround time on an arrest was down to an hour. Bratton also insisted that a check be run on all those arrested. Sure enough, one out of seven arrestees had an outstanding warrant for a previous crime, and one out of twenty was carrying a weapon of some sort. Suddenly it wasn't hard to convince police officers that tackling fare-beating made sense. "For the cops it was a bonanza," Bratton writes. "Every arrest was like opening a box of Cracker Jack. What kind of toy am I going to get? Got a gun? Got a knife? Got a warrant? Do we have a murderer here? . . . After a while the bad guys wised up and began to leave their weapons home and pay their fares." Under Bratton, the number of ejections from subway stations—for drunkenness, or improper behavior—tripled within his first few months in office. Arrests for misdemeanors, for the kind of minor offenses that had gone unnoticed in the past, went up fivefold between 1990 and 1994. Bratton turned the transit police into an organization focused on the smallest infractions, on the details of life underground.

After the election of Rudolph Giuliani as mayor of New York in 1994, Bratton was appointed head of the New York City Police Department, and he applied the same strategies to the city at large. He instructed his officers to crack down on quality-of-life crimes: on the "squeegee men" who came up to drivers at New York City intersections and demanded money for washing car windows, for example, and on all the other above-ground equivalents of turnstile-jumping and graffiti. "Previous police administration had been handcuffed by restrictions," Bratton says. "We took the handcuffs off. We stepped up enforcement of the laws against public drunkenness and public urination and arrested repeat violators, including those who threw empty bottles on the street or were involved in even relatively minor damage to property. . . . If you peed in the street, you were going to jail." When crime began to fall in the city—as quickly and dramatically as it had in the subways—Bratton and Giuliani pointed to the same cause. Minor, seemingly insignificant quality-of-life crimes, they said, were Tipping Points for violent crime.

Broken Windows theory and the Power of Context are one and the same. They are both based on the premise that an epidemic can be reversed, can be tipped, by tinkering with the smallest details of the immediate environment. This is, if you think about it, quite a radical idea. Think back, for instance, to the encounter between Bernie Goetz and those four youths on the subway: Allen, Ramseur, Cabey, and Canty. At least two of them, according to some reports, appear to have been on drugs at the time of the incident. They all came from the Claremont Village housing project in one of the worst parts of the South Bronx. Cabey was, at the time, under indictment for armed robbery. Canty had a prior felony arrest for possession of stolen property. Allen had been previously arrested for attempted assault. Allen, Canty, and Ramseur also all had misdemeanor convictions, ranging from criminal mischief to petty larceny. Two years after the Goetz shooting, Ramseur was sentenced to twenty-five years in prison for rape, robbery, sodomy, sexual abuse, assault, criminal use of a firearm, and possession of stolen property. It's hard to be surprised when people like this wind up in the middle of a violent incident.

Then there's Goetz. He did something that is completely anomalous. White professionals do not, as a rule, shoot young black men on the subway. But if you look closely at who he was, he fits the stereotype of the kind of person who ends up in violent situations. His father was a strict disciplinarian with a harsh temper, and Goetz was often the focus of his father's rage. At school, he was the one teased by classmates, the last one picked for school games, a lonely child who would often leave school in tears. He worked, after graduating from college, for Westinghouse, building nuclear submarines. But he didn't last long. He was constantly clashing with his superiors over what he saw as shoddy practices and corner-cutting, and sometimes broke company and union rules by doing work that he was contractually forbidden to do. He took an apartment on Fourteenth Street in Manhattan, near Sixth Avenue, on a stretch of city block that was then heavy with homelessness and drug dealing. One of the doormen in the building, with whom Goetz was close, was beaten badly by muggers. Goetz became obsessed with cleaning up the neighborhood. He complained endlessly about a vacant newsstand near his building, which was used by vagrants as a trash bin and stank of urine. One night, mysteriously, it burned down, and the next day Goetz was out on the street sweeping away the debris. Once at a community meeting, he said, to the shock of others in the room, "The only way we're going to clean up this street is to get rid of the spics and niggers." In 1981, Goetz was mugged by three black youths as he entered the Canal Street station one afternoon. He ran out of the station with the three of them in pursuit. They grabbed the electronics equipment he was carrying, beat him, and threw him up against a plate-glass door, leaving him with permanent damage to his chest. With the help of an off-duty sanitation worker, Goetz managed to subdue one of his three attackers. But the experience left him embittered. He had to spend six hours in the station house, talking to police, while his assailant was released after two hours and charged, in the end, with only a misdemeanor. He applied to the city for a gun permit. He was turned down. In September 1984, his father died. Three months later, he sat down next to four black youths on the subway and started shooting.

Here, in short, was a man with an authority problem, with a strong sense that the system wasn't working, who had been the recent target of humiliation. Lillian Rubin, Goetz's biographer, writes that his choice to live on Fourteenth Street could hardly have been an accident. "For Bernie," she writes, "there seems to be something seductive about the setting. Precisely because of its deficits and discomforts, it provided him with a comprehensible target for the rage that lives inside him. By focusing it on the external world, he need not deal with his internal one. He rails about the dirt, the noise, the drunks, the crime, the pushers, the junkies. And all with good reason." Goetz's bullets, Rubin concludes, were "aimed at targets that existed as much in his past as in the present."

If you think of what happened on the number two train this way, the shooting begins to feel inevitable. Four hoodlums confront a man with apparent psychological problems. That the shooting took place on the subway seems incidental. Goetz would have shot those four kids if he had been sitting in a Burger King. Most of the formal explanations we use for criminal behavior follow along the same logic. Psychiatrists talk about criminals as people with stunted psychological development, people who have had pathological relationships with their parents, who lack adequate role models. There is a relatively new literature that talks about genes that may or may not dispose certain individuals to crime. On the popular side, there are endless numbers of books by conservatives talking about crime as a consequence of moral failure—of communities and schools and parents who no longer raise children with a respect for right and wrong. All of those theories are essentially ways of saying that the criminal is a personality type—a personality type distinguished by an insensitivity to the norms of normal society. People with stunted psychological development don't understand how to conduct healthy relationships. People with genetic predispositions to violence fly off the handle when normal people keep their cool. People who aren't taught right from wrong are oblivious to what is and what is not appropriate behavior. People who grow up poor, fatherless, and buffeted by racism don't have the same commitment to social norms as those from healthy middle-class homes. Bernie Goetz and those four thugs on the subway were, in this sense, prisoners of their own, dysfunctional, world.

But what do Broken Windows and the Power of Context suggest? Exactly the opposite. They say that the criminal—far from being someone who acts for fundamental, intrinsic reasons and who lives in his own world—is actually someone acutely sensitive to his environment, who is alert to all kinds of cues, and who is prompted to commit crimes based on his perception of the world around him. That is an incredibly radical—and in some sense unbelievable—idea. There is an even more radical dimension here. The Power of Context is an environmental argument. It says that behavior is a function of social context. But it is a very strange kind of environmentalism. In the 1960s, liberals made a similar kind of argument, but when they talked about the importance of environment they were talking about the importance of fundamental social factors: crime, they said, was the result of social injustice, of structural economic inequities, of unemployment, of racism, of decades of institutional and social neglect, so that if you wanted to stop crime you had to undertake some fairly heroic steps. But the Power of Context says that what really matters is little things. The Power of Context says that the showdown on the subway between Bernie Goetz and those four youths had very little to do, in the end, with the tangled psychological pathology of Goetz, and very little as well to do with the background and poverty of the four youths who accosted him, and everything to do with the message sent by the graffiti on the walls and the disorder at the turnstiles. The Power of Context says you don't have to solve the big problems to solve crime. You can prevent crimes just by scrubbing off graffiti and arresting fare-beaters. . . . This is what I meant when I called the Power of Context a radical theory. Giuliani and Bratton—far from being conservatives, as they are commonly identified—actually represent on the question of crime the most extreme liberal position imaginable, a position so extreme that it is almost impossible to accept. How can it be that what was going on in Bernie Goetz's head doesn't matter? And if it is really true that it doesn't matter, why is that fact so hard to believe?

4.

[Elsewhere], . . . I talked about two seemingly counterintuitive aspects of persuasion. One was the study that showed how people who watched Peter Jennings on ABC were more likely to vote Republican than people who watched either Tom Brokaw or Dan Rather because, in some unconscious way, Jennings was able to signal his affection for Republican candidates. The second study showed how people who were charismatic could—without saying anything and with the briefest of exposures—infect others with their emotions. The implications of those two studies go to the heart of the Law of the Few, because they suggest that what we think of as inner states—preferences and emotions—are actually powerfully and imperceptibly influenced by seemingly inconsequential personal influences, by a newscaster we watch for a few minutes a day or by someone we sit next to, in silence, in a two-minute experiment. The essence of the Power of Context is that the same thing is true for certain kinds of environments—that in ways that we don't necessarily appreciate, our inner states are the result of our outer circumstances. The field of psychology is rich with experiments that demonstrate this fact. . . .

In the early 1970s, a group of social scientists at Stanford University, led by Philip Zimbardo, decided to create a mock prison in the basement of the university's psychology building. They took a thirty-five-foot section of corridor and created a cell block with a prefabricated wall. Three small, six- by nine-foot cells were created from laboratory rooms and given steel-barred, black-painted doors. A closet was turned into a solitary confinement cell. The group then advertised in the local papers for volunteers, men who would agree to participate in the experiment. Seventy-five people applied, and from those Zimbardo and his colleagues picked the 21 who appeared the most normal and healthy on psychological tests. Half of the group were chosen, at random, to be guards, and were given uniforms and dark glasses and told that their responsibility was to keep order in the prison. The other half were told that they were to be prisoners. Zimbardo got the Palo Alto Police Department to "arrest" the prisoners in their homes, cuff them, bring them to the station house, charge them with a fictitious crime, fingerprint them, then blindfold them and bring them to the prison Psychology Department basement. Then they were stripped and given a prison uniform to wear, with a number on the front and back that was to serve as their only means of identification for the duration of their incarceration.

The purpose of the experiment was to try to find out why prisons are such nasty places. Was it because prisons are full of nasty people, or was it because prisons are such nasty environments that they make people nasty? In the answer to that question is obviously the answer to the question posed by Bernie Goetz and the subway cleanup, which is how much influence does immediate environment have on the way people behave? What Zimbardo found out shocked him. The guards, some of whom had previously identified themselves as pacifists, fell quickly into the role of hard-bitten disciplinarians. The first night they woke up the prisoners at two in the morning and made them do pushups, line up against the wall, and perform other arbitrary tasks. On the morning of the second day, the prisoners rebelled. They ripped off their numbers and barricaded themselves in their cells. The guards responded by stripping them, spraying them with fire extinguishers, and throwing the leader of the rebellion into solitary confinement. "There were times when we were pretty abusive, getting right in their faces and yelling at them," one guard remembers. "It was part of the whole atmosphere of terror." As the experiment progressed, the guards got systematically crueler and more sadistic. "What we were unprepared for was the intensity of the change and the speed at which it happened," Zimbardo says. The guards were making the prisoners say to one another they loved each other, and making them march down the hallway, in handcuffs, with paper bags over their heads. "It was completely the opposite from the way I conduct myself now," another guard remembers. "I think I was positively creative in terms of my mental cruelty." After 36 hours, one prisoner began to get hysterical, and had to be released. Four more then had to be released because of "extreme emotional depression, crying, rage, and acute anxiety." Zimbardo had originally intended to have the experiment run for two weeks. He called it off after six days. "I realize now," one prisoner said after the experiment was over, "that no matter how together I thought I was inside my head, my prisoner behavior was often less under my control than I realized." Another said: "I began to feel that I was losing my identity, that the person I call ———, the person who volunteered to get me into this prison (because it was a prison to me, it still is a prison to me, I don't regard it as an experiment or a simulation . . .) was distant from me, was remote, until finally I wasn't that person. I was 416. I was really my number and 416 was really going to have to decide what to do."

Zimbardo's conclusion was that there are specific situations so powerful that they can overwhelm our inherent predispositions. The key word here is "situation." Zimbardo isn't talking about environment, about the major external influences on all of our lives. He's not denying that how we are raised by our parents affects who we are, or that the kinds of schools we went to, the friends we have, or the neighborhoods we live in affect our behavior. All of these things are undoubtedly important. Nor is he denying that our genes play a role in determining who we are. Most psychologists believe that nature—genetics—accounts for about half of the reason why we tend to act the way we do. His point is simply that there are certain times and places and conditions when much of that can be swept away, that there are instances where you can take normal people from good schools and happy families and good neighborhoods and powerfully affect their behavior merely by changing the immediate details of their situation. . . .

The mistake we make in thinking of character as something unified and all-encompassing is very similar to a kind of blind spot in the way we process information. Psychologists call this tendency the Fundamental Attribution Error (FAE), which is a fancy way of saying that when it comes to interpreting other people's behavior, human beings invariably make the mistake of overestimating the importance of fundamental character traits and underestimating the importance of the situation and context. We will always reach for a "dispositional" explanation for events, as opposed to a contextual explanation. In one experiment, for instance, a group of people are told to watch two sets of similarly talented basketball players, the first of whom are shooting baskets in a well-lighted gym and the second of whom are shooting baskets in a badly lighted gym (and obviously missing a lot of shots). Then they are asked to judge how good the players were. The players in the well-lighted gym were considered superior. In another example, a group of people are brought in for an experiment and told they are going to play a quiz game. They are paired off and they draw lots. One person gets a card that says he or she is going to be the "Contestant." The other is told he or she is going to be the "Questioner." The Questioner is then asked to draw up a list of ten "challenging but not impossible" questions based on areas of particular interest or expertise, so someone who is into Ukrainian folk music might come up with a series of questions based on Ukrainian folk music. The questions are posed to the Contestant, and after the quiz is over, both parties are asked to estimate the level of general knowledge of the other. Invariably, the Contestants rate the Questioners as being a lot smarter than they themselves are.

You can do these kinds of experiments a thousand different ways and the answer almost always comes out the same way. This happens even when you give people a clear and immediate environmental explanation of the behavior they are being asked to evaluate: that the gym, in the first case, has few lights on; that the Contestant is being asked to answer the most impossibly biased and rigged set of questions. In the end, this doesn't make much difference. There is something in all of us that makes us instinctively want to explain the world around us in terms of people's essential attributes: he's a better basketball player, that person is smarter than I am.

We do this because . . . we are a lot more attuned to personal cues than contextual cues. The FAE also makes the world a much simpler and more understandable place. . . . The psychologist Walter Mischel argues that the human mind has a kind of "reducing valve" that "creates and maintains the perception of continuity even in the face of perpetual observed changes in actual behavior." He writes:

> When we observe a woman who seems hostile and fiercely independent some of the time but passive, dependent and feminine on other occasions, our reducing valve usually makes us choose between the two syndromes. We decide that one pattern is in the service of the other, or that both are in the service of a third motive. She must be a really castrating lady with a façade of passivity—or perhaps she is a warm, passive-dependent woman with a surface defense of aggressiveness. But perhaps nature is bigger than our concepts and it is possible for the lady to be a hostile, fiercely independent, passive, dependent, feminine, aggressive, warm, castrating person all-in-one. Of course which of these she is at any particular moment would not be random or capricious—it would depend on who she is with, when, how, and much, much more. But each of these aspects of her self may be a quite genuine and real aspect of her total being.

Character, then, isn't what we think it is or, rather, what we want it to be. It isn't a stable, easily identifiable set of closely related traits, and it only seems that way because of a glitch in the way our brains are organized. Character is more like a bundle of habits and tendencies and interests, loosely bound together and dependent, at certain times, on circumstance and context. The reason that most of us seem to have a consistent character is that most of us are really good at controlling our environment. . . .

5.

Some years ago two Princeton University psychologists, John Darley and Daniel Batson, decided to conduct a study inspired by the biblical story of the Good Samaritan. As you may recall, that story, from the New Testament Gospel of Luke, tells of a traveler who has been beaten and robbed and left for dead by the side of the road from Jerusalem to Jericho. Both a priest and a Levite—worthy, pious men—came upon the man but did not stop, "passing by on the other side." The only man to help was a Samaritan—the member of a despised minority—who "went up to him and bound up his wounds" and took him to an inn. Darley and Batson decided to replicate that study at the Princeton Theological Seminary. This was an experiment very much in the tradition of the FAE, and it is an important demonstration of how the Power of Context has implications for the way we think about social epidemics of all kinds, not just violent crime.

Darley and Batson met with a group of seminarians, individually, and asked each one to prepare a short, extemporaneous talk on a given biblical theme, then walk over to a nearby building to present it. Along the way to the presentation, each student ran into a man slumped in an alley, head down, eyes closed, coughing and groaning. The question was, who would stop and help? Darley and Batson introduced three variables into the experiment, to make its results more meaningful. First, before the experiment even started, they gave the students a questionnaire about why they had chosen to study theology. Did they see religion as a means of personal and spiritual fulfillment? Or were they looking for a practical tool for finding meaning in everyday life? Then they varied the subject of the theme the students were asked to talk about. Some were asked to speak on the relevance of the professional clergy to the religious vocation. Others were given the parable of the Good Samaritan. Finally, the instructions given by the experimenters to each student varied as well. In some of the cases, as he sent the students on their way, the experimenter would look at his watch and say, "Oh, you're late. They were expecting you a few minutes ago. We'd better get moving." In other cases, he would say, "It will be a few minutes before they're ready for you, but you might as well head over now."

If you ask people to predict which seminarians played the Good Samaritan (and subsequent studies have done just this) their answers are highly consistent. They almost all say that the students who entered the ministry to help people and those reminded of the importance of compassion by having just read the parable of the Good Samaritan will be the most likely to stop. Most of us, I think, would agree with those conclusions. In fact, neither of those factors made any difference. "It is hard to think of a context in which norms concerning helping those in distress are more salient than for a person thinking about the Good Samaritan, and yet it did not significantly increase helping behavior," Darley and Batson concluded. "Indeed, on several occasions, a seminary student going to give his talk on the parable of the Good Samaritan literally stepped over the victim as he hurried on his way." The only thing that really mattered was whether the student was in a rush. Of the group that was, 10 percent stopped to help. Of the group who knew they had a few minutes to spare, 63 percent stopped.

What this study is suggesting, in other words, is that the convictions of your heart and the actual contents of your thoughts are less important, in the end, in guiding your actions than the immediate context of your behavior. The words "Oh, you're late" had the effect of making someone who was ordinarily compassionate into someone who was indifferent to suffering— of turning someone, in that particular moment, into a different person. Epidemics are, at their root, about this very process of transformation. When we are trying to make an idea or attitude or product tip, we're trying to change our audience in some small yet critical respect: we're trying to infect them, sweep them up in our epidemic, convert them from hostility to acceptance. That can be done through the influence of special kinds of people, people of extraordinary personal connection. That's the Law of the Few. It can be done by changing the content of communication, by making a message so memorable that it sticks in someone's mind and compels them to action. That is the Stickiness Factor. I think that both of those laws make intuitive sense. But we need to remember that small changes in context can be just as important in tipping epidemics, even though that fact appears to violate some of our most deeply held assumptions about human nature.

This does not mean that our inner psychological states and personal histories are not important in explaining our behavior. An enormous percentage of those who engage in violent acts, for example, have some kind of psychiatric disorder or come from deeply disturbed backgrounds. But there is a world of difference between being inclined toward violence and actually committing a violent act. A crime is a relatively rare and aberrant event. For a crime to be committed, something extra, something additional, has to happen to tip a troubled person toward violence, and what the Power of Context is saying is that those Tipping Points may be as simple and trivial as everyday signs of disorder like graffiti and fare-beating. The implications of this idea are enormous. The previous notion that disposition is everything— that the cause of violent behavior is always "sociopathic personality" or "deficient superego" or the inability to delay gratification or some evil in the genes—is, in the end, the most passive and reactive of ideas about crime. It says that once you catch a criminal you can try to help him get better—give him Prozac, put him in therapy, try to rehabilitate him—but there is very little you can do to prevent crime from happening in the first place. . . .

Once you understand that context matters, however, that specific and relatively small elements in the environment can serve as Tipping Points, that defeatism is turned upside down. Environmental Tipping Points are things that we can change: we can fix broken windows and clean up graffiti and change the signals that invite crime in the first place. Crime can be more than understood. It can be prevented. There is a broader dimension to this. Judith Harris has convincingly argued that peer influence and community influence are more important than family influence in determining how children turn out. Studies of juvenile delinquency and high school drop-out rates, for example, demonstrate that a child is better off in a good neighborhood and a troubled family than he or she is in a troubled neighborhood and a good family. We spend so much time celebrating the importance and power of family influence that it may seem, at first blush, that this can't be true. But in reality it is no more than an obvious and commonsensical extension of the Power of Context, because it says simply that children are powerfully shaped by their external environment, that the features of our immediate social and physical world—the streets we walk down, the people we encounter—play a huge role in shaping who we are and how we act. It isn't just serious criminal behavior, in the end, that is sensitive to environmental cues, it is all behavior. Weird as it sounds, if you add up the meaning of the Stanford prison experiment and the New York subway experiment, they suggest that it is possible to be a better person on a clean street or in a clean subway than in one littered with trash and graffiti.

"In a situation like this, you're in a combat situation," Goetz told his neighbor Myra Friedman, in an anguished telephone call just days after the shooting. "You're not thinking in a normal way. Your memory isn't even working normally. You are so hyped up. Your vision actually changes. Your field of view changes. Your capabilities change. What you are capable of changes." He acted, Goetz went on, "viciously and savagely. . . . If you corner a rat and you are about to butcher it, okay? The way I responded was viciously and savagely, just like that, like a rat."

Of course he did. He was in a rat hole.   ■

■ *QUESTIONS FOR MAKING CONNECTIONS WITHIN THE READING* ■

1. "The Power of Context" is one of the middle chapters in Malcolm Gladwell's book, *The Tipping Point: How Little Things Can Make a Big Difference.* In "The Power of Context," Gladwell refers to the three principles that govern what he calls "the epidemic transmission" of an idea: the Law of the Few, the Stickiness Factor, and the Power of Context. He provides thumbnail

sketches of the first two principles in this chapter, along with an elaboration of the Power of Context. What is "the law of the few"? What is "the Stickiness Factor"? How much can you piece together about the first two principles from what Gladwell presents in "The Power of Context"?

2. Gladwell states that the "Broken Windows theory and the Power of Context are one and the same." What is the "Broken Windows theory" of crime? How would one go about testing this theory? What other theories are available to explain the cause of crime? Does it matter which theory one accepts?

3. Why is it a mistake to think of "character as something unified and all-encompassing"? If we accept the alternative, namely, that character is fragmented and situation specific, what follows? How is this meant to change one's understanding of criminals and their behavior? Of law-abiding citizens and their behavior?

■ *QUESTIONS FOR WRITING* ■

1. Toward the end of "The Power of Context," Gladwell asserts that his discussion of the relationship between criminal activity and local context has implications that "are enormous." Gladwell leaves it to his readers to spell out these implications. How would our social structure, our criminal system, our modes of education have to change if we abandoned what Gladwell terms our "most passive and reactive ideas about crime"?

2. Gladwell argues that "small changes in context" can play a major role in determining whether an idea takes off or disappears without a trace. This fact, he goes on, "appears to violate some of our most deeply held assumptions about human nature." What does "human nature" mean, if one accepts the argument Gladwell makes in "The Power of Context"? Is it possible to create any form of human behavior just by manipulating the contextual background? Does Gladwell's view suggest that humans are freer than previously thought or that their behavior is more fully determined than previously thought possible?

■ *QUESTIONS FOR MAKING CONNECTIONS BETWEEN READINGS* ■

1. "Down with Dualism" concludes with Frans de Waal's assertion "that distress at the sight of another's pain is an impulse over which we exert no control." Is compassion an intrinsic part of humans, or is it subject to the "power of context" that Gladwell has described? Does Gladwell's discussion of human character reinforce de Waal's argument about human evolution, or does it call that argument into question? Does sensitivity to context have any necessary selective value for the evolution of the species?

2. In "The Naked Citadel," Susan Faludi provides a rich description of how lives are lived in an alternate social structure—the military academy. Does Malcolm Gladwell's account help to explain why Shannon Faulkner wasn't welcomed into the academy? Did Faulkner's appearance cause the academy to "tip"? Does Gladwell's theory have any predictive value? That is, could it tell us, ahead of time, whether the academy would be transformed by being required to admit women?

www **For additional suggestions about making connections between readings, visit the Link-O-Mat and More Sample Assignments at <www.newhum.com>.**

STEPHEN JAY GOULD

PERHAPS MORE THAN any other contemporary American scientist, Stephen Jay Gould committed himself to communicating the goals, processes, and achievements of science to the public. Gould's high visibility, distinctive critical voice, and marked enthusiasm for making science accessible to the general public led him to contribute to debates surrounding creationist science, evolutionary psychology, and biological determinations of race and intelligence. The essay included here, "What Does the Dreaded 'E' Word *Mean,* Anyway?" is part of Gould's lifelong project of explaining Darwin's evolutionary theory, a project that involved clarifying what "survival of the fittest" means and addressing the notion that evolutionary development involves progress toward perfection. As Gould's opening discussion of the Kansas City school board's treatment of evolutionary theory shows, Darwin's ideas and their significance remain largely misunderstood to this day, more than 150 years after they were first voiced.

Undoubtedly the most prolific scientific writer of the twentieth century, Gould published more than twenty books, including *The Mismeasure of Man* (1982), which criticized pseudoscientific justifications for racism and won a National Book Critics Circle Award; *The Panda's Thumb* (1980), which won the American Book Award; and *Wonderful Life: The Burgess Shale and the Nature of History* (1990), which was a finalist for the Pulitzer Prize and winner of the Science Book Prize. Just prior to his death in 2002, Gould published his magnum opus, *The Structure of Evolutionary Theory,* which was described in a review in *Scientific American* as "a monumental work, both in size (1,400-plus pages) and in scope—it sets out to do nothing less than reformulate Darwin's theory of evolution." Professor of Geology and Zoology at Harvard University and also the curator of the Invertebrate Paleontology collection at the Museum of Comparative Zoology there, Gould was the recipient of many academic awards and dis-

Gould, Stephen Jay. "What Does the Dreaded 'E' Word *Mean,* Anyway? A Reverie for the Opening of the New Hayden Planetarium." *Natural History.* February 2000. 28–44.

Quotation drawn from Stephen Jay Gould's interview with AnnOnLine, 9 October 1996 <http://www.annonline.com/interviews/961009/>.

tinctions, including a MacArthur "Genius Grant," the Glenn T. Seaborg Award for contribution to public interest in science, the Distinguished Service Award from the National Association of Biology Teachers, and the Distinguished Service Award from the American Humanists Association.

Gould wrote that "Humans are not the end result of predictable evolutionary progress, but rather a fortuitous cosmic afterthought, a tiny little twig on the enormously arborescent bush of life, which if replanted from seed, would almost surely not grow this twig again." At first glance such a worldview may appear rather bleak. But Gould saw the emergence of *homo sapiens* as wonderful— literally an occasion for wonder—precisely because it uniquely expressed the forces that are at work throughout the universe in every variety of living thing.

www **To learn more about Stephen Jay Gould and the evolutionary process, visit the Link-O-Mat at <www.newhum.com>.**

What Does the Dreaded "E" Word *Mean*, Anyway?

A Reverie for the Opening of the New Hayden Planetarium

Evolution posed no terrors in the liberal constituency of New York City when I studied biology at Jamaica High School in 1956. But our textbooks didn't utter the word either—a legacy of the statutes that had brought William Jennings Bryan and Clarence Darrow to legal blows at Tennessee's trial of John Scopes in 1925. The subject remained doubly hidden within my textbook—covered only in chapter 63 (of 66) and described in euphemism as "the hypothesis of racial development."

The antievolution laws of the Scopes era, passed during the early 1920s in several southern and border states, remained on the books until 1968, when the Supreme Court declared them unconstitutional. The laws were never strictly enforced, but their existence cast a pall over American education, as textbook publishers capitulated to produce "least common denominator" versions acceptable in all states—so schoolkids in New York got short shrift because the statutes of some distant states had labeled evolution dangerous and unteachable.

Ironically, at the very end of this millennium (I am writing this essay in late November 1999), demotions, warnings, and anathemas have again come into vogue in several regions of our nation. The Kansas school board has reduced evolution, the central and unifying concept of the life sciences, to an optional subject within the state's biology curriculum—an educational ruling akin to stating that English will still be taught but that grammar may henceforth be regarded as a peripheral frill, permitted but not mandated as a classroom subject. Two states now require that warning labels be pasted (literally) into all biology textbooks, alerting students that they might wish to consider alternatives to evolution (although no other well-documented scientific concept evokes similar caution). Finally, at least two states have retained all their Darwinian material in official pamphlets and curricula but have replaced the dreaded "e" word with a circumlocution, thus reviving the old strategy of my high school text.

As our fight for good (and politically untrammeled) public education in science must include our forceful defense of a key word—for inquisitors have always understood that an idea can be extinguished most effectively by suppressing all memory of a defining word or an inspirational person—we might consider an interesting historical irony that, properly elucidated, might even aid us in our battle. We must not compromise *our* showcasing of the "e" word, for we give up the game before we start if we grant our opponents control over basic terms. But we should also note that Darwin himself never used the word "evolution" in his epochal book of 1859. In *Origin of Species,* he calls this fundamental biological process "descent with modification." Darwin, needless to say, did not shun "evolution" from motives of fear, conciliation, or political savvy but rather for an opposite and principled reason that can help us appreciate the depth of the intellectual revolution that he inspired and some of the reasons (understandable if indefensible) for the persistent public unease.

Pre-Darwinian terminology for evolution—a widely discussed, if unorthodox, view of life in early nineteenth-century biology—generally used such names as transformation, transmutation, or the development hypothesis. In choosing a label for his own, very different account of genealogical change, Darwin would never have considered "evolution" as a descriptor, because that vernacular English word implied a set of consequences contrary to the most distinctive features of his proposed revolutionary mechanism of change.

"Evolution," from the Latin *evolvere,* literally means "an unrolling"—and clearly implies an unfolding in time of a predictable or prepackaged sequence in an inherently progressive, or at least directional, manner (the "fiddlehead" of a fern unrolls and expands to bring forth the adult plant—a true evolution of preformed parts). The *Oxford English Dictionary* traces the word "evolution" to seventeenth-century English poetry. Here the word's key meaning—the sequential exposure of prepackaged potential—inspired the first recorded usages in our language. For example, Henry More (1614–87), the British philosopher responsible for several of the seventeenth-century citations in the *OED* entry, stated in 1664, "I have not yet evolved all the intangling superstitions that may be wrapt up."

The few pre-Darwinian English citations of genealogical change as "evolution" all employ the word as a synonym for predictable progress. For example, in describing Lamarck's theory for British readers (in the second volume of his *Principles of Geology,* 1832), Charles Lyell generally uses the neutral term "transmutation"—except in one passage, where he wishes to highlight a claim for progress: "The testacea of the ocean existed first, until some of them by gradual evolution were improved into those inhabiting the land."

Although the word "evolution" does not appear in the first edition of *Origin of Species,* Darwin does use the verbal form "evolved," clearly in the vernacular sense and in an especially crucial spot: the very last word of the book! Most students have failed to appreciate the incisive and intended "gotcha" of these closing lines, which have generally been read as a poetic reverie, a harmless linguistic flourish essentially devoid of content, however rich in imagery. In fact, the canny Darwin used this maximally effective location to make a telling point about the absolute glory and comparative importance of natural history as a calling.

We usually regard planetary physics as the paragon of rigorous science, while dismissing natural history as a lightweight exercise in dull, descriptive cataloging that any person with sufficient patience might accomplish. But Darwin, in his closing passage, identified the primary phenomenon of planetary physics as a dull and simple cycling to nowhere, in sharp contrast with life's history, depicted as a dynamic and upwardly growing tree. The Earth *revolves* in uninteresting sameness, but life *evolves* by unfolding its potential for ever expanding diversity along admittedly unpredictable, but wonderfully various, branchings:

> Whilst this planet has gone cycling on according to the fixed law of gravity, from so simple a beginning endless forms most beautiful and most wonderful have been, and are being, evolved.

But Darwin could not have described the process regulated by his mechanism of natural selection as "evolution" in the vernacular meaning then conveyed by the word. For the mechanism of natural selection yields only increasing adaptation to changing local environments, not predictable progress in the usual sense of cosmic or general betterment expressed as growing complexity, augmented mentality, or whatever. In Darwin's causal world, an anatomically degenerate parasite, reduced to a formless clump of feeding and reproductive cells within the body of a host, may be just as well adapted to its surroundings, and just as well endowed with prospects for evolutionary persistence, as is the most intricate creature, exquisitely adapted in all parts to a complex and dangerous external environment. Moreover, since natural selection can adapt organisms only to local circumstances, and since local circumstances change in an effectively random manner through geological time, the pathways of adaptive evolution cannot be predicted.

Thus, on these two fundamental grounds—lack of inherent directionality and lack of predictability—the process regulated by natural selection could scarcely have suggested, to Darwin, the label "evolution," an ordinary English word for sequences of predictable and directional unfolding. We must then, and obviously, ask how "evolution" achieved its coup in becoming the name for Darwin's process—a takeover so complete that the word has now almost (but not quite, as we shall soon see) lost its original English meaning of "unfolding" and has transmuted (or should we say "evolved"?) into an effective synonym for biological change through time.

This interesting shift, despite Darwin's own reticence, occurred primarily because a great majority of his contemporaries, while granting the overwhelming evidence for evolution's factuality, could not accept Darwin's radical views about the causes and patterns of biological change. Most important, they could not bear to surrender the comforting and traditional view that human consciousness must represent a predictable (if not a divinely intended) summit of biological existence. If scientific discoveries enjoined an evolutionary reading of human superiority, then one must bow to the evidence. But Darwin's contemporaries (and many people today as well) would not surrender their traditional view of human domination, and therefore could conceptualize genealogical transmutation only as a process defined by predictable progress toward a human acme—in short, as a process well described by the term "evolution" in its vernacular meaning of "unfolding an inherent potential."

Herbert Spencer's progressivist view of natural change probably exerted the greatest influence in establishing "evolution" as the general name for Darwin's process, for Spencer held a dominating status as Victorian pundit and grand panjandrum of nearly everything conceptual. In any case, Darwin had too many other fish to fry and didn't choose to fight a battle about words rather than things. He felt confident that his views would eventually prevail, even over the contrary etymology of a word imposed upon his process by popular will. (He knew, after all, that meanings of words can transmute within new climates of immediate utility, just as species transform under new local environments of life and ecology!) Darwin never used the "e" word extensively in his writings, but he did capitulate to a developing consensus by referring to his process as evolution for the first time in *Descent of Man*, published in 1871. (Still, Darwin never used the word "evolution" in the title of any book—and he chose, in his book on human history, to emphasize the genealogical "descent" of our species, not our "ascent" to higher levels of consciousness.)

When I was a young boy, growing up on the streets of New York City, the American Museum of Natural History became my second home and inspiration. I loved two exhibits most of all—the *Tyrannosaurus* skeleton on the fourth floor and the star show at the adjacent Hayden Planetarium. I juggled these two passions for many years and eventually became a paleontologist; Carl Sagan, my near-contemporary from the neighboring neverland of Brooklyn (I grew up in Queens) weighed the same two interests in the same building but opted for astronomy as a calling. (I have always suspected a basic biological determinism behind our opposite choices. Carl was tall and looked up toward the heavens; I am shorter than average and tend to look down at the ground.)

My essays may be known for their tactic of selecting odd little tidbits as illustrations of general themes. But why, to mark the reopening of the Hayden Planetarium, would I highlight such a quirky and apparently irrelevant subject as the odyssey of the term "evolution" in scientific, and primarily biological, use—thus seeming, once again, to reject the cosmos in favor of the dinosaurs? Method does inhere in my apparent madness (whether or not I succeed in conveying this reasoning to my readers). I am writing about the term "evolution" in the domain I know in order to explicate its strikingly different meaning in the profession that I put aside but still love avocationally. A discussion of the contrast between biological evolution and cosmological evolution might offer some utility as a commentary about alternative worldviews and as a reminder that many supposed debates in science arise from confusion engendered by differing uses of words and not from deep conceptual muddles about the nature of things.

Interdisciplinary unification represents a grand and worthy goal of intellectual life, but greater understanding can often be won by principled separation and mutual respect, based on clear definitions and distinctions among truly disparate processes, rather than by false unions forged with superficial similarities and papered over by a common terminology. In our understandable desire to unify the sciences of temporal change, we have too often followed the Procrustean strategy of enforcing a common set of causes and explanations upon the history of a species and the life of a star—partly, at least, for the very bad reason that both professions use the term "evolution" to denote change through time. In this case, the fundamental differences trump the superficial similarities—and true unity will be achieved only when we acknowledge the disparate substrates that, taken together, probe the range of possibilities for theories of historical order.

The Darwinian principle of natural selection yields temporal change—evolution in the biological definition—by the twofold process of producing copious and undirected variation within a population and then passing along only a biased (selected) portion of this variation to the next generation. In this manner, the variation within a population at any moment can be converted into differences in mean values (average size, average braininess) among successive populations through time. For this fundamental reason, we call such theories of change *variational* as opposed to the more conventional, and more direct, models of *transformational* change imposed by natural laws that mandate a particular trajectory based on inherent (and therefore predictable) properties of substances and environments. (A ball rolling down an inclined plane does not reach the bottom because selection has favored the differential propagation of moving versus stable elements of its totality but because gravity dictates this result when round balls roll down smooth planes.)

To illustrate the peculiar properties of variational theories like Darwin's in an obviously caricatured, but not inaccurate, description: Suppose that a population of elephants inhabits Siberia during a warm interval before the advance of an ice sheet. The elephants vary, at random and in all directions, in their amount of body hair. As the ice advances and local conditions become colder, elephants with more hair will tend to cope better, by the sheer good fortune of their superior adaptation to changing climates—and they will leave more surviving offspring on average. (This differential reproductive success must be conceived as broadly statistical and not guaranteed in every case: in any generation, the hairiest elephant of all may fall into a crevasse and die.) Because offspring inherit their parents' degree of hairiness, the next generation will contain a higher proportion of more densely clad elephants (who will continue to be favored by natural selection as the climate becomes still colder). This process of increasing average hairiness may continue for many generations, leading to the evolution of woolly mammoths.

This little fable can help us understand how peculiar and how contrary to all traditions of Western thought and explanation of the Darwinian theory of evolution, and variational theories of historical change in general, must sound to the common ear. All the odd and fascinating properties of Darwinian evolution—the sensible and explainable but quite unpredictable nature of the outcome (dependent upon complex and contingent changes in local environments), the nonprogressive character of the alteration (adaptive only to these unpredictable local circumstances and not inevitably building a "better" elephant in any cosmic or general sense)—flow from the variational basis of natural selection.

Transformational theories work in a much simpler and more direct manner. If I want to go from A to B, I will have so much less conceptual (and actual) trouble if I can postulate a mechanism that will just push me there directly than if I must rely upon the selection of "a few good men" from a random cloud of variation about point A, then constitute a new generation around an average point one step closer to B, then generate a new cloud of random variation about this new point, then select "a few good men" once again from this new array—and then repeat this process over and over until I finally reach B.

When one adds the oddity of variational theories in general to our strong cultural and psychological resistance against their application to our own evolutionary origin (as an unpredictable and not necessary progressive little twig on life's luxuriant tree), then we can better understand why Darwin's revolution surpassed all other scientific discoveries in reformatory power and why so many people still fail to understand, and may even actively resist, its truly liberating content. (I must leave the issue of liberation for another time, but once we recognize that the specification of morals and the search for a meaning to our lives cannot be accomplished by scientific study in any case, then Darwin's variational mechanism will no longer seem threatening and may even become liberating in teaching us to look within ourselves for answers to these questions and to abandon a chimerical search for the purpose of our lives, and for the source of our ethical values, in the external workings of nature.)

These difficulties in grasping Darwin's great insight became exacerbated when our Victorian forebears made their unfortunate choice of a defining word—"evolution"—with its vernacular meaning of "directed unfolding." We would not face this additional problem today if "evolution" had undergone a complete transformation to become a strict and exclusive definition of biological change—with earlier and etymologically more appropriate usages then abandoned and forgotten. But important words rarely undergo such a clean switch of meaning, and "evolution" still maintains its original definition of "predictable unfolding" in several nonbiological disciplines—including astronomy.

When astronomers talk about the evolution of a star, they clearly do not have a variational theory like Darwin's in mind. Stars do not change through time because mama and papa stars generate broods of varying daughter stars, followed by the differential survival of daughters best adapted to their particular region of the cosmos. Rather, theories of stellar "evolution" could not be more relentlessly transformational in positing a definite and predictable sequence of changes unfolding as simple consequences of physical laws. (No biological process operates in exactly the same manner, but the life cycle of an organism certainly works better than the evolution of a species as a source of analogy.)

Ironically, astronomy undeniably trumps biology in faithfulness to the etymology and the vernacular definition of "evolution"—even though the term now holds far wider currency under the radically altered definition of the biological sciences. In fact, astronomers have been so true to the original definition that they confine "evolution" to historical sequences of predictable unfolding and resolutely shun the word when describing cosmic changes exhibiting the key features of biological evolution—unpredictability and lack of inherent directionality.

As an illustration of this astronomical usage, consider the most standard and conventional of all sources—the *Encyclopedia Britannica* article "Stars and Star Clusters" (15th edition, 1990 printing). The section entitled "Star Formation and Evolution" begins by analogizing stellar "evolution" to a preprogrammed life cycle, with the degree of evolution defined as the position along the predictable trajectory:

> Throughout the Milky Way Galaxy . . . astronomers have discovered stars that are well evolved or even approaching extinction, or both, as well as occasional stars that must be very young or still in the process of formation. Evolutionary effects on these stars are not negligible.

The fully predictable and linear sequence of stages in a stellar lifetime (evolution, to astronomers) records the consequences of a defining physical process in the construction and history of stars: the conversion of mass to energy by nuclear reactions deep within stars, leading to the transformation of hydrogen into helium.

> The spread of luminosities and colors of stars within the main sequence can be understood as a consequence of evolution . . . As the stars evolve, they adjust to the increase in the helium-to-hydrogen ratio in their cores . . . When the core fuel is exhausted, the internal structure of the star changes rapidly; it quickly leaves the main sequence and moves towards the region of giants and supergiants.

The same basic sequence unfolds through stellar lives, but the rate of change (evolution, to astronomers) varies as a predictable consequence of differences in mass:

> Like the rate of formation of a star, the subsequent rate of evolution on the main sequence is proportional to the mass of the star; the greater the mass, the more rapid the evolution.

More complex factors may determine variation in some stages of the life cycle, but the basic directionality (evolution, to astronomers) does not alter, and predictability from natural law remains precise and complete:

> The great spread in luminosities and colors of giant, supergiant, and subgiant stars is also understood to result from evolutionary events. When a star leaves the main sequence, its future evolution is precisely determined by its mass, rate of rotation (or angular momentum), chemical composition, and whether or not it is a member of a close binary system.

In the most revealing verbal clue of all, the discourse of this particular scientific culture seems to shun the word "evolution" when historical sequences become too meandering, too nondirectional, or too complex to explain as simple consequences of controlling laws—even though the end result may be markedly different from the beginning state, thus illustrating significant change through time. For example, the same *Britannica* article on stellar evolution notes that one can often reach conclusions about the origin of a star or a planet from the relative abundance of chemical elements in its present composition.

Earth, however, has become so modified during its geological history that we cannot use this inferential method to reconstruct the initial state of our own planet. Because the current configuration of Earth's surface developed through complex contingencies and could not have been predicted from simple laws, this style of change apparently does not rank as evolution—but only, in astronomical parlance, as being "affected."

> The relative abundances of the chemical elements provide significant clues regarding their origin. The Earth's crust has been affected severely by erosion, fractionation, and other geologic events, so that its present varied composition offers few clues as to its early stages.

I don't mention these differences to lament, to complain, or to criticize astronomers in any way. After all, their use of "evolution" remains more faithful to etymology and the original English definition, whereas our Darwinian reconstruction has virtually reversed the original meaning. In this case, since neither side will or should give up its understanding of "evolution" (astronomers because they have retained an original and etymologically correct meaning, and evolutionists because their redefinition expresses the very heart of their central and revolutionary concept of life's history), our best solution lies simply in exposing the legitimate differences and explaining the good reasons behind the disparity in usage.

In this way, at least, we may avoid confusion and also the special frustration generated when prolonged wrangles arise from misunderstandings of words rather than from genuine disputes about things and causes in nature. We evolutionary biologists must remain especially sensitive to this issue, because we still face considerable opposition, based on conventional hopes and fears, to our insistence that life evolves in unpredictable directions, with no inherent goal. Since astronomical evolution upholds both contrary positions—predictability and directionality—evolutionary biologists need to emphasize their own distinctive meaning, especially since the general public feels much more comfortable with the astronomical sense and will therefore impose this more congenial definition upon the history of life if we do not clearly explain the logic, the evidence, and the sheer fascination of our challenging conclusion.

Two studies published within the past month led me to this topic, because each discovery confirms the biological, variational, and Darwinian "take" on evolution while also, and quite explicitly, refuting a previous, transformational interpretation—rooted in our culturally established prejudices for the more comforting, astronomical view—that had blocked our understanding and skewed our thoughts about an important episode in life's history:

1. *Vertebrates "all the way down."* In one of the most crucial and enigmatic episodes in the history of life—and a challenge to the older, more congenial idea that life has progressed in a basically stately, linear manner through the ages—nearly all animal phyla made their first appearance in the fossil record at essentially the same time, an interval of some 5 million years (about 525 million to 530 million years ago) called the Cambrian explosion. (Geological firecrackers have long fuses when measured by the inappropriate scale of human time.) Only one major phylum with prominent and fossilizable hard parts did not appear in this incident or during the Cambrian period at all—the Bryozoa, a group of colonial marine organisms unknown to most nonspecialists today (although still relatively common in shallow oceanic waters) but prominent in the early fossil record of animal life.

One other group, until last month, also had no record within the Cambrian explosion, although late Cambrian representatives (well after the explosion itself) have been known for some time. Whereas popular texts have virtually ignored the Bryozoa, the absence of this other group has been prominently showcased and proclaimed highly significant. No vertebrates had ever been recovered from deposits of the Cambrian explosion, although close relatives within our phylum (the Chordata), if not technically vertebrates, had been collected (the Chordata includes three major subgroups: the tunicates, *Amphioxus* and its relatives, and the vertebrates proper).

This absence of vertebrates from strata bearing nearly all other fossilizable animal phyla provided a strong ray of hope for people who wished to view our own group as "higher" or more evolved in a more predictable direction. If evolution implies linear progression, then later is better—and uniquely later (or almost uniquely, given those pesky bryozoans) can only enhance the distinction. But the November 4, 1999, issue of *Nature* includes a persuasive article ("Lower Cambrian Vertebrates from South China," by D-G. Shu, H-L. Luo, S. Conway Morris, X-L. Zhang, S-X. Hu, L. Chen, J. Han, M. Zhu, Y. Li, and L-Z. Chen) reporting the discovery of two vertebrate genera within the Lower Cambrian Chengjiang formation of southern China, right within the temporal heart of the Cambrian explosion. (The Burgess Shale of western Canada, the celebrated site for most previous knowledge of early Cambrian animals, postdates the actual explosion by several million years. The recently discovered Chengjiang fauna, with equally exquisite preservation of soft anatomy, has been yielding comparable or even greater treasures for more than a decade. See "On Embryos and Ancestors," *Natural History,* July–August 1998.)

These two creatures—each only an inch or so in length and lacking both jaws and a backbone and in fact possessing no bony skeleton at all—might not strike a casual student as worthy of inclusion within our exalted lineage. But these features, however much they may command our present focus, arose later in the history of vertebrates and do not enter the central and inclusive taxonomic definition of our group. The vertebrate jaw, for example, evolved from hard parts that originally fortified the gill openings and then moved forward to surround the mouth. All early fishes—and two modern survivors of this initial radiation, the lampreys and the hagfishes—lacked jaws.

The two Chengjiang genera possess all the defining features of vertebrates: the stiff dorsal supporting rod, or notochord (subsequently lost in adults after the vertebal column evolved); the arrangement of flank musculature in a series of zigzag elements from front to back; the set of paired openings piercing the pharynx (operating primarily as respiratory gills in later fishes but used mostly for filter feeding in ancestral vertebrates). In fact, the best reconstruction of branching order on the vertebrate tree places the origin of these two new genera after the inferred ancestors of modern hagfishes but before the presumed forebears of lampreys. If this inference holds, then vertebrates already existed in substantial diversity within the Cambrian explosion. In any case, we now have two distinct and concrete examples of vertebrates "all the way down"—that is, in the very same strata that include the first known fossils of nearly all phyla of modern multicellular animals. We vertebrates do not stand higher and later than our invertebrate cousins, for all "advanced" animal phyla made their first appearance in the fossil record at essentially the same time. The vaunted complexity of vertebrates did not require a special delay to accommodate a slow series of progressive steps, predictable from the general principles of evolution.

2. *An ultimate parasite, or "how are the mighty fallen."* The phyla of complex multicellular animals enjoy a collective designation as Metazoa (literally, "higher animals"). Mobile, single-celled creatures bear the name Protozoa ("first animals"—actually a misnomer, since many of these creatures, in terms of genealogical branching, rank as close to multicellular plants and fungi as to multicellular animals). In a verbal in-between stand the Mesozoa ("middle animals"). Many taxonomic and evolutionary schemes for the organization of life rank the Mesozoa by the literal implication of their name—that is, as a persistently primitive group intermediate between the single-celled and the multicellular animals and illustrating a necessary transitional step in a progressivist reading of life's history.

But the Mesozoa have always been viewed as enigmatic, primarily because they live as parasites within truly multicellular animals, and parasites often adapt to their protected surroundings by evolving an extremely simplified anatomy, sometimes little more than a glob of absorptive and reproductive tissue cocooned within the body of a host. Thus, the extreme simplicity of parasitic anatomy could represent the evolutionary degeneration of a complex, free-living ancestor rather than the maintenance of a primitive state.

The major group of mesozoans, the Dicyemida, live as microscopic parasites in the renal organs of squid and octopuses. Their adult anatomy could hardly be simpler: a single axial cell (which generates the reproductive cells) in the center, enveloped by a single layer of ciliated outer cells (some ten to forty in number) arranged in a spiral around the axial cell, except at the front end [. . .].

The zoological status of the dicyemids has always been controversial. Some scientists, including Libbie H. Hyman, who wrote the definitive, multi-volume text on invertebrate anatomy for her generation, regarded their simplicity as primitive and their evolutionary status as intermediate in the rising complexity of evolution. As she noted in 1940, "Their characters are in the main primitive and not the result of parasitic degeneration." But even those researchers who viewed the dicyemids as parasitic descendants of more complex free-living ancestors never dared to derive these ultimately simple multicellular creatures from a very complex metazoan. For example, Horace W. Stunkard, the leading student of dicyemids in the generation of my teachers, thought that these mesozoans had descended from the simplest of all Metazoa above the grade of sponges and corals—the platyhelminth flatworms.

Unfortunately, the anatomy of dicyemids has become so regressed and specialized that no evidence remains to link them firmly with other animal groups, so the controversy of persistently primitive versus degeneratively parasitic could never be settled until now. But newer methods of gene sequencing can solve this dilemma, because even though visible anatomy may fade or transform into something unrecognizable, evolution can hardly erase all traces of complex gene sequences. If genes known only from advanced Metazoa—and known to operate only in the context of organs and functions unique to Metazoa—also exist in dicyemids, then these creatures are probably degenerated metazoans. But if, after extensive search, no sign of distinctive metazoan genomes can be detected in dicyemids, then the Mesozoa may well be intermediate between single and multicelled life after all.

In the October 21, 1999, issue of *Nature,* M. Kobayashi, H. Furuya, and P.W.H. Holland present an elegant solution to this old problem ("Dicyemids Are Higher Animals"). These researchers located a *Hox* gene—a member of a distinctive subset known only from metazoans and operating in the differentiation of body structures along the antero-posterior (front to back) axis—in *Dicyema orientale.* These particular *Hox* genes occur only in triploblastic, or "higher," metazoans with body cavities and three cell layers, and not in any of the groups (such as the Porifera, or sponges, and the Cnidaria, or corals and their relatives) traditionally placed "below" triploblasts. Thus, the dicyemids are descended from "higher," triploblastic animals and have become maximally simplified in anatomy by adaptation to their parasitic lifestyle. They do not represent primitive vestiges of an early stage in the linear progress of life.

In short, if the traditionally "highest" of all triploblasts—the vertebrate line, including our exalted selves—appears in the fossil record at the same time as all other triploblastic phyla in the Cambrian explosion, and if the most anatomically simplified of all parasites can evolve (as an adaptation to local ecology) from a free-living lineage within the "higher," triploblastic phyla, then the biological, variational, and Darwinian meaning of "evolution" as unpredictable and nondirectional gains powerful support from two cases that, in a former and now disproven interpretation, once bolstered an opposite set of transformational prejudices.

As a final thought to contrast the predictable unfolding of stellar evolution with the contingent nondirectionality of biological evolution, I should note that Darwin's closing line about "this planet . . . cycling on according to the fixed law of gravity," while adequate for now, cannot hold for all time. Stellar evolution will, one day, enjoin a predictable end, at least to life on Earth. Quoting one more time from *Britannica:*

> The Sun is destined to perish as a white dwarf. But before that happens, it will evolve into a red giant, engulfing Mercury and Venus in the process. At the same time, it will blow away the earth's atmosphere and boil its oceans, making the planet uninhabitable.

The same predictability also allows us to specify the timing of this catastrophe—about 5 billion years from now! A tolerably distant future, to be sure, but consider the issue another way, in comparison with the very different style of change known as biological evolution. Earth originated about 4.6 billion years ago. Thus, half of our planet's potential history unfolded before contingent biological evolution produced even a single species with consciousness sufficient to muse over such matters. Moreover, this single lineage arose within a marginal group of mammals—the primates, which include about 200 of the 4,000 or so mammalian species. By contrast, the world holds at least half a million species of beetles. If a meandering process consumed half of all available time to build such an adaptation even once, then mentality at a human level certainly doesn't seem to rank among the "sure bets," or even the mild probabilities, of history.

We must therefore contrast the good fortune of our own evolution with the inexorable evolution of our nurturing Sun toward a spectacular climax that might make our further evolution impossible. True, the time may be too distant to inspire any practical concern, but we humans do like to muse and to wonder. The contingency of our evolution offers no guarantees against the certainties of the Sun's evolution. We shall probably be long gone by then, perhaps taking a good deal of life with us and perhaps leaving those previously indestructible bacteria as the highest mute witnesses to a stellar expansion that will finally unleash a unicellular Armageddon. Or perhaps we, or our successors, will have colonized the universe by then and will shed only a brief tear for the destruction of a little cosmic exhibit entitled "the museum of our geographic origins." Somehow I prefer the excitement of wondering and cogitation—not to mention the power inherent in acting upon things that *can* be changed—to the certainty of distant dissolution.   ■

■ *QUESTIONS FOR MAKING CONNECTIONS WITHIN THE READING* ■

1. What is at stake in changing the meaning of the word *evolution*? What does the word mean to the Kansas school board? To biologists? To astronomers? To nonscientists?

2. Gould states that "All the odd and fascinating properties of Darwinian evolution . . . flow from the variational basis of natural selection." What is the "variational basis"? What are the "odd and fascinating properties" that it gives to Darwinian evolution?

3. Gould makes the following observation:

> [O]nce we recognize that the specification of morals and the search for a meaning to our lives cannot be accomplished by scientific study in any case, then Darwin's variational mechanism will no longer seem threatening and may even become liberating in teaching us to look within ourselves for answers to these questions and to abandon a chimerical search for the purpose of our lives, and for the source of our ethical values, in the external workings of nature.

Is Gould's point that life has no purpose or meaning? What does he consider to be the appropriate relation between moral and ethical questions and scientific research? Do these observations have anything to do with the history surrounding the idea of evolution? How about with events like the decision by the Kansas school board?

■ *QUESTIONS FOR WRITING* ■

1. Is it really possible for ordinary people to take science into account when posing ethical and moral questions? How can we believe in human moral or technological progress, for example, if we believe that biological life "evolves in unpredictable directions, with no inherent goal"? If people generally believed that life has no inherent goal, would this necessarily have destructive consequences? Does society have a right to protect itself from destructive values even when these values have their basis in good science?

2. Some recent thinkers have argued that words predetermine what we see and say. According to these thinkers, we can never know the world directly but must always view it through the "screen" of language. The only way to learn anything new is to change our use of words, and only after we have changed them can changes on the level of experience take place. In this spirit, writers have tried to encourage gender equality by substituting "humanity" for "man" or "mankind," and by using the plural pronoun "their" instead of the masculine pronoun "his." For similar reasons,

political conservatives have managed to turn the word "liberal"—which once connoted generosity and broad-mindedness—into a disparaging epithet. Does Gould's historical account of the word "evolution" confirm, contradict, or complicate this view of the role played by language?

■ *QUESTIONS FOR MAKING CONNECTIONS BETWEEN READINGS* ■

1. In "The Enhanced and the Unenhanced," Gregory Stock describes a near future when humans will routinely engage in "therapeutic enhancement" to improve embryos. Is this an example of Darwinian evolution, as Gould describes it? Is it possible to argue, from a Darwinian perspective, that human manipulation of the genetic code is unnatural? Will the term "unnatural" have meaning to the posthumans Stock imagines? Does it have meaning to Gould?

2. When Gould encourages us "to abandon a chimerical search for the purpose of our lives, and for the source of our ethical values, in the external workings of nature," where would he have us turn instead? Would you say that Frans de Waal's hypothesis about the evolution of altruism provides a more congenial basis than Gould's essay for discussing the purpose of our lives and the source of our ethical values? Does de Waal take us beyond a view of nature as totally value-free? Would he agree with Gould's view of evolution as entirely random? Would de Waal accept Gould's distinction between human values and natural processes?

www **For additional suggestions about making connections between readings, visit the Link-O-Mat and More Sample Assignments at <www.newhum.com>.**

WILLIAM GREIDER

WILLIAM GREIDER, PROMINENT political journalist and author, has spent much of
the past two decades writing about politics and the economy. A former editor at
Rolling Stone and *The Washington Post,* Greider now writes regularly on economic matters for *The Nation.* To date, he has published six books that challenge
mainstream assumptions about how the economy works: *The Education of David
Stockman and Other Americans* (1982); *Secrets of the Temple: How the Federal Reserve
Runs the Country* (1987); *Who Will Tell the People: The Betrayal of American Democracy* (1992); *One World, Ready or Not: The Manic Logic of Global Capitalism* (1997);
Fortress America: The American Military and the Consequences of Peace (1999); and,
most recently, *The Soul of Capitalism: Opening Paths to a Moral Economy* (2003),
from which the following chapter is drawn.

Whether his topic is the Federal Reserve, the news media's coverage of economic policy, the spread of global capitalism, or the workings of the military's
large-scale acquisitions programs, Greider writes with an eye toward exposing
the tensions that exist between the theory of a free market and the actual practices of the regulatory agencies, bankers, and financial investors who drive the
capitalist enterprise. More interested in reform than revolution, Greider has consistently sought to use his work as a reporter to educate his readers about the excesses of capitalism and to argue for changes in policy and practice that will
allow for the creation of what he terms a "moral economy." In bidding us to consider the human consequences of the economy's inequities, Greider seeks not to
dismantle capitalism but rather, as he puts it, to show that it is still possible for
citizens to "change the economic system's operating values."

www **To learn more about William Greider and unionism, please visit the
Link-O-Mat at <www.newhum.com>.**

Greider, William. "Work Rules." *The Soul of Capitalism: Opening Paths to a Moral Economy.* New
York: Simon and Schuster, 2003. 49–74.

Biographical information and quote drawn from William Greider's home page <http://
www.williamgreider.com/about/>.

Work Rules

Yes, the country is fabulously rich in material terms, but are Americans really free? The question itself sounds like civic heresy. It offends national pride and the promise of liberty expressed in our founding documents, but also runs counter to the twentieth-century history of political accomplishments that greatly expanded individual rights to cover once excluded groups. Yet the disturbing contradictions are visible everyday when people go to work. The loss of freedom goes largely unnoticed because it is so routinely part of their lives.

In pursuit of "earning a living" most Americans go to work for someone else and thereby accept the employer's right to command their behavior in intimate detail. At the factory gate or the front office, people implicitly forfeit claims to self-direction and are typically barred from participating in the important decisions that govern their daily efforts. Most employees lose any voice in how the rewards of the enterprise are distributed, the surplus wealth their own work helped to create. Basic rights the founders said were inalienable—free speech and freedom of assembly, among others—are effectively suspended, consigned to the control of others. In some ways, the employee also surrenders essential elements of self.

This stark imbalance of power is embedded in the standard terms of employment and properly described as a master-servant relationship, as economist David Ellerman puts it. Stripped of social coloring and modern legal restraints, the arrangement for work in contemporary America resembles the same terms that functioned during feudalism. But this is more than an echo from distant times. The employment system is the defining structure for maintaining a still dominant hierarchy among citizens, those with stunted rights and those with expansive power over others. Centuries ago, the feudal lord owned the land and all who worked or lived on his land were subject to his rule. In the present, these terms are typically assumed, less bluntly and brutally, by the firm that operates the factory, shop or office. Individual freedom, equitable relationships, and self-empowered lives are severely compromised still.

The description sounds too harsh, of course, because people in workplaces develop their own informal accommodations that soften the everyday interactions among them. The actual circumstances of work vary dramatically across different companies and sectors, from free-spirited and highly collaborative firms to the harsh systems of clockwork supervision that oppressively monitor every move and moment in a worker's day. For most Americans, nevertheless, the underlying reality is this: The terms of their rights, the quality of their work life, the tangible and intangible rewards are determined at the discretion of the employer. For better and for worse. Under feudalism, there were kind and caring lords and there were abusive lords. Either way, no one doubted his power to command the serfs.

Anyone may test this proposition for themselves. Ask yourself if it sounds right, ask others. Is work in America organized around a master-servant relationship? In my occasional random samplings, I have yet to encounter anyone who thinks the premise is wrong. Some pause to ponder the matter. Others respond instantly, of course. Isn't that obvious? I have put the question to managers and owners as well as rank-and-file employees; neither group wishes to argue the basic point. A recognition of these underlying terms seems jarring only because the relationship is so deeply internalized in nearly everyone's life expectations, just the way things are and probably immutable (unless one aspires to become the boss). Thus, despite great leaps forward in technological invention and productive efficiency, despite the rising abundance and various civil protections, the economic realm of work continues to function in distinctly premodern terms—master and servant—an arrangement that sets limits on human liberty as surely as the laws and the Constitution.

I start from this fundamental proposition because it is a bedrock source for so many of the largest discontents and disorders that continue to accompany the capitalist process in America, despite the presence of general prosperity. It is from this malformed power relationship that workers encounter often cruel confinements on their larger lives, the inequities and inequalities that warp and divide. The authorities typically attribute these consequences to "market forces," an abstraction that sounds neutral and objective. But the outcomes also emanate, more concretely, from a top-heavy structure of command and control in which those down below have little or no capacity to appeal or resist.

This feudal remnant helps to explain a lot about American life. It is an important subtext, though not the only one, for the persistent and growing inequalities of income and wealth, a lopsided and self-interested distribution of rewards by those in charge that redundantly favors those who already have great accumulations. It produces many stunting effects on people's life experiences that show up as stressful demands and insecurities imposed upon workers, often ensnaring well-paid professionals as well. A lack of voice and influence obviously injures people in the lower tiers most severely, but also spreads general damage—beyond the money—for many others who experience the deteriorating content of their own work. The inherent qualities and challenges in one's work—the source of much personal satisfaction and self-meaning—often are reengineered for greater efficiency, thereby degrading and sometimes destroying the coherence and integrity of what people do. The inner narrative of one's life often is embedded in one's work, in the satisfying routines and sense of fulfillment, in the sheer pleasure of doing things well. For many Americans, that story has been obliterated in the present age.

Social consequences flow from these conditions in many different directions: the longer working hours that tear up family life and weaken community; a broadening sense of sullen resignation that may feed social resentments and acquisitive envy; the continuing conflicts pitting workers against coworkers or against larger interests of the community. The most serious consequence, however, is political, not personal. It is the deleterious influence upon democracy itself.

Elaine Bernard of Harvard's trade union program explained the connection: "As power is presently distributed, workplaces are factories of authoritarianism polluting our democracy. Citizens cannot spend eight hours a day obeying orders and being shut out of important decisions affecting them, and then be expected to engage in a robust, critical dialogue about the structure of our society. Indeed, in the latter part of this [past] century, instead of the workplace becoming more democratic, the hierarchical corporate workplace model [came] to dominate the rest of society."

Where did citizens learn the resignation and cynicism that leads them to withdraw as active citizens? They learned it at the office; they learned it on the shop floor. This real-life education in who has power and who doesn't creates a formidable barrier to ever establishing an authentic democracy in which Americans are genuinely represented and engaged. The socialization of powerlessness is probably far more damaging to politics than the special-interest campaign money or the emptiness of television advertising. Indeed, both of those malign influences feed off the disillusionment.

Statistics do not capture the texture of these confinements very well. And sweeping generalizations are always misleading or wrong, given the vast diversity in Americans' work experiences. To make the point concretely, let me flash through some snapshots from American workplaces.

In Baltimore, Maryland, a service technician named Joseph Bryant is fired after twenty-four years with Bell Atlantic (now Verizon) because he refuses to work overtime on weekdays. Bryant couldn't stay late on the job. As a single parent, he had to pick up his kids from school by 6:00 P.M. His supervisors are unyielding. Bell Atlantic "rationalized" its workforce, reduced employment by 15 percent, and instructed the others to pick up the slack by working longer hours. Overtime pay is actually cheaper (more efficient) for a firm than hiring additional workers who collect full benefits. Bryant's union, the Communications Workers of America, wins his job back—one small victory for family life.

Middle-level managers, though presumably more powerful, frequently resent their unionized subordinates who seem to enjoy better job security and protections, according to Professor Russell L. Ackoff of the Wharton School of Business. When managements attempt to encourage greater teamwork—the celebrated Quality of Work Life movement—reforms are often sabotaged by midlevel personnel who were ignored in the discussions. "Their quality of work life is often worse than that of production workers," Ackoff explains. While genuine progress has been achieved by many companies, Ackoff cautions: "The QWL movement has not died, but it is in a coma."

In Georgetown, Kentucky, a young "team leader" at Toyota's plant denounces inhumane conditions at the factory, regularly rated the most efficient auto assembly plant in North America. "What I think we have here is a high-priced sweatshop," Tracy Giles tells me. "Four team members in my area were out of work for shoulder surgery. If you're a temp worker and you're injured, which happens a lot, you are sent home and there's another person waiting in line to get the job." At one point, a new time-motion study raised the output goals and speeded up assembly at his workstation where the workers lift forty-pound modules sixty-five times an hour. "We couldn't keep up, and my team members were practically passing out," he says. "I can't stand it; it makes me sick to my stomach. For me, as team leader, it's more of a moral dilemma than anything else."

In the little town of Martinsville, Virginia, one man announces that he has held forty-six jobs in the last three years. He has the pay stubs to prove it. He is a temp worker and the town of 14,000 has nine temporary employment agencies that hire out labor for a few days, a few weeks or months, to do low-wage assembly and packaging jobs. The transaction is more like a short-term rental, only it involves human labor instead of equipment, because the agency collects an overhead fee for each hour of work, ranging from 35 to 45 percent of the wage. Employers are willing to pay a higher cost for temp laborers because they are disposable. "We call it pimping people out," says Suzie Qusenberry, "because that's really what it is. 'I'm going to pimp you out for $8 an hour and all you're going to get is $5.35.' They take the money and you do the work. Isn't that just like pimping?"

If one jumps from a depressed backwater in Virginia to the leading edge of American industry, the fabulous, wealth-creating center known as Silicon Valley, there is a similar snapshot in high-tech production. Temp jobs are the valley's sixth-largest job sector. Major names like Hewlett Packard, Sun, and Apple "outsource" work to smaller component suppliers where the average wages are 30 percent lower. Until the high-tech bust halted expansion, the "virtual employer" was the area's second-fastest-growing source of employment. At one time, Microsoft in Seattle had a third of its employees on temp status, long-term employees who call themselves "permatemps" and wear orange badges instead of the regulars' corporate blue. Nearly 30 percent of American workers are now employed in so-called "nonstandard" jobs: temp workers, part-timers, contract employees, on-call and day laborers, or the self-employed. A minor portion have skill specialties and high-end wages. Most experience the opposite.

Efficiency obliterates identity, the sense of self-meaning in work, and not just for temp jobs or assembly lines. In Puget Sound, Boeing's 20,000 engineers and technicians staged a successful forty-day strike, but the central issue was not money. "Why the heck did we strike? At the highest level, it really was about respect, respect for what engineers do," says Charles Bofferding, executive director of the Seattle Professional Engineer Employees Association. A new, computerized design system was gumming up production. The white-collar engineers weren't consulted, though they possess intimate, problem-solving knowledge of how to build jet aircraft. "They did it the old-school way, brought in a big plan and said this is how it's going to be," Bofferding recalls. "We tried to insert ourselves and, well, we failed." The engineers, hurt personally and professionally, turn uncharacteristically belligerent. "We're not fighting to hurt Boeing, we're fighting to save it," the union leader explains. "It's all short-term thinking, everybody's focused on what the stock price is doing. You're not respected any more. The employees get squeezed. The reason we have design-built teams, integrative product teams, is because we know there are varying perspectives in the company and, unless you honor them all, you're going to come up with a suboptimized product. People matter. Our professionalism matters as well."

Doctors, pro athletes, airline pilots, graduate students—these and other esteemed professionals seek protection from rigid work structures or exploitative terms of employment. It is one of the perverse twists of modern prosperity that many who have very high incomes and the supposed leverage of highly specialized talents employ the collective power of unionization at a time when the older industrial unions are declining in size, some perilously. An AFL-CIO survey focused on the attitudes of young workers, union and nonunion, but uncovered a startling point about their elders: Most young people have hopeful expectations, as they should, but most employees over thirty-five years old have concluded that "working hard isn't enough any more because employers are not loyal." The longer one is employed, the more one knows about the masters. Social trust is among the casualties of work.

These snapshots suggest, among other things, that the brilliant technologies of modern life, while potentially empowering and democratizing, may be employed just as readily to deepen the confinements. Automation displaces workers, of course, but that is the idea: Labor-saving devices raise human productivity. For many firms, however, the new machines allowed them to disembowel the content of work, dumbing down the tasks and challenges by reducing workers to robotic functions. The electronic devices, likewise, enable managers to adopt oppressive systems of intimate control. A survey of business organizations by the American Management Association found that 78 percent use surveillance mechanisms to monitor their employees' communications and performance. "It's got to add stress when everyone knows their production is being monitored," one employer said. "I don't apologize for that."

The contemporary workplace is where energetic capitalism collides, most visibly, with the softer values of human existence. At a large Boston bakery, sociologist Richard Sennett found a grim contrast between the 1970s, when he first observed workers there, and the modernized bakery twenty years later. "In this high-tech, flexible workplace, where everything is user friendly, the workers felt personally demeaned by the way they work. . . . Operationally, everything is so clear; emotionally so illegible," Sennett wrote. He found the workers confused and sullen, indifferent to their work and colleagues, also with much lower wages. Punching computer icons is easier work, but it robs them of the logic and consequences in their actions. They no longer know how to bake bread; many never even see it. The automated ovens also produce lots of waste, daily mounds of misbaked, blackened loaves. Sennett found only one worker in the bakery resisting these "improvements," a Jamaican-born foreman who seemed perpetually angry, frustrated by the wastefulness and also by his fellow workers. "He told me he believed many of these problems could be sorted out if the workers owned the bakery," Sennett reported.

To recapitulate, the snapshots convey that the confinements on human dignity, equity, and self-worth are not restricted to the lower tiers of employment. The deteriorated quality and discontents are far more inclusive now. Their impact stretches upward on the ladder of occupational status and incomes, even to much admired and supposedly privileged stations. The reengineering of work has left many white-collar workers feeling bereft of security and satisfaction. The purposeful efficiencies of downsizing and restructuring are blind to the human identity of a chemical engineer as much as to that of a machinist or casual laborer.

The essential economic transaction modern management has performed, especially in larger companies where the leaders are more distant from the followers, is to shift the burdens of risk and cost from the firm to the employees, economic risks in many forms, but also the personal costs that cannot be counted up. "We did a lot of violence to the expectations of the American workforce," an executive vice president of General Electric acknowledged upon retirement.

Still, it is important to acknowledge the countervailing reality: Many Americans, myself included, are lucky enough to have found jobs we love, work so fulfilling and important to our identity we can't seem to get enough of it (family and friends sometimes see this devotion to work as an addictive disorder). In a perfect world, everyone would find satisfying work—regardless of skills or income—useful tasks that are rewarding in everyday, routine ways and draw out the best of what is within us. But envisioning an economic system where such satisfaction becomes broadly possible for all collides with our deep cultural prejudices. A condescending bias prevails in

American life, especially strong among the well-educated elites but also internalized by many working people, that presumes those who do "brain work" are somehow more meritorious than those who work with their hands.

"Our culture says, if your hands are involved, you can't have a brain," Ronald Blackwell, an AFL-CIO official and former clothing-union leader, observed. "The seamstress and the machinist and nearly every kind of job involves brain as well as hands, but the intellectual content of working with your hands is ignored."

Anyone who has closely observed a carpenter at work—or a seamstress, a machinist, or a truck driver, for that matter—will recognize Blackwell's point. Doing any job well requires abstract reasoning and a continuous process of thinking through choices, just as most intellectual work involves patterns of familiar repetitions and reflexive responses. A skillful brain surgeon might, for instance, be a less creative thinker than a skillful carpenter. A capable trash collector who performs his job effectively may experience greater satisfaction at work than an overwrought bond trader. If we had to decide which occupations the society cannot do without, some of us might choose trash collectors and carpenters over bond traders and brain surgeons.

The point is, the cultural stereotypes attached to work are arbitrary and create their own destructive social divisions. They are generally wrong—inferences made at a distance about people whom we do not know, based upon their status in the occupational hierarchies. Industrial capitalism organizes jobs and work in a broad-based, layered pyramid with a commanding pinnacle, just as feudalism did, though with more productive logic, the division of labor. The pecking order of work is a convenient artifact of capitalism, not the natural order of human existence.

These observations may simply deepen the despair for some readers. If white-collar professionals are as voiceless as blue-collar workers in influencing the conditions of their work, it seems even harder to imagine that anything can change. The first step toward remedy and action, however, is the recognition that there exists a broader, unacknowledged unity among very different working people in the nature of their shared powerlessness. To see this is not easy. It means backing off the familiar conceits and biases about one's status and abilities compared to others. It means accepting the possibility that people have a common self-interest deeper than class or income. It suggests fellow employees need to start talking with one another, despite the vast differences in their jobs and status.

The fundamental solution can be bluntly summarized: People must figure out how to "own" their own work. That is, individually and jointly, they own the place where they work. They accept responsibility, collectively, for the well-being of the firm. They authorize the managers who direct things, but all participate in the rule making and other important policy decisions.

They share the returns from the enterprise and agree upon the terms for sharing. None of these structural changes exempts anyone from the harrowing competition of capitalism or the demand for effective practices and productivity. Nor would this protect anyone from the normal human folly and error—the risks of loss and failure.

But does anyone doubt that, if employees acquired such self-governing powers, the terms of work would be reformed drastically in American business? Or that, if they owned the enterprise together, the rewards and risks would be reallocated in more equitable ways?

What follows is an exploration of this idea of self-ownership—the promise and the difficulties. The concept seems utterly remote to the standard terms of enterprise (and it is), but it is not utopian. Millions of Americans already work in such circumstances, or at least possess important aspects of shared control and responsibility. They are mutual owners of the firm and have a voice in running it. They work in employee-owned companies and cooperatives and partnerships or hybrid variations of all three. Some are highly paid professionals, some are assembly-line workers, some are clerks or janitors. They make it work—together—or they fail. The vision is most difficult to achieve, but many do succeed in practical reality. Running a successful business is difficult, and self-ownership is more so, because people must also alter their own attitudes and aspirations and develop new, more trusting relations among themselves. Profound change is always difficult, yet it is always required to reach the next important stage in human fulfillment.

The master-servant legacy embedded in modern enterprise poses a fundamental question: How can genuine individual freedom ever flourish except for a privileged few—or democracy ever be reconciled with capitalism—so long as the economic system functions along opposite principles, depriving people of rights and responsibilities, even denying their uniqueness as human beings? David Ellerman, an economist with the rare ability to apply moral philosophy to the underlying structure of economic life, has answered the question with an uncompromising argument. This power relationship is inherently illegitimate as a matter of natural law, Ellerman reasons, and is based upon "a legalized fraud." The "fraud" is the economic pretense that people can be treated as things, as commodities or machines, as lifeless property that lacks the qualities inseparable from the human self, the person's active deliberation and choices, the personal accountability for one's actions.

The fact that human beings have accepted this arrangement over the centuries—or were compelled to accept it—does not alter the unnaturalness. The fact that some people prefer mindless subservience to responsibility and self-realization does not confer legitimacy on their masters. Ellerman, formerly a staff economist at the World Bank, has devoted years to constructing a multilayered brief for "economic democracy," melding philosophy, law, and economics to illuminate long-existing fallacies. This discussion does not do justice to the rich complexity of his case but follows his lead in sorting out the fundamental terms. The ideological underpinnings are important to understand because they make clear why the structure of capitalism confines human existence illegitimately and how this might be transformed.*

The subservient nature of the work relationship has been papered over by myth and comforting metaphors, inherited "wisdom" generally accepted by society and firmly codified in its laws. But Ellerman poses an awkward question: What exactly makes the modern system so different from serfdom? The American republic, remember, originated in a Constitution that explicitly recognized the right to own people as private property. The institution of slavery, as a productive capital asset protected by law, was not abolished until the thirteenth amendment, less than 150 years ago. Social traces of the iniquity linger still.

Formal economics has an answer for Ellerman's question, though not one that satisfies his objection. "Workers may not be bought and sold, only rented and hired," Alfred Marshall, a preeminent economist in his time, wrote in 1920. Paul Samuelson, author of a standard textbook for present-day Economics 101, sticks to the same distinction. "Since slavery was abolished, human earning power is forbidden by law to be capitalized [bought and sold as property]," he wrote. "A man is not even free to sell himself; he must rent himself at a wage." The "rented" worker is certainly much better off than the "owned" worker, no question. Yet, as their language suggests, the distinction between slavery and freedom is narrower than supposed, and aspects of property still heavily influence the transaction. Human labor is treated as an input of production no different from the other inputs—machines, raw materials, buildings, capital itself—and these inputs are interchanged routinely in organizing the elements of production. Employees are now described as "human resources," the oddly dehumanizing usage adopted by modern corporations.

The trouble is, people are not things. They are autonomous human actors, not mere "resources." They cannot be reduced to physical inputs, even if they assent, because they are conscious, responsible agents of self, endowed with inalienable rights and inescapably liable for their behavior, legally and otherwise. Ellerman put the point in a way anyone can grasp: "Guns and burglary tools, no matter how efficacious and 'productive' they may be in the commission of a crime, will never be hauled into court and charged with the crime." Human beings, on the other hand, will be held accountable for their behavior

*David Ellerman's principal text is *Property & Contract in Economics: The Case for Economic Democracy*, Blackwell, 1992. Still largely unheralded, his work is beginning to draw respectful consideration among philosophers, though not yet from many economists.

in myriad ways because their actions carry a presumption of individual will and decision. "A hired killer is still a murderer even though he sold his labor," Ellerman observed. Thus, people cannot be "rented" anymore than they can be "sold" without presuming to detach them from the core of what makes them human. This point of collision with capitalism is what makes life and liberty seem incomplete to many Americans.

The violation of natural rights, Ellerman explained, is needed to sustain the fictitious relationship within a company that allows it to exclude the employees from any claim to the new wealth their labor creates—the product and profit of the enterprise. "The capitalist, like the slave owner, has used a legalized fraud, which pretends the worker is an instrument, to arrive at the position of being the 'owner of both instruments of production' [labor and capital] so he can then make a legally defensible claim on the positive product," Ellerman wrote. Workers collect "rent" on their time and exertions but, in most situations, the terms of employment do not allow them to share in the company profits—the surplus wealth their contributions have produced. This contractual reality helps explain the great redundancy of concentrated wealth that persists in American society, why the rich get richer. As the firm's insiders and investors, they own the entire output, both finished product and profit. The "rented" employees whose lives and knowledge are intimately engaged in the firm's functionings are entitled to none (unless the insiders decide to share).

The employment system is thus a main engine generating American inequality, and perhaps the most powerful one. Its functional structure effectively guarantees that the gross inequalities of income and wealth will endure in our society, largely unaltered and replicated for each new generation, despite any ameliorative actions by the government. The system is designed to produce this outcome. The steep ladder of personal incomes, from top to bottom, is reflected by the enormous and growing wage disparities in which the CEO earns more than five hundred times more than the company's average workers. But it is the harvesting of the profits exclusively by insiders and distant owners, instead of by the working employees, that has the greatest impact. This arrangement is not logically inevitable in capitalism—workers might own their own work and harvest the surpluses for themselves—but this is the format that blanketed American life a century ago as Americans moved from farm to factory, from self-employed work to the contract terms of wages and hours.

The contract for employment, its explicit and implied terms, determines these outcomes, but its central impact is obscured and mystified by the aura of property rights, a convenient veil inherited from the feudal order that lends a sense of customary correctness to the domination of labor by the owners of capital. The man who owns the factory, it is generally assumed, commands the workforce and collects the profits as a function of his rights as the property owner. This is an historical myth, in Ellerman's analysis, one that must be demolished if people are to see the situation clearly and recognize the opportunity for changing their condition.

"Marx bought the myth," Ellerman explained. That is, Karl Marx started from the same premise of property's mythological power over others. Whoever owns "the means of production" will rule under capitalism, he asserted (and gave the system its name). Thus, his theoretical solution involved abolishing private property and establishing state ownership of the productive assets. In theory, this would make everyone a "virtual" owner, though in fact they were in charge of neither their work nor their lives, as history has amply demonstrated. The idea that workers "rented" by a government-owned enterprise would be better off somehow—empowered—compared to workers "rented" by private capital was a central fallacy of communism. It failed the test of reality—spectacularly.

The fallacy is easier to recognize in modern capitalism than it was in Marx's time. Many large and successful companies today actually do not own great assets themselves. Their control derives from the insiders' role in organizing the contractual relationships among all of the various elements that contribute to production: the employees; the suppliers; the providers of capital; and the firm's controlling insiders, who may or may not own the factory or contribute much of their own capital to the enterprise. A firm's organizers, if they choose, may "hire" the land and buildings, "lease" the machines, "borrow" the capital or "sell" shares in their ownership, just as they "rent" the workforce. Property ownership, if things are organized shrewdly, is superfluous to their claim on the final product and profits.

The real basis for the insiders' power and their legal claim to the profits is their acceptance of responsibility for the firm, their contractual commitments to pay the costs of production and to absorb the negative consequences of losses and liabilities as well as the positive results. Employees, in a sense, are awarded an opposite status: irresponsibility in the fortunes of the company and, thus, no share in its success unless the management decides to grant one. In exchange for this privileged irresponsibility, workers are rendered powerless. They accept the master-servant status, are subject to the command of others, and have no voice in the company's management or any claim to its returns.

Stated in those stark terms, it does not sound like such a good deal. But understanding the basic contractual relationship prompts a liberating thought: Contracts can be changed. If the power is derived from the employment contract and not from inherited notions of property rights, then the active participants in a company might renegotiate their roles and responsibilities or even create a new firm that reflects a different balance of power. Ellerman describes the opportunity: "Instead of capital hiring labor, labor hires capital."

Labor hires capital? The role reversal seems beyond the plausible until one remembers that this transaction is approximately what does occur in many existing enterprises. The workers, in fact, borrow the capital to own and operate the firm themselves, then pay back their loans from the returns of the enterprise, an arrangement known as the employee-owned company. The ESOP transaction (for employee stock ownership plan) resembles a leveraged buyout in which company insiders borrow capital to take over a controlling position in company stock, then pay back creditors with the company's profits. Or workers form partnerships, like a law firm, collectively assuming responsibility and thus sharing in the governance and the returns. Or they create a cooperative enterprise that, roughly speaking, blends some elements of partnership and employee ownership.

The same essential reversal is present in all three cases: the workers are the "insiders" who organize the firm's contractual relationships; they accept shared responsibility for the firm and allocate the profits among themselves, not with absentee stockholders. The result, in Ellerman's words, is "people jointly working for themselves in democratic firms." Quite literally, they own their own work.

At the start of this new century, around 10 million Americans are worker-owners in some 11,000 employee-owned companies, with total assets of more than $400 billion. Thousands of cooperative enterprises also operate around the country, ranging from some 300 worker cooperatives in manufacturing and services to cooperative day-care centers and small banks to the mammoth agricultural marketing cooperatives owned collectively by the farmers who produce the foodstuffs. The professional partnerships— lawyers, doctors, architects, and others—incorporate similar principles, as do many small firms of the self-employed. These are the meaningful exceptions, however. Most Americans have no ownership of enterprise whatever. For those who do own stock shares, the "owners" are typically confined to a weak and attenuated status.

Self-ownership was the road not taken in American history. The cultural memory still enshrines independent yeomanry—the small farmer toiling in his own fields—but the modern organization of work largely obliterated those values.

It seems odd but necessary to point out that Americans did not always live like this. Just as my grandfather McClure proudly reported himself "unemployed" to the census taker in 1900, workers during the nineteenth century regarded wage employment as alien and inferior to their independent lives. They typically called it "wage slavery" because, as sociologist Charles Perrow has explained, "slavery was the closest thing to factory bureaucracy that people could conceive of; it was the closest precedent in history. Another precedent was also invoked—the military—and people referred to the 'industrial army' in attempting to describe the new situation." For a time, machinists and other craftsmen maintained independent worker-owned shops that sold their output to larger manufacturing firms, but these were gradually pushed aside. Just as the cultural meaning of "unemployed" changed, "free labor" was replaced in the language by "labor supply."

During the explosive rise of industrial capitalism in the second half of the nineteenth century, some organizations of workers, like the Knights of Labor and the American Federation of Labor's early formation, did fight for a larger vision based on worker and community ownership of enterprises, described as the alternative to "wage slavery." But those efforts were overwhelmed by the force and effectiveness of the emerging national corporations, both their scale and deft management of divisions of labor in industrial processes. Advocates of worker ownership lacked the means and resources to carry it out, or their vision seemed insufficiently militant for the ferocious fight underway with capitalists of that era. Led by guilds of skilled craftsmen, unions did fight for control of the workplace (and still do in some sectors), but the contest between labor and capital gradually devolved to the narrower conflicts over wages and job benefits. Labor's victories on these issues were an essential element in creating the broad middle-class prosperity of modern times.

Organized labor, which built the model for collective action in the first half of the twentieth century and mobilized workers to secure political rights for collective bargaining, has since withered greatly in size and power. Its ranks are reduced to 13.5 percent of the workforce overall and to only 9 percent in the private economy. Federal labor law is now archaic and confines workers rather than liberates them. It is used routinely by employers as a blunt instrument to thwart efforts to organize a collective voice, that is, a union. If union members tried to open conversations with middle managers about their shared discontents with the employer such talk would violate the National Labor Relations Act, which imposes legalistic and unnatural divisions upon the broad ranks of employees (in any case, the middle managers likely would be fired for consorting privately with union members). The companies' preferred antiunion weapon is fear—fear of being fired—and the NLRA provides very weak penalties that companies ignore with little consequence (20,000 U.S. workers are fired illegally for union organizing every year, according to Human Rights Watch). Management lawyers game the technicalities for years. When the fines are finally imposed, the fired workers are long gone, the organizing campaign has already been broken. Yet labor lacks the political power to reform the laws.

Labor's weakened position is reflected in the deteriorated terms and conditions of work for union and nonunion members alike. It suggests another discomforting acknowledgment: The mobilization of organized labor, at least as we have known it, has not proved an adequate response to the confining powers of American capitalism. Unions still do win important victories in many arenas, and renewed organizing energies in some unions may yet produce a turnaround in labor's strength. But, to prevail at this point in history, the ethos and spirit of collective action requires, ironically, a much more ambitious vision, one that might reignite sympathies and energies among Americans at large.

That agenda would start from a more fundamental perspective: attacking the compromised civil rights of working people and articulating a critique of the deteriorated conditions of work that speaks also for employees in the many occupations not covered by union protections. The case for self-ownership is a much better fit with present circumstances than it was for struggling workers a century ago. Employee ownership and self-management provide a plausible route toward eventually achieving greater wage equity, reforming the quality of work, and fostering accumulation of financial wealth among the many instead of the few. Eliminating the artificial dividing line between master and servant would open a vast new horizon of possibilities for individual fulfillment. The obvious problem with this approach is that it requires commitment to the long term—and enormous patience—at a time when most unions are embattled on many defensive fronts at once. Some unions are dispirited bureaucracies without hope or ambition and alienated from their rank-and-file members. Some union leaders assume, condescendingly, that their members are not interested in ownership and that the issue would merely undermine class consciousness, confusing the old labor refrain: Which side are you on?

The redeeming fact, however, is that some forward-looking labor leaders, often driven by necessity, have swung around impressively on the subject of ownership during the last few decades. Led by former president Lynn R. Williams, the United Steelworkers of America, one of the most embattled "old industry" unions, became the pioneer twenty years ago in engineering employee takeovers of troubled companies, retaining viable plants that larger corporations were discarding and saving thousands of jobs as well as valuable productive assets. Unions now actively engaged in employee ownership and worker takeovers range from machinists to papermakers, from autos to clothing and textiles. The largest employee-owned company is the troubled United Airlines that along with other major airlines filed for bankruptcy in 2002. The machinists' and pilots' unions are together the majority shareholders with seats on the board, but United got into deep financial trouble for approximately the same reasons as its competitors. The unions ostensibly have controlling power, but they have not yet figured out how to assert their power effectively or to reform United's corporate strategy and management behavior.

On the fringes of organized labor some rank-and-file activists are searching for a larger vision. "Imagine that in place of our half-century-old labor law . . . we had a labor law based on the constitutional rights of free speech, assembly and labor freedom," the Labor Party, an allied political group, declared. The new labor law, the party suggested, would be based on legal principles found in the thirteenth amendment abolishing involuntary servitude.

In any case, the idea of self-ownership no longer belongs to labor alone, and unions are not present in the overwhelming majority of employee-owned firms. Given the many obstacles that burden unions, this transformation is often led by managers and owners. The idea does not belong to either left or right. Indeed, in an earlier era, some enlightened leaders of capitalism shared the progressive vision that corporations might someday be owned entirely by their employees. Owen D. Young was CEO of General Electric in the 1920s when he described the dream: "Perhaps someday we may be able to organize the human beings in a particular undertaking so that they truly will be the employer buying capital as a commodity in the market at the lowest possible price. It will be necessary for them to provide an adequate guarantee fund in order to buy the capital at all. If that is realized, the human beings will be entitled to all the profits over the cost of capital. I hope that day may come when the great business organizations will truly belong to the men who are giving their lives and their efforts to them, I care not in what capacity." Labor hires capital. Workers reap the new wealth. General Electric was a very different company in those days.

The temporary employment agency called Solidarity provides a dramatic illustration of what can happen to ordinary people when they assume the role of owners (so dramatic, in fact, some readers may find it hard to believe). The temp agency operates in Baltimore, Maryland, and is organized as a cooperative. It belongs to the same temp workers it sends out everyday to fill various short-term jobs. They work at the city convention center arranging chairs and setting tables for huge banquets or do light manufacturing jobs or rehab old buildings or fill temps slots at small businesses, hotels, and construction sites. These men come from the "inner city" and the loose pool of workers once known as "casual labor"—the very bottom of the American job ladder. The vast majority of them are recovering narcotics addicts and/or have criminal records and time in prison.

Their firm is thriving and expanding. They earn wages a dollar or two an hour higher than rates paid by competing temp agencies plus they have health insurance coverage. When a new client seeks to hire their labor, Solidarity workers go out to check the employer first and inspect the terms and conditions of work. At year's end the regulars will receive a bonus check from the firm's profits, typically several thousand dollars each. None of these men expect to get rich (some saw a lot more cash when they were dealing drugs), but the idea of owning something themselves is a powerful experience.

"Naturally, when it's your company, your productivity is bound to go up—it belongs to you," said Curtis Brown, a forty-seven-year-old worker who had scuffled in low-wage jobs since he was seventeen. "It's not us against them; it's all us. You're all fighting against the same thing. I've seen guys, I know myself, glad to go to work, happy to go to work. Everybody's working to get the job right."

Oddly enough, their personal troubles turned out to be an asset for the firm. Workers know each other from the streets, but mainly from attending the same Narcotics Anonymous meetings. "How I would I describe it? It's almost like a spiritual thing among the guys," Brown explains. "A lot of us knew each other. When a new guy comes in, we usually recognize him. We seen him in the rooms." "In the rooms" is their phrase for identifying a fellow Narcotics Anonymous member who attends meetings, someone who's been through the same fire and is working on the struggle for personal redemption. Within the cooperative, this powerful subculture has been a source of trust and teamwork, but also for self-discipline. Nobody cons others who are also "in the rooms."

Avis Ransom, an idealistic MBA graduate who left her business consulting career to manage Solidarity, found the firm has competitive advantage in its shared ethos of "self-policing in the workplace—one employee going to another and telling him, 'You're goofing off; start working.' When we started out, our members would come to work and get in prayer circles outside the convention center. Workers from the other [temp] agencies would join them, sometimes even managers. We began to see how easy it was to take workers and jobs from our competitors." Solidarity regularly trains workers and pays the seasoned ones to serve as teachers. It increases the level of training as the firm gains better jobs—do simple math, swing a hammer, read a shop-floor plan. Workers meet every two weeks to air out complaints and share ideas. Not all of them survive the self-criticism. They are not ready to meet the cooperative's standards.

"The greatest problems," Ransom explains, "are workers don't show up on time. They don't show up in the numbers ordered. The client orders ten; eight show up. Or they don't show up work ready. They're sleepy or high or badly dressed or unclean. We called a meeting of workers, maybe twenty or so, and explained these problems. They said, We can fix that. If we have to start work at two, tell us to report at one. If they need twenty people, send twenty-five and, if they don't need the extra workers, send them home with two hours' pay. Now we call it show-up pay. They said, We don't want our clients to see us as not work ready, so you screen us at the work site. Pick out the ones who aren't ready and send them home. We started doing that for every job and it got to the point where we were regularly sending extra people and they would get hired because people from the other agencies didn't show up. We've got an excellent reputation with our clients."

Solidarity made a profit its second year—$50,000—and Ransom called the members together to announce the good news. "The workers made it clear to me: This was *their* money; they had already earned it," she said. "But they wanted to keep the money in the company to develop more alliances with businesses and get a stronger foothold in the industry. For folks who are making eight dollars an hour, that's a phenomenal decision." Profits rose fourfold in the third year and workers collected profit shares based on how many hours they had worked.

It should be obvious that, in these humble circumstances, the workers could not have launched this alone. They had an experienced and influential sponsor in BUILD, a community organization that for twenty-five years has mobilized Baltimore's citizens and neighborhoods, drawn together from black and white churches across the city, to push their own civic agenda of housing, education, and other concerns. BUILD launched the nation's first "living wage" campaign and won a city ordinance boosting incomes for low-wage employees of public contractors and suppliers, an idea that has since spread across the country. Affiliated with the Industrial Areas Foundation's nationwide network of sixty-three grassroots organizations, BUILD adheres to the IAF's "iron rule": "Never do anything for people that they can do for themselves—never." In this case, the organizers patiently canvassed the city's powerless temp workers and helped some of them take the leap to a self-owned firm. BUILD provided a $35,000 line of credit and used its political clout to persuade some public agencies and private employers to become the first clients.

Solidarity, though still fragile like any small start-up, is expanding laterally into new fields of employment and moving workers upward in skills and income. An environmental consultant trained the workers to do the work on a major contract refitting public buildings for energy efficiency: caulking, weather stripping, and other tasks. In exchange, the workers "carried" the contractor for a few weeks during his own early cash-flow problems by temporarily deferring half their pay. Rehab work on church-sponsored halfway houses (a place these men had passed through themselves) is being done by Solidarity members as both workers and contractors.

This is small stuff, to be sure, but it illustrates how, with self-ownership, the work itself can become a leveraging asset. One by one they were hapless temp workers tumbling in and out of jobs. Collectively they possess a little bargaining power to open more doors for the cooperative and to ratchet up the content and value of their own work. This sort of transaction requires business savvy, but also a strong foundation of trust. Solidarity draws inspiration and a model from Mondragon, a much-celebrated network of more than one hundred cooperatives in the Basque region of northern Spain, where workers share ownership and returns in scores of affiliated enterprises, from small manufacturing companies to a major supermarket chain. Mondragon has no stockholders, but relies upon its own self-financing bank and a strong fabric of mutual support among its many small parts.

Collectively, Mondragon resembles a powerful business corporation with more than 20,000 employees.

Solidarity's lead organizers, Arnold Graf and Jonathon Lange, have a larger, less tangible vision: changing the culture of work in Baltimore, starting from the bottom up and eventually affecting others far up the line. They have been scouting for a building convenient to main bus lines that BUILD could turn into a "workers center," a service center and social hall for low-wage workers and their families, equipped with recreational materials and a library, computers and a chapel, music and art, a barbershop and banking services. BUILD may not have the resources to start its own bank like Mondragon, but they are talking to local bankers about forming a self-interested alliance—a worker-friendly bank.

"There's such a terrific breakdown in community places, nowhere for people to come together and call it their own," Graf says. "What excites me is trying to change the culture of what people expect from the economy, what they consider the nature of work. Do I have a right to a living wage and a job where I have something to say about decisions? Or is it just the boss? These are concrete ways of rebuilding community through different aspects of work. We had originally thought about community in terms of the neighborhoods, but we are beginning to see a different kind of vision—the community that is based in work." Solidarity's organizing activities resemble what aggressive labor unions in garment making and other sectors did for low-wage and immigrant members three generations ago. "Somebody accused us of trying to reinvent the wheel," Lange said, "but we take pride in that."

Actually, the example of Solidarity makes the cooperative process seem easier than it is. These working men, after all, may have needed some outside help, but they did not need to create a culture of trust and self-criticism. They already had absorbed that "in the rooms." Mondragon, likewise, is a brilliant model of successful cooperatives but draws power from the unique separateness of the Basque people, an embattled minority struggling to preserve its cultural integrity while also achieving prosperity. In the American experience, immigrant groups similarly rely upon ethnic solidarity—pooling their meager resources and sacrifices—to build something real for themselves. Muslims and Koreans today, Irish, Italian, and Jews in yesteryear.

Given the splintered condition of America's social relations, this is very hard work in most circumstances—constructing a social texture that binds people together in mutual trust and endeavors—and it is especially difficult within large, complicated business organizations. Teamwork is an elusive quality and cannot be faked (nor bought and sold). Modern Americans are remarkably capable people, skillful and inventive in many ways, but they are not so good at talking to one another across their vast differences of social class and economic status. Shared ownership may make it easier to have

such conversations and encourage trust but, paradoxically, shared ownership is unlikely to succeed unless the trust becomes real.   ■

■ QUESTIONS FOR MAKING CONNECTIONS WITHIN THE READING ■

1. Using your own reading of "Work Rules" rather than a dictionary, explain
   what Greider means by "the socialization of powerlessness"? What does
   "socialization" involve, and how do people become "socialized" into one
   way of life or another? If most people are indeed powerless on the job,
   why do so many of them indicate high rates of job satisfaction in polls? Is
   job satisfaction the same thing as autonomy? Is job satisfaction inconsistent with a master-servant relationship?

2. After paying particular attention to Greider's discussion of Karl Marx,
   would you say that Greider is a Marxist? Does Greider make an argument
   in favor of private property, or against it? Are worker-owned businesses
   less consistent with the free market than corporations owned by entrepreneurs and stockholders? Are corporations in some ways less consistent
   with free market ideals than worker-owned companies?

3. The subtitle to the book from which this excerpt was taken is "Opening
   Paths to a Moral Economy." In what ways might the treatment of people
   as things—which David Ellerman refers to on p. 220—contribute to the
   erosion of ethical codes that healthy societies depend on? What might
   Greider have in mind when he argues for a "moral economy"? Aren't all
   economies "amoral," that is, morally neutral? What would be the characteristics of an "immoral" economy?

■ QUESTIONS FOR WRITING ■

1. Greider refers to his grandfather McClure, who "proudly reported himself 'unemployed' to the census taker in 1900." Investigate the work history of your own family. If you can, find out something about what your
   grandparents did for a living, and also about the conditions under which
   they labored. Would you say that you enjoy more prosperity than they
   did? More personal freedom? More security? Does your family's experience confirm, complicate, or contradict Greider's argument?

2. Will worker-owned businesses really solve the problem of citizens' powerlessness? Drawing on the examples that Greider provides—United Airlines and Solidarity—discuss the economic obstacles that stand in the
   way of workplace equality. In a worker-owned company, will employees
   still need to "rent" themselves? If one purpose of a business is to compete
   with other businesses, what pressures work against the achievement of

worker equality? In what ways might worker equality provide a competitive advantage?

■ *QUESTIONS FOR MAKING CONNECTIONS BETWEEN READINGS* ■

1. In "America's Other Drug Problem," Arnold Relman and Marcia Angell
   describe the economic forces that drive innovation in the pharmaceuticals
   industry. If drug companies were transferred to worker ownership,
   would that arrangement make any difference in the behavior of the companies in the marketplace? In other words, would the company be able to
   say no to highly profitable innovations that might actually be less effective than the older drugs they replace?

2. Judging from Greider's discussion, would you say that worker-owned
   businesses would help to make society more democratic? In what ways
   might they help to rectify the problems that Lani Guinier describes in
   "Second Proms and Second Primaries: The Limits of Majority Rule"? To
   what degree might worker-owned businesses have problems closely comparable to those that Guinier describes? If worker-owned businesses operate according to the principle of "majority rule," are they likely to be
   any more empowering than privately owned corporations?

www **For additional suggestions about making connections between readings,
visit the Link-O-Mat and More Sample Assignments at <www.newhum.com>.**

LANI GUINIER

LANI GUINIER [gwen-'ēr] rose to national prominence in 1993 when she was nominated by President Bill Clinton to fill the post of Assistant Attorney General for Civil Rights in the U.S. Justice Department. At the time of her nomination, Guinier was a professor at the University of Pennsylvania Law School and was primarily known in academic circles for having written extensively on how the electoral system might be reformed to better represent all of the nation's citizens in local, state, and national governing bodies. Within weeks of being nominated, however, Guinier found herself regularly pilloried in the press as the "quota queen" and, eventually, had her nomination withdrawn by Clinton who declared her ideas to be "undemocratic."

In an interview that followed shortly afterward, Guinier reflected on the experience of having had her ideas distorted and of having been deprived a chance to defend her positions: "I would like to think that I stood on principle and that I didn't lose. I lost a job, . . . but I have a job for life [as a professor with tenure]. So [having the nomination withdrawn] really wasn't about my personal story but about the larger story of what my experience meant for the American people and our inability to have a genuine, meaningful conversation about race without name-calling and finger-pointing." Guinier has subsequently published a series of books that outline her commitment to what she terms in "Second Proms and Second Primaries" "the ideal of democracy," including *The Tyranny of the Majority: Fundamental Fairness in Representative Democracy* (1995); *Lift Every Voice: Turning a Civil Rights Setback into a New Vision of Social Justice* (1998); and with Gerald Torres, *The Miner's Canary: Enlisting Race, Resisting Power, Transforming Democracy* (2002).

The first African American woman to be appointed to the faculty at Harvard University Law School, Guinier is particularly sensitive to the limits of

Guinier, Lani. "Second Proms and Second Primaries: The Limits of Majority Rule," *Boston Review*. Oct./Nov. 1992. 32–34.

Quotations and biographical information from Lani Guinier, "An Interview with Brian Lamb," 26 June 1994 <http://www.booknotes.org/transcripts/10199.htm>; Lani Guinier, "A 'Commonplace' Conversation with Lani Guinier," interview by Lise Funderburg. *African American Review*, 30(1996):196–204.

a political system that embraces "the worst excesses of the adversarial model of litigation, the 'winner take all' model of sports, and the 'only one of you is going to be left standing' model of war." By focusing on race, voting rights, and representation, Guinier has sought to revive national discussion about the meaning of democracy in an increasingly heterogeneous world: What is the meaning of democracy, Guinier asks, if voting minorities have no way to make their voices heard?

`www` **To learn more about Lani Guinier and the Civil Rights movement, visit the Link-O-Mat at <www.newhum.com>.**

Second Proms and Second Primaries: The Limits of Majority Rule

Brother Rice High School held two senior proms last spring. It was not planned that way. The members of the prom committee at Brother Rice, a boy's Catholic high school in Chicago, expected just one prom when they hired a disc jockey, picked a rock band, and selected music for the prom by consulting student preferences. Each senior was asked to list his three favorite songs, with the understanding that the band would play the songs that appear most frequently on the lists.

Sounds attractively democratic. But Brother Rice is predominantly white, and last year's senior prom committee was all white. That's why they ended up with two proms. The black seniors at Brother Rice felt so shut out by the "democratic process" that they organized their own prom. As one black student put it: "For every vote we had, there were eight votes for what they wanted. . . . [W]ith us being in the minority we're always outvoted. It's as if we don't count." Some embittered white seniors saw things differently. They complained that the black students should have gone along with the majority: "The majority makes a decision. That's the way it works."

In a way, both groups were right: with majority rule and a racially organized majority, "we don't count" is the "way it works" for minorities. In a racially divided society majority rule is not a reliable instrument of democracy. That's a large claim, and one I don't base solely on the actions of the prom committee in one Chicago high school.

In a recent voting rights suit in Arkansas, I represented some black plaintiffs in a case that turned, in the end, less on legal technicalities than on the relationship between democracy and majority rule. The failure to challenge traditional assumptions about that relationship—to show that majority rule is sometimes unfair—sealed the defeat of the plaintiffs. With the Arkansas case as background, I will discuss the standard remedy that courts use when black plaintiffs win in voting rights cases—to establish a majority black electoral district. This strategy of "race conscious districting" is, I believe, an inadequate method for representing minority interests.

But if a group is unfairly treated when it forms a racial minority within a single district, and, if we cannot combat the unfairness by setting up a new district in which the racial minority is now a majority, then what is to be done? The answer is that we need an alternative to majoritarianism: a "principle of proportionality" that transcends winner-take-all majority rule and better accommodates the values of self-government, fairness, deliberation, compromise, and consensus that lie at the heart of the democratic ideal.

The Case of the Majority Vote Run-off

Phillips County is a predominantly rural, economically depressed county in Arkansas. Majority black in population, it is majority white both in voting age population and in registered voters. According to the 1980 census, 53 percent of the 34,772 residents are black; but blacks constitute only 47 percent of the county voting age population. Despite this representation in the population, blacks in the county have never had much political power. In fact, since Reconstruction, no black has ever been nominated to any countywide office in Phillips County.

According to Sam Whitfield and the other plaintiffs in the case of *Whitfield, et al.* vs. *State Democratic Party,* the Arkansas law regulating primary elections bears a significant share of the responsibility for the lack of black political power. The law requires that a candidate receive a "majority of all the votes cast for candidates for the office" in order to win the party's nomination. If no candidate wins a majority in the first round of primaries, then the two leading candidates face each other in a run-off election two weeks later. The plaintiffs alleged that the majority requirement deprived black voters in Phillips County of an equal opportunity to elect the candidates of their choice—a violation of Section 2 of the Voting Rights Act of 1965 (as amended in 1982).

The cornerstone of their argument was the historical pattern of racially polarized voting in Phillips County: white voters vote exclusively for white candidates and black voters for black candidates. So if more than one white candidate sought a nomination, the white vote would be divided and the black candidate might win the support of a plurality by winning all the votes cast by black voters. But there would be no chance for a black candidate to win a majority of the votes for nomination. The majority requirement would, then, force a run-off two weeks later. And in the run-off, the whites would close ranks and defeat the black candidate.

In 1986 and 1988, for example, four blacks came in first as plurality winners in preferential primaries, only to be defeated by racially polarized voting in run-offs. In neither the first or second primary did any white person publicly support or endorse a black candidate. In fact, Rev. Julius McGruder, black political candidate and former school board member, testified on the basis of 15 years working in elections that "no white candidate or white person has came out and supported no black." When Sam Whitfield won a first primary and requested support from Kenneth Stoner, a white candidate he defeated in the first round, Stoner told him that "He could not support a black man. He lives in this town. He is a farmer. His wife teaches school here and that there is just no way that he could support a black candidate."

But racially polarized voting is only one of the political disadvantages for blacks in Phillips County. Blacks also suffer disproportionately from poverty, and that poverty works to impede their effective participation in the run-off primary. For example, 42 percent of blacks lack any vehicle, while only nine percent of the white population are similarly handicapped; and 30 percent of blacks—compared to 11 percent of whites—have no telephone. Isolated by this poverty, black voters are less able to maneuver around such obstacles as frequent, last minute changes in polling places—moving them to locations up to twelve to fifteen miles away, over dirt and gravel roads. Moreover, because of the number of blacks without cars, the lack of public transportation in the county, and the expense of taxis, the run-off election campaigns of black candidates must include "a get-out-and-vote kind of funding effort where we try to have cars to drive people to the polls."

Getting people to the polls a second time within a two-week period severely limits the resources of black candidates, who have difficulty raising money a second time, paying for advertisements, notifying their supporters of the run-off election, and then convincing their supporters to go back to the polls a second time. Rev. McGruder testified that the run-off "just kill[s] all of the momentum, all of the hope, all of the faith, the belief in the system." According to McGruder, many voters "really can't understand the situation where you say 'You know, Brother Whitfield won last night' and then come up to a grandma or my uncle, auntie and say 'Hey, you know, we're going to have to run again in the next 10 days and—because we've got a run-off.'"

In fact, between the first and second primary, turn-out drops precipitously, so that the so-called majority winner in the run-off may receive fewer votes than the black plurality winner in the first primary. For example, 1,893 fewer people voted in the run-off for County Judge in 1986 than in the first primary; and 1,725 fewer people voted in the 1986 circuit clerk run-off. In fact, in all three black/white run-off contests in 1986, the white run-off victor's majority occurred only because the number of people who came out to vote in the second primary went down.

The District Court that heard the 1988 challenge to the Arkansas law did not dispute the facts: that no black candidate had ever been elected to county-wide or state legislative office from Phillips County, and that "race has frequently dominated over qualifications and issues" in elections. Nevertheless, the court rejected the challenge to the majority requirement.

In the first place, the Court argued that the run-off requirement could not itself be blamed for the dilution of black voting strength. To be sure, bloc-voting by the white majority consistently prevented a relatively cohesive black population from nominating or electing their chosen representatives. But, the Court argued, that problem could not be solved by eliminating the run-off. On the contrary, if white candidates were stripped of the protection provided by the run-off, they would simply limit their numbers in the first round, self-selecting one white to run head-to-head against a black. So eliminating the run-off would "tend to perpetuate racial polarization and bloc-voting."

More fundamentally, however, the Court's decision was based more on its enthusiasm for the majority vote requirement than on its skepticism about the benefits of removing that requirement. Majority rule lies at "the very heart of our political system"; the requirement in the primaries was "not tenuous but, to the contrary, strong, laudable, reasonable, and fair to all." For a court to invalidate a majority vote requirement would undermine the operation of democratic systems of representation because "Americans have traditionally been schooled in the notion of majority rule. . . . [A] majority vote gives validation and credibility and invites acceptance; a plurality vote tends to lead to a lack of acceptance and instability."

The central place of majoritarianism in the Court's perception of the case can be highlighted with one more piece of background. Courts do, of course, sometimes invalidate voting schemes on the ground that those schemes deny a minority "an equal opportunity" to nominate or elect "candidates of their choice." In such cases, the court aims to ensure that all groups have some opportunity to have their interests represented in the governing body. For example, when an existing district has a black minority the standard remedy is to establish a subdistrict with a black majority in which blacks can elect representatives of their choice. By creating pockets in which minorities are majorities, race conscious districting provides a remedy for underrepresentation that respects the concerns of minorities while affirming the dominance of the majority principle.

But there was a problem with the standard remedy in Phillips County: the majority vote requirement applied to elections for seven county-wide positions. So each position represented the *entire* electorate. In such a circumstance, several courts have said that the statute does not apply. There can be no equal opportunity to elect because there is "no share" of a single-person office. Modifying an electoral structure to create alternative subdistrict majorities is not plausible where the majority vote rule applies to single-person offices.

With subdistricting ruled out, the only possible remedy then, would have been for the court to require the replacement of the majority require- ment with a plurality system. And that is precisely what the plaintiffs asked the Court to do. But—and here we return to the main point—the Court would not require a plurality scheme because of its own conception of the central place of majoritarianism in democracy. While a plurality win in many cases is quite conventional, to order it as a remedy opened up possi- bilities of non-majoritarianism that the Court found quite threatening. With a plurality system unacceptable, and subdistricting unavailable, the Court had no remedy for the plaintiffs. Absent a remedy, the Court found no violation.

At bottom then, the case was about democracy and majority rule. The Court denied relief because it identified democracy with majority rule. In fact, the Court actually suggested that if plaintiffs lost an election, their in- terpretation of the Act would require the Court simply to suspend elections. Where the Court saw democracy, however, the plaintiffs saw rule by a white numerical majority. As a numerical and stigmatized minority, they regarded the majority vote requirement as simply a white tool to "steal the election"— a tool that had the effect of demobilizing black political participation, en- hancing polarization rather than fostering debate and, in general, excluding black interests from the political process.

In short, the Court's conclusions were supported less by the evidence in Phillips County than by the Court's own majoritarian conception of democ- racy. To win the case then, the plaintiffs needed directly to challenge this premise about the intimate link between majority rule and democracy.

For example, they might have argued that majority rule is legitimate only when it is fair, and not simply because it is desirable to make decisions whose supporters outnumber their opponents. The conventional case for the fairness of majority rule, however, is that it is not really the rule of a fixed group—The Majority—on all issues; instead it is the rule of shifting majori- ties, as the losers at one time or on one issue join with others and become part of the governing coalition at another time or on another issue. So the argument for the majority principle connects it with the value of reciprocity: you cooperate when you lose in part because members of the current major- ity will cooperate when you win and they lose. The result will be a fair system of mutually beneficial cooperation.

But when a prejudiced majority excludes, refuses to inform itself about, or even seeks to thwart the preferences of the minority, then majority rule loses its link with the ideal of reciprocity, and so its moral authority. As the plaintiffs' evidence conclusively demonstrated, this was precisely the situa- tion in Phillips County, where the fairness of the majority requirement was destroyed by the extreme racial polarization, the absence of reciprocity, and the artificial majorities created in the run-offs.

Racial Districting

Under conditions of sharp racial division then, majority rule can serve as an instrument to suppress a minority. It is not a fair way to resolve disagreements because it no longer promises reciprocity. That is what we learn from Brother Rice High School and Phillips County, Arkansas.

How can this unfairness be remedied? Perhaps through a more vigorous application of the conventional remedy of race-conscious districting. As indicated earlier, this remedy is not applied when—as in Phillips County—there is a system of district-wide, single-person offices rather than a collective decision-making body with multiple seats. But in the face of evidence of racial subordination, courts could simply reject such arrangements, require a system of subdistricts, and then ensure that some subdistricts have, for example, a black majority.

This strategy of judicially imposing alternative electoral constituencies is in fact consistent with some understandings of the Voting Rights Act. But instead of dwelling on legal issues, since race-conscious districting is, like any system of winner-take-all, flawed as a method for ensuring a fair system of political representation—I'll argue and evaluate the conventional remedy on three tests of political fairness from the perspective of minority interests: Does a system mobilize or discourage participation? Does it encourage genuine debate or foster polarization? Does it promise real inclusion or only token representation? Race-conscious districting does not do well on any of these three dimensions. While it may be true that no election structure alone can do all that I envision, we need to consider alternatives to single-member districts—in particular, to consider systems of proportional representation, which promise politically cohesive minorities both potential electoral success *and proportionate influence* throughout the extended political process. But I'm jumping ahead. First we need to see the problems with establishing geographically defined, race-conscious districts, each of which elects a single member to a representative body.

Firstly, *districting fails to mobilize sustained voter participation.* Districting systems rely on geography as a tool for identifying voter interests. Voters are assigned to territorial constituencies, the assumption being that territorial contiguity is associated with a community of interest.

Moreover, districting assumes that smaller political units best fulfill the political empowerment and equality norms of American constitutional jurisprudence. With smaller units, it's easier for constituents to identify political leaders, easier to recognize communities of interest, and easier to participate. Also, safe black districts enable blacks to get elected and then re-elected leading to positions of seniority and status within the elected body.

At the same time, however, single member districts emphasize individual candidacies, and for this reason may demobilize poor black and Latino

voters. Turn-out generally goes up in response to first time election opportunities for the candidate of choice of the minority community. But the mobilization efforts for these break-through elections are generally not repeated. As the black pioneer becomes the incumbent, turn-out drops.

Moreover, politics in geographically organized, winner-take-all electoral
districts tend to develop an exclusively electoral focus. The result is that the
core constituency becomes alienated given the absence of local, alternative
community organizations to educate and mobilize constituent participation
outside of elections. Indeed, once elected, incumbents may demobilize constituents by not maintaining a genuine, community-based political organization to provide feedback, ideas, and reinforcement to the elected official
while in office.

Furthermore, given racially-polarized voting, single-member districts
give rise to real gains only to the extent there is substantial residential segre-
gation at the appropriate geographic scale. Thus, for Latinos who live in dispersed barrios, districting does not capture either their real or potential
power. In addition, it may exacerbate intergroup conflict as minorities are
pitted against each other in a fight to be "the group" who gets the district. In
jurisdictions with a complicated racial, ethnic, and linguistic mix, the redistricting struggle often becomes a source of conflict between blacks and other
minority voters. These groups may compete over how many minority districts should be created and who should control them. Each group is encouraged to assert its superior moral, historic, and pragmatic claim. But in the
lottery of competing oppression, no one wins.

Single-member districts also tend to under-represent minority voters,
even where some race-conscious districts are created. Unless minority voters are both large enough and concentrated "just right," they will not enjoy
representation in proportion to their presence in the population. Thus after
a decade of race-conscious districting, blacks are not proportionately represented in any of the Southern legislatures.

Districting then, is limited as a strategy of empowerment. It is also troubling because it denies the connection between empowerment and voluntary participation. Districts are drawn by professionals without any involvement by voters. The presumption is that their political interests can be
identified by their residential choices. The process of creating districts,
which may be accompanied by extensive but perfunctory public hearings, is
dominated by incumbent self-interest or court-appointed experts with no
particular tie to grassroots concerns. By removing the issue from the voter,
the districting process is antithetical to empowerment strategies based on
voter participation and voter choice.

Furthermore, districting assumes that even where voters' interests are
not represented by the ultimate district winner, their real interests will somehow indirectly get represented. Consider an earlier Supreme Court case,
UJO v. Carey. Hasidic Jews in Brooklyn challenged a legislative plan on the

grounds that it discriminated against them by employing race-conscious districting. The Court denied the claim, holding that the challenged plan conveyed no stigma or disadvantage and so was not unconstitutional. In arriving at this conclusion, the Court in effect treated the Hasidim as just another group of white voters. The Court argued that white voters were proportionately represented state-wide, so drawing districts to represent blacks did not disadvantage whites—even a white, Hasidic minority within a majority black district. This argument assumes that voters are interchangeable, that the courts can override voters' self-categorizations, and that the courts know better than the voters when their real interests are represented.

Secondly, *districting fails to foster genuine debate about issues.* In geographic districts, the threshold of representation is put close to 50 percent because districts are winner-take-all. The idea is that the winning candidate must demonstrate significant support to justify gaining *all* the power, but this pushes candidates toward the middle of the political spectrum where most of the votes are. The focus on developing consensus prior to the election means that issues are often not fully articulated or debated. Candidates avoid controversial positions and instead offer palliatives designed to offend no one.

Furthermore, the fact that interests within the district are only represented to the extent they garner majority support dooms third political parties to perpetual defeat. Because parties only win anything if they win a majority, and because it is difficult for a third party to win a majority, voters are reluctant to "throw away" their votes on third party candidates. And this in turn narrows the scope of political debate.

By promoting only two real choices, winner-take-all districting also has created an environment conducive to negative campaigning. A system that fosters two-way races is the "basis for such tried-and-true strategies as driving up the negatives of [an opponent] without worrying that the defecting voters will turn to a relatively unsullied third candidate," a common occurrence in three-way races. Negative campaign tactics contribute to voter alienation and apathy.

And thirdly, *districting fails to promote opportunities for more than token inclusion.* Proponents of race-conscious districting believe that separate can be made equal, or at least that poor blacks are empowered when provided a choice to elect a representative accountable only to them. Thus, they assume that electoral control works as a proxy for interest.

Creating majority black, predominantly poor districts is one way to ensure at least physical representation of black interests. This makes sense to the extent that electoral control insures accountability and influence. But racial districting also means that the electoral success of white legislators in white districts is not dependent on black votes. The direct consequence of majority black districts is that fewer white legislators are directly accountable to black interests. In this way, districting may reproduce within the legislature the polarization experienced at the polls; token electoral presence is replaced by token legislative presence.

Where blacks and whites are geographically separate, race-conscious districting isolates blacks from potential white allies—for example, white women—who are not geographically concentrated. It "wastes" the votes of white liberals who may be submerged within white, Republican districts. Thus it suppresses the potential development of issue-based campaigning and cross-racial coalitions.

As a consequence, race-conscious districting does not give blacks proportional legislative influence. Because majority black districts are necessarily accompanied by majority white districts, black representatives may be isolated in the governing body. Some conservative critics of race-conscious districting argue that such districts quarantine poor blacks in inner-city ghettoes. For example, critics of newly-drawn majority black congressional districts claim that the districts ultimately benefit white Republicans. In Alabama, for example, one critic claims such a district "yokes together by violence" areas as geographically different but racially similar as a large section of industrial Birmingham and vast expanses of the rural Black Belt, thus leaving other districts whiter and more Republican.

What these and related difficulties underscore is that proportionate influence requires something that winner-take-all districts simply cannot provide to numerically-weak minority voters: a basis of inclusion and representation that does not require winning more than 50 percent of the votes in a politically-imposed and geographically-defined constituency.

Proportionality

Let's now consider a system of proportional representation that drops the majority requirement. There are many such systems, but here I will focus on a scheme used in corporate governance called "cumulative voting." Under cumulative voting, voters cast multiple votes up to the number fixed by the number of open seats. If there are five seats on the city council, then each voter gets to cast five votes; if there are thirty songs at the senior prom, then each senior gets thirty votes. But they may choose to express the intensity of their preferences by concentrating all of their votes on a single candidate or a single song.

Let's return now to the three tests sketched earlier, and consider how cumulative voting fares in mobilizing participation, encouraging debate, and fostering inclusion.

Cumulative Voting and Participation. If voting is polarized along racial lines, as voting rights litigation cases hypothesize, then a system of cumulative voting would likely operate to provide at least a minimal level of minority representation. Unlike race-conscious districting, however, cumulative voting allows minority group members to identify their own allegiances and their preferences based on their strategic use of multiple voting possibilities. Instead of having the government authoritatively assign people to groups and districts, cumulative voting allows voluntary interest constituencies to form and regroup at each election; voters in effect "redistrict" themselves at every election. By abandoning geographic districting, it also permits a fair representation of minority voters who do not enjoy the numerical strength to become a district electoral majority or who—as in my earlier example of Latinos living in dispersed barrios—are so geographically separated within a large metropolitan area that their strength cannot be maximized within one or more single-member districts.

In all of these ways, cumulative voting would likely encourage greater electoral participation.

Cumulative Voting and Political Debate. Cumulative voting also looks good as a way to encourage genuine debate rather than foster polarization. Cumulative voting lowers the barriers to entry for third parties since supporters of such parties can concentrate all their votes on the candidates from their party. With those barriers reduced, minority political parties might reclaim, at a newly invigorated grassroots level, the traditional party role of mobilizing voter participation, expanding the space of organized alternatives, and so stretching the limits of political debate. Additionally, locally-based political parties might then organize around issues or issue-based coalitions. Since the potential support for the minority political party is not confined by a geographic or necessarily racial base, cross-racial coalitions are possible.

Cumulative Voting and Inclusion. Cumulative voting is more inclusive than winner-take-all race-conscious districting. Cumulative voting begins with the proposition that a consensus model of power sharing is preferable to a majoritarian model of centralized, winner-take-all accountability and popular sovereignty. It takes the idea of democracy by consensus and compromise and structures it in a deliberative, collective decision-making body in which the prejudiced white majority is "disaggregated." The majority is disaggregated both because the threshold for participation and representation is lowered to something less than 51 percent and because minorities are not simply shunted into "their own districts." These changes would encourage and reward efforts to build electoral alliances with minorities.

To get the full benefits of cumulative voting, however, it would also be necessary to change the process of governmental decision-making itself, away from a majoritarian model toward one of proportional power. In particular, efforts to centralize authority in a single executive would be discouraged in favor of power-sharing alternatives that emphasize collective decision-making. Within the legislature, rules would be preferred that require super-majorities for the enactment of certain decisions so that minority groups have an effective veto, thus forcing the majority to bargain with them and include them in any winning coalition, and with other devices for minority incorporation such as rotation in legislative office. Other electoral and legislative decision-making alternatives also exist such as legislative cumulative voting, that are fair and legitimate and that preserve representational authenticity, yet are more likely than current practices to promote just results.

The principle of proportionality is molded by the hope that a more co-operative political style of deliberation and ultimately a more equal basis for preference satisfaction is possible when authentic minority representatives are reinforced by structures to empower them at every stage of the political process. Ultimately however, representation and participation based on principles of proportionality are also an attempt to reconceptualize the ideal of political equality, and so the ideal of democracy itself.

The aim of that reconstruction should be to re-orient our political imagination away from the chimera of achieving a physically integrated legislature in a color-blind society and toward a clearer vision of a fair and just society. In the debate over competing claims to democratic legitimacy based on the value of minority group representation, I side with the advocates of an integrated, diverse legislature. A homogeneous legislature in a heterogeneous society is simply not legitimate.

But while black legislative visibility is an important measure of electoral fairness, taken by itself it represents an anemic approach to political fairness and justice. A vision of fairness and justice must begin to imagine a full and effective voice for disadvantaged minorities, a voice that is accountable to self-identified community interests, a voice that persuades, and a voice that is included in and resonates throughout the political process. That voice will not be achieved by majoritarian means or by enforced separation into winner-take-all racial districts. For in the end democracy is not about rule by the powerful—even a powerful majority—nor is it about arbitrarily separating groups to create separate majorities in order to increase their share. Instead, the ideal of democracy promises a fair discussion among self-defined equals about how to achieve our common aspirations. To redeem that promise, we need to put the idea of proportionality at the center of our conception of representation.   ■

■ *QUESTIONS FOR MAKING CONNECTIONS WITHIN THE READING* ■

1. Lani Guinier distinguishes among three different models for governance: the winner-take-all majority rule; an electoral system that awards victory to the candidate who has received a plurality of the votes; and, finally, a system based on a "principle of proportionality." What are the differences

among these three systems? Is one system more democratic than the others? More fair? More just? Are the terms—"fair" and "just"—interchangeable?

2. The primary solution to the problem of minority underrepresentation in the political process has been to redraw the lines that establish voting districts. What's wrong with this as a solution? Why can't redistricting lead to the kind of proportional representation that Guinier favors?

3. At the end of her essay, Guinier calls for us to move "away from the chimera of achieving a physically integrated legislature in a color-blind society and toward a clearer vision of a fair and just society." Why is "achieving a physically integrated legislature in a color-blind society" a "chimera"? And what would a "fair and just society" look like if it abandoned this chimera? How would it differ from the society we have today?

■ *QUESTIONS FOR WRITING* ■

1. Lani Guinier sets out, in "Second Proms and Second Primaries," to redefine democracy. What is the difference between her vision of democracy and a democracy based on majoritarianism? How do fairness and justice get defined in each of these understandings of democracy? What are the dangers you see in each of these understandings?

2. "[W]hen a prejudiced majority excludes, refuses to inform itself about, or even seeks to thwart the preferences of the minority," Guinier writes, "then majority rule loses its link with the ideal of reciprocity, and so its moral authority." Why is Guinier concerned with reciprocity and moral authority? What do these ideas have to do with elections and the democratic process? Does democracy depend on the ideal of reciprocity?

■ *QUESTIONS FOR MAKING CONNECTIONS BETWEEN READINGS* ■

1. Guinier argues that "[a] homogeneous legislature in a heterogeneous society is simply not legitimate." In making this case, Guinier focuses on underrepresented minorities. In so doing has she fallen into the "anti-universalist" trap that Martha Nussbaum describes in "Women and Cultural Universals"? Does Guinier's approach support, diverge from, or conflict with Nussbaum's argument that the goal of public planning should be to enhance universal human capabilities? Is a commitment to basic human rights compatible with the differential voting plan Guinier proposes?

2. Throughout "Second Proms and Second Primaries," Guinier argues that changing the electoral process will improve the quality of communication

between the races, between constituencies, and across parties. What would Deborah Tannen make of Guinier's call to "encourage genuine debate"? Is the ideal of democracy that Guinier refers to approached through dialogue, debate, or some other mode of communication? What is the best way for citizens in a democracy to resolve their disagreements?

www For additional suggestions about making connections between readings, visit the Link-O-Mat and More Sample Assignments at <www.newhum.com>.

STEVEN JOHNSON

STEVEN JOHNSON IS the founder and editor of one of the Web's earliest magazines, *Feed*, and the author of *Interface Culture: How New Technology Transforms the Way We Create and Communicate* (1997); *Emergence: The Connected Lives of Ants, Brains, Cities, and Software* (2001), from which "The Myth of the Ant Queen" is drawn, and, most recently, *Mind Wide Open: Your Brain and the Neuroscience of Everyday Life* (2004). Johnson's preoccupation throughout these works is with rethinking the nature of intelligence. Although it is common to think of intelligence as located in the individual—the outstanding student, the creative genius, the scientist at work in his lab—Johnson invites us to consider intelligence not as the property of an individual, but as a characteristic that emerges out of a system working as a whole. To illustrate this reconceptualization of intelligence, Johnson looks at complex systems, like ant colonies, cities, and software programs, and argues that in these contexts "intelligence" emerges in the absence of any central form of leadership or authority; the intelligence of the whole is created, rather, by individual agents—ants, people, subroutines—following what Johnson terms "local rules." By showing how decentralized, adaptive, self-organizing systems use lower-level thinking to solve higher-order problems, Johnson asks his readers to see the advent of the Internet itself not simply as an extension of human intelligence, but as a new frontier where the very nature of human intelligence is being transformed, one hyperlink at a time.

Johnson acknowledges the difficulties involved in imagining intelligence in these terms. When filmmakers try to depict artificial intelligence, they envision a future where cyborgs look and think just like humans. Johnson predicts, though, that when there is a significant breakthrough in the effort to create artificial intelligence, the result "won't quite look like human intelligence. It'll have other properties in it, and it may be hard for us to pick up on the fact that it is intelligent because our criteria [are] different." In the current political environment, the importance of developing new criteria for describing intelligence

Johnson, Steven. "The Myth of the Ant Queen." *Emergence: The Connected Lives of Ants, Brains, Cities, and Software*. New York: Scribners, 2001. 29–57.

Quote drawn from <http://www.oreillynet.com/pub/a/network/2002/02/22/johnson.html>.

should be clear: Decentralized terrorist networks work in the emergent ways Johnson describes, as did the residents of New York City in the wake of the attacks on the Twin Towers.

www **To learn more about Steven Johnson and intelligence, please visit the Link-O-Mat at <www.newhum.com>.**

The Myth of the Ant Queen

It's early fall in Palo Alto, and Deborah Gordon and I are sitting in her office in Stanford's Gilbert Biological Sciences building, where she spends three-quarters of the year studying behavioral ecology. The other quarter is spent doing fieldwork with the native harvester ants of the American Southwest, and when we meet, her face still retains the hint of a tan from her last excursion to the Arizona desert.

I've come here to learn more about the collective intelligence of ant colonies. Gordon, dressed neatly in a white shirt, cheerfully entertains a few borderline-philosophical questions on group behavior and complex systems, but I can tell she's hankering to start with a hands-on display. After a few minutes of casual rumination, she bolts up out of her chair. "Why don't we start with me showing you the ants that we have here," she says. "And then we can talk about what it all means."

She ushers me into a sepulchral room across the hallway, where three long tables are lined up side by side. The initial impression is that of an underpopulated and sterilized pool hall, until I get close enough to one of the tables to make out the miniature civilization that lives within each of them. Closer to a Habitrail than your traditional idea of an ant farm, Gordon's contraptions house an intricate network of plastic tubes connecting a dozen or so plastic boxes, each lined with moist plaster and coated with a thin layer of dirt.

"We cover the nests with red plastic because some species of ants don't see red light," Gordon explains. "That seems to be true of this species too." For a second, I'm not sure what she means by "this species"—and then my eyes adjust to the scene, and I realize with a start that the dirt coating the plastic boxes is, in fact, thousands of harvester ants, crammed so tightly into their quarters that I had originally mistaken them for an undifferentiated mass. A second later, I can see that the whole simulated colony is wonderfully alive, the clusters of ants pulsing steadily with movement. The tubing and cramped conditions and surging crowds bring one thought immediately to mind: the New York subway system, rush hour.

At the heart of Gordon's work is a mystery about how ant colonies develop, a mystery that has implications extending far beyond the parched earth of the Arizona desert to our cities, our brains, our immune systems—and increasingly, our technology. Gordon's work focuses on the connection between the microbehavior of individual ants and the overall behavior of the colonies themselves, and part of that research involves tracking the life cycles of individual colonies, following them year after year as they scour the desert floor for food, competing with other colonies for territory, and—once a year—mating with them. She is a student, in other words, of a particular kind of emergent, self-organizing system.

Dig up a colony of native harvester ants and you'll almost invariably find that the queen is missing. To track down the colony's matriarch, you need to examine the bottom of the hole you've just dug to excavate the colony: you'll find a narrow, almost invisible passageway that leads another two feet underground, to a tiny vestibule burrowed out of the earth. There you will find the queen. She will have been secreted there by a handful of ladies-in-waiting at the first sign of disturbance. That passageway, in other words, is an emergency escape hatch, not unlike a fallout shelter buried deep below the West Wing.

But despite the Secret Service–like behavior, and the regal nomenclature, there's nothing hierarchical about the way an ant colony does its thinking. "Although *queen* is a term that reminds us of human political systems," Gordon explains, "the queen is not an authority figure. She lays eggs and is fed and cared for by the workers. She does not decide which worker does what. In a harvester ant colony, many feet of intricate tunnels and chambers and thousands of ants separate the queen, surrounded by interior workers, from the ants working outside the nest and using only the chambers near the surface. It would be physically impossible for the queen to direct every worker's decision about which task to perform and when." The harvester ants that carry the queen off to her escape hatch do so not because they've been ordered to by their leader; they do it because the queen ant is responsible for giving birth to all the members of the colony, and so it's in the colony's best interest—and the colony's gene pool—to keep the queen safe. Their genes instruct them to protect their mother, the same way their genes instruct them to forage for food. In other words, the matriarch doesn't train her servants to protect her, evolution does.

Popular culture trades in Stalinist ant stereotypes—witness the authoritarian colony regime in the animated film *Antz*—but in fact, colonies are the exact opposite of command economies. While they are capable of remarkably coordinated feats of task allocation, there are no Five-Year Plans in the ant kingdom. The colonies that Gordon studies display some of nature's most mesmerizing decentralized behavior: intelligence and personality and learning that emerges from the bottom up.

I'm still gazing into the latticework of plastic tubing when Gordon directs my attention to the two expansive white boards attached to the main colony space, one stacked on top of the other and connected by a ramp. (Imagine a two-story parking garage built next to a subway stop.) A handful of ants meander across each plank, some porting crumblike objects on their back, others apparently just out for a stroll. If this is the Central Park of Gordon's ant metropolis, I think, it must be a workday.

Gordon gestures to the near corner of the top board, four inches from the ramp to the lower level, where a pile of strangely textured dust—littered with tiny shells and husks—presses neatly against the wall. "That's the midden," she says. "It's the town garbage dump." She points to three ants marching up the ramp, each barely visible beneath a comically oversize shell. "These ants are on midden duty: they take the trash that's left over from the food they've collected—in this case, the seeds from stalk grass—and deposit it in the midden pile."

Gordon takes two quick steps down to the other side of the table, at the far end away from the ramp. She points to what looks like another pile of dust. "And this is the cemetery." I look again, startled. She's right: hundreds of ant carcasses are piled atop one another, all carefully wedged against the table's corner. It looks brutal, and yet also strangely methodical.

I know enough about colony behavior to nod in amazement. "So they've somehow collectively decided to utilize these two areas as trash heap and cemetery," I say. No individual ant defined those areas, no central planner zoned one area for trash, the other for the dead. "It just sort of happened, right?"

Gordon smiles, and it's clear that I've missed something. "It's better than that," she says. "Look at what actually happened here: they've built the cemetery at exactly the point that's furthest away from the colony. And the midden is even more interesting: they've put it at precisely the point that maximizes its distance from both the colony *and* the cemetery. It's like there's a rule they're following: put the dead ants as far away as possible, and put the midden as far away as possible without putting it near the dead ants."

I have to take a few seconds to do the geometry myself, and sure enough, the ants have got it right. I find myself laughing out loud at the thought: it's as though they've solved one of those spatial math tests that appear on standardized tests, conjuring up a solution that's perfectly tailored to their environment, a solution that might easily stump an eight-year-old human. The question is, who's doing the conjuring?

It's a question with a long and august history, one that is scarcely limited to the collective behavior of ant colonies. We know the answer now because we have developed powerful tools for thinking about—and model-ing—the emergent intelligence of self-organizing systems, but that answer was not always so clear. We know now that systems like ant colonies don't have real leaders, that the very idea of an ant "queen" is misleading. But the desire to find pacemakers in such systems has always been powerful—in both the group behavior of the social insects, and in the collective human be-havior that creates a living city.

Records exist of a Roman fort dating back to A.D. 76 situated at the conflu-ence of the Medlock and Irwell Rivers, on the northwestern edge of modern England, about 150 miles from London. Settlements persisted there for three centuries, before dying out with the rest of the empire around A.D. 400. His-torians believe that the site was unoccupied for half a millennium, until a town called Manchester began to take shape there, the name derived from the Roman settlement Mamucium—Latin for "place of the breastlike hill."

Manchester subsisted through most of the millennium as a nondescript northern-England borough: granted a charter in 1301, the town established a college in the early 1400s, but remained secondary to the neighboring town of Salford for hundreds of years. In the 1600s, the Manchester region became a node for the wool trade, its merchants shipping goods to the Con-tinent via the great ports of London. It was impossible to see it at the time, but Manchester—and indeed the entire Lancashire region—had planted it-self at the very center of a technological and commercial revolution that would irrevocably alter the future of the planet. Manchester lay at the con-fluence of several world-historical rivers: the nascent industrial technologies of steam-powered looms; the banking system of commercial London; the global markets and labor pools of the British Empire. The story of that con-vergence has been told many times, and the debate over its consequences continues to this day. But beyond the epic effects that it had on the global economy, the industrial takeoff that occurred in Manchester between 1700 and 1850 also created a new kind of city, one that literally exploded into existence.

The statistics on population growth alone capture the force of that ex-plosion: a 1773 estimate had 24,000 people living in Manchester; the first of-ficial census in 1801 found 70,000. By the midpoint of the century, there were more than 250,000 people in the city proper—a tenfold increase in only seventy-five years. That growth rate was as unprecedented and as violent as the steam engines themselves. In a real sense, the city grew too fast for the authorities to keep up with it. For five hundred years, Manchester had tech-nically been considered a "manor," which meant, in the eyes of the law, it was run like a feudal estate, with no local government to speak of—no city planners, police, or public health authorities. Manchester didn't even send representatives to Parliament until 1832, and it wasn't incorporated for an-other six years. By the early 1840s, the newly formed borough council finally began to institute public health reforms and urban planning, but the British government didn't officially recognize Manchester as a city until 1853. This constitutes one of the great ironies of the industrial revolution, and it captures just how dramatic the rate of change really was: the city that most defined the future of urban life for the first half of the nineteenth century didn't legally become a city until the great explosion had run its course.

The result of that discontinuity was arguably the least planned and most chaotic city in the six-thousand-year history of urban settlements. Noisy, polluted, massively overcrowded, Manchester attracted a steady stream of intellectuals and public figures in the 1830s, traveling north to the industrial magnet in search of the modern world's future. One by one, they returned with stories of abject squalor and sensory overload, their words straining to convey the immensity and uniqueness of the experience. "What I have seen has disgusted and astonished me beyond all measure," Dickens wrote after a visit in the fall of 1838. "I mean to strike the heaviest blow in my power for these unfortunate creatures." Appointed to command the northern districts in the late 1830s, Major General Charles James Napier wrote: "Manchester is the chimney of the world. Rich rascals, poor rogues, drunken ragamuffins and prostitutes form the moral. . . . What a place! The entrance to hell, realized." De Tocqueville visited Lancashire in 1835 and described the landscape in language that would be echoed throughout the next two centuries: "From this foul drain the greatest stream of human industry flows out to fertilize the whole world. From this filthy sewer pure gold flows. Here humanity attains its most complete development and its most brutish; here civilization works its miracles, and civilized man is turned back almost into a savage."

But Manchester's most celebrated and influential documentarian was a young man named Friedrich Engels, who arrived in 1842 to help oversee the family cotton plant there, and to witness firsthand the engines of history bringing the working class closer to self-awareness. While Engels was very much on the payroll of his father's firm, Ermen and Engels, by the time he arrived in Manchester he was also under the sway of the radical politics associated with the Young Hegelian school. He had befriended Karl Marx a few years before and had been encouraged to visit Manchester by the socialist Moses Hess, whom he'd met in early 1842. His three years in England were thus a kind of scouting mission for the revolution, financed by the capitalist class. The book that Engels eventually wrote, *The Condition of the Working Class in England,* remains to this day one of the classic tracts of urban history and stands as the definitive account of nineteenth-century Manchester life in all its tumult and dynamism. Dickens, Carlyle, and Disraeli had all attempted to capture Manchester in its epic wildness, but their efforts were outpaced by a twenty-four-year-old from Prussia.

But *The Condition* is not, as might be expected, purely a document of Manchester's industrial chaos, a story of all that is solid melting into air, to borrow a phrase Engels's comrade would write several years later. In the midst of the city's insanity, Engels's eye is drawn to a strange kind of order, in a wonderful passage where he leads the reader on a walking tour of the industrial capital, a tour that reveals a kind of politics built into the very topography of the city's streets. It captures Engels's acute powers of observation, but I quote from it at length because it captures something else as well—how difficult it is to think in models of self-organization, to imagine a world without pacemakers.

> The town itself is peculiarly built, so that someone can live in it for years and travel into it and out of it daily without ever coming into contact with a working-class quarter or even with workers—so long, that is to say, as one confines himself to his business affairs or to strolling about for pleasure. This comes about mainly in the circumstances that through an unconscious, tacit agreement as much as through conscious, explicit intention, the working-class districts are most sharply separated from the parts of the city reserved for the middle class. . . .
>
>   I know perfectly well that this deceitful manner of building is more or less common to all big cities. I know as well that shopkeepers must in the nature of the business take premises on the main thoroughfares. I know in such streets there are more good houses than bad ones, and that the value of land is higher in their immediate vicinity than in neighborhoods that lie at a distance from them. But at the same time I have never come across so systematic a seclusion of the working class from the main streets as in Manchester. I have never elsewhere seen a concealment of such fine sensibility of everything that might offend the eyes and nerves of the middle classes. And yet it is precisely Manchester that has been built less according to a plan and less within the limitations of official regulations—and indeed more through accident—than any other town. Still . . . I cannot help feeling that the liberal industrialists, the Manchester "bigwigs," are not so altogether innocent of this bashful style of building.

You can almost hear the contradictions thundering against each other in this passage, like the "dark satanic mills" of Manchester itself. The city has built a *cordon sanitaire* to separate the industrialists from the squalor they have unleashed on the world, concealing the demoralization of Manchester's working-class districts—and yet that disappearing act comes into the world without "conscious, explicit intention." The city seems artfully planned to hide its atrocities, and yet it "has been built less according to a plan" than any city in history. As Steven Marcus puts it, in his history of the young Engels's sojourn in Manchester, "The point to be taken is that this astonishing and outrageous arrangement cannot fully be understood as the result of a plot, or even a deliberate design, although those in whose interests it works also control it. It is indeed too huge and too complex a state of organized affairs ever to have been *thought up* in advance, to have preexisted as an idea."

Those broad, glittering avenues, in other words, suggest a Potemkin village without a Potemkin. That mix of order and anarchy is what we now call emergent behavior. Urban critics since Lewis Mumford and Jane Jacobs have known that cities have lives of their own, with neighborhoods clustering into place without any Robert Moses figure dictating the plan from above. But that understanding has entered the intellectual mainstream only in recent years—when Engels paced those Manchester streets in the 1840s, he was left groping blindly, trying to find a culprit for the city's fiendish organization, even as he acknowledged that the city was notoriously unplanned. Like most intellectual histories, the development of that new understanding—the sciences of complexity and self-organization—is a complicated, multithreaded tale, with many agents interacting over its duration. It is probably better to think of it as less a linear narrative and more an interconnected web, growing increasingly dense over the century and a half that separates us from Engels's first visit to Manchester.

Complexity is a word that has frequently appeared in critical accounts of metropolitan space, but there are really two kinds of complexity fundamental to the city, two experiences with very different implications for the individuals trying to make sense of them. There is, first, the more conventional sense of complexity as sensory overload, the city stretching the human nervous system to its very extremes, and in the process teaching it a new series of reflexes—and leading the way for a complementary series of aesthetic values, which develop out like a scab around the original wound. The German cultural critic Walter Benjamin writes in his unfinished masterpiece, *The Arcades Project:*

> Perhaps the daily sight of a moving crowd once presented the eye with a spectacle to which it first had to adapt. . . . [T]hen the assumption is not impossible that, having mastered this task, the eye welcomed opportunities to confirm its possession of its new ability. The method of impressionist painting, whereby the picture is assembled through a riot of flecks of color, would then be a reflection of experience with which the eye of a big-city dweller has become familiar.

There's a long tributary of nineteenth- and twentieth-century urban writing that leads into this passage, from the London chapters of Wordsworth's *Prelude* to the ambulatory musings of Joyce's *Dubliners:* the noise and the senselessness somehow transformed into an aesthetic experience. The crowd is something you throw yourself into, for the pure poetry of it all. But complexity is not solely a matter of sensory overload. There is also the sense of complexity as a self-organizing system—more Santa Fe Institute than Frankfurt School. This sort of complexity lives up one level: it describes the system of the city itself, and not its experiential reception by the city dweller. The city is complex because it overwhelms, yes, but also because it has a coherent personality, a personality that self-organizes out of millions of individual decisions, a global order built out of local interactions. This is the "systematic" complexity that Engels glimpsed on the boulevards of Manchester: not the overload and anarchy he documented elsewhere, but instead a strange kind of order, a pattern in the streets that furthered the political values of Manchester's elite without being deliberately planned by them. We know now from computer models and sociological studies—as well as from the studies of comparable systems generated by the social insects, such as Gordon's harvester ants—that larger patterns can emerge out of uncoordinated local actions. But for Engels and his contemporaries, those unplanned urban shapes must have seemed like a haunting. The city appeared to have a life of its own.

A hundred and fifty years later, the same techniques translated into the language of software . . . trigger a similar reaction: the eerie sense of something lifelike, something organic forming on the screen. Even those with sophisticated knowledge about self-organizing systems still find these shapes unnerving—in their mix of stability and change, in their capacity for open-ended learning. The impulse to build centralized models to explain that behavior remains almost as strong as it did in Engels's day. When we see repeated shapes and structure emerging out of apparent chaos, we can't help looking for pacemakers.

Understood in the most abstract sense, what Engels observed are *patterns* in the urban landscape, visible because they have a repeated structure that distinguishes them from the pure noise you might naturally associate with an unplanned city. They are patterns of human movement and decision-making that have been etched into the texture of city blocks, patterns that are then fed back to the Manchester residents themselves, altering their subsequent decisions. (In that sense, they are the very opposite of the traditional sense of urban complexity—they are signals emerging where you would otherwise expect only noise.) A city is a kind of pattern-amplifying machine: its neighborhoods are a way of measuring and expressing the repeated behavior of larger collectivities—capturing information about group behavior, and sharing that information with the group. Because those patterns are fed back to the community, small shifts in behavior can quickly escalate into larger movements: upscale shops dominate the main boulevards, while the working class remains clustered invisibly in the alleys and side streets; the artists live on the Left Bank, the investment bankers in the Eighth Arrondissement. You don't need regulations and city planners deliberately creating these structures. All you need are thousands of individuals and a few simple rules of interaction. The bright shop windows attract more bright shop windows and drive the impoverished toward the hidden core. There's no need for a Baron Haussmann in this world, just a few repeating patterns of movement, amplified into larger shapes that last for lifetimes: clusters, slums, neighborhoods.

Not all patterns are visible to every city dweller, though. The history of urbanism is also the story of more muted signs, built by the collective behavior of smaller groups and rarely detected by outsiders. Manchester harbors several such secret clusters, persisting over the course of many generations, like a "standing wave in front of a rock in a fast-moving stream." One of them lies just north of Victoria University, at a point where Oxford Road becomes Oxford Street. There are reports dating back to the mid-nineteenth century of men cruising other men on these blocks, looking for casual sex, more lasting relationships, or even just the camaraderie of shared identity at a time when that identity dared not speak its name. Some historians speculate that Wittgenstein visited these streets during his sojourn in Manchester in 1908. Nearly a hundred years later, the area has christened itself the Gay Village and actively promotes its coffee bars and boutiques as a must-see Manchester tourist destination, like Manhattan's Christopher Street and San Francisco's Castro. The pattern is now broadcast to a wider audience, but it has not lost its shape.

But even at a lower amplitude, that signal was still loud enough to attract the attention of another of Manchester's illustrious immigrants: the British polymath Alan Turing. As part of his heroic contribution to the war effort, Turing had been a student of mathematical patterns, designing the equations and the machines that cracked the "unbreakable" German code of the Enigma device. After a frustrating three-year stint at the National Physical Laboratory in London, Turing moved to Manchester in 1948 to help run the university's embryonic computing lab. It was in Manchester that Turing began to think about the problem of biological development in mathematical terms, leading the way to the "Morphogenesis" paper, published in 1952, that Evelyn Fox Keller would rediscover more than a decade later. Turing's war research had focused on detecting patterns lurking within the apparent chaos of code, but in his Manchester years, his mind gravitated toward a mirror image of the original code-breaking problem: how complex patterns could come into being by following simple rules. How does a seed know how to build a flower?

Turing's paper on morphogenesis—literally, "the beginning of shape"—turned out to be one of his seminal works, ranking up there with his more publicized papers and speculations: his work on Gödel's undecidability problem, the Turing Machine, the Turing Test—not to mention his contributions to the physical design of the modern digital computer. But the morphogenesis paper was only the beginning of a shape—a brilliant mind sensing the outlines of a new problem, but not fully grasping all its intricacies. If Turing had been granted another few decades to explore the powers of self-assembly—not to mention access to the number-crunching horsepower of non-vacuum-tube computers—it's not hard to imagine his mind greatly enhancing our subsequent understanding of emergent behavior. But the work on morphogenesis was tragically cut short by his death in 1954.

Alan Turing was most likely a casualty of the brutally homophobic laws of postwar Britain, but his death also intersected with those discreet patterns of life on Manchester's sidewalks. Turing had known about that stretch of Oxford Road since his arrival in Manchester; on occasion, he would drift down to the neighborhood, meeting other gay men—inviting some of them back to his flat for conversation, and presumably some sort of physical contact. In January of 1952, Turing met a young man named Arnold Murray on those streets, and the two embarked on a brief relationship that quickly turned sour. Murray—or a friend of Murray's—broke into Turing's house and stole a few items. Turing reported the theft to the police and, with his typical forthrightness, made no effort to conceal the affair with Murray when the police visited his flat. Homosexuality was a criminal offense according to British law, punishable by up to two years' imprisonment, and so the police promptly charged both Turing and Murray with "gross indecency."

On February 29, 1952, while the Manchester authorities were preparing their case against him, Turing finished the revisions to his morphogenesis paper, and he argued over its merits with Ilya Prigogine, the visiting Belgian chemist whose work on nonequilibrium thermodynamics would later win him a Nobel prize. In one day, Turing had completed the text that would help engender the discipline of biomathematics and inspire Keller and Segel's slime mold discoveries fifteen years later, and he had enjoyed a spirited exchange with the man who would eventually achieve world fame for his research into self-organizing systems. On that winter day in 1952, there was no mind on the face of the earth better prepared to wrestle with the mysteries of emergence than Alan Turing's. But the world outside that mind was conspiring to destroy it. That very morning, a local paper broke the story that the war-hero savant had been caught in an illicit affair with a nineteen-year-old boy.

Within a few months Turing had been convicted of the crime and placed on a humiliating estrogen treatment to "cure" him of his homosexuality. Hounded by the authorities and denied security clearance for the top-secret British computing projects he had been contributing to, Turing died two years later, an apparent suicide.

Turing's career had already collided several times with the developing web of emergence before those fateful years in Manchester. In the early forties, during the height of the war effort, he had spent several months at the legendary Bell Laboratories on Manhattan's West Street, working on a number of encryption schemes, including an effort to transmit heavily encoded waveforms that could be decoded as human speech with the use of a special key. Early in his visit to Bell Labs, Turing hit upon the idea of using another Bell invention, the Vocoder—later used by rock musicians such as Peter Frampton to combine the sounds of a guitar and the human voice—as a way of encrypting speech. (By early 1943, Turing's ideas had enabled the first secure voice transmission to cross the Atlantic, unintelligible to German eavesdroppers.) Bell Labs was the home base for another genius, Claude Shannon, who would go on to found the influential discipline of information theory, and whose work had explored the boundaries between noise and information. Shannon had been particularly intrigued by the potential for machines to detect and amplify patterns of information in noisy communication channels—a line of inquiry that promised obvious value to a telephone company, but could also save thousands of lives in a war effort that relied so heavily on the sending and breaking of codes. Shannon and Turing immediately recognized that they had been working along parallel tracks: they were both code-breakers by profession at that point, and in their attempts to build automated machines that could recognize patterns in audio signals or numerical sequences, they had both glimpsed a future populated by even more intelligence machines. Shannon and Turing passed many an extended lunchtime at the Bell Labs, trading ideas on an "electronic brain" that might be capable of humanlike feats of pattern recognition.

Turing had imagined his thinking machine primarily in terms of its logical possibilities, its ability to execute an infinite variety of computational routines. But Shannon pushed him to think of the machine as something closer to an actual human brain, capable of recognizing more nuanced patterns. One day over lunch at the lab, Turing exclaimed playfully to his colleagues, "Shannon wants to feed not just data to a brain, but *cultural* things! He wants to play music to it!" Musical notes were patterns too, Shannon recognized, and if you could train an electronic brain to understand and respond to logical patterns of zeros and ones, then perhaps sometime in the future we could train our machines to appreciate the equivalent patterns of minor chord progressions and arpeggios. The idea seemed fanciful at the time—it was hard enough getting a machine to perform long division, much less savor Beethoven's Ninth. But the pattern recognition that Turing and Shannon envisioned for digital computers has, in recent years, become a central part of our cultural life, with machines both generating music for our entertainment and recommending new artists for us to enjoy. The connection between musical patterns and our neurological wiring would play a central role in one of the founding texts of modern artificial intelligence, Douglas Hofstadter's *Gödel, Escher, Bach.* Our computers still haven't developed a genuine ear for music, but if they ever do, their skill will date back to those lunchtime conversations between Shannon and Turing at Bell Labs. And that learning too will be a kind of emergence, a higher-level order forming out of relatively simple component parts.

Five years after his interactions with Turing, Shannon published a long essay in the *Bell System Technical Journal* that was quickly repackaged as a book called *The Mathematical Theory of Communication*. Dense with equations and arcane chapter titles such as "Discrete Noiseless Systems," the book managed to become something of a cult classic, and the discipline it spawned—information theory—had a profound impact on scientific and technological research that followed, on both a theoretical and practical level. *The Mathematical Theory of Communication* contained an elegant, layman's introduction to Shannon's theory, penned by the esteemed scientist Warren Weaver, who had early on grasped the significance of Shannon's work. Weaver had played a leading role in the Natural Sciences division of the Rockefeller Foundation since 1932, and when he retired in the late fifties, he composed a long report for the foundation, looking back at the scientific progress that had been achieved over the preceding quarter century. The occasion suggested a reflective look backward, but the document that Weaver produced (based loosely on a paper he had written for *American Scientist*) was far more prescient, more forward-looking. In many respects, it deserves to be thought of as the founding text of complexity theory—the point at which the study of complex systems began to think of itself as a unified field. Drawing upon research in molecular biology, genetics, physics, computer science, and Shannon's information theory, Weaver divided the last few centuries of scientific inquiry into three broad camps. First, the study of simple systems: two or three variable problems, such as the rotation of planets, or the connection between an electric current and its voltage and resistance. Second, problems of "disorganized complexity": problems characterized by millions or billions of variables that can only be approached by the methods of statistical mechanics and probability theory. These tools helped explain not only the behavior of molecules in a gas, or the patterns of heredity in a gene pool, but also helped life insurance companies turn a profit despite their limited knowledge about any individual human's future health. Thanks to Claude Shannon's work, the statistical approach also helped phone companies deliver more reliable and intelligible long-distance service.

But there was a third phase to this progression, and we were only beginning to understand. "This statistical method of dealing with disorganized complexity, so powerful an advance over the earlier two-variable methods, leaves a great field untouched," Weaver wrote. There was a middle region between two-variable equations and problems that involved billions of variables. Conventionally, this region involved a "moderate" number of variables, but the size of the system was in fact a secondary characteristic:

> Much more important than the mere number of variables is the fact that these variables are all interrelated. . . . These problems, as contrasted with

the disorganized situations with which statistics can cope, *show the essential feature of organization.* We will therefore refer to this group of problems as those of *organized complexity.*

Think of these three categories of problems in terms of [a] billiards table analogy. . . . A two- or three-variable problem would be an ordinary billiards table, with balls bouncing off one another following simple rules: their velocities, the friction of the table. That would be an example of a "simple system"—and indeed, billiard balls are often used to illustrate basic laws of physics in high school textbooks. A system of disorganized complexity would be that same table enlarged to include a million balls, colliding with one another millions of times a second. Making predictions about the behavior of any individual ball in that mix would be difficult, but you could make some accurate predictions about the overall behavior of the table. Assuming there's enough energy in the system at the outset, the balls will spread to fill the entire table, like gas molecules in a container. It's complex because there are many interacting agents, but it's disorganized because they don't create any higher-level behavior other than broad statistical trends. Organized complexity, on the other hand, is like [a] motorized billiards table, where the balls follow specific rules and through their various interactions create a distinct macrobehavior, arranging themselves in a specific shape, or forming a specific pattern over time. That sort of behavior, for Weaver, suggested a problem of organized complexity, a problem that suddenly seemed omnipresent in nature once you started to look for it:

> What makes an evening primrose open when it does? Why does salt water fail to satisfy thirst? . . . What is the description of aging in biochemical terms? . . . What is a gene, and how does the original genetic constitution of a living organism express itself in the developed characteristics of the adult?
>
> All these are certainly complex problems. But they are not problems of disorganized complexity, to which statistical methods hold the key. They are all problems which involve dealing simultaneously with a sizable number of factors which are interrelated into an organic whole.

Tackling such problems required a new approach: "The great central concerns of the biologist . . . are now being approached not only from *above,* with the broad view of the natural philosopher who scans the whole living world, but also from *underneath,* by the quantitative analyst who measures the underlying facts." This was a genuine shift in the paradigm of research, to use Thomas Kuhn's language—a revolution not so much in the interpretations that science built in its attempt to explain the world, but rather in the types of questions it asked. The paradigm shift was more than just a new mind-set, Weaver recognized; it was also a by-product of new tools that were appearing on the horizon. To solve the problems of organized complexity, you needed a machine capable of churning through thousands, if not millions, of calculations per second—a rate that would have been unimaginable for individual brains running the numbers with the limited calculating machines of the past few centuries. Because of his connection to the Bell Labs group, Weaver had seen early on the promise of digital computing, and he knew that the mysteries of organized complexity would be much easier to tackle once you could model the behavior in close-to-real time. For millennia, humans had used their skills at observation and classification to document the subtle anatomy of flowers, but for the first time they were perched on the brink of answering a more fundamental question, a question that had more to do with patterns developing over time than with static structure: Why does an evening primrose open when it does? And how does a simple seed know how to make a primrose in the first place? . . .

"Organized complexity" proved to be a constructive way of thinking . . . but . . . was it possible to model and explain the behavior of self-organizing systems using more rigorous methods? Could the developing technology of digital computing be usefully applied to this problem? Partially thanks to Shannon's work in the late forties, the biological sciences . . . made a number of significant breakthroughs in understanding pattern recognition and feedback. . . . Shortly after his appointment to the Harvard faculty in 1956, the entomologist Edward O. Wilson convincingly proved that ants communicate with one another—and coordinate overall colony behavior—by recognizing patterns in pheromone trails left by fellow ants. . . . At the Free University of Brussels in the fifties, Ilya Prigogine was making steady advances in his understanding of nonequilibrium thermodynamics, environments where the laws of entropy are temporarily overcome, and higher-level order may spontaneously emerge out of underlying chaos. And at MIT's Lincoln Laboratory, a twenty-five-year-old researcher named Oliver Selfridge was experimenting with a model for teaching a computer how to learn.

There is a world of difference between a computer that passively receives the information you supply and a computer that actively learns on its own. The very first generation of computers such as ENIAC had processed information fed to them by their masters, and they had been capable of performing various calculations with that data, based on the instruction sets programmed into them. This was a startling enough development at a time when "computer" meant a person with a slide rule and an eraser. But even in those early days, the digital visionaries had imagined a machine capable of more open-ended learning. Turing and Shannon had argued over the future musical tastes of the "electronic brain" during lunch hour at Bell Labs, while their colleague Norbert Wiener had written a best-selling paean to the self-regulatory powers of feedback in his 1949 manifesto *Cybernetics*.

"Mostly my participation in all of this is a matter of good luck for me," Selfridge says today, sitting in his cramped, windowless MIT office. Born in

England, Selfridge enrolled at Harvard at the age of fifteen and started his doctorate three years later at MIT, where Norbert Wiener was his dissertation adviser. As a precocious twenty-one-year-old, Selfridge suggested a few corrections to a paper that his mentor had published on heart flutters, corrections that Wiener graciously acknowledged in the opening pages of *Cybernetics*. "I think I now have the honor of being one of the few living people mentioned in that book," Selfridge says, laughing.

After a sojourn working on military control projects in New Jersey, Selfridge returned to MIT in the midfifties. His return coincided with an explosion of interest in artificial intelligence (AI), a development that introduced him to a then-junior fellow at Harvard named Marvin Minsky. "My concerns in AI," Selfridge says now, "were not so much the actual processing as they were in how systems change, how they evolve—in a word, how they learn." Exploring the possibilities of machine learning brought Selfridge back to memories of his own education in England. "At school in England I had read John Milton's *Paradise Lost*," he says, "and I'd been struck by the image of Pandemonium—it's Greek for 'all the demons.' Then after my second son, Peter, was born, I went over *Paradise Lost* again, and the shrieking of the demons awoke something in me." The pattern recognizer in Selfridge's brain had hit upon a way of teaching a computer to recognize patterns.

"We are proposing here a model of a process which we claim can adaptively improve itself to handle certain pattern-recognition problems which cannot be adequately specified in advance." These were the first words Selfridge delivered at a symposium in late 1958, held at the very same National Physical Laboratory from which Turing had escaped a decade before. Selfridge's presentation had the memorable title "Pandemonium: A Paradigm for Learning," and while it had little impact outside the nascent computer-science community, the ideas Selfridge outlined that day would eventually become part of our everyday life—each time we enter a name in our Palm-Pilots or use voice-recognition software to ask for information over the phone. Pandemonium, as Selfridge outlined it in his talk, was not so much a specific piece of software as it was a way of approaching a problem. The problem was an ambitious one, given the limited computational resources of the day: how to teach a computer to recognize patterns that were ill-defined or erratic, like the sound waves that comprise spoken language.

The brilliance of Selfridge's new paradigm lay in the fact that it relied on a distributed, bottom-up intelligence, and not a unified, top-down one. Rather than build a single smart program, Selfridge created a swarm of limited miniprograms, which he called demons. "The idea was, we have a bunch of these demons shrieking up the hierarchy," he explains. "Lower-level demons shrieking to higher-level demons shrieking to higher ones."

To understand what that "shrieking" means, imagine a system with twenty-six individual demons, each trained to recognize a letter of the alphabet. The pool of demons is shown a series of words, and each demon "votes" as to whether each letter displayed represents its chosen letter. If the first letter is *a*, the *a*-recognizing demon reports that it is highly likely that it has recognized a match. Because of the similarities in shape, the *o*-recognizer might report a possible match, while the *b*-recognizer would emphatically declare that the letter wasn't intelligible to it. All the letter-recognizing demons would report to a master demon, who would tally up the votes for each letter and choose the demon that expressed the highest confidence. Then the software would move on to the next letter in the sequence, and the process would begin again. At the end of the transmission, the master demon would have a working interpretation of the text that had been transmitted, based on the assembled votes of the demon democracy.

Of course, the accuracy of that interpretation depended on the accuracy of the letter recognizers. If you were trying to teach a computer how to read, it was cheating to assume from the outset that you could find twenty-six accurate letter recognizers. Selfridge was after a larger goal: How do you teach a machine to recognize letters—or vowel sounds, minor chords, fingerprints—in the first place? The answer involved adding another layer of demons, and a feedback mechanism whereby the various demon guesses could be graded. This lower level was populated by even less sophisticated miniprograms, trained only to recognize raw physical shapes (or sounds, in the case of Morse code or spoken language). Some demons recognized parallel lines, others perpendicular ones. Some demons looked for circles, others for dots. None of these shapes were associated with any particular letter; these bottom-dwelling demons were like two-year-old children—capable of reporting on the shapes they witnessed, but not perceiving them as letters or words.

Using these minimally equipped demons, the system could be trained to recognize letters, without "knowing" anything about the alphabet in advance. The recipe was relatively simple: Present the letter *b* to the bottom-level demons, and see which ones respond, and which ones don't. In the case of the letter *b*, the vertical-line recognizers might respond, along with the circle recognizers. Those lower-level demons would report to a letter-recognizer one step higher in the chain. Based on the information gathered from its lieutenants, that recognizer would make a guess as to the letter's identity. Those guesses are then "graded" by the software. If the guess is wrong, the software learns to dissociate those particular lieutenants from the letter in question; if the guess happens to be right, it *strengthens* the connection between the lieutenants and the letter.

The results are close to random at first, but if you repeat the process a thousand times, or ten thousand, the system learns to associate specific assembles of shape-recognizers with specific letters and soon enough is capable of translating entire sentences with remarkable accuracy. The system doesn't come with any predefined conceptions about the shapes of letters— you train the system to associate letters with specific shapes in the grading phase. (This is why handwriting-recognition software can adapt to so many different types of penmanship, but *can't* adapt to penmanship that changes day to day.) That mix of random beginnings organizing into more complicated results reminded Selfridge of another process, whose own underlying code was just then being deciphered in the form of DNA. "The scheme sketched is really a natural selection on the processing demons," Selfridge explained. "If they serve a useful function they survive and perhaps are even the source for other subdemons who are themselves judged on their merits. It is perfectly reasonable to conceive of this taking place on a broader scale . . . instead of having but one Pandemonium we might have some crowd of them, all fairly similarly constructed, and employ natural selection on the crowd of them."

The system Selfridge described—with its bottom-up learning, and its evaluating feedback loops—belongs in the history books as the first practical description of an emergent software program. The world now swarms with millions of his demons.   ∎

■ *QUESTIONS FOR MAKING CONNECTIONS WITHIN THE READING* ■

1. Do you accept Johnson's analogy between the behavior of harvester ants and the emergence of cities like Manchester? Does Johnson mean that instinct guides human builders in much the same way as it guides the ants? Does he mean that in both cases an order has emerged entirely by accident? Or does he mean that there is something about "systems" in general—ant colonies as well as sprawling conurbations—that makes them self-organizing? What exactly is a self-organizing system, and how do both the ant colony and the city qualify as equally appropriate examples? How does each system organize itself?

2. The idea of self-organizing systems might seem to suggest that order automatically and smoothly arises as ants and human beings go about their private business. Can Manchester in the nineteenth century, when Napier, Dickens, and Engels each observed it, be described as orderly? Was there an order behind the apparent disorder? How can we distinguish between a self-organizing system and the results that are produced entirely by chance?

3. One could say that there are three different parts to "The Myth of the Ant Queen." The first deals with the colony of harvester ants. The second deals with the city of Manchester. The third deals with the emergence of complexity theory. In what ways are these three parts connected? Why doesn't Johnson make the connections more explicit—why does he leave them for the reader to work out? Could the structure of his chapter in some way reflect the nature of his argument about self-organization?

■ *QUESTIONS FOR WRITING* ■

1. What role does intelligence play in self-organizing systems? This question might be more complex than it seems at first because intelligence may exist on multiple levels. The intelligence demonstrated by an ant colony may be much greater than the intelligence of an individual ant. On any particular day during the 1880s, life in Manchester must have seemed to many people very close to absolute chaos, but could it be said that the city as a whole possessed a certain intelligence? Does Johnson mean to suggest that the ideas and aspirations of individuals do not matter? Are we, from the standpoint of complexity theory, intelligent beings? What is intelligence, anyway?

2. Families, communities, schools, religious groups, circles of friends, political parties, public service organizations—all of these qualify as social institutions, and there are many others. Choose one institution and, drawing on Johnson's chapter, decide whether it qualifies as truly self-organizing. If it does not, can you imagine how it might be reorganized in a bottom-up fashion? In what ways do our customs and traditions encourage or discourage self-organization? What do you conclude from the importance of kings, presidents, generals, CEOs, bosses, coaches, principals, and other leaders in our culture?

■ *QUESTIONS FOR MAKING CONNECTIONS*
BETWEEN READINGS ■

1. Do self-organizing systems manage, as time goes on, to insulate themselves from the influence of chance? Does chance continue to play a role, or does it actually become even more important? To explore these questions, you might consider the examples that Johnson provides—the ant colony, the city, and the development of the science of complexity. But you might also consider Edward Tenner's discussion of technology and unintended consequences. Although technology appears to make life safer and more stable, it also exposes us to "revenge effects." Does self-organization protect us from these effects, or might it make them more likely?

2. At first glance, Robert Thurman's claim that we have no permanent or essential self may seem like sheer nonsense, since, clearly, each of us is a self or has one. But does "the self," as we call it, actually represent a self-organizing system, more like an ant colony than a single ant, or more like a city than a single neighborhood? As you work through this question, you should move beyond the two texts to consider your own experience. Are you always the same person from one moment to the next? To what degree is your identity at any particular time shaped by your interactions

with others? Can you accurately predict what you will be like ten years from now? Ten months? Ten days?

www   **For additional suggestions about making connections between readings, visit the Link-O-Mat and More Sample Assignments at <www.newhum.com>.**

MARY KALDOR

FOLLOWING THE DESTRUCTION of the World Trade Center on September 11, 2001, people have come to understand the dangers posed by unofficial warfare—that is, conflicts not waged by governments but by paramilitary organizations that are often international and clandestine. While the dangers have become clear, the most effective ways to respond to this kind of warfare are far less obvious. Few writers in our time have addressed the problem more thoughtfully than Mary Kaldor. In the aftermath of September 11, Kaldor wrote in *The Nation* about just how different this new kind of warfare is: "What we have learned about this kind of war is that the only possible exit route is political. There has to be a strategy of winning hearts and minds to counter the strategy of fear and hate. There has to be an alternative politics based on tolerance and inclusiveness, which is capable of defeating the politics of intolerance and exclusion and capable of preserving the space for democratic politics. In the case of the current new war, what is needed is an appeal for global—not American—justice and legitimacy, aimed at establishing the rule of law in place of war and at fostering understanding between communities in place of terror."

Currently the director of the Center for the Study of Global Governance at the London School of Economics, Kaldor has spent her professional life studying globalization and the transformation of modern warfare. In the 1980s, she helped to cofound European Nuclear Disarmament (END), a nongovernmental organization dedicated to convincing Western European states to refuse to stockpile a nuclear arsenal. Subsequently, Kaldor cochaired the Helsinki Citizen's Assembly, an international consortium of nongovernmental organizations promoting global peace and human rights; she was also a member of the Independent International Commission to Investigate the Kosovo Crisis. The author of numerous books on global and European politics, her most recent work, *New*

Kaldor, Mary. "Beyond Militarism, Arms Races, and Arms Control." Talk delivered at the Nobel Peace Prize Centennial Symposium, Oslo, Norway, 6 December 2001.

Biographical information from the London School of Economics and Political Science Web site <http://www.lse.ac.uk/experts/display?xml=experts.xml&xsl=experts.xsl&xslparam=person%3dm.h.kaldor>; quotation from "Wanted: Global Politics," *The Nation*, 5 November 2001 <http://www.thenation.com/doc.mhtml?i=20011105&s=kaldor>.

and Old Wars: Organized Violence in a Global Era (1999), documents the shifts from an earlier form of warfare between armed combatants, where eighty percent of the casualties were soldiers, to the current form of organized violence, where eighty percent of the casualties are civilians. In the public talk reproduced here, Kaldor draws on this research to describe the challenges that unofficial warfare poses in the twenty-first century and to argue for the necessity of developing an international, humanitarian response to contain such conflicts.

www   **To learn more about Mary Kaldor and the practice of unofficial warfare, please visit the Link-O-Mat at <www.newhum.com>.**

Beyond Militarism, Arms Races, and Arms Control

Since the end of the Cold War, a profound restructuring of armed forces has taken place. During the Cold War period, armed forces tended to resemble each other all over the world. They were disciplined, hierarchical, and technology intensive. There were, of course, guerrilla and/or terrorist groups but they were considered marginal and their demand for weapons was small in relation to the overall demand for weapons.

The Cold War could be described as the final stage of what has come to be known as modernity, or to use Anthony Giddens' terminology, the final stages of the first phase of modernity. By *modernity,* I mean that period of human development that began somewhere between the fifteenth and the eighteenth centuries, characterized by the development of science and technology, the nation state, modern industry, and, I would argue, Clausewitzean[1] or modern war. By *modern war,* I mean war between states, fought by armed forces, for state interest; the type of war that was theorized so brilliantly by Clausewitz. The development of modern war cannot be disentangled from the development of modern states. It was in war that European states, which were to provide the model for other states, established their monopoly of organized violence within the territorial confines of the state; they eliminated competitors, centralized administration, increased taxation and forms of borrowing, and above all, created an idea of the state as the organization responsible for protection of borders against other states and for upholding a rule of law within the state. The sharp distinctions between the military and civilians, public and private, internal and external, are a product of these developments. As Charles Tilly put it in a famous phrase: "States made war and war made the state."

After 1945, the whole world was parceled up into individual states, each with their own currency and their own armed forces. Each state was a member of a bloc (West, East and non-aligned) and within each bloc, there were transfers of weapons and other types of military assistance according to a very similar model of warfare. The idea of war and of preparations for war was bound up with the ways in which states established their political legitimacy.

Since the end of the Cold War, military spending by governments has fallen substantially. But what we have witnessed is less a contraction of military forces than a restructuring and increased diversity of types of military forces. There is a parallel with the pre-modern period, which was also characterized by a diversity of military forces—feudal levies, citizens' militias, mercenaries, pirates, for example—and by a corresponding variety of types of warfare.

Two interlinked developments have been critical, in my view, in bringing about these changes. One is the sheer destructiveness of modern warfare. As all types of weapons have become more lethal and/or more accurate, decisive military victory has become more and more difficult. The scale of destruction in World War II (some 50 million dead) is almost unbearable to contemplate. The Cold War could be understood as a way of evading or psychologically suppressing the implications of that destructiveness. Through the system of deterrence, the idea of modern war was kept alive in the imagination and helped to sustain the legitimacy and discipline of modern states. The military planners and scenario builders imagined wars, even more destructive than World War II, and developed competitive new technologies that, in theory, would be used in such wars. There were, of course, real wars and some 5 million people have died in wars in every decade since 1945 but, among the dominant powers, these were regarded as 'not-war' or marginal to the main contingency—a global inter-state clash. With the end of the Cold War, we have to come to terms with the impossibility of wars of the modern type.

The second development is the process known as globalization. By *globalization*, I mean increasing interconnectedness, the shrinking of distance and time, as a result of the combination of Information and Communications Technology (ICT) and air travel. A central issue for theorists of globalization has to do with the implications for the modern state (Held, 1999). Some argue that the state has become an anachronism and that we are moving towards a single world community. Some take the opposite view, that globalization is an invention of the state and can easily be reversed. Yet others insist that globalization does not mean the end of the state but rather its transformation. I share the last position but I would argue that there is no single method of transformation. States are changing in a variety of ways and, moreover, these changes, I shall argue, are bound up with changes in the types of armed forces and the forms of warfare.

The terms *militarism, arms races,* and *arms control* are expressions drawn from the Cold War era and before. *Militarism* refers to excessive levels of military spending by the state and excessive influence of armed forces over civilian life. *Arms races* refer to the competition between similar types of military forces. *Arms control* refers to the process of treaty making between states based on the assumption that stability can best be preserved through a "balance of power (or terror)" between states.

In this essay, I shall distinguish between the different types of armed forces that are emerging in the post–Cold War world, only some of which can be characterized in terms of militarism and arms races, and discuss how they are loosely associated with different modes of state transformation and different forms of warfare. I have identified four different types of armed forces. They could be described as Weberian ideal types. They are probably not comprehensive, and no single example exactly fits a particular type. There is also a lot of overlap. The point is to provide a schematic account of what is happening in the field of warfare so as to be able to offer some new ways of thinking about the possibilities for controlling or limiting the means of warfare and why we need a new terminology beyond militarism, arms races, and arms control. I shall suggest that the emphasis that has been increasingly accorded to international law, particularly humanitarian law, offers a possible way forward.

Netforce: Informal or Privatized Armed Forces

A typical new phenomenon is armed networks of non-state and state actors. They include: para-military groups organized around a charismatic leader, warlords who control particular areas, terrorist cells, fanatic volunteers like the Mujahadeen, organized criminal groups, units of regular forces or other security services, as well as mercenaries and private military companies.

The form of warfare that is waged by these networks is what I call "new war" (Kaldor, 1999). New wars, which take place in the Balkans, Africa, Central Asia and other places, are sometimes called internal or civil wars to distinguish them from intra-state or Clausewitzean war. I think this terminology is inappropriate for a number of reasons. First, the networks cross borders. One of the typical features of the "new wars" is the key role played by Diaspora groups either far away (Sudanese or Palestinian workers in the Gulf states, former Yugoslav workers in Western Europe, immigrant groups in the new "melting pot" nations like North America or Oceania) or in neighboring states (Serbs in Croatia and Bosnia, Tutsis in Burundi or the DRC). Secondly, the wars involve an array of global actors—foreign mercenaries and volunteers, Diaspora supporters, neighboring states, not to mention the humanitarian actors such as aid agencies, NGOs or reporters.

And thirdly, and most importantly, the "new wars" tend to be concentrated in areas where the modern state is unraveling and where the distinctions between internal and external, public and private, no longer have the same meaning. Such areas are characterized by what are called frail or failing states, quasi or shadow states. These are states, formally recognized by the outside world, with some of the trappings of statehood—an incomplete administrative apparatus, a flag, sometimes a currency—but where those trappings do not express control over territory and where access to the state apparatus is about private gain, not public policy. In particular these are states where the monopoly of legitimate organized violence is eroding.

In many of the areas where new wars take place, it is possible to observe a process that is almost the reverse of the process through which modern states were constructed. Taxes fall because of declining investment and production, increased corruption and clientilism, or declining legitimacy. The declining tax revenue leads to growing dependence both on external sources and on private sources, through, for example, rent seeking or criminal activities. Reductions in public expenditure as a result of the shrinking fiscal base as well as pressures from external donors for macro-economic stabilization and liberalization (which also may reduce export revenues) further erode legitimacy. A growing informal economy associated with increased inequalities, unemployment and rural-urban migration, combined with the loss of legitimacy, weakens the rule of law and may lead to the re-emergence of privatized forms of violence: organized crime and the substitution of "protection" for taxation; vigilantes; private security guards protecting economic facilities, especially international companies; or para-military groups associated with particular political factions. In particular, reductions in security expenditure, often encouraged by external donors for the best of motives, may lead to breakaway groups of redundant soldiers and policemen seeking alternative employment.

Of course, the networks that engage in new wars are not all to be found in these failing states. They include nodes in advanced industrial countries and, in the inner cities of the West, it is possible to observe gang warfare that has many of the characteristics of "new wars." Nevertheless, this type of state provides a fertile environment for these types of network.

There are three main characteristics of the "new wars." First of all, I use the term *war* to emphasize the political character of the new wars, even though they could also be described as organized crime (illegal or private violence) or as massive violations of human rights (violence against civilians). Because networks are loose horizontal coalitions, unlike vertical disciplined armies of the past, a shared narrative, often based on a common identity, ethnic or religious, is an important organizing mechanism. In the case of the netforce, the networks engaged in the new wars, what holds them together is generally an extreme political ideology based on the exclusive claim to state power on the basis of identity—ethnic chauvinism or religious communalism. I stress access to state power because these ideologies are not about substantive grievances, such as language rights or religious rights, although these may be indirectly important; rather they are about control of power and resources for an exclusively defined group of people.

I take the view that these ideologies are politically constituted. Even though they are based on pre-existing cleavages of tribe, nation and religion, and even though they may make use of memories and experiences of past injustices, they are constructed or accentuated for the purpose of political mobilization.

Modern communications are important for the new networks both as a way of organizing the network and as a form of mobilization. Constructions of the past are developed and disseminated through radio, videos and television. Thus hate radio was of key importance in Rwanda. In Serbia, television was effectively used to remind people of the injustices of the past—the defeat of the Serbs by the Turks in 1389 and the fascist Croat treatment of Serbs during World War II. In the Middle East, videocassettes of Bin Laden's speeches circulate widely. The effect of television and radio in speeding up mobilization especially in the countryside or among newly arrived urban migrants, who do not have the reading habit, should not be underestimated. There is an important contrast here with nineteenth century "imagined communities" which were propagated through the print media and involved the intellectual classes. The more populist electronic media are designed to appeal primarily to the least educated members of the public. In general, it is states that control the radio and television. But non-state groups can make use of other forms of media: Diaspora broadcasts through satellite television, which were important in Kosovo; the circulation of videos; or local radio in areas under political control.

A second characteristic of the "new wars" is that war itself is a form of political mobilization. In what I have called wars between states, the aim of war was, to quote Clausewitz, "to compel an opponent to fulfil our will." In general this was achieved through the military capture of territory and victory in battle. People were mobilized to participate in the war effort—to join the army or to produce weapons and uniforms. In the new wars, mobilizing people is the aim of the war effort; the point of the violence is not so much directed against the enemy; rather the aim is to expand the networks of extremism. Generally the strategy is to control territory through political means, and military means are used to kill, expel, or silence those who might challenge control. This is why the warring parties use techniques of terror, ethnic cleansing, or genocide as deliberate war strategies. In the new wars, battles are rare and violence is directed against civilians. Violations of humanitarian and human rights law are not a side effect of war but the central methodology of new wars. Over 90 percent of the casualties in the new wars are civilian, and the number of refugees and displaced persons per conflict has risen steadily.

The strategy is to gain political power through sowing fear and hatred, to create a climate of terror, to eliminate moderate voices, and to defeat tolerance. The political ideologies of exclusive nationalism or religious communalism are generated through violence. It is generally assumed that extreme ideologies, based on exclusive identities—Serb nationalism, for example, or fundamentalist Islam—are the cause of war. Rather, the spread and strengthening of these ideologies are the consequence of war. "The war had to be so bloody," Bosnians will tell you, "because we did not hate each other; we had to be taught to hate each other."

A third characteristic of the new wars is the type of economy they generate. Because these networks flourish in states where systems of taxation have collapsed and where little new wealth is being created, and where the wars destroy physical infrastructure, cut off trade, and create a climate of insecurity that prohibits investment, they have to seek alternative, exploitative forms of financing. They raise money through loot and plunder, through illegal trading in drugs, illegal immigrants, cigarettes and alcohol, through "taxing" humanitarian assistance, through support from sympathetic states, and through remittances from members of the networks. All of these types of economic activity are predatory and depend on an atmosphere of insecurity. Indeed, the new wars can be described as a central source of the globalized informal economy—the transnational criminal and semi-legal economy that represents the underside of globalization.

The logical conclusion that can be drawn from these three characteristics is that the new wars are very difficult to contain and very difficult to end. They spread through refugees and displaced persons, through criminal networks, and through the extremist viruses they nurture. We can observe growing clusters of warfare in Africa, the Middle East, Central Asia or the Caucasus. The wars represent a defeat for democratic politics, and each bout of warfare strengthens those networks with a vested political and economic interest in continued violence. There are no clear victories or defeats because the warring parties are sustained both politically and economically by continuing violence. The wars speed up the process of state unraveling; they destroy what remains of productive activities, they undermine legitimacy, and they foster criminality. The areas where conflicts have lasted longest have generated cultures of violence, as in the jihad culture taught in religious schools in Pakistan and Afghanistan or among the Tamils of Sri Lanka, where young children are taught to be martyrs and where killing is understood as an offering to God. In the instructions found in the car of the hijackers in Boston's Logan Airport, it is written: "If God grants any one of you a slaughter, you should perform it as an offering on behalf of your father and mother, for they are owed by you. If you slaughter, you should plunder those you slaughter, for that is a sanctioned custom of the Prophet's."

It should be noted that there are other private or informal forces that do not correspond to this analysis. For example, in many of the new wars, villages or municipalities establish citizens' militias to defend local people—this was the case in some groups in Rwanda and also in Tuzla and Zenica during the Bosnian war. There are also more traditional guerrilla groups, whose strategy is to gain political control through winning hearts and minds rather than through sowing fear and hatred; hence they attack agents of the state and not civilians, at least in theory. Finally, there are numerous private security companies, often established to protect multinational companies in difficult places, and mercenaries, who fight for money; tactics and forms of warfare, in these cases, depend largely on the paymasters.

The New American Militarism

It could be argued that if September 11 had not happened, the American military-industrial complex might have had to invent it. Indeed, what happened on September 11 could have come out of what seemed to be the wild fantasies of "asymmetric threats" that were developed by American strategic analysts as they sought a new military role for the United States after the end of the Cold War. A reporter for the *London Observer* claimed to have found in one of the headquarters for terrorist training in Afghanistan, a photocopy of the "terrorist cookbook" which circulates among the American fundamentalist right.

World military spending declined by one third in the decade after 1989. American military spending also declined but by less than the global average and began to rise again after 1998. As of the year 2000, American military spending in real terms is equivalent to its spending in 1980, just before the Reagan military build-up. More importantly, what took place during the 1990s was a radical shift in the structure of U.S. military expenditure. Spending on military research and development declined less than overall military spending and has increased faster since 1998. As of 2000, U.S. military R&D spending is 47 percent higher in real terms than in 1980 (SIPRI, 2001). Instead of ushering in a period of downsizing, disarmament and conversion (although some of that did take place at local levels in the U.S.), the end of the Cold War led to a feverish technological effort to apply information technology to military purposes, known as the Revolution in Military Affairs (RMA). . . .

The Gulf war provided a model for what can be described as casualty-free war—that is to say the use of high-technology either directly to attack an enemy or to support a proxy, say the KLA in Kosovo or the Northern Alliance in Afghanistan. The idea now is that this high-tech warfare can be used against "rogue states" sponsoring terrorists. The same techniques were used against Iraq in December 1998, in Yugoslavia in 1999 and now in Afghanistan. They satisfy a confluence of interests. They fulfill the needs of the scientists, engineers and companies that provide an infrastructure for the American military effort. They allow for a continuation of the imaginary war of the Cold War period from the point of view of Americans. They do not involve American casualties, and they can be watched on television and demonstrate the determination and power of the United States government—the "spectacles" as Der Derian has put it, that "serve to deny imperial decline." It is this imaginary character from an American perspective that explains Jean Baudrillard's famous remark that the Gulf War did not happen.

The program for national missile defense has to be understood in the same vein. Even if the system cannot work, it provides imaginary protection for the United States, allowing the United States to engage in casualty-free war without fear of retaliation. This notion is evident from the way in which Donald Rumsfeld, the U.S. defense secretary, talks about how NMD will enhance deterrence through a combination of defensive and offensive measures. The weakness of deterrence was always the problem of credibility; a problem that leads to more and more useable nuclear weapons. With casualty-free war, the credibility of U.S. action is more convincing; after all, it is said, that the attack on the World Trade Towers was equivalent to the use of a sub-strategic nuclear weapon. NMD, at least psychologically, extends the possibilities for casualty-free war.

However, from the point of view of the victims, these wars are very real and not so different from old wars. However precise the strikes, it is impossible to avoid "mistakes" or "collateral damage." It does not make civilian casualties any more palatable to be told they were not intended. Moreover, the destruction of physical infrastructure and the support for one side in the conflict, as in the case of proxies, results in many more indirect casualties. In the case of the Gulf War, direct Iraqi casualties . . . numbered in the tens of thousands but the destruction of physical infrastructure and the ensuing wars with the Kurds and the Shiites caused hundreds of thousands of further casualties and seem to have entrenched the vicious and dangerous rule of Saddam Hussein. In the . . . war in Afghanistan, there [were] thousands of casualties, both civilian and military, as well as thousands of people fleeing their homes and a humanitarian disaster because aid agencies [were unable] to enter the country. . . . Far from extending support for democratic values, casualty-free war shows that American lives are privileged over the lives of others and contributes to a perception of the United States as a global bully.

Terms like *imperialism* are, however, misleading. The United States is best characterized not as an imperial power but as the "last nation state." It is the only state, in this globalized world, that still has the capacity to act unilaterally. Its behavior is determined less by imperial considerations than by concerns about its own domestic public opinion. Casualty-free war is also in a sense a form of political mobilization. It is about satisfying various domestic constituencies, not about influencing the rest of the world, even though such actions have a profound impact on the rest of the world.

Neo-Modern Militarism

Neo-modern militarism refers to the evolution of classical military forces in large transition states. These are states that are undergoing a transition from a centralized economy to a more internationally open market-oriented system and, yet, which are large enough to retain a sizeable state sector. Typical examples are Russia, India and China. They are not large enough to challenge the U.S. and they are constrained by many of the imperatives of globalization, subject to many of the pressures that are experienced by frail or failing states. They tend to adopt extreme ideologies that resemble the ideologies of the "new wars"—Russian or Hindu chauvinism, for example. And there are often direct links to and even co-operation with the shadier networks, especially in Russia. Israel should probably also be included in this category, although its capacity to retain a sizeable military sector is due less to its size than to its dependence on the United States.

These states have retained their military forces, including nuclear weapons. In the case of India, there has been a significant increase in military spending throughout the 1990s and it could be argued that the term *arms race* could be applied to India and Pakistan, especially after the 1998 nuclear tests. Pakistan, however, could be said to be closer to the networks of the new wars with its links to militants in Kashmir and Afghanistan; in other words somewhere between netforce and neo-modern militarism. In the case of Russia, there was a dramatic contraction of military spending after the break-up of the Soviet Union and a deep crisis in the military-industrial complex. But pressure to increase military spending has increased and the demands of the war in Chechnya are leading to a reassessment of the relative importance of conventional versus nuclear weapons. The proposed cuts in nuclear weapons discussed between Putin and Bush will release funds for conventional improvements. China is also engaged in military expansion, especially since 1998, when the military were prohibited from engaging in commercial activities. Given the reductions in Russian nuclear capabilities and the new generation of Chinese systems, China will come to look more like a competitor to Russia, especially in the nuclear field.

The type of warfare that is associated with neo-modern militarism is either limited inter-state warfare or counter-insurgency. These states envisage wars on the classic Clausewitzean model. They engage in counter-insurgency in order to defeat extremist networks as in Chechnya or Kashmir. Or they prepare for the defense of borders against other states, as in the case of the Kargil war between India and Pakistan in 1998. Unlike the United States, these states are prepared to risk casualties and, in the case of the Chechen war, Russian casualties have been extremely high. The typical tactics used against the networks are shelling from tanks, helicopters, or artillery, as well as population displacement to "clean" areas of extremists or "terrorists." The impact on civilians is thus very similar to the impact of the "new wars." Yet precisely because of the growing destructiveness of all types of weapons and the consequent difficulty of overcoming defensive positions, military victory against an armed opponent is very hard to achieve. Grozny has virtually been reduced to rubble. Yet still resistance persists.

The networks have understood that they cannot take territory militarily, only through political means, and the point of the violence is to contribute to those political means. The states engaged in neo-modern militarism are still under the illusion that they can win militarily. The consequence is either self-imposed limits, as in the case of inter-state war, or exacerbation of "new wars" as in the case of Kashmir, Chechnya or Palestine, where counter-insurgency merely contributes to the political polarizing process of fear and hate. In other words, the utility of modern military force, the ability to "compel an opponent to fulfill our will" is open to question nowadays.

Protectionforce: Peacekeeping/Peace-Enforcement

An important trend in the last decade has been the increase in peacekeeping operations. At the start of the decade, there were only eight United Nations peacekeeping operations; they involved some 10,000 troops. As of the end of 2000, there were fifteen United Nations operations involving some 38,000 military troops (Global Civil Society, 2001). In addition, a number of regional organizations were engaged in peacekeeping: NATO in Bosnia, Kosovo and Macedonia; the Commonwealth of Independent States (CIS), mainly Russia, in Tajikistan, Transdinestr, Abkhazia, and South Ossetia; the Economic Community of West African States (ECOWAS) in Sierra Leone, Liberia and Guinea.

Peacekeeping has not only increased in scale; there have been important changes in the tasks peacekeepers are asked to perform and in the way we think about peacekeeping. During the Cold War period, peacekeeping was based on the assumption that wars were of the Clausewitzean type. The job of peacekeepers was to separate the warring parties and to monitor cease-fires on the basis of agreements. Peacekeeping was sharply distinguished from peace enforcement, which was equated with war fighting, i.e., intervening in a war on one side, authorized under Chapter VIII of the UN Charter.

In terms of organization, peacekeeping has more in common with the networks than with classic military forces. Peacekeeping forces are generally loose transnational coalitions. Although they usually have a clearly defined multinational command system, peacekeepers are also subject to national commands, which erodes the vertical character of the command system. Because they are often far away from the decision-makers and because of the nature of their tasks, individual initiative is often more important than unquestioning obedience. Moreover, peacekeepers have to work together with a range of other agencies, international organizations like UNHCR or UNDP and also NGOs involved in humanitarian assistance or conflict resolution. A shared normative narrative based on humanitarian principles is critical in holding the networks together.

The new tasks for peacekeepers include the protection of safe havens, where civilians can find refuge, the protection of convoys delivering humanitarian assistance, disarmament and demobilization, providing a secure environment for elections or for the return of refugees and displaced persons, or capturing war criminals. These tasks reflect the changes in the nature of the warfare. New terms like *second-generation peacekeeping, wider peacekeeping* or *robust peacekeeping* have been used to describe these new roles. Peacekeepers nowadays operate in the context of continuing wars or insecure post-conflict situations, and they are more likely to risk casualties than were traditional peacekeepers.

A number of recent reports have emphasized that the new role of peacekeeping is, first and foremost, the protection of civilians since they are the main targets of the new wars (Brahimi, 2000). The new peacekeeping is indeed somewhere between traditional peacekeeping (separating sides) and peace enforcement (taking sides). I have argued that outright military victory is very, very difficult nowadays, at least if we are unwilling to contemplate mass destruction. The job of the new protectionforce is not to defeat an enemy but to protect civilians and stabilize war situations so that non-extremist tolerant politics has space to develop. The task is thus more like policing than warfighting although it involves the use of military forces. Techniques like safe havens or humanitarian corridors are ways of protecting civilians and also of increasing the international presence on the ground so as to influence political outcomes.

In practice, peacekeeping has not lived up to this description. Partly this is due to lack of resources. Not nearly enough has been invested in peacekeeping and in providing appropriate training and equipment. More importantly, international lives are still privileged over the lives of the civilians they are supposed to protect. OSCE monitors left Kosovo hurriedly when the bombing of Yugoslavia began, leaving behind a terrified population who had believed rightly or wrongly that the orange vans of the OSCE monitors were some protection; the local OSCE staff left behind were all killed. Likewise, Dutch peacekeepers handed over the 8000 men and boys of Srebrenica to Serb forces in July 1995 and they were all massacred. In Rwanda, UN forces were withdrawn just as the genocide of 800,000 Tutsis began, despite the impassioned plea of the Canadian UN Commander, General Dallaire, to establish safe havens. There are, of course, also moments of heroism, like the Ukrainian peacekeepers in Zepa or the British in Goradze, or the UN staff in East Timor who refused to evacuate their headquarters unless the people who had sought refuge there were also saved. But, as yet, these moments are insufficient to be seen to justify the commitment in resources and will that would be necessary for a serious and sustained use of peacekeeping.

Peacekeeping/peace-enforcement is associated with states that could be described as post-modern (Cooper, 2000) or globalizing (Clark, 1999). These are states that have come to terms with the erosion of their autonomy (their ability to retain control over what happens in their territory), in the context of growing interconnectedness. They have thus adopted a deliberate strategy of multilateralism, of trying to influence the formation of global rules and participating actively in the enforcement of those rules. The British Prime Minister Tony Blair attempted to articulate this position in his speech on the "Doctrine of the International Community" during the Kosovo war. "We are all internationalists now whether we like it or not," he told an audience in Chicago. "We cannot refuse to participate in global markets if we want to prosper. We cannot ignore new political ideas in other countries if we want to innovate. We cannot turn our backs on conflicts and the violation of human rights in other countries if we still want to be secure" (Blair, 1999).

The states that fit this category include most European states, Canada, South Africa, Japan, as well as a number of others. Of course, most states, including the United States and Russia, engage in this type of peace operation. But it is not viewed as the main contingency for which they prepare. The new globalizing states are reorienting their military doctrines along these lines. The wars in the Balkans have had a profound impact in Europe, where concern about Balkan stability and experience in the region is shaping military thinking.

Controlling War?

During the Cold War period, the main concern was how to prevent a war of global annihilation. Arms control was seen as one of the most important methods of prevention; it was a way of stabilizing the perception of a balance of power. A true balance of power is a war that no side can win. Because armed forces were roughly similar during the Cold War period, it was possible to estimate a surrogate balance of power based on quantitative estimates of military forces, which could be codified in arms control treaties. This surrogate balance of power was seen as a way of preventing perceptions of imbalance, which might have tempted one or the other side to start a war. In practice, of course, numbers are irrelevant since any nuclear war is likely to lead to global annihilation but the exercise of measuring a balance of power shored up the notion of an imaginary war that could not be won.

The danger of a war of global annihilation has, thankfully, receded since the end of the Cold War. What we are now witnessing, however, is a series of real wars that cannot be won. There are no surrogate balances, except perhaps between the neo-modern military forces. The U.S. no longer has what is known in the jargon as a "peer competitor," and other types of armed forces are too varied to be compared. What I have tried to argue is that the first three types of armed forces (the networks, the new American military forces, and the neo-modern military forces) all engage in real wars with very similar consequences—indiscriminate suffering for civilians (even though the Americans claim that their greater precision and discriminateness minimizes such suffering). Nowadays, therefore, the emphasis of those who are concerned about such suffering has to be directly with the ways to control war. Limitations on weapons may be part of that wider goal but have to be viewed from a different perspective than in the Cold War period.

Perhaps the most hopeful approach to the contemporary problem of controlling war, nowadays, is not through arms control but through the extension and application of international humanitarian law (the "laws of war") and human rights law. During the 1990s, much greater importance was accorded to humanitarian norms—the notion that the international community has a duty to prevent genocide, violations of humanitarian law (war crimes) and massive violations of human rights (crimes against humanity). The idea of overriding state sovereignty in the case of humanitarian crises became much more widely accepted. The establishment of the Yugoslav and Rwanda Tribunals paved the way for the establishment of an International Criminal Court. The Pinochet and Ariel Sharon cases removed the principle of sovereign immunity.

Humanitarian law is not, of course, new. Its origins lie in the codification of "laws of war," especially under the auspices of the International Red Cross, in the late nineteenth century. The aim was to limit what we now call "collateral damage" or the side effects of war, above all, to prevent the indiscriminate suffering of civilians, and to ensure humane treatment for the wounded and for prisoners of war. These laws codified rules in Europe, which dated back to the Middle Ages and underlay a notion of "civilized" warfare, which was important in order to define the role of the soldier as the legitimate agent of the state, as a hero, not a criminal. (Of course, these rules were not applied outside Europe against "barbarians" or the "rude nations").

Humanitarian law was greatly extended after World War II. The Nuremberg and Tokyo trials marked the first enforcement of war crimes and, indeed, crimes against humanity. The Genocide Convention of 1948 as well as further extension of the Geneva Conventions, and the newly developing human rights law all represented further strengthening of humanitarian law, albeit marginalized by the dominant Cold War confrontation.

What has changed in the last decades is the change in the nature of warfare, even though some aspects were presaged in the Holocaust and the bombing of civilians in the Second World War. As argued above, violations of humanitarian law and human rights law are no longer "side effects" of war; they represent the core of the new warfare. Therefore taking seriously humanitarian law is one way of controlling the new warfare.

This is the context in which the limitation of armaments should also be understood. Recent efforts to limit or eliminate categories of weapons, like the Land Mines Convention or the protocol to the Biological Weapons Convention, or the efforts to control small arms, are not based on the assumption of a balance between states. Rather they are the outcome of pressure by global civil society to uphold humanitarian norms and prevent indiscriminate harm to civilians. The 1996 International Court of Justice decision about nuclear weapons, as well as several recent cases in Scotland, is based on the same line of thinking.

Taken seriously, a humanitarian approach would outlaw netforce and would restructure legitimate, i.e., state, military forces from classic war-fighting tasks to a new and extended form of protectionforce. It would outlaw WMD as well as weapons like land mines that cause indiscriminate harm. Peacekeeping and peace-enforcement could be reconceptualized as humanitarian law enforcement, with appropriate equipment and training.

Such an approach would be consistent with the transformation of states along the lines of the post-modern or globalizing states. It would imply a strengthening of global rules and greater participation in the enforcement of rules. All three of the other types of warfare I have described are based on particularist assumptions about the need to protect particular communities, networks or states, and to privilege their lives over others. There is no reason why growing interconnectedness cannot be combined with particularism and fragmentation; indeed that is the characteristic of the contemporary world. But it is no longer possible to insulate particular communities or states; even the United States is now vulnerable to transnational networks. If we are to find ways to cope with the uneven impact of globalization and to deal with the criminal and violent underside of globalization, then the main task is to construct some form of legitimate set of global rules. This is not the same as a global state; rather it is about establishing a set of global regimes underpinned by states, international institutions and global civil society. The humanitarian regime would be at the heart of such a set of rules because of the legitimacy that derives from the assumption of human equality.

If the legitimacy of modern states derived from their ability to protect borders against external enemies and to uphold the law domestically, then the legitimacy of global governance is likely to be greatly enhanced by a humanitarian regime that takes ultimate responsibility for the protection of individuals and for upholding international law. I am not implying a single world security organization. Rather, I am talking about a collective commitment by states, international organizations, and civil society to act when individual states fail to sustain these norms and to do so within a framework of international law.

How would this approach have changed the reaction to the events of September 11? What happened on September 11 was a crime against humanity. It was interpreted, however, in the U.S. as an attack on the U.S. and a parallel has been repeatedly drawn with Pearl Harbor. Bush talks about a "war on terrorism" and has said that "you are either with us or with the terrorists." . . . We do not know how many people have died as a result of the [American forces'] strikes or have fled their homes but it undoubtedly numbers in hundreds if not thousands. . . . While the Taliban has been overthrown [in Afghanistan] and, hopefully, bin Laden may be caught, there is unlikely to be any clear military victory. As I have argued, the political narrative, in this case of jihad against America, is central to the functioning of the network. [The current U.S. approach] confirms the political narrative and sets up exactly the kind of war envisaged by the Al-Qaeda network.

A humanitarian approach would have defined September 11 as a crime against humanity. It would have sought United Nations authorization for any action and it would have adopted tactics aimed at increasing trust and confidence on the ground, for example through the establishment of safe havens in the North as well as humanitarian corridors. It would have established an International Court to try terrorists. It would have adopted some of the means already adopted to put pressure on terrorist networks through squeezing financial assets, for example, as well as efforts to catch the criminals. Such an approach would also have to eschew double standards. Catching Mladic and Karadic, the perpetrators of the Srebrenica massacre, is just as important as catching bin Laden. Human rights violations in Palestine and Chechnya are no less serious than in Kosovo or Afghanistan.

A humanitarian approach, of course, has to be part of a wider political approach. In wars, in which no military victory is possible, political approaches are key. An alternative political narrative, based on the idea of global justice, is the only way to minimize the exclusive political appeal of the networks. I am aware that all this sounds impossibly utopian. Unfortunately, the humanitarian approach may be seen in retrospect as a brief expression of the interregnum between the end of the Cold War and September 11, 2001. We are, I fear, on the brink of a global new war, something like the wars in the Balkans or the Israel-Palestine war, on a global scale with no outsiders to constrain its course. Sooner or later, the impossibility of winning such a war must become evident and that is why we need to keep the humanitarian approach alive. Even if it cannot solve these conflicts, it can offer some hope to those caught in the middle. ■

NOTES

1. Carl Clausewitz (1780–1831) was a Prussian general who advocated "total war," which involved attacking the enemy's territory, property, and citizens.

REFERENCES

H. Anheier, M. Glasius, M. Kaldor (Eds.), *Global Civil Society 2001*, Oxford University Press, Oxford, England.

Blair, T. (1999), 'Doctrine of the International Community,' (23 April), http://www.primeminister.gov.uk.

Brahimi (2000), *Report of the Panel on United Nations Peace Operations*, (UN Doc.A/55/305S/2000/809, 21 August), New York, United Nations.

Clark, Ian (1999), *Globalisation and International Relations Theory,* Oxford, England, Oxford University Press.

Cooper, Robert (2000), *The Postmodern State and the World Order,* Demos/Foreign Policy Centre, London, 2nd edition.

Der Derian, J. and Shapiro, M. (1989) (Eds.), *International/Intertextual Relations: Postmodern Readings of World Politics,* Lexington, Mass.: Lexington Books.

Freedman, L. (1998), 'The Revolution in Strategic Affairs,' *Adelphi Paper 318,* London, International Institute of Strategic Affairs.

Giddens, A. (1990), *The Consequences of Modernity,* Polity Press, 1990.

Held, David et al. (1999), *Global Transformations,* Polity Press, Cambridge.

Kaldor, M. (1999), *New and Old Wars: Organized Violence in a Global Era,* Cambridge, England: Polity Press.

SIPRI (2001), Stockholm International Peace Research Institute, *SIPRI Yearbook 2001: Armaments, Disarmament and International Security,* Oxford, England, Oxford University Press.

Tilly, C. (1992), *Coercion, Capital and European States AD 990–1992,* Blackwell, Oxford.

■ QUESTIONS FOR MAKING CONNECTIONS WITHIN THE READING ■

1. What does Charles Tilly mean when he writes, "States made war and war made the state"? Is it true that war is primarily what defines us as Americans today? How about in the past? In what ways have wars played a decisive role in shaping our national identity?

2. What forces are responsible for the idea of "casualty-free war"? Is the expectation on the part of Americans that war should be casualty free, or as close to this goal as possible, simply a consequence of technological innovations, or are there other causes as well? What kinds of wars do you feel that most Americans are prepared to support? What kinds might they object to?

3. Why doesn't Kaldor use the term *terrorism* to cover all forms of non-state-sponsored violence? In what ways does her alternative term, *new war,* complicate our thinking about "unofficial" conflicts? Would you say that her terminology runs the risk of legitimizing terrorism? Alternately, does it free us from the arbitrariness that some might see in the use of that term?

■ QUESTIONS FOR WRITING ■

1. Is there a contradiction between "the new American militarism" and Kaldor's view that "the most hopeful approach to the contemporary problem of controlling war . . . is not through arms control but through the extension and application of international humanitarian law . . . and human rights law"? Does our country's "new militarism" contribute to, or detract from, the advancement of human rights and international order?

2. What is the difference between viewing the events of September 11 as an act of "terrorism" or "moral evil" and viewing them instead as "a political act"? What are the advantages and disadvantages of each approach to the event? Why, do you think, has a political interpretation of the events of September 11 received so little attention from the popular press? To say that readers and viewers "want something else" is not really an answer. Please consider the *culture* of the popular press: Does it rely on a nationalist perspective or globalist one?

■ *QUESTIONS FOR MAKING CONNECTIONS BETWEEN READINGS* ■

1. In "A World on the Edge," Amy Chua argues that "market-dominant minorities are the Achilles' heel of free-market democracy" because their success inspires resentment that leads to instability and violence. In such a context, is it advisable for First World countries like the United States to move "beyond militarism," as Kaldor recommends? If the U.S. began to support a greater degree of international cooperation, would this approach to political unrest also help to defuse the tensions created by economic inequality, or might it actually worsen those tensions by making America's wealth and power even more frustratingly obvious? Would Chua agree with Kaldor's proposals for responding to netforce threats?

2. Is Kaldor's view of human rights consistent with Martha Nussbaum's? If the United States were to adopt Nussbaum's ethical programs as the basis of its foreign policy, would the result be a higher level of integration between states, or an increased degree of international tension? In what ways might disagreements over basic moral issues stand in the way of global mechanisms for conflict resolution? Would the Taliban, for example, have bowed voluntarily to world pressure to improve the status of Afghan women? If globalization is inevitable, are wars over basic values inevitable as well, given the world's cultural diversity?

www **For additional suggestions about making connections between readings, visit the Link-O-Mat and More Sample Assignments at <www.newhum.com>.**

Jon Krakauer

Jon Krakauer, a regular contributor to *Outside Magazine,* rose to national prominence with the publication of *Into the Wild,* his investigative account of the life and death of Chris McCandless, a young man who disappeared after graduating from college in Georgia in the early 1990s and whose body was discovered two years later in an abandoned school bus in the wilds of Alaska. In an interview, Krakauer explained why he was driven to pursue McCandless's story in such detail:

> I was haunted by the particulars of the boy's starvation and by vague, unsettling parallels between events in his life and those in my own. Unwilling to let McCandless go, I spent more than a year retracing the convoluted path that led to his death in the Alaskan taiga, chasing down details of his peregrinations with an interest that bordered on obsession. In trying to understand McCandless, I inevitably came to reflect on other, larger subjects as well: the grip wilderness has on the American imagination, the allure high-risk activities hold for young men of a certain mind, the complicated, highly charged bond that exists between fathers and sons.

Retracing McCandless's journey, Krakauer meditates not only on what it means to be a man at the end of the twentieth century but also, more generally, on the place of the natural world in contemporary society.

After completing *Into the Wild,* Krakauer set off to study the tourist industry's guided climbs up Mount Everest. *Into Thin Air,* which also became an instant bestseller, is Krakauer's firsthand account of his experiences on a disastrous trip up Mount Everest that left nine climbers dead. The fact that this tragedy could easily have been avoided by staying down off the mountain has not escaped Krakauer's attention: "[W]hen I got back from Everest, I couldn't help but think that maybe I'd devoted my life to something that isn't just selfish

Krakauer, Jon. "The Alaska Interior" and "The Stampede Trail," *Into the Wild.* New York: Random House, 1996. 157–199.

Quotations from Jon Krakauer, "Everest a Year Later: Lessons in Futility," *Outside Magazine,* May 1997 <http://www.outsidemag.com/magazine/0597/9705krakauer.html> and Jon Krakauer's Author Introduction, *Outside Magazine* <http://www.outsidemag.com/disc/guest/krakauer/bookintro.html>.

and vainglorious and pointless, but actually wrong. There's no way to defend it, even to yourself, once you've been involved in something like this disaster. And yet I've continued to climb." Why do people embark on such adventures? What are they looking for? What is it they hope to achieve? These are the questions that animate Krakauer's writing; they are also the questions that he continues to try to answer for himself.

www   **To learn more about Jon Krakauer and adventure writing, visit the Link-O-Mat at <www.newhum.com>.**

Selections from
Into the Wild

The Alaska Interior

I wished to acquire the simplicity, native feelings, and virtues of savage life; to divest myself of the factitious habits, prejudices and imperfections of civilization; . . . and to find, amidst the solitude and grandeur of the western wilds, more correct views of human nature and of the true interests of man. The season of snows was preferred, that I might experience the pleasure of suffering, and the novelty of danger.

Estwick Evans,
A Pedestrious Tour, of Four Thousand Miles,
Through the Western States and Territories,
During the Winter and Spring of 1818

Wilderness appealed to those bored or disgusted with man and his works. It not only offered an escape from society but also was an ideal stage for the Romantic individual to exercise the cult that he frequently made of his own soul. The solitude and total freedom of the wilderness created a perfect setting for either melancholy or exultation.

Roderick Nash,
Wilderness and the American Mind

On April 15, 1992, Chris McCandless departed Carthage, South Dakota, in the cab of a Mack truck hauling a load of sunflower seeds. His "great Alaskan odyssey" was under way. Three days later he crossed the Canadian border at Roosville, British Columbia, and thumbed north through Skookumchuck and Radium Junction, Lake Louise and Jasper, Prince George and Dawson Creek—where, in the town center, he took a snapshot of the signpost marking the official start of the Alaska Highway. MILE "0," the sign reads, FAIRBANKS 1,523 MILES.

Hitchhiking tends to be difficult on the Alaska Highway. It's not unusual, on the outskirts of Dawson Creek, to see a dozen or more doleful-looking men and women standing along the shoulder with extended thumbs. Some of them may wait a week or more between rides. But McCandless experienced no such delay. On April 21, just six days out of Carthage, he arrived at Liard River Hotsprings, at the threshold of the Yukon Territory.

There is a public campground at Liard River, from which a boardwalk leads half a mile across a marsh to a series of natural thermal pools. It is the most popular way-stop on the Alaska Highway, and McCandless decided to pause there for a soak in the soothing waters. When he finished bathing and attempted to catch another ride north, however, he discovered that his luck had changed. Nobody would pick him up. Two days after arriving, he was still at Liard River, impatiently going nowhere.

At six-thirty on a brisk Thursday morning, the ground still frozen hard, Gaylord Stuckey walked out on the boardwalk to the largest of the pools, expecting to have the place to himself. He was surprised, therefore, to find someone already in the steaming water, a young man who introduced himself as Alex.

Stuckey—bald and cheerful, a ham-faced sixty-three-year-old Hoosier—was en route from Indiana to Alaska to deliver a new motor home to a Fairbanks RV dealer, a part-time line of work in which he'd dabbled since retiring after forty years in the restaurant business. When he told McCandless his destination, the boy exclaimed, "Hey, that's where I'm going, too! But I've been stuck here for a couple of days now, trying to get a lift. You mind if I ride with you?"

"Oh, jiminy," Stuckey replied. "I'd love to, son, but I can't. The company I work for has a strict rule against picking up hitchhikers. It could get me canned." As he chatted with McCandless through the sulfurous mist, though, Stuckey began to reconsider: "Alex was clean-shaven and had short hair, and I could tell by the language he used that he was a real sharp fella. He wasn't what you'd call a typical hitchhiker. I'm usually leery of 'em. I figure there's probably something wrong with a guy if he can't even afford a bus ticket. So anyway, after about half an hour I said, 'I tell you what, Alex: Liard is a thousand miles from Fairbanks. I'll take you five hundred miles, as far as Whitehorse; you'll be able to get a ride the rest of the way from there.'"

A day and a half later, however, when they arrived in Whitehorse—the capital of the Yukon Territory and the largest, most cosmopolitan town on the Alaska Highway—Stuckey had come to enjoy McCandless's company so much that he changed his mind and agreed to drive the boy the entire distance. "Alex didn't come out and say too much at first," Stuckey reports. "But it's a long, slow drive. We spent a total of three days together on those washboard roads, and by the end he kind of let his guard down. I tell you what: He was a dandy kid. Real courteous, and he didn't cuss or use a lot of that there slang. You could tell he came from a nice family. Mostly he talked about his sister. He didn't get along with his folks too good, I guess. Told me his dad was a genius, a NASA rocket scientist, but he'd been a bigamist at one time—and that kind of went against Alex's grain. Said he hadn't seen his parents in a couple of years, since his college graduation."

McCandless was candid with Stuckey about his intent to spend the summer alone in the bush, living off the land. "He said it was something he'd wanted to do since he was little," says Stuckey. "Said he didn't want to see a single person, no airplanes, no sign of civilization. He wanted to prove to himself that he could make it on his own, without anybody else's help."

Stuckey and McCandless arrived in Fairbanks on the afternoon of April 25. The older man took the boy to a grocery store, where he bought a big bag of rice, "and then Alex said he wanted to go out to the university to study up on what kind of plants he could eat. Berries and things like that. I told him, 'Alex, you're too early. There's still two foot, three foot of snow on the ground. There's nothing growing yet.' But his mind was pretty well made up. He was chomping at the bit to get out there and start hiking." Stuckey drove to the University of Alaska campus, on the west end of Fairbanks, and dropped McCandless off at 5:30 P.M.

"Before I let him out," Stuckey says, "I told him, 'Alex, I've driven you a thousand miles. I've fed you and fed you for three straight days. The least you can do is send me a letter when you get back from Alaska.' And he promised he would.

"I also begged and pleaded with him to call his parents. I can't imagine anything worse than having a son out there and not knowing where he's at for years and years, not knowing whether he's living or dead. 'Here's my credit card number,' I told him. '*Please* call them!' But all he said was 'Maybe I will and maybe I won't.' After he left, I thought, 'Oh, why didn't I get his parents' phone number and call them myself?' But everything just kind of happened so quick."

After dropping McCandless at the university, Stuckey drove into town to deliver the RV to the appointed dealer, only to be told that the person responsible for checking in new vehicles had already gone home for the day and wouldn't be back until Monday morning, leaving Stuckey with two days to kill in Fairbanks before he could fly home to Indiana. On Sunday morning, with time on his hands, he returned to the campus. "I hoped to find Alex and spend another day with him, take him sightseeing or something. I looked for a couple of hours, drove all over the place, but didn't see hide or hair of him. He was already gone."

After taking his leave of Stuckey on Saturday evening, McCandless spent two days and three nights in the vicinity of Fairbanks, mostly at the university. In the campus book store, tucked away on the bottom shelf of the Alaska section, he came across a scholarly, exhaustively researched field guide to the region's edible plants, *Tanaina Plantlore/Dena'ina K'et'una: An Ethnobotany of the Dena'ina Indians of Southcentral Alaska* by Priscilla Russell Kari. From a postcard rack near the cash register, he picked out two cards of a polar bear, on which he sent his final messages to Wayne Westerberg and Jan Burres from the university post office.

Perusing the classified ads, McCandless found a used gun to buy, a semiautomatic .22-caliber Remington with a 4-x-20 scope and a plastic stock. A model called the Nylon 66, no longer in production, it was a favorite of Alaska trappers because of its light weight and reliability. He closed the deal in a parking lot, probably paying about $125 for the weapon, and then purchased four one-hundred-round boxes of hollow-point long-rifle shells from a nearby gun shop.

At the conclusion of his preparations in Fairbanks, McCandless loaded up his pack and started hiking west from the university. Leaving the campus, he walked past the Geophysical Institute, a tall glass-and-concrete building capped with a large satellite dish. The dish, one of the most distinctive landmarks on the Fairbanks skyline, had been erected to collect data from satellites equipped with synthetic aperture radar of Walt McCandless's design. Walt had in fact visited Fairbanks during the start-up of the receiving station and had written some of the software crucial to its operation. If the Geophysical Institute prompted Chris to think of his father as he tramped by, the boy left no record of it.

Four miles west of town, in the evening's deepening chill, McCandless pitched his tent on a patch of hard-frozen ground surrounded by birch trees, not far from the crest of a bluff overlooking Gold Hill Gas & Liquor. Fifty yards from his camp was the terraced road cut of the George Parks Highway, the road that would take him to the Stampede Trail. He woke early on the morning of April 28, walked down to the highway in the predawn gloaming, and was pleasantly surprised when the first vehicle to come along pulled over to give him a lift. It was a gray Ford pickup with a bumper sticker on the back that declared, I FISH THEREFORE I AM. PETERSBURG, ALASKA. The driver of the truck, an electrician on his way to Anchorage, wasn't much older than McCandless. He said his name was Jim Gallien.

Three hours later Gallien turned his truck west off the highway and drove as far as he could down an unplowed side road. When he dropped McCandless off on the Stampede Trail, the temperature was in the low thirties—it would drop into the low teens at night—and a foot and a half of crusty spring snow covered the ground. The boy could hardly contain his excitement. He was, at long last, about to be alone in the vast Alaska wilds.

As he trudged expectantly down the trail in a fake-fur parka, his rifle slung over one shoulder, the only food McCandless carried was a ten-pound bag of long-grained rice—and the two sandwiches and bag of corn chips that Gallien had contributed. A year earlier he'd subsisted for more than a month beside the Gulf of California on five pounds of rice and a bounty of fish caught with a cheap rod and reel, an experience that made him confident he could harvest enough food to survive an extended stay in the Alaska wilderness, too.

The heaviest item in McCandless's half-full backpack was his library: nine or ten paperbound books, most of which had been given to him by Jan Burres in Niland. Among these volumes were titles by Thoreau and Tolstoy and Gogol, but McCandless was no literary snob: He simply carried what he thought he might enjoy reading, including mass-market books by Michael Crichton, Robert Pirsig, and Louis L'Amour. Having neglected to pack writing paper, he began a laconic journal on some blank pages in the back of *Tanaina Plantlore.*

The Healy terminus of the Stampede Trail is traveled by a handful of dog mushers, ski tourers, and snow-machine enthusiasts during the winter months, but only until the frozen rivers begin to break up, in late March or early April. By the time McCandless headed into the bush, there was open water flowing on most of the larger streams, and nobody had been very far down the trail for two or three weeks; only the faint remnants of a packed snow-machine track remained for him to follow.

McCandless reached the Teklanika River his second day out. Although the banks were lined with a jagged shelf of frozen overflow, no ice bridges spanned the channel of open water, so he was forced to wade. There had been a big thaw in early April, and breakup had come early in 1992, but the weather had turned cold again, so the river's volume was quite low when McCandless crossed—probably thigh-deep at most—allowing him to splash to the other side without difficulty. He never suspected that in so doing, he was crossing his Rubicon. To McCandless's inexperienced eye, there was nothing to suggest that two months hence, as the glaciers and snowfields at the Teklanika's headwater thawed in the summer heat, its discharge would multiply nine or ten times in volume, transforming the river into a deep, violent torrent that bore no resemblance to the gentle brook he'd blithely waded across in April.

From his journal we know that on April 29, McCandless fell through the ice somewhere. It probably happened as he traversed a series of melting beaver ponds just beyond the Teklanika's western bank, but there is nothing to indicate that he suffered any harm in the mishap. A day later, as the trail crested a ridge, he got his first glimpse of Mt. McKinley's high, blinding-white bulwarks, and a day after that, May 1, some twenty miles down the trail from where he was dropped by Gallien, he stumbled upon the old bus beside the Sushana River. It was outfitted with a bunk and a barrel stove, and previous visitors had left the improvised shelter stocked with matches, bug dope, and other essentials. "Magic Bus Day," he wrote in his journal. He decided to lay over for a while in the vehicle and take advantage of its crude comforts.

He was elated to be there. Inside the bus, on a sheet of weathered plywood spanning a broken window, McCandless scrawled an exultant declaration of independence:

> *TWO YEARS HE WALKS THE EARTH. NO PHONE, NO POOL, NO PETS, NO CIGARETTES. ULTIMATE FREEDOM. AN EXTREMIST. AN AESTHETIC VOYAGER WHOSE HOME IS <u>THE ROAD</u>. ESCAPED FROM ATLANTA. THOU SHALT NOT RETURN, 'CAUSE "THE WEST <u>IS</u> THE BEST." AND NOW AFTER TWO RAMBLING YEARS COMES THE FINAL AND GREATEST ADVENTURE. THE CLIMACTIC BATTLE TO KILL THE FALSE BEING WITHIN AND VICTORIOUSLY CONCLUDE THE SPIRITUAL PILGRIMAGE. TEN DAYS AND NIGHTS OF FREIGHT TRAINS AND HITCHHIKING BRING HIM TO THE GREAT WHITE NORTH. NO LONGER TO BE POISONED BY CIVILIZATION HE FLEES, AND WALKS ALONE UPON THE LAND TO BECOME LOST <u>IN THE WILD</u>.*
>
> *Alexander Supertramp*
> *May 1992*

Reality, however, was quick to intrude on McCandless's reverie. He had difficulty killing game, and the daily journal entries during his first week in the bush include "Weakness," "Snowed in," and "Disaster." He saw but did not shoot a grizzly on May 2, shot at but missed some ducks on May 4, and finally killed and ate a spruce grouse on May 5; but he didn't shoot anything else until May 9, when he bagged a single small squirrel, by which point he'd written "4th day famine" in the journal.

But soon thereafter his fortunes took a sharp turn for the better. By mid-May the sun was circling high in the heavens, flooding the taiga with light. The sun dipped below the northern horizon for fewer than four hours out of every twenty-four, and at midnight the sky was still bright enough to read by. Everywhere but on the north-facing slopes and in the shadowy ravines, the snowpack had melted down to bare ground, exposing the previous season's rose hips and lingonberries, which McCandless gathered and ate in great quantity.

He also became much more successful at hunting game and for the next six weeks feasted regularly on squirrel, spruce grouse, duck, goose, and porcupine. On May 22, a crown fell off one of his molars, but the event didn't seem to dampen his spirits much, because the following day he scrambled up the nameless, humplike, three-thousand-foot butte that rises directly north of the bus, giving him a view of the whole icy sweep of the Alaska Range and mile after mile of uninhabited country. His journal entry for the day is characteristically terse but unmistakably joyous: "CLIMB MOUNTAIN!"

McCandless had told Gallien that he intended to remain on the move during his stay in the bush. "I'm just going to take off and keep walking west," he'd said. "I might walk all the way to the Bering Sea." On May 5, after pausing for four days at the bus, he resumed his perambulation. From the snapshots recovered with his Minolta, it appears that McCandless lost (or intentionally left) the by now indistinct Stampede Trail and headed west and north through the hills above the Sushana River, hunting game as he went.

It was slow going. In order to feed himself, he had to devote a large part of each day to stalking animals. Moreover, as the ground thawed, his route turned into a gauntlet of boggy muskeg and impenetrable alder, and McCandless belatedly came to appreciate one of the fundamental (if counterintuitive) axioms of the North: winter, not summer, is the preferred season for traveling overland through the bush.

Faced with the obvious folly of his original ambition, to walk five hundred miles to tidewater, he reconsidered his plans. On May 19, having traveled no farther west than the Toklat River—less than fifteen miles beyond the bus—he turned around. A week later he was back at the derelict vehicle, apparently without regret. He'd decided that the Sushana drainage was plenty wild to suit his purposes and that Fairbanks bus 142 would make a fine base camp for the remainder of the summer.

Ironically, the wilderness surrounding the bus—the patch of overgrown country where McCandless was determined "to become lost in the wild"— scarcely qualifies as wilderness by Alaska standards. Less than thirty miles to the east is a major thoroughfare, the George Parks Highway. Just sixteen miles to the north, beyond an escarpment of the Outer Range, hundreds of tourists rumble daily into Denali Park over a road patrolled by the National Park Service. And unbeknownst to the Aesthetic Voyager, scattered within a six-mile radius of the bus are four cabins (although none happened to be occupied during the summer of 1992).

But despite the relative proximity of the bus to civilization, for all practical purposes McCandless was cut off from the rest of the world. He spent nearly four months in the bush all told, and during that period he didn't encounter another living soul. In the end the Sushana River site was sufficiently remote to cost him his life.

In the last week of May, after moving his few possessions into the bus, McCandless wrote a list of housekeeping chores on a parchmentlike strip of birch bark: collect and store ice from the river for refrigerating meat, cover the vehicle's missing windows with plastic, lay in a supply of firewood, clean the accumulation of old ash from the stove. And under the heading "LONG TERM" he drew up a list of more ambitious tasks: map the area, improvise a bathtub, collect skins and feathers to sew into clothing, construct a bridge across a nearby creek, repair mess kit, blaze a network of hunting trails.

The diary entries following his return to the bus catalog a bounty of wild meat. May 28: "Gourmet Duck!" June 1: "5 Squirrel." June 2: "Porcupine, Ptarmigan, 4 Squirrel, Grey Bird." June 3: "Another Porcupine! 4 Squirrel, 2 Grey Bird, Ash Bird." June 4: "A THIRD PORCUPINE! Squirrel, Grey Bird." On June 5, he shot a Canada goose as big as a Christmas turkey. Then, on June 9, he bagged the biggest prize of all: "MOOSE!" he recorded in the journal. Overjoyed, the proud hunter took a photograph of himself kneeling over his trophy, rifle thrust triumphantly overhead, his features distorted in a rictus of ecstasy and amazement, like some unemployed janitor who'd gone to Reno and won a million-dollar jackpot.

Although McCandless was enough of a realist to know that hunting game was an unavoidable component of living off the land, he had always been ambivalent about killing animals. That ambivalence turned to remorse soon after he shot the moose. It was relatively small, weighing perhaps six hundred or seven hundred pounds, but it nevertheless amounted to a huge quantity of meat. Believing that it was morally indefensible to waste any part of an animal that has been shot for food, McCandless spent six days toiling to preserve what he had killed before it spoiled. He butchered the carcass under a thick cloud of flies and mosquitoes, boiled the organs into a stew, and then laboriously excavated a burrow in the face of the rocky stream bank directly below the bus, in which he tried to cure, by smoking, the immense slabs of purple flesh.

Alaskan hunters know that the easiest way to preserve meat in the bush is to slice it into thin strips and then air-dry it on a makeshift rack. But McCandless, in his naïveté, relied on the advice of hunters he'd consulted in South Dakota, who advised him to smoke his meat, not an easy task under the circumstances. "Butchering extremely difficult," he wrote in the journal on June 10. "Fly and mosquito hordes. Remove intestines, liver, kidneys, one lung, steaks. Get hindquarters and leg to stream."

June 11: "Remove heart and other lung. Two front legs and head. Get rest to stream. Haul near cave. Try to protect with smoker."

June 12: "Remove half rib-cage and steaks. Can only work nights. Keep smokers going."

June 13: "Get remainder of rib-cage, shoulder and neck to cave. Start smoking."

June 14: "Maggots already! Smoking appears ineffective. Don't know, looks like disaster. I now wish I had never shot the moose. One of the greatest tragedies of my life."

At that point he gave up on preserving the bulk of the meat and abandoned the carcass to the wolves. Although he castigated himself severely for this waste of a life he'd taken, a day later McCandless appeared to regain some perspective, for his journal notes, "henceforth will learn to accept my errors, however great they be."

Shortly after the moose episode, McCandless began to read Thoreau's *Walden*. In the chapter titled "Higher Laws," in which Thoreau ruminates on the morality of eating, McCandless highlighted, "when I had caught and cleaned and cooked and eaten my fish, they seemed not to have fed me essentially. It was insignificant and unnecessary, and cost more than it came to."

"THE MOOSE," McCandless wrote in the margin. And in the same passage he marked,

> The repugnance to animal food is not the effect of experience, but is an instinct. It appeared more beautiful to live low and fare hard in many respects; and though I never did so, I went far enough to please my imagination. I believe that every man who has ever been earnest to preserve his higher or poetic faculties in the best condition has been particularly inclined to abstain from animal food, and from much food of any kind. . . .
>
> It is hard to provide and cook so simple and clean a diet as will not offend the imagination; but this, I think, is to be fed when we feed the body; they should both sit down at the same table. Yet perhaps this may be done. The fruits eaten temperately need not make us ashamed of our appetites, nor interrupt the worthiest pursuits. But put an extra condiment into your dish, and it will poison you.

"YES," wrote McCandless and, two pages later, "*Consciousness* of food. Eat and cook with *concentration*. . . . Holy Food." On the back pages of the book that served as his journal, he declared:

> I am reborn. This is my dawn. Real life has just begun.
>
> *Deliberate Living:* Conscious attention to the basics of life, and a constant attention to your immediate environment and its concerns, example ➔ A job, a task, a book; anything requiring efficient concentration (Circumstance has no value. It is how one *relates* to a situation that has value. All true meaning resides in the personal relationship to a phenomenon, what it means to you).
>
> The Great Holiness of **FOOD**, the Vital Heat.
>
> *Positivism*, the Insurpassable Joy of the Life Aesthetic.
>
> Absolute Truth and Honesty.
>
> Reality.
>
> Independence.
>
> Finality—Stability—Consistency.

As McCandless gradually stopped rebuking himself for the waste of the moose, the contentment that began in mid-May resumed and seemed to continue through early July. Then, in the midst of this idyll, came the first of two pivotal setbacks.

Satisfied, apparently, with what he had learned during his two months of solitary life in the wild, McCandless decided to return to civilization: It was time to bring his "final and greatest adventure" to a close and get himself back to the world of men and women, where he could chug a beer, talk philosophy, enthrall strangers with tales of what he'd done. He seemed to have moved beyond his need to assert so adamantly his autonomy, his need to separate himself from his parents. Maybe he was prepared to forgive their imperfections; maybe he was even prepared to forgive some of his own. McCandless seemed ready, perhaps, to go home.

Or maybe not; we can do no more than speculate about what he intended to do after he walked out of the bush. There is no question, however, that he intended to walk out.

Writing on a piece of birch bark, he made a list of things to do before he departed: "Patch Jeans, Shave!, Organize pack. . . ." Shortly thereafter he propped his Minolta on an empty oil drum and took a snapshot of himself brandishing a yellow disposable razor and grinning at the camera, clean-shaven, with new patches cut from an army blanket stitched onto the knees of his filthy jeans. He looks healthy but alarmingly gaunt. Already his cheeks are sunken. The tendons in his neck stand out like taut cables.

On July 2, McCandless finished reading Tolstoy's "Family Happiness," having marked several passages that moved him:

> He was right in saying that the only certain happiness in life is to live for others. . . .

> I have lived through much, and now I think I have found what is needed for happiness. A quiet secluded life in the country, with the possibility of being useful to people to whom it is easy to do good, and who are not accustomed to have it done to them; then work which one hopes may be of some use; then rest, nature, books, music, love for one's neighbor—such is my idea of happiness. And then, on top of all that, you for a mate, and children, perhaps—what more can the heart of a man desire?

Then, on July 3, he shouldered his backpack and began the twenty-mile hike to the improved road. Two days later, halfway there, he arrived in heavy rain at the beaver ponds that blocked access to the west bank of the Teklanika River. In April they'd been frozen over and hadn't presented an obstacle. Now he must have been alarmed to find a three-acre lake covering the trail. To avoid having to wade through the murky chest-deep water, he scrambled up a steep hillside, bypassed the ponds on the north, and then dropped back down to the river at the mouth of the gorge.

When he'd first crossed the river, sixty-seven days earlier in the freezing temperatures of April, it had been an icy but gentle knee-deep creek, and he'd simply strolled across it. On July 5, however, the Teklanika was at full flood, swollen with rain and snowmelt from glaciers high in the Alaska Range, running cold and fast.

If he could reach the far shore, the remainder of the hike to the highway would be easy, but to get there he would have to negotiate a channel some one hundred feet wide. The water, opaque with glacial sediment and only a few degrees warmer than the ice it had so recently been, was the color of wet concrete. Too deep to wade, it rumbled like a freight train. The powerful current would quickly knock him off his feet and carry him away.

McCandless was a weak swimmer and had confessed to several people that he was in fact afraid of the water. Attempting to swim the numbingly cold torrent or even to paddle some sort of improvised raft across seemed too risky to consider. Just downstream from where the trail met the river, the Teklanika erupted into a chaos of boiling whitewater as it accelerated through the narrow gorge. Long before he could swim or paddle to the far shore, he'd be pulled into these rapids and drowned.

In his journal he now wrote, "Disaster. . . . Rained in. River look impossible. Lonely, scared." He concluded, correctly, that he would probably be swept to his death if he attempted to cross the Teklanika at that place, in those conditions. It would be suicidal; it was simply not an option.

If McCandless had walked a mile or so upstream, he would have discovered that the river broadened into a maze of braided channels. If he'd scouted carefully, by trial and error he might have found a place where these braids were only chest-deep. As strong as the current was running, it would have certainly knocked him off his feet, but by dog-paddling and hopping along the bottom as he drifted downstream, he could conceivably have made it across before being carried into the gorge or succumbing to hypothermia.

But it would still have been a very risky proposition, and at that point McCandless had no reason to take such a risk. He'd been fending for himself quite nicely in the country. He probably understood that if he was patient and waited, the river would eventually drop to a level where it could be safely forded. After weighing his options, therefore, he settled on the most prudent course. He turned around and began walking to the west, back toward the bus, back into the fickle heart of the bush.

The Stampede Trail

Nature was here something savage and awful, though beautiful. I looked with awe at the ground I trod on, to see what the Powers had made there, the form and fashion and material of their work. This was that Earth of which we have heard, made out of Chaos and Old Night. Here was no man's garden, but the unhandselled globe. It was not lawn, nor pasture, nor mead, nor woodland, nor lea, nor arable, nor waste land. It was the fresh and natural surface of the planet Earth, as it was made forever and ever,—to be the dwelling of man, we say,—so Nature made it, and man may use it if he can. Man was not to be associated with it. It was Matter, vast, terrific,—not his Mother Earth that we have heard of, not for him to tread on, or to be buried in,—no, it were being too familiar even to let his bones lie there,—the home, this, of Necessity and Fate. There was clearly felt the presence of a force not bound to be kind to man. It was a place of heathenism and superstitious rites,—

to be inhabited by men nearer of kin to the rocks and to wild animals than we. . . . What is it to be admitted to a museum, to see a myriad of particular things, compared with being shown some star's surface, some hard matter in its home! I stand in awe of my body, this matter to which I am bound has become so strange to me. I fear not spirits, ghosts, of which I am one,—that my body might,—but I fear bodies, I tremble to meet them. What is this Titan that has possession of me? Talk of mysteries! Think of our life in nature,—daily to be shown matter, to come in contact with it,—rocks, trees, wind on our cheeks! the solid earth! the actual world! the common sense! Contact! Contact! Who are we? where are we?

Henry David Thoreau, "Ktaadn"

A year and a week after Chris McCandless decided not to attempt to cross the Teklanika River, I stand on the opposite bank—the eastern side, the highway side—and gaze into the churning water. I, too, hope to cross the river. I want to visit the bus. I want to see where McCandless died, to better understand why.

It is a hot, humid afternoon, and the river is livid with runoff from the fast-melting snowpack that still blankets the glaciers in the higher elevations of the Alaska Range. Today the water looks considerably lower than it looks in the photographs McCandless took twelve months ago, but to try to ford the river here, in thundering midsummer flood, is nevertheless unthinkable. The water is too deep, too cold, too fast. As I stare into the Teklanika, I can hear rocks the size of bowling balls grinding along the bottom, rolled downstream by the powerful current. I'd be swept from my feet within a few yards of leaving the bank and pushed into the canyon immediately below, which pinches the river into a boil of rapids that continues without interruption for the next five miles.

Unlike McCandless, however, I have in my backpack a 1:63,360-scale topographic map (that is, a map on which one inch represents one mile). Exquisitely detailed, it indicates that half a mile downstream, in the throat of the canyon, is a gauging station that was built by the U.S. Geological Survey. Unlike McCandless, too, I am here with three companions: Alaskans Roman Dial and Dan Solie and a friend of Roman's from California, Andrew Liske. The gauging station can't be seen from where the Stampede Trail comes down to the river, but after twenty minutes of fighting our way through a snarl of spruce and dwarf birch, Roman shouts, "I see it! There! A hundred yards farther."

We arrive to find an inch-thick steel cable spanning the gorge, stretched between a fifteen-foot tower on our side of the river and an outcrop on the far shore, four hundred feet away. The cable was erected in 1970 to chart the Teklanika's seasonal fluctuations; hydrologists traveled back and forth above the river by means of an aluminum basket that is suspended from the cable with pulleys. From the basket they would drop a weighted plumb line to measure the river's depth. The station was decommissioned nine years ago for lack of funds, at which time the basket was supposed to be chained and locked to the tower on our side—the highway side—of the river. When we climbed to the top of the tower, however, the basket wasn't there. Looking across the rushing water, I could see it over on the distant shore—the bus side—of the canyon.

Some local hunters, it turns out, had cut the chain, ridden the basket across, and secured it to the far side in order to make it harder for outsiders to cross the Teklanika and trespass on their turf. When McCandless tried to walk out of the bush one year ago the previous week, the basket was in the same place it is now, on his side of the canyon. If he'd known about it, crossing the Teklanika to safety would have been a trivial matter. Because he had no topographic map, however, he had no way of conceiving that salvation was so close at hand.

Andy Horowitz, one of McCandless's friends on the Woodson High cross-country team, had mused that Chris "was born into the wrong century. He was looking for more adventure and freedom than today's society gives people." In coming to Alaska, McCandless yearned to wander uncharted country, to find a blank spot on the map. In 1992, however, there were no more blank spots on the map—not in Alaska, not anywhere. But Chris, with his idiosyncratic logic, came up with an elegant solution to this dilemma: He simply got rid of the map. In his own mind, if nowhere else, the *terra* would thereby remain *incognita*.

Because he lacked a good map, the cable spanning the river also remained incognito. Studying the Teklanika's violent flow, McCandless thus mistakenly concluded that it was impossible to reach the eastern shore. Thinking that his escape route had been cut off, he returned to the bus—a reasonable course of action, given his topographical ignorance. But why did he then stay at the bus and starve? Why, come August, didn't he try once more to cross the Teklanika, when it would have been running significantly lower, when it would have been safe to ford?

Puzzled by these questions, and troubled, I am hoping that the rusting hulk of Fairbanks bus 142 will yield some clues. But to reach the bus, I, too, need to cross the river, and the aluminum tram is still chained to the far shore.

Standing atop the tower anchoring the eastern end of the span, I attach myself to the cable with rock-climbing hardware and begin to pull myself across, hand over hand, executing what mountaineers call a Tyrolean traverse. This turns out to be a more strenuous proposition than I had anticipated. Twenty minutes after starting out, I finally haul myself onto the outcrop on the other side, completely spent, so wasted I can barely raise my arms. After at last catching my breath, I climb into the basket—a rectangular aluminum car two feet wide by four feet long—disconnect the chain, and head back to the eastern side of the canyon to ferry my companions across.

The cable sags noticeably over the middle of the river; so when I cut loose from the outcrop, the car accelerates quickly under its own weight, rolling faster and faster along the steel strand, seeking the lowest point. It's a thrilling ride. Zipping over the rapids at twenty or thirty miles per hour, I hear an involuntary bark of fright leap from my throat before I realize that I'm in no danger and regain my composure.

After all four of us are on the western side of the gorge, thirty minutes of rough bushwhacking returns us to the Stampede Trail. The ten miles of trail we have already covered—the section between our parked vehicles and the river—were gentle, well marked, and relatively heavily traveled. But the ten miles to come have an utterly different character.

Because so few people cross the Teklanika during the spring and summer months, much of the route is indistinct and overgrown with brush. Immediately past the river the trail curves to the southwest, up the bed of a fast-flowing creek. And because beavers have built a network of elaborate dams across this creek, the route leads directly through a three-acre expanse of standing water. The beaver ponds are never more than chest deep, but the water is cold, and as we slosh forward, our feet churn the muck on the bottom into a foul-smelling miasma of decomposing slime.

The trail climbs a hill beyond the uppermost pond, then rejoins the twisting, rocky creek bed before ascending again into a jungle of scrubby vegetation. The going never gets exceedingly difficult, but the fifteen-foot-high tangle of alder pressing in from both sides is gloomy, claustrophobic, oppressive. Clouds of mosquitoes materialize out of the sticky heat. Every few minutes the insects' piercing whine is supplanted by the boom of distant thunder, rumbling over the taiga from a wall of thunderheads rearing darkly on the horizon.

Thickets of buckbrush leave a crosshatch of bloody lacerations on my shins. Piles of bear scat on the trail and, at one point, a set of fresh grizzly tracks—each print half again as long as a size-nine boot print—put me on edge. None of us has a gun. "Hey, Griz!" I yell at the undergrowth, hoping to avoid a surprise encounter. "Hey, bear! Just passing through! No reason to get riled!"

I have been to Alaska some twenty times during the past twenty years—to climb mountains, to work as a carpenter and a commercial salmon fisherman and a journalist, to goof off, to poke around. I've spent a lot of time alone in the country over the course of my many visits and usually relish it. Indeed, I had intended to make this trip to the bus by myself, and when my friend Roman invited himself and two others along, I was annoyed. Now, however, I am grateful for their company. There is something disquieting about this Gothic, overgrown landscape. It feels more malevolent than other, more remote corners of the state I know—the tundra-wrapped slopes of the Brooks Range, the cloud forests of the Alexander Archipelago, even the frozen, gale-swept heights of the Denali massif. I'm happy as hell that I'm not here alone.

* * *

At 9:00 P.M. we round a bend in the trail, and there, at the edge of a small clearing, is the bus. Pink bunches of fireweed choke the vehicle's wheel wells, growing higher than the axles. Fairbanks bus 142 is parked beside a coppice of aspen, ten yards back from the brow of a modest cliff, on a shank of high ground overlooking the confluence of the Sushana River and a smaller tributary. It's an appealing setting, open and filled with light. It's easy to see why McCandless decided to make this his base camp.

We pause some distance away from the bus and stare at it for a while in silence. Its paint is chalky and peeling. Several windows are missing. Hundreds of delicate bones litter the clearing around the vehicle, scattered among thousands of porcupine quills: the remains of the small game that made up the bulk of McCandless's diet. And at the perimeter of this boneyard lies one much larger skeleton: that of the moose he shot, and subsequently agonized over.

When I'd questioned Gordon Samel and Ken Thompson shortly after they'd discovered McCandless's body, both men insisted—adamantly and unequivocally—that the big skeleton was the remains of a caribou, and they derided the greenhorn's ignorance in mistaking the animal he killed for a moose. "Wolves had scattered the bones some," Thompson had told me, "but it was obvious that the animal was a caribou. The kid didn't know what the hell he was doing up here."

"It was definitely a caribou," Samel had scornfully piped in. "When I read in the paper that he thought he'd shot a moose, that told me right there he wasn't no Alaskan. There's a big difference between a moose and a caribou. A real big difference. You'd have to be pretty stupid not to be able to tell them apart."

Trusting Samel and Thompson, veteran Alaskan hunters who've killed many moose and caribou between them, I duly reported McCandless's mistake in the article I wrote for *Outside,* thereby confirming the opinion of countless readers that McCandless was ridiculously ill prepared, that he had no business heading into any wilderness, let alone into the big-league wilds of the Last Frontier. Not only did McCandless die because he was stupid, one Alaska correspondent observed, but "the scope of his self-styled adventure was so small as to ring pathetic—squatting in a wrecked bus a few miles out of Healy, potting jays and squirrels, mistaking a caribou for a moose (pretty hard to do). . . . Only one word for the guy: incompetent."

Among the letters lambasting McCandless, virtually all those I received mentioned his misidentification of the caribou as proof that he didn't know the first thing about surviving in the back country. What the angry letter writers didn't know, however, was that the ungulate McCandless shot was exactly what he'd said it was. Contrary to what I reported in *Outside,* the animal was a moose, as a close examination of the beast's remains now indicated and several of McCandless's photographs of the kill later confirmed beyond all doubt. The boy made some mistakes on the Stampede Trail, but confusing a caribou with a moose wasn't among them.

Walking past the moose bones, I approach the vehicle and step through an emergency exit at the back. Immediately inside the door is the torn mattress, stained and moldering, on which McCandless expired. For some reason I am taken aback to find a collection of his possessions spread across its ticking: a green plastic canteen; a tiny bottle of water-purification tablets; a used-up cylinder of Chap Stick; a pair of insulated flight pants of the type sold in military-surplus stores; a paperback copy of the bestseller *0 Jerusalem!*, its spine broken; wool mittens; a bottle of Muskol insect repellent; a full box of matches; and a pair of brown rubber work boots with the name Gallien written across the cuffs in faint black ink.

Despite the missing windows, the air inside the cavernous vehicle is stale and musty. "Wow," Roman remarks. "It smells like dead birds in here." A moment later I come across the source of the odor: a plastic garbage bag filled with feathers, down, and the severed wings of several birds. It appears that McCandless was saving them to insulate his clothing or perhaps to make a feather pillow.

Toward the front of the bus, McCandless's pots and dishes are stacked on a makeshift plywood table beside a kerosene lamp. A long leather scabbard is expertly tooled with the initials R. F.: the sheath for the machete Ronald Franz gave McCandless when he left Salton City.

The boy's blue toothbrush rests next to a half-empty tube of Colgate, a packet of dental floss, and the gold molar crown that, according to his journal, fell off his tooth three weeks into his sojourn. A few inches away sits a skull the size of a watermelon, thick ivory fangs jutting from its bleached maxillae. It is a bear skull, the remains of a grizzly shot by someone who visited the bus years before McCandless's tenure. A message scratched in Chris's tidy hand brackets a cranial bullet hole: ALL HAIL THE PHANTOM BEAR, THE BEST WITHIN US ALL. ALEXANDER SUPERTRAMP, MAY 1992.

Looking up, I notice that the sheet-metal walls of the vehicle are covered with graffiti left by numerous visitors over the years. Roman points out a message he wrote when he stayed in the bus four years ago, during a traverse of the Alaska Range: NOODLE EATERS EN ROUTE TO LAKE CLARK 8/89. Like Roman, most people scrawled little more than their names and a date. The longest, most eloquent graffito is one of several inscribed by McCandless, the proclamation of joy that begins with a nod to his favorite Roger Miller song: TWO YEARS HE WALKS THE EARTH, NO PHONE, NO POOL, NO PETS, NO CIGARETTES. ULTIMATE FREEDOM. AN EXTREMIST. AN AESTHETIC VOYAGER WHOSE NAME IS THE ROAD. . . .

Immediately below this manifesto squats the stove, fabricated from a rusty oil drum. A twelve-foot section of a spruce trunk is jammed into its open doorway, and across the log are draped two pairs of torn Levi's, laid out as if to dry. One pair of jeans—waist thirty, inseam thirty-two—is patched crudely with silver duct tape; the other pair has been repaired more carefully, with scraps from a faded bedspread stitched over gaping holes in the knees and seat. This latter pair also sports a belt fashioned from a strip of blanket. McCandless, it occurs to me, must have been forced to make the belt after growing so thin that his pants wouldn't stay up without it.

Sitting down on a steel cot across from the stove to mull over this eerie tableau, I encounter evidence of McCandless's presence wherever my vision rests. Here are his toenail clippers, over there his green nylon tent spread over a missing window in the front door. His Kmart hiking boots are arranged neatly beneath the stove, as though he'd soon be returning to lace them up and hit the trail. I feel uncomfortable, as if I were intruding, a voyeur who has slipped into McCandless's bedroom while he is momentarily away. Suddenly queasy, I stumble out of the bus to walk along the river and breathe some fresh air.

An hour later we build a fire outside in the fading light. The rain squalls, now past, have rinsed the haze from the atmosphere, and distant, backlit hills stand out in crisp detail. A stripe of incandescent sky burns beneath the cloud base on the northwestern horizon. Roman unwraps some steaks from a moose he shot in the Alaska Range last September and lays them across the fire on a blackened grill, the grill McCandless used for broiling his game. Moose fat pops and sizzles into the coals. Eating the gristly meat with our fingers, we slap at mosquitoes and talk about this peculiar person whom none of us ever met, trying to get a handle on how he came to grief, trying to understand why some people seem to despise him so intensely for having died here.

By design McCandless came into the country with insufficient provisions, and he lacked certain pieces of equipment deemed essential by many Alaskans: a large-caliber rifle, map and compass, an ax. This has been regarded as evidence not just of stupidity but of the even greater sin of arrogance. Some critics have even drawn parallels between McCandless and the Arctic's most infamous tragic figure, Sir John Franklin, a nineteenth-century British naval officer whose smugness and hauteur contributed to some 140 deaths, including his own.

In 1819, the Admiralty assigned Franklin to lead an expedition into the wilderness of northwestern Canada. Two years out of England, winter overtook his small party as they plodded across an expanse of tundra so vast and empty that they christened it the Barrens, the name by which it is still known. Their food ran out. Game was scarce, forcing Franklin and his men to subsist on lichens scraped from boulders, singed deer hide, scavenged animal bones, their own boot leather, and finally one another's flesh. Before the ordeal was over, at least two men had been murdered and eaten, the suspected murderer had been summarily executed, and eight others were dead from sickness and starvation. Franklin was himself within a day or two of expiring when he and the other survivors were rescued by a band of métis.

An affable Victorian gentleman, Franklin was said to be a good-natured bumbler, dogged and clueless, with the naïve ideals of a child and a disdain for acquiring backcountry skills. He had been woefully unprepared to lead an Arctic expedition, and upon returning to England, he was known as the

Man Who Ate His Shoes—yet the sobriquet was uttered more often with awe than with ridicule. He was hailed as a national hero, promoted to the rank of captain by the Admiralty, paid handsomely to write an account of his ordeal, and, in 1825, given command of a second Arctic expedition.

That trip was relatively uneventful, but in 1845, hoping finally to discover the fabled Northwest Passage, Franklin made the mistake of returning to the Arctic for a third time. He and the 128 men under his command were never heard from again. Evidence unearthed by the forty-odd expeditions sent to search for them eventually established that all had perished, the victims of scurvy, starvation, and unspeakable suffering.

When McCandless turned up dead, he was likened to Franklin not simply because both men starved but also because both were perceived to have lacked a requisite humility; both were thought to have possessed insufficient respect for the land. A century after Franklin's death, the eminent explorer Vilhjalmur Stefansson pointed out that the English explorer had never taken the trouble to learn the survival skills practiced by the Indians and the Eskimos—peoples who had managed to flourish "for generations, bringing up their children and taking care of their aged" in the same harsh country that killed Franklin. (Stefansson conveniently neglected to mention that many, many Indians and Eskimos have starved in the northern latitudes, as well.)

McCandless's arrogance was not of the same strain as Franklin's, however. Franklin regarded nature as an antagonist that would inevitably submit to force, good breeding, and Victorian discipline. Instead of living in concert with the land, instead of relying on the country for sustenance as the natives did, he attempted to insulate himself from the northern environment with ill-suited military tools and traditions. McCandless, on the other hand, went too far in the opposite direction. He tried to live entirely off the country—and he tried to do it without bothering to master beforehand the full repertoire of crucial skills.

It probably misses the point, though, to castigate McCandless for being ill prepared. He was green, and he overestimated his resilience, but he was sufficiently skilled to last for sixteen weeks on little more than his wits and ten pounds of rice. And he was fully aware when he entered the bush that he had given himself a perilously slim margin for error. He knew precisely what was at stake.

It is hardly unusual for a young man to be drawn to a pursuit considered reckless by his elders; engaging in risky behavior is a rite of passage in our culture no less than in most others. Danger has always held a certain allure. That, in large part, is why so many teenagers drive too fast and drink too much and take too many drugs, why it has always been so easy for nations to recruit young men to go to war. It can be argued that youthful derring-do is in fact evolutionarily adaptive, a behavior encoded in our genes. McCandless, in his fashion, merely took risk-taking to its logical extreme.

He had a need to test himself in ways, as he was fond of saying, "that mattered." He possessed grand—some would say grandiose—spiritual ambitions. According to the moral absolutism that characterizes McCandless's beliefs, a challenge in which a successful outcome is assured isn't a challenge at all.

It is not merely the young, of course, who are drawn to hazardous undertakings. John Muir is remembered primarily as a no-nonsense conservationist and the founding president of the Sierra Club, but he was also a bold adventurer, a fearless scrambler of peaks, glaciers, and waterfalls whose best-known essay includes a riveting account of nearly falling to his death, in 1872, while ascending California's Mt. Ritter. In another essay Muir rapturously describes riding out a ferocious Sierra gale, by choice, in the uppermost branches of a one-hundred-foot Douglas fir:

> [N]ever before did I enjoy so noble an exhilaration of motion. The slender tops fairly flapped and swished in the passionate torrent, bending and swirling backward and forward, round and round, tracing indescribable combinations of vertical and horizontal curves, while I clung with muscles firm braced, like a bobolink on a reed.

He was thirty-six years old at the time. One suspects that Muir wouldn't have thought McCandless terribly odd or incomprehensible.

Even staid, prissy Thoreau, who famously declared that it was enough to have "traveled a good deal in Concord," felt compelled to visit the more fearsome wilds of nineteenth-century Maine and climb Mt. Katahdin. His ascent of the peak's "savage and awful, though beautiful" ramparts shocked and frightened him, but it also induced a giddy sort of awe. The disquietude he felt on Katahdin's granite heights inspired some of his most powerful writing and profoundly colored the way he thought thereafter about the earth in its coarse, undomesticated state.

Unlike Muir and Thoreau, McCandless went into the wilderness not primarily to ponder nature or the world at large but, rather, to explore the inner country of his own soul. He soon discovered, however, what Muir and Thoreau already knew: An extended stay in the wilderness inevitably directs one's attention outward as much as inward, and it is impossible to live off the land without developing both a subtle understanding of, and a strong emotional bond with, that land and all it holds.

The entries in McCandless's journal contain few abstractions about wilderness or, for that matter, few ruminations of any kind. There is scant mention of the surrounding scenery. Indeed, as Roman's friend Andrew Liske points out upon reading a photocopy of the journal, "These entries are almost entirely about what he ate. He wrote about hardly anything except food."

Andrew is not exaggerating: The journal is little more than a tally of plants foraged and game killed. It would probably be a mistake, however, to conclude thereby that McCandless failed to appreciate the beauty of the country around him, that he was unmoved by the power of the landscape. As cultural ecologist Paul Shepard has observed,

> *The nomadic Bedouin does not dote on scenery, paint landscapes, or compile a nonutilitarian natural history. . . . [H]is life is so profoundly in transaction with nature that there is no place for abstraction or esthetics or a "nature philosophy" which can be separated from the rest of his life. . . . Nature and his relationship to it are a deadly-serious matter, prescribed by convention, mystery, and danger. His personal leisure is aimed away from idle amusement or detached tampering with nature's processes. But built into his life is awareness of that presence, of the terrain, of the unpredictable weather, of the narrow margin by which he is sustained.*

Much the same could be said of McCandless during the months he spent beside the Sushana River.

It would be easy to stereotype Christopher McCandless as another boy who felt too much, a loopy young man who read too many books and lacked even a modicum of common sense. But the stereotype isn't a good fit. McCandless wasn't some feckless slacker, adrift and confused, racked by existential despair. To the contrary: His life hummed with meaning and purpose. But the meaning he wrested from existence lay beyond the comfortable path: McCandless distrusted the value of things that came easily. He demanded much of himself—more, in the end, than he could deliver.

Trying to explain McCandless's unorthodox behavior, some people have made much of the fact that like John Waterman, he was small in stature and may have suffered from a "short man's complex," a fundamental insecurity that drove him to prove his manhood by means of extreme physical challenges. Others have posited that an unresolved Oedipal conflict was at the root of his fatal odyssey. Although there may be some truth in both hypotheses, this sort of posthumous off-the-rack psychoanalysis is a dubious, highly speculative enterprise that inevitably demeans and trivializes the absent analysand. It's not clear that much of value is learned by reducing Chris McCandless's strange spiritual quest to a list of pat psychological disorders.

Roman and Andrew and I stare into the embers and talk about McCandless late into the night. Roman, thirty-two, inquisitive and outspoken, has a doctorate in biology from Stanford and an abiding distrust of conventional wisdom. He spent his adolescence in the same Washington, D.C., suburbs as McCandless and found them every bit as stifling. He first came to Alaska as a nine-year-old, to visit a trio of uncles who mined coal at Usibelli, a big strip-mine operation a few miles east of Healy, and immediately fell in love with everything about the North. Over the years that followed, he returned repeatedly to the forty-ninth state. In 1977, after graduating from high school as a sixteen-year-old at the top of his class, he moved to Fairbanks and made Alaska his permanent home.

These days Roman teaches at Alaska Pacific University, in Anchorage, and enjoys statewide renown for a long, brash string of backcountry escapades: He has—among other feats—traveled the entire 1,000-mile length of the Brooks Range by foot and paddle, skied 250 miles across the Arctic National Wildlife Refuge in subzero winter cold, traversed the 700-mile crest of the Alaska Range, and pioneered more than thirty first ascents of northern peaks and crags. And Roman doesn't see a great deal of difference between his own widely respected deeds and McCandless's adventure, except that McCandless had the misfortune to perish.

I bring up McCandless's hubris and the dumb mistakes he made—the two or three readily avoidable blunders that ended up costing him his life. "Sure, he screwed up," Roman answers, "but I admire what he was trying to do. Living completely off the land like that, month after month, is incredibly difficult. I've never done it. And I'd bet you that very few, if any, of the people who call McCandless incompetent have ever done it either, not for more than a week or two. Living in the interior bush for an extended period, subsisting on nothing except what you hunt and gather—most people have no idea how hard that actually is. And McCandless almost pulled it off."

"I guess I just can't help identifying with the guy," Roman allows as he pokes the coals with a stick. "I hate to admit it, but not so many years ago it could easily have been me in the same kind of predicament. When I first started coming to Alaska, I think I was probably a lot like McCandless: just as green, just as eager. And I'm sure there are plenty of other Alaskans who had a lot in common with McCandless when they first got here, too, including many of his critics. Which is maybe why they're so hard on him. Maybe McCandless reminds them a little too much of their former selves."

Roman's observation underscores how difficult it is for those of us preoccupied with the humdrum concerns of adulthood to recall how forcefully we were once buffeted by the passions and longings of youth. As Everett Ruess's father mused years after his twenty-year-old son vanished in the desert, "The older person does not realize the soul-flights of the adolescent. I think we all poorly understood Everett."

Roman, Andrew, and I stay up well past midnight, trying to make sense of McCandless's life and death, yet his essence remains slippery, vague, elusive. Gradually, the conversation lags and falters. When I drift away from the fire to find a place to throw down my sleeping bag, the first faint smear of dawn is already bleaching the rim of the northeastern sky. Although the mosquitoes are thick tonight and the bus would no doubt offer some refuge, I decide not to bed down inside Fairbanks 142. Nor, I note before sinking into a dreamless sleep, do the others.   ■

■ *QUESTIONS FOR MAKING CONNECTIONS WITHIN THE READING* ■

1. Jon Krakauer is telling the story of Chris McCandless, who was interested in, among other things, recording the adventures of "Alexander Supertramp." What is the relationship between McCandless and Supertramp?

What does writing under a different name allow McCandless to do that he wouldn't otherwise be able to do?

2. Most everyone at one time or another has dreamed of getting away from it all. Chris McCandless actually did so. Would he have been able to have the adventure he was looking for if he'd done more research? Would his story be more or less compelling if he had brought along a map? If he had survived?

3. One of Krakauer's central concerns in *Into the Wild* is to determine what drove McCandless to embark on such a dangerous journey and to speculate on what McCandless's motives were when he sought to make his way back out of the wild. How does Krakauer go about trying to uncover the answers to these questions? What is his method? What counts as evidence for him? When does Krakauer know—or feel—that he has found what he was looking for?

▪ QUESTIONS FOR WRITING ▪

1. At the end of this reading, Krakauer asserts that one reason adults have so much difficulty understanding McCandless's actions is that they struggle "to recall how forcefully [they] were once buffeted by the passions and longings of youth." To understand this observation, one must be able to define what "the passions and longings of youth" are. What do these passions and longings have to do with escape? With the natural world? And if one can recall such passions and longings, how might this change one's understanding of the import of McCandless's death?

2. In providing a narrative of McCandless's journey, Krakauer draws on the writings Chris left behind in the blank pages and margins of his books and on the walls of the bus where he spent his final months. What does all this writing tell Krakauer about McCandless's motives for heading off into the wild? Is it possible to escape from civilization in the twenty-first century? Does it make sense to try?

▪ QUESTIONS FOR MAKING CONNECTIONS BETWEEN READINGS ▪

1. In "The Naked Citadel," Susan Faludi sets out to study how young men are turned into soldiers at a military academy and to record how this training process was upended when the academy was required to admit young women into its ranks. In detailing McCandless's journey into the wild, Krakauer provides a glimpse into another ritualized way of "becoming a man." Would you argue that McCandless's journey is consistent with The Citadel's efforts to create a certain kind of man? Or was McCandless's journey an attempt to escape from the masculine ideals embodied

by The Citadel's students? What, if anything, do these two stories suggest about how masculinity will be defined and experienced in the twenty-first century?

2. Toward the end of this reading, Krakauer cites the cultural ecologist Paul Shepard's observations about how the nomadic Bedouin relates to the natural world. According to Shepard: "The nomadic Bedouin does not dote on scenery, paint landscapes, or compile a nonutilitarian natural history. . . . [H]is life is so profoundly in transaction with nature that there is no place for abstraction or esthetics or a 'nature philosophy' which can be separated from the rest of his life." This, Krakauer argues, is the kind of relationship with nature that McCandless achieved at the end of his travels. And yet, with Lila Abu-Lughod's depiction of Bedouin culture in mind, what are we to make of the fact that Chris fled the world that Kamla rushes to embrace? Is McCandless's view of the natural world a form of nostalgia available only to the privileged? Is Kamla's view of city life a fantasy available only to those on the margins?

www   **For additional suggestions about making connections between readings, visit the Link-O-Mat and More Sample Assignments at <www.newhum.com>.**

BETH LOFFREDA

How do the media decide which stories to cover on any given day? And what gets left out when the stories chosen get transformed into a three-minute segment on the nightly news or a column of print in the daily paper? These are some of the issues that Beth Loffreda takes up in *Losing Matt Shepard: Life and Politics in the Aftermath of Anti-Gay Murder,* her book-length study of how the residents of Wyoming responded when Shepard, a young gay student at the university in Laramie, was brutally beaten and left to die by the side of the road in the fall of 1998. Both an ethnographic study and a cultural critique, *Losing Matt Shepard* explores and carefully details the limits of the media's representation of the complexities of life in Wyoming after Shepard's highly publicized murder. In his review of *Losing Matt Shepard* for the *Lambda Book Report,* Malcolm Farley wrote: "Anyone who cares about the gay experience in America—or about America in general—should read Loffreda's fiercely intelligent account of the causes and consequences of Matt Shepard's murder."

Beth Loffreda is an associate professor of English and adjunct professor of Women's Studies at the University of Wyoming, where she also serves as an adviser to the university's Gay, Lesbian, Bisexual, and Transgendered student group. Since the publication of *Losing Matt Shepard,* which was selected as a finalist for the American Library Association's Gay, Lesbian, Bisexual, and Transgendered Round Table Award in 2000, Loffreda has become a national spokesperson in discussions about hate crimes legislation and gay rights. She was also recognized as one of the University of Wyoming's top teachers in 1999. In the selection from *Losing Matt Shepard* included here, Loffreda shows just how varied the response to Shepard's murder was at the University of Wyoming, in the surrounding communities of Laramie, and across the nation. As she does so, she asks her readers to consider the following question: Why is it that, when there are so many murders every year, this one in particular captured the nation's attention?

www **To learn more about Beth Loffreda and hate crimes legislation, please visit the Link-O-Mat at <www.newhum.com>.**

Loffreda, Beth. Selections from *Losing Matt Shepard.* New York: Columbia University Press, 2000. 1–31.

Biographical information drawn from Beth Loffreda, *Losing Matt Shepard.* New York: Columbia University Press, 2000.

■   ■

Selections from
Losing Matt Shepard
Life and Politics in the Aftermath of Anti-Gay Murder

Perhaps the first thing to know about Laramie, Wyoming, is that it is beautiful. On most days the high-altitude light is so precise and clear that Laramie appears some rarefied place without need of an atmosphere. We were having a stretch of days like that in early October 1998, as the news began to trickle in that a man had been found beaten somewhere on the edge of town. We'd later sort out the key facts: that Matt Shepard had encountered Russell Henderson and Aaron McKinney late Tuesday night in the Fireside Bar; that he'd left with them; that they had driven him in a pickup truck to the edge of town; that Henderson had tied him to a fence there and McKinney had beaten him viciously and repeatedly with a .357 Magnum; that they had taken his shoes and wallet and intended to rob his apartment but instead returned to town and got into a fight with two other young men, Jeremy Herrera and Emiliano Morales (McKinney clubbed Morales on the head with the same gun, still covered in Matt's blood; Herrera retaliated by striking McKinney's head with a heavy stick); that the police, responding to the altercation, picked up Henderson—McKinney had fled—and saw the gun, Matt's credit card, and his shoes in the truck but didn't yet know the fatal meaning of those objects; that after being released later that night, Henderson and his girlfriend, Chasity Pasley, and McKinney and his girlfriend, Kristen Price, began to hatch their false alibis; and that through all this Matt remained tied to the fence and wouldn't be found until Wednesday evening, after an entire night and most of a day had passed. We'd learn all that, and learn that Matt's sexuality was woven through all of it. Those facts reached us swiftly, but making sense of them took much longer.

Jim Osborn, a recent graduate of the university's education program, was the chair of the Lesbian Gay Bisexual Transgender Association that October, a group that Matt, a freshman, had just recently joined. The LGBTA is the sole gay organization on campus and in Laramie itself. While students make up most of its membership, it welcomes university staff and townspeople as well, although only a few have joined. The group has been active since 1990; before that, another gay campus organization, Gays and Lesbians of Wyoming—GLOW—had an intermittent but vivid life in the 1970s and early 1980s. Women typically outnumber men at LGBTA meetings, although not by a significant margin; altogether, attendance on any given night usually hovers between ten and twenty members. The group's email list, however, reaches far more. There's no single reason for that discrepancy; it most likely arises from a combination of factors, including the familiar reluctance of many college students to join groups and, more specifically in this case, the anxiety some gay or questioning students might feel attending a public meeting.

The LGBTA gathers weekly in a nondescript, carpeted seminar room on the second floor of the university union. It has no office space of its own. (When hundreds of letters arrived after Matt's murder, the group stored them in the corner of the Multicultural Resource Center downstairs.) Meetings are usually hourlong sessions, punctuated by bursts of laughter, during which the group plans upcoming events—speakers, dances, potlucks. The LGBTA juggles numerous, sometimes contradictory roles as it tries to be a public face for gay and lesbian issues on campus (organizing events, running panels about sexuality for many courses) and at the same time create a comfortable, safe space for socializing in a town without a gay bar or bookstore. It also serves as something of a gay news exchange, sharing information about what teachers might be supportive or not, what places in town and elsewhere might be safe or not, what's happening that might not show up in the campus paper, *The Branding Iron*.

That last role mattered on Tuesday, October 6th. As the members handled the last-minute details of Gay Awareness Week, scheduled to begin the following Monday, Jim Osborn warned the group to be careful. The week before, he had been harassed while walking across campus. A young man— Jim thinks he was probably a university student—had come up behind him, said, "You're one of those faggots, aren't you?" and thrown a punch. Jim is a big, strapping white man from northern Wyoming; he blocked the punch and hit his attacker. They then took off in opposite directions. Jim didn't report the attack to the police but did want to alert members of the LGBTA that it had happened. Matt was among those there to hear Jim's story. After the meeting, members of the group, including Matt and Jim, went out for coffee at the College Inn, something of a Tuesday-night LGBTA tradition. Jim remembers that Matt sat at the other end of a crowded table. It was the last Jim would see of him.

Jim can talk an eloquent blue streak and is something of an organizational genius—at LGBTA meetings I've listened to him recall the minutiae of university regulations and budget protocols as if they were fond personal memories. He also has a staggeringly large network of friends and acquaintances. On Thursday morning, he got an email from Tina Labrie, a friend of his and Matt's; she had introduced them in August, when Matt, new to Laramie, wanted to learn about the LGBTA. The message said that Matt had been found near death the evening before and was hospitalized in Fort Collins, Colorado. (Matt had initially been taken to Ivinson Memorial Hospital in Laramie and was then transferred to Poudre Valley Hospital's more sophisticated trauma unit. While Matt was being treated in the Ivinson Memorial ER, McKinney was a few curtains down, admitted earlier for the head wound he had received from Herrera; like Matt, McKinney would also be transferred to Poudre Valley.) Horrified, Jim phoned Tina and learned that the police were trying to reconstruct Matt's whereabouts on Tuesday evening. When he called the Laramie Police to tell them what he knew, an officer informed him that Matt wasn't going to make it. Matt was suffering from hypothermia, and there was severe trauma to the brain stem. The officer told Jim that one side of Matt's head had been beaten in several inches and that the neurosurgeon was quite frankly surprised that he was still alive.

Bob Beck, news director for Wyoming Public Radio, also got word of the attack on Thursday. Beck has lived in Laramie since 1984; he's a tall, lanky midwesterner with a serious jones for Chicago Bulls basketball. On the radio he speaks in the sedated tones cultivated by NPR reporters everywhere, but in person he displays a vinegary wit and a likably aggravated demeanor. "It was a strange thing," he told me. "I teach a class, and one of my students called up and told me he needed to miss class that day because one of his friends had got beaten up very badly and was taken to the hospital in Fort Collins." That student was Phil Labrie, Tina's husband. Worried when they couldn't reach Matt, they had called the police on Wednesday, shortly after Matt was found, and learned what had happened. "[Phil] didn't tell me a lot of details because he said the cops had told him not to really tell anyone. But then he said I will know about it later and it will be a big story. . . . So I right away thought I better follow up on this immediately." He contacted the Albany County Sheriff's Office and learned that a press conference would be held later that day.

Beck attended the press conference that day—typically a routine exercise, but one that in this case would unexpectedly and profoundly shape public reaction to the attack. According to Beck, the sheriff:

> indicated that there was a young man who had been very badly beaten, was on life support, had been taken to Poudre Valley Hospital. During the questioning, the sheriff at the time, Gary Puls, indicated that they thought he may have been beaten because he was gay. And when he described this situation to us he told us that [Shepard] was found by a mountain bike rider, tied to a fence like a scarecrow. My recollection is there was discussion of exactly what do you mean, "tied like a scarecrow," and I think every single one of us who were in the room got the impression certainly of being tied up spread-eagled, splayed out.

Matt hadn't actually been tied like a scarecrow; when he was approached first by the mountain biker, Aaron Kreifels, and then by Reggie Fluty, the sheriff's deputy who answered Kreifels's emergency call, Matt lay on his back, head propped against the fence, legs outstretched. His hands were lashed behind him and tied barely four inches off the ground to a fencepost.

In dramatic and widely reported testimony, Fluty would later state that at first she thought Matt could have been no older than thirteen, he was so small (Matt was only five feet two inches, barely over one hundred pounds). And when she described Matt's brutally disfigured face, she said that the only spots not covered in blood were the tracks cleansed by his tears—an enduring image that continues to appear in essays, poetry, and songs dedicated to Shepard. It is most likely that Kreifels was the source of Puls's press-conference description. Kreifels told police and reporters that he at first thought Matt was a scarecrow flopped on the ground, maybe some kind of Halloween joke staged a few weeks early. No matter its provenance, the notion that Matt had been strung up in something akin to a crucifixion became the starting point for the reporting and reaction to come.

Beck says, "I know that's how we all reported it, and that was never corrected."[1] The vicious symbolism of that image, combined with Puls's early acknowledgment that the beating might have been an anti-gay hate crime, drew instant attention. Attending the press conference were the Associated Press, members of the Wyoming and Colorado media, Beck, and two friends of Matt, Walt Boulden and Alex Trout. According to press reports, Boulden and Trout, afraid that the attack might go unnoticed, had already begun to alert the media earlier that day. Boulden had had plans with Matt for Tuesday night; Matt had canceled and later, apparently, had decided to head off to the Fireside alone. Boulden was not shy about seizing the attack as a political opportunity, linking the assault to the Wyoming legislature's failure to pass a hate crimes bill: he told reporters that "they said nothing like that happens in Wyoming because someone is gay, but we've always known someone would have to get killed or beaten before they finally listened. I just can't believe it happened to someone I cared so much about." By Friday morning, when the police already had McKinney, Henderson, Price, and Pasley in custody (Beck says "the investigation was one of the better I've seen"), the media interest, spurred by Thursday's press conference, had increased exponentially.

At the same time, Laramie's gay residents were learning what had happened. Stephanie and Lisa, a lesbian couple active in the LGBTA, heard the news from Jim on Thursday evening. Lisa, a striking redhead and a good friend of Jim's, talked to him first: "He told me Matt had been beaten. And I said, well, shit, how badly? Is he okay? And Jim said no—he's in critical condition, had to be airlifted to Poudre Valley." Both Stephanie and Lisa knew Matt only slightly, although Stephanie had expected to have the chance to grow closer. She had just agreed to be Matt's mentor in a program the LGBTA was considering as a way to welcome new students to the gay community. Like Lisa, Steph has an edgy, witty charisma, but it deserted her that night, as she, Lisa, and Jim watched the first TV news reports. "There was this horrifying feeling that we were standing on the brink of learning something really, really awful," she says of that Thursday. "Like the part in the horror movie just before she opens the closet and finds the dead cat. It was that moment. For a day. And then we got the facts . . . and everything started happening at this tremendous speed. The next day was the day the story broke. And there were newspaper reporters and cameras all over the place." Steph had called me early that Friday morning, spreading word of the attack and warning people associated with the LGBTA to watch their backs: "I can remember wanting to tell everybody, absolutely everybody, wanting to physically grab people by their lapels and make them listen."

An atmosphere of genuine shock permeated the university; most students and faculty I encountered that day wore stunned and distraught expressions that I imagine mirrored my own; they seemed absorbed simply in trying to understand how something so brutal could have happened within a short walk of their daily lives. Gay and lesbian members of the university that I spoke to felt a wrenching mix of fear and sadness; many, including Stephanie and Lisa, were also immediately and intensely angry. A number of students in my morning American Literature course, after a long discussion in which they sought answers for how to publicly express their repugnance for the crime, decided that the university's homecoming parade, coincidentally scheduled for the following morning, would be an ideal site for that response. Finding like-minded students in the United Multicultural Council, the LGBTA, and the student government, they began printing flyers, making hundreds of armbands, and arranging permits to join the parade.[2] Their unjaded eagerness to publicly involve themselves in the case contrasted sharply with the university administration's first official response, much of which had concerned itself with pointing out that the attack happened off campus and was committed by nonstudents.

On Friday afternoon—as Jim Osborn began to field what would eventually become an overwhelming flood of media requests for interviews—the four accused appeared in court for the first time. Bob Beck attended the initial appearance: "That's where you bring in the people, read them formal charges, and we then get their names, backgrounds—which is important for us." Beck had left for the courthouse a half hour early; initial appearances are typically held in a small room in the courthouse basement, and Beck thought it might be more full than usual. He was right. "It was sold out. It was wall-to-wall cameras." Residents of Laramie—professors and LGBTA members in particular—had also come to witness the proceedings. So many attended that the reading of the charges had to be delayed while everyone moved upstairs to the much larger district court. Beck remembers, "I went in—in fact it was so crowded I got shoved by where the jury box is located— and I stood behind the defendants when they came in. I got a really good look at everybody, and I was actually surprised at how young they looked, how scared they looked, and how little they were." Only Henderson, McKinney, and Chasity Pasley were charged that day; separate proceedings had been arranged for Kristen Price. Pasley wept throughout. She was someone Jim Osborn knew well and liked. She worked in the campus activities center and had helped Jim countless times when the LGBTA needed photocopying or assistance setting up for an event. "She was very supportive of the group," Jim says. Often when he saw her on a Wednesday, she'd ask, "Hey, how'd it go last night?" In the past, he had seen her wearing one of the group's "Straight But Not Narrow" buttons.

I was in the courtroom that afternoon and can remember the professional flatness with which the county judge, Robert Castor, read the charges aloud. Castor had arrived in the courtroom to find a cameraman sitting at the prosecution's table, an early symbol of the persistent media invasion, Bob Beck believes, that frustrated the court and the prosecutor, Cal Rerucha, and led them to sharply limit information about the case thereafter. Castor charged McKinney and Henderson with three identical counts of kidnapping, aggravated robbery, and attempted first-degree murder; Pasley he charged with a count of accessory after the fact to attempted first-degree murder (in addition to providing false alibis for their boyfriends, she and Price had also helped dispose of evidence, including Henderson's bloody clothing). After each count, Castor recited "the essential facts" supporting the charge, in what became a truly grim ritual of repetition. In language I've condensed from the court documents, the essential facts were these: "On or between October 6, 1998, and the early morning hours of October 7, 1998, Aaron McKinney and Russell Henderson met Matthew Shepard at the Fireside Bar, and after Mr. Shepard confided he was gay, the subjects deceived Mr. Shepard into leaving with them in their vehicle to a remote area near Sherman Hills subdivision in Albany County. En route to said location, Mr. Shepard was struck in the head with a pistol." (McKinney, we'd later learn, had apparently told Matt, "We're not gay, and you just got jacked," before striking him.) "Upon arrival at said location, both subjects tied their victim to a buck fence, robbed him, and tortured him, while beating him with the butt of a pistol. During the incident, the victim was begging for his life. The subjects then left the area, leaving the victim for dead." By the third time Castor read that Matt had begged for his life, the courtroom had become choked with sickness and grief. The true darkness of the crime had become impossible to flee.

The next morning—Saturday—began with the university's homecoming parade. As the parade kicked off, one hundred students, university employees, and townspeople lined up at the end of the long string of floats and marching bands. They had quietly gathered in the morning chill to protest the attack on Matt. The leaders of the march carried a yellow banner painted with green circles, symbols of peace chosen by the UMC. They were followed by a silent crowd wearing matching armbands and holding signs that read "No Hate Crimes in Wyoming," "Is This What Equality Feels Like?" and "Straight But Not Stupid." I walked a few yards from the front, watching

Carly Laucomer, a university student holding the middle of the banner, field questions from reporters walking backward a single pace in front of her. Beside me, Cat, another university student, muttered that she wished the marchers weren't so sparse. Cat, like Carly, was then a student in my American Literature course, a smart young woman usually prepared to be disappointed by the world around her. Laramie surprised her. As the march moved west down Ivinson Avenue, spectators began to join, walking off sidewalks into the street. By the time the march reached downtown (where a giant second-story banner proclaimed, "Hate Is Not a Wyoming Value") and circled back toward campus, it had swelled beyond even Cat's demanding expectations; final estimates ranged from five to eight hundred participants. It didn't seem like much—just a bunch of people quietly walking—but it was a genuinely spontaneous, grassroots effort to protest the attack and express the community's profound dismay, and in that sense it was unforgettable.

A very different sort of tribute to Matt appeared in the Colorado State University homecoming parade the same day in the city of Fort Collins. As Matt lay in the hospital just a few miles away, a float in the parade carried a scarecrow draped in anti-gay epithets. While the papers were reluctant to report the full range of insults, I heard that the signs read "I'm Gay" and "Up My Ass." Colorado State University acted quickly to punish the sorority and fraternity responsible for the float (the censured students blamed vandalism committed by an unknown third party), but still it is worth pausing for a moment to consider the degree of dehumanization such an act required, how much those responsible must have felt, however fleetingly or unconsciously, that Matt was not a fellow human being, their age, with his future torn away from him. Fort Collins is home to a visible and energetic community of gay activists, and the float was widely denounced. Still, a week later Fort Collins would vote down, by nearly a two-to-one margin, City Ordinance 22, a proposal to expand the city's antidiscrimination statute to include protections for gays and lesbians.

Later that Saturday, a moment of silence for Matt was held before the University of Wyoming's football game; players wore the UMC's symbols on their helmets. And, impossibly, the media presence continued to grow. Bob Beck, juggling requests for interviews with his own reporting, was in the thick of it and felt a growing frustration at the sloppiness of what he saw around him. "Right away it was horrible. Part of that, in fairness, was that we didn't have all the information we needed. While the sheriff was very up front at first, next thing you know, nobody's talking." City officials, naturally unprepared (in a town with barely a murder a year) for the onslaught, focused their resources on the investigation and, angry that Laramie was being depicted as a hate crimes capital, began to restrict press access. But the media, especially the TV tabloids, Beck says, needed to turn things around quickly, and since they were getting stonewalled by the city and by many

Laramie residents, "it seemed like the place they went to interview every-body was in bars. As we all know who are in the media, if you want to get somebody to be very glib, give you a few quick takes, you want to go to a bar. And you certainly are going to meet a segment of our population that will have more interesting things to say." I remember watching for footage of the Saturday morning march later that evening and seeing instead pre-cisely the sort of bar interview Beck describes, a quick and dirty media tactic I heard many residents mock in the coming months.

Beck also remembers one of the first television news reports he saw: "It was this woman reporter outside the Fireside doing what we call a bridge, a stand-up: 'Hate: it's a common word in Wyoming.'" Beck couldn't believe it, but that mirrored precisely the assumptions of most of the media repre-sentatives he encountered that week. Journalists who interviewed him began with comments like, "Well, this kind of thing probably happens a lot up there," or, "You have that cowboy mentality in Wyoming, so this was bound to happen." Reporters criticized Laramie, he says, for not having a head trauma unit, not having gay bars, not pushing back homecoming. The tone of the questioning was hostile; Jim Osborn, speaking to journalists from locations as far-flung as Australia and the Netherlands, encountered it too. Jim says the press he spoke to wanted to hear that this was a hateful, red-neck town, that Wyoming was, in the inane rhyming of some commentators, "the hate state." But Jim insisted on what he considered accurate: "Nobody expects murder here—nobody. This is not a place where you kill your neigh-bor, and we see each other as neighbors. This is a good place."

But the crime, and Laramie, had already begun to take on a second life, a broadcast existence barely tethered to the truths of that night or this place, an existence nourished less by facts and far more by the hyperboles of tabloid emotion. Such a development should be unsurprising to even the most novice of cultural critics, yet to be in the middle of it, to watch rumor become myth, to see the story stitched out of repetition rather than investi-gation, was something else entirely. Beck told me, "Right away I saw pack journalism like I have not seen pack journalism in a while. It was really something. I remember going to the courthouse, and somebody would say, 'Hey I understand he got burned'—which wasn't true by the way—'where did he get burned?' And somebody would say, 'Oh, on his face,' and they're all taking notes, and they were sources for each other. They would never say where it came from or who had the information—it was just 'there were burns on his face.'" As Beck watched, the mistakes multiplied. One journal-ist would announce, "'I did an interview with one of the deputies, and he told me this,' and they would all go with it; no one [else] went and inter-viewed the deputy. Now part of this is that the deputies and other officials weren't available to us . . . and the same stuff got continually reported." The lead investigator on the case, Sergeant Rob DeBree of the Sheriff's Office, held a press conference early on in an attempt to correct the errors, but, he told me, it didn't seem to make much of a difference—the media had become a closed loop, feeding off their own energies.

As the fall wore on, the distance between Laramie and its broadcast image would become unbridgeable. The court increasingly limited press access to the case and eventually, in the spring, issued a gag order. In response, the Wyoming Press Association wrangled with the court throughout that year over access to hearings and records, suggesting that the court model its treatment of the media on press access guidelines in the Timothy McVeigh trial. Beck assessed Wyoming Public Radio's own performance for me: "I'm not saying we didn't make any mistakes, because we probably did. But I finally got so weary of it I said, 'You know what? If we can't confirm it ourselves, we don't go with it.' It was just too wild."

As the weekend continued, vigils for Matt were held across the nation. By the end of the week, we'd heard word of vigils in Casper, Cheyenne, and Lander (Wyoming towns), Colorado, Idaho, Montana, Iowa, Arizona, Rhode Island, and Pennsylvania. A memorial in Los Angeles attracted an estimated five thousand participants; a "political funeral" in New York City that ended in civil disobedience and hundreds of arrests, about the same. Several hundred mourners lit candles at a vigil outside Poudre Valley Hospital, and a Web site set up by the hospital to give updates about Matt's condition eventually drew over 815,000 hits from around the world.

In Laramie, we held two vigils of our own Sunday night. Jim spoke at the first, held outside the St. Paul's Newman Catholic Center. Father Roger Schmit, the organizer of the event, had contacted him earlier that weekend and asked him to speak. Jim remembers, "I'm sitting here thinking, 'Catholic Church . . . this is not exactly the scene I want to get into.'" But the priest told him, Jim says, "This is such a powerful opportunity—people need to hear from you, and it will help them." Jim thought, "I want to hate him, I want to disagree with him, but I can't." Indeed, such bedfellows would become less strange in the coming months. Matt's death triggered yearlong conversations in several Laramie churches; the Newman Center, the Episcopal church, and the Unitarian-Universalist Fellowship each began discussion groups devoted to questions of sexual orientation and religious doctrine. Father Schmit, the priest Jim regarded with such initial suspicion, would in particular become a vocal advocate for gay tolerance.

I attended that first vigil, which drew nearly one thousand people, a sizable fraction of Laramie's total population. As I crossed Grand Avenue, dodging traffic, the vigil already under way, I was struck by the size and murmurous intensity of the crowd. The speakers included friends of Matt, student leaders, and university officials. Father Schmit had also invited every religious leader in town but found many reluctant to come. The event was genuinely affecting and rightly given over to the desire, as Jim put it, to think of Matt "the person" and not the newly created symbol. While speakers did indeed condemn the homophobia that slid Matt from complicated human being to easy target, others, including Jim, also tried to rehumanize Matt by offering up small details—the nature of his smile, the clothes he liked to wear. The press was there too, of course, and—perhaps inevitably under such circumstances—a faint odor of PR hung in the air. University president Phil Dubois told the assembled, "Nothing could match the sorrow and revulsion we feel for this attack on Matt. It is almost as sad, however, to see individuals and groups around the country react to this event by stereotyping an entire community, if not an entire state."

Stephanie sensed another trouble, a hypocrisy, at work that night:

> There was a tremendous outpouring of support—the vigils, the parade—and a lot of those people—not all of them, not even a substantial portion, but some of those people—if they had known that Matt was gay while he was alive, would have spit on him. But now it was a cause, and that made me upset. Not that I think you can't grieve over this because you're straight or anything like that, but I just questioned the sincerity of some people. And I grew to be very angry at the vigil Sunday night, because it was so like the one I had attended for Steve.

She meant Steve Heyman, a gay man who had been a psychology professor and LGBTA faculty adviser at the university. Heyman was found dead on November 1, 1993, on the edge of Route 70 in Denver. He appeared to have been tossed from a moving car. The case was never solved. To Stephanie, who had known and adored Heyman, the coincidence was unbearable. "It was the same candles, the same fucking hymns. I will never sing 'We are a gentle, angry people' again, because it doesn't change anything. And I'm not going to sing 'We are not afraid today deep in my heart' because I am afraid, and I will always be afraid, and that's what they want, that's why they kill us."

Driven by that anger, Stephanie spoke at the second vigil that night. Much smaller—perhaps one hundred people were in attendance—it was held on the edge of town, at the Unitarian Fellowship. People who went that night tell me it was different from the first. Instead of a lengthy list of official speakers, community members were invited to testify to their mourning, and to their experiences of anti-gay discrimination in Laramie. It was more intense, more ragged, more discomfiting. But both vigils held the same fragile promise of a changed Laramie, a town that—whether it much wanted to or not—would think hard and publicly and not in unison about the gay men and women in its midst, about their safety and comfort and rights.

Later that Sunday night, as the participants in that second vigil left for home, thought about the events of the day, and got ready for bed, Matt Shepard's blood pressure began to drop. He died in the early hours of Monday, October 12th. It was the first day of Gay Awareness Week at the University of Wyoming.

* * *

Monday, flags were flown at half-staff on the university campus. Later that week, in Casper, flags were lowered on the day of Matt's funeral to signal a "day of understanding." (According to local newspapers, Wyoming governor Jim Geringer was criticized by the Veterans of Foreign Wars for not following "proper flag etiquette.") That Monday eight hundred people gathered for a memorial service held on Prexy's Pasture, a patch of green in the middle of campus encircled by parking spaces and university buildings and anchored by a statue of "the university family," a happy heterosexual unit of father, mother, and child that one lesbian student, in a letter to the student newspaper, longingly imagined detonating. The memorial service was another exercise in what was becoming a familiar schizophrenia for Laramie residents. Even the layout of the event expressed it: speakers stood in a small clump ringed by sidewalk; spread beyond them was the far larger, shaggy-edged group of listeners. In between the two was an encampment of reporters, flourishing microphones and tape recorders, pivoting cameras back and forth, capturing clips of the speakers and reaction shots of the crowd. It was hard to see past the reporters to the event that had drawn us in the first place, and it was hard to know to a certainty whether we were all there simply to mourn Matt or to make sure that mourning was represented. Not that the second urge was itself necessarily a hypocrisy or a contradiction of the first. It was instead an early manifestation of Laramie's new double consciousness. We didn't simply live here anymore: we were something transmitted, watched, evaluated for symbolic resonance; something available for summary. I suspect a few people naturally sought that televised attention, felt authenticated and confirmed, even thrilled, by the opportunity to be representative; and others seized it, as Walt Boulden had, as a chance to articulate political goals that might otherwise go unheard. Mostly, though, it just pissed people off. As the memorial drew to a close, I walked past satellite vans and the professional autism of TV reporters practicing their opening lines and switching on their solemn expressions and talking to no one in particular.

I was on my way to the first event of Gay Awareness Week. Shortly after the memorial, Leslea Newman, scheduled long before the murder to give the keynote talk, spoke about her gay-themed children's books, which include the oft-censored *Heather Has Two Mommies*. The week's events would be held despite Matt's death, but attendance that evening hadn't necessarily swelled in response—there were maybe seventy folks scattered around in the darkened auditorium. Newman spoke with a bracing, funny, New York brusqueness that scuffed up the audience as she briskly detailed her skirmishes with religious conservatives, and she spoke as well of her sorrow over Matt and her friends' fearful pleading that she cancel her visit to Laramie. They weren't alone in feeling that anxiety; many of the members of the LGBTA were tensed for a backlash as they passed out pro-gay trinkets and "heterosexual questionnaires" at the "Straight But Not Narrow" table in the student union during Awareness Week. They knew the statistics: that anti-gay violence tends to rise sharply in the aftermath of a publicized bashing. But instead, as consoling letters and emails flooded the offices of *The Branding Iron,* the LGBTA, and Wyoming newspapers, supporters flocking to the union tables quickly ran through the association's supplies of buttons and stickers.

As the week dragged on, Laramie residents hung in their windows and cars flyers decrying hate provided by the Wyoming Grassroots Project (a year and a half later, you can still find a few examples around town, stubbornly hanging on). Yellow sashes fluttered from student backpacks; local businesses announced, on signs usually reserved for information about nightly rates, indoor pools, and bargain lunches, their dismay with the crime. The Comfort Inn: "Hate and Violence Are Not Our Way of Life." The University Inn: "Hate Is Not a Laramie Value." Arby's: "Hate and Violence Are Not Wyoming Values 5 Regulars $5.95." Obviously, those signs suggested a typically American arithmetic, promiscuously mixing moral and economic registers. Underneath the sentiment lingered a question: what will his death cost us? But it would be wrong, I think, to see all those gestures as merely cynical calculation, a self-interested weighing of current events against future tourism. We were trying to shape the media summary of Laramie all right, but we were also talking to each other, pained and wondering, through such signs.

Late Monday, about the same time as the Prexy's Pasture memorial, the charges against McKinney, Henderson, and Pasley were upgraded in a closed hearing to reflect Matt's death. Price's charge, the same as Pasley's— accessory after the fact to first-degree murder—was announced at her individual arraignment on Tuesday. In a *20/20* interview that week, Price offered her defense of McKinney and Henderson. She claimed Shepard approached McKinney and Henderson and "said that he was gay and wanted to get with Aaron and Russ." They intended, she said, "to teach a lesson to him not to come on to straight people"—as if torture and murder were reasonable responses to the supposed humiliation of overtures from a gay man. McKinney's father, speaking to the *Denver Post,* argued that no one would care about the crime if his son had killed a heterosexual, which struck me as not exactly on point, even as a media critique. Wyoming's Libertarian gubernatorial candidate (it was an election year) had his own unique twist: he told reporters, "If two gays beat and killed a cowboy, the story would have never been reported by the national media vultures."

Fred Phelps, a defrocked minister, leader of the tiny Kansas Westboro Baptist Church, and author of the Internet site GodHatesFags.com, announced that Monday that he intended to picket Matthew's funeral, scheduled for the coming Friday at St. Mark's Episcopal Church in Casper. His Web site also promised a visit to Laramie on October 19th, but in the end he didn't show. Phelps had made a name for himself in the 1990s as a virulently anti-gay activist, notorious for protesting at the funerals of AIDS victims. Never one to shy from media attention, Phelps faxed reporters images of the signs he and his followers intended to carry at the funeral: "Fag Matt in Hell," "God Hates Fags," "No Tears for Queers." On his Web site, Phelps wrote that "the parents of Matt Shepard did not bring him up in the nature and admonition of the Lord, or he would not have been trolling for perverted sex partners in a cheap Laramie bar." He also, to the bitter laughter of members of the LGBTA, deemed the University of Wyoming "very militantly pro-gay." "The militant homosexual agenda is vigorously pursued" at the university, he proclaimed. At the time of Phelps's statement, the university's equal employment and civil rights regulations did not include sexual orientation as a protected category, nor did the university offer insurance benefits to same-sex partners. President Dubois and the board of trustees, in response to Matt's death, eventually rectified the former failure in September 1999; the latter still remains true to this day. Apparently none of that mattered much in Phelps's estimation, and he would become a familiar figure in Laramie in the months to come.

The Westboro Church's announcement was only one manifestation of the murder's parallel national life, its transmutation into political and religious currency. Matt himself might have been dead, but his image was resurrected by Phelps as well as by his antagonists, and those resurrections, while not invariably hypocritical or grotesque, nevertheless struck me as always risky. Not because we shouldn't talk about Matt, about the murder, looking hard at the facts of it, as well as at its contexts. The risk, it seemed to me, lay in what his image was so often used for in the coming months—the rallying of quick and photogenic outrage, sundered from the hard, slow work for local justice.

On Wednesday, October 14th, the national gay organization the Human Rights Campaign held a candlelight vigil on the steps of the U.S. Capitol, noteworthy if only for the incongruity of an event that paired the likes of Ted Kennedy and Ellen DeGeneres. Jim Osborn was also there—Cathy Renna, a member of GLAAD (Gay and Lesbian Alliance Against Defamation), who had arrived in Laramie the previous weekend to monitor events for her organization, had asked Jim to participate and taken him to Washington. That night, DeGeneres declared that "this is what she was trying to stop" with her television sitcom *Ellen*. The proportions of that statement—the belief that a sitcom could breathe in the same sentence as the brutal vortex of murder—seemed out of kilter to say the least, but it is the age of celebrity politics, after all: Elton John would send flowers to Matt's funeral, Barbra Streisand would phone the Albany County Sheriffs office to demand quick action on the case, and Madonna would call up an assistant to UW president Dubois to complain about what had happened to Matt. Jim Osborn remembers standing next to Dan Butler, an actor on *Frasier,* during the vigil; later, he spotted Kristen Johnston (of *Third Rock from the Sun*) smoking backstage. Attended by numerous federal legislators, the vigil was skipped by Wyoming's two senators, who had announced their sorrow and condemned intolerance in press releases the previous day. The disconnect worked both ways: the Human Rights Campaign, for all its sustained rallying on the national level, never, according to Jim, sent a representative to Laramie until the following summer.

Back in Laramie, on the same day as the D.C. vigil, the university initiated a three-day series of teach-ins on "prejudice, intolerance, and violence" to begin, according to the announcement, "the healing process." The ideas expressed that day were valuable, the sympathies genuine, but I remember feeling overloaded by premature talk of closure. It may have seemed easy for straight mourners to move so quickly, but as Stephanie told me that week, she'd barely begun to realize the extent of her anger. In the face of that, the swiftness of the official move to "healing" seemed at best a well-intended deafness, and indeed, in their outrage by proxy, denunciations of hatred, and exhortations for tolerance, most of the speakers seemed to be talking implicitly and exclusively to straight members of the audience who already agreed.

Many professors on campus also made time in their classes that week to let their students talk about Matt; the university provided a list of teachers willing to facilitate such discussions if individual faculty were uncomfortable raising such an emotionally fraught issue. It was indeed, as Jim Osborn put it, a "teachable moment," and those conversations undoubtedly did real good. One student, who spoke to me on the condition I didn't use his name, told me that before Matt's death he "straight-up hated fags." It hadn't occurred to him that there actually were any gays or lesbians around (a surprisingly common assumption at the university, not to mention in Wyoming generally)—"fag" was a word handy mainly for demeaning other guys in his dorm for "being pussy" (a typical but still depressing conflation of slurs). After seeing students cry in one of his classes as they discussed Matt's death, he had what he called, with a defensive grin, a real breakthrough: he felt a little sick, he told me, that he had thought things about gays that the two killers had probably been thinking about Shepard.

It's impossible to quantify such changes in attitude, but clearly they were happening in many classrooms around campus. Those developments were heartening, but it would be wrong to imply that the changes were immediate or seismic; several students in the coming weeks would describe to me overhearing others saying Matt "got what he deserved." One woman told me that during a class devoted to discussing the murder, "There was a really ugly incident with a couple of guys in the back who were like 'I hate gays and I'm not changing my opinion.'" "People really think that way here," she finished with a resigned expression. In the coming year students and faculty checking out books on gay topics sometimes found them defaced, and in the spring of 1999 vandals defecated on the university's copies of *The Advocate,* a gay magazine.

It would be wrong too to imply that the faculty were perfectly equipped to handle the events of October. When Matt died, there was only one openly gay faculty member on the university campus—Cathy Connelly, a professor of sociology. Since her arrival in 1991, Professor Connelly had periodically taught graduate courses on gay and lesbian issues, but other than Connelly and the small Safe Zone diversity-training group, the university had few resources in place to respond to what had happened. Troubling as well were the reactions of more than one professor I spoke to that week, whose primary responses were to comment on their own uselessness, their own irrelevance—as scholars of obscure fields of inquiry—to such primal issues of life and death. Academics tend to be fairly skilled at self-lacerating narcissism, but it seemed to me at the time an appalling luxury, an indulgence in a kind of intellectual self-pity at a moment when the basic skills of education—critical thinking, articulation, self-reflection—could be so concretely valuable. I wondered about that, and I wondered too when we'd stop talking about how we felt and begin talking about what to do.

Not that public political gestures are always more meaningful than private, emotional ones. On October 15th, the day before Shepard's funeral, the U.S. House of Representatives approved a resolution condemning the murder. Sponsored by Wyoming's sole representative, Barbara Cubin, it struck me as an essentially empty gesture. The nonbinding resolution stated that the House would "do everything in its power" to fight intolerance, and Cubin herself announced that "our country must come together to condemn these types of brutal, nonsensical acts of violence. We cannot lie down, we cannot bury our heads, and we cannot sit on our hands." Stirring stuff, but she also told reporters that day that she opposes federal hate crimes legislation and suggested such things be left up to individual states. So much for "our country coming together." Cubin was not alone, of course, in her contradictory patriotic embrace of Matt; flags were lowered, resolutions passed, in a nation otherwise happy to express its loathing of gays by closeting them in the military, refusing them antidiscrimination protection in most cities and states, repressing their presence in school curricula, faculty, and clubs, and denouncing them in churches. Meanwhile, back in Wyoming that afternoon, a bewildered and frustrated Casper City Council grappled with more concrete resolutions than those that faced the United States Congress. At an emergency meeting to address Phelps's intended picketing of Matt's funeral, the council decided that protesters must stay at least fifty feet from the church. Casper's SWAT team and the Street Drug Unit would be in attendance outside St. Mark's. Streets would be closed nearby the church, the Casper *Star-Tribune* reported, to allow "media satellite vehicles to position themselves."

The funeral on Friday unfurled as a heavy, wet snow fell on Casper. The storm ripped down power lines, cutting electricity in and around Casper; hundreds of cottonwoods and elms lost their branches. Phelps and his handful of protesters (along with another anti-gay protester, W. N. Orwell of En-terprise, Texas) were penned inside black plastic barricades, taunting the huge crowd of mourners, which included strangers, gay and straight alike, drawn to the scene from Cheyenne, Denver, Laramie, and elsewhere. As Charles Levendosky put it a few days later in the *Star-Tribune,* "One thou-sand others from Wyoming and surrounding states flew or drove into Wyoming to mourn for Matt Shepard, the symbol." While a few mourners engaged in heated debate with the picketers—one carrying a sign reading "Get Back in Your Damn Closet"—most turned their backs to them, the um-brellas pulled out for the snow acting as a fortuitous blockade. To protect the Shepard family from hearing Phelps, the assembled crowd sang "Amazing Grace" to drown out his anti-gay preaching. (The family's loss would inten-sify that day—Shepard's great uncle suffered what would be a fatal heart at-tack in the church shortly before the service began.) The funeral inside St. Mark's remained restricted to friends and family of Matt, but a live audio feed carried the service to the First Presbyterian Church nearby. Outside St. Mark's, more mourners ("some wearing black leather," the *Star-Tribune* ob-served) listened to a KTWO radio broadcast of the service. At the funeral, Matt's cousin Ann Kirch, a minister in Poughkeepsie, New York, delivered the sermon. Emphasizing Matt's gentleness and desire "to help, to nurture, to bring joy to others," she echoed a statement made by Matt's father earlier in the day at a press conference outside city hall: "A person as caring and loving as our son Matt would be overwhelmed by what this incident has done to the hearts and souls of people around the world."

Three days later, the university held yet another memorial service. Around one thousand people heard songs by a multicultural chorus, psalms read by Geneva Perry of the university's Office of Minority Affairs, and statements by Tina Labrie, Jim Osborn, and Trudy McCraken, Laramie's mayor. Rounding out the service was university president Dubois, who made a passionate, personal plea for hate crimes legislation—the political issue that had already, only one week after his death, come to dominate dis-cussions of Matt's murder. "No hate crime statute, even had it existed, would have saved Matt," Dubois read. "But Matt Shepard was not merely robbed, and kidnapped, and murdered. This was a crime of humiliation. This crime was all about being gay. . . . We must find a way to commemorate this awful week in a way that will say to the entire state and nation that we will not forget what happened here."

On Tuesday, October 20th, the Wyoming Lodging and Restaurant Asso-ciation offered one such response to the nation by passing a resolution in favor of hate crimes legislation. The association was up front about its moti-vations: to curry favor among tourists who might seek recreation elsewhere. The director was quoted in the Casper *Star-Tribune:* "We want them to know this was an isolated case and could happen anywhere."

* * *

Could happen anywhere indeed. While that oft-repeated phrase was the quick defense offered by many who felt Laramie was being unfairly vilified, it also bumped up against an undeniable truth: in the late 1990s, homosexuality and vehement opposition to it were everywhere in American public culture and politics. Gays in the military, gays in the schools, gays in church, gays in marriage—the place of gay men and lesbians in American culture seemed to be debated in every way possible. For example, on October 14th, two days before Matt's funeral, the Supreme Court upheld a Cincinnati ordinance that denied gays and lesbians legal protection from discrimination in housing, employment, and other public accommodations. Later that autumn Ohio hosted a conference, organized by Focus on the Family, on how to prevent childhood homosexuality; one speaker there, John Paulk, became notorious during the summer of 1998 when he posed with his wife for national newspaper ads announcing that they were former homosexuals "cured" by their faith in God. About the same time the Supreme Court ruled on the city ordinance, the Roman Catholic Archdiocese of Cincinnati announced a deeply contradictory attempt to "reconcile church teachings that denounce homosexual sex as immoral but encourage the loving acceptance of gays." As long as they're celibate, that is—as long as they "live chaste lives." "Hate the sin, love the sinner"—that idea was invoked again and again in Laramie, in church congregations and letters to the editor. But it seems to me that in such visions sexuality slides so intimately close to identity itself that in the end such exhortations call for moral acrobatics requiring an impossible and fundamentally hypocritical kind of dexterity.

Religious justifications were everywhere, of course, in the attacks on homosexuality. Senate Majority Leader Trent Lott, in June 1998, said he learned from the Bible that "you should try to show them a way to deal with [homosexuality] just like alcohol . . . or sex addiction . . . or kleptomaniacs." Pat Robertson announced that "the acceptance of homosexuality is the last step in the decline of Gentile civilization." Bob Jones University in South Carolina instituted a rule banning gay alumni from returning to campus. The religious right boycotted Disney and American Airlines for having policies that refused to discriminate against gays and lesbians. Salt Lake City banned all student clubs rather than allow a gay-straight alliance to continue at one public high school. The Mormon Church donated roughly half a million dollars to supporters of Alaska's Proposition 2, an initiative banning same-sex marriage that succeeded in the fall of 1998. Bans on gay marriage would also pass in Hawaii, California, and West Virginia in the next year and a half. Vermont, with its legalization of gay "civil unions" early in 2000, would be one of the few bright spots.

That Matt's death occurred in the midst of such pervasive anxiety and upheaval might begin to explain why the nation paid attention, but it doesn't stretch very far—his was only one of thirty-three anti-gay murders that year, followed by, in the first months of 1999, a beheading in Virginia and a vicious beating in Georgia. Here in Laramie, we asked a version of that question too: Why Matt, when no one in the media seemed to take a second glance at the other truly awful recent murders we had the grim distinction of claiming? Why Matt, and not Daphne Sulk, a fifteen-year-old pregnant girl stabbed seventeen times and dumped in the snow far from town? Why Matt, and not Kristin Lamb, an eight-year-old Laramie girl who was kidnapped while visiting family elsewhere in Wyoming and then raped, murdered, and thrown in a landfill? Governor Geringer asked those very questions in an October 9th press release, and we asked them too, in Laramie—in letters to the editor, in private conversation. But we didn't always mean the same thing. To some, the media attention to Matt seemed to imply that his death was somehow worse than the deaths of the two girls, and such an implication was genuinely offensive. To some, like Val Pexton, a graduate student in creative writing, it had something to do with the politics of gender: "What happened to [Lamb] was certainly as violent, as hateful, as horrible; and I guess one of my first thoughts was, if [Henderson and McKinney] had done that to a woman, would this have made it into the news outside of Laramie, outside of Wyoming?" And to some, like Jim Osborn, the comparison of Matt to Kristin and Daphne sometimes masked a hostility to gays: "They became incensed—why didn't Kristin Lamb get this kind of coverage, why didn't Daphne Sulk get this kind of coverage? That was the way people could lash out who very much wanted to say, fuck, it was just a gay guy. But they couldn't say it was just a gay guy, so they said, what about these two girls?"

In some ways, it's easy to understand why the media industry seized upon Matt, and why so many responded to the image it broadcast (Judy Shepard, Matt's mother, told *The Advocate* magazine in March 1999 that the family had received "about 10,000 letters and 70,000 emails," as well as gifts, stuffed animals, blankets, and food). Matt was young (and looked younger), small, attractive; he had been murdered in a particularly brutal fashion. The mistaken belief that he had been strung up on the fence provided a rich, obvious source of symbolism: religious leaders, journalists, and everyday people saw in it a haunting image of the Crucifixion, and at the memorial services and vigils for Matt here and elsewhere, that comparison was often drawn. And while Matt had not in reality been put on display in that fashion, the idea that he had been resonated deeply with America's bitter history of ritual, public violence against minorities—many, including *Time* magazine, compared the attack to a lynching. But Matt seemed to provide a source of intense, almost obsessive interest whose explanation lies well beyond these considerations. Perhaps it was merely the insistent repetition of his image in those early days. In the few snapshots that circulated in the press, Matt appeared boyish, pensive, sweet, charmingly vulnerable in oversized wool sweaters—a boy who still wore braces when he died, a boy who looked innocent of sex, a boy who died because he was gay but whose unthreatening image allowed his sexuality to remain an abstraction for many. In my darker moods, I wonder too if Matt invited such sympathy and political outrage precisely because he was dead—if, for many of the straight people who sincerely mourned his murder, he would nevertheless have been at best invisible while alive. To Jim Osborn, the explanation was less dark and more simple: Matt was "someone we can identify with. Matt was the boy next door. He looked like everybody's brother and everybody's neighbor. He looked like he could have been anyone's son."

"He was the nuclear son of the nuclear family." Jay, a Shoshone-Northern Arapahoe-Navajo American Indian born on the Wind River Reservation in the center of Wyoming, is talking to me about the limits of identification. "If that was me hung on the fence, they'd just say, oh, another drunk Indian. No one would have paid much attention." Jay is gay (he uses the Navajo term *nádleeh*—which he translates as "one who loves his own kind"—to describe himself), and while he feels sympathy for Matt, he doesn't feel much kinship. To Jay, the reason why the nation seized upon Matt is just as simple as Jim Osborn's reason but radically different: to Jay, it was as if white, middle-class America finally had its own tragedy. His argument makes some undeniable sense: in a media culture consecrated to repetition, to the endless recopying of the supposed center of American life—white, moneyed, male— Matt did indeed fit the bill, did suit the recycled homogeneities of a still-myopic national culture. For Jay, the tremendous public outpouring of grief, no matter how sincere, remained essentially alienating. When I ask him how people he knows back on the reservation reacted to the murder, he sums up what he describes as a common response, which he himself shared: "Well, at least now one of them"—whites—"knows what we live through every day." Matt learned it, he says. "And one mother now knows, for a little while anyway, what our lives have always been." As he speaks, defiance, resignation, bitterness, and pride mingle in his voice. "Now people might know what our lives are like," what forms of violence—physical, political, cultural—native people experience in the still-hostile territories of the American West.

Jay's home on the reservation was without running water or electricity, but that never felt like deprivation or unusual circumstance to him—"It's just the way it was." When he was nine, Jay moved to Laramie with his family. They arrived after dark. "Laramie looked so beautiful—all these lights spread out—[it] seemed huge to me." He laughs as he describes how he has learned to love the materialism of life off the reservation—"I really, really like having things now," he admits in simultaneous mockery of himself and Anglo consumerism. When I ask him what white residents here don't know about their town, he replies that "Laramie's a nice town"—he likes life here fine—with a pointed caveat: "White people always say there's no bias in Laramie, no racism, but they just don't want to see." Jay has long black hair pulled back in a braid and a round, lived-in face; he's frequently mistaken for Hispanic. As a child, it didn't take him long to stumble across the racial fault lines he describes. In his first year in Laramie, as he walked home from school near the university campus, a college-aged man spit on him. And on the day we talked, a white woman hissed "spic" at Jay minutes before we met. A student at the university, Jay says there is a reason why the October vigils held for Matt were mostly attended by whites: when Matt died and then later, during the legal proceedings against Henderson and McKinney, Jay observes, "you never saw a minority alone on campus—they either left town, or stayed home, or walked in pairs or groups." They were, he and others say, afraid of a backlash—if "someone got killed for being gay, then someone might get killed for being black or Hispanic or native—that's how we felt." In Jay's opinion, the surprise and horror expressed at the vigils—not to mention simply attending them—was almost something of a white luxury: "They felt shock," Jay says, but "I wasn't shocked—I knew this was coming, since I was in high school, seeing the white and Hispanic kids fight. I knew sooner or later someone was going to die." To Jay, risk, the risk of visible difference, didn't seem all that unfamiliar.

Other minority students on campus confirm Jay's point, however melodramatic it might seem to some. Carina Evans, a young woman of Latino and African-American heritage, told me that when the minority community on campus heard that two Latino teenagers had also been attacked by Henderson and McKinney that night, "the immediate response was, oh my God, what about my safety? How safe am I here? And I think our way of dealing with it was just to not talk about it, because I think we figured the less we drew attention to ourselves, the less the chance that something else was going to happen. Which was a sorry response, but a lot of people left town, just did not feel safe, went away for the week or the weekend."[3] She and others thought, "I'm not going to make myself a target—I'm going to get out of here." No such retaliation was ever reported, but the fact that minority members of the community so feared its possibility that it felt logical to leave town—at the same time that so many white residents could unquestionably consider the attack an isolated incident—reveals something about the complexities of daily life in Laramie.

The divides that run through Jay's and Carina's lives became harder for many in Laramie to ignore in the aftermath of Matt's death. But it was nevertheless a town made defensive by such half-unearthed truths. "Hate is not a Wyoming value," residents kept telling each other, telling visitors, telling the press. "We really take care of each other here," a woman told me one day in a coffee shop, echoing a dearly held ethos I've heard from many in Laramie and that strikes me as generally true. That defensiveness intensified as it encountered the first, clumsy journalistic attempts to offer sociological explanations for the roots of Henderson and McKinney's violence, attempts that implied—to us here, anyway—that Laramie was to blame. Perhaps the most locally reviled version was an article written by Todd Lewan and

Steven K. Paulson for the Associated Press that appeared in October, an occasionally persuasive attempt at class analysis hamstrung by bad facts and a love affair with the thuddingly clichéd symbolic density of the railroad tracks that cut through town. Here is their Laramie:

> On the east side is the University of Wyoming's ivy-clad main campus, where students drive sports cars or stroll and bike along oak-shaded sidewalks. On the opposite side of town, a bridge spans railroad tracks to another reality, of treeless trailer parks baking in the heavy sun, fenced-off half-acre lots, stray dogs picking for scraps among broken stoves, refrigerators, and junked pickups. Unlike the university students, youths on the west side have little in the way of entertainment: no malls, no organized dance troupes, no theater or playing fields.

Blowing holes in this picture is still a local sport, more than a year after the murder. Bob Beck, for example, takes fairly comprehensive aim at the story:

> They decided that the reason a murder like this happened was because those of us, including me, who live in west Laramie, the "other side of the tracks," are underprivileged, don't have benefits, all this stuff. Because we're over there, we're obviously looking to get even with the good side of the tracks and are going to commit a crime like this. [They] basically blamed the fact that some of us who live in west Laramie don't have a mall (meanwhile there isn't a mall on the east side either); so we don't have a mall, we don't have paved streets, apparently don't have trees. And this is the reason for all this violence? That was one of the most damaging stories in retrospect, because it got picked up by just about every major paper. A lot of people got their impressions of the case from that.

The list of mistakes could continue: Henderson and McKinney didn't even live in west Laramie; oaks rarely grow at seven thousand feet; and few university students drive fancy sports cars—more likely, like many of the students I've encountered, they're working fifteen to thirty hours a week to pay their tuition, maybe at the same Taco Bell where Henderson worked as a teenager. It's hard to choose, but my personal favorite is the anguished handwringing over west Laramie's lack of organized dance troupes. Organized dance troupes?

Plenty of folks I've spoken to volunteer that they live on the west side and are quick to say they're "not trash," that they like the rustic character of west Laramie's unpaved streets, that they don't necessarily feel excluded from "Laramie proper," despite, for example, the west side's usual lack of representation on the city council. And I've found few residents who weren't offended by such shallow press characterizations of Laramie, who didn't argue that status doesn't matter much here, that Laramie is friendly and easygoing and safe, that most folks don't even bother to lock their doors. All their points of rebuttal are well taken, and indeed they're reasons why many love to live here. But nevertheless I think the eager rapidity with which so many of us rejected such examples of journalistic ineptitude masked at times a certain unease—and sometimes a hardworking amnesia—about the subtle realities of class, sexuality, and race here in Laramie. Those realities may be too complicated to sum up through the convenient shorthand of railroad tracks and trailer parks, but they still flow, hushed yet turbulent, beneath daily life in this town.   ■

NOTES

1. Melanie Thernstrom's essay on the murder in the March 1999 issue of *Vanity Fair* notes that Matt was not strung up, but only in a parenthetical remark near the end of the piece, and the article itself has the title "The Crucifixion of Matthew Shepard." JoAnn Wypijewski's tough-minded essay "A Boy's Life," which appeared in the September 1999 issue of *Harper's Magazine,* was the first thorough demystification of this myth in the national media, but many people still believe it. For example, Melissa Etheridge's song "Scarecrow" on her 1999 album *Breakdown* relies on it, as well as on other early misstatements of fact, including the false report that Shepard had been burned by his killers.

2. While the United Multicultural Council did good work that day, and while some strong connections have been made between the UMC and the LGBTA since Matt's death, it would be wrong to imply that those ties have been built without friction. Carina Evans, a university student who worked in the Minority Affairs Office that year, observed that at the time some members of the "diversity clubs" represented by the UMC "would not deal with the gay issue. The United Multicultural Council had no representation from the LGBTA, had no representation of openly gay students—and I think that's not at all multicultural. But they don't want to handle that. It's not like they're hostile about it, but they just don't encourage it." The tension flows both ways: Jay, a gay American Indian now active in the UMC, told me that some gay students of color he knows are uncomfortable attending LGBTA meetings because they feel that some members are not sensitive to racial differences.

3. A Mexican-American student, Lindsey Gonzales, spoke to me as well about the attack on Morales and Herrera. Lindsey knew Morales quite well (they'd hung out together in the past). She thinks neither the media nor the public cared much about the attack on Morales and Herrera compared to Matt because "they didn't die." But if they had, she speculates, people probably wouldn't have cared much more. When I ask her why, she says she's not sure, but she speculates that racial prejudice is simply more "familiar," something with a longer and better-known history in America, whereas "we're all just getting used to" homosexuality right now, and "that made it a big deal."

■ *QUESTIONS FOR MAKING CONNECTIONS WITHIN THE READING* ■

1. As Beth Loffreda works to unpack the significance of Matt Shepard's murder, she finds herself confronting a wide array of prejudices, not only about gays, but about Wyoming, the West, and Native Americans. Create

a chart that details all of the prejudices that Loffreda uncovers. What are the relationships among these prejudices? Does Loffreda have any prejudices, or is her view unbiased?

2. In detailing the responses to Shepard's murder, Loffreda refers to many different individuals by name. Who are the most important people in the story that Loffreda has to tell? Which responses had more weight at the time of the murder? Which responses have the most weight with Loffreda? With you?

3. How is this selection from *Losing Matt Shepard* organized? Is it a series of observations or an argument? Does it build to a point? Does it have a structure? How does the structure that Loffreda has chosen influence what she has to say?

▪ QUESTIONS FOR WRITING ▪

1. One of Loffreda's arguments in *Losing Matt Shepard* is that Matt Shepard, the individual, got lost in the media frenzy that followed his murder: part of the shock of Shepard's death, Loffreda reports, was "to watch rumor become myth, to see the story stitched out of repetition rather than investigation." If the media got Shepard's murder wrong, what are we to make of how and why they got it wrong? What would it take to provide "better coverage" of such tragedies? Are the print and visual media capable of providing nuanced understandings of unfolding events?

2. In describing how her colleagues at the University of Wyoming responded to Shepard's death, Loffreda records her own frustration at hearing teachers speak of their own "uselessness" and "irrelevance" in the face of such a tragedy. Such remarks struck Loffreda as "an appalling luxury, an indulgence in a kind of intellectual self-pity at a moment when the basic skills of education—critical thinking, articulation, self-reflection—could be so concretely valuable. I wondered about that, and I wondered too when we'd stop talking about how we felt and begin talking about what to do." What is it that teachers can or should do at such times? What role should secular institutions play in trying to shape the way their students see and understand the world?

▪ QUESTIONS FOR MAKING CONNECTIONS BETWEEN READINGS ▪

1. This selection from *Losing Matt Shepard* closes with Loffreda's discussion of what she terms "the limits of identification." In a sense, Susan Faludi's "The Naked Citadel" could also be described as a piece centrally concerned

with "the limits of identification." What are these limits? How are they discovered? Can they be changed?

2. In exploring the responses to Matt Shepard's murder, has Loffreda gained access to what James C. Scott terms "the hidden transcript," or are homophobia and its violent consequences better considered part of the nation's public transcript?

www **For additional suggestions about making connections between readings, visit the Link-O-Mat and More Sample Assignments at <www.newhum.com>.**

Azar Nafisi

AZAR NAFISI ROSE to international prominence in 2003, with the publication of her critically acclaimed bestseller *Reading Lolita in Tehran: A Memoir in Books*. A professor of aesthetics, culture, and literature, Dr. Nafisi was expelled from the University of Tehran in 1981 for refusing to wear the *chador,* or Islamic veil, as mandated by the Ayatollah Khomeini. Nafisi resumed teaching again in 1987, but resigned eight years later in protest over the harsh treatment of women by the Iranian government. *Reading Lolita* provides an account of the seminar that Nafisi then went on to hold in her home from 1995 to 1997, where seven of her best students joined her to discuss some of the classic texts of Western literature. Nafisi saw the change in her circumstances as an opportunity to fulfill a dream of working with "a group of students who just love literature—who are in it not for the grades, not to just graduate and get a job but just want to read Nabokov or Austen." That Nafisi and her students persisted in this activity, despite the obvious dangers it posed, has come to symbolize, for readers around the world, how the struggle against totalitarianism is waged on the level of everyday human experience.

Currently a Visiting Fellow and professorial lecturer at the Foreign Policy Institute of the Johns Hopkins University's School of Advanced International Studies (SAIS) in Washington, D.C., Nafisi directs The Dialogue Project, "a multi-year initiative designed to promote—in a primarily cultural context—the development of democracy and human rights in the Muslim world." At the same time, The Dialogue Project is also engaged in a program of education and outreach designed to provide knowledge about the Muslim world to Western policymakers, scholars, development professionals, media workers, and citizens.

For Nafisi, our freedom to talk and think together in small groups, in a context where the ideas raised and the topics covered are not determined in ad-

Nafisi, Azar. Excerpt from *Reading Lolita in Tehran: A Memoir in Books.* New York: Random House, 2003. 3–26.

Biographical information drawn from Azar Nafisi's home page at <http://dialogueproject .sais-jhu.edu/anafisi.php>; the extended quote about The Dialogue Project is drawn from <http://dialogueproject.sais-jhu.edu/aboutDP.php>.

vance, is the litmus test for a true democracy; to engage in this act, she believes, is to embrace a humanity that transcends national and religious differences.

`www` **To learn more about Azar Nafisi and Islamic culture in Iran, please visit the Link-O-Mat at <www.newhum.com>.**

Selections from
Reading Lolita in Tehran
A Memoir in Books

1

In the fall of 1995, after resigning from my last academic post, I decided to in-dulge myself and fulfill a dream. I chose seven of my best and most commit-ted students and invited them to come to my home every Thursday morning to discuss literature. They were all women—to teach a mixed class in the pri-vacy of my home was too risky, even if we were discussing harmless works of fiction. One persistent male student, although barred from our class, in-sisted on his rights. So he, Nima, read the assigned material, and on special days he would come to my house to talk about the books we were reading.

I often teasingly reminded my students of Muriel Spark's *The Prime of Miss Jean Brodie* and asked, Which one of you will finally betray me? For I am a pessimist by nature and I was sure at least one would turn against me. Nassrin once responded mischievously, You yourself told us that in the final analysis we are our own betrayers, playing Judas to our own Christ. Manna pointed out that I was no Miss Brodie, and they, well, they were what they were. She reminded me of a warning I was fond of repeating: *do not,* under *any* circumstances, belittle a work of fiction by trying to turn it into a carbon copy of real life; what we search for in fiction is not so much reality but the epiphany of truth. Yet I suppose that if I were to go against my own recommendation and choose a work of fiction that would most resonate with our lives in the Islamic Republic of Iran, it would not be *The Prime of Miss Jean Brodie* or even *1984* but perhaps Nabokov's *Invitation to a Beheading* or better yet, *Lolita.*

A couple of years after we had begun our Thursday-morning seminars, on the last night I was in Tehran, a few friends and students came to say good-bye and to help me pack. When we had deprived the house of all its items, when the objects had vanished and the colors had faded into eight gray suitcases, like errant genies evaporating into their bottles, my students and I stood against the bare white wall of the dining room and took two photographs.

I have the two photographs in front of me now. In the first there are seven women, standing against a white wall. They are, according to the law of the land, dressed in black robes and head scarves, covered except for the oval of their faces and their hands. In the second photograph the same group, in the same position, stands against the same wall. Only they have taken off their coverings. Splashes of color separate one from the next. Each has become distinct through the color and style of her clothes, the color and the length of her hair; not even the two who are still wearing their head scarves look the same.

The one to the far right in the second photograph is our poet, Manna, in a white T-shirt and jeans. She made poetry out of things most people cast aside. The photograph does not reflect the peculiar opacity of Manna's dark eyes, a testament to her withdrawn and private nature.

Next to Manna is Mahshid, whose long black scarf clashes with her delicate features and retreating smile. Mahshid was good at many things, but she had a certain daintiness about her and we took to calling her "my lady." Nassrin used to say that more than defining Mahshid, we had managed to add another dimension to the word *lady*. Mahshid is very sensitive. She's like porcelain, Yassi once told me, easy to crack. That's why she appears fragile to those who don't know her too well; but woe to whoever offends her. As for me, Yassi continued good-naturedly, I'm like good old plastic; I won't crack no matter what you do with me.

Yassi was the youngest in our group. She is the one in yellow, bending forward and bursting with laughter. We used to teasingly call her our comedian. Yassi was shy by nature, but certain things excited her and made her lose her inhibitions. She had a tone of voice that gently mocked and questioned not just others but herself as well.

I am the one in brown, standing next to Yassi, with one arm around her shoulders. Directly behind me stands Azin, my tallest student, with her long blond hair and a pink T-shirt. She is laughing like the rest of us. Azin's smiles never looked like smiles; they appeared more like preludes to an irrepressible and nervous hilarity. She beamed in that peculiar fashion even when she was describing her latest trouble with her husband. Always outrageous and outspoken, Azin relished the shock value of her actions and comments, and often clashed with Mahshid and Manna. We nicknamed her the wild one.

On my other side is Mitra, who was perhaps the calmest among us. Like the pastel colors of her paintings, she seemed to recede and fade into a paler register. Her beauty was saved from predictability by a pair of miraculous dimples, which she could and did use to manipulate many an unsuspecting victim into bending to her will.

Sanaz, who, pressured by family and society, vacillated between her desire for independence and her need for approval, is holding on to Mitra's arm. We are all laughing. And Nima, Manna's husband and my one true literary critic—if only he had had the perseverance to finish the brilliant essays he started to write—is our invisible partner, the photographer.

There was one more: Nassrin. She is not in the photographs—she didn't make it to the end. Yet my tale would be incomplete without those who could not or did not remain with us. Their absences persist, like an acute pain that seems to have no physical source. This is Tehran for me: its absences were more real than its presences.

When I see Nassrin in my mind's eye, she's slightly out of focus, blurred, somehow distant. I've combed through the photographs my students took with me over the years and Nassrin is in many of them, but always hidden behind something—a person, a tree. In one, I am standing with eight of my students in the small garden facing our faculty building, the scene of so many farewell photographs over the years. In the background stands a sheltering willow tree. We are laughing, and in one corner, from behind the tallest student, Nassrin peers out, like an imp intruding roguishly on a scene it was not invited to. In another I can barely make out her face in the small V space behind two other girls' shoulders. In this one she looks absentminded; she is frowning, as if unaware that she is being photographed.

How can I describe Nassrin? I once called her the Cheshire cat, appearing and disappearing at unexpected turns in my academic life. The truth is I can't describe her: she was her own definition. One can only say that Nassrin was Nassrin.

For nearly two years, almost every Thursday morning, rain or shine, they came to my house, and almost every time, I could not get over the shock of seeing them shed their mandatory veils and robes and burst into color. When my students came into that room, they took off more than their scarves and robes. Gradually, each one gained an outline and a shape, becoming her own inimitable self. Our world in that living room with its window framing my beloved Elburz Mountains became our sanctuary, our self-contained universe, mocking the reality of black-scarved, timid faces in the city that sprawled below.

The theme of the class was the relation between fiction and reality. We read Persian classical literature, such as the tales of our own lady of fiction, Scheherazade, from *A Thousand and One Nights,* along with Western classics—*Pride and Prejudice, Madame Bovary, Daisy Miller, The Dean's December* and, yes, *Lolita.* As I write the title of each book, memories whirl in with the wind to disturb the quiet of this fall day in another room in another country.

Here and now in that other world that cropped up so many times in our discussions, I sit and reimagine myself and my students, my girls as I came to call them, reading *Lolita* in a deceptively sunny room in Tehran. But to steal the words from Humbert, the poet/criminal of *Lolita,* I need you, the reader, to imagine us, for we won't really exist if you don't. Against the tyranny of time and politics, imagine us the way we sometimes didn't dare to imagine ourselves: in our most private and secret moments, in the most extraordinarily ordinary instances of life, listening to music, falling in love, walking down the shady streets or reading *Lolita* in Tehran. And then imagine us again with all this confiscated, driven underground, taken away from us.

If I write about Nabokov today, it is to celebrate our reading of Nabokov in Tehran, against all odds. Of all his novels I choose the one I taught last, and the one that is connected to so many memories. It is of *Lolita* that I want to write, but right now there is no way I can write about that novel without also writing about Tehran. This, then, is the story of *Lolita* in Tehran, how *Lolita* gave a different color to Tehran and how Tehran helped redefine Nabokov's novel, turning it into this *Lolita*, our *Lolita*.

2

And so it happened that one Thursday in early September we gathered in my living room for our first meeting. Here they come, one more time. First I hear the bell, a pause, and the closing of the street door. Then I hear footsteps coming up the winding staircase and past my mother's apartment. As I move towards the front door, I register a piece of sky through the side window. Each girl, as soon as she reaches the door, takes off her robe and scarf, sometimes shaking her head from side to side. She pauses before entering the room. Only there is no room, just the teasing void of memory.

More than any other place in our home, the living room was symbolic of my nomadic and borrowed life. Vagrant pieces of furniture from different times and places were thrown together, partly out of financial necessity, and partly because of my eclectic taste. Oddly, these incongruous ingredients created a symmetry that the other, more deliberately furnished rooms in the apartment lacked.

My mother would go crazy each time she saw the paintings leaning against the wall and the vases of flowers on the floor and the curtainless windows, which I refused to dress until I was finally reminded that this was an Islamic country and windows needed to be dressed. I don't know if you really belong to me, she would lament. Didn't I raise you to be orderly and organized? Her tone was serious, but she had repeated the same complaint for so many years that by now it was an almost tender ritual. Azi—that was my nickname—Azi, she would say, you are a grown-up lady now; act like one. Yet there was something in her tone that kept me young and fragile and obstinate, and still, when in memory I hear her voice, I know I never lived up to her expectations. I never did become the lady she tried to will me into being.

That room, which I never paid much attention to at that time, has gained a different status in my mind's eye now that it has become the precious object of memory. It was a spacious room, sparsely furnished and decorated.

At one corner was the fireplace, a fanciful creation of my husband, Bijan. There was a love seat against one wall, over which I had thrown a lace cover, my mother's gift from long ago. A pale peach couch faced the window, accompanied by two matching chairs and a big square glass-topped iron table.

My place was always in the chair with its back to the window, which opened onto a wide cul-de-sac called Azar. Opposite the window was the former American Hospital, once small and exclusive, now a noisy, overcrowded medical facility for wounded and disabled veterans of the war. On "weekends"—Thursdays and Fridays in Iran—the small street was crowded with hospital visitors who came as if for a picnic, with sandwiches and children. The neighbor's front yard, his pride and joy, was the main victim of their assaults, especially in summer, when they helped themselves to his beloved roses. We could hear the sound of children shouting, crying and laughing, and, mingled in, their mothers' voices, also shouting, calling out their children's names and threatening them with punishments. Sometimes a child or two would ring our doorbell and run away, repeating their perilous exercise at intervals.

From our second-story apartment—my mother occupied the first floor, and my brother's apartment, on the third floor, was often empty, since he had left for England—we could see the upper branches of a generous tree and, in the distance, over the buildings, the Elburz Mountains. The street, the hospital and its visitors were censored out of sight. We felt their presence only through the disembodied noises emanating from below.

I could not see my favorite mountains from where I sat, but opposite my chair, on the far wall of the dining room, was an antique oval mirror, a gift from my father, and in its reflection, I could see the mountains capped with snow, even in summer, and watch the trees change color. That censored view intensified my impression that the noise came not from the street below but from some far-off place, a place whose persistent hum was our only link to the world we refused, for those few hours, to acknowledge.

That room, for all of us, became a place of transgression. What a wonderland it was! Sitting around the large coffee table covered with bouquets of flowers, we moved in and out of the novels we read. Looking back, I am amazed at how much we learned without even noticing it. We were, to borrow from Nabokov, to experience how the ordinary pebble of ordinary life could be transformed into a jewel through the magic eye of fiction.

3

Six A.M.: the first day of class. I was already up. Too excited to eat breakfast, I put the coffee on and then took a long, leisurely shower. The water caressed my neck, my back, my legs, and I stood there both rooted and light. For the first time in many years, I felt a sense of anticipation that was not marred by tension: I would not need to go through the torturous rituals that had marked my days when I taught at the university—rituals governing what I was forced to wear, how I was expected to act, the gestures I had to remember to control. For this class, I would prepare differently.

Life in the Islamic Republic was as capricious as the month of April, when short periods of sunshine would suddenly give way to showers and storms. It was unpredictable: the regime would go through cycles of some tolerance, followed by a crackdown. Now, after a period of relative calm and so-called liberalization, we had again entered a time of hardships. Universities had once more become the targets of attack by the cultural purists who were busy imposing stricter sets of laws, going so far as to segregate men and women in classes and punishing disobedient professors.

The University of Allameh Tabatabai, where I had been teaching since 1987, had been singled out as the most liberal university in Iran. It was rumored that someone in the Ministry of Higher Education had asked, rhetorically, if the faculty at Allameh thought they lived in Switzerland. *Switzerland* had somehow become a byword for Western laxity: any program or action that was deemed un-Islamic was reproached with a mocking reminder that Iran was by no means Switzerland.

The pressure was hardest on the students. I felt helpless as I listened to their endless tales of woe. Female students were being penalized for running up the stairs when they were late for classes, for laughing in the hallways, for talking to members of the opposite sex. One day Sanaz had barged into class near the end of the session, crying. In between bursts of tears, she explained that she was late because the female guards at the door, finding a blush in her bag, had tried to send her home with a reprimand.

Why did I stop teaching so suddenly? I had asked myself this question many times. Was it the declining quality of the university? The ever-increasing indifference among the remaining faculty and students? The daily struggle against arbitrary rules and restrictions?

I smiled as I rubbed the coarse loofah over my skin, remembering the reaction of the university officials to my letter of resignation. They had harassed and limited me in all manner of ways, monitoring my visitors, controlling my actions, refusing a long-overdue tenure; and when I resigned, they infuriated me by suddenly commiserating and by refusing to accept my resignation. The students had threatened to boycott classes, and it was of some satisfaction to me to find out later that despite threats of reprisals, they in fact did boycott my replacement. Everyone thought I would break down and eventually return.

It took two more years before they finally accepted my resignation. I remember a friend told me, You don't understand their mentality. They won't accept your resignation because they don't think you have the right to quit. *They* are the ones who decide how long you should stay and when you should be dispensed with. More than anything else, it was this arbitrariness that had become unbearable.

What will you do? my friends had asked. Will you just stay home now? Well, I could write another book, I would tell them. But in truth I had no definite plans. I was still dealing with the aftershocks of a book on Nabokov I had just published, and only vague ideas, like vapors, formed when I turned to consider the shape of my next book. I could, for a while at least, continue the pleasant task of studying Persian classics, but one particular project, a notion I had been nurturing for years, was uppermost in my mind. For a long time I had dreamt of creating a special class, one that would give me the freedoms denied me in the classes I taught in the Islamic Republic. I wanted to teach a handful of selected students wholly committed to the study of literature, students who were not handpicked by the government, who had not chosen English literature simply because they had not been accepted in other fields or because they thought an English degree would be a good career move.

Teaching in the Islamic Republic, like any other vocation, was subservient to politics and subject to arbitrary rules. Always, the joy of teaching was marred by diversions and considerations forced on us by the regime—how well could one teach when the main concern of university officials was not the quality of one's work but the color of one's lips, the subversive potential of a single strand of hair? Could one really concentrate on one's job when what preoccupied the faculty was how to excise the word *wine* from a Hemingway story, when they decided not to teach Brontë because she appeared to condone adultery?

I was reminded of a painter friend who had started her career by depicting scenes from life, mainly deserted rooms, abandoned houses and discarded photographs of women. Gradually, her work became more abstract, and in her last exhibition, her paintings were splashes of rebellious color, like the two in my living room, dark patches with little droplets of blue. I asked about her progress from modern realism to abstraction. Reality has become so intolerable, she said, so bleak, that all I can paint now are the colors of my dreams.

The colors of my dreams, I repeated to myself, stepping out of the shower and onto the cool tiles. I liked that. How many people get a chance to paint the colors of their dreams? I put on my oversize bathrobe—it felt good to move from the security of the embracing water to the protective cover of a bathrobe wrapped around my body. I walked barefoot into the kitchen, poured some coffee into my favorite mug, the one with red strawberries, and sat down forgetfully on the divan in the hall.

This class was the color of my dreams. It entailed an active withdrawal from a reality that had turned hostile. I wanted very badly to hold on to my rare mood of jubilance and optimism. For in the back of my mind, I didn't know what awaited me at the end of this project. You are aware, a friend had said, that you are more and more withdrawing into yourself, and now that you have cut your relations with the university, your whole contact with the outside world will be mainly restricted to one room. Where will you go from here? he had asked. Withdrawal into one's dreams could be dangerous, I reflected, padding into the bedroom to change; this I had learned from Nabokov's crazy dreamers, like Kinbote and Humbert.

In selecting my students, I did not take into consideration their ideological or religious backgrounds. Later, I would count it as the class's great achievement that such a mixed group, with different and at times conflicting backgrounds, personal as well as religious and social, remained so loyal to its goals and ideals.

One reason for my choice of these particular girls was the peculiar mixture of fragility and courage I sensed in them. They were what you would call loners, who did not belong to any particular group or sect. I admired their ability to survive not despite but in some ways because of their solitary lives. We can call the class "a space of our own," Manna had suggested, a sort of communal version of Virginia Woolf's room of her own.

I spent longer than usual choosing my clothes that first morning, trying on different outfits, until I finally settled on a red-striped shirt and black corduroy jeans. I applied my makeup with care and put on bright red lipstick. As I fastened my small gold earrings, I suddenly panicked. What if it doesn't work? What if they won't come?

Don't, don't do that! Suspend all fears for the next five or six hours at least. Please, please, I pleaded with myself, putting on my shoes and going into the kitchen.

4

I was making tea when the doorbell rang. I was so preoccupied with my thoughts that I didn't hear it the first time. I opened the door to Mahshid. I thought you weren't home, she said, handing me a bouquet of white and yellow daffodils. As she was taking off her black robe, I told her, There are no men in the house—you can take that off, too. She hesitated before uncoiling her long black scarf. Mahshid and Yassi both observed the veil, but Yassi of late had become more relaxed in the way she wore her scarf. She tied it with a loose knot under her throat, her dark brown hair, untidily parted in the middle, peeping out from underneath. Mahshid's hair, however, was meticulously styled and curled under. Her short bangs gave her a strangely old-fashioned look that struck me as more European than Iranian. She wore a deep blue jacket over her white shirt, with a huge yellow butterfly embroidered on its right side. I pointed to the butterfly: did you wear this in honor of Nabokov?

I no longer remember when Mahshid first began to take my classes at the university. Somehow, it seems as if she had always been there. Her father, a devout Muslim, had been an ardent supporter of the revolution. She wore the scarf even before the revolution, and in her class diary, she wrote about the lonely mornings when she went to a fashionable girls' college, where she felt neglected and ignored—ironically, because of her then-conspicuous attire. After the revolution, she was jailed for five years because of her affiliation with a dissident religious organization and banned from continuing her education for two years after she was out of jail.

I imagine her in those pre-revolutionary days, walking along the uphill street leading to the college on countless sunny mornings. I see her walking alone, her head to the ground. Then, as now, she did not enjoy the day's brilliance. I say "then, as now" because the revolution that imposed the scarf on others did not relieve Mahshid of her loneliness. Before the revolution, she could in a sense take pride in her isolation. At that time, she had worn the scarf as a testament to her faith. Her decision was a voluntary act. When the revolution forced the scarf on others, her action became meaningless.

Mahshid is proper in the true sense of the word: she has grace and a certain dignity. Her skin is the color of moonlight, and she has almond-shaped eyes and jet-black hair. She wears pastel colors and is soft-spoken. Her pious background should have shielded her, but it didn't. I cannot imagine her in jail.

Over the many years I have known Mahshid, she has rarely alluded to her jail experiences, which left her with a permanently impaired kidney. One day in class, as we were talking about our daily terrors and nightmares, she mentioned that her jail memories visited her from time to time and that she had still not found a way to articulate them. But, she added, everyday life does not have fewer horrors than prison.

I asked Mahshid if she wanted some tea. Always considerate, she said she'd rather wait for the others and apologized for being a little early. Can I help? she asked. There's really nothing to help with. Make yourself at home, I told her as I stepped into the kitchen with the flowers and searched for a vase. The bell rang again. I'll get it, Mahshid cried out from the living room. I heard laughter; Manna and Yassi had arrived.

Manna came into the kitchen holding a small bouquet of roses. It's from Nima, she said. He wants to make you feel bad about excluding him from the class. He says he'll carry a bouquet of roses and march in front of your house during class hours, in protest. She was beaming; a few brief sparkles flashed in her eyes and died down again.

Putting the pastries onto a large tray, I asked Manna if she envisioned the words to her poems in colors. Nabokov writes in his autobiography that he and his mother saw the letters of the alphabet in color, I explained. He says of himself that he is a painterly writer.

The Islamic Republic coarsened my taste in colors, Manna said, fingering the discarded leaves of her roses. I want to wear outrageous colors, like shocking pink or tomato red. I feel too greedy for colors to see them in carefully chosen words of poetry. Manna was one of those people who would experience ecstasy but not happiness. Come here, I want to show you something, I said, leading her into our bedroom. When I was very young, I was obsessed with the colors of places and things my father told me about in his nightly stories. I wanted to know the color of Scheherazade's dress, her bedcover, the color of the genie and the magic lamp, and once I asked him about the color of paradise. He said it could be any color I wanted it to be. That was not enough. Then one day when we had guests and I was eating my soup in the dining room, my eyes fell on a painting I had seen on the wall ever since I could remember, and I instantly knew the color of my paradise. And here it is, I said, proudly pointing to a small oil painting in an old wooden frame: a green landscape of lush, leathery leaves with two birds, two deep red apples, a golden pear and a touch of blue.

My paradise is swimming-pool blue! Manna shot in, her eyes still glued to the painting. We lived in a large garden that belonged to my grandparents, she said, turning to me. You know the old Persian gardens, with their fruit trees, peaches, apples, cherries, persimmons and a willow or two. My best memories are of swimming in our huge irregularly shaped swimming pool. I was a swimming champion at our school, a fact my dad was very proud of. About a year after the revolution, my father died of a heart attack, and then the government confiscated our house and our garden and we moved into an apartment. I never swam again. My dream is at the bottom of that pool. I have a recurring dream of diving in to retrieve something of my father's memory and my childhood, she said as we walked to the living room, for the doorbell had rung again.

Azin and Mitra had arrived together. Azin was taking off her black kimonolike robe—Japanese-style robes were all the rage at the time—revealing a white peasant blouse that made no pretense of covering her shoulders, big golden earrings and pink lipstick. She had a branch of small yellow orchids—from Mitra and myself, she said in that special tone of hers that I can only describe as a flirtatious pout.

Nassrin came in next. She had brought two boxes of nougats: presents from Isfahan, she declared. She was dressed in her usual uniform—navy robe, navy scarf and black heelless shoes. When I had last seen her in class, she was wearing a huge black chador, revealing only the oval of her face and two restless hands, which, when she was not writing or doodling, were constantly in motion, as if trying to escape the confines of the thick black cloth. More recently, she had exchanged the chador for long, shapeless robes in navy, black or dark brown, with thick matching scarves that hid her hair and framed her face. She had a small, pale face, skin so transparent you could count the veins, full eyebrows, long lashes, lively eyes (brown), a small straight nose and an angry mouth: an unfinished miniature by some master who had suddenly been called away from his job and left the meticulously drawn face imprisoned in a careless splash of dark color.

We heard the sound of screeching tires and sudden brakes. I looked out the window: a small old Renault, cream-colored, had pulled up on the curb. Behind the wheel, a young man with fashionable sunglasses and a defiant profile rested his black-sleeved arm on the curve of the open window and gave the impression that he was driving a Porsche. He was staring straight in front of him as he talked to the woman beside him. Only once did he turn his head to his right, with what I could guess was a cross expression, and that was when the woman got out of the car and he angrily slammed the door behind her. As she walked to our front door, he threw his head out and shouted a few words, but she did not turn back to answer. The old Renault was Sanaz's; she had bought it with money saved from her job.

I turned towards the room, blushing for Sanaz. That must be the obnoxious brother, I thought. Seconds later the doorbell rang and I heard Sanaz's hurried steps and opened the door to her. She looked harassed, as if she had been running from a stalker or a thief. As soon as she saw me, she adjusted her face into a smile and said breathlessly: I hope I am not too late?

There were two very important men dominating Sanaz's life at the time. The first was her brother. He was nineteen years old and had not yet finished high school and was the darling of their parents, who, after two girls, one of whom had died at the age of three, had finally been blessed with a son. He was spoiled, and his one obsession in life was Sanaz. He had taken to proving his masculinity by spying on her, listening to her phone conversations, driving her car around and monitoring her actions. Her parents had tried to appease Sanaz and begged her, as the older sister, to be patient and understanding, to use her motherly instincts to see him through this difficult period.

The other was her childhood sweetheart, a boy she had known since she was eleven. Their parents were best friends, and their families spent most of their time and vacations together. Sanaz and Ali seemed to have been in love forever. Their parents encouraged this union and called it a match made in heaven. When Ali went away to England six years ago, his mother took to calling Sanaz his bride. They wrote to each other, sent photographs, and recently, when the number of Sanaz's suitors increased, there were talks of engagement and a reunion in Turkey, where Iranians did not require entrance visas. Any day now it might happen, an event Sanaz looked forward to with some fear and trepidation.

I had never seen Sanaz without her uniform, and stood there almost transfixed as she took off her robe and scarf. She was wearing an orange T-shirt tucked into tight jeans and brown boots, yet the most radical transformation was the mass of shimmering dark brown hair that now framed her face. She shook her magnificent hair from side to side, a gesture that I later noticed was a habit with her; she would toss her head and run her fingers through her hair every once in a while, as if making sure that her most prized possession was still there. Her features looked softer and more radiant—the black scarf she wore in public made her small face look emaciated and almost hard.

I'm sorry I'm a little late, she said breathlessly, running her fingers through her hair. My brother insisted on driving me, and he refused to wake up on time. He never gets up before ten, but he wanted to know where I was going. I might be off on some secret tryst, you know, a date or something.

I have been worrying in case any of you would get into trouble for this class, I said, inviting them all to take their seats around the table in the living room. I hope your parents and spouses feel comfortable with our arrangement.

Nassrin, who was wandering around the room, inspecting the paintings as if seeing them for the first time, paused to say offhandedly, I mentioned the idea very casually to my father, just to test his reaction, and he vehemently disapproved.

How did you convince him to let you come? I asked. I lied, she said. You lied? What else can one do with a person who's so dictatorial he won't let his daughter, at *this age,* go to an all-female literature class? Besides, isn't this how we treat the regime? Can we tell the Revolutionary Guards the truth? We lie to them; we hide our satellite dishes. We tell them we don't have illegal books and alcohol in our houses. Even my venerable father lies to them when the safety of his family is at stake, Nassrin added defiantly.

What if he calls me to check on you? I said, half teasingly. He won't. I gave a brilliant alibi. I said Mahshid and I had volunteered to help translate Islamic texts into English. And he believed you? Well, he had no reason not to. I hadn't lied to him before—not really—and it was what he wanted to believe. And he trusts Mahshid completely.

So if he calls me, I should lie to him? I persisted. It's up to you, Nassrin said after a pause, looking down at her twisting hands. Do *you* think you should tell him? By now I could hear a note of desperation in her voice. Am I getting you into trouble?

Nassrin always acted so confident that sometimes I forgot how vulnerable she really was under that tough-girl act. Of course I would respect your confidence, I said more gently. As you said, you are a big girl. You know what you're doing.

I had settled into my usual chair, opposite the mirror, where the mountains had come to stay. It is strange to look into a mirror and see not yourself but a view so distant from you. Mahshid, after some hesitation, had taken the chair to my right. On the couch, Manna settled to the far right and Azin to the far left; they instinctively kept their distance. Sanaz and Mitra were perched on the love seat, their heads close together as they whispered and giggled.

At this point Yassi and Nassrin came in and looked around for seats. Azin patted the empty part of the couch, inviting Yassi with her hand. Yassi hesitated for a moment and then slid between Azin and Manna. She slumped into place and seemed to leave little room for her two companions, who sat upright and a little stiff in their respective corners. Without her robe, she looked a little overweight, as if she had not as yet lost her baby fat. Nassrin had gone to the dining room in search of a chair. We can squeeze you in here, said Manna. No, thank you, I actually prefer straight-backed chairs. When she returned, she placed her chair between the couch and Mahshid.

They kept that arrangement, faithfully, to the end. It became representative of their emotional boundaries and personal relations. And so began our first class.

5

"Upsilamba!" I heard Yassi exclaim as I entered the dining room with a tray of tea. Yassi loved playing with words. Once she told us that her obsession with words was pathological. As soon as I discover a new word, I have to use it, she said, like someone who buys an evening gown and is so eager that she wears it to the movies, or to lunch.

Let me pause and rewind the reel to retrace the events leading us to Yassi's exclamation. This was our first session. All of us had been nervous and inarticulate. We were used to meeting in public, mainly in classrooms and in lecture halls. The girls had their separate relationships with me, but except for Nassrin and Mahshid, who were intimate, and a certain friendship between Mitra and Sanaz, the rest were not close; in many cases, in fact, they would never have chosen to be friends. The collective intimacy made them uncomfortable.

I had explained to them the purpose of the class: to read, discuss and respond to works of fiction. Each would have a private diary, in which she should record her responses to the novels, as well as ways in which these works and their discussions related to her personal and social experiences. I explained that I had chosen them for this class because they seemed dedicated to the study of literature. I mentioned that one of the criteria for the books I had chosen was their authors' faith in the critical and almost magical power of literature, and reminded them of the nineteen-year-old Nabokov, who, during the Russian Revolution, would not allow himself to be diverted by the sound of bullets. He kept on writing his solitary poems while he heard the guns and saw the bloody fights from his window. Let us see, I said, whether seventy years later our disinterested faith will reward us by transforming the gloomy reality created of this other revolution.

The first work we discussed was *A Thousand and One Nights*, the familiar tale of the cuckolded king who slew successive virgin wives as revenge for his queen's betrayal, and whose murderous hand was finally stayed by the entrancing storyteller Scheherazade. I formulated certain general questions for them to consider, the most central of which was how these great works of imagination could help us in our present trapped situation as women. We were not looking for blueprints, for an easy solution, but we did hope to find a link between the open spaces the novels provided and the closed ones we were confined to. I remember reading to my girls Nabokov's claim that "readers were born free and ought to remain free."

What had most intrigued me about the frame story of *A Thousand and One Nights* were the three kinds of women it portrayed—all victims of a king's unreasonable rule. Before Scheherazade enters the scene, the women in the story are divided into those who betray and then are killed (the queen) and those who are killed before they have a chance to betray (the virgins). The virgins, who, unlike Scheherazade, have no voice in the story, are mostly ignored by the critics. Their silence, however, is significant. They surrender their virginity, and their lives, without resistance or protest. They do not quite exist, because they leave no trace in their anonymous death. The queen's infidelity does not rob the king of his absolute authority; it throws him off balance. Both types of women—the queen and the virgins—tacitly accept the king's public authority by acting within the confines of his domain and by accepting its arbitrary laws.

Scheherazade breaks the cycle of violence by choosing to embrace different terms of engagement. She fashions her universe not through physical force, as does the king, but through imagination and reflection. This gives her the courage to risk her life and sets her apart from the other characters in the tale.

Our edition of *A Thousand and One Nights* came in six volumes. I, luckily, had bought mine before it was banned and sold only on the black market, for exorbitant prices. I divided the volumes among the girls and asked them, for the next session, to classify the tales according to the types of women who played central roles in the stories.

Once I'd given them their assignment, I asked them each to tell the rest of us why they had chosen to spend their Thursday mornings here, discussing Nabokov and Jane Austen. Their answers were brief and forced. In order to break the ice, I suggested the calming distraction of cream puffs and tea.

This brings us to the moment when I enter the dining room with eight glasses of tea on an old and unpolished silver tray. Brewing and serving tea is an aesthetic ritual in Iran, performed several times a day. We serve tea in transparent glasses, small and shapely, the most popular of which is called slim-waisted: round and full at the top, narrow in the middle and round and full at the bottom. The color of the tea and its subtle aroma are an indication of the brewer's skill.

I step into the dining room with eight slim-waisted glasses whose honey-colored liquid trembles seductively. At this point, I hear Yassi shout triumphantly, "Upsilamba!" She throws the word at me like a ball, and I take a mental leap to catch it.

Upsilamba!—the word carries me back to the spring of 1994, when four of my girls and Nima were auditing a class I was teaching on the twentieth-century novel. The class's favorite book was Nabokov's *Invitation to a Beheading.* In this novel, Nabokov differentiates Cincinnatus C., his imaginative and lonely hero, from those around him through his originality in a society where uniformity is not only the norm but also the law. Even as a child, Nabokov tells us, Cincinnatus appreciated the freshness and beauty of language, while other children "understood each other at the first word, since they had no words that would end in an unexpected way, perhaps in some archaic letter, an upsilamba, becoming a bird or catapult with wondrous consequences."

No one in class had bothered to ask what the word meant. No one, that is, who was properly taking the class—for many of my old students just stayed on and sat in on my classes long after their graduation. Often, they were more interested and worked harder than my regular students, who were taking the class for credit. Thus it was that those who audited the class—including Nassrin, Manna, Nima, Mahshid and Yassi—had one day gathered in my office to discuss this and a number of other questions.

I decided to play a little game with the class, to test their curiosity. On the midterm exam, one of the questions was "Explain the significance of the word *upsilamba* in the context of *Invitation to a Beheading.* What does the word mean, and how does it relate to the main theme of the novel?" Except for four or five students, no one had any idea what I could possibly mean, a point I did not forget to remind them of every once in a while throughout the rest of that term.

The truth was that *upsilamba* was one of Nabokov's fanciful creations, possibly a word he invented out of *upsilon,* the twentieth letter in the Greek alphabet, and *lambda,* the eleventh. So that first day in our private class, we let our minds play again and invented new meanings of our own.

I said I associated *upsilamba* with the impossible joy of a suspended leap. Yassi, who seemed excited for no particular reason, cried out that she always thought it could be the name of a dance—you know, "C'mon, baby, do the Upsilamba with me." I proposed that for the next time, they each write a sentence or two explaining what the word meant to them.

Manna suggested that *upsilamba* evoked the image of small silver fish leaping in and out of a moonlit lake. Nima added in parentheses, Just so you won't forget me, although you have barred me from your class: an upsilamba to you too! For Azin it was a sound, a melody. Mahshid described an image of three girls jumping rope and shouting "Upsilamba!" with each leap. For Sanaz, the word was a small African boy's secret magical name.

Mitra wasn't sure why the word reminded her of the paradox of a blissful sigh. And to Nassrin it was the magic code that opened the door to a secret cave filled with treasures.

Upsilamba became part of our increasing repository of coded words and expressions, a repository that grew over time until gradually we had created a secret language of our own. That word became a symbol, a sign of that vague sense of joy, the tingle in the spine Nabokov expected his readers to feel in the act of reading fiction; it was a sensation that separated the good readers, as he called them, from the ordinary ones. It also became the code word that opened the secret cave of remembrance.

6

In his foreword to the English edition of *Invitation to a Beheading* (1959), Nabokov reminds the reader that his novel does not offer *"tout pour tous."* Nothing of the kind. "It is," he claims, "a violin in the void." And yet, he goes on to say, "I know . . . a few readers who will jump up, ruffling their hair." Well, absolutely. The original version, Nabokov tells us, was published in installments in 1935. Almost six decades later, in a world unknown and presumably unknowable to Nabokov, in a forlorn living room with windows looking out towards distant white-capped mountains, time and again I would stand witness to the unlikeliest of readers as they lost themselves in a madness of hair-ruffling.

Invitation to a Beheading begins with the announcement that its fragile hero, Cincinnatus C., has been sentenced to death for the crime of "gnostic turpitude": in a place where all citizens are required to be transparent, he is opaque. The principal characteristic of this world is its arbitrariness; the condemned man's only privilege is to know the time of his death—but the executioners keep even this from him, turning every day into a day of execution. As the story unfolds, the reader discovers with increasing discomfort the artificial texture of this strange place. The moon from the window is fake; so is the spider in the corner, which, according to convention, must become the prisoner's faithful companion. The director of the jail, the jailer and the defense lawyer are all the same man, and keep changing places. The most important character, the executioner, is first introduced to the prisoner under another name and as a fellow prisoner: M'sieur Pierre. The executioner and the condemned man must learn to love each other and cooperate in the act of execution, which will be celebrated in a gaudy feast. In this staged world, Cincinnatus's only window to another universe is his writing.

The world of the novel is one of empty rituals. Every act is bereft of substance and significance, and even death becomes a spectacle for which the good citizens buy tickets. It is only through these empty rituals that brutality becomes possible. In another Nabokov novel, *The Real Life of Sebastian*

Knight, Sebastian's brother discovers two seemingly incongruous pictures in his dead brother's library: a pretty, curly-haired child playing with a dog and a Chinese man in the act of being beheaded. The two pictures remind us of the close relation between banality and brutality. Nabokov had a special Russian term for this: *poshlust.*

Poshlust, Nabokov explains, "is not only the obviously trashy but mainly the falsely important, the falsely beautiful, the falsely clever, the falsely attractive." Yes, there are many examples you can bring from everyday life, from the politicians' sugary speeches to certain writers' proclamations to chickens. Chickens? You know, the ones the street vendors sell nowadays—if you lived in Tehran, you couldn't possibly miss them. The ones they dip in paint—shocking pink, brilliant red or turquoise blue—in order to make them more attractive. Or the plastic flowers, the bright pink-and-blue artificial gladiolas carted out at the university both for mourning and for celebration.

What Nabokov creates for us in *Invitation to a Beheading* is not the actual physical pain and torture of a totalitarian regime but the nightmarish quality of living in an atmosphere of perpetual dread. Cincinnatus C. is frail, he is passive, he is a hero without knowing or acknowledging it: he fights with his instincts, and his acts of writing are his means of escape. He is a hero because he refuses to become like all the rest.

Unlike in other utopian novels, the forces of evil here are not omnipotent; Nabokov shows us their frailty as well. They are ridiculous and they can be defeated, and this does not lessen the tragedy—the waste. *Invitation to a Beheading* is written from the point of view of the victim, one who ultimately sees the absurd sham of his persecutors and who must retreat into himself in order to survive.

Those of us living in the Islamic Republic of Iran grasped both the tragedy and absurdity of the cruelty to which we were subjected. We had to poke fun at our own misery in order to survive. We also instinctively recognized poshlust—not just in others, but in ourselves. This was one reason that art and literature became so essential to our lives: they were not a luxury but a necessity. What Nabokov captured was the texture of life in a totalitarian society, where you are completely alone in an illusory world full of false promises, where you can no longer differentiate between your savior and your executioner.

We formed a special bond with Nabokov despite the difficulty of his prose. This went deeper than our identification with his themes. His novels are shaped around invisible trapdoors, sudden gaps that constantly pull the carpet from under the reader's feet. They are filled with mistrust of what we call everyday reality, an acute sense of that reality's fickleness and frailty.

There was something, both in his fiction and in his life, that we instinctively related to and grasped, the possibility of a boundless freedom when all options are taken away. I think that was what drove me to create the class. My main link with the outside world had been the university, and now that I had severed that link, there on the brink of the void, I could invent the violin or be devoured by the void.

7

The two photographs should be placed side by side. Both embody the "fragile unreality"—to quote Nabokov on his own state of exile—of our existence in the Islamic Republic of Iran. One cancels the other, and yet without one, the other is incomplete. In the first photograph, standing there in our black robes and scarves, we are as we had been shaped by someone else's dreams. In the second, we appear as we imagined ourselves. In neither could we feel completely at home.

The second photograph belonged to the world inside the living room. But outside, underneath the window that deceptively showcased only the mountains and the tree outside our house, was the other world, where the bad witches and furies were waiting to transform us into the hooded creatures of the first.

The best way I can think of explaining this self-negating and paradoxical inferno is through an anecdote, one that, like similar anecdotes, defies fiction to become its own metaphor.

The chief film censor in Iran, up until 1994, was blind. Well, nearly blind. Before that, he was the censor for theater. One of my playwright friends once described how he would sit in the theater wearing thick glasses that seemed to hide more than they revealed. An assistant who sat by him would explain the action onstage, and he would dictate the parts that needed to be cut.

After 1994, this censor became the head of the new television channel. There, he perfected his methods and demanded that the scriptwriters give him their scripts on audiotape; they were forbidden to make them attractive or dramatize them in any way. He then made his judgments about the scripts based on the tapes. More interesting, however, is the fact that his successor, who was not blind—not physically, that is—nonetheless followed the same system.

Our world under the mullahs' rule was shaped by the colorless lenses of the blind censor. Not just our reality but also our fiction had taken on this curious coloration in a world where the censor was the poet's rival in rearranging and reshaping reality, where we simultaneously invented ourselves and were figments of someone else's imagination.

We lived in a culture that denied any merit to literary works, considering them important only when they were handmaidens to something seemingly more urgent—namely ideology. This was a country where all gestures, even the most private, were interpreted in political terms. The colors of my head scarf or my father's tie were symbols of Western decadence and imperialist tendencies. Not wearing a beard, shaking hands with members of the opposite sex, clapping or whistling in public meetings, were likewise considered Western and therefore decadent, part of the plot by imperialists to bring down our culture.

A few years ago some members of the Iranian Parliament set up an investigative committee to examine the content of national television. The committee issued a lengthy report in which it condemned the showing of *Billy Budd,* because, it claimed, the story promoted homosexuality. Ironically, the Iranian television programmers had mainly chosen that film because of its lack of female characters. The cartoon version of *Around the World in Eighty Days* was also castigated, because the main character—a lion—was British and the film ended in that bastion of imperialism, London.

Our class was shaped within this context, in an attempt to escape the gaze of the blind censor for a few hours each week. There, in that living room, we rediscovered that we were also living, breathing human beings; and no matter how repressive the state became, no matter how intimidated and frightened we were, like Lolita we tried to escape and to create our own little pockets of freedom. And like Lolita, we took every opportunity to flaunt our insubordination: by showing a little hair from under our scarves, insinuating a little color into the drab uniformity of our appearances, growing our nails, falling in love and listening to forbidden music.

An absurd fictionality ruled our lives. We tried to live in the open spaces, in the chinks created between that room, which had become our protective cocoon, and the censor's world of witches and goblins outside. Which of these two worlds was more real, and to which did we really belong? We no longer knew the answers. Perhaps one way of finding out the truth was to do what we did: to try to imaginatively articulate these two worlds and, through that process, give shape to our vision and identity.

8

How can I create this other world outside the room? I have no choice but to appeal once again to your imagination. Let's imagine one of the girls, say Sanaz, leaving my house and let us follow her from there to her final destination. She says her good-byes and puts on her black robe and scarf over her orange shirt and jeans, coiling her scarf around her neck to cover her huge gold earrings. She directs wayward strands of hair under the scarf, puts her notes into her large bag, straps it on over her shoulder and walks out into the hall. She pauses a moment on top of the stairs to put on thin lacy black gloves to hide her nail polish.

We follow Sanaz down the stairs, out the door and into the street. You might notice that her gait and her gestures have changed. It is in her best interest not to be seen, not be heard or noticed. She doesn't walk upright, but bends her head towards the ground and doesn't look at passersby. She walks quickly and with a sense of determination. The streets of Tehran and other Iranian cities are patrolled by militia, who ride in white Toyota patrols, four gun-carrying men and women, sometimes followed by a minibus. They are called the Blood of God. They patrol the streets to make sure that women like Sanaz wear their veils properly, do not wear makeup, do not walk in public with men who are not their fathers, brothers or husbands. She will pass slogans on the walls, quotations from Khomeini and a group called the Party of God: MEN WHO WEAR TIES ARE U.S. LACKEYS. VEILING IS A WOMAN'S PROTECTION. Beside the slogan is a charcoal drawing of a woman: her face is featureless and framed by a dark chador. MY SISTER, GUARD YOUR VEIL. MY BROTHER, GUARD YOUR EYES.

If she gets on a bus, the seating is segregated. She must enter through the rear door and sit in the back seats, allocated to women. Yet in taxis, which accept as many as five passengers, men and women are squeezed together like sardines, as the saying goes, and the same goes with minibuses, where so many of my students complain of being harassed by bearded and God-fearing men.

You might well ask, What is Sanaz thinking as she walks the streets of Tehran? How much does this experience affect her? Most probably, she tries to distance her mind as much as possible from her surroundings. Perhaps she is thinking of her brother, or of her distant boyfriend and the time when she will meet him in Turkey. Does she compare her own situation with her mother's when she was the same age? Is she angry that women of her mother's generation could walk the streets freely, enjoy the company of the opposite sex, join the police force, become pilots, live under laws that were among the most progressive in the world regarding women? Does she feel humiliated by the new laws, by the fact that after the revolution, the age of marriage was lowered from eighteen to nine, that stoning became once more the punishment for adultery and prostitution?

In the course of nearly two decades, the streets have been turned into a war zone, where young women who disobey the rules are hurled into patrol cars, taken to jail, flogged, fined, forced to wash the toilets and humiliated, and as soon as they leave, they go back and do the same thing. Is she aware, Sanaz, of her own power? Does she realize how dangerous she can be when her every stray gesture is a disturbance to public safety? Does she think how vulnerable the Revolutionary Guards are who for over eighteen years have patrolled the streets of Tehran and have had to endure young women like herself, and those of other generations, walking, talking, showing a strand of hair just to remind them that they have not converted?

We have reached Sanaz's house, where we will leave her on her doorstep, perhaps to confront her brother on the other side and to think in her heart of her boyfriend.

These girls, my girls, had both a real history and a fabricated one. Although they came from very different backgrounds, the regime that ruled them had tried to make their personal identities and histories irrelevant. They were never free of the regime's definition of them as Muslim women.

Whoever we were—and it was not really important what religion we belonged to, whether we wished to wear the veil or not, whether we observed certain religious norms or not—we had become the figment of someone else's dreams. A stern ayatollah, a self-proclaimed philosopher-king, had come to rule our land. He had come in the name of a past, a past that, he claimed, had been stolen from him. And he now wanted to re-create us in the image of that illusory past. Was it any consolation, and did we even wish to remember, that what he did to us was what we allowed him to do?   ■

■ QUESTIONS FOR CONNECTIONS WITHIN THE READING ■

1. Why does Nafisi spend so much time describing the members of her reading group? What different motives may have brought these readers to Nafisi's apartment? We may normally think of reading as a solitary activity, unlike watching movies or sports; why was it so important for the women to meet together as a group?

2. Judging from the information that Nafisi provides, why do you think her reading group selected the particular works she mentions: *A Thousand and One Nights,* as well as *Invitation to a Beheading, Lolita,* and other novels by Nabokov? Why might religious authorities, not only in Iran but also in the United States, object to the teaching of such works?

3. Early in Chapter 10 of *Reading Lolita in Tehran,* Nafisi writes, "*Lolita* was *not* a critique of the Islamic Republic, but it went against the grain of all totalitarian perspectives." Without consulting a dictionary, and drawing instead on Nafisi's account, define "totalitarian." What social and psychological effects does the totalitarian regime have on Nafisi and her students? In what sense might *Lolita* provide a "critique" of totalitarianism?

■ QUESTIONS FOR WRITING ■

1. Does Nafisi present a theory of interpretation? In other words, what does she see as the "real" or "correct" meaning of a work of art? Does she accept Nabokov's claims that "readers were born free and ought to remain free"? Would Nafisi say a work of art can mean anything we want? What

is the value of art if it has no determinate or "correct" meaning? If art has a value, is its value simply personal? Does it also have social, political, and cultural value?

2. Nafisi and her students read Nabokov against the backdrop of the Islamic Republic of Iran. In that setting, what does the experience offer them? Would their reading of the novel provide the same experience if it took place in the United States? Does literature serve a different social function in our society? How might reading a novel in a private group differ from the experience of reading the same novel in an American high school or college classroom?

■ QUESTIONS FOR MAKING CONNECTIONS BETWEEN READINGS ■

1. Would you say that Nafisi calls into question Eric Schlosser's negative portrayal of American culture overseas? Do we export more than Big Macs and the culture of Las Vegas? On the other hand, is it conceivable that a market-driven society can be as one-dimensional as the Islamic Republic of Iran, albeit without the use of force? In Iran, no one can escape the power of the mullahs. In the United States, is it any easier to escape the power of the market—or should we reject any analogy between the two?

2. Toward the close of his essay "The Mind's Eye," Oliver Sacks asks, "Do any of us, finally, know how we think?" Assuming that the answer to this question is no, what conclusions can we reach about the ways that each of us interprets our individual worlds? If everyone makes things meaningful in his or her own way, what purpose might be served by an activity such as meeting to discuss a work of literature? What does the individual gain from the communal reading of a work of fiction? Do the blind subjects of Sacks's essay have anything in common with Nafisi's students? Do Sacks and Nafisi, taken together, show that there is ultimately only one way to achieve "a rich and full realization" of an inner life?

www For additional suggestions about making connections between the readings, visit the Link-O-Mat and More Sample Assignments at <www.newhum.com>.

MARTHA NUSSBAUM

MARTHA NUSSBAUM is the Ernst Freund Distinguished Service Professor of Law and Ethics at the University of Chicago, where she has appointments in the Philosophy Department, the Law School, the Divinity School, and the Classics Department. A philosopher, a critic, an activist, and a feminist, Nussbaum is equally at home discussing ancient Greek philosophy and contemporary moral and political philosophy. She has written at length about the connections between philosophy and literature, arguing that literature is the best means we have for exploring the consequences of moral choices. She has testified about homosexuality in Ancient Greece before the Supreme Court when it was deliberating a Colorado law that forbade extending civil rights to gays and lesbians. And, as a research adviser for the United Nations' World Institute for Development Economics Research for many years, she has committed herself to improving the status of women in the politics of international development.

Although Nussbaum has long had an interest in liberal education, it has been her work with the United Nations group researching the problems women face in developing countries that has most profoundly shaped her current thoughts about what education is for and what it takes to actually help people from other cultures. As she describes it, after joining this project, "I realized all of a sudden that my own education had not acquainted me at all with the fundamentals. . . . I knew nothing about Hinduism, nothing about Islam, nothing about Buddhism, nothing about the history of Africa or of India, so in short I was just very ill equipped to play the role that I was playing."

In learning more about these other cultures, traditions, and histories, Nussbaum came to see the needs of women in developing countries in a different light. While Nussbaum sees American academic feminists as largely satisfied by

Nussbaum, Martha. "Women and Cultural Universals." *Sex and Social Justice.* New York: Oxford University Press, 1999. 29–54.

Biographical information from Martha Nussbaum's home page at the University of Chicago Law School <http://www.law.uchicago.edu/faculty/nussbaum/>; quotations from Martha Nussbaum, interview by Barry Clark, for ABC's radio series, "Globally Speaking: The Politics of Globalization," on global citizenship <http://www.abc.net.au/global/radio/nussbaum .htm>.

playing games with language, she believes that international feminists must be committed to establishing the basic conditions for self-determination discussed in "Women and Cultural Universals." In order to act ethically in the global economy, Nussbaum argues, it is not sufficient just to learn some facts about other exotic cultures; it is necessary to cultivate "the ability to imagine what it might be like to be in the shoes of someone who's different from yourself." As Nussbaum sees it, her role as a teacher, scholar, and activist is to help foster such acts of critical imagination.

www **To learn more about Martha Nussbaum and women's rights in an international context, visit the Link-O-Mat at <www.newhum.com>.**

Women and Cultural Universals

We shall only solve our problems if we see them as human problems arising out of a special situation; and we shall not solve them if we see them as African problems, generated by our being somehow unlike others.

—*Kwame Anthony Appiah,*
Africa in the Philosophy of Cultures

Being a woman is not yet a way of being a human being.

—*Catharine MacKinnon*

I. A Matter of Survival

"I may die, but still I cannot go out. If there's something in the house, we eat. Otherwise, we go to sleep." So Metha Bai, a young widow in Rajasthan, India, with two young children, described her plight as a member of a caste whose women are traditionally prohibited from working outside the home—even when, as here, survival itself is at issue. If she stays at home, she and her children may shortly die. If she attempts to go out, her in-laws will beat her and abuse her children. For now, Metha Bai's father travels from 100 miles away to plow her small plot of land. But he is aging, and Metha Bai fears that she and her children will shortly die with him.[1]

In this case, as in many others throughout the world, cultural traditions pose obstacles to women's health and flourishing. Depressingly, many traditions portray women as less important than men, less deserving of basic life support or of fundamental rights that are strongly correlated with quality of life, such as the right to work and the right to political participation. Sometimes, as in the case of Metha Bai, the women themselves resist these traditions. Sometimes, on the other hand, the traditions have become so deeply internalized that they seem to record what is "right" and "natural," and women themselves endorse their own second-class status.

Such cases are hardly confined to non-Western or developing countries. As recently as 1873, the U.S. Supreme Court upheld a law that forbade women to practice law in the state of Illinois, on the grounds that "[t]he constitution of the family organization, which is founded in the divine ordinance, as well as in the nature of things, indicates the domestic sphere as that which properly belongs to the domain and functions of womanhood."[2] And in 1993, a woman who was threatened and grossly harassed by her male coworkers, after becoming the first woman to work in the heavy metal shop in the General Motors plant in Indiana, was described by a federal district judge as having provoked the men's conduct by her "unladylike" behavior—behavior that consisted in using a four-letter word a few times in a five-year period.[3] Clearly our own society still appeals to tradition in its own way to justify women's unequal treatment.

What should people concerned with justice say about this? And should they say anything at all? On the one hand, it seems impossible to deny that traditions, both Western and non-Western, perpetrate injustice against women in many fundamental ways, touching on some of the most central elements of a human being's quality of life—health, education, political liberty and participation, employment, self-respect, and life itself. On the other hand, hasty judgments that a tradition in some distant part of the world is morally retrograde are familiar legacies of colonialism and imperialism and are correctly regarded with suspicion by sensitive thinkers in the contemporary world. To say that a practice endorsed by tradition is bad is to risk erring by imposing one's own way on others, who surely have their own ideas of what is right and good. To say that a practice is all right whenever local tradition endorses it as right and good is to risk erring by withholding critical judgment where real evil and oppression are surely present. To avoid the whole issue because the matter of proper judgment is so fiendishly difficult is tempting but perhaps the worst option of all. It suggests the sort of moral collapse depicted by Dante when he describes the crowd of souls who mill around in the vestibule of hell, dragging their banner now one way, now another, never willing to set it down and take a definite stand on any moral or political question. Such people, he implies, are the most despicable of all. They cannot even get into hell because they have not been willing to stand for anything in life, one way or another. To express the spirit of this chapter

very succinctly, it is better to risk being consigned by critics to the "hell" reserved for alleged Westernizers and imperialists—however unjustified such
criticism would in fact be—than to stand around in the vestibule waiting for
a time when everyone will like what we are going to say. And what we are
going to say is: that there are universal obligations to protect human functioning and its dignity, and that the dignity of women is equal to that of men.
If that involves assault on many local traditions, both Western and non-
Western, so much the better, because any tradition that denies these things is
unjust. Or, as a young Bangladeshi wife said when local religious leaders
threatened to break the legs of women who went to the literacy classes conducted by a local NGO (nongovernmental organization), "We do not listen to
the *mullahs* any more. They did not give us even a quarter kilo of rice."[4]

The situation of women in the contemporary world calls urgently for
moral standtaking. Women, a majority of the world's population, receive
only a small proportion of its opportunities and benefits. According to the
Human Development Report, in no country in the world is women's quality of
life equal to that of men, according to a complex measure that includes life
expectancy, educational attainment, and GDP (gross domestic product) per
capita.[5] Some countries have much larger gender disparities than others.
(Among prosperous industrial countries, for example, Spain and Japan perform relatively poorly in this area; Sweden, Denmark, and New Zealand
perform relatively well.[6]) If we now examine the Gender Empowerment
Measure, which uses variables chosen explicitly to measure the relative empowerment of men and women in political and economic activity,[7] we find
even more striking signs of gender disparity. Once again, the Scandinavian
nations do well; Japan and Spain do relatively poorly.[8]

If we turn our attention to the developing countries we find uneven
achievements but, in the aggregate, a distressing situation. On average, employment participation rates of women are only 50% those of men (in South
Asia 29%; in the Arab states only 16%).[9] Even when women are employed,
their situation is undercut by pervasive wage discrimination and by long
hours of unpaid household labor. (If women's unpaid housework were
counted as productive output in national income accounts, global output
would increase by 20–30%.) Outside the home, women are generally employed in a restricted range of jobs offering low pay and low respect. The percentage of earned income that goes to women is rarely higher than 35%. In
many nations it is far lower: in Iran, 16%; Belize, 17%; Algeria, 16%; Iraq,
17%; Pakistan, 19%. (China at 38% is higher than Japan at 33%; highest in the
world are Sweden at 45%, Denmark at 42%, and the extremely impoverished
Rwanda at 41%, Burundi at 42%, and Mozambique at 42%.) The situation of
women in the workplace is frequently undermined by sex discrimination
and sexual harassment.

Women are much less likely than men to be literate. In South Asia, female literacy rates average around 50% those of males. In some countries the
rate is still lower: in Nepal, 35%; Sierra Leone, 37%; Sudan, 27%;

Afghanistan, 32%.[10] Two-thirds of the world's illiterate people are women. In higher education, women lag even further behind men in both developing and industrial nations.[11]

Although some countries allowed women the vote early in this century, some still have not done so. And there are many informal obstacles to women's effective participation in political life. Almost everywhere, they are underrepresented in government: In 1980, they made up only around 10% of the world's parliamentary representatives and less than 4% of its cabinet officials.[12]

As Metha Bai's story indicates, employment outside the home has a close relationship to health and nutrition. So too, frequently, does political voice. And if we now turn to the very basic issue of health and survival, we find compelling evidence of discrimination against females in many nations of the world. It appears that when equal nutrition and health care are present women live, on average, slightly longer than men—even allowing for a modest level of maternal mortality. Thus, in Europe the female/male ratio in 1986 was 105/100, in North America 104.7/100.[13] But it may be objected that for several reasons it is inappropriate to compare these developed countries with countries in the developing world. Let us, therefore, with Jean Drèze and Amartya Sen, take as our baseline the ratio in sub-Saharan Africa, where there is great poverty but little evidence of gender discrimination in basic nutrition and health.[14] The female/male ratio in 1986 was 102.2/100. If we examine the sex ratio in various other countries and ask the question, "How many more women than are now in country C would be there if its sex ratio were the same as that of sub-Saharan Africa?," we get a number that Sen has graphically called the number of "missing women." The number of missing women in Southeast Asia is 2.4 million; in Latin America, 4.4; in North Africa, 2.4; in Iran, 1.4; in China, 44.0; in Bangladesh, 3.7; in India, 36.7; in Pakistan, 5.2; in West Asia, 4.3. If we now consider the ratio of the number of missing women to the number of actual women in a country, we get, for Pakistan, 12.9%; for India, 9.5%; for Bangladesh, 8.7%; for China, 8.6%; for Iran, 8.5%; for West Asia, 7.8%; for North Africa, 3.9%; for Latin America, 2.2%; for Southeast Asia, 1.2%. In India, not only is the mortality differential especially sharp among children (girls dying in far greater numbers than boys), the higher mortality rate of women compared to men applies to all age groups until the late thirties.[15]

Poverty alone does not cause women to die in greater numbers than men. This is abundantly clear from comparative regional studies in India, where some of the poorest regions, for example, Kerala, have the most equal sex ratios, and some far richer regions perform very poorly.[16] When there is scarcity, custom and political arrangement frequently decree who gets to eat the little there is and who gets taken to the doctor. And custom and political arrangement are always crucial in deciding who gets to perform wage labor outside the home, an important determinant of general status in the family and the community. As Sen has argued, a woman's perceived contribution to the well-being of the family unit is often determined by her ability to work outside, and this determines, in turn, her bargaining position within the family unit.[17] Custom and politics decree who gets access to the education that would open job opportunities and make political rights meaningful. Custom and politics decree who can go where in what clothing in what company. Custom and politics decree who gets to make what sorts of protests against ill treatment both inside and outside the family and whose voice of protest is likely to be heard.

Customs and political arrangements, in short, are important causes of women's misery and death. It seems incumbent on people interested in justice, and aware of the information about women's status that studies such as the *Human Development Reports* present, to ask about the relationship between culture and justice and between both of these and legal-political arrangements. It then seems incumbent on them to try to work out an account of the critical assessment of traditions and political arrangements that is neither do-gooder colonialism or an uncritical validation of the status quo.

One might suppose that any approach to the question of quality of life assessment in development economics would offer an account of the relationship between tradition and women's equality that would help us answer these questions. But in fact such an account is sorely lacking in the major theoretical approaches that, until recently, dominated the development scene. (Here I do not even include what has been the most common practical approach, which has been simply to ask about GNP (gross national product) per capita. This crude approach does not even look at the distribution of wealth and income; far less does it ask about other constituents of life quality, for example, life expectancy, infant mortality, education, health, and the presence or absence of political liberties, that are not always well correlated with GNP per capita.[18] The failure to ask these questions is a particularly grave problem when it is women's quality of life we want to consider. For women have especially often been unable to enjoy or control the fruits of a nation's general prosperity.)

The leading economic approach to the family is the model proposed by Nobel Prize–winning economist Gary Becker. Becker assumes that the family's goal is the maximization of utility, construed as the satisfaction of preference or desire, and that the head of the household is a beneficent altruist who will adequately take thought for the interests of all family members.[19] In real life, however, the economy of the family is characterized by pervasive "cooperative conflicts," that is, situations in which the interests of members of a cooperative body split apart, and some individuals fare well at the expense of others.[20] Becker deserves great credit for putting these issues on the agenda of the profession in the first place. But his picture of male motivation does not fit the evidence, and in a way substantial enough to affect the model's predictive value—especially if one looks not only at women's stated satisfactions and preferences, which may be deformed by intimidation, lack of information, and habit,[21] but at their actual functioning.[22] Furthermore, the model prevents those who use it from even getting the information about individual family members on which a more adequate account might be based.[23]

Suppose we were to retain a utilitarian approach and yet to look at the satisfactions of all family members—assuming, as is standardly done in economics, that preferences and tastes are exogenous and independent of laws, traditions, and institutions rather than endogenously shaped by them. Such an approach—frequently used by governments polling citizens about well-being—has the advantage of assessing all individuals one by one. But the evidence of preference endogeneity is great, and especially great when we are dealing with people whose status has been persistently defined as second class in laws and institutions of various sorts. There are many reasons to think that women's perception even of their health status is shaped by traditional views, such as the view that female life is worth less than male life, that women are weaker than men, that women do not have equal rights, and so forth. In general, people frequently adjust their expectations to the low level of well-being they think they can actually attain.[24] This approach, then, cannot offer a useful account of the role of tradition in well-being, because it is bound by its very commitments to an uncritical validation of the status quo.

More promising than either Becker's model or the standard utilitarian approach is one suggested by John Rawls's liberalism, with its account of the just distribution of a small list of basic goods and resources.[25] This approach does enable us to criticize persistent inequalities, and it strongly criticizes the view that preferences are simply given rather than shaped by society's basic structure. But in one way the Rawlsian approach stops short. Rawls's list of "primary goods," although it includes some capacity-like items, such as liberty and opportunity, also includes thing-like items, particularly income and wealth, and it measures who is least well off simply in terms of the amount of these thing-like resources an individual can command. But people have varying needs for resources: a pregnant woman, for example, needs more calories than a nonpregnant woman, a child more protein than an adult. They also have different abilities to convert resources into functioning. A person in a wheelchair will need more resources to become mobile than a person with unimpaired limbs; a woman in a society that has defined employment outside the home as off limits to women needs more resources to become a productive worker than one who does not face such struggles. In short, the Rawlsian approach does not probe deeply enough to show us how resources do or do not go to work in making people able to function. Again, at least some of our questions about the relationship between tradition and quality of life cannot be productively addressed.

Workers on such issues have therefore increasingly converged on an approach that is now widely known as "the capabilities approach." This approach to quality-of-life measurement and the goals of public policy[26] holds that we should focus on the question: What are the people of the group or country in question actually able to do and to be? Unlike a focus on opulence (say, GNP per capita), this approach asks about the distribution of resources and opportunities. In principle, it asks how each and every individual is doing with respect to all the functions deemed important. Unlike Becker's approach, the capability approach considers people one by one, not as parts of an organic unit; it is very interested in seeing how a supposed organic unit such as the family has constructed unequal capabilities for various types of functioning. Unlike a standard utilitarian approach, the capability approach maintains that preferences are not always reliable indicators of life quality, as they may be deformed in various ways by oppression and deprivation. Unlike the type of liberal approach that focuses only on the distribution of resources, the capability approach maintains that resources have no value in themselves, apart from their role in promoting human functioning. It therefore directs the planner to inquire into the varying needs individuals have for resources and their varying abilities to convert resources into functioning. In this way, it strongly invites a scrutiny of tradition as one of the primary sources of such unequal abilities.[27]

But the capabilities approach raises the question of cultural universalism, or, as it is often pejoratively called, "essentialism." Once we begin asking how people are actually functioning, we cannot avoid focusing on some components of lives and not others, some abilities to act and not others, seeing some capabilities and functions as more central, more at the core of human life, than others. We cannot avoid having an account, even if a partial and highly general account, of what functions of the human being are most worth the care and attention of public planning the world over. Such an account is bound to be controversial.

II. Anti-Universalist Conversations

The primary opponents of such an account of capability and functioning will be "antiessentialists" of various types, thinkers who urge us to begin not with sameness but with difference—both between women and men and across groups of women—and to seek norms defined relatively to a local context and locally held beliefs. This opposition takes many forms, and I shall be responding to several distinct objections. But I can begin to motivate the enterprise by telling several true stories of conversations that have taken place at the World Institute for Development Economics Research (WIDER), in which the anti-universalist position seemed to have alarming implications for women's lives.[28]

At a conference on "Value and Technology," an American economist who has long been a leftwing critic of neoclassical economics delivers a paper urging the preservation of traditional ways of life in a rural area of Orissa, India, now under threat of contamination from Western development projects. As evidence of the excellence of this rural way of life, he points to the fact that whereas we Westerners experience a sharp split between the values that prevail in the workplace and the values that prevail in the home, here, by contrast, exists what the economist calls "the embedded way of life," the same values obtaining in both places. His example: Just as in the home a menstruating woman is thought to pollute the kitchen and therefore may not enter it, so too in the workplace a menstruating woman is taken to pollute the loom and may not enter the room where looms are kept. Some feminists object that this example is repellant rather than admirable; for surely such practices both degrade the women in question and inhibit their freedom. The first economist's collaborator, an elegant French anthropologist (who would, I suspect, object violently to a purity check at the seminar room door), replies: Don't we realize that there is, in these matters, no privileged place to stand? This, after all, has been shown by both Derrida and Foucault. Doesn't he know that he is neglecting the otherness of Indian ideas by bringing his Western essentialist values into the picture?[29]

The same French anthropologist now delivers her paper. She expresses regret that the introduction of smallpox vaccination to India by the British eradicated the cult of Sittala Devi, the goddess to whom one used to pray to avert smallpox. Here, she says, is another example of Western neglect of difference. Someone (it might have been me) objects that it is surely better to be healthy rather than ill, to live rather than to die. The answer comes back; Western essentialist medicine conceives of things in terms of binary oppositions: life is opposed to death, health to disease.[30] But if we cast away this binary way of thinking, we will begin to comprehend the otherness of Indian traditions.

At this point Eric Hobsbawm, who has been listening to the proceedings in increasingly uneasy silence, rises to deliver a blistering indictment of the traditionalism and relativism that prevail in this group. He lists historical examples of ways in which appeals to tradition have been politically engineered to support oppression and violence.[31] His final example is that of National Socialism in Germany. In the confusion that ensues, most of the relativist social scientists—above all those from far away, who do not know who Hobsbawm is—demand that Hobsbawm be asked to leave the room. The radical American economist, disconcerted by this apparent tension between his relativism and his affiliation with the left, convinces them, with difficulty, to let Hobsbawm remain.

We shift now to another conference two years later, a philosophical conference on the quality of life.[32] Members of the quality-of-life project are speaking of choice as a basic good, and of the importance of expanding women's sphere of choices. We are challenged by the radical economist of my first story, who insists that contemporary anthropology has shown that non-Western people are not especially attached to freedom of choice. His example: A book on Japan has shown that Japanese males, when they get home from work, do not wish to choose what to eat for dinner, what to wear, and so on. They wish all these choices to be taken out of their hands by their wives. A heated exchange follows about what this example really shows. I leave it to your imaginations to reconstruct it. In the end, the confidence of the radical economist is unshaken: We are victims of bad universalist thinking, who fail to respect "difference."[33]

The phenomenon is an odd one. For we see here highly intelligent people, people deeply committed to the good of women and men in developing countries, people who think of themselves as progressive and feminist and antiracist, people who correctly argue that the concept of development is an evaluative concept requiring normative argument[34]—effectively eschewing normative argument and taking up positions that converge, as Hobsbawm correctly saw, with the positions of reaction, oppression, and sexism. Under the banner of their fashionable opposition to universalism march ancient religious taboos, the luxury of the pampered husband, educational deprivation, unequal health care, and premature death.

Nor do these anti-universalists appear to have a very sophisticated conception of their own core notions, such as "culture," "custom," and "tradition." It verges on the absurd to treat India as a single culture, and a single visit to a single Orissan village as sufficient to reveal its traditions. India, like all extant societies, is a complex mixture of elements[35]: Hindu, Muslim, Parsi, Christian, Jewish, atheist; urban, suburban, rural; rich, poor, and middle class; high caste, low caste, and aspiring middle caste; female and male; rationalist and mystical. It is renowned for mystical religion but also for achievements in mathematics and for the invention of chess. It contains intense, often violent sectarianism, but it also contains Rabindranath Tagore's cosmopolitan humanism and Mahatma Gandhi's reinterpretation of Hinduism as a religion of universal nonviolence. Its traditions contain views of female whorishness and childishness that derive from the Laws of Manu[36]; but it also contains the sexual agency of Draupadi in the *Mahabharata,* who solved the problem of choice among Pandava husbands by taking all five, and the enlightened sensualism and female agency of the *Kama Sutra,* a sacred text that foreign readers wrongly interpret as pornographic. It contains women like Metha Bai, who are confined to the home; it also contains women like Amita Sen (mother of Amartya Sen), who fifty years ago was among the first middle-class Bengali women to dance in public, in Rabindranath Tagore's musical extravaganzas in Santiniketan. It contains artists who disdain the foreign, preferring, with the Marglins, the "embedded" way of life, and it also contains Satyajit Ray, that great Bengali artist and lover of local traditions, who could also write, "I never ceased to regret that while I had stood in the scorching summer sun in the wilds of Santiniketan sketching *simul* and *palash* in full bloom, *Citizen Kane* had come and gone, playing for just three days in the newest and biggest cinema in Calcutta."[37]

What, then, is "the culture" of a woman like Metha Bai? Is it bound to be that determined by the most prevalent customs in Rajasthan, the region of her marital home? Or, might she be permitted to consider with what traditions or groups she wishes to align herself, perhaps forming a community of solidarity with other widows and women, in pursuit of a better quality of life? What is "the culture" of Chinese working women who have recently been victims of the government's "women go home" policy, which appeals to Confucian traditions about woman's "nature"?[38] Must it be the one advocated by Confucius, or may they be permitted to form new alliances—with one another, and with other defenders of women's human rights? What is "the culture" of General Motors employee Mary Carr? Must it be the one that says women should be demure and polite, even in the face of gross insults, and that an "unladylike" woman deserves the harassment she gets? Or might she be allowed to consider what norms are appropriate to the situation of a woman working in a heavy metal shop, and to act accordingly? Real cultures contain plurality and conflict, tradition, and subversion. They borrow good things from wherever they find them, none too worried about purity. We would never tolerate a claim that women in our own society must embrace traditions that arose thousands of years ago—indeed, we are proud that we have no such traditions. Isn't it condescending, then, to treat Indian and Chinese women as bound by the past in ways that we are not?

Indeed, as Hobsbawm suggested, the vision of "culture" propounded by the Marglins, by stressing uniformity and homogeneity, may lie closer to artificial constructions by reactionary political forces than to any organic historical entity. Even to the extent to which it is historical, one might ask, exactly how does that contribute to make it worth preserving? Cultures are not museum pieces, to be preserved intact at all costs. There would appear, indeed, to be something condescending in preserving for contemplation a way of life that causes real pain to real people.

Let me now, nonetheless, describe the most cogent objections that might be raised by a relativist against a normative universalist project.

III. The Attack on Universalism

Many attacks on universalism suppose that any universalist project must rely on truths eternally fixed in the nature of things, outside human action and human history. Because some people believe in such truths and some do not, the objector holds that a normative view so grounded is bound to be biased in favor of some religious/metaphysical conceptions and against others.[39]

But universalism does not require such metaphysical support.[40] For universal ideas of the human do arise within history and from human experience, and they can ground themselves in experience. Indeed, those who take all human norms to be the result of human interpretation can hardly deny that universal conceptions of the human are prominent and pervasive among such interpretations, hardly to be relegated to the dustbin of metaphysical history along with recondite theoretical entities such as phlogiston. As Aristotle so simply puts it, "One may observe in one's travels to distant countries the feelings of recognition and affiliation that link every human being to every other human being."[41] Kwame Anthony Appiah makes the same point, telling the story of his bicultural childhood. A child who visits one set of grandparents in Ghana and another in rural England, who has a Lebanese uncle and who later, as an adult, has nieces and nephews from more than seven different nations, finds, he argues, not unbridgeable alien "otherness," but a great deal of human commonality, and comes to see the world as a "network of points of affinity."[42] But such a metaphysically agnostic, experiential and historical universalism is still vulnerable to some, if not all, of the objections standardly brought against universalism.

Neglect of Historical and Cultural Differences

The opponent charges that any attempt to pick out some elements of human life as more fundamental than others, even without appeal to a transhistorical reality, is bound to be insufficiently respectful of actual historical and cultural differences. People, it is claimed, understand human life and humanness in widely different ways, and any attempt to produce a list of the most fundamental properties and functions of human beings is bound to enshrine certain understandings of the human and to demote others. Usually, the objector continues, this takes the form of enshrining the understanding of a dominant group at the expense of minority understandings. This type of objection, frequently made by feminists, can claim support from many historical examples in which the human has indeed been defined by focusing on actual characteristics of males.

It is far from clear what this objection shows. In particular it is far from clear that it supports the idea that we ought to base our ethical norms, instead, on the current preferences and the self-conceptions of people who are living what the objector herself claims to be lives of deprivation and oppression. But it does show at least that the project of choosing one picture of the human over another is fraught with difficulty, political as well as philosophical.

Neglect of Autonomy

A different objection is presented by liberal opponents of universalism. The objection is that by determining in advance what elements of human life have most importance, the universalist project fails to respect the right of people to choose a plan of life according to their own lights, determining what is central and what is not.[43] This way of proceeding is "imperialistic." Such evaluative choices must be left to each citizen. For this reason, politics must refuse itself a determinate theory of the human being and the human good.

Prejudicial Application

If we operate with a determinate conception of the human being that is meant to have some normative moral and political force, we must also, in applying it, ask which beings we take to fall under the concept. And here the objector notes that, all too easily—even if the conception itself is equitably and comprehensively designed—the powerless can be excluded. Aristotle himself, it is pointed out, held that women and slaves were not full-fledged human beings, and because his politics were based on his view of human functioning, the failure of these beings (in his view) to exhibit the desired mode of functioning contributed to their political exclusion and oppression.

It is, once again, hard to know what this objection is supposed to show. In particular, it is hard to know how, if at all, it is supposed to show that we would be better off without such determinate universal concepts. For it could be plausibly argued that it would have been even easier to exclude women and slaves on a whim if one did not have such a concept to combat.[44] On the other hand, it does show that we need to think not only about getting the concept right but also about getting the right beings admitted under the concept.

Each of these objections has some merit. Many universal conceptions of the human being have been insular in an arrogant way and neglectful of differences among cultures and ways of life. Some have been neglectful of choice and autonomy. And many have been prejudicially applied. But none of this shows that all such conceptions must fail in one or more of these ways. At this point, however, we need to examine a real proposal, both to display its merits and to argue that it can in fact answer these charges.

IV. A Conception of the Human Being: The Central Human Capabilities

The list of basic capabilities is generated by asking a question that from the start is evaluative: What activities[45] characteristically performed by human beings are so central that they seem definitive of a life that is truly human? In other words, what are the functions without which (meaning, without the availability of which) we would regard a life as not, or not fully, human?[46] We can get at this question better if we approach it via two somewhat more concrete questions that we often really ask ourselves. First is a question about personal continuity. We ask ourselves which changes or transitions are compatible with the continued existence of that being as a member of the human kind and which are not. Some functions can fail to be present without threatening our sense that we still have a human being on our hands; the absence of others seems to signal the end of a human life. This question is asked regularly, when we attempt to make medical definitions of death in a situation in which some of the functions of life persist, or to decide, for others or (thinking ahead) for ourselves, whether a certain level of illness or impairment means the end of the life of the being in question.[47]

The other question is a question about kind inclusion. We recognize other humans as human across many differences of time and place, of custom and appearance. We often tell ourselves stories, on the other hand, about anthropomorphic creatures who do not get classified as human, on account of some feature of their form of life and functioning. On what do we base these inclusions and exclusions? In short, what do we believe must be there, if we are going to acknowledge that a given life is human?[48] The answer to these questions points us to a subset of common or characteristic human functions, informing us that these are likely to have a special importance for everything else we choose and do.

Note that the procedure through which this account of the human is derived is neither ahistorical nor a priori. It is the attempt to summarize empirical findings of a broad and ongoing cross-cultural inquiry. As such, it is both open-ended and humble; it can always be contested and remade. Nor does it claim to read facts of "human nature" from biological observation; it takes biology into account as a relatively constant element in human experience.[49] It is because the account is evaluative from the start that it is called a conception of the good.

It should also be stressed that, like John Rawls's account of primary goods in *A Theory of Justice*,[50] this list of good functions, which is in some ways more comprehensive than his own list, is proposed as the object of a specifically political consensus.[51] The political is not understood exactly as Rawls understands it because the nation state is not assumed to be the basic unit, and the account is meant to have broad applicability to cross-cultural deliberations. This means, given the current state of world politics, that many of the obligations to promote the adequate distribution of these goods must rest with individuals rather than with any political institution, and in that way its role becomes difficult to distinguish from the role of other norms and goals of the individual. Nonetheless, the point of the list is the same as that of Rawlsian primary goods: to put forward something that people from many different traditions, with many different fuller conceptions of the good, can agree on, as the necessary basis for pursuing their good life. That is why the list is deliberately rather general.[52] Each of its components can be more concretely specified in accordance with one's origins, religious beliefs, or tastes. In that sense, the consensus that it hopes to evoke has many of the features of the "overlapping consensus" described by Rawls.[53]

Having isolated some functions that seem central in defining the very presence of a human life, we do not rest content with mere bare humanness. We want to specify a life in which fully human functioning, or a kind of basic human flourishing, will be available. For we do not want politics to take mere survival as its goal; we want to describe a life in which the dignity of the human being is not violated by hunger or fear or the absence of opportunity. (The idea is very much Marx's idea, when he used an Aristotelian notion of functioning to describe the difference between a merely animal use of one's faculties and a "truly human use."[54]) The following list of central human functional capabilities is an attempt to specify this basic notion of the good: All citizens should have these capabilities, whatever else they have and pursue.[55] I introduce this as a list of capabilities rather than of actual functionings, because I shall argue that capability, not actual functioning, should be the goal of public policy.

Central Human Functional Capabilities

1. *Life.* Being able to live to the end of a human life of normal length[56]; not dying prematurely or before one's life is so reduced as to be not worth living
2. *Bodily health and integrity.* Being able to have good health, including reproductive health; being adequately nourished[57]; being able to have adequate shelter[58]
3. *Bodily integrity.* Being able to move freely from place to place; being able to be secure against violent assault, including sexual assault, marital rape, and domestic violence; having opportunities for sexual satisfaction and for choice in matters of reproduction
4. *Senses, imagination, thought.* Being able to use the senses; being able to imagine, to think, and to reason—and to do these things in a "truly human" way, a way informed and cultivated by an adequate education, including, but by no means limited to, literacy and basic mathematical and scientific training; being able to use imagination and thought in connection with experiencing and producing expressive works and events of one's own choice (religious, literary, musical, etc.); being able to use one's mind in ways protected by guarantees of freedom of expression with respect to both political and artistic speech and freedom of religious exercise; being able to have pleasurable experiences and to avoid nonbeneficial pain
5. *Emotions.* Being able to have attachments to things and persons outside ourselves; being able to love those who love and care for us; being able to grieve at their absence; in general, being able to love, to grieve, to experience longing, gratitude, and justified anger; not having one's emotional developing blighted by fear or anxiety. (Supporting this capability means supporting forms of human association that can be shown to be crucial in their development.[59])
6. *Practical reason.* Being able to form a conception of the good and to engage in critical reflection about the planning of one's own life. (This entails protection for the liberty of conscience.)
7. *Affiliation.* (a) Being able to live for and in relation to others, to recognize and show concern for other human beings, to engage in various forms of social interaction; being able to imagine the situation of another and to have compassion for that situation; having the capability for both

justice and friendship. (Protecting this capability means, once again, protecting institutions that constitute such forms of affiliation, and also protecting the freedoms of assembly and political speech.) (b) Having the social bases of self-respect and nonhumiliation; being able to be treated as a dignified being whose worth is equal to that of others. (This entails provisions of nondiscrimination.)

8. *Other species.* Being able to live with concern for and in relation to animals, plants, and the world of nature[60]

9. *Play.* Being able to laugh, to play, to enjoy recreational activities

10. *Control over one's environment.* (a) *Political:* being able to participate effectively in political choices that govern one's life; having the rights of political participation, free speech, and freedom of association (b) *Material:* being able to hold property (both land and movable goods); having the right to seek employment on an equal basis with others; having the freedom from unwarranted search and seizure.[61] In work, being able to work as a human being, exercising practical reason and entering into meaningful relationships of mutual recognition with other workers.

The "capabilities approach," as I conceive it,[62] claims that a life that lacks any one of these capabilities, no matter what else it has, will fall short of being a good human life. Thus it would be reasonable to take these things as a focus for concern, in assessing the quality of life in a country and asking about the role of public policy in meeting human needs. The list is certainly general—and this is deliberate, to leave room for plural specification and also for further negotiation. But like (and as a reasonable basis for) a set of constitutional guarantees, it offers real guidance to policymakers, and far more accurate guidance than that offered by the focus on utility, or even on resources.[63]

The list is, emphatically, a list of separate components. We cannot satisfy the need for one of them by giving a larger amount of another one. All are of central importance and all are distinct in quality. This limits the trade-offs that it will be reasonable to make and thus limits the applicability of quantitative cost-benefit analysis. At the same time, the items on the list are related to one another in many complex ways. Employment rights, for example, support health, and also freedom from domestic violence, by giving women a better bargaining position in the family. The liberties of speech and association turn up at several distinct points on the list, showing their fundamental role with respect to several distinct areas of human functioning.

V. Capability as Goal

The basic claim I wish to make—concurring with Amartya Sen—is that the central goal of public planning should be the *capabilities* of citizens to perform various important functions. The question that should be asked when assessing quality of life in a country—and of course this is a central part of assessing the quality of its political arrangements—is, How well have the people of the country been enabled to perform the central human functions? And, have they been put in a position of mere human subsistence with respect to the functions, or have they been enabled to live well? Politics, we argue (here concurring with Rawls), should focus on getting as many people as possible into a state of capability to function, with respect to the interlocking set of capabilities enumerated by that list.[64] Naturally, the determination of whether certain individuals and groups are across the threshold is only as precise a matter as the determination of the threshold. I have left things deliberately somewhat open-ended at this point, in keeping with the procedures of the *Human Development Report,* believing that the best way to work toward a more precise determination, at present, is to focus on comparative information and to allow citizens to judge for themselves whether their policymakers have done as well as they should have. Again, we will have to answer various questions about the costs we are willing to pay to get all citizens above the threshold, as opposed to leaving a small number below and allowing the rest a considerably above-threshold life quality. It seems likely, at any rate, that moving all citizens above a basic threshold of capability should be taken as a central social goal. When citizens are across the threshold, societies are to a great extent free to choose the other goals they wish to pursue. Some inequalities, however, will themselves count as capability failures. For example, inequalities based on hierarchies of gender or race will themselves be inadmissible on the grounds that they undermine self-respect and emotional development.

The basic intuition from which the capability approach starts, in the political arena, is that human capabilities exert a moral claim that they should be developed. Human beings are creatures such that, provided with the right educational and material support, they can become fully capable of the major human functions. That is, they are creatures with certain lower-level capabilities (which I call "basic capabilities"[65]) to perform the functions in question. When these capabilities are deprived of the nourishment that would transform them into the high-level capabilities that figure on my list, they are fruitless, cut off, in some way but a shadow of themselves. They are like actors who never get to go on the stage, or a person who sleeps all through life, or a musical score that is never performed. Their very being makes forward reference to functioning. Thus, if functioning never arrives on the scene they are hardly even what they are. This may sound like a metaphysical idea, and in a sense it is (in that it is an idea discussed in Aristotle's *Metaphysics*). But that does not mean it is not a basic and pervasive empirical idea, an idea that underwrites many of our daily practices and judgments in many times and places. Just as we hold that a child who dies before getting to maturity has died especially tragically—for her activities of growth and preparation for adult activity now have lost their point—so too with capability and functioning more generally: We believe that certain basic and central human endowments have a claim to be assisted in developing, and exert that claim on others, and especially, as Aristotle saw, on government. Without some such notion of the basic worth of human capacities, we have a hard time arguing for women's equality and for basic human rights. Think, for example, of the remark of Catharine MacKinnon that I quoted as my epigraph. If women were really just trees or turtles or filing cabinets, the fact that their current status in many parts of the world is not a fully human one would not be, as it is, a problem of justice. In thinking of political planning we begin, then, from a notion of the basic capabilities and their worth, thinking of them as claims to a chance for functioning, which give rise to correlated political duties.

I have spoken both of functioning and of capability. How are they related? Getting clear about this is crucial in defining the relation of the capabilities approach to liberalism. For if we were to take functioning itself as the goal of public policy, the liberal would rightly judge that we were precluding many choices that citizens may make in accordance with their own conceptions of the good. A deeply religious person may prefer not to be well nourished but to engage in strenuous fasting. Whether for religious or for other reasons, a person may prefer a celibate life to one containing sexual expression. A person may prefer to work with an intense dedication that precludes recreation and play. Am I saying that these are not fully human or flourishing lives? Does the approach instruct governments to nudge or push people into functioning of the requisite sort, no matter what they prefer?

Here we must answer: No, capability, not functioning, is the political goal. This is so because of the very great importance the approach attaches to practical reason, as a good that both suffuses all the other functions, making them human rather than animal,[66] and figures, itself, as a central function on the list. It is perfectly true that functionings, not simply capabilities, are what render a life fully human: If there were no functioning of any kind in a life, we could hardly applaud it, no matter what opportunities it contained. Nonetheless, for political purposes it is appropriate for us to shoot for capabilities, and those alone. Citizens must be left free to determine their course after that. The person with plenty of food may always choose to fast, but there is a great difference between fasting and starving, and it is this difference we wish to capture. Again, the person who has normal opportunities for sexual satisfaction can always choose a life of celibacy, and we say nothing against this. What we do speak against, for example, is the practice of female genital mutilation, which deprives individuals of the opportunity to choose sexual functioning (and indeed, the opportunity to choose celibacy as well).[67] A person who has opportunities for play can always choose a workaholic life; again, there is a great difference between that chosen life and a life constrained by insufficient maximum-hour protections and/or the "double day" that makes women in many parts of the world unable to play.

The issue will be clearer if we recall that there are three different types of capabilities that figure in the analysis.[68] First, there are *basic capabilities:* the innate equipment of individuals that is the necessary basis for developing the more advanced capability. Most infants have from birth the basic capability for practical reason and imagination, though they cannot exercise such functions without a lot more development and education. Second, there are *internal capabilities:* states of the person herself that are, as far as the person herself is concerned, sufficient conditions for the exercise of the requisite functions. A woman who has not suffered genital mutilation has the internal capability for sexual pleasure; most adult human beings everywhere have the internal capability to use speech and thought in accordance with their own conscience. Finally, there are *combined capabilities,* which we define as internal capabilities *combined with* suitable external conditions for the exercise of the function. A woman who is not mutilated but is secluded and forbidden to leave the house has internal but not combined capabilities for sexual expression (and work and political participation). Citizens of repressive nondemocratic regimes have the internal but not the combined capability to exercise thought and speech in accordance with their conscience. The aim of public policy is the production of *combined capabilities.* This means promoting the states of the person by providing the necessary education and care; it also means preparing the environment so that it is favorable for the exercise of practical reason and the other major functions.[69]

This clarifies the position. The approach does not say that public policy should rest content with *internal capabilities* but remain indifferent to the struggles of individuals who have to try to exercise these in a hostile environment. In that sense, it is highly attentive to the goal of functioning, and instructs governments to keep it always in view. On the other hand, we are not pushing individuals into the function: Once the stage is fully set, the choice is up to them.

The approach is therefore very close to Rawls's approach using the notion of primary goods. We can see the list of capabilities as like a long list of opportunities for life functioning, such that it is always rational to want them whatever else one wants. If one ends up having a plan of life that does not make use of all of them, one has hardly been harmed by having the chance to choose a life that does. (Indeed, in the cases of fasting and celibacy it is the very availability of the alternative course that gives the choice its moral value.) The primary difference between this capabilities list and Rawls's list of primary goods is its length and definiteness, and in particular its determination to place on the list the social basis of several goods that Rawls has called "natural goods," such as "health and vigor, intelligence and imagination."[70] Since Rawls has been willing to put the social basis of self-respect on his list, it is not at all clear why he has not made the same move with imagination and health.[71] Rawls's evident concern is that no society can guarantee health to its individuals—in that sense, saying that our goal is full combined capability may appear unreasonably idealistic. Some of the capabilities (e.g., some of the political liberties) can be fully guaranteed by society, but many others involve an element of chance and cannot be so guaranteed. We respond to this by saying that the list is an enumeration of political *goals* that should be useful as a benchmark for aspiration and comparison. Even though individuals with adequate health support often fall ill, it still makes sense to compare societies by asking about actual health capabilities, because we assume that the comparison will reflect the different inputs of human planning and can be adjusted to take account of more and less favorable natural situations.

Earlier versions of the list appeared to diverge from the approach of Rawlsian liberalism by not giving as central a place as Rawls does to the traditional political rights and liberties—although the need to incorporate them was stressed from the start.[72] This version of the list corrects that defect of emphasis. These political liberties have a central importance in making well-being human. A society that aims at well-being while overriding these has delivered to its members a merely animal level of satisfaction.[73] As Amartya Sen has recently written, "Political rights are important not only for the fulfillment of needs, they are crucial also for the formulation of needs. And this idea relates, in the end, to the respect that we owe each other as fellow human beings."[74] This idea has recently been echoed by Rawls: Primary goods specify what citizens' needs are from the point of view of political justice.[75]

The capability view justifies its elaborate list by pointing out that choice is not pure spontaneity, flourishing independently of material and social conditions. If one cares about people's powers to choose a conception of the good, then one must care about the rest of the form of life that supports those powers, including its material conditions. Thus the approach claims that its more comprehensive concern with flourishing is perfectly consistent with the impetus behind the Rawlsian project, which has always insisted that we are not to rest content with merely formal equal liberty and opportunity but must pursue their fully equal worth by ensuring that unfavorable economic and social circumstances do not prevent people from availing themselves of liberties and opportunities that are formally open to them.

The guiding thought behind this Aristotelian enterprise is, at its heart, a profoundly liberal idea,[76] and one that lies at the heart of Rawls's project as well: the idea of the citizen as a free and dignified human being, a maker of choices. Politics has an urgent role to play here, getting citizens the tools they need, both to choose at all and to have a realistic option of exercising the most valuable functions. The choice of whether and how to use the tools, however, is left up to them, in the conviction that this is an essential aspect of respect for their freedom. They are seen not as passive recipients of social planning but as dignified beings who shape their own lives.[77]

Let us now return to the Marglins and to Metha Bai. What would this universalist approach have to say about these concrete cases? Notice how close the Marglin approach is, in its renunciation of critical normative argument, to the prevailing economic approaches of which it presents itself as a radical critique. A preference-based approach that gives priority to the preferences of dominant males in a traditional culture is likely to be especially subversive of the quality of life of women, who have been on the whole badly treated by prevailing traditional norms. And one can see this clearly in the Marglins's own examples. For menstruation taboos, even if endorsed by habit and custom, impose severe restrictions on women's power to form a plan of life and to execute the plan they have chosen.[78] They are members of the same family of traditional attitudes that make it difficult for women like Metha Bai to sustain the basic functions of life. Vulnerability to smallpox, even if someone other than an anthropologist should actually defend it as a good thing, is even more evidently a threat to human functioning. And the Japanese husband who allegedly renounces freedom of choice actually shows considerable attachment to it, in the ways that matter, by asking the woman to look after the boring details of life. What should concern us is whether the woman has a similar degree of freedom to plan her life and to execute her plan.

As for Metha Bai, the absence of freedom to choose employment outside the home is linked to other capability failures, in the areas of health, nutrition, mobility, education, and political voice. Unlike the type of liberal view that focuses on resources alone, my view enables us to focus directly on the obstacles to self-realization imposed by traditional norms and values and thus to justify special political action to remedy the unequal situation. No male of Metha Bai's caste would have to overcome threats of physical violence in order to go out of the house to work for life-sustaining food.

The capabilities approach insists that a woman's affiliation with a certain group or culture should not be taken as normative for her unless, on due consideration, with all the capabilities at her disposal, she makes that norm her own. We should take care to extend to each individual full capabilities to pursue the items on the list—and then see whether they want to avail themselves of those opportunities. Usually they do, even when tradition says they should not. Martha Chen's work with widows like Metha Bai reveals that they are already deeply critical of the cultural norms that determine their life quality. One week at a widows' conference in Bangalore was sufficient to cause these formerly secluded widows to put on forbidden colors and to apply for loans; one elderly woman, "widowed" at the age of seven, danced for the first time in her life, whirling wildly in the center of the floor.[79] In other cases, especially when a woman must negotiate a relationship with a surviving husband, it takes longer for her real affiliations and preferences to emerge. Chen's related study of a rural literacy project in Bangladesh[80] shows that it took a good deal of time for women previously illiterate to figure out, in consultation with development workers, that literacy might offer something to their own concrete lives. Nonetheless, what we do not see in any of these cases is the fantasy that the Marglins describe, a cultural monolith univocally repudiating the outsider and clinging to an "embedded way of life." Why should women cling to a tradition, indeed, when it is usually not their voice that speaks or their interests that are served?   ∎

NOTES

I have discussed the capabilities approach in several other papers, to which I shall refer: "Nature, Function, and Capability: Aristotle on Political Distribution," *Oxford Studies in Ancient Philosophy* Supplementary Volume 1 (1988), 145–84, hereafter NFC; "Aristotelian Social Democracy," in *Liberalism and the Good*, ed. R. B. Douglass *et al.* (New York: Routledge, 1990), 203–52, hereafter ASD; "Non-Relative Virtues: An Aristotelian Approach," in *The Quality of Life*, ed. M. Nussbaum and A. Sen (Oxford: Clarendon Press, 1993), hereafter NRV; "Aristotle on Human Nature and the Foundations of Ethics," in *World, Mind and Ethics: Essays on the Ethical Philosophy of Bernard Williams*, ed. J. E. J. Altham and Ross Harrison (Cambridge: Cambridge University Press, 1995), 86–131, hereafter HN; "Human Functioning and Social Justice: In Defense of Aristotelian Essentialism," *Political Theory 20* (1992), 202–46, hereafter HF; "Human Capabilities, Female Human Beings," in *Women, Culture, and Development*, ed. M. Nussbaum and J. Glover (Oxford: Clarendon Press, 1995), 61–104, hereafter HC; "The Good as Discipline, the Good as Freedom," in *The Ethics of Consumption and Global Stewardship*, ed. D. Crocker and T. Linden (Lanham, MD: Rowman and Littlefield, 1998), 312–41, hereafter GDGF; "Capabilities and Human Rights," *Fordham Law Review 66* (1997), 273–300, hereafter CHR.

1. For this case and others like it, see Martha Chen, "A Matter of Survival: Women's Rights to Employment in India and Bangladesh," in *Women, Culture, and Development* (hereafter WCD), ed. M. Nussbaum and J. Glover (Oxford: Clarendon Press, 1995), 37–57. See also M. Chen, *Perpetual Mourning: Widowhood in Rural India* (Delhi: Oxford University Press, 2000).

2. *Bradwell v. Illinois*, 83 U.S. (16 Wall.) 130 (1873).

3. *Carr v. Allison Gas Turbine Division, General Motors Corp.*, 32 F.3d 1007 (1994). Mary Carr won her case on appeal.

4. Martha Chen, *A Quiet Revolution: Women in Transition in Rural Bangladesh* (Cambridge, MA: Schenkman, 1983), 176.

5. *Human Development Report* (New York: United Nations Development Program, 1996) (hereafter *Report*); see also the 1995 *Report*, which focuses on gender. The countries in which women do best in life quality, according to the Gender Development Index (GDI), a measure using the same variables as the HDI (Human Development Index) but adjusted according to disparities between the sexes (see *Report*, 107, for the technical formulation) are, in order, Sweden, Canada, Norway, the United States, Finland, Iceland, Denmark, France, Australia, New Zealand, the Netherlands, Japan, Austria, the United Kingdom, and Belgium.

6. If we subtract the GDI rank from the HDI rank, we get –10 for Spain, –9 for Japan, 8 for Sweden, 10 for Denmark, and 4 for New Zealand.

7. These variables include percentage shares of administrative and managerial positions, percentage shares of professional and technical jobs, and percentage shares of parliamentary seats.

8. The ranking at the top: Norway, Sweden, Denmark, Finland, New Zealand, Canada, Germany, the Netherlands, the United States, Austria, Barbados, and Switzerland. Spain ranks 25; Japan, 37; France, 40; and Greece, 60.

9. These data are from the 1993 report; later reports disaggregate employment data into jobs of various specific kinds and no longer count unpaid agricultural labor as employment.

10. Again, these are 1993 data; the 1996 report gives the absolute percentages, which are, for these examples, Sierra Leone, 16.7%; Afghanistan, 13.5%; Sudan, 32%; Nepal, 13%. Nations in which the female literacy rate is strikingly out of step with the general level of economic development include Saudi Arabia, 47.6%; Algeria, 45.8%; Egypt, 37.0%; Iraq, 42.3%; Pakistan, 23.0%; and India, 36.0%. Striking progress in female literacy, on the other hand, if one can rely on the figures, has been made in Cuba, 94.6%; Sri Lanka, 86.2%; Philippines, 93.9%; and most of the former constituent states of the Soviet Union, in the 90s; Vietnam, 89.5%; and China, 70.9%. On the disparity of achievement between China and India, see Jean Drèze and Amartya Sen, *India: Economic Development and Social Opportunity* (Oxford: Clarendon Press, 1996).

11. Numbers of female students in tertiary education per 100,000 people: Hong Kong, 1,022; Barbados, 1,885; Republic of Korea, 2,866; Philippines, 3,140; Egypt, 499; China, 132; Iran, 764; Laos, 60; Pakistan, 149; Ethiopia, 24; and Rwanda, 19.

12. Countries where women hold a high percentage of parliamentary seats: Norway, 39.4%; Sweden, 40.4%; and Denmark, 33.0%. Bangladesh at 10.6% is ahead of the United States at 10.4%, and India at 8.0% is ahead of Japan at 6.7%.

13. The statistics in this paragraph are taken from Jean Drèze and Amartya Sen, *Hunger and Public Action* (Oxford: Clarendon Press, 1989).

14. This is very likely due to the central role women play in productive economic activity. For a classic study of this issue, see Esther Boserup, *Women's Role in Economic Development* (New York: St. Martin's Press, 1970), 2nd ed. (Aldershot: Gower Publishing, 1986). For a set of valuable responses to Boserup's work, see *Persistent Inequalities*, ed. Irene Tinker (New York: Oxford University Press, 1990).

15. See Drèze and Sen, 52.

16. See Drèze and Sen, *India*.

17. See Sen, "Gender and Cooperative Conflicts," in Tinker, 123–49.

18. See Drèze and Sen, *India*, for graphic evidence of the relative independence of educational and health attainment from economic growth, in comparative regional studies.

19. Gary Becker, *A Treatise on the Family* (Cambridge, MA: Harvard University Press, 1981; 2nd ed. 1991).

20. See Sen, "Gender and Cooperative Conflicts"; Partha Dasgupta, *An Inquiry Into Well-Being and Destitution* (Oxford: Clarendon Press, 1993), chap. 11; on food allocation, see Lincoln C. Chen, E. Huq, and S. D'Souza, "Sex Bias in the Family Allocation of Food and Health Care in Rural Bangladesh," *Population and Development Review* 7 (1981), 55–70. Bargaining models of the family are now proliferating; for two valuable recent examples, see Shelly Lundberg and Robert A. Pollak, "Bargaining and Distribution in Marriage," *Journal of Economic Perspectives* 10 (1996), 139–58, and S. Lundberg, R. Pollak, and T. J. Wales, "Do Husbands and Wives Pool Their Resources? Evidence from the U.K. Child Benefit," *Journal of Human Resources* (forthcoming).

21. See, now, Gary Becker, "The Economic Way of Looking at Behavior," the Nobel Address 1992, in *The Essence of Becker*, ed. Ramón Febrero and Pedro S. Schwartz (Stanford, CA: Hoover Institution Press, 1995), 647, on the role of childhood experiences in shaping preferences.

22. Sen, "Gender and Cooperative Conflicts," argues that Becker's account is much stronger as an account of actual preferences in the household than as an account of the real interests (life and death, good and bad health, good and bad nutrition) that underlie the preferences. (He provides evidence that people's perception of their health and nutritional status may be severely distorted by informational deficiencies.)

23. Becker now admits deficiencies in the model: "Many economists, including me, have excessively relied on altruism to tie together the interests of family members." Motives of "obligation, anger, and other attitudes usually neglected by theories of rational behavior" should be added to the models. Becker, "The Economic Way of Looking at Behavior," 648. Elsewhere, Becker mentions guilt, affection, and fear—his example being a woman's habitual fear of physical abuse from men. Ibid., 647. It is unclear whether he still supports an organic one-actor model, with a more complicated motivational structure, or a "bargaining model," of the sort increasingly used by family economists. See Becker, *A Treatise on the Family.*

24. See Sen, "Gender and Cooperative Conflicts"; Jon Elster, *Sour Grapes* (Cambridge: Cambridge University Press, 1993).

25. See John Rawls, *A Theory of Justice* (hereafter TJ) (Cambridge, MA: Harvard University Press, 1970); *Political Liberalism* (hereafter PL) (New York: Columbia University Press, 1993, paper ed. 1996).

26. The "capabilities approach" was pioneered within economics by Amartya Sen and has been developed by both Sen and me in complementary but not identical ways. For an overview, see David Crocker, "Functioning and Capability: the Foundations of Sen's and Nussbaum's Development Ethic," in WCD, 152–98.

27. See Amartya Sen, "Equality of What?," in *Choice, Welfare, and Measurement* (Oxford: Basil Blackwell, 1982), 353–72; and Nussbaum, ASD.

28. Much of the material described in these examples is now published in *Dominating Knowledge: Development, Culture, and Resistance,* ed. Frédérique Apffel Marglin and Stephen A. Marglin (Oxford: Clarendon Press, 1990). The issue of "embeddedness" and menstruation taboos is discussed in S. A. Marglin, "Losing Touch: The Cultural Conditions of Worker Accommodation and Resistance," 217–82, and related issues are discussed in S. A. Marglin, "Toward the Decolonization of the Mind," 1–28. On Sittala Devi, see F. A. Marglin, "Smallpox in Two Systems of Knowledge," 102–44; and for related arguments see Ashis Nandy and Shiv Visvanathan, "Modern Medicine and Its Non-Modern Critics," 144–84. I have in some cases combined two conversations into one; otherwise things happened as I describe them.

29. For Sen's own account of the plurality and internal diversity of Indian values, one that strongly emphasizes the presence of a rationalist and critical strand in Indian traditions, see M. Nussbaum and A. Sen, "Internal Criticism and Indian Relativist Traditions, in *Relativism: Interpretation and Confrontation,* ed. M. Krausz (Notre Dame: Notre Dame University Press, 1989), 299–325 (an essay originally presented at the same WIDER conference and refused publication by the Marglins in its proceedings); and A. Sen, "India and the West," *The New Republic,* June 7, 1993. See also Bimal K. Matilal, *Perception* (Oxford: Clarendon Press, 1995) (a fundamental study of Indian traditions regarding knowledge and logic); and B. K. Matilal, "Ethical Relativism and the Confrontation of Cultures," in Krausz, ed., *Relativism,* 339–62.

30. S. A. Marglin, "Toward the Decolonization," 22–3, suggests that binary thinking is peculiarly Western. But such oppositions are pervasive in Indian, Chinese, and African traditions (see HC). To deny them to a culture is condescending: for how can one utter a definite idea without bounding off one thing against another?

31. See Eric Hobsbawm and Terence Ranger, eds., *The Invention of Tradition* (Cambridge: Cambridge University Press, 1983). In his *New Republic* piece, Sen makes a similar argument about contemporary India: The Western construction of India as mystical and "other" serves the purposes of the fundamentalist Bharatiya Janata Party (BJP), who are busy refashioning history to serve the ends of their own political power. An eloquent critique of the whole notion of the "other" and of the associated "nativism," where Africa is concerned, can be found in Kwame Anthony Appiah, *In My Father's House: Africa in the Philosophy of Cultures* (New York: Oxford University Press, 1991).

32. The proceedings of this conference are now published as M. Nussbaum and A. Sen, eds., *The Quality of Life* (Oxford: Clarendon Press, 1993).

33. Marglin has since published this point in "Toward the Decolonization." His reference is to Takeo Doi, *The Anatomy of Dependence* (Tokyo: Kodansha, 1971).

34. See S. A. Marglin, "Toward the Decolonization."

35. See Nussbaum and Sen, "Internal Criticism," and A. Sen, "Human Rights and Asian Values," *The New Republic*, July 10/17, 1997, 33–40.

36. See Roop Rekha Verma, "Femininity, Equality, and Personhood," in WCD.

37. Satyajit Ray, "Introduction," *Our Films, Their Films* (Bombay: Orient Longman, 1976, reprinted New York: Hyperion, 1994), 5.

38. Personal communication, scholars in women's studies at the Chinese Academy of Social Sciences, June 1995.

39. Note that this objection itself seems to rely on some universal values such as fairness and freedom from bias.

40. See HF for a longer version of this discussion.

41. Aristotle, *Nicomachean Ethics* VIII.I. I discuss this passage in HN and NRV.

42. "If my sisters and I were 'children of two worlds,' no one bothered to tell us this; we lived in one world, in two 'extended' families divided by several thousand miles and an allegedly insuperable cultural distance that never, so far as I can recall, puzzled or perplexed us much." Appiah, vii–viii. Appiah's argument does not neglect distinctive features of concrete histories; indeed, one of its purposes is to demonstrate how varied, when concretely seen, histories really are. But his argument, like mine, seeks a subtle balance between perception of the particular and recognition of the common.

43. This point is made by the Marglins, as well as by liberal thinkers, but can they consistently make it while holding that freedom of choice is just a parochial Western value? It would appear not; on the other hand, F. A. Marglin (here differing, I believe, from S. A. Marglin) also held in oral remarks delivered at the 1986 conference that logical consistency is simply a parochial Western value.

44. See Noam Chomsky, in *Cartesian Linguistics* (New York: Harper and Row, 1966). Chomsky argues that Cartesian rationalism, with its insistence on innate essences, was politically more progressive, more hostile to slavery and imperialism, than empiricism, with its insistence that people were just what experience had made of them.

45. The use of this term does not imply that the functions all involve doing something especially "active." See here A. Sen, "Capability and Well-Being," in *The Quality of Life*, ed. M. Nussbaum and A. Sen (Oxford: Clarendon Press, 1993), 30–53. In Aristotelian terms, and in mine, being healthy, reflecting, and being pleased are all "activities."

46. For further discussion of this point, and for examples, see HN.

47. Could one cease to be one's individual self without ceasing to be human? Perhaps, in cases of profound personality or memory change, but I shall leave such cases to one

side here. This is ruled out, I think, in Aristotle's conception but is possible in some other metaphysical conceptions.

48. See HN for a more extended account of this procedure and how it justifies.

49. Nor does it deny that experience of the body is shaped by culture. See NRV.

50. Rawls, TJ, 90–95, 396–7.

51. This was implicit in ASD but has become more prominent in recent essays. See A. Sen, "Freedoms and Needs," *New Republic*, January 10/17, 1994, 31–38; Nussbaum, GDGF.

52. In ASD I call it "the thick vague theory of the good."

53. Rawls, PL. Note that the consensus is defined in terms of a normative notion of reasonableness. Thus, the failure of some real individuals to agree will not be fatal to the view.

54. On this relationship, see HN.

55. The current version of this list reflects changes suggested to me by discussions during my visits to women's development projects in India. These include a new emphasis on bodily integrity, on employment, on property rights, and on dignity and nonhumiliation.

56. Although "normal length" is clearly relative to current human possibilities and may need, for practical purposes, to be to some extent relativized to local conditions, it seems important to think of it—at least at a given time in history—in universal and comparative terms, as the *Human Development Report* does, to give rise to complaint in a country that has done well with some indicators of life quality but badly on life expectancy. And although some degree of relativity may be put down to the differential genetic possibilities of different groups (the "missing women" statistics, for example, allow that on the average women live somewhat longer than men), it is also important not to conclude prematurely that inequalities between groups—for example, the growing inequalities in life expectancy between blacks and whites in the United States—are simply genetic variation, not connected with social injustice.

57. The precise specification of these health rights is not easy, but the work currently being done on them in drafting new constitutions in South Africa and Eastern Europe gives reasons for hope that the combination of a general specification of such a right with a tradition of judicial interpretation will yield something practicable. It should be noticed that I speak of health, not just health care; and health itself interacts in complex ways with housing, with education, with dignity. Both health and nutrition are controversial as to whether the relevant level should be specified universally, or relatively to the local community and its traditions. For example, is low height associated with nutritional practices to be thought of as "stunting" or as felicitous adaptation to circumstances of scarcity? For an excellent summary of this debate, see S. R. Osmani, ed., *Nutrition and Poverty* (Oxford: Clarendon Press, WIDER series, 1990), especially the following papers on: the relativist side, T. N. Srinivasan, "Undernutrition: Concepts, Measurements, and Policy Implications," 97–120; on the universalist side, C. Gopalan, "Undernutrition: Measurement and Implications," 17–48; for a compelling adjudication of the debate, coming out on the universalist side, see Osmani, "On Some Controversies in the Measurement of Undernutrition," 121–61.

58. There is a growing literature on the importance of shelter for health; for example, that the provision of adequate housing is the single largest determinant of health status for HIV-infected persons. Housing rights are increasingly coming to be constitutionalized, at least in a negative form—giving squatters grounds for appeal, for example, against a landlord who would bulldoze their shanties. On this as a constitutional

right, see proposed Articles 11, 12, and 17 of the South African Constitution, in a draft put forward by the African National Congress (ANC) committee adviser Albie Sachs, where this is given as an example of a justiciable housing right.

59. Some form of intimate family love is central to child development, but this need not be the traditional Western nuclear family. In the development of citizens it is crucial that the family be an institution characterized by justice as well as love. See Susan Moller Okin, *Justice, Gender, and the Family* (New York: Basic Books, 1989).

60. In terms of cross-cultural discussion, this item has proven the most controversial and elusive on the list. It also properly raises the question whether the list ought to be anthropocentric at all, or whether we should seek to promote appropriate capabilities for all living things. I leave further argument on these questions for another occasion.

61. ASD argues that property rights are distinct from, for example, speech rights, in the sense that property is a tool of human functioning and not an end in itself. See also Nussbaum, CHR.

62. Sen has not endorsed any such specific list of the capabilities.

63. See Sen, "Gender Inequality and Theories of Justice," in WCD, 259–73; Becker, "The Economic Way of Looking at Behavior."

64. With Sen, I hold that the capability set should be treated as an interlocking whole. For my comments on his arguments, see NFC.

65. See ibid., with reference to Aristotle.

66. See HN. This is the core of Marx's reading of Aristotle.

67. See chapter 4 in *Sex and Social Justice* (New York: Oxford University Press, 1999).

68. See NFC, referring to Aristotle's similar distinctions.

69. This distinction is related to Rawls's distinction between social and natural primary goods. Whereas he holds that only the social primary goods should be on the list, and not the natural (such as health, imagination), we say that *the social basis of* the natural primary goods should most emphatically be on the list.

70. TJ, 62.

71. Rawls comments that "although their possession is influenced by the basic structure, they are not so directly under its control." TJ, 62. This is of course true if we are thinking of health, but if we think of the social basis of health, it is not true. It seems to me that the case for putting these items on the political list is just as strong as the case for the social basis of self-respect. In "The Priority of Right and Ideas of the Good," *Philosophy and Public Affairs* 17 (1988), 251–76, Rawls suggests putting health on the list.

72. See ASD and GDGF.

73. See HN. For the relation of capabilities to human rights, see CHR.

74. Sen, "Freedoms and Needs," 38.

75. PL, 187–8.

76. Though in one form Aristotle had it too. See also GDGF; and CHR.

77. Compare Sen, "Freedoms and Needs," 38: "The importance of political rights for the understanding of economic needs turns ultimately on seeing human beings as people with rights to exercise, not as parts of a 'stock' or a 'population' that passively exists and must be looked after. What matters, finally, is how we see each other."

78. Chapter 3 (in *Sex and Social Justice*) argues that religious norms should not be imposed without choice on individuals who may not have opted for that religious tradition. In that sense, any religiously based employment restriction is questionable.

79. Chen, *The Lives of Widows in Rural India.* Girls in some regions of India are betrothed at a very young age and at that point become members of their husband's family, although the marriage will not be consummated until puberty. Such a girl is treated as widowed even if the male dies before consummation.

80. Chen, *A Quiet Revolution.*

■ *QUESTIONS FOR MAKING CONNECTIONS WITHIN THE READING* ■

1. Martha Nussbaum takes issue with the ideas of "tradition," "custom," and "culture." To what, specifically, does she object about these ideas? Does she want simply to define the terms themselves in a rather different way, or does she actually believe that there really are no such things as traditions, customs, and cultures?

2. In Nussbaum's discussion of several recent academic conferences, she goes out of her way to emphasize that her opponents are "leftists" or "leftwing." What does the term *left* mean in the context of her argument? Is Nussbaum philosophically unsympathetic to the goals of the left? Would you describe her as a rightist—that is, a political or cultural conservative?

3. Why would anyone object to universalism? Some readers may find Nussbaum's argument so compelling that the position of her opponents might sound unreasonable, even absurd. What arguments might be offered in defense of "otherness"? When considered sympathetically, are the arguments for "otherness" as flat-footed as Nussbaum implies? Can we safely infer from the success of our society's values that they will offer the same good service in all other places at all other times? Does Nussbaum say that they will?

■ *QUESTIONS FOR WRITING* ■

1. Nussbaum often uses the pronoun *we*, as she does in this passage:

    We recognize other humans as human across many differences of time and place, of custom and appearance. We often tell ourselves stories, on the other hand, about anthropomorphic creatures who do not get classified as human, on account of some feature of their form of life and functioning. On what do we base these inclusions and exclusions? In short, what do we believe must be there, if we are going to acknowledge that a given life is human?

    Who is Nussbaum's "we," here and throughout the selection? Nussbaum's opponents would allege that her "we" is a false universal: it ostensibly represents everyone but actually represents only educated, white, and relatively wealthy people living in the West. Does this argument seem fair to you? Does such a criticism make it impossible to offer general insights of any kind about human experience?

2. What does Nussbaum mean when she says that her list of "Central Human Functional Capabilities" is "proposed as the object of a specifically political consensus"? Why a *political* consensus? What difference does it make if we understand our obligations to others as political in nature rather than as, say, the product of divine revelation or pure reason? Does Nussbaum imply that the list can grow or shrink over time? If the items on the list can change, in what sense does it remain "universal"?

■*QUESTIONS FOR MAKING CONNECTIONS BETWEEN READINGS* ■

1. What might Nussbaum learn from reading Deborah Tannen? One question that might arise for Nussbaum is whether our own institutions—especially the educational system—discourage in unacknowledged ways the growth of the "central capabilities." Drawing from your own experience as well as from Tannen's observations, would you conclude that the "argument culture" poses a significant barrier to the achievement of a good life? As you explore this question, consider as well the character of Nussbaum's reasoning. Does she participate in the argument culture? If Nussbaum does, would you say that she undermines her own credibility? Or could it be that the argument culture is less damaging than Tannen assumes?

2. Once we begin to take full advantage of "germinal choice technology," as Gregory Stock predicts we will in his essay "The Enhanced and the Unenhanced," will it still make sense to talk about "central human functional capabilities"? Once we enter the age of the "posthuman," will it ever be possible to refer once again to any common humanity? Does Nussbaum's argument for the importance of "central human functional capabilities" require that we take steps to curtail germinal choice technology? Or might it be the case instead that this technology will actually help to develop and extend our capabilities?

www **For additional suggestions about making connections between readings, visit the Link-O-Mat and More Sample Assignments at <www.newhum.com>.**

TIM O'BRIEN

IN 1968, DURING the war in Vietnam, Tim O'Brien graduated from college and was served a draft notice. An avowed opponent of the war, he considered fleeing to Canada but ultimately reported for basic training and was stationed near My Lai a year after the infamous massacre there. O'Brien returned to the United States in 1970, having received injuries that earned him a Purple Heart. Since then he has published dozens of stories and books, both fiction and nonfiction, including the National Book Award Winner *Going After Cacciato* (1978). O'Brien has received many other prestigious awards as well; among them are the O. Henry Award, the National Book Critics Circle Award, and the Pulitzer Prize. He is currently a Writer in Residence at Texas State University, in San Marcos, Texas.

"How to Tell a True War Story," one of the stories collected in *The Things They Carried*, is actually a work of fiction even though it reads like a memoir. O'Brien's decision to present his narrative in this ambiguous fashion reflects concerns that have shaped his work for almost three decades. For him, the line between reality and fiction is always a fuzzy one, especially in accounts of war, where the experience outstrips the resources of language. Faced with the complexity of war, O'Brien is trying, not to "close the books" on a painful past, but to keep the books from ever getting closed by those who might prefer to forget the high price that war always exacts. And in O'Brien's work, the high price is not just the loss of life, but also a permanent loss of moral certainty. In response to a question about why he keeps returning to incidents that took place in the 1960s, O'Brien has said, "The war occurred half a lifetime ago, and yet the remembering makes it now. And sometimes remembering will lead to a story, which makes it forever. That's what stories are for. Stories are for joining the past to the future. Stories are for those late hours in the night when you can't remember how you got from where you were to where you are. Stories are for eternity, when memory is erased, when there is nothing to remember except the story."

`www` **To learn more about Tim O'Brien and his fiction, please visit the Link-O-Mat at <www.newhum.com>.**

O'Brien, Tim. "How to Tell a True War Story." *The Things They Carried*. New York: Broadway Books, 1998. 67–85.
Biographical information drawn from <http://www.utsa.edu/lc/commonreading/Biography.cfm>. Closing quote drawn from <http://www.illyria.com/tobhp.html>.

How to Tell a True War Story

This is true.

I had a buddy in Vietnam. His name was Bob Kiley, but everybody called him Rat.

A friend of his gets killed, so about a week later Rat sits down and writes a letter to the guy's sister. Rat tells her what a great brother she had, how together the guy was, a number one pal and comrade. A real soldier's soldier, Rat says. Then he tells a few stories to make the point, how her brother would always volunteer for stuff nobody else would volunteer for in a million years, dangerous stuff, like doing recon or going out on these really badass night patrols. Stainless steel balls, Rat tells her. The guy was a little crazy, for sure, but crazy in a good way, a real daredevil, because he liked the challenge of it, he liked testing himself, just man against gook. A great, great guy, Rat says.

Anyway, it's a terrific letter, very personal and touching. Rat almost bawls writing it. He gets all teary telling about the good times they had together, how her brother made the war seem almost fun, always raising hell and lighting up villes and bringing smoke to bear every which way. A great sense of humor, too. Like the time at this river when he went fishing with a whole damn crate of hand grenades. Probably the funniest thing in world history, Rat says, all that gore, about twenty zillion dead gook fish. Her brother, he had the right attitude. He knew how to have a good time. On Halloween, this real hot spooky night, the dude paints up his body all different colors and puts on this weird mask and hikes over to a ville and goes trick-or-treating almost stark naked, just boots and balls and an M-16. A tremendous human being, Rat says. Pretty nutso sometimes, but you could trust him with your life.

And then the letter gets very sad and serious. Rat pours his heart out. He says he loved the guy. He says the guy was his best friend in the world. They were like soul mates, he says, like twins or something, they had a whole lot in common. He tells the guy's sister he'll look her up when the war's over.

So what happens?

Rat mails the letter. He waits two months. The dumb cooze never writes back.

A true war story is never moral. It does not instruct, nor encourage virtue, nor suggest models of proper human behavior, nor restrain men from doing the things men have always done. If a story seems moral, do not believe it. If at the end of a war story you feel uplifted, or if you feel that some small bit of rectitude has been salvaged from the larger waste, then you have been made the victim of a very old and terrible lie. There is no rectitude whatsoever. There is no virtue. As a first rule of thumb, therefore, you can tell a true war story by its absolute and uncompromising allegiance to obscenity and evil. Listen to Rat Kiley. Cooze, he says. He does not say bitch. He certainly does not say woman, or girl. He says cooze. Then he spits and stares. He's nineteen years old—it's too much for him—so he looks at you with those big sad gentle killer eyes and says cooze, because his friend is dead, and because it's so incredibly sad and true: she never wrote back.

You can tell a true war story if it embarrasses you. If you don't care for obscenity, you don't care for the truth; if you don't care for the truth, watch how you vote. Send guys to war, they come home talking dirty.

Listen to Rat: "Jesus Christ, man, I write this beautiful fuckin' letter, I slave over it, and what happens? The dumb cooze never writes back."

The dead guy's name was Curt Lemon. What happened was, we crossed a muddy river and marched west into the mountains, and on the third day we took a break along a trail junction in deep jungle. Right away, Lemon and Rat Kiley started goofing. They didn't understand about the spookiness. They were kids; they just didn't know. A nature hike, they thought, not even a war, so they went off into the shade of some giant trees—quadruple canopy, no sunlight at all—and they were giggling and calling each other yellow mother and playing a silly game they'd invented. The game involved smoke grenades, which were harmless unless you did stupid things, and what they did was pull out the pin and stand a few feet apart and play catch under the shade of those huge trees. Whoever chickened out was a yellow mother. And if nobody chickened out, the grenade would make a light popping sound and they'd be covered with smoke and they'd laugh and dance around and then do it again.

It's all exactly true.

It happened, to *me*, nearly twenty years ago, and I still remember that trail junction and those giant trees and a soft dripping sound somewhere beyond the trees. I remember the smell of moss. Up in the canopy there were tiny white blossoms, but no sunlight at all, and I remember the shadows spreading out under the trees where Curt Lemon and Rat Kiley were playing catch with smoke grenades. Mitchell Sanders sat flipping his yo-yo. Norman Bowker and Kiowa and Dave Jensen were dozing, or half dozing, and all around us were those ragged green mountains.

Except for the laughter things were quiet.

At one point, I remember, Mitchell Sanders turned and looked at me, not quite nodding, as if to warn me about something, as if he already *knew*, then after a while he rolled up his yo-yo and moved away.

It's hard to tell you what happened next.

They were just goofing. There was a noise, I suppose, which must've been the detonator, so I glanced behind me and watched Lemon step from the shade into bright sunlight. His face was suddenly brown and shining. A handsome kid, really. Sharp gray eyes, lean and narrow-waisted, and when he died it was almost beautiful, the way the sunlight came around him and lifted him up and sucked him high into a tree full of moss and vines and white blossoms.

In any war story, but especially a true one, it's difficult to separate what happened from what seemed to happen. What seems to happen becomes its own happening and has to be told that way. The angles of vision are skewed. When a booby trap explodes, you close your eyes and duck and float outside yourself. When a guy dies, like Curt Lemon, you look away and then look back for a moment and then look away again. The pictures get jumbled; you tend to miss a lot. And then afterward, when you go to tell about it, there is always that surreal seemingness, which makes the story seem untrue, but which in fact represents the hard and exact truth as it *seemed*.

In many cases a true war story cannot be believed. If you believe it, be skeptical. It's a question of credibility. Often the crazy stuff is true and the normal stuff isn't, because the normal stuff is necessary to make you believe the truly incredible craziness.

In other cases you can't even tell a true war story. Sometimes it's just beyond telling.

I heard this one, for example, from Mitchell Sanders. It was near dusk and we were sitting at my foxhole along a wide muddy river north of Quang Ngai. I remember how peaceful the twilight was. A deep pinkish red spilled out on the river, which moved without sound, and in the morning we would cross the river and march west into the mountains. The occasion was right for a good story.

"God's truth," Mitchell Sanders said. "A six-man patrol goes up into the mountains on a basic listening-post operation. The idea's to spend a week up there, just lie low and listen for enemy movement. They've got a radio along, so if they hear anything suspicious—anything—they're supposed to call in artillery or gunships, whatever it takes. Otherwise they keep strict field discipline. Absolute silence. They just listen."

Sanders glanced at me to make sure I had the scenario. He was playing with his yo-yo, dancing it with short, tight little strokes of the wrist.

His face was blank in the dusk.

"We're talking regulation, by-the-book LP. These six guys, they don't say boo for a solid week. They don't got tongues. *All* ears."

"Right," I said.

"Understand me?"

"Invisible."

Sanders nodded.

"Affirm," he said. "Invisible. So what happens is, these guys get themselves deep in the bush, all camouflaged up, and they lie down and wait and that's all they do, nothing else, they lie there for seven straight days and just listen. And man, I'll tell you—it's spooky. This is mountains. You don't *know* spooky till you been there. Jungle, sort of, except it's way up in the clouds and there's always this fog—like rain, except it's not raining—everything's all wet and swirly and tangled up and you can't see jack, you can't find your own pecker to piss with. Like you don't even have a body. Serious spooky. You just go with the vapors—the fog sort of takes you in . . . And the sounds, man. The sounds carry forever. You hear stuff nobody should *ever* hear."

Sanders was quiet for a second, just working the yo-yo, then he smiled at me.

"So after a couple days the guys start hearing this real soft, kind of wacked-out music. Weird echoes and stuff. Like a radio or something, but it's not a radio, it's this strange gook music that comes right out of the rocks. Faraway, sort of, but right up close, too. They try to ignore it. But it's a listening post, right? So they listen. And every night they keep hearing that crazyass gook concert. All kinds of chimes and xylophones. I mean, this is wilderness—no way, it can't be real—but there it *is*, like the mountains are tuned in to Radio fucking Hanoi. Naturally they get nervous. One guy sticks Juicy Fruit in his ears. Another guy almost flips. Thing is, though, they can't report music. They can't get on the horn and call back to base and say, 'Hey, listen, we need some firepower, we got to blow away this weirdo gook rock band.' They can't do that. It wouldn't go down. So they lie there in the fog and keep their mouths shut. And what makes it extra bad, see, is the poor dudes can't horse around like normal. Can't joke it away. Can't even talk to each other except maybe in whispers, all hush-hush, and that just revs up the willies. All they do is listen."

Again there was some silence as Mitchell Sanders looked out on the river. The dark was coming on hard now, and off to the west I could see the mountains rising in silhouette, all the mysteries and unknowns.

"This next part," Sanders said quietly, "you won't believe."

"Probably not," I said.

"You won't. And you know why?" He gave me a long, tired smile. "Because it happened. Because every word is absolutely dead-on true."

Sanders made a sound in his throat, like a sigh, as if to say he didn't care if I believed him or not. But he did care. He wanted me to feel the truth, to believe by the raw force of feeling. He seemed sad, in a way.

"These six guys," he said, "they're pretty fried out by now, and one night they start hearing voices. Like at a cocktail party. That's what it sounds like, this big swank gook cocktail party somewhere out there in the fog. Music and chitchat and stuff. It's crazy, I know, but they hear the champagne corks. They hear the actual martini glasses. Real hoity-toity, all very civilized, except this isn't civilization. This is Nam.

"Anyway, the guys try to be cool. They just lie there and groove, but after a while they start hearing—you won't believe this—they hear chamber

music. They hear violins and cellos. They hear this terrific mama-san so-
prano. Then after a while they hear gook opera and a glee club and the
Haiphong Boys Choir and a barbershop quartet and all kinds of weird
chanting and Buddha-Buddha stuff. And the whole time, in the background,
there's still that cocktail party going on. All these different voices. Not
human voices, though. Because it's the mountains. Follow me? The rock—
it's *talking*. And the fog, too, and the grass and the goddamn mongooses.
Everything talks. The trees talk politics, the monkeys talk religion. The
whole country: Vietnam. The place talks. It talks. Understand? Nam—it
truly *talks*.

"The guys can't cope. They lose it. They get on the radio and report
enemy movement—a whole army, they say—and they order up the firepower. They get arty and gunships. They call in air strikes. And I'll tell you,
they fuckin' crash that cocktail party. All night long, they just smoke those
mountains. They make jungle juice. They blow away trees and glee clubs and
whatever else there is to blow away. Scorch time. They walk napalm up and
down the ridges. They bring in the Cobras and F-4s, they use Willie Peter
and HE and incendiaries. It's all fire. They make those mountains burn.

"Around dawn things finally get quiet. Like you never even *heard* quiet
before. One of those real thick, real misty days—just clouds and fog, they're
off in this special zone—and the mountains are absolutely dead-flat silent.
Like *Brigadoon*—pure vapor, you know? Everything's all sucked up inside
the fog. Not a single sound, except they still *hear* it.

"So they pack up and start humping. They head down the mountain,
back to base camp, and when they get there they don't say diddly. They
don't talk. Not a word, like they're deaf and dumb. Later on this fat bird
colonel comes up and asks what the hell happened out there. What'd they
hear? Why all the ordnance? The man's ragged out, he gets down tight on
their case. I mean, they spent six trillion dollars on firepower, and this fatass
colonel wants answers, he wants to know what the fuckin' story is.

"But the guys don't say zip. They just look at him for a while, sort of
funny like, sort of amazed, and the whole war is right there in that stare. It
says everything you can't ever say. It says, man, you got *wax* in your ears. It
says, poor bastard, you'll never know—wrong frequency—you don't *even*
want to hear this. Then they salute the fucker and walk away, because certain stories you don't ever tell."

You can tell a true war story by the way it never seems to end. Not then, not
ever. Not when Mitchell Sanders stood up and moved off into the dark.

It all happened.

Even now, at this instant, I remember that yo-yo. In a way, I suppose,
you had to be there, you had to hear it, but I could tell how desperately
Sanders wanted me to believe him, his frustration at not quite getting the
details right, not quite pinning down the final and definitive truth.

And I remember sitting at my foxhole that night, watching the shadows of Quang Ngai, thinking about the coming day and how we would cross the river and march west into the mountains, all the ways I might die, all the things I did not understand.

Late in the night Mitchell Sanders touched my shoulder. "Just came to me," he whispered. "The moral, I mean. Nobody listens. Nobody hears nothin'. Like that fatass colonel. The politicians, all the civilian types. Your girlfriend. My girlfriend. Everybody's sweet little virgin girlfriend. What they need is to go out on LP. The vapors, man. Trees and rocks—you got to *listen* to your enemy."

And then again, in the morning, Sanders came up to me. The platoon was preparing to move out, checking weapons, going through all the little rituals that preceded a day's march. Already the lead squad had crossed the river and was filing off toward the west.

"I got a confession to make," Sanders said. "Last night, man, I had to make up a few things."

"I know that."

"The glee club. There wasn't any glee club."

"Right."

"No opera."

"Forget it, I understand."

"Yeah, but listen, it's still true. Those six guys, they heard wicked sound out there. They heard sound you just plain won't believe."

Sanders pulled on his rucksack, closed his eyes for a moment, then almost smiled at me. I knew what was coming.

"All right," I said, "what's the moral?"

"Forget it."

"No, go ahead."

For a long while he was quiet, looking away, and the silence kept stretching out until it was almost embarrassing. Then he shrugged and gave me a stare that lasted all day.

"Hear that quiet, man?" he said. "That quiet—just listen. There's your moral."

In a true war story, if there's a moral at all, it's like the thread that makes the cloth. You can't tease it out. You can't extract the meaning without unraveling the deeper meaning. And in the end, really, there's nothing much to say about a true war story, except maybe "Oh."

True war stories do not generalize. They do not indulge in abstraction or analysis.

For example: War is hell. As a moral declaration the old truism seems perfectly true, and yet because it abstracts, because it generalizes, I can't believe it with my stomach. Nothing turns inside.

It comes down to gut instinct. A true war story, if truly told, makes the stomach believe.

This one does it for me. I've told it before—many times, many versions—but here's what actually happened.

We crossed that river and marched west into the mountains. On the third day, Curt Lemon stepped on a booby-trapped 105 round. He was playing catch with Rat Kiley, laughing, and then he was dead. The trees were thick; it took nearly an hour to cut an LZ for the dustoff.

Later, higher in the mountains, we came across a baby VC water buffalo. What it was doing there I don't know—no farms or paddies—but we chased it down and got a rope around it and led it along to a deserted village where we set up for the night. After supper Rat Kiley went over and stroked its nose.

He opened up a can of C rations, pork and beans, but the baby buffalo wasn't interested.

Rat shrugged.

He stepped back and shot it through the right front knee. The animal did not make a sound. It went down hard, then got up again, and Rat took careful aim and shot off an ear. He shot it in the hindquarters and in the little hump at its back. He shot it twice in the flanks. It wasn't to kill; it was to hurt. He put the rifle muzzle up against the mouth and shot the mouth away. Nobody said much. The whole platoon stood there watching, feeling all kinds of things, but there wasn't a great deal of pity for the baby water buffalo. Curt Lemon was dead. Rat Kiley had lost his best friend in the world. Later in the week he would write a long personal letter to the guy's sister, who would not write back, but for now it was a question of pain. He shot off the tail. He shot away chunks of meat below the ribs. All around us there was the smell of smoke and filth and deep greenery, and the evening was humid and very hot. Rat went to automatic. He shot randomly, almost casually, quick little spurts in the belly and butt. Then he reloaded, squatted down, and shot it in the left front knee. Again the animal fell hard and tried to get up, but this time it couldn't quite make it. It wobbled and went down sideways. Rat shot it in the nose. He bent forward and whispered something, as if talking to a pet, then he shot it in the throat. All the while the baby buffalo was silent, or almost silent, just a light bubbling sound where the nose had been. It lay very still. Nothing moved except the eyes, which were enormous, the pupils shiny black and dumb.

Rat Kiley was crying. He tried to say something, but then cradled his rifle and went off by himself.

The rest of us stood in a ragged circle around the baby buffalo. For a time no one spoke. We had witnessed something essential, something brand-new and profound, a piece of the world so startling there was not yet a name for it.

Somebody kicked the baby buffalo.

It was still alive, though just barely, just in the eyes.

"Amazing," Dave Jensen said. "My whole life, I never seen anything like it."

"Never?"

"Not hardly. Not once."

Kiowa and Mitchell Sanders picked up the baby buffalo. They hauled it across the open square, hoisted it up, and dumped it in the village well.

Afterward, we sat waiting for Rat to get himself together.

"Amazing," Dave Jensen kept saying. "A new wrinkle. I never seen it before."

Mitchell Sanders took out his yo-yo. "Well, that's Nam," he said. "Garden of Evil. Over here, man, every sin's real fresh and original."

How do you generalize?

War is hell, but that's not the half of it, because war is also mystery and terror and adventure and courage and discovery and holiness and pity and despair and longing and love. War is nasty; war is fun. War is thrilling; war is drudgery. War makes you a man; war makes you dead.

The truths are contradictory. It can be argued, for instance, that war is grotesque. But in truth war is also beauty. For all its horror, you can't help but gape at the awful majesty of combat. You stare out at tracer rounds unwinding through the dark like brilliant red ribbons. You crouch in ambush as a cool, impassive moon rises over the nighttime paddies. You admire the fluid symmetries of troops on the move, the harmonies of sound and shape and proportion, the great sheets of metal-fire streaming down from a gunship, the illumination rounds, the white phosphorus, the purply orange glow of napalm, the rocket's red glare. It's not pretty, exactly. It's astonishing. It fills the eye. It commands you. You hate it, yes, but your eyes do not. Like a killer forest fire, like cancer under a microscope, any battle or bombing raid or artillery barrage has the aesthetic purity of absolute moral indifference—a powerful, implacable beauty—and a true war story will tell the truth about this, though the truth is ugly.

To generalize about war is like generalizing about peace. Almost everything is true. Almost nothing is true. At its core, perhaps, war is just another name for death, and yet any soldier will tell you, if he tells the truth, that proximity to death brings with it a corresponding proximity to life. After a firefight, there is always the immense pleasure of aliveness. The trees are alive. The grass, the soil—everything. All around you things are purely living, and you among them, and the aliveness makes you tremble. You feel an intense, out-of-the-skin awareness of your living self—your truest self, the human being you want to be and then become by the force of wanting it. In the midst of evil you want to be a good man. You want decency. You want justice and courtesy and human concord, things you never knew you wanted. There is a kind of largeness to it, a kind of godliness. Though it's odd, you're never more alive than when you're almost dead. You recognize what's valuable. Freshly, as if for the first time, you love what's best in yourself and in the world, all that might be lost. At the hour of dusk you sit at your foxhole and look out on a wide river turning pinkish red, and at the mountains beyond, and although in the morning you must cross the river and go into the mountains and do terrible things and maybe die, even so, you find yourself studying the fine colors on the river, you feel wonder and awe at the setting of the sun, and you are filled with a hard, aching love for how the world could be and always should be, but now is not.

Mitchell Sanders was right. For the common soldier, at least, war has the feel—the spiritual texture—of a great ghostly fog, thick and permanent. There is no clarity. Everything swirls. The old rules are no longer binding, the old truths no longer true. Right spills over into wrong. Order blends into chaos, love into hate, ugliness into beauty, law into anarchy, civility into savagery. The vapors suck you in. You can't tell where you are, or why you're there, and the only certainty is overwhelming ambiguity.

In war you lose your sense of the definite, hence your sense of truth itself, and therefore it's safe to say that in a true war story nothing is ever absolutely true.

Often in a true war story there is not even a point, or else the point doesn't hit you until twenty years later, in your sleep, and you wake up and shake your wife and start telling the story to her, except when you get to the end you've forgotten the point again. And then for a long time you lie there watching the story happen in your head. You listen to your wife's breathing. The war's over. You close your eyes. You smile and think, Christ, what's the *point?*

This one wakes me up.

In the mountains that day, I watched Lemon turn sideways. He laughed and said something to Rat Kiley. Then he took a peculiar half step, moving from shade into bright sunlight, and the booby-trapped 105 round blew him into a tree. The parts were just hanging there, so Dave Jensen and I were ordered to shinny up and peel him off. I remember the white bone of an arm. I remember pieces of skin and something wet and yellow that must've been the intestines. The gore was horrible, and stays with me. But what wakes me up twenty years later is Dave Jensen singing "Lemon Tree" as we threw down the parts.

You can tell a true war story by the questions you ask. Somebody tells a story, let's say, and afterward you ask, "Is it true?" and if the answer matters, you've got your answer.

For example, we've all heard this one. Four guys go down a trail. A grenade sails out. One guy jumps on it and takes the blast and saves his three buddies.

Is it true?

The answer matters.

You'd feel cheated if it never happened. Without the grounding reality, it's just a trite bit of puffery, pure Hollywood, untrue in the way all such stories are untrue. Yet even if it did happen—and maybe it did, anything's possible—even then you know it can't be true, because a true war story does not depend upon that kind of truth. Absolute occurrence is irrelevant. A thing may happen and be a total lie; another thing may not happen and be truer than the truth. For example: Four guys go down a trail. A grenade sails out. One guy jumps on it and takes the blast, but it's a killer grenade and everybody dies anyway. Before they die, though, one of the dead guys says, "The fuck you do *that* for?" and the jumper says, "Story of my life, man," and the other guy starts to smile but he's dead.

That's a true story that never happened.

Twenty years later, I can still see the sunlight on Lemon's face. I can see him turning, looking back at Rat Kiley, then he laughed and took that curious half step from shade into sunlight, his face suddenly brown and shining, and when his foot touched down, in that instant, he must've thought it was the sunlight that was killing him. It was not the sunlight. It was a rigged 105 round. But if I could ever get the story right, how the sun seemed to gather around him and pick him up and lift him high into a tree, if I could somehow re-create the fatal whiteness of that light, the quick glare, the obvious cause and effect, then you would believe the last thing Curt Lemon believed, which for him must've been the final truth.

Now and then, when I tell this story, someone will come up to me afterward and say she liked it. It's always a woman. Usually it's an older woman of kindly temperament and humane politics. She'll explain that as a rule she hates war stories; she can't understand why people want to wallow in all the blood and gore. But this one she liked. The poor baby buffalo, it made her sad. Sometimes, even, there are little tears. What I should do, she'll say, is put it all behind me. Find new stories to tell.

I won't say it but I'll think it.

I'll picture Rat Kiley's face, his grief, and I'll think, *You dumb cooze.*

Because she wasn't listening.

It *wasn't* a war story. It was a *love* story.

But you can't say that. All you can do is tell it one more time, patiently, adding and subtracting, making up a few things to get at the real truth. No Mitchell Sanders, you tell her. No Lemon, no Rat Kiley. No trail junction. No baby buffalo. No vines or moss or white blossoms. Beginning to end, you tell her, it's all made up. Every goddamn detail—the mountains and the river and especially that poor dumb baby buffalo. None of it happened. *None* of it. And even if it did happen, it didn't happen in the mountains, it happened in this little village on the Batangan Peninsula, and it was raining like crazy, and one night a guy named Stink Harris woke up screaming with a leech on his tongue. You can tell a true war story if you just keep on telling it.

And in the end, of course, a true war story is never about war. It's about sunlight. It's about the special way that dawn spreads out on a river when you know you must cross the river and march into the mountains and do things you are afraid to do. It's about love and memory. It's about sorrow. It's about sisters who never write back and people who never listen.

■ *QUESTIONS FOR MAKING CONNECTIONS*
WITHIN THE READING ■

1. Tim O'Brien's "How to Tell a True War Story" is part of a collection of stories by the author entitled *The Things They Carried*. Although the ostensible subject of this particular short story is a series of events that may have actually happened, the subtitle of the entire collection is "A Work of Fiction." "How to Tell a True War Story" begins with the explicit statement "This is true," but what sort of truth does it manage to convey? As you consider possible answers, please remember that the narrator warns us, "In many cases a true war story cannot be believed. If you believe it, be skeptical." Why is the issue of truth so important to a story about what happens in war? Does O'Brien really mean that there is no such thing as truth when we are talking about this issue? If everything about war is subjective, then is it ever possible for one person to judge another person's military conduct?

2. Why does Rat Kiley write a letter to Curt Lemon's sister? What do you make of the details of his letter? Conventionally, such a letter would praise a fallen fellow combatant as a "hero," someone of exemplary character who had chosen to make the "ultimate sacrifice." Instead, Rat writes about the times he and Curt were "raising hell and lighting up villes and bringing smoke to bear every which way." Is Rat trying to insult the sister? Seduce her? Destroy her positive memories of her brother? When she fails to write back to him, why does Rat refer to her as a "dumb cooze"? For that matter, why does he refer to the Vietnamese as "gooks"? Is this simply an example of crude prejudice? If Rat thought of the Vietnamese as people, much like his own family back home, how would such a change influence his behavior? If he thought of Lemon's sister as nothing more than a "cooze," why did he bother to write to her at all?

3. Why does Rat Kiley kill the baby water buffalo? And why is it that "the whole platoon stood there watching, feeling all kinds of things, but [not] a great deal of pity for the baby water buffalo"? How do you explain the reaction of Mitchell Sanders: "Well, that's Nam. Garden of Evil. Over here . . . every sin's fresh and original"? If the men view Rat's killing of the buffalo as a "sin," why do they make no effort to stop him? Why do they appear to feel no remorse afterward? Do they displace onto the buffalo their desire to get back at the Vietnamese, or is their behavior even more complicated? When they kill the buffalo, are they killing something in themselves? What part of themselves might they be killing, and why might they want to do so?

■ *QUESTIONS FOR WRITING* ■

1. Readers might perceive O'Brien's story to be a powerfully realistic evocation of war as people actually live it. On the other hand, in spite of its realistic qualities, the story sometimes becomes highly poetic, as in passages like this one:

   Twenty years later, I can still see the sunlight on Lemon's face. I can see him turning, looking back at Rat Kiley, then he laughed and took the curious half step from shade into sunlight, his face suddenly brown and shining, and when his foot touched down, in that instant, he must've thought it was the sunlight that was killing him.

   Is O'Brien guilty of aestheticizing war—that is, of making it seem more beautiful, romantic, or exotic than it really is? Do you think that your reading of his account has made you less likely or more likely to regard war as necessary and noble? Has O'Brien's account made it less likely or more likely that you will think of war as a natural and even indispensable part of life as a human being?

2. What is the connection in O'Brien's short story between experience and language? Does he believe that our language predetermines the nature of our experience, or does he suggest, instead, that our experience is often more complex than our language can accommodate? Toward the end of the story, the narrator describes the kind of exchange he has, after reading his short stories in public, often with "an older woman of kindly temperament and humane politics." What sense can you make of the narrator's remarks about this exchange? Is it ever possible to describe our experience to others? Would listeners who had served in Vietnam be more likely to understand the narrator's account than those who had never been there? How about someone who had served in a different war? How much experience must people share in order to understand one another?

■ *QUESTIONS FOR MAKING CONNECTIONS BETWEEN READINGS* ■

1. Would O'Brien's narrator be comfortable at The Citadel as described by Susan Faludi? Does the form of camaraderie we find at The Citadel correspond to the "love" felt by the men who served with the narrator of O'Brien's story? Can we understand the rituals performed at The Citadel as forging bonds similar to those forged by war, or do you see significant differences? In what ways does O'Brien's story suggest that the culture of The Citadel is likely to prove more enduring than Faludi suggests? Is the culture of The Citadel really the culture of war itself? If you think so, then why have some distinguished military leaders tried to reform that institution?

2. Would Christopher McCandless, as described by Jon Krakauer, have fit in with the soldiers O'Brien describes? Would they value the same things, and were they looking for the same forms of satisfaction? In what ways might the soldiers' experience of war have been shaped by attitudes and outlooks they already held as Americans even before they arrived in Vietnam—attitudes and outlooks expressed by Chris McCandless's journey "into the wild"? Did Vietnam become the "wilderness" for the American soldiers there? In what ways might the values we sometimes think of as closest to nature—values like independence and toughness—be the product of centuries of war? Is there really such a thing as "wilderness"? How is wilderness different from a battlefield? Is the real wilderness inside us?

www For additional suggestions about making connections between readings, visit the Link-O-Mat and More Sample Assignments at <www.newhum.com>.

MICHAEL POLLAN

IN HIS RECENT BOOK, *The Botany of Desire: A Plant's-Eye View of the World* (2001), the environmental journalist Michael Pollan has written the "biographies" of four everyday plants—apples, tulips, cannabis, and the potato—that he feels embody the way humans fulfill their desires through nature. The idea of assuming a plant's point of view first came to Pollan when he was working in his garden and realized that he and the bees swarming around him were doing essentially the same thing: they were both at work manipulating the environment to better serve the needs of the plants in his garden. And, in a paradigm shift, Pollan found himself wondering about the degree to which the plants themselves determined his actions by influencing his decisions over what seeds to put down, what to pull out, what to water, and what to cut back.

Pollan explains his shift in perspective as follows: "Think of all the trees that have been cut down to make room for the grasses. It makes just as much sense to a Darwinian to say that agriculture was something that the grasses came up with to get us to cut down the trees." With this insight into the ways that humans and certain plants have coevolved, Pollan realized that one could read in domesticated plants a record of human desire: in the effort to refine the apple, Pollan discerns a partial history of human longings for sweetness; in the tulip, the search for beauty; in cannabis, the call of intoxication; and in the lowly potato, the subject of "Playing God in the Garden," the yearning for control. "Seeing these plants . . . as willing partners in an intimate and reciprocal relationship with us means looking at ourselves a little differently," Pollan believes. We must see ourselves, he goes on to say, "as the objects of other species' designs and desires, as one of the newer bees in Darwin's garden—ingenious, sometimes reckless, and remarkably unself-conscious."

The author of *Second Nature: A Gardener's Education* (1991) and *A Place of My Own: The Education of an Amateur Builder* (1997), Pollan has published widely on

Pollan, Michael. "Playing God in the Garden." *The New York Times Magazine.* 25 October 1998. 6–44.

Quotations from Michael Pollan, "Books: In Person," interview by Maria Hong, *The Austin Chronicle,* 25 May 2001, and Michael Pollan, introduction to *The Botany of Desire* (New York: Random House, 2000).

gardening, environmentalism, and architecture and has served as an editor-at-large for *Harper's Magazine* and a contributing editor at *The New York Times Magazine*. Michael Pollan is currently the Knight Professor of Journalism and Director of the Knight Program in Science and Environmental Journalism at the University of California–Berkeley.

www **To learn more about Michael Pollan and the biotechnology industry, visit the Link-O-Mat at <www.newhum.com>.**

Playing God in the Garden

Planting

Today I planted something new in my vegetable garden—something very new, as a matter of fact. It's a potato called the New Leaf Superior, which has been genetically engineered—by Monsanto, the chemical giant recently turned "life sciences" giant—to produce its own insecticide. This it can do in every cell of every leaf, stem, flower, root and (here's the creepy part) spud. The scourge of potatoes has always been the Colorado potato beetle, a handsome and voracious insect that can pick a plant clean of its leaves virtually overnight. Any Colorado potato beetle that takes so much as a nibble of my New Leafs will supposedly keel over and die, its digestive tract pulped, in effect, by the bacterial toxin manufactured in the leaves of these otherwise ordinary Superiors. (Superiors are the thin-skinned white spuds sold fresh in the supermarket.) You're probably wondering if I plan to eat these potatoes, or serve them to my family. That's still up in the air; it's only the first week of May, and harvest is a few months off.

Certainly my New Leafs are aptly named. They're part of a new class of crop plants that is rapidly changing the American food chain. This year, the fourth year that genetically altered seed has been on the market, some 45 million acres of American farmland have been planted with biotech crops, most of it corn, soybeans, cotton and potatoes that have been engineered to either produce their own pesticides or withstand herbicides. Though Americans have already begun to eat genetically engineered potatoes, corn and soybeans, industry research confirms what my own informal surveys suggest: hardly any of us knows it. The reason is not hard to find. The biotech industry, with the concurrence of the Food and Drug Administration, has

decided we don't need to know it, so biotech foods carry no identifying labels. In a dazzling feat of positioning, the industry has succeeded in depicting these plants simultaneously as the linchpins of a biological revolution—
part of a "new agricultural paradigm" that will make farming more
sustainable, feed the world and improve health and nutrition—and, oddly
enough, as the same old stuff, at least so far as those of us at the eating end
of the food chain should be concerned.

This convenient version of reality has been roundly rejected by both
consumers and farmers across the Atlantic. Last summer, biotech food
emerged as the most explosive environmental issue in Europe. Protesters
have destroyed dozens of field trials of the very same "frankenplants" (as
they are sometimes called) that we Americans are already serving for dinner, and throughout Europe the public has demanded that biotech food be
labeled in the market.

By growing my own transgenic crop—and talking with scientists and
farmers involved with biotech—I hoped to discover which of us was crazy.
Are the Europeans overreacting, or is it possible that we've been underreact-
ing to genetically engineered food?

After digging two shallow trenches in my garden and lining them with
compost, I untied the purple mesh bag of seed potatoes that Monsanto had
sent and opened up the Grower Guide tied around its neck. (Potatoes, you
may recall from kindergarten experiments, are grown not from seed but
from the eyes of other potatoes.) The guide put me in mind not so much of
planting potatoes as booting up a new software release. By "opening and
using this product," the card stated, I was now "licensed" to grow these
potatoes, but only for a single generation; the crop I would water and tend
and harvest was mine, yet also not mine. That is, the potatoes I will harvest
come August are mine to eat or sell, but their genes remain the intellectual
property of Monsanto, protected under numerous United States patents, including Nos. 5,196,525, 5,164,316, 5,322,938 and 5,352,605. Were I to save
even one of them to plant next year—something I've routinely done with
potatoes in the past—I would be breaking Federal law. The small print in the
Grower Guide also brought the news that my potato plants were themselves
a pesticide, registered with the Environmental Protection Agency.

If proof were needed that the intricate industrial food chain that begins
with seeds and ends on our dinner plates is in the throes of profound change,
the small print that accompanied my New Leaf will do. That food chain has
been unrivaled for its productivity—on average, a single American farmer
today grows enough food each year to feed 100 people. But this accomplishment has come at a price. The modern industrial farmer cannot achieve such
yields without enormous amounts of chemical fertilizer, pesticide, machinery and fuel, a set of capital-intensive inputs, as they're called, that saddle the
farmer with debt, threaten his health, erode his soil and destroy its fertility,
pollute the ground water and compromise the safety of the food we eat.

We've heard all this before, of course, but usually from environmentalists and organic farmers; what is new is to hear the same critique from conventional farmers, government officials and even many agribusiness corporations, all of whom now acknowledge that our food chain stands in need of reform. Sounding more like Wendell Berry than the agribusiness giant it is, Monsanto declared in its most recent annual report that "current agricultural technology is not sustainable."

What is supposed to rescue the American food chain is biotechnology— the replacement of expensive and toxic chemical inputs with expensive but apparently benign genetic information: crops that, like my New Leafs, can protect themselves from insects and disease without being sprayed with pesticides. With the advent of biotechnology, agriculture is entering the information age, and more than any other company, Monsanto is positioning itself to become its Microsoft, supplying the proprietary "operating systems"—the metaphor is theirs—to run this new generation of plants.

There is, of course, a second food chain in America: organic agriculture. And while it is still only a fraction of the size of the conventional food chain, it has been growing in leaps and bounds—in large part because of concerns over the safety of conventional agriculture. Organic farmers have been among biotechnology's fiercest critics, regarding crops like my New Leafs as inimical to their principles and, potentially, a threat to their survival. That's because Bt, the bacterial toxin produced in my New Leafs (and in many other biotech plants) happens to be the same insecticide organic growers have relied on for decades. Instead of being flattered by the imitation, however, organic farmers are up in arms: the widespread use of Bt in biotech crops is likely to lead to insect resistance, thus robbing organic growers of one of their most critical tools; that is, Monsanto's version of sustainable agriculture may threaten precisely those farmers who pioneered sustainable farming.

Sprouting

After several days of drenching rain, the sun appeared on May 15, and so did my New Leafs. A dozen deep-green shoots pushed up out of the soil and commenced to grow—faster and more robustly than any of the other potatoes in my garden. Apart from their vigor, though, my New Leafs looked perfectly normal. And yet as I watched them multiply their lustrous dark-green leaves those first few days, eagerly awaiting the arrival of the first doomed beetle, I couldn't help thinking of them as existentially different from the rest of my plants.

All domesticated plants are in some sense artificial—living archives of both cultural and natural information that we in some sense "design." A given type of potato reflects the values we've bred into it—one that has been selected to yield long, handsome french fries or unblemished round potato chips is the expression of a national food chain that likes its potatoes highly processed. At the same time, some of the more delicate European fingerlings I'm growing alongside my New Leafs imply an economy of small market growers and a taste for eating potatoes fresh. Yet all these qualities already existed in the potato, somewhere within the range of genetic possibilities presented by *Solanum tuberosum*. Since distant species in nature cannot be crossed, the breeder's art has always run up against a natural limit of what a potato is willing, or able, to do. Nature, in effect, has exercised a kind of veto on what culture can do with a potato.

My New Leafs are different. Although Monsanto likes to depict biotechnology as just another in an ancient line of human modifications of nature going back to fermentation, in fact genetic engineering overthrows the old rules governing the relationship of nature and culture in a plant. For the first time, breeders can bring qualities from anywhere in nature into the genome of a plant—from flounders (frost tolerance), from viruses (disease resistance) and, in the case of my potatoes, from *Bacillus thuringiensis,* the soil bacterium that produces the organic insecticide known as Bt. The introduction into a plant of genes transported not only across species but whole phyla means that the wall of that plant's essential identity—its irreducible wildness, you might say—has been breached.

But what is perhaps most astonishing about the New Leafs coming up in my garden is the human intelligence that the inclusion of the Bt gene represents. In the past, that intelligence resided outside the plant, in the mind of the organic farmers who deployed Bt (in the form of a spray) to manipulate the ecological relationship of certain insects and a certain bacterium as a way to foil those insects. The irony about the New Leafs is that the cultural information they encode happens to be knowledge that resides in the heads of the very sort of people—that is, organic growers—who most distrust high technology.

One way to look at biotechnology is that it allows a larger portion of human intelligence to be incorporated into the plant itself. In this sense, my New Leafs are just plain smarter than the rest of my potatoes. The others will depend on my knowledge and experience when the Colorado potato beetles strike; the New Leafs, knowing what I know about bugs and Bt, will take care of themselves. So while my biotech plants might seem like alien beings, that's not quite right. They're more like us than like other plants because there's more of us in them.

Growing

To find out how my potatoes got that way, I traveled to suburban St. Louis in early June. My New Leafs are clones of clones of plants that were first engineered seven years ago in Monsanto's $150 million research facility, a long, low-slung brick building on the banks of the Missouri that would look like any other corporate complex were it not for the 26 greenhouses that crown its roof like shimmering crenellations of glass.

Dave Stark, a molecular biologist and co-director of Naturemark, Monsanto's potato subsidiary, escorted me through the clean rooms where potatoes are genetically engineered. Technicians sat at lab benches before petri dishes in which fingernail-size sections of potato stem had been placed in a nutrient mixture. To this the technicians added a solution of agrobacterium, a disease bacterium whose *modus operandi* is to break into a plant cell's nucleus and insert some of its own DNA. Essentially, scientists smuggle the Bt gene into the agrobacterium's payload, and then the bacterium splices it into the potato's DNA. The technicians also add a "marker" gene, a kind of universal product code that allows Monsanto to identify its plants after they leave the lab.

A few days later, once the slips of potato stem have put down roots, they're moved to the potato greenhouse up on the roof. Here, Glenda DeBrecht, a horticulturist, invited me to don latex gloves and help her transplant pinky-size plantlets from their petri dish to small pots. The whole operation is performed thousands of times, largely because there is so much uncertainty about the outcome. There's no way of telling where in the genome the new DNA will land, and if it winds up in the wrong place, the new gene won't be expressed (or it will be poorly expressed) or the plant may be a freak. I was struck by how the technology could at once be astoundingly sophisticated and yet also a shot in the genetic dark.

"There's still a lot we don't understand about gene expression," Stark acknowledged. A great many factors influence whether, or to what extent, a new gene will do what it's supposed to, including the environment. In one early German experiment, scientists succeeded in splicing the gene for redness into petunias. All went as planned until the weather turned hot and an entire field of red petunias suddenly and inexplicably lost their pigment. The process didn't seem nearly as simple as Monsanto's cherished software metaphor would suggest.

When I got home from St. Louis, I phoned Richard Lewontin, the Harvard geneticist, to ask him what he thought of the software metaphor. "From an intellectual-property standpoint, it's exactly right," he said. "But it's a bad one in terms of biology. It implies you feed a program into a machine and get predictable results. But the genome is very noisy. If my computer made as many mistakes as an organism does"—in interpreting its DNA, he meant—"I'd throw it out."

I asked him for a better metaphor. "An ecosystem," he offered. "You can always intervene and change something in it, but there's no way of knowing what all the downstream effects will be or how it might affect the environment. We have such a miserably poor understanding of how the organism develops from its DNA that I would be surprised if we don't get one rude shock after another."

Flowering

My own crop was thriving when I got home from St. Louis; the New Leafs were as big as bushes, crowned with slender flower stalks. Potato flowers are actually quite pretty, at least by vegetable standards—five-petaled pink stars with yellow centers that give off a faint rose perfume. One sultry afternoon I watched the bumblebees making their lazy rounds of my potato blossoms, thoughtlessly powdering their thighs with yellow pollen grains before lumbering off to appointments with other blossoms, other species.

Uncertainty is the theme that unifies much of the criticism leveled against biotech agriculture by scientists and environmentalists. By planting millions of acres of genetically altered plants, we have introduced something novel into the environment and the food chain, the consequences of which are not—and at this point, cannot be—completely understood. One of the uncertainties has to do with those grains of pollen bumblebees are carting off from my potatoes. That pollen contains Bt genes that may wind up in some other, related plant, possibly conferring a new evolutionary advantage on that species. "Gene flow," the scientific term for this phenomenon, occurs only between closely related species, and since the potato evolved in South America, the chances are slim that my Bt potato genes will escape into the wilds of Connecticut. (It's interesting to note that while biotechnology depends for its power on the ability to move genes freely among species and even phyla, its environmental safety depends on the very opposite phenomenon: on the integrity of species in nature and their rejection of foreign genetic material.)

Yet what happens if and when Peruvian farmers plant Bt potatoes? Or when I plant a biotech crop that does have local relatives? A study reported in *Nature* [in September 1998] found that plant traits introduced by genetic engineering were more likely to escape into the wild than the same traits introduced conventionally.

Andrew Kimbrell, director of the Center for Technology Assessment in Washington, told me he believes such escapes are inevitable. "Biological pollution will be the environmental nightmare of the 21st century," he said when I reached him by phone. "This is not like chemical pollution—an oil spill—that eventually disperses. Biological pollution is an entirely different model, more like a disease. Is Monsanto going to be held legally responsible when one of its transgenes creates a superweed or resistant insect?"

Kimbrell maintains that because our pollution laws were written before the advent of biotechnology, the new industry is being regulated under an ill-fitting regime designed for the chemical age. Congress has so far passed no environmental law dealing specifically with biotech. Monsanto, for its part, claims that it has thoroughly examined all the potential environmental and health risks of its biotech plants, and points out that three regulatory agencies—the U.S.D.A., the E.P.A. and the F.D.A.—have signed off on its products. Speaking of the New Leaf, Dave Stark told me, "This is the most intensively studied potato in history."

Significant uncertainties remain, however. Take the case of insect resistance to Bt, a potential form of "biological pollution" that could end the effectiveness of one of the safest insecticides we have—and cripple the organic farmers who depend on it. The theory, which is now accepted by most entomologists, is that Bt crops will add so much of the toxin to the environment that insects will develop resistance to it. Until now, resistance hasn't been a worry because the Bt sprays break down quickly in sunlight and organic farmers use them only sparingly. Resistance is essentially a form of co-evolution that seems to occur only when a given pest population is threatened with extinction; under that pressure, natural selection favors whatever chance mutations will allow the species to change and survive.

Working with the E.P.A., Monsanto has developed a "resistance-management plan" to postpone that eventuality. Under the plan, farmers who plant Bt crops must leave a certain portion of their land in non-Bt crops to create "refuges" for the targeted insects. The goal is to prevent the first Bt-resistant Colorado potato beetle from mating with a second resistant bug, unleashing a new race of superbeetles. The theory is that when a Bt-resistant bug does show up, it can be induced to mate with a susceptible bug from the refuge, thus diluting the new gene for resistance.

But a lot has to go right for Mr. Wrong to meet Miss Right. No one is sure how big the refuges need to be, where they should be situated or whether the farmers will cooperate (creating havens for a detested pest is counter-intuitive, after all), not to mention the bugs. In the case of potatoes, the E.P.A. has made the plan voluntary and lets the companies themselves implement it; there are no E.P.A. enforcement mechanisms. Which is why most of the organic farmers I spoke to dismissed the regulatory scheme as window dressing.

Monsanto executives offer two basic responses to criticism of their Bt crops. The first is that their voluntary resistance-management plans will work, though the company's definition of success will come as small consolation to an organic farmer: Monsanto scientists told me that if all goes well, resistance can be postponed for 30 years. (Some scientists believe it will come in three to five years.) The second response is more troubling. In St. Louis, I met with Jerry Hjelle, Monsanto's vice president for regulatory affairs. Hjelle told me that resistance should not unduly concern us since "there are a thousand other Bts out there"—other insecticidal proteins. "We can handle this problem with new products," he said. "The critics don't know what we have in the pipeline."

And then Hjelle uttered two words that I thought had been expunged from the corporate vocabulary a long time ago: "Trust us."

"Trust" is a key to the success of biotechnology in the marketplace, and while I was in St. Louis, I asked Hjelle and several of his colleagues why they thought the Europeans were resisting biotech food. Austria, Luxembourg and Norway, risking trade war with the United States, have refused to accept imports of genetically altered crops. Activists in England have been staging sit-ins and "decontaminations" in biotech test fields. A group of French farmers broke into a warehouse and ruined a shipment of biotech corn seed by urinating on it. The Prince of Wales, who is an ardent organic gardener, waded into the biotech debate last June, vowing in a column in *The Daily Telegraph* that he would never eat, or serve to his guests, the fruits of a technology that "takes mankind into realms that belong to God and to God alone."

Monsanto executives are quick to point out that mad cow disease has made Europeans extremely sensitive about the safety of their food chain and has undermined confidence in their regulators. "They don't have a trusted agency like the F.D.A. looking after the safety of their food supply," said Phil Angell, Monsanto's director of corporate communications. Over the summer, Angell was dispatched repeatedly to Europe to put out the P.R. fires; some at Monsanto worry these could spread to the United States.

I checked with the F.D.A. to find out exactly what had been done to insure the safety of this potato. I was mystified by the fact that the Bt toxin was not being treated as a "food additive" subject to labeling, even though the new protein is expressed in the potato itself. The label on a bag of biotech potatoes in the supermarket will tell a consumer all about the nutrients they contain, even the trace amounts of copper. Yet it is silent not only about the fact that those potatoes are the product of genetic engineering but also about their containing an insecticide.

At the F.D.A., I was referred to James Maryanski, who oversees biotech food at the agency. I began by asking him why the F.D.A. didn't consider Bt a food additive. Under F.D.A. law, any novel substance added to a food must— unless it is "generally regarded as safe" ("GRAS," in F.D.A. parlance)—be thoroughly tested and if it changes the product in any way, must be labeled.

"That's easy," Maryanski said. "Bt is a pesticide, so it's exempt" from F.D.A. regulation. That is, even though a Bt potato is plainly a food, for the purposes of Federal regulation it is not a food but a pesticide and therefore falls under the jurisdiction of the E.P.A.

Yet even in the case of those biotech crops over which the F.D.A. does have jurisdiction, I learned that F.D.A. regulation of biotech food has been largely voluntary since 1992, when Vice President Dan Quayle issued regulatory guidelines for the industry as part of the Bush Administration's campaign for "regulatory relief." Under the guidelines, new proteins engineered into foods are regarded as additives (unless they're pesticides), but as Maryanski explained, "the determination whether a new protein is GRAS can be made by the company." Companies with a new biotech food decide for themselves whether they need to consult with the F.D.A. by following a series of "decision trees" that pose yes or no questions like this one: "Does . . . the introduced protein raise any safety concern?"

Since my Bt potatoes were being regulated as a pesticide by the E.P.A. rather than as a food by the F.D.A., I wondered if the safety standards are the same. "Not exactly," Maryanski explained. The F.D.A. requires "a reasonable certainty of no harm" in a food additive, a standard most pesticides could not meet. After all, "pesticides are toxic to something," Maryanski pointed out, so the E.P.A. instead establishes human "tolerances" for each chemical and then subjects it to a risk-benefit analysis.

When I called the E.P.A. and asked if the agency had tested my Bt potatoes for safety as a human food, the answer was . . . not exactly. It seems the E.P.A. works from the assumption that if the original potato is safe and the Bt protein added to it is safe, then the whole New Leaf package is presumed to be safe. Some geneticists believe this reasoning is flawed, contending that the process of genetic engineering itself may cause subtle, as yet unrecognized changes in a food.

The original Superior potato is safe, obviously enough, so that left the Bt toxin, which was fed to mice, and they "did fine, had no side effects," I was told. I always feel better knowing that my food has been poison-tested by mice, though in this case there was a small catch: the mice weren't actually eating the potatoes, not even an extract from the potatoes, but rather straight Bt produced in a bacterial culture.

So are my New Leafs safe to eat? Probably, assuming that a New Leaf is nothing more than the sum of a safe potato and a safe pesticide, and further assuming that the E.P.A.'s idea of a safe pesticide is tantamount to a safe food. Yet I still had a question. Let us assume that my potatoes are a pesticide—a very safe pesticide. Every pesticide in my garden shed—including the Bt sprays—carries a lengthy warning label. The label on my bottle of Bt says, among other things, that I should avoid inhaling the spray or getting it in an open wound. So if my New Leaf potatoes contain an E.P.A.-registered pesticide, why don't they carry some such label?

Maryanski had the answer. At least for the purposes of labeling, my New Leafs have morphed yet again, back into a food: the Food, Drug and Cosmetic Act gives the F.D.A. sole jurisdiction over the labeling of plant foods, and the F.D.A. has ruled that biotech foods need be labeled only if they contain known allergens or have otherwise been "materially" changed.

But isn't turning a potato into a pesticide a material change?

It doesn't matter. The Food, Drug and Cosmetic Act specifically bars the F.D.A. from including any information about pesticides on its food labels.

I thought about Maryanski's candid and wondrous explanations the next time I met Phil Angell, who again cited the critical role of the F.D.A. in assuring Americans that biotech food is safe. But this time he went even further. "Monsanto should not have to vouchsafe the safety of biotech food," he said. "Our interest is in selling as much of it as possible. Assuring its safety is the F.D.A.'s job."

Meeting the Beetles

My Colorado potato beetle vigil came to an end the first week of July, shortly before I went to Idaho to visit potato growers. I spied a single mature beetle sitting on a New Leaf leaf; when I reached to pick it up, the beetle fell drunkenly to the ground. It had been sickened by the plant and would soon be dead. My New Leafs were working.

From where a typical American potato grower stands, the New Leaf looks very much like a godsend. That's because where the typical potato grower stands is in the middle of a bright green field that has been doused with so much pesticide that the leaves of his plants wear a dull white chemical bloom that troubles him as much as it does the rest of us. Out there, at least, the calculation is not complex: a product that promises to eliminate the need for even a single spraying of pesticide is, very simply, an economic and environmental boon.

No one can make a better case for a biotech crop than a potato farmer, which is why Monsanto was eager to introduce me to several large growers. Like many farmers today, the ones I met feel trapped by the chemical inputs required to extract the high yields they must achieve in order to pay for the chemical inputs they need. The economics are daunting: a potato farmer in south-central Idaho will spend roughly $1,965 an acre (mainly on chemicals, electricity, water and seed) to grow a crop that, in a good year, will earn him maybe $1,980. That's how much a french-fry processor will pay for the 20 tons of potatoes a single Idaho acre can yield. (The real money in agriculture—90 percent of the value added to the food we eat—is in selling inputs to farmers and then processing their crops.)

Danny Forsyth laid out the dismal economics of potato farming for me one sweltering morning at the coffee shop in downtown Jerome, Idaho. Forsyth, 60, is a slight blue-eyed man with a small gray ponytail; he farms 3,000 acres of potatoes, corn and wheat, and he spoke about agricultural chemicals like a man desperate to kick a bad habit. "None of us would use them if we had any choice," he said glumly.

I asked him to walk me through a season's regimen. It typically begins early in the spring with a soil fumigant; to control nematodes, many potato farmers douse their fields with a chemical toxic enough to kill every trace of microbial life in the soil. Then, at planting, a systemic insecticide (like Thimet) is applied to the soil; this will be absorbed by the young seedlings and, for several weeks, will kill any insect that eats their leaves. After planting, Forsyth puts down an herbicide—Sencor or Eptam—to "clean" his field of all weeds. When the potato seedlings are six inches tall, an herbicide may be sprayed a second time to control weeds.

Idaho farmers like Forsyth farm in vast circles defined by the rotation of a pivot irrigation system, typically 135 acres to a circle; I'd seen them from 30,000 feet flying in, a grid of verdant green coins pressed into a desert of scrubby brown. Pesticides and fertilizers are simply added to the irrigation system, which on Forsyth's farm draws most of its water from the nearby Snake River. Along with their water, Forsyth's potatoes may receive 10 applications of chemical fertilizer during the growing season. Just before the rows close—when the leaves of one row of plants meet those of the next— he begins spraying Bravo, a fungicide, to control late blight, one of the biggest threats to the potato crop. (Late blight, which caused the Irish potato famine, is an airborne fungus that turns stored potatoes into rotting mush.) Blight is such a serious problem that the E.P.A. currently allows farmers to spray powerful fungicides that haven't passed the usual approval process. Forsyth's potatoes will receive eight applications of fungicide.

Twice each summer, Forsyth hires a crop duster to spray for aphids. Aphids are harmless in themselves, but they transmit the leafroll virus, which in Russet Burbank potatoes causes net necrosis, a brown spotting that will cause a processor to reject a whole crop. It happened to Forsyth last year. "I lost 80,000 bags"—they're a hundred pounds each—"to net necrosis," he said. "Instead of getting $4.95 a bag, I had to take $2 a bag from the dehydrator, and I was lucky to get that." Net necrosis is a purely cosmetic defect; yet because big buyers like McDonald's believe (with good reason) that we don't like to see brown spots in our fries, farmers like Danny Forsyth must spray their fields with some of the most toxic chemicals in use, including an organophosphate called Monitor.

"Monitor is a deadly chemical," Forsyth said. "I won't go into a field for four or five days after it's been sprayed—even to fix a broken pivot." That is, he would sooner lose a whole circle to drought than expose himself or an employee to Monitor, which has been found to cause neurological damage.

It's not hard to see why a farmer like Forsyth, struggling against tight margins and heartsick over chemicals, would leap at a New Leaf—or, in his case, a New Leaf Plus, which is protected from leafroll virus as well as beetles. "The New Leaf means I can skip a couple of sprayings, including the Monitor," he said. "I save money, and I sleep better. It also happens to be a nice-looking spud." The New Leafs don't come cheaply, however. They cost between $20 and $30 extra per acre in "technology fees" to Monsanto.

Forsyth and I discussed organic agriculture, about which he had the usual things to say ("That's all fine on a small scale, but they don't have to feed the world"), as well as a few things I'd never heard from a conventional farmer: "I like to eat organic food, and in fact I raise a lot of it at the house. The vegetables we buy at the market we just wash and wash and wash. I'm not sure I should be saying this, but I always plant a small area of potatoes without any chemicals. By the end of the season, my field potatoes are fine to eat, but any potatoes I pulled today are probably still full of systemics. I don't eat them."

Forsyth's words came back to me a few hours later, during lunch at the home of another potato farmer. Steve Young is a progressive and prosperous potato farmer—he calls himself an agribusinessman. In addition to his 10,000 acres—the picture window in his family room gazes out on 85 circles, all computer-controlled—Young owns a share in a successful fertilizer distributorship. His wife prepared a lavish feast for us, and after Dave, their 18-year-old, said grace, adding a special prayer for me (the Youngs are devout Mormons), she passed around a big bowl of homemade potato salad. As I helped myself, my Monsanto escort asked what was in the salad, flashing me a smile that suggested she might already know. "It's a combination of New Leafs and some of our regular Russets," our hostess said proudly. "Dug this very morning."

After talking to farmers like Steve Young and Danny Forsyth, and walking fields made virtually sterile by a drenching season-long rain of chemicals, you could understand how Monsanto's New Leaf potato does indeed look like an environmental boon. Set against current practices, growing New Leafs represents a more sustainable way of potato farming. This advance must be weighed, of course, against everything we don't yet know about New Leafs—and a few things we do: like the problem of Bt resistance I had heard so much about back East. While I was in Idaho and Washington State, I asked potato farmers to show me their refuges. This proved to be a joke.

"I guess that's a refuge over there," one Washington farmer told me, pointing to a cornfield.

Monsanto's grower contract never mentions the word "refuge" and only requires that farmers grow no more than 80 percent of their fields in New Leaf. Basically, any field not planted in New Leaf is considered a refuge, even if that field has been sprayed to kill every bug in it. Farmers call such acreage a clean field; calling it a refuge is a stretch at best.

It probably shouldn't come as a big surprise that conventional farmers would have trouble embracing the notion of an insect refuge. To insist on real and substantial refuges is to ask them to start thinking of their fields in an entirely new way, less as a factory than as an ecosystem. In the factory, Bt is another in a long line of "silver bullets" that work for a while and then get replaced; in the ecosystem, all bugs are not necessarily bad, and the relationships between various species can be manipulated to achieve desired ends—like the long-term sustainability of Bt.

This is, of course, precisely the approach organic farmers have always taken to their fields, and after my lunch with the Youngs that afternoon, I paid a brief visit to an organic potato grower. Mike Heath is a rugged, laconic man in his mid-50's; like most of the organic farmers I've met, he looks as though he spends a lot more time out of doors than a conventional farmer, and he probably does: chemicals are, among other things, labor-saving devices. While we drove around his 500 acres in a battered old pickup, I asked him about biotechnology. He voiced many reservations—it was synthetic, there were too many unknowns—but his main objection to planting a biotech potato was simply that "it's not what my customers want."

That point was driven home last December when the Department of Agriculture proposed a new "organic standards" rule that, among other things, would have allowed biotech crops to carry an organic label. After receiving a flood of outraged cards and letters, the agency backed off. (As did Monsanto, which asked the U.S.D.A. to shelve the issue for three years.) Heath suggested that biotech may actually help organic farmers by driving worried consumers to the organic label.

I asked Heath about the New Leaf. He had no doubt resistance would come—"the bugs are always going to be smarter than we are"—and said it was unjust that Monsanto was profiting from the ruin of Bt, something he regarded as a "public good."

None of this particularly surprised me; what did was that Heath himself resorted to Bt sprays only once or twice in the last 10 years. I had assumed that organic farmers used Bt or other approved pesticides in much the same way conventional farmers use theirs, but as Heath showed me around his farm, I began to understand that organic farming was a lot more complicated than substituting good inputs for bad. Instead of buying many inputs at all, Heath relied on long and complex crop rotations to prevent a buildup of crop-specific pests—he has found, for example, that planting wheat after spuds "confuses" the potato beetles.

He also plants strips of flowering crops on the margins of his potato fields—peas or alfalfa, usually—to attract the beneficial insects that eat beetle larvae and aphids. If there aren't enough beneficials to do the job, he'll introduce ladybugs. Heath also grows eight varieties of potatoes, on the theory that biodiversity in a field, as in the wild, is the best defense against any imbalances in the system. A bad year with one variety will probably be offset by a good year with the others.

"I can eat any potato in this field right now," he said, digging Yukon Golds for me to take home. "Most farmers can't eat their spuds out of the field. But you don't want to start talking about safe food in Idaho."

Heath's were the antithesis of "clean" fields, and, frankly, their weedy margins and overall patchiness made them much less pretty to look at. Yet it was the very complexity of these fields—the sheer diversity of species, both in space and time—that made them productive year after year without many inputs. The system provided for most of its needs.

All told, Heath's annual inputs consisted of natural fertilizers (compost and fish powder), ladybugs and a copper spray (for blight)—a few hundred dollars an acre. Of course, before you can compare Heath's operation with a conventional farm, you've got to add in the extra labor (lots of smaller crops means more work; organic fields must also be cultivated for weeds) and time—the typical organic rotation calls for potatoes every fifth year, in contrast to every third on a conventional farm. I asked Heath about his yields. To my astonishment, he was digging between 300 and 400 bags per acre—just as many as Danny Forsyth and only slightly fewer than Steve Young.

Heath was also getting almost twice the price for his spuds: $8 a bag from an organic processor who was shipping frozen french fries to Japan.

On the drive back to Boise, I thought about why Heath's farm remained the exception, both in Idaho and elsewhere. Here was a genuinely new paradigm that seemed to work. But while it's true that organic agriculture is gaining ground (I met a big grower in Washington who had just added several organic circles), few of the mainstream farmers I met considered organic a "realistic" alternative. For one thing, it's expensive to convert: organic certifiers require a field to go without chemicals for three years before it can be called organic. For another, the U.S.D.A., which sets the course of American agriculture, has long been hostile to organic methods.

But I suspect the real reasons run deeper, and have more to do with the fact that in a dozen ways a farm like Heath's simply doesn't conform to the requirements of a corporate food chain. Heath's type of agriculture doesn't leave much room for the Monsantos of this world: organic farmers buy remarkably little—some seed, a few tons of compost, maybe a few gallons of ladybugs. That's because the organic farmer's focus is on a process, rather than on products. Nor is that process readily systematized, reduced to, say, a prescribed regime of sprayings like the one Forsyth outlined for me—regimes that are often designed by companies selling chemicals.

Most of the intelligence and local knowledge needed to run Mike Heath's farm resides in the head of Mike Heath. Growing potatoes conventionally requires intelligence, too, but a large portion of it resides in laboratories in distant places like St. Louis, where it is employed in developing sophisticated chemical inputs. That sort of centralization of agriculture is unlikely to be reversed, if only because there's so much money in it; besides, it's much easier for the farmer to buy prepackaged solutions from big companies. "Whose Head Is the Farmer Using? Whose Head Is Using the Farmer?" goes the title of a Wendell Berry essay.

Organic farmers like Heath have also rejected what is perhaps the cornerstone of industrial agriculture: the economies of scale that only a monoculture can achieve. Monoculture—growing vast fields of the same crop year after year—is probably the single most powerful simplification of modern agriculture. But monoculture is poorly fitted to the way nature seems to work. Very simply, a field of identical plants will be exquisitely vulnerable to insects, weeds and disease. Monoculture is at the root of virtually every problem that bedevils the modern farmer, and that virtually every input has been designed to solve.

To put the matter baldly, a farmer like Heath is working very hard to adjust his fields and his crops to the nature of nature, while farmers like Forsyth are working equally hard to adjust nature in their fields to the requirement of monoculture and, beyond that, to the needs of the industrial food chain. I remember asking Heath what he did about net necrosis, the bane of Forsyth's existence. "That's only really a problem with Russet Burbanks," he said. "So I plant other kinds." Forsyth can't do that. He's part of a food chain—at the far end of which stands a long, perfectly golden McDonald's fry—that demands he grow Russet Burbanks and little else.

This is where biotechnology comes in, to the rescue of Forsyth's Russet Burbanks and, if Monsanto is right, to the whole food chain of which they form a part. Monoculture is in trouble—the pesticides that make it possible are rapidly being lost, either to resistance or to heightened concerns about their danger. Biotechnology is the new silver bullet that will save monoculture. But a new silver bullet is not a new paradigm—rather, it's something that will allow the old paradigm to survive. That paradigm will always construe the problem in Forsyth's fields as a Colorado potato beetle problem, rather than as a problem of potato monoculture.

Like the silver bullets that preceded them—the modern hybrids, the pesticides and the chemical fertilizers—the new biotech crops will probably, as advertised, increase yields. But equally important, they will also speed the process by which agriculture is being concentrated in a shrinking number of corporate hands. If that process has advanced more slowly in farming than in other sectors of the economy, it is only because nature herself—her complexity, diversity and sheer intractibility in the face of our best efforts at control—has acted as a check on it. But biotechnology promises to remedy this "problem," too.

Consider, for example, the seed, perhaps the ultimate "means of production" in any agriculture. It is only in the last few decades that farmers have begun buying their seed from big companies, and even today many farmers still save some seed every fall to replant in the spring. Brown-bagging, as it is called, allows farmers to select strains particularly well adapted to their needs; since these seeds are often traded, the practice advances the state of the genetic art—indeed, has given us most of our crop plants. Seeds by their very nature don't lend themselves to commodification: they produce more of themselves ad infinitum (with the exception of certain modern hybrids), and for that reason the genetics of most major crop plants have traditionally been regarded as a common heritage. In the case of the potato, the genetics of most important varieties—the Burbanks, the Superiors, the Atlantics— have always been in the public domain. Before Monsanto released the New Leaf, there had never been a multinational seed corporation in the potato-seed business—there was no money in it.

Biotechnology changes all that. By adding a new gene or two to a Russet Burbank or Superior, Monsanto can now patent the improved variety. Legally, it has been possible to patent a plant for many years, but biologically, these patents have been almost impossible to enforce. Biotechnology partly solves that problem. A Monsanto agent can perform a simple test in my garden and prove that my plants are the company's intellectual property. The contract farmers sign with Monsanto allows company representatives to perform such tests in their fields at will. According to *Progressive*

Farmer, a trade journal, Monsanto is using informants and hiring Pinkertons to enforce its patent rights; it has already brought legal action against hundreds of farmers for patent infringement.

Soon the company may not have to go to the trouble. It is expected to acquire the patent to a powerful new biotechnology called the Terminator, which will, in effect, allow the company to enforce its patents biologically. Developed by the U.S.D.A. in partnership with Delta and Pine Land, a seed company in the process of being purchased by Monsanto, the Terminator is a complex of genes that, theoretically, can be spliced into any crop plant, where it will cause every seed produced by that plant to be sterile. Once the Terminator becomes the industry standard, control over the genetics of crop plants will complete its move from the farmer's field to the seed company—to which the farmer will have no choice but to return year after year. The Terminator will allow companies like Monsanto to privatize one of the last great commons in nature—the genetics of the crop plants that civilization has developed over the past 10,000 years.

At lunch on his farm in Idaho, I had asked Steve Young what he thought about all this, especially about the contract Monsanto made him sign. I wondered how the American farmer, the putative heir to a long tradition of agrarian independence, was adjusting to the idea of field men snooping around his farm, and patented seed he couldn't replant. Young said he had made his peace with corporate agriculture, and with biotechnology in particular: "It's here to stay. It's necessary if we're going to feed the world, and it's going to take us forward."

Then I asked him if he saw any downside to biotechnology, and he paused for what seemed a very long time. What he then said silenced the table. "There is a cost," he said. "It gives corporate America one more noose around my neck."

Harvest

A few weeks after I returned home from Idaho, I dug my New Leafs, harvesting a gorgeous-looking pile of white spuds, including some real lunkers. The plants had performed brilliantly, though so had all my other potatoes. The beetle problem never got serious, probably because the diversity of species in my (otherwise organic) garden had attracted enough beneficial insects to keep the beetles in check. By the time I harvested my crop, the question of eating the New Leafs was moot. Whatever I thought about the soundness of the process that had declared these potatoes safe didn't matter. Not just because I'd already had a few bites of New Leaf potato salad at the Youngs but also because Monsanto and the F.D.A. and the E.P.A. had long ago taken the decision of whether or not to eat a biotech potato out of my—out of all of our—hands. Chances are, I've eaten New Leafs already, at McDonald's or in a bag of Frito-Lay chips, though without a label there can be no way of knowing for sure.

So if I've probably eaten New Leafs already, why was it that I kept putting off eating mine? Maybe because it was August, and there were so many more-interesting fresh potatoes around—fingerlings with dense, luscious flesh, Yukon Golds that tasted as though they had been pre-buttered—that the idea of cooking with a bland commercial variety like the Superior seemed beside the point.

There was this, too: I had called Margaret Mellon at the Union of Concerned Scientists to ask her advice. Mellon is a molecular biologist and lawyer and a leading critic of biotech agriculture. She couldn't offer any hard scientific evidence that my New Leafs were unsafe, though she emphasized how little we know about the effects of Bt in the human diet. "That research simply hasn't been done," she said.

I pressed. Is there any reason I shouldn't eat these spuds?

"Let me turn that around. Why would you want to?"

It was a good question. So for a while I kept my New Leafs in a bag on the porch. Then I took the bag with me on vacation, thinking maybe I'd sample them there, but the bag came home untouched.

The bag sat on my porch till the other day, when I was invited to an end-of-summer potluck supper at the town beach. Perfect. I signed up to make a potato salad. I brought the bag into the kitchen and set a pot of water on the stove. But before it boiled I was stricken by this thought: I'd have to tell people at the picnic what they were eating. I'm sure (well, almost sure) the potatoes are safe, but if the idea of eating biotech food without knowing it bothered me, how could I possibly ask my neighbors to? So I'd tell them about the New Leafs—and then, no doubt, lug home a big bowl of untouched potato salad. For surely there would be other potato salads at the potluck and who, given the choice, was ever going to opt for the bowl with the biotech spuds?

So there they sit, a bag of biotech spuds on my porch. I'm sure they're absolutely fine. I pass the bag every day, thinking I really should try one, but I'm beginning to think that what I like best about these particular biotech potatoes—what makes them different—is that I have this choice. And until I know more, I choose not.   ■

■ *QUESTIONS FOR MAKING CONNECTIONS WITHIN THE READING* ■

1. Michael Pollan asserts at the opening of his essay that "the intricate industrial food chain that begins with seeds and ends on our dinner plates is in the throes of profound change." How is the food chain being changed by biotechnology? Why does Pollan believe this change to be "profound" rather than, say, "incremental," or just a part of the natural flow of progress?

2. Pollan discusses three governmental regulatory agencies: the USDA, the FDA, and the EPA. What do these agencies do? Why haven't any of these

agencies been able to control the growth of the biogenetic engineering industry?

3. At the end of "Playing God in the Garden," Pollan decides not to eat the New Leaf Superiors that he has grown in his own garden. Why doesn't he? Is there an answer to the question that is posed to Pollan at the end of his essay: That is, why would someone want to eat biogenetically engineered food?

■ *QUESTIONS FOR WRITING* ■

1. "Biological pollution will be the environmental nightmare of the 21st century." This is one of the darker pronouncements in Pollan's essay. What is biological pollution, and how does it differ from other forms of pollution? If it is safe to assume that there is no turning back and biogenetically engineered foods are with us to stay, what can be done to control the spread of biological pollution? Who is best equipped to address this problem: the individual, the local community, state or federal government, farmers, or food corporations?

2. Why does Pollan title his essay "Playing God in the Garden"? Does this title signal Pollan's disapproval of or his admiration for Monsanto's biotechnological research? Does research of this kind violate something sacred? Is it "unnatural" for humans to try to control their environment in this way? On the basis of what principle or principles can questions of this kind be answered?

■ *QUESTIONS FOR MAKING CONNECTIONS BETWEEN READINGS* ■

1. In "Another Look Back, and a Look Ahead," Edward Tenner describes what he terms "the revenge effects" of technology and the unintended consequences that follow from these acts of "revenge." Do you think that Tenner would be likely to share Pollan's concerns about genetic engineering? What "revenge effects" might we expect to see? While innovations like the New Leaf potato could affect the larger ecosystem in undesirable ways, is it possible that we might also reap benefits other than those intended by the Monsanto Corporation? What might those benefits be? On the basis of the evidence that Pollan provides, does it make sense to maintain "technological optimism" about the biotech industry?

2. In "What Does the Dreaded 'E' Word *Mean*, Anyway?" Stephen Jay Gould provides an extended discussion of what the word *evolution* means in the life sciences. Does genetic engineering, as Pollan describes it, disrupt the evolutionary process Gould describes? Does it participate in that evolu-

tionary process? Does Gould's argument suggest that we should be concerned about genetic engineering or that there is nothing to worry about? That is, does the definition of evolution used in the life sciences put to rest the concerns Pollan has raised about genetic engineering or does it heighten those concerns?

www **For additional suggestions about making connections between readings, visit the Link-O-Mat and More Sample Assignments at <www.newhum.com>.**

VIRGINIA POSTREL

THE CRITIC CAMILLE PAGLIA HAS described Virginia Postrel, the author of *The Future and Its Enemies* (1998), and *The Substance of Style* (2003), as "one of the smartest women in America [who] for years . . . has demonstrated her daunting gift for cutting-edge social and economic analysis as well as her admirable command of lean, lucid prose." Now one of the nation's most sought-after public speakers on contemporary developments involving business, technology, and culture, Postrel began her career as a journalist with reporting stints at *Inc.* and *The Wall Street Journal,* and then served as editor of the Libertarian magazine *Reason* from 1989 to 2000. Postrel has a column that appears regularly in the *New York Times* and maintains a highly trafficked weblog at <http://www.dynamist .com/weblog/index.html>, where she provides on-the-spot responses both to weighty and to seemingly trivial developments on the national and international news scene.

In *The Future and Its Enemies,* Postrel challenges those who see the spread of technology, the advent of the global economy, and the increasing influence of popular culture as threatening to undermine our nation's fundamental values and to imperil the country's future. Arguing against those on both the right and the left side of the political spectrum who see change in these areas as inevitably leading to decline, Postrel proposes an alternate, "dynamist" model in which the direction of progress is understood always to be unpredictable, open-ended, and contingent. She believes that embracing this model makes it possible to rethink everything from standard business practices to the search for truth and beauty. Postrel picks up this discussion in *The Substance of Style: How the Rise of Aesthetic Value Is Remaking Commerce, Culture, and Consciousness.* Here, she focuses on the liberating power that is afforded by individual choice in the marketplace. Bringing together her research into fields as diverse as fashion, real estate, politics, de-

Postrel, Virginia. "Surface and Substance." *The Substance of Style: How the Rise of Aesthetic Value Is Remaking Commerce, Culture, and Consciousness.* New York: HarperCollins, 2003.

Camille Paglia's quote is drawn from "How the Demos Lost the White House in Seattle," Salon.com, December 8, 1999 <http://www.salon.com/people/col/pagl/1999/12/08/ cp1208/print.html>. Additional biographical information drawn from Virginia Postrel's home page <http://www.vpostrel.com/contact/biography.html>.

sign, and economics, Postrel seeks to establish that the biologically driven search for beauty expresses itself in all these areas, profoundly influencing the future of human culture. To this way of thinking, a seemingly trivial matter, like a political candidate's hairstyle, is understood to have a deeper significance, and the nation's preoccupation with style is seen not as a cause for concern but as a sign that the future belongs to those who appreciate the driving power of the desire for beauty.

www **To learn more about Virginia Postrel and the theory of dynamism, please visit the Link-O-Mat at <www.newhum.com>.**

Surface and Substance

To the chagrin of designers, it's hard to measure the value of aesthetics, even in a straightforward business context. Often look and feel change at the same time as other factors, making the specific advantages of each new characteristic hard to isolate. Some companies, such as Apple Computer, are good at design but less adept at other business operations, muffling whatever success their fine styling might bring. And in many markets, competition tends to wipe out any hope of direct gain; the benefits of aesthetic investment go to consumers, not producers. In these cases, spending on aesthetics is just a cost of staying in business, not a profit-increasing investment.

We know that people generally don't want something that's otherwise worthless just because it comes in a pretty package and, conversely, that valuable goods and services are worth even more in attractive wrappings. Beyond these generalities, it's often hard to tell exactly how surface and substance interact. Occasionally, however, we get a fairly pure example of how much people value aesthetics.

In the early 1990s, Motorola came out with an updated version of its most popular pager. The new version had enhanced features, but what really made it special was the pager's colorful face. Managers bored with the old look had replaced basic black with bright green, making the new-and-improved pager unlike anything on the market in those pre-iMac days. Buyers thought the green pager was cool, and they were willing to pay a premium to get it. "The moral of the story, which I repeat many, many times to engineers, is that all the fancy-ass technological engineering in the world couldn't get us a nickel more for the product," says the former head of

Motorola's pager division. "But squirt-gun green plastic, which actually cost us nothing, could get us fifteen bucks extra per unit."[1]

Is this anecdote an innocent example of creativity in action, with a few laughs at the expense of technologically earnest, aesthetically clueless geeks? Or does the story provide a glimpse at just what's wrong with an age of look and feel—an era in which a bright plastic face is as important as real technological improvements? Should the success of the squirt-gun green pager give us the creeps?

An appealing pager face may delight customers, but it upsets many critics, who question the value of form without function. Surface and substance are opposites, they believe. Surface is irrelevant at best and often downright deceptive. If people pay more for mere aesthetics, goes the reasoning, then those consumers are being tricked. A squirt-gun green pager is simply not worth more than a black one. The two pagers have the same features! Paying more for green plastic is stupid, and only a dupe would do it. Function, not form, creates legitimate value.

The idea that surface itself has genuine value, for which consumers willingly pay extra when other characteristics are the same, appalls these critics. They "see that view as tantamount to advocating cannibalism of infants or something," says graphic designer Michael Bierut.[2] In one such case, he recalls, a critic berated a conference of designers "for creating meaningless distinctions between identical products like Coke and Pepsi. After some back and forth I asked him whether there was any inherent virtue in variety and beauty for their own sake. He sort of fumbled around and then more or less said that things could not exist 'for their own sake' and then invoked the example of Leni Riefenstahl's work for Hitler. That was as quick a ride from Pepsi to Nazis as I've had in a long time."

To such critics, form is dangerously seductive, because it allows the sensory to override the rational. An appealing package can make you believe that Nazis are good, or that colas are distinguishable. The very power of aesthetics makes its value suspect. "In advertising, packaging, product design, and corporate *identity*, the power of provocative surfaces speaks to the eye's mind, overshadowing matters of quality or substance," writes Stuart Ewen, the critic with whom Bierut sparred.[3] "Provocative surfaces" have no legitimate value of their own, he suggests, and they inevitably hide the truth. Contemplating the rise of streamlining in the 1930s, Ewen declares that "a century that began with a heady vision of moving beyond the ornament and uncovering the beauty of essential truth had rediscovered the lie." Aesthetics, in this view, is nothing more than a tool for manipulation and deceit.

Ewen is not alone. Sociologist Daniel Bell, in the twentieth-anniversary edition of his influential book *The Cultural Contradictions of Capitalism*, points to the prominence of cosmetics in department stores as a sign of the pervasive falsehood oiling "the machinery of gratification and instant desire" that is contemporary capitalism.[4] Women's fashion and fashion photography exemplify for Bell the same falsehood as advertising: "this task of selling illusions, the persuasions of the witches' craft," which he deems one of the contradictions that will ultimately bring down capitalism by eroding its Puritan foundation. To Bell, consumers are too susceptible to illusion and luxury, embracing hedonistic values that undermine bourgeois virtue. "The world of hedonism," he writes, "is the world of fashion, photography, advertising, television, travel. It is a world of make-believe."

Informing many such critiques is a naïve mid-twentieth-century view of how business operates: that producers can simply decree what consumers will buy, in a foolproof "circle of manipulation and retroactive need," as the Frankfurt School Marxists Theodor Adorno and Max Horkheimer put it in an influential 1944 essay.[5] In commercial products at least, such critics see ornament and variety not as goods that we value for their own sakes but as tools for creating false desire. Where the gullible public finds pleasure and meaning, the expert observer perceives deception. "That the difference between the Chrysler range and General Motors products is basically illusory strikes every child with a keen interest in varieties," declare Adorno and Horkheimer. "What connoisseurs discuss as good or bad points serve only to perpetuate the semblance of competition and range of choice."

In this view, modern commerce, because it appeals to consumers as visual, tactile creatures, is deceptive and decadent. The claim is unfalsifiable, since the more we try to proclaim the real value we attach to look and feel, the more we demonstrate just how duped we are. Legitimate value must come from objective characteristics—the taste (or, preferably, the nutritional value) of colas, the fuel-efficiency and power of cars, the cooking quality of toasters, the warmth of clothing—not through the associations and pleasures added by graphic imagery, streamlining, or fashionable cuts.

Although tinged with Marxism, this analysis is not all that different from the engineering vision of archcapitalist Scott McNealy of Sun Microsystems, who declared PowerPoint presentations wasteful because they consume more computer memory than handwritten slides—even though memory is abundant and virtually free. Hardheaded realists have no patience for the triviality of surfaces. If "content," rather than "packaging," is the only real value, then any attention to aesthetics furthers a lie, and resources spent on aesthetics are obviously wasted. This reasoning combines the oversimplified Maslovian idea, "aesthetics is a luxury," with a puritanical conviction that luxury is waste.

Just as the aesthetic imperative is not something only businesses feel, the fear that surfaces dissemble, distract, and distort is not limited to commerce and its critics. A conservative minister worries that evangelical churches, in their efforts to attract and hold members, have sacrificed the substance of preaching and prayer for mere spectacle. Today's services feature giant video screens, professionally lit stages, and high-energy rock bands. "The worship of God is increasingly presented as a spectator event of visual and sensory power rather than a verbal event in which we engage in a deep soul dialogue with the Triune God," he writes,[6] adding that

"Aesthetics, be they artistic or musical, are given a priority over holiness. More and more is seen, less and less is heard. There is a sensory feast but a famine of hearing. . . . Now there must be color, movement, audiovisual effects, or God cannot be known, loved, praised and trusted for his own sake."

Here, the "sensory feast" is less a lie than a distraction, diverting worshipers' attention and ministers' efforts from more important matters. As aesthetic expectations rise, in this view, congregants too easily forget the purpose of the spectacle. They become addicted to sensory stimulus, losing the ability to worship without it. They come to expect an experience of "color, movement, [and] audiovisual effects," an immersive environment rather than a cognitive exchange. As the aesthetic overrides the verbal, the feeling of worship overwhelms the message.

This critique reflects the widespread fear that surface and substance cannot coexist, that artifice inevitably detracts from truth. It is a fitting argument for a traditional Calvinist minister, whose dissenting forebears stripped churches of many of their aesthetic trappings. Before ornament was crime, it was idolatry. The whitewashed Puritan meetinghouse is as devoid of decoration as any modernist box.

You don't have to be a religious leader to worry that the spectacular may cancel out the verbal. The same anxieties arise even for pure entertainment. One sign of the "age of falsification," writes a critic, is "the blockbuster movie in which story line and plausibility are sacrificed to digital effects and Dolby Sound."[7] In this pessimistic vision, substance—"story line and plausibility"—will not survive the rise of surface. We cannot have movies that have both good stories and special effects. Our love of sensory delights is crowding out more cognitive pleasures. And it is creating a world of falsehoods.

Even worse, we fear, the aesthetic imperative is disguising who we really are. From Loos to Bell, and for centuries before them, critics of ornament have aimed some of their sharpest attacks at bodily decoration—at all the ways in which individuals create "false" selves and at the temptation to judge people by their appearances. In the seventeenth century, writers and preachers warned against women's makeup, which "takes the pencill out of God's hand," defying nature and divine will.[8] "What a contempt of God is this, to preferre the worke of thine owne finger to the worke of God?" exclaimed one writer condemning cosmetics.

The idea that unadorned faces and bodies are more virtuous and real than those touched by artifice persists to this day, usually in a secular, often political, form. In *The Beauty Myth*, Naomi Wolf advocates "civil rights for women that will entitle a woman to say that she'd rather look like herself than some 'beautiful' young stranger."[9] Wolf praises the "female identity" affirmed by women who refuse to alter their appearance with makeup, hair dye, or cosmetic surgery: "a woman's determination to show her loyalty—

in the face of a beauty myth as powerful as myths about white supremacy—to her age, her shape, her self, her life." Except those born with exceptional natural beauty, authenticity and aesthetics are, in this vision, inevitably at odds. Remaining true to oneself means eschewing artifice.

The preachers—secular and religious, contemporary and historical—tell us that surfaces are meaningless, misleading distractions of no genuine value. But our experience and intuition suggest otherwise. Viscerally, if not intellectually, we're convinced that style does matter, that look and feel add something important to our lives. We ignore the preachers and behave as if aesthetics does have real value. We cherish streamlined artifacts, unconcerned that they do not really move through space. We find spiritual uplift in pageantry and music. We prefer PowerPoint typefaces and color to plain, handwritten transparencies. We define our real selves as the ones wearing makeup and high heels. We judge people, places, and things at least in part by how they look. We care about surfaces.

But we are not only aesthetic consumers. We are also producers, subject to the critical eyes of others. And that makes us worry.

We worry that other people will judge us by our flawed appearances, rather than our best selves. We worry that minding our looks will detract from more important, or more enjoyable, pursuits. We worry that we will lack the gifts or skills to measure up. And we worry that our stylistic choices will be misinterpreted. Businesses making pagers, creating sales brochures, and designing trade show booths face all the same problems, but without the emotional anguish that comes when the surface and substance are personal.

"If you look like you spend too much time on your clothes, there are people who will assume that you haven't put enough energy into your mind," says an English professor who advises aspiring humanities scholars on their appearance and manners.[10] Still, she warns that the wrong clothes can be catastrophic: "If you don't know how to dress, then what else don't you know? Do you know how to advise students or grade papers? The clothes *are* part of the judgment of the mind." Even to people ostensibly concerned only with substance, surface matters. And getting it right is hard.

Speaking to Yale University's 2001 graduating class, Hillary Rodham Clinton, just a few months into her first term as a U.S. senator, bundled these anxieties into a bitter joke. "The most important thing that I have to say today is that hair matters," she said.[11] "This is a life lesson my family did not teach me, Wellesley and Yale failed to instill in me: the importance of your hair. Your hair will send very important messages to those around you. It will tell people who you are and what you stand for. What hopes and dreams you have for the world . . . and especially what hopes and dreams you have for your hair. Likewise, your shoes. But really, more your hair. So, to sum up. Pay attention to your hair. Because everyone else will."

Beneath the humor is a sense of betrayal. *Why are you so obsessed with my hair? Why won't you take me seriously?* It wasn't supposed to be this way, not for ambitious public women. Hair is just surface stuff. And surfaces aren't supposed to be important, at least not in a postfeminist era in which women can be more than decorators and decoration. Yet Hillary Clinton's hair is so famous that there used to be a Web site, hillaryshair.com, devoted to its many changing styles.[12] Countless column inches and television minutes have chronicled her various hairdos and probed their meaning, seeking those "very important messages." Clinton is a polarizing figure, so her enemies and her allies have identified radically different messages. But both camps have opined about the meaning of her hair.

Taken literally, Clinton's joke offers another reading, equally marked by betrayal. *Somebody should have warned me. My education ripped me off.* Looks matter, and Wellesley and Yale and the Rodham family sent Hillary into the world without teaching her how to manage her appearance. They instead told her that serious people, especially serious women, don't waste precious attention on anything as trivial as hair. Inculcated with the idea that surfaces are false and unimportant, she lacked the presentation skills for an aesthetic age and had to learn them in public.

The joke simultaneously expresses three contradictory beliefs: that appearance matters and should be given due attention (the unironic reading); that appearance shouldn't matter (the ironic reading); and that appearance matters for its own aesthetic pleasures rather than for any message it sends ("what hopes and dreams you have for your hair"). These sentiments are hardly original or unique to Hillary Clinton. Most of us hold all three views at least some of the time. Untangling them—figuring out when each is true and how they relate to each other—is essential to understanding how to live in our age of look and feel.

As emotionally satisfying as it may sometimes be, declaring surfaces false and worthless is merely another form of deception. That sort of cheap dismissal not only ignores obvious realities. It also makes us a little crazy. Rather than deny that aesthetics conveys both pleasure and meaning—and, thus, has value to human beings—we need to better understand how pleasure and meaning relate to each other and to other, nonaesthetic values. What is the substance of surface?

When they aren't denouncing surfaces as lies and illusion, cultural critics typically have one explanation for why we devote time, attention, and, most of all, money to aesthetics: It's all about status. The intrinsic pleasures of look and feel are irrelevant. We're simply attracted to anything that helps us compete for recognition and dominance.

In *Luxury Fever*, a self-described "book about waste," economist Robert Frank treats the aesthetic ratchet effect as entirely status-driven.[13] We want ever-more appealing things because our neighbors have them. True enough. But in Frank's world, finding out that our neighbors are enjoying some new luxury functions only as a competitive spur, not as information about what's possible. We aren't happy for the neighbors. We don't want to share the same pleasures. We don't identify with them and want to imitate their taste. We just want to show them up. To Frank, rising expectations reflect only a desperate struggle to keep up with the Joneses.

Larger, better appointed homes are not, in this view, an enjoyable effect of prosperity but the outcome of a race to have the biggest and best on the block—a race that can have only one winner. We buy fancy clothes and luxury furnishings because we want to "stand out from the crowd," not because we like these things. Hence Frank's argument that "if, within each social group, everyone were to spend a little less on shoes, the same people who stand out from the crowd now would continue to do so. And because that outcome would free up resources to spend in other ways, people would have good reasons to prefer it."[14]

The argument depends on the conviction that we do not want those expensive shoes or large homes because of any intrinsic qualities. Frank assumes that we do not value the luxuries themselves—the soft leather of the shoes, the smooth granite countertop, the sculptural lines of the car, the drape and fit of the jacket—but just want to stand out, or at least not look bad, compared to other people. He also imagines only rivalry, not identification, a desire to stand out from the crowd, never to fit in with our friends. In Frank's world, aesthetics provides no pleasure and only the most desiccated and antisocial meaning.

Not surprisingly, he sees aesthetic competition as almost entirely wasteful, making everyone worse off. "If I buy a custom-tailored suit for my job interview," Frank writes, "I reduce the likelihood that others will land the same job; and in the process, I create an incentive for them to spend more than they planned on their own interview suits. . . . In situations like these, individual spending decisions are the seeds of a contagious process." In this view, we would all benefit if men could agree to wear cheap, ugly suits and spend their money on more important, more substantial things—a vision of fashion not unlike the British Utility scheme that took the ornament out of furniture and declared bookcases more essential than easy chairs.

Why, then, is the process contagious? Frank thinks it's just a matter of status-oriented one-upmanship, focused almost entirely on how much things cost. But consider why Frank's ideal world would require a cartel, in which everyone agreed to follow a drab standard. What would happen if every restaurant looked like a functional school cafeteria—but one establishment started to decorate with colored paint and table linens, background music, and special lighting? What if every product came in a plain black-and-white box—but one company invested in graphics and color? What if everyone wore drab Mao suits—but one person dressed with color, tailoring, and flair? People would, of course, be drawn to the aesthetic deviant, even though that nonconformity might well offend the reigning status hierarchy.

This thought experiment suggests something at work besides status and one-upmanship. Sensory pleasure works to commercial and personal advantage because aesthetics has intrinsic value. People seek it out, they reward those who offer new-and-improved pleasures, and they identify with those who share their tastes. If a nice suit helps someone win a job, that's because the interviewer finds it more enjoyable to talk with someone dressed that way. The aesthetic ratchet effect, whether it demands deodorant and clean hair or well-cut clothes and attractive shoes, rewards what we find pleasing to the senses. But there's more at work than Frank's money-oriented status pursuit. If you show up for an interview in a custom-tailored suit only to find your prospective boss wearing khakis and a polo shirt, the mismatch in aesthetic identities will cancel out any imagined status gains. You and the boss obviously have different ideas of what's enjoyable and appropriate.

Status competition is part of human life, of course. But cultural analysts like Frank are so determined to see status as the only possible value, and money as the only source of status, that they often ignore the very evidence they cite. Frank writes that "the status symbol of the 1990s has been the restaurant stove."[15] Fancy stoves are, in his opinion, entirely about keeping up with the neighbors' kitchens. To bolster his argument, he quotes a woman who owns a $7,000 stove, despite rarely cooking at home. Does she say she felt social pressure to buy an overpriced appliance? Does she say she wanted to stand out from the crowd? No, she describes the stove as a *work of art:* "You think of it as a painting that makes the kitchen look good." The supposedly damning quotation demonstrates the opposite of what Frank maintains: The woman sees the stove primarily not as a status symbol but as an aesthetic pleasure.

The manufacturers intended as much. "I was convinced that if I built something beautiful and powerful and safe, there were people out there who'd buy it," says the founder of the Viking Range Corp.[16] The company admits that most buyers are "look, don't cook" customers. Even an employee who was given a range says she never uses it, preferring to microwave something quick. "But I love looking at my Viking," she says. "Sometimes, I turn it on just to feel its power." Obviously the stoves serve something besides functional needs. But that "something" is more complex and sensual than status, combining a vision of an ideal life of home cooking with the immediate pleasures of beauty and power. Whatever status a fancy range conveys comes less from its cost than from its ability to show off the owner's discerning eye.

Even analysts who do not view luxury goods as waste do not necessarily credit the goods' intrinsic sensory appeal. In *Living It Up*, a mostly sympathetic analysis of what he calls "opuluxe," James Twitchell examines the spread of luxury goods, which he describes as "objects as rich in meaning as they are low in utility."[17] Opuluxe demonstrates the openness of today's social structure, he argues. Anyone can buy into the signs of wealth, so "making it" is no longer a matter of joining a socially exclusive club. Twitchell thus sees the profusion of luxury goods as tacky but benign.

Like Frank, however, Twitchell has a hard time noticing any qualities beyond status badges and advertising-created brand personas. And, like Frank, he unconsciously offers clues that more is going on. He tells us, for instance, that in the Beverly Hills Armani store, "I saw something I hadn't seen before. I saw customers patting the clothes, fondling the fabrics, touching the buttons. . . . It was like being in a petting zoo."[18] People pet Armani clothes because the fabrics feel so good. Those clothes attract us as visual, tactile creatures, not because they are "rich in meaning" but because they are rich in pleasure. The garments' utility includes the way they look and feel.

Twitchell's twenty-two-year-old daughter, Liz, accompanies him on his tour of Rodeo Drive, pretending to be a spoiled daddy's girl being bribed with presents to stay in college. This false persona reflects Twitchell's preconceptions about why people buy luxury goods, and what sort of people those buyers are. Only a superficial young woman, he assumes, would be wowed by luxury, not his intellectual Liz.

After a day at the act, however, Liz finally breaks down in tears, forcing the pair to make an abrupt exit from Tiffany. She explains why: "I believe myself to be everything the woman in Tiffany thought I wasn't: intelligent, self-sufficient, not given over to the whimsical spending of large amounts of money."[19] But Liz is sucked in. She wants the stuff her father is pretending he might buy for her. And she wants it not so she can impress anyone else or feel affiliated with prestigious brands. She wants those luxuries because they are aesthetically appealing, because they are, in a word, *beautiful*.

"Watching the woman in Armani try on the $20,000 beaded dress, I was momentarily entranced—and more than slightly jealous," she writes after the experiment collapses.

> The stuff was just so BEAUTIFUL, and when I looked down at my Old Navy sweater, I couldn't help but feel a bit wanting. . . . I wanted to leave Rodeo Drive for the same reason I often avoid fashion magazines: not because I don't care about such trivial stuff, but because I DO care, and when I look at these beautiful things, I'm left with an aching feeling of desire and a slight dissatisfaction with my current life. Luxury is incredibly powerful, and it gets to almost all of us, even when we're told it's meaningless.

The status critique does not actually say luxury is meaningless. To the contrary, the critics' usual argument is that such goods are *only* about meaning; they are "objects as rich in meaning as they are low in utility." The status critique sees only two possible sources of value: function and meaning; and it reduces meaning to a single idea: "I'm better than you." It denies the existence or importance of aesthetic pleasure and the many meanings and associations that can flow from that pleasure.

Luxuries, in this view, offer no intrinsic appeal beyond their social signals. But only superficial people, filled with status-anxiety and insecure about their own worth, would care about those meanings. By circular reasoning, then, to be attracted to such goods is to be a superficial person. So a serious young woman like Liz must avoid contact with fashion magazines and luxurious clothes—not simply because she would ache at the unattainable, but because wanting those things would call her identity into question. Her desire would imply that she's the sort of superficial, insecure person who cares about "such trivial stuff." To affirm that she's a young woman of substance, she must ignore the appeal of surfaces.

If surfaces are "trivial stuff," surfaces that change for no good reason are even less worthy. Hence, those who see aesthetics as "illusion" and "make-believe" are particularly vitriolic toward fashion. *Fashion* in this sense applies not just to clothing and related products but to anything whose aesthetic form evolves continuously, from typefaces and car bodies to musical styles and popular colors. Fashion is the process by which form seems exhausted and then refreshed, without regard to functional improvements.

Critics often portray fashion as entirely the product of commercial manipulation. "Typewriters and telephones came out in a wide range of colors in 1956, presumably to make owners dissatisfied with their plain old black models," sniffed the influential social critic Vance Packard in his 1957 book *The Hidden Persuaders*.[20] Nearly a half century later, many people still imagine that the world works the way Packard portrayed it. Aesthetic changes, in his view, were merely forms of deception, ways of creating artificial obsolescence. Packard offered no evidence that the colorful typewriters and telephones performed any worse than the plain old black models; rather, he objected to purely aesthetic upgrades, deeming them wasteful.

Today an engineer similarly condemns the latest iMac for using behind-the-curve chips and mocks buyers who've "been seduced by the case plastic":

> After people get over the *oh, cool!* and start really looking at this, the only real reason for getting it will be to impress people, just as was the case with the Cube, because what is *really* innovative about this is the case. And you can't actually get any work done with a fancy case[21]

Missing the effects of the technological progress he sees as legitimate innovation, the engineer doesn't consider the trade-offs. For a long time, ever-greater computing power was indeed what people looked for in a new machine. But computers are so capable these days that most customers don't need the absolutely fastest chip. To someone who doesn't plan to tax the machine's processing speed, a beautiful case may be worth more than cutting-edge technology, not just for status ("to impress people") but for personal enjoyment. At a given price, adding style will be more valuable, at least to some people, than adding power. True, you can't get any more work done with a fancy case, but you can enjoy the same work more.

From the buyer's point of view, greater aesthetic variety in an equally functional product is an unequivocal improvement, possibly (as with the green pager) one for which consumers will gladly pay a premium. If the goal is happiness rather than expert-determined "efficiency," form is itself a function. Pleasure is as real as meaning or usefulness, and its value is as subjective. Of course, aesthetic experimentation does not preclude other improvements. A new pager may have both enhanced features and a stylish face.

Fashion exists because novelty is itself an aesthetic pleasure. Even when the general form of something has reached an enduring ideal—the layout of book pages, the composition of men's suits, the structure of automobiles, the shapes of knives, forks, and spoons—we crave variation within that classic type. Colors and shapes that looked great a couple of years ago begin to seem dull. We're attracted to fresher, newer forms. The same never-ending tinkering that gives us more functional, better-looking toilet brushes also gives us new looks to replace the old.

The changes are usually incremental, moving gradually in one direction over a long period until that form's aesthetic possibilities are exhausted and something new suddenly feels right. That new look has often evolved without much notice, also building slowly, so that what seems like an abrupt shift actually represents a switch from one incremental process to another.

Consider a story told by Anne Bass, a wealthy patron of the arts and haute couture.[22] She describes her taste in clothes as classic, not "so much embellishment as beautiful lines, beautiful tailoring, things that are constructed in clever ways." In the flamboyant 1980s, her fashion choices were relatively restrained, but she did buy evening clothes "that had a bit of the 'costume' about them." Bass recalls the moment when those clothes suddenly felt obsolete. In August 1989, she attended a Paris fashion show and dinner given by Giorgio Armani:

> I remember wearing a Saint Laurent evening suit that paired a heavily embroidered jacket with a tangerine charmeuse sarong, and that was the last time I recall putting on something that made that kind of statement. Because, suddenly, that night, it felt completely wrong. It felt like Armani was modern, was what was happening. Before that night, I didn't really get Armani. I thought he was a nonevent. But I remember that evening, that party, as the end of an era. . . . I don't think it was long afterward that I opened my closet in New York, and noticed that everything was either beige or black.

The shift Bass observed had been going on for some time. Otherwise no one would have been interested in attending an Armani event in the first place. The designer had in fact come to prominence in the early 1980s. But Bass and her fashion-savvy friends could not have known in advance when one man's vision of what clothes should look like would go from a stylistic "nonevent" to a newly dominant aesthetic. Exactly what sort of variation will seem appealing at a given time is uncertain and can be discovered only through trial and error.

The fashion process is not mechanical but contingent; which changes will fit the moment depends on a host of unarticulated desires and unnoticed influences, making shifts hard to predict. A fashion writer refers to "fashion's X-factor, the unknown quantity that makes an item seem hot to a consumer."[23] The decrees of would-be style makers—that mauve is back but in a "more sophisticated" form, that gray is the "new black," that velvet furniture is in again—suggest a sort of dictatorial authority. But this rhetoric is just a combination of bravado and best guesses. The sales racks are full of aesthetic experiments that failed to capture the public imagination, and every such item is an argument against the notion that authorities can dictate style. Now more than ever, that is not how fashion works.

Besides, there is more to fashion than profit-seeking "built-in obsolescence." We find fashion patterns in goods for which there is no commercial market. Historian Anne Hollander notes that fashion in clothing has existed for eight hundred years, centuries longer than the apparel business. "The shifty character of what looks right is not new, and was never a thing deliberately created to impose male will on females, or capitalist will on the population, or designers' will on public taste," she writes.[24] "Long before the days of industrialized fashion, stylistic motion in Western dress was enjoying a profound emotional importance, giving a dynamically poetic visual cast to people's lives, and making Western fashion hugely compelling all over the world." Pleasure, not manipulation, drives changes in look and feel.

Even intangible, noncommercial "goods" exhibit similar patterns. Sociologist Stanley Lieberson has studied how tastes in children's names change over time.[25] Nobody runs ads to convince parents to choose *Emily* or *Joshua* for their newborns. No magazine editors authoritatively dictate that "*Ryan* is the new *Michael*." But names still shift according to fashion. Name choices, like clothing choices, are influenced by the desire to be different but not too different; the ideal balance varies from person to person. Like designers experimenting with new ideas in ignorance of what their competitors are trying, parents have to choose their babies' names without knowing exactly what other parents are choosing. The result is a complex, often surprising, dynamic. Parents frequently find that the name they "just liked" is suddenly widely popular, expressing aesthetic preferences that are somehow in the air. Contrary to common assumptions about how fashion works, Lieberson finds that names don't trickle down in a simple way from high-income, well-educated parents to lower-income, less-educated parents. Newly popular names tend to catch on with everyone at about the same time.

External influences, such as the names of celebrities or fictional characters, do play a role in what's popular. But cause and effect are complicated. Fictional characters don't just publicize possible names; their creators, like new parents, select those names from the current milieu. And whether a famous name spreads partly depends on internal, purely aesthetic factors. Harrison Ford, Arnold Schwarzenegger, and Wesley Snipes are all action stars, but their stardom hasn't translated into millions of little Harrisons, Arnolds, or Wesleys—in part because their names just don't *sound* all that appealing.

What does sound appealing itself changes over time, as particular phonemes go in and out of style. In recent years, for instance, the ending *schwa* sound has been popular for girls' names, such as Hannah, Samantha, Sarah, and Jessica; in the era of Susan and Kimberly other endings seemed equally feminine. African-American parents are more likely than whites to invent completely new names for their babies; those unique names follow clear patterns that indicate gender, and they show fashion cycles in the popularity of component syllables. *La-* used to be a popular first syllable for black girls' names. Now *-eisha* is a popular ending. Names associated with living old people often seem dated, like out-of-style clothing; popular names from generations who have passed on, by contrast, may seem classic and resonant, like vintage fashion. Even in this completely noncommercial context, we see fashion cycles of distinctiveness, popularity, and obsolescence, driven by the quest for aesthetic satisfaction. That satisfaction combines purely sensory components with meaningful associations.

Whether for names or clothes, fashion reflects the primacy of individual taste over inherited custom. The freer people feel to choose names they like, rather than, say, names of relatives or saints, the more rapidly baby names go through fashion cycles. As Hollander observes, "Fashion has its own manifest virtue, not unconnected with the virtues of individual freedom and uncensored imagination that still underlie democratic ideals."[26] Fashion pervades open, dynamic societies. Through markets, media, and migration, such societies offer more outlets for creativity, more sources of new aesthetic ideas, and more chances for individuals to find and adopt the forms that please them. Our age of look and feel reflects the increasing openness of our social and economic life, which both enhances and takes advantage of aesthetic abundance. As a result, we see fashion appearing in new areas, with much greater fluidity of form. The more influence accorded individual preferences, the greater the importance of fashion—and, in many cases, the more accelerated its pace.

This dynamic perturbs critics. Static, customary forms, they suggest, are more authentic. Thus Daniel Bell worries about the rise of syncretism, "the jumbling of styles in modern art, which absorbs African masks or Japanese prints into its modes of depicting spatial perceptions; or the merging of Oriental and Western religions, detached from their histories, in a modern meditative consciousness. Modern culture is defined by this extraordinary freedom to ransack the world storehouse and to engorge any and every style it comes upon."[27] And Ewen, again equating style with illusion, writes that "modern style speaks to a world where change is the rule of the day, where one's place in the social order is a matter of perception, the product of diligently assembled illusions."[28] Although he might recoil from the implications, Ewen seems to assume that "one's place in the social order" would be more valid if it were determined not by perception and individual effort but by something more impersonal and objective—bloodlines, perhaps, or skin color.

Even when he cites the advantages of the shift to a more open society, Ewen casts it in terms of false identity: "On the one hand, style speaks for the rise of a democratic society, in which who one wishes to become is often seen as more consequential than who one is. On the other hand, style speaks for a society in which coherent meaning has fled to the hills, and in which drift has provided a context of continual discontent."[29] This analysis scorns the search for individual satisfaction and self-definition—the pursuit of happiness—as no more than a source of "continual discontent." The traditionalist conservative argument against the disruptions of an open social and economic order has transmogrified into a left-wing attack on fashion.

Genuine value, such critics suggest, ought to reflect something more permanent and substantial than ever-shifting tastes. The ephemeral nature of style, in this view, confirms its fundamental falsehood. "As style reached out to a more broadly defined 'middle class' of consumers" in the nineteenth century, Ewen complains,

> the value of objects was less and less associated with workmanship, material quality, and rarity, and more and more derived from the abstract and increasingly malleable factor of aesthetic appeal. Durable signs of style were being displaced by signs that were ephemeral: shoddy goods with elaborately embossed surfaces, advertising cards, product labels. If style had once been a device by which individuals tried to surround themselves with symbols of perpetuity, now it was becoming something of the moment, to be employed for effect, and then displaced by a new device of impression.

Value in this view should approximate static, universal standards instead of fluctuating with fickle individual preferences. Hence Ewen's dislike of the "abstract and malleable factor of aesthetic appeal," which is all too subjective and personal.

The old "symbols of perpetuity" were in fact products of a traditional, fairly static social order. These goods demonstrated inherited social position; only a family that had maintained wealth and rank over generations would possess homes, portraits, furnishings, or silverware with the patina of age. You could show off your grandfather's portrait or your great-grandmother's silver only if your family was in fact one of long-standing status. Surface patina demonstrated social substance. As anthropologist Grant McCracken notes, "The patina of an object allows it to serve as the medium for a vitally important status message. The purpose of this message is not to claim status. It is to verify status claims."[30] Arrivistes could be identified by the shine of their possessions, avoiding the sixteenth-century fear of the "tailor or barber [who] in the excess of apparel [would] counterfeit and be like a gentleman."[31] (Clothes, rather than acquiring patina, wear out over time; that's why they're more subject to fashion and why status-oriented societies try to impose sumptuary laws.)

The ephemeral nineteenth-century merchandise that Ewen condemns spread new aesthetic pleasures to people of limited means. Made possible by new forms of production and distribution, these goods were cheap in both senses of the word. Embossed paper doodads might be short-lived, but they were also accessible and fun. They had little to do with social status and much to do with personal enjoyment. A world of pretty product labels is more delightful than a world of generic barrels, and it is a world in which style no longer belongs only to an elite. These new and shifting forms of aesthetic pleasure befit a fluid social order.

Fashion itself can, of course, be a source of status. As anyone who has been a teenager knows, the right style can determine who's in, while the wrong look can mean social oblivion. Early-twentieth-century social critics worried about the social pressures created by newly affordable ready-to-wear clothes when respectability depended greatly on the proper appearance. Writing in 1929, one essayist complained that "crops may fail, silkworms suffer blight, weavers may strike, tariffs may hamper, but the mass-gesture of the feminine neck bending to the yoke of each new season's fashion goes on."[32] Garment makers, she complained, made sure "that last year's wardrobe shall annually be made as obsolete as possible," placing a severe financial burden on poor women who wanted to look current. Here is an earlier version of the Packard and Ewen critiques: Fashion represents the tyranny of commercial manipulation.

Such critics exaggerated both year-to-year fashion shifts and the response of consumers; as we know from survey data, families with moderate incomes did not own large or frequently changing wardrobes. But these criticisms expressed genuine anxiety. By making fashionable clothes available to people who a generation earlier would have had no such choice, the apparel industry increased not just pleasure but aspiration. And with aspiration came, inevitably, the disappointment of limits. In industrialized countries, working women had access to new forms of self-expression and adornment, the sorts of aesthetic pleasures once reserved for the social elite. But, like Liz Twitchell in Beverly Hills, they would also ache for the unattainable.

We do not know, of course, that traditional peasant women experienced no such pangs. Folktales like "Cinderella" suggest that they did. What was different by the nineteenth century was that social critics cared, and that fashionable attire had taken on symbolic importance for average people. Dressing in style was a new sort of personal achievement, especially if you weren't rich enough to buy someone else's good taste, and it was a source of social prestige. Self-presentation had become a valuable skill, at all social levels.

That is all the more true today, and the task is far more difficult. Although the financial cost of putting on a good appearance has dropped, the trickiness of the challenge has increased. As Hillary Clinton can testify, the more technological and social choices we have about how we look, the more ways we can go wrong—and the more meaning people are likely to read into our choices. The challenges of fashion have also spread to previously fashion-free areas of life. When law firms eschewed graphic design and followed long-standing customs, no one judged them by their letterhead. Now they have to think about the connotations of typefaces and logos; sticking to the plain old style is itself an indicative choice. "Fashion," observes Hollander, "is a perpetual test of character and self-knowledge, as well as taste, whereas traditional dress"—or any other custom-bound aesthetic expression—"is not."[33]

The "character" Hollander sees tested by fashion's demands is not moral character but a combination of self-awareness, confidence, taste, and affiliation. How we deal with fashion's flux suggests something about our inner life. Can we enjoy its pleasures, using them to create an aesthetic identity that reflects who we are, including what we enjoy? Can we find a happy balance between look and feel and other values? Or do we feel compelled either to subordinate the rest of our life to appearance or to ignore appearance altogether—to treat look and feel either as the ultimate value or as entirely without value?

Much of the rhetoric surrounding appearance offers this false choice. From well-intended mothers to scathing social commentators, authorities tell us that surfaces are "meaningless." That might be true if they meant that the value of aesthetics lies in its own pleasures, not in what it says about something else. But that's not at all what they intend. Authorities call aesthetics "meaningless" to suggest that it is worthless and unimportant, that it doesn't matter. Thus, Liz Twitchell says she's been taught that luxury is "meaningless," so its pleasures shouldn't affect her. Ewen excoriates graphic designers for creating "meaningless distinctions" between products, denying the value of aesthetic pleasures and associations. "I try to help her not judge herself against the prevailing criteria of how she's supposed to be," says a father whose thirteen-year-old daughter thinks she's too skinny. "I tell her all this is meaningless."[34]

When a father tells his teenage daughter that looks are "meaningless," he is not assuring her that she's attractive or will become so over time. He is saying that she's loved and valued for her other traits, regardless of how she looks—a loving but irrelevant affirmation. Her looks do mean something important to her. They don't match her sense of who she is or would like to be. By changing the subject, her father is inadvertently agreeing that she looks bad, exacerbating her sense of failure. We do not respond similarly to teenagers who wish they were stronger, more musical, or better in school; we coach them on how to build on their natural gifts. Yet somehow we believe that looks are different, that appearance must be worth either everything or nothing.

Denying that we care about appearance for its own sake leads us to exaggerate its deeper significance, in order to justify our natural interest. Consider some of the commentary surrounding the 2000 election. When Florida Secretary of State Katherine Harris appeared with heavy makeup, wags compared her to a drag queen and Cruella De Vil.[35] Al Gore got similar treatment after he wore bad makeup in his first debate with George W. Bush. Commentators called him, among other things, "Herman Munster doing a bad Ronald Reagan impression"[36] and "a big, orange, waxy, wickless candle."[37]

In both cases, commentators appealed to their readers' interest in how other people look. To give their criticisms a respectable mask, however, many pundits treated these cosmetic problems as symbols of more serious flaws. One interpreted Harris's blue eye shadow as evidence that "she failed to think for herself" and declared that "one wonders how this Republican woman, who can't even use restraint when she's wielding a mascara wand, will manage to use it and make sound decisions in this game of partisan one-upmanship."[38] Amid the Florida recount, a Gore critic harked back to his excessive makeup to suggest that he was a phony: "While Gore yammered about [the voters'] 'will,' it was clear to my houseplants that the man who looks like he raids Katherine Harris' pancake makeup supply was really gloating about the Florida Supreme Court decision in his favor."[39]

These commentators went well beyond the idea that self-presentation may say something about the "judgment of the mind," reflecting a person's self-awareness and taste. They damned Harris and Gore not for bad judgment but for bad character. They invoked the old tradition that equates cosmetics with deception and decadence. Someone who wears a lot of makeup, they suggested, is not to be trusted.

In fact, someone who wears a lot of makeup may just have a sunburn (Gore) or out-of-date style (Harris). Surface may not say much at all about substance. Being able to separate the two is the first step toward avoiding the deception that critics of aesthetics so fear. But to do so we have to admit that aesthetics has value in and of itself instead of pretending that it is "meaningless" or trying to justify our interest in looks by freighting them with unwarranted symbolism. All other things being equal, we prefer beauty, just as we prefer intelligence, charm, eloquence, or talent. But beauty can coexist with stupidity, rudeness, or cruelty. All other things may not be equal. What's true for people is true for places and things. All other things being equal, we prefer attractive computers. That does not mean, as Apple discovered with its beautiful Cube, that we will ignore price and performance to get aesthetics.[40]

The challenge is to learn to accept that aesthetic pleasure is an autonomous good, not the highest or the best but one of many plural, sometimes conflicting, and frequently unconnected sources of value. Not all sources of value, including aesthetic and moral worth, line up in one-to-one correspondence. Rhetoric that treats aesthetic quality as a mark of goodness and truth—or as a sign of evil and deception—is profoundly misleading.

The values of design itself—function, meaning, and pleasure—can exist independently of each other. It's incorrect to argue in defense of Wal-Mart's big-box stores that "a Wal-Mart is 'ugly' only because we either ignore or devalue what it does best."[41] The value of Wal-Mart's design comes from its function. Ugliness diminishes pleasure, a different good. Function may coexist with pleasure, and increasingly it does, but it does not have to. Saying a store is ugly does not mean it has no value, only that its value must lie outside aesthetics. Just as we may value a green pager more highly than a black one entirely because of its looks, we may value Wal-Mart for its convenience and efficiency, while acknowledging that it's ugly. And we can tell nothing about the moral worth of either the green pager or the store by judging its looks.

A bad person can be beautiful or create beautiful things. A good person can be ugly or make bad art. Goodness does not create or equal beauty. The problem with Leni Riefenstahl's films is not that they're aesthetically powerful—that achievement is, considered in isolation, valuable. But aesthetic quality does not trump or cancel out other considerations. Beauty is not a moral defense, merely an autonomous value. Just as a plain face does not make a young woman bad, so artistic achievement does not justify serving an evil cause. Aesthetic pleasure and moral virtue are independent goods. They may complement or contradict each other, or operate entirely independently. Colas are neither good nor evil, and neither is their packaging. The packaging design adds pleasure and meaning, and thus value, to morally neutral products.

When evil deeds come to be associated with otherwise attractive images, the images lose their attraction. Meaning arises from association, in this case canceling out pleasure. A black swastika in a circle of white on a red background may be graphically appealing, but we do not evaluate its form independently of its historic meaning. For two generations after Hitler, well-muscled Nordic men looked like villains, not Adonises. Only recently, under the influence of gay aesthetics, has that ideal of masculine beauty begun to lose its Nazi connotations. Riefenstahl's artistic achievements, and her images, are permanently polluted by the cause she served. Film students may study her techniques, but they do not forget or forgive her moral failings. Form has its own power and worth, but it does not inevitably trump content. Aesthetics is not a psychological superweapon, capable of blinding us to all other values.

When terrorists slammed two passenger jets into the World Trade Center on September 11, 2001, Michael Bierut had his own moment of Nazis-to-Pepsi self-doubt. He was in London and returned home to Manhattan a few days after the attack. "As a designer," he wrote me, "I am still reeling from the images of 9/11."[42] The act had been horrifying, but the images it created could not have been better designed: "The timing of the collisions, the angle of the second plane, the colors of the explosions, the slow-motion collapsing of the towers: could the terrorists ever dream how nightmarishly vivid this would be to the vast viewing audience?"

Amid the trauma of mid-September, this terrible juxtaposition—striking images in the service of death—recalled all the attacks ever made on surface for its own sake, and on the designers who create surface appeal. If an event so awful could look so vivid, even beautiful in a purely formal sense, how could we trust aesthetic pleasure? How could designers like Bierut justify their work, except when surface serves some grander substance? The attack, wrote Bierut, "makes me think about all the times I've worked on purposeless assignments and put meaningless content into beautiful packages. I will not approach my work the same way from now on."

He knew better. The destruction of the World Trade Center was not a carefully composed movie scene, designed to arouse pity and terror within the safe frame of fiction. It was the all-too-real murder of thousands. It was entirely substance. The attack was not packaging, not surface, not performance art. It had both meaning and political purpose. The striking images produced led viewers not to praise but to condemn the attackers who created them. Only those who embraced the murderers' cause rejoiced in those images. Aesthetics did not prove a superweapon, justifying slaughter. To the contrary, the media images that followed were attempts to capture the events—and the horror and grief—of the day. Those images were valuable because they could say more than words. But the images were not the act itself.

In the horror of the moment, Bierut had forgotten the meaning and value of his work, falling into the puritanical mind-set that denies the value of aesthetic pleasure and seeks always to link it with evil. To wrap meaningless, as opposed to vicious, content in beautiful packaging does no harm. To the contrary, such creativity enriches the world and affirms the worth of the individuals whose pleasure it serves. Colas are not genocide.

Bierut soon had second thoughts. "One of the signatures of any repressive regime," he wrote the following day, "is their need to control not just meaningful differences—the voices of dissent, for instance—but ostensibly 'meaningless' ones as well, like dress. It will take some time for people to realize that creating the difference between Coke and Pepsi is not just an empty pastime but one of many signs of life in a free society."[43] The Afghan women who risked the Taliban's prisons to paint their faces and style their hair in underground beauty shops, and who celebrated the liberation of Kabul by coloring their nails with once-forbidden polish, would agree.[44] Surface may take on meaning, but it has a value all its own. ∎

NOTES

1. Iain Morris, quoted in Eric Nee, "Open Season on Carly Fiorina," *Fortune*, July 23, 2001, p. 120.

2. Michael Bierut interview with the author, November 11, 2000, and e-mail to the author, May 9, 2001.

3. Stuart Ewen, *All Consuming Images*, pp. 22, 149.

4. Daniel Bell, *The Cultural Contradictions of Capitalism*, 2nd ed. (New York: Basic Books, 1996), pp. 283, 293–94, 70. Bell's 1996 critique is heavily influenced by Warner Sombart's *Luxury and Capitalism*, which in Bell's words "made the idiosyncratic argument that illicit love and the style of life it produced gave rise to luxury— and capitalism." He also cites Rousseau on adornment's origins in falsehood: "Rousseau related what happened in that mythical moment when young men and women, growing up, began to meet around a large tree or campfire, to sing and dance and be 'true children of love and leisure.' But when 'each one began to look at the others and wanted to be looked at himself,' public esteem became a value. 'The one who sang or danced the best, the handsomest, the strongest, the most adroit, or the most eloquent, became the most highly considered; and *that was the first step toward inequality and, at the same time, toward vice.*' Those who had lost out, so to speak, began to dissemble, to adorn themselves, to wear plumage, to be sly or boisterous; in short, 'for one's own advantage to appear to be other than what one in fact was, to be and seem to become two altogether different things; and from this distinction [arise] conspicuous ostentation, deceptive cunning, and all the vices that follow from them,'" pp. 294–95.

5. Theodor W. Adorno and Max Horkheimer, "The Culture Industry: Enlightenment as Mass Deception," in Juliet B. Schor and Douglas B. Holt, eds., *The Consumer Society Reader* (New York: The New Press, 2000), pp. 4–5.

6. Sinclair B. Ferguson, "'Repent,' Said Jesus; Do Evangelicals Hear Him?" *The Dallas Morning News*, January 27, 2001, p. 4G. Ferguson is a minister in the Church of Scotland.

7. Kenneth Brower, "Photography in the Age of Falsification," *The Atlantic Monthly*, May 1998, p. 93. In Platonic thought, of course, storytelling itself is a suspect act, creating falsehoods.

8. The first quote is from a sermon by John Donne; the second is from Thomas Tuke's 1616 tract *A Treatise against Painting and Tincturing of Men and Women*. Both are quoted in Frances E. Dolan, "Taking the Pencil out of God's Hand: Art, Nature, and the Face-Painting Debate in Early Modern England," *PMLA*, March 1993, pp. 224–39.

9. Naomi Wolf, *The Beauty Myth: How Images of Beauty Are Used Against Women* (New York: Anchor Books, 1992), pp. 55–66.

10. Emily Toth, quoted in Alison Schneider, "Frumpy or Chic? Tweed or Kente? Sometimes Clothes Make the Professor," *The Chronicle of Higher Education*, January 23, 1998, p. A12.

11. Hillary Rodham Clinton, "Remarks of Senator Hillary Rodham Clinton," Class Day, Yale University, May 20, 2001, http://clinton.senate.gov/~clinton/speeches/010520.html.

12. The domain name hillaryshair.com now belongs to an unrelated pornography site that draws traffic from the many links still aimed at the old site.

13. Robert Frank, *Luxury Fever: Why Money Fails to Satisfy in an Era of Excess* (New York: The Free Press, 1999), p. 9.

14. Robert Frank, *Luxury Fever*, p. 9.

15. Robert Frank, *Luxury Fever*, p. 24.

16. Fred Carl and Tawana Thompson, quoted in Molly O'Neill, "The Viking Invasion," *The New Yorker*, July 29, 2002, pp. 40–45.

17. James B. Twitchell, *Living It Up: Our Love Affair with Luxury* (New York: Columbia University Press, 2002), p. 1.

18. James B. Twitchell, *Living It Up*, p. 91.

19. James B. Twitchell, *Living It Up*, pp. 102–3. Twitchell has his wife play a similarly degraded role on a shopping trip in Palm Beach. Her equally unexpected rebellion takes a different form; she takes off and goes shopping without him, buying luxuries, such as Paloma Picasso earrings, that she likes and can afford on her own salary.

20. Vance Packard, *The Hidden Persuaders* (New York: David McKay, 1957), p. 172.

21. Steven Den Beste, *USS Clueless*, January 7, 2002, http://denbeste.nu/cd_log_entries/2002/01/fog/0000000118.shtml.

22. Anne Bass, "The 1980s," *Vogue*, November 1999, pp. 492, 542.

23. Amy M. Spindler, "Are Retail Consultants Missing Fashion's X-Factor?" *The New York Times*, June 13, 1996, p. B8.

24. Anne Hollander, *Sex and Suits* (New York: Kodansha, 1994), pp. 11–12.

25. Stanley Lieberson, *A Matter of Taste: How Names, Fashions, and Culture Change* (New Haven: Yale University Press, 2000).

26. Anne Hollander, *Sex and Suits*, p. 12.

27. Daniel Bell, *The Cultural Contradictions of Capitalism*, pp. 13–14.

28. Stuart Ewen, *All Consuming Images*, p. 23.

29. Stuart Ewen, *All Consuming Images*, p. 38.

30. Grant McCracken, *Culture and Consumption* (Bloomington: Indiana University Press, 1988), p. 35.

31. Sir Thomas Elyot, quoted in Grant McCracken, *Culture and Consumption*, p. 33. Spelling has been modernized.

32. Jenna Weissman Joselit, *A Perfect Fit: Clothes, Character, and the Promise of America* (New York: Metropolitan Books, 2001), p. 33.

33. Anne Hollander, *Sex and Suits*, p. 21.

34. Jeffrey Leder, quoted in Abby Ellin, "How Fathers Can Help Daughters in the Body-Image Battle," *The New York Times*, September 18, 2000, p. B7.

35. *When Florida Secretary of State* Janny Scott, "When First Impressions Count," *The New York Times*, December 3, 2000, sec. 4, p. 3. Kim Folstad, "She Monitors Election, We Monitor Her," *The Palm Beach Post*, November 18, 2000, p. 1D. Hayley Kaufman, "Fashion Victim," *The Boston Globe*, November 16, 2000, p. D2.

36. Mark Steyn, "Game Face Otherwise Occupied," *Chicago Sun-Times*, October 15, 2000, p. 48.

37. Maureen Dowd, "Dead Heat Humanoids," *The New York Times*, October 5, 2000, p. A35.

38. Robin Givhan, "The Eyelashes Have It," *The Washington Post*, November 18, 2000, p. C1.

39. Andrea Peyser, "Oh, How I Wish That I'd Never Voted for Gore," *The New York Post*, November 24, 2000, p. 5.

40. Virginia Postrel, "Can Good Looks Guarantee a Product's Success?" *The New York Times*, July 12, 2001, p. C2.

41. Dan Hansen, "The Beauty of Wal-Mart," *Happy Fun Pundit*, August 9, 2002, http://happyfunpundit.blogspot.com/2002_08_04_happyfunpundit_archive.html.

42. Michael Bierut, e-mail to the author, September 18, 2001.

43. Michael Bierut, e-mail to the author, September 19, 2001.

44. Saira Shah, "Beneath the Veil: The Taliban's Harsh Rule of Afghanistan," *CNN Presents*, September 22, 2001. Virginia Postrel, "Free Hand," *Reason*, March 2002, p. 82.

■ *QUESTIONS FOR MAKING CONNECTIONS WITHIN THE ESSAY* ■

1. A key word in Postrel's argument is "value." What exactly does she mean by this word? What are the different kinds of value that she acknowledges in her essay? Why is it so important for her that we grant to the aesthetic a special value all its own? Postrel argues that we have failed to see the value of aesthetics, but is it possible to value aesthetics too highly? Does Postrel's chapter implicitly present a theory about the ways that different kinds of values should be related to one another?

2. In her piece, Postrel takes on a number of arguments against aesthetics. On what assumptions do these varied arguments rest? Pay attention to the values and concerns that might motivate the critics she responds to. Daniel Bell is an American sociologist. Theodor Adorno and Max Horkheimer were social theorists inspired by Karl Marx. Other critics of the aesthetic named by Postrel include Sun Microsystems CEO Scott McNealy, an unnamed "conservative minister," Senator Hillary Rodham Clinton, the economist Robert Frank, and the English professor James Twitchell. What might lie behind their attitudes toward aesthetics? Given the diversity of the critics, what might we conclude about our society's prevailing attitudes toward beauty, pleasure, and so on?

3. In her final paragraph, Postrel writes that "creating the difference between Coke and Pepsi is not just an empty pastime but one of the many signs of life in a free society." In what ways might aesthetics be connected to freedom, either for individuals or for society as a whole? In what ways may aesthetics help to heighten or intensify our sense of being alive? Is there a difference between "living" form and "dead" form? If there is, do people tend to agree about the forms that seem most alive? We may ordinarily assume that our experiences of beauty, harmony, and energy are entirely subjective, but are they really? If our perception of "life" in things

is entirely subjective, then why did so many customers buy the same "squirt-gun green pagers"?

■ QUESTIONS FOR WRITING ■

1. What are the larger implications of Postrel's argument? One way to answer this question is to ask if she has ultimately done nothing more than defend crass commercialism. Has Postrel simply devised a clever argument in defense of a life dedicated to superficiality and acquisitiveness? Or does she point the way to alternative forms of intellectual depth and personal integrity? If most people were to think and act in the way that Postrel would like them to, would our society be any different—or any better—than it is right now?

2. Is the "surface" of Postrel's chapter consistent with its "substance"? Is the *way* she makes her point appropriate to the point she makes? In order to answer this question, you might look carefully at the formal qualities of her argument, starting with a paragraph-by-paragraph outline. Would you describe Postrel's chapter in the main as "polemical" or as "affirmative"? What do you notice about the tone of the chapter? Would you call it "adversarial" or "conciliatory," "genial" or "strident"? Would you describe Postrel's treatment of other writers as "balanced" or "tendentious"? If you regard the surface of Postrel's argument as inconsistent with its substance, can you think of a more effective way to get the same point across?

■ QUESTIONS FOR MAKING CONNECTIONS BETWEEN READINGS ■

1. How might Postrel respond to Eric Schlosser's "Global Realization"? Would she put Schlosser in the same company as Bell, Adorno, Twitchell, and the other detractors of aesthetics, or might she respond sympathetically to some aspects of Schlosser's critique? Would you say that criticism of McDonald's is symptomatic of a disrespect for the aesthetic? Or might a world that valued aesthetics more highly be one in which McDonald's would go broke? McDonald's is sometimes seen as synonymous with materialism, but if people were true materialists—if they truly valued the qualities of material things—what would they think of fast food?

2. Postrel offers a spirited defense of aesthetics, but she never looks carefully at the ways people actually experience beauty, pleasure, novelty, excitement, and so on. We might find clues to the nature of aesthetic experience, however, in Robert Thurman's "Wisdom." Take a look in particular at the section entitled "Practice: Trying to Find Your 'I.'" When we cultivate awareness in the way that Thurman describes, does every moment

become an aesthetic experience? Could it be that our awareness of aesthetics is in some way similar to an experience like meditation? What happens to the "I" when we become aware of beauty, novelty, order, or energy in the world around us?

www For additional suggestions about making connections between readings, visit the Link-O-Mat and More Sample Assignments at <www.newhum.com>.

Arnold S. Relman and Marcia Angell

Arnold S. Relman is professor emeritus of Medicine and of Social Medicine at the Harvard Medical School. Dr. Relman served as the editor of the *Journal of Clinical Investigation* from 1962 to 1967 and as editor of the *New England Journal of Medicine* from 1977 to 1991. Over the course of his career, he has served on the faculty of the Boston University School of Medicine, Boston City Hospital, and the University of Pennsylvania School of Medicine. He has written extensively on the economic, ethical, legal, and social aspects of health care.

A board-certified pathologist, Dr. Marcia Angell joined the editorial staff of the *New England Journal of Medicine* in 1979 and was promoted to Executive Editor in 1988 and interim Editor-in-Chief in 1999. Currently Senior Lecturer in the Department of Social Medicine at Harvard Medical School, Angell writes and speaks publicly on medical ethics, health policy, and the nature of medical evidence. In 1997, *Time* magazine named Marcia Angell one of the 25 most influential Americans.

Angell is the author of the critically acclaimed *Science on Trial: The Clash of Medical Evidence and the Law in the Breast Implant Case* (1996), which explores the influence that junk science has in the court system and in the public sphere more generally. Arguing that the value of science resides in its commitment to assessing evidence objectively, Angell details the ways in which this commitment is undermined in the courts, where scientists are tempted to sell their expert opinions to the highest bidder. Angell's more recent work, *The Truth About the Drug Companies: How They Deceive Us and What to Do About It* (2004), explores how conflicts of interest in the scientific community are further undermining the unfettered pursuit of truth. As Angell sees the issue, it is the responsibility of scientific journals like the *New England Journal of Medicine* and of academic medical centers to conduct objective research and to subject the findings of such research to rigorous and unbiased analysis. Fulfilling this responsibility has become

——

Relman, Arnold, and Angell, Marcia. "America's Other Drug Problem: How the Drug Industry Distorts Medicine and Politics." *The New Republic* 227(25), Dec. 16, 2002: 27–41.

Quotation taken from Angell's remarks at the Health and Human Services Conference on Financial Conflicts of Interest <http://aspe.hhs.gov/sp/coi/angell.htm>. Additional biographical information taken from <http://www.healthcoalition.ca/arnold-relman.html>.

increasingly difficult, Angell believes, precisely because the doctors, scientists, and technicians who carry out the research rely on medical and pharmaceutical corporations to fund their work. This is a problem because

> the mission of investor-owned companies is quite different from the mission of academic medical centers. The primary purpose of the former is to increase the value of their shareholders' stock, which they do by securing patents and marketing their products. Their purpose is not to educate, nor even to carry out research, except secondarily or as a means to their primary end. I believe academics often forget this, and allow themselves to believe that marketing is really education.

In "America's Other Drug Problem," we find Relman and Angell asking a similar set of questions: What ethical standards should scientists be held to? What role should science have in a civil society? And is it possible to preserve science's commitment to "service and disinterestedness" once scientists move out of the lab and into the courtroom and the marketplace?

www **To learn more about Arnold Relman, Marcia Angell, and scientific objectivity, please visit the Link-O-Mat at <www.newhum.com>.**

America's Other Drug Problem:

How the Drug Industry Distorts Medicine and Politics

The American health care system cannot live without the pharmaceutical industry, but it may not be able to live with it either, unless the industry is greatly reformed. For better and for worse, this enormous and hugely profitable enterprise has become a dominating presence in American life. It uses its great wealth and influence to ensure favorable government policies. It has also, with the acquiescence of a medical profession addicted to drug company largesse, assumed a role in directing medical treatment, clinical research, and physician education that is totally inappropriate for a profit-driven industry. Like most other for-profit corporations, drug companies are impelled primarily by the financial aspirations of their investors and executives. This incentive may serve useful social purposes in the distribution of ordinary goods in most markets, but prescription drugs are not like ordinary goods, and the market for drugs is not like other markets. The misconception that drugs and their market are like other goods and markets explains most of the serious problems with the pharmaceutical industry today.

Drug Costs

The rising costs of drugs are the immediate public issue. Expenditures on prescription drugs—now roughly $170 billion per year—constitute a rapidly growing fraction of our $1.4 trillion health care bill. Greater overall use of drugs, higher prices for new drugs, and steady increases in the prices of existing drugs all contribute to an annual inflation in drug expenditures of 14 percent (down from a high of 18 percent in 1999). Within a few years, this surge in costs will probably make drugs the second largest component of our national health care budget, after hospitalization. According to statistics kept by the Center for Medicare and Medicaid Services, American expenditures on prescription drugs, expressed as a percentage of GDP, were virtually steady between 1960 and 1980 but increased rapidly soon thereafter, and by 2000 they had almost tripled.

Last year, a prescription for one of the twenty top-selling brand-name drugs—which is usually for a one-month supply—cost on average about $100. Prices for prescription drugs are on average much higher in the United States than anywhere else in the world. Many patients, particularly the elderly, take several drugs, so drug costs have become a heavy burden for them; but the costs of prescription drugs are now a major problem for all who must pay for them. That includes government and private insurance plans, and uninsured and partly insured individuals.

Resistance to escalating drug expenditures is growing among all the purchasers, and the media are full of critical stories and commentaries. So far, however, none of this has had a noticeable impact on rising drug expenditures. The pharmaceutical industry has been fighting effectively against all efforts to control prices or to limit the markets for its expensive new brand-name drugs. It channels these efforts and most of its public relations and lobbying activities through its trade association, the Pharmaceutical Research and Manufacturers of America (PhRMA). PhRMA's membership includes virtually all American manufacturers of brand-name drugs, and many foreign manufacturers as well. With a full-time staff of 120 in its Washington offices and hundreds of lobbyists working the halls of federal and state government, and with a core budget of some $60 million and large additional subsidies from the industry for special projects, PhRMA conducts an extensive, virtually nonstop campaign on behalf of its clients. This is in addition to the millions spent in Washington by individual pharmaceutical firms promoting their own business objectives.

PhRMA adamantly opposes any regulation of expenditures for brand-name drugs. It argues that high prices simply reflect the very high costs of discovering and developing new drugs. Any form of price control, it claims, would eat into the industry's research and development budget, and thereby choke off the pipeline that brings the public important new drugs. Generic drugs are different, it points out, because they are merely copies of brand-name drugs whose exclusive marketing rights have expired, and therefore their manufacturers do not have high research costs. Moreover, PhRMA contends that high profits are a necessary incentive for undertaking the risky and arduous business of discovering innovative drugs. These drugs are vital to the health of Americans, according to the industry, and it would be disastrously shortsighted to lessen the incentives to find them. PhRMA also maintains that, whatever the expenditures for prescription drugs, we get more than our money's worth. According to this argument, the output of the industry's research laboratories not only cures disease and extends and improves people's lives, but probably even saves money by avoiding hospitalizations and other more expensive kinds of treatment. In sum, the industry portrays itself as an exemplar of science-based free enterprise, primarily dedicated to discovering—through costly and risky research—new treatments for disease. It wants the public to believe the catchy slogan of the pharmaceutical giant Pfizer: "Life is our life's work."

The rhetoric is stirring, but the arguments simply do not hold up. First, research and development (R&D) constitutes a relatively small part of the budgets of the large drug companies. Their marketing and advertising expenditures are much greater than their investment in R&D. Furthermore, they make more in profits than they spend on R&D. In fact, their profits are consistently much higher than those of any other American industry. Prices (which bear little relation to the costs of developing and manufacturing a drug) could be lowered substantially without coming close to threatening the R&D budgets of drug companies, much less their economic survival.

Second, the pharmaceutical industry is not particularly innovative, and it is growing less so each year. The great majority of new drugs coming to market these days, although patented, are not new at all. They are variations on older drugs already on the market. These are called "me-too" drugs, and they represent attempts to capitalize on the success of "blockbuster" drugs. (Blockbusters are defined here as drugs with over $500 million in annual sales.) The few drugs that are truly innovative have usually been based on taxpayer-supported research done in nonprofit academic medical centers or at the National Institutes of Health. In fact, many drugs now sold by drug companies were licensed to them by academic medical centers or small biotechnology companies.

Third, while there is no doubt that the best of the new drugs have greatly improved or saved many lives, this is certainly not true of all of them; most add little or no medical value. The use of some drugs has saved money by reducing hospitalizations or the need for expensive procedures, but whether prescription drugs reduce total expenditures for health care in the long run is an imponderable question. As expenditures on drugs continue to rise, the answer becomes more uncertain, the industry's insistence to the contrary notwithstanding.

Far from being a "research-based industry," as it likes to call itself, the pharmaceutical industry now devotes most of its resources to functioning as a vast marketing and advertising enterprise whose best products were discovered and often partially developed elsewhere—usually at public expense. And this industry is hardly a model of free enterprise. It may be free to decide which drugs to develop and to set its own prices, but its lifeblood is government-granted monopolies—in the form of patents and FDA-approved exclusive marketing rights. Drug companies apparently see no contradiction in manipulating existing laws and regulations to stave off competition from generic and foreign manufacturers and lobbying for even more governmental protections while at the same time using free-market rhetoric to demand less government involvement in the pricing and the marketing of drugs.

The industry wants to obscure a basic fact: there is not and there cannot be anything like a free market in prescription drugs. The pharmaceutical business is, for many reasons, critically dependent on government help. That is why it spends so much on lobbying. Moreover, its sales are not determined primarily by price or by consumer choice, but by the physicians who prescribe drugs. And that is why it spends so much more to influence the behavior of doctors.

R&D Costs: How High Are They Really?

Before discussing the costs of bringing a new drug to market, we must first explain the steps in that process. The discovery of a drug candidate is usually the result of research into the molecular basis of disease, which is done primarily in academic or government laboratories. The next step is the preclinical phase of the R&D work, which is usually done by industry—although not necessarily by the company that ultimately sells the drug. This involves biological screening and pharmacological testing in laboratory animals to determine how the drug is absorbed, metabolized, and excreted, and to learn about its toxicity. According to PhRMA's annual report, approximately one-quarter to one-third of all pharmaceutical R&D expenditures are involved in finding or acquiring a new drug candidate and taking it through the pre-clinical screening phase. The industry claims that only about one in one thousand screened compounds makes it through the pre-clinical phase to the clinical phase—that is, to testing in human subjects.

To begin clinical testing, a drug must be registered with the Food and Drug Administration (FDA), which by law must ultimately approve all drugs for safety and effectiveness before they can be sold. There are four phases of clinical testing. In Phase I, the new drug is given to a few human volunteers to establish safe dosage levels and to study its metabolism and side effects. If the drug looks promising, it moves into Phase II, which involves small clinical trials at various doses in patients with the relevant medical condition. Finally, if all goes well, Phase III clinical trials are undertaken. These evaluate the safety and the effectiveness of the drug in much larger numbers of patients (hundreds or thousands of them), with the expectation of gaining FDA approval if the trials are successful. No more than one in five drug candidates entering clinical testing makes it through to FDA approval and reaches the market, so the chances that a drug candidate, once selected, will ever get to the market are said to be less than one in five thousand.

The total time from the beginning of pre-clinical testing of a candidate drug to FDA approval ranges from about six to ten years. That includes the time the FDA spends on review of the application for approval (called a new drug application, or NDA), which averages about 16 months. But these times are quite variable, and in special cases they can be greatly shortened. After approval of a drug, the FDA requires the manufacturer to continue its surveillance of the drug and to report unanticipated side effects. The company may also want to do additional clinical studies to gain approval for new uses or formulations of the drug. All clinical studies after the initial approval are designated as Phase IV trials.

According to PhRMA's annual report, the large drug companies last year spent approximately 15 to 17 percent of their income on R&D (before adjustment for tax deductions and credits). This figure is necessarily soft, since in general the industry's accounting for its R&D expenses leaves a lot to be desired, and there are also differing estimates of total income. Much R&D information is considered proprietary. Individual companies report total R&D expenditures in their Securities and Exchange Commission (SEC) filings, and PhRMA's annual report gives industry-wide averages for total R&D as well as average figures for the breakdown of expenses by general R&D functions. But the companies do not make available most of the really interesting details, such as what each company spends, and for what purposes, on the development of each drug. We also do not know how much marketing is concealed under the rubric of "development," particularly in Phase IV post-approval studies. Still, one financial detail of R&D expenses has been widely publicized by the industry: the estimated average total

R&D cost of each new drug brought to market. That figure is currently said to be $802 million (in year 2000 dollars), including the amount spent on the many failures and false starts. This huge outlay, which we are told is rising rapidly with the growing expense of clinical trials, is said to justify—indeed to require—the high prices of new drugs.

Pre-clinical and clinical testing and the other tasks required before a drug can be brought to the FDA for approval can be long, difficult, and very expensive. But $802 million apiece? To put it in the kindest terms, that is an imaginary number. It is based on debatable accounting theory and it is premised on blind faith in the confidential information supplied by the industry to its economic consultants at the Tufts Center for the Study of Drug Development, the University of Rochester Graduate School of Business Administration, and the Department of Economics at Duke University, who arrived at this number. Over the years, these consultants have analyzed the costs of new drug development, and the $802 million estimate represents an updating of their work.

Although this latest analysis has not yet been formally published, it was announced at a forum and a press conference last year in Philadelphia. PhRMA, leaders of the industry, and its defenders in the media have been trumpeting the results ever since. Joseph DiMasi of Tufts University, the senior author of this work, kindly sent us a draft of the manuscript describing the analysis, and he discussed his views with us in several telephone conversations. He also shared his opinions about a critical analysis of this work that was released last year by Public Citizen, the Washington-based consumer watch group. Among Public Citizen's objections to the work of DiMasi's group, we consider the following to be most important.

First, the analysis concerns the costs only of new molecular entities (NMEs), sometimes called new chemical entities (NCEs). These are drugs whose active ingredients are newly discovered or synthesized molecules. The analysis was also restricted to NMEs developed entirely within the drug companies. The 68 drugs selected for study are never named; nor are the manufacturers or the individual costs. But NMEs are only a minority of the drugs that are newly approved. As we already noted, most are new dosage forms or combinations of drugs already on the market. Moreover, an increasing number of drugs are simply licensed from academic medical centers or biotechnology companies, and are not entirely developed in the drug companies. So, despite the implication by the industry that the DiMasi calculations tell us the average cost of the R&D needed for all the new drugs sold, these estimates seem to be based on sampling from a highly selected group of drugs. Full disclosure of the data, including the identity of the drugs selected for study and the costs for each, would have been important for the evaluation of the significance of this economic analysis.

Second, the final estimate of the cost per drug is not the actual out-of-pocket cost, but what the authors call the "capitalized" cost—that is, it includes the estimated revenue that might have been generated over the long development period if the money spent on R&D had instead been invested in the equity market. This theoretically lost revenue is known as the "opportunity cost," and it is added to the industry's out-of-pocket costs of R&D. The authors seem to justify this interesting accounting maneuver on the grounds that from the perspective of investors, a pharmaceutical company is really just one kind of investment, which they chose among other possible investment options. But while this may be true for investors, surely it is not true for the pharmaceutical companies themselves. The latter have no choice but to spend money on R&D if they wish to be in the pharmaceutical business, so they have no "opportunity costs." To add the investors' opportunity costs to the company's out-of-pocket cost of developing a drug seems rather odd. DiMasi assures us that this calculation conforms with standard economic thought and accounting practice, but recent events on Wall Street make such reassurance less comforting than it might once have been. In any case, when DiMasi and his colleagues add the "opportunity cost" to their calculated out-of-pocket cost of pharmaceutical R&D ($403 million per drug), the final estimate is approximately doubled.

Finally, the Public Citizen analysis points out that since R&D expenses are deductible from a firm's tax base, calculation of the cost of R&D should be reduced by the amount of corporate tax avoided. This tax saving would reduce the net cost of R&D by a percentage equal to the corporate tax rate (currently about 34 percent). DiMasi says that the corporate tax applies to net income, and since the latter is already reduced by the R&D expenditures, there is, properly speaking, no tax saving and no need to adjust the calculation of the R&D cost that he and his colleagues are making. We are not qualified to debate the accounting terminology, but it seems to us only common sense that were it not for the full deductibility of R&D from the tax base, the pharmaceutical industry's taxes would be higher and its after-tax income would be lower. Why is it not reasonable, therefore, to deduct this difference—whether it is called a "tax saving" or not—from the out-of-pocket expenditures on R&D when calculating the net cost of R&D to a pharmaceutical firm? The Office for Technology Assessment, whose report on this subject in 1993 is often cited incorrectly as supporting the DiMasi analysis because it also considers opportunity costs, agrees with Public Citizen's position on tax deductions.

In sum, we believe that Public Citizen's criticisms are substantially correct, and we agree with the group's conclusion that even if one were blindly to accept the reliability of the unrevealed data used in the calculations, the $802 million estimate of "capitalized" cost produced by the industry's economic consultants should be reduced to an after-tax net of less than $266 million. But remember, that would be the average out-of-pocket R&D cost only for the new molecular entities developed entirely in-house, not the average cost of all of the drugs approved each year. Most approved drugs entering the market are not really new, or they are licensed from other sources, or both. Such drugs probably have lower R&D costs, although there are no good data on this point. We conclude that the average out-of-pocket, after-tax R&D cost of most of the drugs upon which the industry's revenue now depends was probably much lower than $266 million (in year 2000 dollars). Tax credits for certain types of R&D would probably reduce that estimate even more.

The suspicion that average R&D costs per drug are not nearly as high as claimed is further supported by other data provided by Public Citizen. If one divides the industry-supplied estimates of total R&D expenses by the total number of drugs entering the market, making appropriate allowances for the lag time between expenditures and the date of entrance into the market, the resulting net out-of-pocket, after-tax costs would probably be less than $100 million for each drug that was approved between 1994 and 2000. That, admittedly, is only a rough approximation, but the general conclusion seems inescapable: that the $802 million estimate now being promoted by the industry and its partisans is much too high.

Whatever the cost of bringing each new drug to market, the total R&D expenditures of the pharmaceutical industry—according to PhRMA, now about $30 billion for all its members in the United States and abroad—are indeed large. But they should be compared with reported expenditures on marketing and administration, which are more than twice as much as R&D expenditures. Moreover, the most important financial fact about the major pharmaceutical firms is that, despite their expenses, they are immensely profitable. The ten American pharmaceutical companies in the Fortune 500 list last year ranked far above all other American industries in average net return, whether as a percentage of revenues (18.5 percent), of assets (16.3 percent), or of shareholders' equity (33.2 percent). (For comparison, the median net return for other industries was only 3.3 percent of revenues.) And this has generally been the case for the past two decades. A business consistently this profitable cannot by any stretch of language be described as "risky" or as needing special protection of its revenues.

How Innovative Is the Pharmaceutical Industry?

The pharmaceutical industry justifies its extraordinary profits largely by the claim that they are necessary as an incentive to continue its vital research. The implication is that if the public wants new cures for diseases, it should give the industry free rein. It is important, then, to ask just how innovative the pharmaceutical industry really is. We think the answer is not very. Drug companies greatly exaggerate their role in the scientific work leading to the discovery of new drugs. As we have already noted, the development of important new drugs is usually the culmination of many discoveries in basic science laboratories outside the pharmaceutical industry. This work increases the understanding of the molecular basis of disease and thereby identifies promising targets and models for the design of new drugs. Most of this groundbreaking research, done with support from the National Institutes of Health (NIH) or other institutions, appears in scientific journals before the big companies become involved. The industry is certainly not the major engine of discovery and medical progress that it would have the public believe. Public investment in research has been primarily responsible for the great medical advances society is enjoying, and this is likely to be so in the future as well.

A general idea of the relative contribution of the pharmaceutical industry to the underlying medical research that leads to the development of new drugs can be gained from a recent study published in the journal *Health Affairs*. The study reported that in 1998 only about 15 percent of the scientific articles cited in patent applications for clinical medicine came from industry research, while 54 percent came from academic centers, 13 percent from government, and the rest from various other public and nonprofit institutions. Remember that these are patent applications for all new drugs and medical innovations, not simply for those ultimately judged to be clinically important. Had the data been limited to only major breakthrough drugs, the industry's role would undoubtedly have looked even smaller.

The relatively small contribution of industry is also clear from an unpublished internal document produced by the NIH in February 2000, which was obtained by Public Citizen through the Freedom of Information Act. The NIH had selected the five top-selling drugs in 1995 (Zantac, Zovirax, Capoten, Vasotec, and Prozac) and found that 16 of the 17 key scientific papers leading to the discovery and development of these drugs came from outside the industry. Looking at all the relevant published research, not just at the key studies, 85 percent came from American taxpayer-supported laboratories or foreign academic laboratories. While it is true that academic scientists may have more incentive to publish their research results than do their colleagues in industry, these data are persuasive: publicly funded medical research is by far the major source of pharmaceutical innovation—not the industry itself.

A more concrete appreciation of the relative contributions of outside scientific laboratories and the drug industry can be gained by considering the histories of three important, groundbreaking drugs that have appeared on the market during the past two decades.

Zidovudine, commonly known as AZT, was first marketed in the United States in 1987 by the company then called Burroughs Wellcome Co., which is now part of a much larger firm called Glaxo-SmithKline. AZT, sold under the brand name Retrovir, was the first drug shown to be effective in suppressing HIV infection. It has recently been joined by several other effective drugs, but it usually remains part of the combination drug therapy still in use. The AZT molecule was first synthesized at the Michigan Cancer Foundation in 1964 as a possible treatment for cancer and was studied in many laboratories for that purpose. In 1974, in a German basic science laboratory, it was found to be effective against experimental viral infections in mice. In 1983–1984, U.S. government-supported research at the NIH and at Duke University showed that this molecule also suppressed the AIDS virus in human cells in test tubes and, later, that it was effective in patients. Encouraged by the Stevenson-Wydler and Bayh-Dole Acts of 1980, NIH-supported scientists began to collaborate with Burroughs Wellcome. By 1985, the company was able to obtain a patent on the use of AZT in the treatment of AIDS and to proceed with clinical trials that enabled it to receive FDA approval after an expedited review that required only four months—one of the shortest on record. This history shows that the drug treatment of AIDS, certainly one of the major public health advances in our time, began with basic preclinical work conducted almost entirely outside the drug industry and largely supported by taxpayers.

Erythropoietin, which is marketed by Amgen under the name Epogen, is a protein hormone normally produced in healthy kidneys that stimulates red blood cell production. Technically, it is a "biological," not a "drug," because it is a natural substance made in the body. We include it in our discussion because Amgen is an important member of PhRMA, and because many pharmaceutical firms sell biologicals as well as drugs. Erythropoietin was discovered through a long series of investigations in academic laboratories that began in the 1960s and was largely supported by the NIH. This work established that the severe anemia characteristic of chronic kidney disease was largely caused by the failure of the damaged kidneys to manufacture erythropoietin. The isolation and the definitive chemical identification of the substance was finally accomplished by a scientist at the University of Chicago in 1976, but the university did not patent the molecule or initiate any efforts to develop it for clinical use.

To use erythropoietin in the treatment of anemia requires a safe, efficient method of biosynthesis, and this was Amgen's contribution. The task of the company's scientists was facilitated by a recombinant gene technique that was developed and patented at Columbia University (again with NIH support). Amgen, then a small biotechnology start-up company, licensed the technique from Columbia, used it to develop a practical method for recombinant synthesis of erythropoietin, and patented the biosynthetic molecule. By 1987, Amgen had completed its first clinical trials and was able to show that Epogen was safe and effective in treating anemia in patients with kidney failure—a major medical advance in the field.

With FDA approval, Epogen has been widely and successfully used, and now generates for Amgen more than $2 billion in annual sales—mainly from

Medicare, which pays for the treatment of kidney failure. Thus, it turns out that taxpayers pay whatever Amgen charges for a drug discovered largely through taxpayer-supported research. For license of its recombinant gene patent, Columbia receives 1 percent of all sales from Amgen.

Imatinib mesylate, marketed as Gleevec, is a new molecule that was synthesized in the early 1990s in the chemistry laboratories of the Swiss pharmaceutical firm Novartis and has recently been shown to be spectacularly successful in the treatment of a type of blood cancer called chronic myeloid leukemia (CML). This form of leukemia affects about 20,000 adults in the United States at any given time, and it is usually fatal after about three to five years. The story of imatinib is particularly instructive and worth telling in some detail.

The long trail of basic scientific research leading to the development of this drug began back in 1960 with the discovery of a characteristic abnormal-looking chromosome in patients with CML. Subsequent work showed that the abnormal-looking chromosome is due to the breakage and the subsequent rejoining of parts of two chromosomes. Later studies from many different laboratories showed that this rejoining creates a new gene that directs the production of an abnormal enzyme, which causes white blood cells to become malignant. Other work had shown that similar types of enzymes were probably involved in a variety of other cancers, although not as directly; so chemists in Israel and in the laboratories of Novartis independently set about synthesizing molecules that would inhibit the action of these abnormal enzymes. Novartis patented several such inhibitor molecules in 1994 and added them to its collection of potentially useful drug candidates.

There was apparently no immediate interest at Novartis in determining whether any of these new inhibitors might be clinically useful in the treatment of CML until Dr. Brian J. Druker, a clinical research physician in hematology at the Oregon Health Sciences University in Portland, became interested in their possible use for this purpose. Much of the rest of this story we learned from Druker. Working with a scientist at Novartis, he obtained a small supply of several of the company's most promising enzyme inhibitors. He found that imatinib was the most potent in suppressing the growth of malignant CML blood cells in culture, and furthermore that it had no effect at all on normal blood cells. Such specific action is almost unheard of in cancer treatment, and Druker urged the company to explore this exciting lead. But there was little corporate enthusiasm for undertaking further clinical work on imatinib. Druker nevertheless persisted, and Novartis finally agreed to support cautious, limited tests of the drug in Druker's clinic and two other sites. By 1999, Druker was able to report spectacularly successful preliminary results before a large national meeting of American hematologists. The news about imatinib's remarkable effectiveness in CML quickly became public, and it aroused great interest. The company then decided to proceed with large-scale clinical trials to determine whether the drug was safe enough and effective enough to warrant FDA approval and general use in CML. Last year, once the positive clinical evidence was in hand, the FDA quickly gave its approval.

So Novartis's R&D investment in testing imatinib for the treatment of CML was made several years after there was already good scientific evidence to suggest that it might be useful. Druker told us that he did not know how much the company's initial reticence was due to its finding that the drug had toxic effects in dogs at high doses; but given the relatively small number of patients with CML, he believes that a purely business calculation of the size of the likely market also played a role. In any case, the great initial success of this new drug in CML has sparked exploration, in clinical centers and laboratories around the world, of a similar approach to the treatment of other cancers. In the meantime, clinical studies to determine imatinib's long-term effects on CML continue. For most patients starting on Gleevec, Novartis now charges $25,000 for a year's supply of the drug, and the current expectation is that these patients will have to be on treatment for at least several years, with or without supplemental therapy.

How did the company decide on Gleevec's walloping price? We do not know, but in this connection it is interesting to consider the comment made last year by Raymond V. Gilmartin, the influential chairman and CEO of Merck, at the press conference announcing the latest R&D cost estimate by DiMasi and his colleagues. Referring to the $802 million per drug estimate, Gilmartin remarked: "The price of medicines isn't determined by their research costs. Instead, it is determined by their value in preventing and treating disease. Whether Merck spends $500 million or $1 billion developing a medicine, it is the doctor, the patient, and those paying for our medicines who will determine its true value." Since those who pay for a drug are not usually able to judge its value in comparison with other drugs or other forms of treatment, and since those who can make that judgment—the doctors—do not pay for the drug, we do not understand Gilmartin's comment. Taken literally, it would mean that the high prices of today's me-too drugs reflect their medical value—which seems very unlikely. Could he really be saying that the price is simply determined by whatever the market will bear?

These three stories about drug development could be multiplied many times and all the stories would make the same point: the discovery of the important and innovative drugs in the past few decades usually began with basic scientific work at NIH or academic research laboratories, supported by government grants. There have been exceptions, but the pharmaceutical industry has so far devoted most of its R&D resources not to scientific discovery, but to the practical application of discoveries generated at taxpayer expense and to the development of variations on or new uses for drugs already on the market.

All of this makes good business sense for the pharmaceutical industry if, like most industries, it is primarily interested in immediate profits. The kind of wide-ranging, open-ended, and relatively undirected basic research into the molecular biology of disease that is done mainly with NIH support is very expensive, and its results are unpredictable. Whether a given line of investigation will quickly (or ever) lead to the development of a new drug cannot be known in advance. But this kind of research is the only way in which genuine medical progress is made. Pharmaceutical companies, pressured by investors to keep delivering profitable new products—whether they are medically important or not—must use less risky strategies. They use their R&D dollars to imitate top-selling drugs already on the market or to find new uses for their own blockbusters.

That me-too's have come to dominate the new drug market is documented very clearly by the FDA, which classifies drugs under review by their likely therapeutic value and by whether they are NMEs or simply reformulations and combinations of old drugs. Over the twelve-year period beginning in 1990, 1,035 drugs were approved, and of these only 23 percent were classified as likely to be a "significant improvement" on products already on the market. (In our own judgment as physicians, even many of these drugs would be more accurately described as modest, incremental improvements.) All the others were classified as appearing to have "therapeutic qualities similar to those of one or more already marketed drugs." Moreover, just 15 percent of the approved drugs were classified as both a significant improvement and an NME. Last year, the FDA approved 66 drugs for the entire drug industry. The agency classified only ten as a significant improvement, and only seven of these were NMEs. So the already small percentage of newly marketed drug products that are really novel and important seems to be dropping still further, with me-too's becoming the rule. This trend has continued during the current year.

Industry spokespeople sometimes justify the growing profusion of brand-name me-too drugs by arguing that they increase market competition and keep prices down. For this reason, they object to the term "monopoly" as applied to the exclusive marketing rights conferred by patents or FDA approval. But me-too drugs are not promoted on the basis of price. Instead, they are marketed as being especially effective—usually in total disregard of the facts. There is little evidence of price competition. Thus, although the availability of multiple similar brand-name drugs may have some modulating effect on prices, it is certainly not nearly as great as the price competition that results when unpatented generic drugs enter the market.

Other apologists claim that in drug therapy one size does not fit all. Very similar drugs, they say, may vary in their effects from patient to patient, so it is important to have choices among them. But there is a paucity of evidence to support the notion that if a particular drug does not work for a patient, a virtually identical one will. It might occasionally be useful to have a new, long-acting version of an identical short-acting drug that is already on the market. But we think most experts would agree that there is little or no rationale for having four or more me-too drugs, as is now the case in many fields. There are now five patented statins (a type of cholesterol-lowering drug) on the market, four patented anti-depressants of the so-called SSRI (selective serotonin reuptake inhibitor) type, and seven patented angiotensin blocking agents (drugs to treat high blood pressure and heart failure). We are aware of no good studies establishing the clinical need for so many.

Blockbusters have one thing in common besides their high sales: they are usually treatments for very common lifelong conditions. The conditions are not so serious that they are lethal, but they do not go away either. Sometimes they are little more than annoyances, like hay fever. Consequently, large numbers of people may take drugs for these conditions for years, and that is why the markets are so large. People with uncommon or acute diseases are generally not of much interest to drug companies. The major difficulty in launching a me-too blockbuster, however, is in persuading doctors and patients that it is better than the others, since the evidence is at best marginal. Unfortunately, the FDA will approve a me-too drug on the basis of clinical trials comparing it not with an older drug of the same type, but with a placebo or a drug of another type. Drug companies would rather not have a head-to-head comparison, because they might lose. To launch a me-too drug successfully, then, requires a lot of marketing, which largely explains the industry's mammoth marketing expenditures.

Testing Drugs on People

The only way to determine a new drug's safety, effectiveness, and—if this important question is asked—its relative efficacy compared with existing drugs is through properly designed and conducted clinical trials, that is, tests on people. These trials represent the third phase of the R&D process that we have described, and they are the most expensive part of clinical development. Before the FDA will consider approving a new drug for marketing, the manufacturer must present the results of at least one (and usually more) Phase III trials for review by the agency as part of the new drug application. Although the FDA usually reviews the results of the trials submitted to it very carefully, it cannot guarantee the integrity of the work, so it is essential that clinical trials be well designed and executed without bias or manipulation of the results.

Until the past decade, around 80 percent of clinical trials were conducted on patients at academic medical centers and teaching hospitals under the direction of medical faculty, who usually initiated the application for support of the trial. Most of these trials were supported by grants from a pharmaceutical company to the academic institution, although some were funded by the NIH. The design and execution of the studies and the collection, interpretation, and reporting of the data were all the primary responsibility of the academic team, made up of experts in the field. They had no financial ties to the company or to the drug being tested, although part of their salary might have been paid from the grant as compensation for the time that they invested in the trial.

As the number and the size of clinical trials have grown and the industry's need for faster results and access to large numbers of patients has rapidly increased, more and more trials (over half of them) have been shifted to private-practice settings outside the academic centers, where pharmaceutical firms or their contractors have assumed direct responsibility for the conduct of the clinical studies. A large new industry has arisen to serve the pharmaceutical firms' needs. It consists mainly of companies called contract research organizations (CROs), which are hired by the drug companies to organize and to conduct clinical trials. Often working through other companies, they employ physicians in private practice to recruit patients as subjects for the studies. There are reportedly now over one thousand CROs worldwide, and they generated an estimated $7 billion in revenues last year from their contracts with the pharmaceutical and biotechnology industries. Although the physicians they hire to recruit patients also help with the conduct of clinical trials, the results of the studies are analyzed and interpreted by the companies. Control over most clinical trials is now largely in the hands of the pharmaceutical industry, and the influence of the academic centers and their clinical faculty is greatly reduced— even in trials conducted at those centers. These dramatic changes have transformed the entire system for the development and the marketing of new drugs, with troubling consequences.

In an effort to recapture income from the pharmaceutical industry, most of the leading academic centers have set up clinical-trials offices to provide the industry with the same quick, comprehensive services that the drug firms have been getting from the CROs and other private research businesses. These centers now openly court the pharmaceutical industry, offering the services of their clinical faculties, access to patients, and help with the design, the conduct, and the analysis of clinical trials. Although some of the stronger academic institutions still insist on faculty control of the studies and the reporting of results, the pendulum of power has shifted. Drug companies have increasing control over the evaluation of their own products. A very recent increase in NIH support of clinical trials may now be starting to reduce the dependence of major academic centers on contracts with the pharmaceutical industry.

Adding to the problem are the growing financial ties of clinical faculty with the pharmaceutical industry. Almost every academic expert who might be qualified to direct a clinical trial now is paid by one or more firms as a consultant or a speaker. Some medical schools have policies limiting these ties and preventing faculty with financial connections to a company from doing clinical research on that company's drugs, but many medical schools do not, and virtually all of them allow exceptions to their generally lenient rules. The consequence is that the public can no longer assume that clinical reports from academic centers are written by physicians who have no vested interests in the results. About the best to be hoped for is that these interests will be disclosed in the published reports, and that any bias resulting from these financial connections will be balanced by reports from other companies and researchers with competing interests. But the point is that the public can no longer be confident that the testing of new drugs is unbiased.

The pervasive connections between the pharmaceutical industry and academia are not limited to clinical trials. Virtually every research-intensive medical center in the country now has contractual ties with one or more drug firms, usually involving subsidies for or collaborations with particular research programs and faculty. In return, the firms gain information about new findings before publication, hands-on laboratory education for their research personnel, and rights of first refusal on patents for the products of this research. Drug companies are even beginning to locate their new research laboratories near academic centers to facilitate such relationships. Merck is now building a large new research facility on land in Boston immediately adjacent to the Harvard Medical School (the first such facility in an area previously reserved for academic and clinical institutions), and Novartis has leased two research facilities in Cambridge close to MIT, joining several biotechnology companies already there.

We do not doubt that collaboration in basic research between academic centers and industry, with appropriate safeguards to preserve the integrity and the independence of academic institutions and their faculties, can be very useful. Yet physical proximity and close economic ties between the industry and the academy have a serious drawback. They can involve academic centers and their faculty too deeply in commercial enterprises, at the expense of their traditional missions of education, patient care, and free-ranging research. They also threaten the objectivity that is the essential hallmark of good scientific research and medical education. Recently the Association of American Medical Colleges (AAMC) suggested guidelines for managing financial conflicts of interest, but these guidelines are not binding, and they do not address the fundamental issue of whether medical schools and their faculties should have such extensive ties with industry in the first place.

Marketing: Where the Action Is

According to data published in their SEC reports for 2001, the big drug companies spent on average about 35 percent of their income on what most of them call "marketing and administration." At least one major company, Novartis, separates these two functions in its report, assigning 36 percent of total income to "marketing and distribution" and 5 percent to "administration and general overhead." It is unlikely that other companies differ very much from Novartis in this relative weighting. Still, not much is known about the exact distribution of expenditures within the "marketing" category. Whatever the exact figures, it seems clear that marketing and related activities account for the largest part of the industry's expenses. They certainly are far greater than the expenses for R&D or manufacturing. By following the money, we conclude that marketing, not the search for new drugs and their development for clinical practice, is the most important focus for the industry. This conclusion is also supported by the distribution of employees as reported by PhRMA. More than one-third of the industry's workforce is employed in marketing, much more than in R&D, manufacturing, or administration.

If the industry argues that drug prices necessarily reflect its high costs for R&D, then what can it say about its much higher costs for sales promotion? Those who pay for prescription drugs are paying for marketing, too. But if the current crop of new drugs were as valuable as the industry would like us to believe, and if there were not so many me-too drugs, surely it would not be necessary to spend so much money pushing them. A genuinely important new drug, such as Gleevec, does not have to be marketed widely. Cancer doctors treating patients with CML will know about this drug and use it. No sales pitch is needed.

Still, the extravagant expenditures on drug marketing and their effect on drug prices are not the worst part of this story. What should be of even greater concern is the effect of the industry's marketing and advertising money on the independence and the trustworthiness of the medical profession. As a learned profession, medicine has a fiduciary responsibility to patients in particular and to society in general to provide expert, unbiased advice on the use of drugs, based on the best available scientific information. Also, the profession has an obligation to educate its own practitioners about the selection and discriminating use of the best and most cost-effective drugs—old and new, patented and generic. This should be largely the responsibility of medical schools, resident training programs in hospitals, and the postgraduate or continuing medical education (CME) courses organized by professional societies, schools, and hospitals. The latter are required for renewal of doctors' licenses.

But the professional bodies that ought to be responsible for CME have been more or less co-opted by the pharmaceutical industry. There are guidelines, agreed to by the industry and the professional institutions, that are supposed to protect against commercial influence on the content of this education, but most of these guidelines are general and vague. They require that the medical institutions accepting industry support merely approve the CME programs, although the company paying the costs usually recommends the speakers—who, more often than not, are consultants for the company. The softness of the guidelines is hardly surprising, given the fact that they were drafted in 1992 by a task force consisting almost equally of representatives of industry and of the medical profession. They were adopted with only minor changes by the American Medical Association (AMA) and the national professional organization responsible for regulating CME.

The drug companies pay the piper, and by one means or another they call the tune; and the tune is keyed to their sales pitch. The results are clearly demonstrated by published studies showing that industry sponsorship of CME is usually followed by increased prescribing of the sponsor's products. Were there not clear marketing and sales benefits for the sponsoring companies, they would not spend the huge sums that they do on supporting these activities. Most companies pay for medical education from their marketing budgets: this fact should speak for itself.

Perhaps the clearest indication that what the industry calls "education" is really intended to promote sales is the growth of "medical education and communication companies," or MECCs. MECCs are for-profit businesses hired by drug companies to prepare teaching programs and procure medical speakers. The drug companies offer these programs to hospitals or medical groups that are accredited to provide CME. Many MECCs are also officially approved by the medical profession's CME accrediting body to award education credits on their own. The MECCs are candid in their advertising to their drug industry clients. They say their purpose is to increase their clients' sales through professional "education"—and that is what they do. If any further demonstration were needed of the true purpose of what the industry calls "medical education," it was clearly supplied by a recent front-page article in *The New York Times*, with an accompanying report on the PBS program *Now with Bill Moyers*. According to these sources, three of the largest advertising agencies handling pharmaceutical accounts are now investing in companies that do contract research and prepare "educational" packages for the drug industry. This astonishingly incestuous arrangement makes it clear that research and education have both become subordinate to sales promotion.

The largest single piece of the known drug-marketing budget is spent on the direct promotion of drugs to doctors by representatives of drug firms. (This is called "detailing.") There are some 88,000 sales representatives through-out the country, who are paid more than $7 billion per year by the drug com-panies to visit doctors in hospitals and offices to pitch their employers' prod-ucts. The number and the ubiquity of these salespeople have increased greatly over the past few years. They roam the halls of almost every sizable hospital in the country seeking opportunities to talk with the medical staff and offering gifts (such as books, golf balls, and tickets to sporting events), drug samples, and free meals. In many teaching hospitals, drug representa-tives regularly provide lunches for the resident staff in order to gain their ear. They attend conferences, they are invited into operating and procedure rooms, and sometimes they are even present when physicians examine pa-tients in clinics or at the bedside.

Sales representatives also regularly visit doctors in their offices, often armed with information about the doctor's prescribing habits obtained from local drugstores. (There are firms that buy this information from pharmacies and sell it to drug companies.) They make themselves welcome by taking practitioners to dinner in fine restaurants, where company-selected and -paid experts sometimes give talks, and they distribute favors and gifts of all kinds to doctors and their office staffs. Free samples of drugs for physicians to give to their patients are a major gift item provided by representatives of large drug companies. Industry sources say they spend about $8 billion per year on free samples. These samples are an effective way to get doctors and patients committed to the continued use of the sampled product—usually an expensive, newly approved drug, with a long period of exclusivity ahead of it.

Sometimes doctors are even paid to prescribe the product and to report on the results, under the guise of participating in a company's continuing "Phase IV" research. How much of this kind of drug promotion masquer-ades as R&D is an interesting but unanswered question. Recently, according to an article in *American Medical News*, at least two new businesses in the Cincinnati area have been established to broker meetings between drug rep-resentatives and physicians in office practice. One such business charges drug firms $105 for each ten-minute meeting with a doctor—of which $50 goes to the doctor and $5 to a charity selected by the doctor from a list of five.

An effective marketing technique used by many drug firms is to focus on so-called "opinion leaders" in a particular medical specialty. These are prominent experts, usually on medical faculties and hospital staffs, who write papers, contribute to textbooks, and give talks at medical meetings—all of which influence the use of drugs in their fields. Companies shower special favors on these physicians, offer them honoraria as consultants and speakers, and often pay for them to attend conferences in posh resorts osten-sibly to seek their advice or to coach them in public speaking. In many med-ical specialties these days, it is almost impossible to find an expert who is not receiving payments from one or more drug companies in the field. Disclosure of these arrangements is said to be an adequate remedy for the conflicts of interest, but many observers worry about the loss of professional objectivity and independence that such financial ties produce, regardless of whether they are disclosed.

At medical meetings, drug companies are allowed to present symposia or other types of educational programs—with free lunches or dinners—to supplement the programs presented under the sponsoring society's auspices. The latter are themselves often supported by drug firms. The atmosphere at many large medical meetings resembles a bazaar, dominated by the presence of garish drug company exhibits and friendly salespeople eager to ply physicians with samples, gifts, and services while they pitch their company's drugs. In the exhibit areas adjacent to the meeting rooms, physicians wander through a carnival-like scene. Many carry large canvas bags, bearing drug company logos, stuffed with goodies. To some senior physicians who have watched the atmosphere at these meetings evolve from the sober professionalism of a few decades ago to the trade-show hucksterism of today, it is a dispiriting spectacle.

The cumulative effect of all of this is to blur the crucial distinction between drug marketing and professional education. Medical education worthy of the name requires an unbiased analysis of all the available evidence, led by experts who have no vested interest in the drugs that they are discussing. That is how medical meetings used to be, and that is how they ought to be, but it is most assuredly not what the companies want to support. They are not philanthropists. They need to sell their drugs; and experience has shown that when they organize "educational programs," when they pay for sales representatives to shower favors on physicians while touting the company's products, and when they spend huge sums on creating trade shows at medical meetings, the sales of their products increase. We would like to know how much all of this costs, but the industry prefers to keep these matters secret.

This kind of promotion masquerading as "education" is what largely accounts for the market success of new and expensive drugs that are not significantly different or better than less expensive existing drugs. And for this both the industry and the medical profession must take responsibility. Although there has been criticism from some members of the profession, medical societies and associations have taken no effective steps to oppose these practices. Most of the profession, it seems, finds it difficult to break the habit of taking money and gifts from the drug industry. Over a decade ago the AMA issued guidelines on accepting gifts from industry, but they were voluntary and quite permissive. They have not been observed in practice nor monitored by the AMA. PhRMA recently issued guidelines of its own, which closely follow those of the AMA, but, not surprisingly, they are also voluntary and permissive. It remains to be seen whether this latest effort will have any significant effect on drug-industry practices or will prove to be just another public relations ploy.

The Office of the Inspector General (OIG) of the Department of Health and Human Services recently placed in *The Federal Register* for comment a draft of proposed guidelines for ethical and legal relationships between the pharmaceutical industry on the one hand and physicians, pharmacists, and various purchasers of drugs on the other. The OIG notes that many of the existing practices involving gifts and payments to physicians are intended to influence the prescribing of a drug company's products and may potentially violate federal anti-kickback laws. It urges drug companies to review existing laws and regulations to avoid civil and criminal penalties. The code recently adopted by industry, to which we have already referred, is a minimum standard that certainly ought to be met, the OIG says, but mere compliance with that code does not guarantee protection against persecution for illegal conduct. Although they are only general recommendations, not regulations, the tone of these proposed guidelines from the OIG is stern. It remains to be seen what will happen to them when the drug industry and other interested parties weigh in. In any event, the introduction of such guidelines suggests a rising concern about the influence of the industry on the prescribing behavior of physicians and the costs of prescription drugs.

About the only organized sector of the medical profession that seems genuinely concerned about this issue is the national organization of medical students, the American Medical Student Association. Last spring, this group voted for a total ban on the acceptance of all drug-industry gifts and favors to medical students. It was a brave and laudable gesture, but its impact on practicing physicians and their organizations is doubtful. Recently we attended the annual meeting of the state medical society of Massachusetts, where student delegates urged their elders to pass a similar resolution that would apply to physicians. It was decisively defeated in favor of a resolution that recommended further study of the issue.

One of the most important developments in the marketing of prescription drugs is the recent explosion in direct-to-consumer (DTC) advertising. In 1997, the FDA changed its policies to allow DTC advertising without the requirement that it include medical details on the side effects of drugs. Since then, DTC advertising has burgeoned and is now estimated to be a nearly $3 billion industry. Drug firms now spend about as much on this advertising as they do on advertising to physicians in medical journals and other professional media. Advertisements for blockbuster drugs that are prescribed for common complaints such as allergy, heartburn, arthritis, "erectile dysfunction," depression, and anxiety are seen everywhere. Often celebrities—former politicians, famous athletes, movie stars—endorse the product. Consumers are urged to "ask your doctor" if a certain drug "would be right for you," and to "be sure to tell your doctor if you have kidney or liver problems" or some other medical condition—something we would hope doctors already knew or could find out for themselves.

A variant on the use of celebrities for the promotion of brand-name pharmaceuticals recently attracted much comment in the news. It seems that celebrities are being paid by drug companies to appear on television news and talk shows and enthusiastically mention their use of a particular drug. Audiences are not informed about the financial arrangement, and are thus allowed to assume that the celebrities are simply volunteering their personal experience. Embarrassed by these revelations, networks are now scrambling to require full disclosure.

Drug companies have been delighted with the effect of DTC advertising on their sales. Advocates like to describe this obvious form of selling as "education," just as they describe their advertising to doctors. But drug companies, owing to their clear conflict of interest, are not the ones to educate people about the drugs that they are selling. DTC ads mainly benefit the bottom line of the drug industry, not the public. They mislead consumers more than they inform them, and they pressure physicians to prescribe new, expensive, and often marginally helpful drugs, although a more conservative option might be better for the patient. That is probably why DTC ads are not permitted in other advanced countries less in the thrall of the pharmaceutical industry. . . .

What Should Be Done?

The pharmaceutical industry dominates just about every aspect of the American health care system that is related to its business interests. It uses its wealth and its political clout to influence all who might check or monitor its activities—including physicians, professional and academic institutions, Congress, and the FDA. Hiding behind a screen of public relations and advertising, it expects consumers to sit still for its excesses, with the clearly implied threat that otherwise it will be forced to stop producing its medical miracles.

What reforms might remedy the situation and direct the industry toward more socially useful behavior? First, the laws and regulations relating to the patenting of drugs and the granting of exclusive marketing rights need to be changed. The U.S. patent system is based on Article I, section 8, of the Constitution: "Congress shall have power . . . to promote the progress of science and useful arts, by securing for limited times to authors and inventors the exclusive right to their respective writings and discoveries." Patents were supposed to protect the intellectual property rights of inventors while enabling them to share information that others might use to advance the field, all in the public interest. But in the modern pharmaceutical business, as we have shown, the system is being grossly abused to allow companies to patent drugs that cannot reasonably be called new inventions, and to permit extensions of exclusivity on the flimsiest of legal pretexts.

The system has allowed the companies to flood the market with expensive me-too drugs and absurdly trivial variations on existing products. The system has also been used by the companies to delay, and sometimes to prevent altogether, competition from generic drugs. There is no question that modifications of [existing law] are needed. [Senators Charles] Schumer and [John] McCain are correct in their criticisms of the system, and we certainly support the general thrust of their proposals for reform. But more is needed. The whole patent system needs a new look, in view of the recent relaxation of standards for both usefulness and originality. The issues are technical and complicated, and the details of the needed changes will require careful consideration by experts to avoid making a bad situation even worse. We suggest study by a commission of experts (free of industry control) before any legislative or regulatory action is taken, but the completion of the study and the enactment of reforms deserve a high congressional priority.

Strengthening the FDA and improving its operations also should be a high priority for Congress. The FDA needs more help from congressional appropriations in meeting its growing responsibilities. Its dependence on user fees from industry should be replaced by adequate government support. This is an agency with an agenda of enormous importance to the public health, and it should not have to depend on the industry it is supposed to be regulating, any more than the SEC, for example, should have to depend on contributions from publicly traded corporations.

Of crucial importance, FDA regulations should be changed to require that new drug applications include evidence not only of the safety and the efficacy of a new drug, but also of the drug's effectiveness in relation to existing products of the same type. Approval should depend in part on whether the new drug adds something useful in terms of greater effectiveness, greater safety, fewer side effects, or substantially greater convenience. The FDA should be allowed reasonable flexibility in its judgments, of course; but it should not approve drugs that on balance offer trivial advantages or no advantages at all over products already available, and may even be worse. That policy change alone would dramatically improve the medical value of new prescription drugs, since drug companies would have no incentive to turn out me-too drugs and would have to shift their R&D emphasis to finding more innovative ones.

The requirements for membership on FDA advisory committees, upon which the agency depends for advice in the evaluation and approval of new drugs, should be strengthened to avoid conflicts of interest. Given the pervasiveness of the financial ties with the drug industry that now exist among clinical experts in most fields, it is admittedly difficult to find qualified consultants without such conflicts. But the task is not impossible, and the agency should be required to show that it is making every reasonable effort. Without unbiased experts, the FDA cannot get the help it needs to withstand the pressures from industry to approve drugs that really ought not to be allowed on the market or to keep drugs on the market that ought to be withdrawn.

We have already explained why we believe that direct-to-consumer ads are not in the public interest. The FDA should reverse its policy and prohibit such ads in the future, or at least greatly restrict their use. The drug industry and the advertising agencies, which have a financial interest in such ads, will strongly resist, so any such action would probably require a congressional mandate. For reasons of public health and safety, however, the FDA is acknowledged to have purview over pharmaceutical advertising, so there is no question of an unfettered "right to commercial free speech" in this case. The issue is how, and how much, it should be regulated.

Reforms are also needed in the current system for conducting clinical trials. The drug industry should not control the medical evaluation of its own products. The industry has a legitimate interest in seeing that these clinical trials are carried out, and it should pay for most of them. But the design and the conduct of the trials, and the collection, the analysis, and the interpretation of the results, should be the responsibility of the independent clinical investigators who do the work—not of the sponsoring drug companies. This will require stringent oversight or elimination of the hired businesses that conduct clinical trials for the drug companies, as well as substantial reforms at the academic centers and teaching hospitals that would then carry out most of the studies. Perhaps drug-company trials might best be monitored through some centralized, not-for-profit institution that could be a repository for contract proposals from the companies and an intermediary for the distribution of funds. What should be avoided in any case is the market competition among academic centers for drug-company business. This threatens to transform our medical centers into commercial enterprises, with the inevitable weakening of their commitments to education, clinical care, and unrestricted research. Guidelines such as those recently promulgated by the AAMC will be helpful in preventing this transformation, but the outright elimination of a commercial market for clinical trials would probably be most effective.

In devising remedies for the problems described here, we must not lose sight of the fact that the prescription-drug industry can sell only the drugs that doctors are willing to prescribe. We have noted the costly and excessive lengths to which drug companies go to influence the prescribing behavior of physicians. But this is done only with the acquiescence of the doctors and their professional associations and educational institutions. If the drug industry presumes to take responsibility for the "education" of physicians, it is because the profession allows—or even invites—the industry to do so. In so doing, the profession abdicates its responsibility to act as fiduciaries and advisers for patients. The profession must take the necessary steps to end its financial and intellectual reliance on the pharmaceutical industry. We believe that many physicians (including medical educators) share this view but hesitate to voice it publicly. The public should be able to get trustworthy expert advice from physicians on what drugs are safe and effective and which of these, if any, are needed for optimal and cost-effective treatment. This is unlikely if much of the profession and its institutions are in the industry's pocket.

Finally, we note that most of the reforms we have suggested are intended to improve the quality of prescription drugs and the discrimination with which they are prescribed. Most would probably also reduce expenditures. But the greatest contribution to the control of prescription-drug costs could come from the bargaining power of large purchasers. The largest potential purchaser is the government—through Medicare, Medicaid, and the Veterans Affairs System. If payment for all the drugs used by the patients in these programs were to be negotiated by the government, there is no doubt that major savings would be achieved, particularly if physicians were also to use formularies that limit the routine use of me-too drugs. Such measures would undoubtedly spread to the private insurance system. However, with Republicans now in control of Congress, federal policies will probably become even friendlier to the pharmaceutical industry.

Prescription drugs are an essential part of modern medical care. Americans need good new drugs at reasonable prices. Yet the pharmaceutical industry is failing to meet that need. There is a widening gap between its rhetoric and its practices. Neither the medical profession nor government has so far done much to remedy the situation, but sooner or later they will have to act. The increased conservative complexion of the new Congress and the growing dependence of physicians on pharmaceutical money will probably delay such action. Nevertheless, the public is aroused and some kind of reform seems ultimately inevitable. The consequences of continuing to allow an essential industry to put profits above the public interest are simply too grave. ∎

▪ QUESTIONS FOR MAKING CONNECTIONS WITHIN THE READING ▪

1. Whenever we read a work of nonfiction, the author's credibility is always a significant concern. Especially in writing on a subject as controversial as pricing in the pharmaceutical industry, much of an argument's success or failure depends on the author's ability to sustain the persona of a true expert or of a well-informed observer. How well do Relman and Angell sustain this persona? In what ways does their concern for credibility shape

both the form and the content of the argument they make? How well have they managed to defend themselves from counterattacks by the big drug companies? What qualities of good writing have Relman and Angell sacrificed in order to showcase their credibility?

2. What arguments do the pharmaceutical companies offer in defense of their high profits? What counterargument do Relman and Angell offer? Have the two been fair in representing the position of the drug companies? What criteria should define "fairness" in such a case? Is agreement the only fair response, or is it possible to disagree with the drug companies in an ethical and well-informed way? If you feel that Relman and Angell have been unfair, what arguments might you regard as more fair? If you feel that the two authors have argued fairly, what arguments might you regard as unethical?

3. Given Relman and Angell's analysis of how the drug industry conducts business, do you regard their solutions as adequate and likely to succeed? In order to explore this question, you might first make an outline of the problems Relman and Angell address. Would you say that all of the problems are equally important, or are some more significant than others? Is it possible to view the problems of drug pricing as *systemic* in origin—reflective of an entire system or industry? Now turn to the solutions proposed by Relman and Angell: Would you say that these solutions get to the heart of the problem?

▪ QUESTIONS FOR WRITING ▪

1. Do the practices of the pharmaceutical industry present a clear and present danger to the health of the American people? In what ways might these practices deform or disable the medical profession? Judging from the evidence, is there a real possibility that doctors will deliver inferior care because of the actions of drug companies? Even if physicians can still deliver effective care to their patients, in what ways might current pricing practices help to deprive other Americans of care by placing it out of financial reach or by draining off the resources of the entire health care system?

2. Write a detailed and well-aimed defense of the drug industry. In doing so, you might look for possible omissions, contradictions, or oversimplifications in Relman and Angell's argument. You should assume that their research is accurate, but you should feel free to question the conclusions they draw from the evidence. "Detailed and well-aimed" means that you cannot ignore the particulars of Relman and Angell's position: You must respond to the argument as a whole, but you should also pay close attention to the logic and evidence they offer in support of that argument.

Keep in mind that an effective defense of the drug industry might concede the truth of some of Relman and Angell's accusations, while at the same time offering a modified view that represents the drug companies in a more favorable light.

■ *QUESTIONS FOR MAKING CONNECTIONS BETWEEN READINGS* ■

1. Does advertising have a place in the pharmaceutical industry? Relman and Angell are deeply concerned about the health care industry's marketing practices and recommend greater regulation in this area, but they leave to other readers the work of imagining what these regulations might be. Is Virginia Postrel's argument about the aesthetic value of surface applicable to this situation? Or is health care an area where the consideration of aesthetics, particularly the aesthetics of advertising, is out of bounds? Does Postrel's argument only apply to "trivial" situations where the items being advertised—shoes or homes—don't have "intrinsic qualities" in quite the same way that drugs do? Write an essay in which you discuss the obstacles and the opportunities for regulating the pharmaceutical industry's future advertising practices.

2. In what ways does the account presented in "America's Other Drug Problem" confirm, contradict, or complicate the reasoning presented by Gregory Stock in "The Enhanced and the Unenhanced"? Stock envisions a genetics industry that will respond in a fairly direct and transparent way to the public's demand for genetic amelioration. But can we be sure that the response will be as direct and transparent as Stock assumes? Is it possible that, as in the drug industry, development costs in the field of genetics—whether these costs are real or not—might justify pricing that excludes large numbers of people, or that limits the range of options for all, regardless of their earning power? If you have doubts about the feasibility of Stock's proposal, what alternative arrangements might distribute in the fairest way innovations in genetic engineering?

www For additional suggestions about making connections between readings, visit the Link-O-Mat and more Sample Questions at <www.newhum.com>.

OLIVER SACKS

W‌HEN O‌LIVER S‌ACKS was awarded the Lewis Thomas Prize by Rockefeller University in 2002 for his life's work of presenting the case histories of patients with neurological diseases, he was praised for his ability to take his readers into the nearly unimaginable mental worlds of those who have suffered brain damage: "Sacks," the awards committee concluded, "presses us to follow him into uncharted regions of human experience—and compels us to realize, once there, that we are confronting only ourselves." This is an extraordinary claim, given that Sacks has written, most famously, about patients who suffered sleeping sickness for decades, about a man who mistook his wife for a hat, and about what it is like to live with Tourette's syndrome, a disease that drives its victims to spew forth curses in public. It has been Sacks's lifelong project to write about the mentally ill in ways that foreground the humanity of those who are suffering from diseases that generate all manner of strange behavior.

Born and educated in England, Sacks has lived in New York since 1965, where he is clinical professor of neurology at the Albert Einstein College of Medicine, adjunct professor of neurology at the NYU School of Medicine, and consultant neurologist to the Little Sisters of the Poor. Sacks explained in a recent interview that his interest in the brain and in neurology arose from his childhood experience of visual migraines. "I would often lose sight to one side, and sometimes one can lose the idea of one side in a migraine, which can be a very, very strange thing. When I was young I was sort of terrified of these things. I asked my mother, who was a doctor herself and also had visual migraines. She was the first to explain to me that we are not just cameras—we are not just given the visual world. We make it to some extent."

The observation of how patients creatively adapt to the challenges an illness poses has shaped Sacks's own approach to medicine, and has led him to create what he has called a "neuroanthropology" of how illness is both perceived and experienced around the world. The author of *Awakenings* (1973), *The Man Who*

Sacks, Oliver. "The Mind's Eye." *The New Yorker*, July 28, 2003. 48–59.

Initial quote drawn from the Rockefeller University Web site <http://www.rockefeller.edu/lectures/sacks031802.html>. Closing quote drawn from the Salon.com interview with Sacks, <http://www.salon.com/dec96/sacks961223.html>.

Mistook His Wife for a Hat (1985), and *An Anthropologist on Mars* (1995), among other works, Sacks brings together biology and biography in the interests of forging a humane medical practice.

www **To learn more about Oliver Sacks and the medical humanities, please visit the Link-O-Mat at <www.newhum.com>.**

The Mind's Eye

What the Blind See

In his last letter, Goethe wrote, "The Ancients said that the animals are taught through their organs; let me add to this, so are men, but they have the advantage of teaching their organs in return." He wrote this in 1832, a time when phrenology was at its height, and the brain was seen as a mosaic of "little organs" subserving everything from language to drawing ability to shyness. Each individual, it was believed, was given a fixed measure of this faculty or that, according to the luck of his birth. Though we no longer pay attention, as the phrenologists did, to the "bumps" on the head (each of which, supposedly, indicated a brain-mind organ beneath), neurology and neuroscience have stayed close to the idea of brain fixity and localization—the notion, in particular, that the highest part of the brain, the cerebral cortex, is effectively programmed from birth: this part to vision and visual processing, that part to hearing, that to touch, and so on.

This would seem to allow individuals little power of choice, of self-determination, let alone of adaptation, in the event of a neurological or perceptual mishap.

But to what extent are we—our experiences, our reactions—shaped, predetermined, by our brains, and to what extent do we shape our own brains? Does the mind run the brain or the brain the mind—or, rather, to what extent does one run the other? To what extent are we the authors, the creators, of our own experiences? The effects of a profound perceptual deprivation such as blindness can cast an unexpected light on this. To become blind, especially later in life, presents one with a huge, potentially overwhelming challenge: to find a new way of living, of ordering one's world, when the old way has been destroyed.

A dozen years ago, I was sent an extraordinary book called "Touching the Rock: An Experience of Blindness." The author, John Hull, was a professor of religious education who had grown up in Australia and then moved to England. Hull had developed cataracts at the age of thirteen, and became completely blind in his left eye four years later. Vision in his right eye remained reasonable until he was thirty-five or so, and then started to deteriorate. There followed a decade of steadily failing vision, in which Hull needed stronger and stronger magnifying glasses, and had to write with thicker and thicker pens, until, in 1983, at the age of forty-eight, he became completely blind.

"Touching the Rock" is the journal he dictated in the three years that followed. It is full of piercing insights relating to Hull's life as a blind person, but most striking for me is Hull's description of how, in the years after his loss of sight, he experienced a gradual attenuation of visual imagery and memory, and finally a virtual extinction of them (except in dreams)—a state that he calls "deep blindness."

By this, Hull meant not only the loss of visual images and memories but a loss of the very idea of seeing, so that concepts like "here," "there," and "facing" seemed to lose meaning for him, and even the sense of objects having "appearances," visible characteristics, vanished. At this point, for example, he could no longer imagine how the numeral 3 looked, unless he traced it in the air with his hand. He could construct a "motor" image of a 3, but not a visual one.

Hull, though at first greatly distressed about the fading of visual memories and images—the fact that he could no longer conjure up the faces of his wife or children, or of familiar and loved landscapes and places—then came to accept it with remarkable equanimity; indeed, to regard it as a natural response to a nonvisual world. He seemed to regard this loss of visual imagery as a prerequisite for the full development, the heightening, of his other senses.

Two years after becoming completely blind, Hull had apparently become so nonvisual as to resemble someone who had been blind from birth. Hull's loss of visuality also reminded me of the sort of "cortical blindness" that can happen if the primary visual cortex is damaged, through a stroke or traumatic brain damage—although in Hull's case there was no direct damage to the visual cortex but, rather, a cutting off from any visual stimulation or input.

In a profoundly religious way, and in language sometimes reminiscent of that of St. John of the Cross, Hull enters into this state, surrenders himself, with a sort of acquiescence and joy. And such "deep" blindness he conceives as "an authentic and autonomous world, a place of its own. . . . Being a whole-body seer is to be in one of the concentrated human conditions."

Being a "whole-body seer," for Hull, means shifting his attention, his center of gravity, to the other senses, and he writes again and again of how these have assumed a new richness and power. Thus he speaks of how the sound of rain, never before accorded much attention, can now delineate a whole landscape for him, for its sound on the garden path is different from its sound as it drums on the lawn, or on the bushes in his garden, or on the fence dividing it from the road. "Rain," he writes, "has a way of bringing out the contours of everything; it throws a coloured blanket over previously invisible things; instead of an intermittent and thus fragmented world, the steadily falling rain creates continuity of acoustic experience . . . presents the fullness of an entire situation all at once . . . gives a sense of perspective and of the actual relationships of one part of the world to another."

With his new intensity of auditory experience (or attention), along with the sharpening of his other senses, Hull comes to feel a sense of intimacy with nature, an intensity of being-in-the-world, beyond anything he knew when he was sighted. Blindness now becomes for him "a dark, paradoxical gift." This is not just "compensation," he emphasizes, but a whole new order, a new mode of human being. With this he extricates himself from visual nostalgia, from the strain, or falsity, of trying to pass as "normal," and finds a new focus, a new freedom. His teaching at the university expands, becomes more fluent, his writing becomes stronger and deeper; he becomes intellectually and spiritually bolder, more confident. He feels he is on solid ground at last.

What Hull described seemed to me an astounding example of how an individual deprived of one form of perception could totally reshape himself to a new center, a new identity.

It is said that those who see normally as infants but then become blind within the first two years of life retain no memories of seeing, have no visual imagery and no visual elements in their dreams (and, in this way, are comparable to those born blind). It is similar with those who lose hearing before the age of two: they have no sense of having "lost" the world of sound, nor any sense of "silence," as hearing people sometimes imagine. For those who lose sight so early, the very concepts of "sight" or "blindness" soon cease to have meaning, and there is no sense of losing the world of vision, only of living fully in a world constructed by the other senses.

But it seemed extraordinary to me that such an annihilation of visual memory as Hull describes could happen equally to an adult, with decades, an entire lifetime, of rich and richly categorized visual experience to call upon. And yet I could not doubt the authenticity of Hull's account, which he relates with the most scrupulous care and lucidity.

Important studies of adaptation in the brain were begun in the nineteen-seventies by, among others, Helen Neville, a cognitive neuroscientist now working in Oregon. She showed that in prelingually deaf people (that is, those who had been born deaf or become deaf before the age of two or so) the auditory parts of the brain had not degenerated or atrophied. These had remained active and functional, but with an activity and a function that were new: they had been transformed, "reallocated," in Neville's term, for processing visual language. Comparable studies in those born blind, or early blinded, show that the visual areas of the cortex, similarly, may be reallocated in function, and used to process sound and touch.

With the reallocation of the visual cortex to touch and other senses, these can take on a hyperacuity that perhaps no sighted person can imagine. Bernard Morin, the blind mathematician who in the nineteen-sixties had shown how a sphere could be turned inside out, felt that his achievement required a special sort of spatial perception and imagination. And a similar sort of spatial giftedness has been central to the work of Geerat Vermeij, a blind biologist who has been able to delineate many new species of mollusk, based on tiny variations in the shapes and contours of their shells.

Faced with such findings and reports, neurologists began to concede that there might be a certain flexibility or plasticity in the brain, at least in the early years of life. But when this critical period was over, it was assumed, the brain became inflexible, and no further changes of a radical type could occur. The experiences that Hull so carefully recounts give the lie to this. It is clear that his perceptions, his brain, did finally change, in a fundamental way. Indeed, Alvaro Pascual-Leone and his colleagues in Boston have recently shown that, even in adult sighted volunteers, as little as five days of being blindfolded produces marked shifts to nonvisual forms of behavior and cognition, and they have demonstrated the physiological changes in the brain that go along with this. And only last month, Italian researchers published a study showing that sighted volunteers kept in the dark for as little as ninety *minutes* may show a striking enhancement of tactile-spatial sensitivity.

The brain, clearly, is capable of changing even in adulthood, and I assumed that Hull's experience was typical of acquired blindness—the response, sooner or later, of everyone who becomes blind, even in adult life.

So when I came to publish an essay on Hull's book, in 1991, I was taken aback to receive a number of letters from blind people, letters that were often somewhat puzzled, and occasionally indignant, in tone. Many of my correspondents, it seemed, could not identify with Hull's experience, and said that they themselves, even decades after losing their sight, had never lost their visual images or memories. One correspondent, who had lost her sight at fifteen, wrote, "Even though I am totally blind . . . I consider myself a very visual person. I still 'see' objects in front of me. As I am typing now I can see my hands on the keyboard. . . . I don't feel comfortable in a new environment until I have a mental picture of its appearance. I need a mental map for my independent moving, too."

Had I been wrong, or at least one-sided, in accepting Hull's experience as a typical response to blindness? Had I been guilty of emphasizing one mode of response too strongly, oblivious to the possibilities of radically different responses?

This feeling came to a head in 1996, when I received a letter from an Australian psychologist named Zoltan Torey. Torey wrote to me not about blindness but about a book he had written on the brain-mind problem and the nature of consciousness. (The book was published by Oxford University Press as "The Crucible of Consciousness," in 1999.) In his letter Torey also spoke of how he had been blinded in an accident at the age of twenty-one, while working at a chemical factory, and how, although "advised to switch from a visual to an auditory mode of adjustment," he had moved in the opposite direction, and resolved to develop instead his "inner eye," his powers of visual imagery, to their greatest possible extent.

In this, it seemed, he had been extremely successful, developing a remarkable power of generating, holding, and manipulating images in his mind, so much so that he had been able to construct an imagined visual world that seemed almost as real and intense to him as the perceptual one he had lost—and, indeed, sometimes more real, more intense, a sort of controlled dream or hallucination. This imagery, moreover, enabled him to do things that might have seemed scarcely possible for a blind man.

"I replaced the entire roof guttering of my multi-gabled home single-handed," he wrote, "and solely on the strength of the accurate and well-focused manipulation of my now totally pliable and responsive mental space." (Torey later expanded on this episode, mentioning the great alarm of his neighbors at seeing a blind man, alone, on the roof of his house—and, even more terrifying to them, at night, in pitch darkness.)

And it enabled him to think in ways that had not been available to him before, to envisage solutions, models, designs, to project himself to the inside of machines and other systems, and, finally, to grasp by visual thought and simulation (complemented by all the data of neuroscience) the complexities of that ultimate system, the human brain-mind.

When I wrote back to Torey, I suggested that he consider writing another book, a more personal one, exploring how his life had been affected by blindness, and how he had responded to this, in the most improbable and seemingly paradoxical of ways. "Out of Darkness" is the memoir he has now written, and in it Torey describes his early memories with great visual intensity and humor. Scenes are remembered or reconstructed in brief, poetic glimpses of his childhood and youth in Hungary before the Second World War: the sky-blue buses of Budapest, the egg-yellow trams, the lighting of gas lamps, the funicular on the Buda side. He describes a carefree and privileged youth, roaming with his father in the wooded mountains above the Danube, playing games and pranks at school, growing up in a highly intellectual environment of writers, actors, professionals of every sort. Torey's father was the head of a large motion-picture studio and would often give his son scripts to read. "This," Torey writes, "gave me the opportunity to visualize stories, plots and characters, to work my imagination—a skill that was to become a lifeline and source of strength in the years ahead."

All of this came to a brutal end with the Nazi occupation, the siege of Buda, and then the Soviet occupation. Torey, now an adolescent, found himself passionately drawn to the big questions—the mystery of the universe, of life, and above all the mystery of consciousness, of the mind. In 1948, nineteen years old, and feeling that he needed to immerse himself in biology, engineering, neuroscience, and psychology, but knowing that there was no chance of study, of an intellectual life, in Soviet Hungary, Torey made his escape and eventually found his way to Australia, where, penniless and without connections, he did various manual jobs. In June of 1951, loosening the plug in a vat of acid at the chemical factory where he worked, he had the accident that bisected his life.

"The last thing I saw with complete clarity was a glint of light in the flood of acid that was to engulf my face and change my life. It was a nanosecond of sparkle, framed by the black circle of the drumface, less than a foot away. This was the final scene, the slender thread that ties me to my visual past."

When it became clear that his corneas had been hopelessly damaged and that he would have to live his life as a blind man, he was advised to rebuild his representation of the world on the basis of hearing and touch and to "forget about sight and visualizing altogether." But this was something that Torey could not or would not do. He had emphasized, in his first letter to me, the importance of a most critical choice at this juncture: "I immediately resolved to find out how far a partially sense-deprived brain could go to rebuild a life." Put this way, it sounds abstract, like an experiment. But in his book one senses the tremendous feelings underlying his resolution—the horror of darkness, "the empty darkness," as Torey often calls it, "the grey fog that was engulfing me," and the passionate desire to hold on to light and sight, to maintain, if only in memory and imagination, a vivid and living visual world. The very title of his book says all this, and the note of defiance is sounded from the start.

Hull, who did not use his potential for imagery in a deliberate way, lost it in two or three years, and became unable to remember which way round a 3 went; Torey, on the other hand, soon became able to multiply four-figure numbers by each other, as on a blackboard, visualizing the whole operation in his mind, "painting" the suboperations in different colors.

Well aware that the imagination (or the brain), unrestrained by the usual perceptual input, may run away with itself in a wildly associative or self-serving way—as may happen in deliria, hallucinations, or dreams—Torey maintained a cautious and "scientific" attitude to his own visual imagery, taking pains to check the accuracy of his images by every means available. "I learned," he writes, "to hold the image in a tentative way, conferring credibility and status on it only when some information would tip the balance in its favor." Indeed, he soon gained enough confidence in the reliability of his visual imagery to stake his life upon it, as when he undertook roof repairs by himself. And this confidence extended to other, purely mental projects. He became able "to imagine, to visualize, for example, the inside of a differential gearbox in action as if from inside its casing. I was able to watch the cogs bite, lock and revolve, distributing the spin as required. I began to play around with this internal view in connection with mechanical and technical problems, visualizing how subcomponents relate in the atom, or in the living cell." This power of imagery was crucial, Torey thought, in enabling him to arrive at a solution of the brain-mind problem by visualizing the brain "as a perpetual juggling act of interacting routines."

In a famous study of creativity, the French mathematician Jacques Hadamard asked many scientists and mathematicians, including Einstein, about their thought processes. Einstein replied, "The physical entities which seem to serve as elements in thought are . . . more or less clear images which can be 'voluntarily' reproduced and combined. [Some are] of visual and some of muscular type. Conventional words or other signs have to be sought for laboriously only in a secondary stage." Torey cites this, and adds, "Nor was Einstein unique in this respect. Hadamard found that almost all scientists work this way, and this was also the way my project evolved."

Soon after receiving Torey's manuscript, I received the proofs of yet another memoir by a blind person: Sabriye Tenberken's "My Path Leads to Tibet." While Hull and Torey are thinkers, preoccupied in their different ways by inwardness, states of brain and mind, Tenberken is a doer; she has travelled, often alone, all over Tibet, where for centuries blind people have been treated as less than human and denied education, work, respect, or a role in the community. Virtually single-handed, Tenberken has transformed their situation over the past half-dozen years, devising a form of Tibetan Braille, establishing schools for the blind, and integrating the graduates of these schools into their communities.

Tenberken herself had impaired vision almost from birth but was able to make out faces and landscapes until she was twelve. As a child in Germany, she had a particular predilection for colors, and loved painting, and when she was no longer able to decipher shapes and forms she could still use colors to identify objects. Tenberken has, indeed, an intense synesthesia. "As far back as I can remember," she writes, "numbers and words have instantly triggered colors in me. . . . The number 4, for example, [is] gold. Five is light green. Nine is vermillion. . . . Days of the week as well as months have their colors, too. I have them arranged in geometrical formations, in circular sectors, a little like a pie. When I need to recall on which day a particular event happened, the first thing that pops up on my inner screen is the day's color, then its position in the pie." Her synesthesia has persisted and been intensified, it seems, by her blindness.

Though she has been totally blind for twenty years now, Tenberken continues to use all her other senses, along with verbal descriptions, visual memories, and a strong pictorial and synesthetic sensibility, to construct "pictures" of landscapes and rooms, of environments and scenes—pictures so lively and detailed as to astonish her listeners. These images may sometimes be wildly or comically different from reality, as she relates in one incident when she and a companion drove to Nam Co, the great salt lake in Tibet. Turning eagerly toward the lake, Tenberken saw, in her mind's eye, "a beach of crystallized salt shimmering like snow under an evening sun, at the edge of a vast body of turquoise water. . . . And down below, on the deep green mountain flanks, a few nomads were watching their yaks grazing." But it then turns out that she has been facing in the wrong direction, not "looking" at the lake at all, and that she has been "staring" at rocks and a gray landscape. These disparities don't faze her in the least—she is happy to have so vivid a visual imagination. Hers is essentially an artistic imagination, which can be impressionistic, romantic, not veridical at all, where Torey's imagination is that of an engineer, and has to be factual, accurate down to the last detail.

I had now read three memoirs, strikingly different in their depictions of the visual experience of blinded people: Hull with his acquiescent descent into imageless "deep blindness," Torey with his "compulsive visualization" and meticulous construction of an internal visual world, and Tenberken with her impulsive, almost novelistic, visual freedom, along with her remarkable and specific gift of synesthesia. Was there any such thing, I now wondered, as a "typical" blind experience?

I recently met two other people blinded in adult life who shared their experiences with me.

Dennis Shulman, a clinical psychologist and psychoanalyst who lectures on Biblical topics, is an affable, stocky, bearded man in his fifties who gradually lost his sight in his teens, becoming completely blind by the time he entered college. He immediately confirmed that his experience was unlike Hull's: "I still live in a visual world after thirty-five years of blindness. I have very vivid visual memories and images. My wife, whom I have never seen—I think of her visually. My kids, too. I see myself visually—but it is as I last saw myself, when I was thirteen, though I try hard to update the image. I often give public lectures, and my notes are in Braille; but when I go over them in my mind, I see the Braille notes visually—they are visual images, not tactile."

Arlene Gordon, a charming woman in her seventies, a former social worker, said that things were very similar for her: "If I move my arms back and forth in front of my eyes, I see them, even though I have been blind for more than thirty years." It seemed that moving her arms was immediately translated for her into a visual image. Listening to talking books, she added, made her eyes tire if she listened too long; she seemed to herself to be reading at such times, the sound of the spoken words being transformed to lines of print on a vividly visualized book in front of her. This involved a sort of cognitive exertion (similar perhaps to translating one language into another), and sooner or later this would give her an eye ache.

I was reminded of Amy, a colleague who had been deafened by scarlet fever at the age of nine but was so adept a lipreader that I often forgot she was deaf. Once, when I absent-mindedly turned away from her as I was speaking, she said sharply, "I can no longer hear you."

"You mean you can no longer see me," I said.

"*You* may call it seeing," she answered, "but I experience it as hearing."

Amy, though totally deaf, still constructed the sound of speech in her mind. Both Dennis and Arlene, similarly, spoke not only of a heightening of visual imagery and imagination since losing their eyesight but also of what seemed to be a much readier transference of information from verbal description—or from their own sense of touch, movement, hearing, or smell—into a visual form. On the whole, their experiences seemed quite similar to Torey's, even though they had not systematically exercised their powers of visual imagery in the way that he had, or consciously tried to make an entire virtual world of sight.

There is increasing evidence from neuroscience for the extraordinarily rich interconnectedness and interactions of the sensory areas of the brain, and the difficulty, therefore, of saying that anything is purely visual or purely auditory, or purely anything. This is evident in the very titles of some recent papers—Pascual-Leone and his colleagues at Harvard now write of "The Metamodal Organization of the Brain," and Shinsuke Shimojo and his group at Caltech, who are also exploring intersensory perceptual phenomena, recently published a paper called "What You See Is What You Hear," and stress that sensory modalities can never be considered in isolation. The world of the blind, of the blinded, it seems, can be especially rich in such in-between states—the intersensory, the metamodal—states for which we have no common language.

Arlene, like Dennis, still identifies herself in many ways as a visual person. "I have a very strong sense of color," she said. "I pick out my own clothes. I think, Oh, that will go with this or that, once I have been told the colors." Indeed, she was dressed very smartly, and took obvious pride in her appearance.

"I love travelling," she continued. "I 'saw' Venice when I was there." She explained how her travelling companions would describe places, and she would then construct a visual image from these details, her reading, and her own visual memories. "Sighted people enjoy travelling with me," she said. "I ask them questions, then they look, and see things they wouldn't otherwise. Too often people with sight don't see anything! It's a reciprocal process—we enrich each other's worlds."

If we are sighted, we build our own images, using our eyes, our visual information, so instantly and seamlessly that it seems to us we are experiencing "reality" itself. One may need to see people who are color-blind, or motion-blind, who have lost certain visual capacities from cerebral injury, to realize the enormous act of analysis and synthesis, the dozens of subsystems involved in the subjectively simple act of seeing. But can a visual image be built using *nonvisual* information—information conveyed by the other senses, by memory, or by verbal description?

There have, of course, been many blind poets and writers, from Homer on. Most of these were born with normal vision and lost their sight in boyhood or adulthood (like Milton). I loved reading Prescott's "Conquest of Mexico" and "Conquest of Peru" as a boy, and feel that I first saw these lands through his intensely visual, almost hallucinogenic descriptions, and I was amazed to discover, years later, that Prescott not only had never visited Mexico or Peru but had been virtually blind since the age of eighteen. Did he, like Torey, compensate for his blindness by developing such powers of visual imagery that he could experience a "virtual reality" of sight? Or were his brilliant visual descriptions in a sense simulated, made possible by the evocative and pictorial powers of language? To what extent can language, a picturing in words, provide a substitute for actual seeing, and for the visual, pictorial imagination? Blind children, it has often been noted, tend to be precocious verbally, and may develop such fluency in the verbal description of faces and places as to leave others (and perhaps themselves) uncertain as to whether they are actually blind. Helen Keller's writing, to give a famous example, startles one with its brilliantly visual quality.

When I asked Dennis and Arlene whether they had read John Hull's book, Arlene said, "I was stunned when I read it. His experiences are so unlike mine." Perhaps, she added, Hull had "renounced" his inner vision. Dennis agreed, but said, "We are only two individuals. You are going to have to talk to dozens of people. . . . But in the meanwhile you should read Jacques Lusseyran's memoir."

Lusseyran was a French Resistance fighter whose memoir, "And There Was Light," deals mostly with his experiences fighting the Nazis and later in Buchenwald but includes many beautiful descriptions of his early adaptations to blindness. He was blinded in an accident when he was not quite eight years old, an age that he came to feel was "ideal" for such an eventuality, for, while he already had a rich visual experience to call on, "the habits of a boy of eight are not yet formed, either in body or in mind. His body is infinitely supple." And suppleness, agility, indeed came to characterize his response to blindness.

Many of his initial responses were of loss, both of imagery and of interests:

> A very short time after I went blind I forgot the faces of my mother and father and the faces of most of the people I loved. . . . I stopped caring whether people were dark or fair, with blue eyes or green. I felt that sighted people spent too much time observing these empty things. . . . I no longer even thought about them. People no longer seemed to possess them. Sometimes in my mind men and women appeared without heads or fingers.

This is similar to Hull, who writes, "Increasingly, I am no longer even trying to imagine what people look like. . . . I am finding it more and more difficult to realize that people look like anything, to put any meaning into the idea that they have an appearance."

But then, while relinquishing the actual visual world and many of its values and categories, Lusseyran starts to construct and to use an imaginary visual world more like Torey's.

This started as a sensation of light, a formless, flooding, streaming radiance. Neurological terms are bound to sound reductive in this almost mystical context. Yet one might venture to interpret this as a "release" phenomenon, a spontaneous, almost eruptive arousal of the visual cortex, now deprived of its normal visual input. This is a phenomenon analogous, perhaps, to tinnitus or phantom limbs, though endowed here, by a devout and precociously imaginative little boy, with some element of the supernal. But then, it becomes clear, he does find himself in possession of great powers of visual imagery, and not just a formless luminosity.

The visual cortex, the inner eye, having now been activated, Lusseyran's mind constructed a "screen" upon which whatever he thought or desired was projected and, if need be, manipulated, as on a computer screen. "This screen was not like a blackboard, rectangular or square, which so quickly reaches the edge of its frame," he writes. "My screen was always as big as I needed it to be. Because it was nowhere in space it was everywhere at the same time. . . . Names, figures and objects in general did not appear on my screen without shape, nor just in black and white, but in all the colors of the rainbow. Nothing entered my mind without being bathed in a certain amount of light. . . . In a few months my personal world had turned into a painter's studio."

Great powers of visualization were crucial to the young Lusseyran, even in something as nonvisual (one would think) as learning Braille (he visualizes the Braille dots, as Dennis does), and in his brilliant successes at school. They were no less crucial in the real, outside world. He describes walks with his sighted friend Jean, and how, as they were climbing together up the side of a hill above the Seine Valley, he could say:

> "Just look! This time we're on top. . . . You'll see the whole bend of the river, unless the sun gets in your eyes!" Jean was startled, opened his eyes wide

and cried: "You're right." This little scene was often repeated between us, in a thousand forms.

"Every time someone mentioned an event," Lusseyran relates, "the event immediately projected itself in its place on the screen, which was a kind of inner canvas. . . . Comparing my world with his, [Jean] found that his held fewer pictures and not nearly as many colors. This made him almost angry. 'When it comes to that,' he used to say, 'which one of us two is blind?'"

It was his supernormal powers of visualization and visual manipulation—visualizing people's position and movement, the topography of any space, visualizing strategies for defense and attack—coupled with his charismatic personality (and seemingly infallible "nose" or "ear" for detecting falsehood, possible traitors), which later made Lusseyran an icon in the French Resistance.

Dennis, earlier, had spoken of how the heightening of his other senses had increased his sensitivity to moods in other people, and to the most delicate nuances in their speech and self-presentation. He could now recognize many of his patients by smell, he said, and he could often pick up states of tension or anxiety which they might not even be aware of. He felt that he had become far more sensitive to others' emotional states since losing his sight, for he was no longer taken in by visual appearances, which most people learn to camouflage. Voices and smells, by contrast, he felt, could reveal people's depths. He had come to think of most sighted people, he joked, as "visually dependent."

In a subsequent essay, Lusseyran inveighs against the "despotism," the "idol worship" of sight, and sees the "task" of blindness as reminding us of our other, deeper modes of perception and their mutuality. "A blind person has a better sense of feeling, of taste, of touch," he writes, and speaks of these as "the gifts of the blind." And all of these, Lusseyran feels, blend into a single fundamental sense, a deep attentiveness, a slow, almost prehensile attention, a sensuous, intimate being at one with the world which sight, with its quick, flicking, facile quality, continually distracts us from. This is very close to Hull's concept of "deep blindness" as infinitely more than mere compensation but a unique form of perception, a precious and special mode of being.

What happens when the visual cortex is no longer limited, or constrained, by any visual input? The simple answer is that, isolated from the outside, the visual cortex becomes hypersensitive to internal stimuli of all sorts: its own autonomous activity; signals from other brain areas—auditory, tactile, and verbal areas; and the thoughts and emotions of the blinded individual. Sometimes, as sight deteriorates, hallucinations occur—of geometrical patterns, or occasionally of silent, moving figures or scenes that appear and disappear spontaneously, without any relation to the contents of consciousness, or intention, or context.

Something perhaps akin to this is described by Hull as occurring almost convulsively as he was losing the last of his sight. "About a year after I was registered blind," he writes, "I began to have such strong images of what people's faces looked like that they were almost like hallucinations."

These imperious images were so engrossing as to preëmpt consciousness: "Sometimes," Hull adds, "I would become so absorbed in gazing upon these images, which seemed to come and go without any intention on my part, that I would entirely lose the thread of what was being said to me. I would come back with a shock . . . and I would feel as if I had dropped off to sleep for a few minutes in front of the wireless." Though related to the context of speaking with people, these visions came and went in their own way, without any reference to his intentions, conjured up not by him but by his brain.

The fact that Hull is the only one of the four authors to describe this sort of release phenomenon is perhaps an indication that his visual cortex was starting to escape from his control. One has to wonder whether this signalled its impending demise, at least as an organ of useful visual imagery and memory. Why this should have occurred with him, and how common such a course is, is something one can only speculate on.

Torey, unlike Hull, clearly played a very active role in building up his visual imagery, took control of it the moment the bandages were taken off, and never apparently experienced, or allowed, the sort of involuntary imagery Hull describes. Perhaps this was because he was already very at home with visual imagery, and used to manipulating it in his own way. We know that Torey was very visually inclined before his accident, and skilled from boyhood in creating visual narratives based on the film scripts his father gave him. We have no such information about Hull, for his journal entries start only when he has become blind.

For Lusseyran and Tenberken, there is an added physiological factor: both were attracted to painting, in love with colors, and strongly synesthetic—prone to visualizing numbers, letters, words, music, etc., as shapes and colors—before becoming blind. They already had an overconnectedness, a "cross talk" between the visual cortex and other parts of the brain primarily concerned with language, sound, and music. Given such a neurological situation (synesthesia is congenital, often familial), the persistence of visual imagery and synesthesia, or its heightening, might be almost inevitable in the event of blindness.

Torey required months of intense cognitive discipline dedicated to improving his visual imagery, making it more tenacious, more stable, more malleable, whereas Lusseyran seemed to do this almost effortlessly from the start. Perhaps this was aided by the fact that Lusseyran was not yet eight when blinded (while Torey was twenty-one), and his brain was, accordingly, more plastic, more able to adapt to a new and drastic contingency.

But adaptability does not end with youth. It is clear that Arlene, becoming blind in her forties, was able to adapt in quite radical ways, too, developing not exactly synesthesia but something more flexible and useful: the ability to "see" her hands moving before her, to "see" the words of books read to her, to construct detailed visual images from verbal descriptions. Did she adapt, or did her brain do so? One has a sense that Torey's adaptation was largely shaped by conscious motive, will, and purpose; that Lusseyran's was shaped by overwhelming physiological disposition; and that Arlene's lies somewhere in between. Hull's, meanwhile, remains enigmatic.

There has been much recent work on the neural bases of visual imagery—this can be investigated by brain imaging of various types (PET scanning, functional MRIs, etc.)—and it is now generally accepted that visual imagery activates the cortex in a similar way, and with almost the same intensity, as visual perception itself. And yet studies on the effects of blindness on the human cortex have shown that functional changes may start to occur in a few days, and can become profound as the days stretch into months or years.

Torey, who is well aware of all this research, attributes Hull's loss of visual imagery and memory to the fact that he did not struggle to maintain it, to heighten and systematize and use it, as Torey himself did. (Indeed, Torey expresses horror at what he regards as Hull's passivity, at his letting himself slide into deep blindness.) Perhaps Torey was able to stave off an otherwise inevitable loss of neuronal function in the visual cortex; but perhaps, again, such neural degeneration is quite variable, irrespective of whether or not there is conscious visualization. And, of course, Hull had been losing vision gradually for many years, whereas for Torey blindness was instantaneous and total. It would be of great interest to know the results of brain imaging in the two men, and indeed to look at a large number of people with acquired blindness, to see what correlations, what predictions could be made.

But what if their differences reflect an underlying predisposition independent of blindness? What of visual imagery in the sighted?

I first became conscious that there could be huge variations in visual imagery and visual memory when I was fourteen or so. My mother was a surgeon and comparative anatomist, and I had brought her a lizard's skeleton from school. She gazed at this intently for a minute, turning it round in her hands, then put it down and without looking at it again did a number of drawings of it, rotating it mentally by thirty degrees each time, so that she produced a series, the last drawing exactly the same as the first. I could not imagine how she had done this, and when she said that she could "see" the skeleton in her mind just as clearly and vividly as if she were looking at it, and that she simply rotated the image through a twelfth of a circle each time, I felt bewildered, and very stupid. I could hardly see anything with my mind's eye—at most, faint, evanescent images over which I had no control.

I did have vivid images as I was falling asleep, and in dreams, and once when I had a high fever—but otherwise I saw nothing, or almost nothing, when I tried to visualize, and had great difficulty picturing anybody or anything. Coincidentally or not, I could not draw for toffee.

My mother had hoped I would follow in her footsteps and become a surgeon, but when she realized how lacking in visual powers I was (and how clumsy, lacking in mechanical skill, too) she resigned herself to the idea that I would have to specialize in something else.

I was, however, to get a vivid idea of what mental imagery could be like when, during the nineteen-sixties, I had a period of experimenting with large doses of amphetamines. These can produce striking perceptual changes, including dramatic enhancements of visual imagery and memory (as well as heightenings of the other senses, as I describe in "The Dog Beneath the Skin," a story in "The Man Who Mistook His Wife for a Hat"). For a period of two weeks or so, I found that I could do the most accurate anatomical drawings. I had only to look at a picture or an anatomical specimen, and its image would remain both vivid and stable, and I could easily hold it in my mind for hours. I could mentally project the image onto the paper before me—it was as clear and distinct as if projected by a camera lucida—and trace its outlines with a pencil. My drawings were not elegant, but they were, everyone agreed, very detailed and accurate, and could bear comparison with some of the drawings in our neuroanatomy textbook. This heightening of imagery attached to everything—I had only to think of a face, a place, a picture, a paragraph in a book to see it vividly in my mind. But when the amphetamine-induced state faded, after a couple of weeks, I could no longer visualize, no longer project images, no longer draw—nor have I been able to do so in the decades since.

A few months ago, at a medical conference in Boston, I spoke of Torey's and Hull's experiences of blindness, and of how "enabled" Torey seemed to be by the powers of visualization he had developed, and how "disabled" Hull was—in some ways, at least—by the loss of his powers of visual imagery and memory. After my talk, a man in the audience came up to me and asked how well, in my estimation, *sighted* people could function if they had no visual imagery. He went on to say that he had no visual imagery whatever, at least none that he could deliberately evoke, and that no one in his family had any, either. Indeed, he had assumed this was the case with everyone, until he came to participate in some psychological tests at Harvard and realized that he apparently lacked a mental power that all the other students, in varying degrees, had.

"And what do you do?" I asked him, wondering what this poor man *could* do.

"I am a surgeon," he replied. "A vascular surgeon. An anatomist, too. And I design solar panels."

But how, I asked him, did he recognize what he was seeing?

"It's not a problem," he answered. "I guess there must be representations or models in the brain that get matched up with what I am seeing and doing. But they are not conscious. I cannot evoke them."

This seemed to be at odds with my mother's experience—she, clearly, did have extremely vivid and readily manipulable visual imagery, though (it now seemed) this may have been a bonus, a luxury, and not a prerequisite for her career as a surgeon.

Is this also the case with Torey? Is his greatly developed visual imagery, though clearly a source of much pleasure, not as indispensable as he takes it to be? Might he, in fact, have done everything he did, from carpentry to roof repair to making a model of the mind, without any conscious imagery at all? He himself raises this question.

The role of mental imagery in thinking was explored by Francis Galton, Darwin's irrepressible cousin, who wrote on subjects as various as fingerprints, eugenics, dog whistles, criminality, twins, visionaries, psychometric measures, and hereditary genius. His inquiry into visual imagery took the form of a questionnaire, with such questions as "Can you recall with distinctness the features of all near relations and many other persons? Can you at will cause your mental image . . . to sit, stand, or turn slowly around? Can you . . . see it with enough distinctness to enable you to sketch it leisurely (supposing yourself able to draw)?" The vascular surgeon would have been hopeless on such tests—indeed, it was questions such as these which had floored him when he was a student at Harvard. And yet, finally, how much had it mattered?

As to the significance of such imagery, Galton is ambiguous and guarded. He suggests, in one breath, that "scientific men, as a class, have feeble powers of visual representation" and, in another, that "a vivid visualizing faculty is of much importance in connection with the higher processes of generalized thoughts." He feels that "it is undoubtedly the fact that mechanicians, engineers and architects usually possess the faculty of seeing mental images with remarkable clearness and precision," but goes on to say, "I am, however, bound to say, that the missing faculty seems to be replaced so serviceably by other modes of conception . . . that men who declare themselves entirely deficient in the power of seeing mental pictures can nevertheless give lifelike descriptions of what they have seen, and can otherwise express themselves as if they were gifted with a vivid visual imagination. They can also become painters of the rank of Royal Academicians." I have a cousin, a professional architect, who maintains that he cannot visualize anything whatever. "How do you think?" I once asked him. He shook his head and said, "I don't know." Do any of us, finally, know how we think?

When I talk to people, blind or sighted, or when I try to think of my own internal representations, I find myself uncertain whether words, symbols, and images of various types are the primary tools of thought or whether there are forms of thought antecedent to all of these, forms of thought essentially amodal. Psychologists have sometimes spoken of "interlingua" or "mentalese," which they conceive to be the brain's own language, and Lev Vygotsky, the great Russian psychologist, used to speak of "thinking in pure meanings." I cannot decide whether this is nonsense or profound truth—it is the sort of reef I end up on when I think about thinking.

Galton's seemingly contradictory statements about imagery—is it antithetical to abstract thinking, or integral to it?—may stem from his failure to distinguish between fundamentally different levels of imagery. Simple visual imagery such as he describes may suffice for the design of a screw, an engine, or a surgical operation, and it may be relatively easy to model these essentially reproductive forms of imagery or to simulate them by constructing video games or virtual realities of various sorts. Such powers may be invaluable, but there is something passive and mechanical and impersonal about them, which makes them utterly different from the higher and more personal powers of the imagination, where there is a continual struggle for concepts and form and meaning, a calling upon all the powers of the self. Imagination dissolves and transforms, unifies and creates, while drawing upon the "lower" powers of memory and association. It is by such imagination, such "vision," that we create or construct our individual worlds.

At this level, one can no longer say of one's mental landscapes what is visual, what is auditory, what is image, what is language, what is intellectual, what is emotional—they are all fused together and imbued with our own individual perspectives and values. Such a unified vision shines out from Hull's memoir no less than from Torey's, despite the fact that one has become "nonvisual" and the other "hypervisual." What seems at first to be so decisive a difference between the two men is not, finally, a radical one, so far as personal development and sensibility go. Even though the paths they have followed might seem irreconcilable, both men have "used" blindness (if one can employ such a term for processes which are deeply mysterious, and far below, or above, the level of consciousness and voluntary control) to release their own creative capacities and emotional selves, and both have achieved a rich and full realization of their own individual worlds.   ■

■ QUESTIONS FOR MAKING CONNECTIONS WITHIN THE READING ■

1. Early in his essay, Sacks poses this question: "Does the mind run the brain or the brain the mind—or, rather, to what extent does one run the other?" Most of the discussion that follows this question, however, concerns the experience of blindness: instead of providing an extended analysis of

mental processing or brain chemistry, Sacks gives us details about people who have lost their vision and then adapted in different ways. How do these accounts of blindness connect to the debate about mind and brain?

2. To what extent are the different responses of the people Sacks discusses attributable to their individual ways of "being in the world"? Do you see any evidence of a continuity in the behavior of his subjects before and after the onset of their blindness? What are the larger implications of their adaptations? Would you say that the world is what we make it, or are there limits to the power of imagination, intelligence, and determination? What does Sacks appear to believe?

3. At one point in his essay, Sacks recalls a period in his life when he was "experimenting with large doses of amphetamines":

> For a period of two weeks or so, I found that I could do the most accurate anatomical drawings. I had only to look at a picture or an anatomical specimen, and its image would remain both vivid and stable, and I could easily hold it in my mind for hours. I could mentally project the image onto the paper before me—it was as clear and distinct as if projected by a camera lucida—and trace its outlines with a pencil. . . . But when the amphetamine-induced state faded, . . . I could no longer visualize, no longer project images, no longer draw—nor have I been able to do so in the decades since.

Why does Sacks include this vignette? What point does he make, and how does the passage extend the argument he develops in the previous pages? Does it matter that the story he tells is personal?

▪ QUESTIONS FOR WRITING ▪

1. Do the discoveries of neuroscience undermine our assumptions about such issues as free will, the uniqueness of each individual, and the importance of creativity? Ordinarily, we might think that if we can explain an emotion like love or the experience of beauty as the product of the brain's hardwiring, something important will be lost. But will it? Is human behavior in any way diminished or degraded by our knowledge of brain science? In what ways might an understanding of neuroscience foster greater understanding and a tolerance for diversities—and uniformities—in human behavior?

2. For the last century or so, thinkers have debated the relative influence of "nature" and "nurture" over human behavior. By "nature," people ordinarily mean biology, chemistry, genetics, and neuroscience. By "nurture," they mean custom, culture, and education. What does Sacks's essay contribute to this debate? Can he be accused of perpetuating "reductionism": Does he, in other words, oversimplify the complexities of human life by reducing everything to one explanation?

3. On the basis of the evidence that Sacks provides, can we ever say that human behavior is entirely "hardwired"? Can we argue, in other words, that the ways in which we act are predetermined by the structure and functioning of our brains? Or are we entitled to say that the brain is flexible enough to adapt to an event like the loss of sight in ways that are infinitely varied? Do the adaptations vary infinitely, or are there biological limits? Are there no commonalities among all the different adaptations that Sacks discusses? Do you think that these commonalities have their origin in the brain, or can they be explained in some other way?

■ *QUESTIONS FOR MAKING CONNECTIONS BETWEEN READINGS* ■

1. In what ways does Sacks's essay complicate or even contradict Gregory Stock's argument in "The Enhanced and the Unenhanced"? On the basis of the evidence that Sacks provides, would you say that intelligence resides primarily in our brains, or is it a product of the ways in which we interact with the world? If intelligence does not reside entirely in our brains, but is also a quality of our behavior, then how likely is it that intelligence might be passed on through or improved by genetic engineering? Is education just as likely as genetic engineering to produce creative, thoughtful, and adaptive people?

2. Sacks suggests that the brain is actually quite flexible in its adaptations to the world. If this is so, then many different ways of organizing experience would seem to be possible. Are all ways of organizing experience equally successful as survival strategies? Did the individuals Sacks studies "choose" their mode of adaptation, or was their mode of adaptation presented to them as the only option, given how their individual minds worked? Is it possible that human consciousness has evolved through trial and error in much the same way as different species have evolved? Drawing on Stephen J. Gould's essay, "What Does the Dreaded 'E' Word Mean, Anyway," or on Frans de Waal's "Selections from *The Ape and the Sushi Master*," explore the possible dynamics behind the evolution of consciousness.

www **For additional suggestions about making connections between readings, visit the Link-O-Mat and More Sample Questions at <www.newhum.com>.**

ERIC SCHLOSSER

IN HIS AWARD-WINNING article, "In the Strawberry Fields," the investigative journalist Eric Schlosser focused attention on workers' rights by recounting the tale
of how strawberries make their way from the fields to the supermarket, exposing in the process the industry's reliance on illegal immigrants. In *Fast Food Nation: The Dark Side of the All-American Meal* (2001), Schlosser pursues a similar approach by telling the story of how the Big Mac and other fast-food products find
their way into the hands of consumers around the world. Who makes this food?
Under what conditions? What societal, environmental, and economic changes
have been produced by the shift in American eating habits? What are the long-
term consequences of the "Americanization" of eating habits around the globe?
These are the questions that animate *Fast Food Nation,* Schlosser's book-length
study of the fast-food industry.

In criticizing the place that fast food has come to occupy in the American
diet, Schlosser aims to go beyond complaining about the architectural tackiness
of fast-food restaurants and the blandness of the food—arguments most readers
would find unsurprising and could, at any rate, generate on their own.
Schlosser's concerns, rather, are with how the fast-food industry treats its workers, what's in the food that those workers sell, and the dramatic changes that
America's new eating habits have produced in the agricultural industry. In raising these issues, Schlosser means to promote an alternative future, one where
people are fed by a "sustainable and largely deindustrialized agriculture, regional production and fast-food restaurants that are locally owned and somehow
connected in a real way to the places where they operate." In "Global Realization," Schlosser details ongoing efforts to make certain that food looks and tastes
the same the world over and the counter-efforts of those who would resist such
attempts to globalize American standards of consumption. Acknowledging that

Schlosser, Eric. "Global Realization." *Fast Food Nation.* Boston: Houghton Mifflin, 2001.
225–252.

Biographical information from Eric Schlosser, interview by Bill Goldstein <http://www
.nytimes.com/books/01/01/21/specials/schlosser.html>. Quotations from Eric Schlosser, interview by Patricia Chui, *The Nation,* <http://www.thenation.com/special/schlosser.mhtml>
and Eric Schlosser, interview by Julia Livshin, *The Atlantic,* 14 December 2000 <http://www
.theatlantic.com/unbound/interviews/ba2000-12-14.html>.

"it's very hard to get readers to care about these subjects," Schlosser nevertheless believes that it is his responsibility to try "to give a voice to people outside of the mainstream."

www **To learn more about Eric Schlosser and the fast-food industry, visit the Link-O-Mat at <www.newhum.com>.**

Global Realization

Whenever I told someone in Berlin that I was planning to visit Plauen, I got the same reaction. It didn't matter whom I told—someone old or young, hip or square, gay, straight, raised in West Germany, raised in the East—there'd always be a laugh, followed by a look of slight amazement. "Plauen?" they'd say. "Why would you ever want to go to Plauen?" The way the name was spoken, the long, drawn-out emphasis on the second syllable, implied that the whole idea was vaguely ridiculous. Located halfway between Munich and Berlin, in a part of Saxony known as the Vogtland, Plauen is a small provincial city surrounded by forests and rolling hills. To Berliners, whose city is the present capital of Germany and perhaps the future capital of Europe, Plauen is a sleepy backwater that sat for decades on the wrong side of the Berlin Wall. Berliners regard the place in much the same way that New Yorkers view Muncie, Indiana. But I found Plauen fascinating. The countryside around it is lush and green. Some of the old buildings have real charm. The people are open, friendly, unpretentious—and yet somehow cursed.

For decades Plauen has been on the margins of history, far removed from the centers of power; nevertheless, events there have oddly foreshadowed the rise and fall of great social movements. One after another, the leading ideologies of modern Europe—industrialism, fascism, communism, consumerism—have passed through Plauen and left their mark. None has completely triumphed or been completely erased. Bits and pieces of these worldviews still coexist uneasily, cropping up in unexpected places, from the graffiti on the wall of an apartment building to the tone of an offhand remark. There is nothing settled yet, nothing that can be assumed. All sorts of things, good and bad, are still possible. In the heart of the Vogtland, without much notice from the rest of the world, the little city of Plauen has been alternately punished, rewarded, devastated, and transformed by the great unifying systems of the twentieth century, by each new effort to govern all of mankind with a single set of rules. Plauen has been a battlefield for these competing ideologies, with their proudly displayed and archetypal symbols: the smokestack, the swastika, the hammer and sickle, the golden arches.

For centuries, Plauen was a small market town where Vogtland farmers came to buy and sell goods. And then, at the end of the nineteenth century, a local weaving tradition gave birth to a vibrant textile industry. Between 1890 and 1914, the city's population roughly tripled, reaching 118,000 on the eve of World War I. Its new textile mills specialized in lace and in embroidered fabrics, exporting most of their output to the United States. The doilies on dinner tables throughout the American Midwest came from Plauen, as well as the intricate lacework that set the tone of many upper-middle-class Victorian homes. Black-and-white postcards from Plauen before the Great War show lovely Art Nouveau and Neo-Romantic buildings that evoke the streets of Paris, elegant cafés and parks, electric streetcars, zeppelins in the air.

Life in Plauen became less idyllic after Germany's defeat. When the Victorian world and its values collapsed, so did the market for lace. Many of Plauen's textile mills closed, and thousands of people were thrown out of work. The social unrest that later engulfed the rest of Germany came early to Plauen. In the 1920s Plauen had the most millionaires per capita in Germany—and the most suicides. It also had the highest unemployment rate. Amid the misery, extremism thrived. Plauen was the first city outside of Bavaria to organize its own chapter of the Nazi party. In May of 1923, the Hitler Youth movement was launched in Plauen, and the following year, the little city became the Nazi headquarters for Saxony. Long before the Nazi reign of terror began elsewhere, union leaders and leftists were murdered in Plauen. Hitler visited the city on several occasions, receiving an enthusiastic welcome. Hermann Göring and Joseph Goebbels visited too, and Plauen became a sentimental favorite of the Nazi leadership. On the night of November 9, 1938, *Kristallnacht,* a crowd eagerly destroyed Plauen's only synagogue, a strikingly modern building designed by Bauhaus architect Fritz Landauer. Not long afterward, Plauen officially became *Juden-frei* (Jew-free).

For most of World War II, Plauen remained strangely quiet and peaceful, an oasis of ordinary life. It provided safe haven to thousands of German refugees fleeing bombed-out cities. All sorts of rumors tried to explain why Plauen was being spared, while other towns in Saxony were being destroyed. On September 19, 1944, American bombers appeared over the city for the first time. Instead of rushing into shelters, people stood in the streets, amazed, watching bombs fall on the railway station and on a factory that built tanks for the German army. A few months later, Plauen appeared alongside Dresden on an Allied bombing list.

Plauen was largely deserted on April 10, 1945, when hundreds of British Lancaster bombers appeared over the city. Its inhabitants no longer felt mysteriously protected; they knew that Dresden had recently been fire-bombed into oblivion. During a single raid the Royal Air Force dropped 2,000 tons of high explosives on Plauen. Four days later, the U.S. Army occupied what was left of the town. The birthplace of the Hitler Youth, the most Nazified city in Saxony, gained another distinction only weeks before the war ended. More bombs were dropped on Plauen, per square mile, than on any other city in eastern Germany—roughly three times as many as were dropped on Dresden. Although the carnage was far worse in Dresden, a larger proportion of Plauen's buildings were destroyed. At the end of the war, about 75 percent of Plauen lay in ruins.

When the Allies divided their spheres of influence in Germany, Plauen's misfortune continued. The U.S Army pulled out of the city, and the Soviet army rolled in. Plauen became part of the communist German Democratic Republic (GDR), but just barely. The new border with West Germany was only nine miles away. Plauen languished under Communist rule. It lost one-third of its prewar population. Sitting in a remote corner of the GDR, it received little attention or investment from the Communist party leadership in East Berlin. Much of Plauen was never rebuilt; parking lots and empty lots occupied land where ornate buildings had once stood. One of the few successful factories, a synthetic wool plant, blanketed Plauen in some of East Germany's worst air pollution. According to historian John Connelly, the polluted air helped give the city an "unusually low quality of life, even for GDR standards."

On October 7, 1989, the first mass demonstration against East Germany's Communist rulers took place in Plauen. Small, scattered protests also occurred that day in Magdeberg, East Berlin, and other cities. The size of Plauen's demonstration set it apart. More than one-quarter of the city's population suddenly took to the streets. The level of unrest greatly surprised local government officials. The Stasi (East Germany's secret police) had expected about four hundred people to appear in the town center that day, the fortieth anniversary of the GDR's founding. Instead, about twenty thousand people began to gather, despite dark skies and a steady drizzle. The demonstration had no leadership, no organizers, no formal plan of action. It grew spontaneously, spreading through word of mouth.

The protesters in other East German cities were mainly college students and members of the intelligentsia; in Plauen they were factory workers and ordinary citizens. Some of the demonstration's most fervent supporters were long-haired, working-class fans of American heavy metal music, known in Plauen as *die Heavies,* who rode their motorcycles through town distributing antigovernment pamphlets. As the crowd grew, people began to chant Mikhail Gorbachev's nickname—"Gorby! Gorby!"—cheering the Soviet leader's policies of *glasnost* and *perestroika,* demanding similar reforms in East Germany, defiantly yelling "Stasi go home!" One large banner bore the words of the German poet Friedrich von Schiller. "We want freedom," it said, "like the freedom enjoyed by our forefathers."

Police officers and Stasi agents tried to break up the demonstration, arresting dozens of people, firing water cannons at the crowd, flying helicopters low over the rooftops of Plauen. But the protesters refused to disperse. They marched to the town hall and called for the mayor to come outside and address their demands. Thomas Küttler, the superintendent of Plauen's Lutheran church, volunteered to act as a mediator. Inside the town hall, he found Plauen's high-ranking officials cowering in fear. None would emerge to face the crowd. The equation of power had fundamentally changed that day. A mighty totalitarian system of rule, erected over the course of four decades, propped up by tanks and guns and thousands of Stasi informers, was crumbling before his eyes, as its rulers nervously chain-smoked in the safety of their offices. The mayor finally agreed to address the crowd, but a Stasi official prevented him from leaving the building. And so Küttler stood on the steps of the town hall with a megaphone, urging the soldiers not to fire their weapons and telling the demonstrators that their point had been made, now it was time to go home. As bells atop the Lutheran church rang, the crowd began to disperse.

A month later, the Berlin Wall fell. And a few months after that extraordinary event, marking the end of the Cold War, the McDonald's Corporation announced plans to open its first restaurant in East Germany. The news provoked a last gasp of collectivism from Ernst Doerfler, a prominent member of the doomed East German parliament, who called for an official ban on "McDonald's and similar abnormal garbage-makers." McDonald's, however, would not be deterred; Burger King had already opened a mobile hamburger cart in Dresden. During the summer of 1990, construction quickly began on the first McDonald's in East Germany. It would occupy an abandoned lot in the center of Plauen, a block away from the steps of the town hall. The McDonald's would be the first new building erected in Plauen since the coming of a new Germany.

Uncle McDonald

As the fast food industry has grown more competitive in the United States, the major chains have looked to overseas markets for their future growth. The McDonald's Corporation recently used a new phrase to describe its hopes for foreign conquest: "global realization." A decade ago, McDonald's had about three thousand restaurants outside the United States; today it has about fifteen thousand restaurants in more than 117 foreign countries. It currently opens about five new restaurants every day, and at least four of them are overseas. Within the next decade, Jack Greenberg, the company's chief executive, hopes to double the number of McDonald's. The chain earns the majority of its profits outside the United States, as does KFC. McDonald's now ranks as the most widely recognized brand in the world, more familiar than Coca-Cola. The values, tastes, and industrial practices of the American fast food industry are being exported to every corner of the globe, helping to create a homogenized international culture that sociologist Benjamin R. Barber has labeled "McWorld."

The fast food chains have become totems of Western economic development. They are often the first multinationals to arrive when a country has opened its markets, serving as the avant-garde of American franchising. Fifteen years ago, when McDonald's opened its first restaurant in Turkey, no other foreign franchisor did business there. Turkey now has hundreds of franchise outlets, including 7-Eleven, Nutra Slim, Re/Max Real Estate, Mail Boxes Etc., and Ziebart Tidy Car. Support for the growth of franchising has even become part of American foreign policy. The U.S. State Department now publishes detailed studies of overseas franchise opportunities and runs a Gold Key Program at many of its embassies to help American franchisors find overseas partners.

The anthropologist Yunxiang Yan has noted that in the eyes of Beijing consumers, McDonald's represents "Americana and the promise of modernization." Thousands of people waited patiently for hours to eat at the city's first McDonald's in 1992. Two years later, when a McDonald's opened in Kuwait, the line of cars waiting at the drive-through window extended for seven miles. Around the same time, a Kentucky Fried Chicken restaurant in Saudi Arabia's holy city of Mecca set new sales records for the chain, earning $200,000 in a single week during Ramadan, the Muslim holy month. In Brazil, McDonald's has become the nation's largest private employer. The fast food chains are now imperial fiefdoms, sending their emissaries far and wide. Classes at McDonald's Hamburger University in Oak Park, Illinois, are taught in twenty different languages. Few places on earth seem too distant or too remote for the golden arches. In 1986, the Tahiti Tourism Promotion Board ran an ad campaign featuring pristine beaches and the slogan "Sorry, No McDonald's." A decade later, one opened in Papeete, the Tahitian capital, bringing hamburgers and fries to a spot thousands of miles, across the Pacific, from the nearest cattle ranches or potato fields.

As the fast food chains have moved overseas, they have been accompanied by their major suppliers. In order to diminish fears of American imperialism, the chains try to purchase as much food as possible in the countries where they operate. Instead of importing food, they import entire systems of agricultural production. Seven years before McDonald's opened its first restaurant in India, the company began to establish a supply network there, teaching Indian farmers how to grow iceberg lettuce with seeds specially developed for the nation's climate. "A McDonald's restaurant is just the window of a much larger system comprising an extensive food-chain, running right up to the farms," one of the company's Indian partners told a foreign journalist.

In 1987, ConAgra took over the Elders Company in Australia, the largest beef company in the country that exports more beef than any other in the world. Over the past decade, Cargill and IBP have gained control of the beef industry in Canada. Cargill has established large-scale poultry operations in China and Thailand. Tyson Foods is planning to build chicken-processing plants in China, Indonesia, and the Philippines. ConAgra's Lamb Weston division now manufactures frozen french fries in Holland, India, and Turkey. McCain, the world's biggest french fry producer, operates fifty processing plants scattered across four continents. In order to supply McDonald's, J. R. Simplot began to grow Russet Burbank potatoes in China, opening that nation's first french fry factory in 1993. A few years ago Simplot bought eleven processing plants in Australia, aiming to increase sales in the East Asian market. He also purchased a 3-million-acre ranch in Australia, where he hopes to run cattle, raise vegetables, and grow potatoes. "It's a great little country," Simplot says, "and there's nobody in it."

As in the United States, the fast food companies have targeted their foreign advertising and promotion at a group of consumers with the fewest attachments to tradition: young children. "Kids are the same regarding the issues that affect the all-important stages of their development," a top executive at the Gepetto Group told the audience at a recent KidPower conference, "and they apply to any kid in Berlin, Beijing, or Brooklyn." The KidPower conference, attended by marketing executives from Burger King and Nickelodeon, among others, was held at the Disneyland outside of Paris. In Australia, where the number of fast food restaurants roughly tripled during the 1990s, a survey found that half of the nation's nine- and ten-year-olds thought that Ronald McDonald knew what kids should eat. At a primary school in Beijing, Yunxiang Yan found that all of the children recognized an image of Ronald McDonald. The children told Yan they liked "Uncle McDonald" because he was "funny, gentle, kind, and . . . he understood children's hearts." Coca-Cola is now the favorite drink among Chinese children, and McDonald's serves their favorite food. Simply eating at a McDonald's in Beijing seems to elevate a person's social status. The idea that you are what you eat has been enthusiastically promoted for years by Den Fujita, the eccentric billionaire who brought McDonald's to Japan three decades ago. "If we eat McDonald's hamburgers and potatoes for a thousand years," Fujita once promised his countrymen, "we will become taller, our skin will become white, and our hair will be blonde."

The impact of fast food is readily apparent in Germany, which has become one of McDonald's most profitable overseas markets. Germany is not only the largest country in Europe, but also the most Americanized. Although the four Allied powers occupied it after World War II, the Americans exerted the greatest lasting influence, perhaps because their nationalism was so inclusive, and their nation so distant. Children in West German schools were required to study English, facilitating the spread of American pop culture. Young people who sought to distance themselves from the wartime behavior of their parents found escape in American movies, music, and novels. "For a child growing up in the turmoil of [postwar] Berlin . . . the Americans were angels," Christa Maerker, a Berlin filmmaker, wrote in an essay on postwar Germany's infatuation with the United States. "Anything from them was bigger and more wonderful than anything that preceded it."

The United States and Germany fought against each other twice in the twentieth century, but the enmity between them has often seemed less visceral than other national rivalries. The recent takeover of prominent American corporations—such as Chrysler, Random House, and RCA Records—by German companies provoked none of the public anger that was unleashed when Japanese firms bought much less significant American assets in the 1980s. Despite America's long-standing "special relationship" with Great Britain, the underlying cultural ties between the United States and Germany, though less obvious, are equally strong. Americans with German ancestors far outnumber those with English ancestors. Moreover, during the past century both American culture and German culture have shown an unusually strong passion for science, technology, engineering, empiricism, social order, and efficiency. The electronic paper-towel dispenser that I saw in a Munich men's room is the spiritual kin of the gas-powered ketchup dispensers at the McDonald's in Colorado Springs.

The traditional German restaurant—serving schnitzel, bratwurst, knackwurst, sauerbraten, and large quantities of beer—is rapidly disappearing in Germany. Such establishments now account for less than one-third of the German foodservice market. Their high labor costs have for the most part been responsible for their demise, along with the declining popularity of schnitzel. McDonald's Deutschland, Inc., is by far the biggest restaurant company in Germany today, more than twice as large as the nearest competitor. It opened the first German McDonald's in 1971; at the beginning of the 1990s it had four hundred restaurants, and now it has more than a thousand. The company's main dish happens to be named after Hamburg, a German city where ground-beef steaks were popular in the early nineteenth century. The hamburger was born when Americans added the bun. McDonald's Deutschland uses German potatoes for its fries and Bavarian dairy cows for its burgers. It sends Ronald McDonald into hospitals and schools. It puts new McDonald's restaurants in gas stations, railway stations, and airports. It battles labor unions and—according to Siegfried Pater, author of *Zum Beispiel McDonald's*—has repeatedly fired union sympathizers. The success of McDonald's, Pizza Hut, and T.G.I. Fridays in Germany has helped spark a franchising boom. Since 1992, the number of franchised outlets there has doubled, and about five thousand more are being added every year. In August of 1999, McDonald's Deutschland announced that it would be putting restaurants in Germany's new Wal-Mart stores. "The partnership scheme will undoubtedly be a success," a German financial analyst told London's *Evening Standard*. "The kiddie factor alone—children urging their parents to shop at Wal-Mart because they have a McDonald's inside the store—could generate an upsurge in customers."

The golden arches have become so commonplace in Germany that they seem almost invisible. You don't notice them unless you're looking for them, or feeling hungry. One German McDonald's, however, stands out from the rest. It sits on a nondescript street in a new shopping complex not far from Dachau, the first concentration camp opened by the Nazis. The stores were built on fields where Dachau's inmates once did forced labor. Although the architecture of the shopping complex looks German and futuristic, the haphazard placement of the buildings on the land seems distinctively American. They would not seem out of place near an off-ramp of I-25 in Colorado. Across the street from the McDonald's there's a discount supermarket. An auto parts store stands a few hundred yards from the other buildings, separated by fields that have not yet vanished beneath concrete. In 1997, protests were staged against the opening of a McDonald's so close to a concentration camp where gypsies, Jews, homosexuals, and political opponents of the Nazis were imprisoned, where Luftwaffe scientists performed medical experiments on inmates and roughly 30,000 people died. The McDonald's Corporation denied that it was trying to profit from the Holocaust and said the restaurant was at least a mile from the camp. After the curator of the Dachau Museum complained that McDonald's was distributing thousands of leaflets among tourists in the camp's parking lot, the company halted the practice. "Welcome to Dachau," said the leaflets, "and welcome to McDonald's."

The McDonald's at Dachau is one-third of a mile from the entrance to the concentration camp. The day I went there, the restaurant was staging a "Western Big Mac" promotion. It was decorated in a Wild West theme, with paper place mats featuring a wanted poster of "Butch Essidie." The restaurant was full of mothers and small children. Teenagers dressed in Nikes, Levis, and Tommy Hilfiger T-shirts sat in groups and smoked cigarettes. Turkish immigrants worked in the kitchen, seventies disco music played, and the red paper cups on everyone's tray said "Always Coca-Cola." This McDonald's was in Dachau, but it could have been anywhere—anywhere in the United States, anywhere in the world. Millions of other people at that very moment were standing at the same counter, ordering the same food from the same menu, food that tasted everywhere the same.

At the Circus

The most surreal experience that I had during three years of research into fast food took place not at the top-secret air force base that got its Domino's pizzas delivered, not at the flavor factory off the New Jersey Turnpike, not at the Dachau McDonald's. It occurred on March 1, 1999, at the Mirage Hotel in Las Vegas. Like an epiphany, it revealed the strange power of fast food in the new world order. The Mirage—with its five-story volcano, its shark tank, dolphin tank, indoor rain forest, Lagoon Saloon, DKNY boutique, and

Secret Garden of Siegfried & Roy—is a fine place for the surreal. Even its name suggests the triumph of illusion over reality, a promise that you won't believe your eyes. On that day in March, as usual, Las Vegas was full of spectacles and name acts. George Carlin was at Bally's, and David Cassidy was at the MGM Grand, starring in *EFX*, a show billed as a high-tech journey through space and time. *The History of Sex* was at the Golden Nugget, *The Number One Fool Contest* was at the Comedy Stop, Joacquin Ayala (Mexico's most famous magician) was at Harrah's, the Radio City Rockettes were at the Flamingo Hilton, "the Dream King" (Elvis impersonator Trent Carlini) was at the Boardwalk. And Mikhail Gorbachev (former president of the Supreme Soviet of the USSR, winner of the Orders of Lenin, the Red Banner of Labor, and the Nobel Peace Prize) was at the Grand Ballroom of the Mirage, giving the keynote speech before a fast food convention.

The convention and its setting were an ideal match. In many ways Las Vegas is the fulfillment of social and economic trends now sweeping from the American West to the farthest reaches of the globe. Las Vegas is the fastest-growing major city in the United States—an entirely man-made creation, a city that lives for the present, that has little connection to its surrounding landscape, that cares little about its own past. Nothing in Las Vegas is built to last, hotels are routinely demolished as soon as they seem out of fashion, and the city limits seem as arbitrary as its location, with plastic bags and garbage littering the open land where the lawns end, the desert not far from the Strip.

Las Vegas began as an overnight camp for travelers going to California on the Old Spanish Trail. It later became a ranching town, notable in the early 1940s mainly for its rodeo, its Wild West tourist attractions, and a nightclub called the Apache Bar. The population was about 8,000. The subsequent growth of Las Vegas was made possible by the federal government, which spent billions of dollars to erect the Hoover Dam and build military bases near the city. The dam supplied water and electricity, while the bases provided the early casinos with customers. When authorities in southern California cracked down on illegal gambling after World War II, the gamblers headed for Nevada. As in Colorado Springs, the real boom in Las Vegas began toward the end of the 1970s. Over the past twenty years the population of Las Vegas has nearly tripled.

Today there are few remaining traces of the city's cowboy past. Indeed, the global equation has been reversed. While the rest of the world builds Wal-Marts, Arby's, Taco Bells, and other outposts of Americana, Las Vegas has spent the past decade re-creating the rest of the world. The fast food joints along the Strip seem insignificant compared to the new monuments towering over them: recreations of the Eiffel Tower, the Statue of Liberty, and the Sphinx, enormous buildings that evoke Venice, Paris, New York, Tuscany, medieval England, ancient Egypt and Rome, the Middle East, the South Seas. Las Vegas is now so contrived and artificial that it has become something authentic, a place unlike any other. The same forces that are homogenizing other cities have made Las Vegas even more unique.

At the heart of Las Vegas is technology: machinery that cools the air, erupts the volcano, and powers the shimmering lights. Most important of all is the machinery that makes money for the casinos. While Las Vegas portrays itself as a free-wheeling, entrepreneurial town where anyone can come and strike it rich, life there is more tightly regulated, controlled, and monitored by hidden cameras than just about anywhere else in the United States. The city's principal industry is legally protected against the workings of the free market, and operates according to strict rules laid down by the state. The Nevada Gaming Control Board determines not only who can own a casino, but who can enter one. In a town built on gambling, where fortunes were once earned with a roll of the dice, it is remarkable how little is now left to chance. Until the late 1960s, about three-quarters of a typical casino's profits came from table games, from poker, blackjack, baccarat, roulette. During the last twenty-five years table games, which are supervised by dealers and offer gamblers the best odds, have been displaced by slot machines. Today about two-thirds of a typical casino's profits now come from slots and video poker—machines that are precisely calibrated to take your money. They guarantee the casino a profit rate of as much as 20 percent—four times what a roulette wheel will bring.

The latest slot machines are electronically connected to a central computer, allowing the casino to track the size of every bet and its outcome. The music, flashing lights, and sound effects emitted by these slots help disguise the fact that a small processor inside them is deciding with mathematical certainty how long you will play before you lose. It is the ultimate consumer technology, designed to manufacture not a tangible product, but something much more elusive: a brief sense of hope. That is what Las Vegas really sells, the most brilliant illusion of all, a loss that feels like winning.

Mikhail Gorbachev was in town to speak at the Twenty-sixth Annual Chain Operators Exchange, a convention sponsored by the International Foodservice Manufacturers Association. Executives from the major fast food companies had gathered to discuss, among other things, the latest labor-saving machinery and the prospects of someday employing a workforce that needed "zero training." Representatives from the industry's leading suppliers—ConAgra, Monfort, Simplot, and others—had come to sell their latest products. The Grand Ballroom at the Mirage was filled with hundreds of middle-aged white men in expensive business suits. They sat at long tables beneath crystal chandeliers, drinking coffee, greeting old friends, waiting for the morning program to begin. A few of them were obviously struggling to recover from whatever they'd done in Las Vegas the night before.

On the surface, Mikhail Gorbachev seemed an odd choice to address a group so resolutely opposed to labor unions, minimum wages, and workplace safety rules. "Those who hope we shall move away from the socialist path will be greatly disappointed," Gorbachev had written in *Perestroika* (1987), at the height of his power. He had never sought the dissolution of the Soviet Union and never renounced his fundamental commitment to Marxism-Leninism. He still believed in the class struggle and "scientific socialism." But the fall of the Berlin Wall had thrown Gorbachev out of power and left him in a precarious financial condition. He was beloved abroad, yet despised in his own land. During Russia's 1996 presidential election he received just 1 percent of the vote. The following year he expressed great praise for America's leading fast food chain. "And the merry clowns, the Big Mac signs, the colourful, unique decorations and ideal cleanliness," Gorbachev wrote in the foreword of *To Russia with Fries*, a memoir by a McDonald's executive, "all of this complements the hamburgers whose great popularity is well deserved."

In December of 1997, Gorbachev appeared in a Pizza Hut commercial, following in the footsteps of Cindy Crawford and Ivana Trump. A group of patrons at a Moscow Pizza Hut thanked him in the ad for bringing the fast food chain to Russia and then shouted "Hail to Gorbachev!" In response Gorbachev saluted them by raising a slice of pizza. He reportedly earned $160,000 for his appearance in the sixty-second spot, money earmarked for his nonprofit foundation. A year later Pizza Hut announced that it was pulling out of Russia as the country's economy collapsed, and Gorbachev told a German reporter that "all my money is gone." For his hour-long speech at the Mirage, Gorbachev was promised a fee of $150,000 and the use of a private jet.

The Twenty-sixth Annual Chain Operators Exchange officially opened with a video presentation of the national anthem. As the song boomed from speakers throughout the Grand Ballroom, two huge screens above the stage displayed a series of patriotic images: the Statue of Liberty, the Lincoln Memorial, amber waves of grain. In one of the morning's first speeches, an executive hailed the restaurant industry's record profits the previous year, adding without irony, "As if things weren't good enough, consumers also dropped all pretense of wanting healthy food." An ongoing industry survey had found that public concerns about salt, fat, and food additives were at their lowest level since 1982, when the survey began—one more bit of news to justify the industry's "current state of bliss." Another executive, a self-described "sensory evaluation specialist," emphasized the importance of pleasant smells. He noted that Las Vegas resorts were now experimenting with "signature scents" in their casinos, hoping the subtle aromas would subconsciously make people gamble more money.

Robert Nugent, the head of Jack in the Box and honorary chairman of the Twenty-sixth Annual Chain Operators Exchange, broke the cheery mood with an ominous, unsettling speech. He essentially accused critics of the fast food industry of being un-American. "A growing number of groups who represent narrow social and political interests," Nugent warned, "have set their sights on our industry in an effort to legislate behavioral change." Enjoying a great meal at a restaurant was "the very essence of freedom," he declared, a ritual now being threatened by groups with an agenda that was "anti-meat, anti-alcohol, anti-caffeine, anti-fat, anti-chemical additives, anti-horseradish, anti-non-dairy creamer." The media played a central role in helping these "activist fearmongers," but the National Restaurant Association had recently launched a counterattack, working closely with journalists to dispel myths and gain better publicity. Nugent called upon the fast food executives to respond even more forcefully to their critics, people who today posed "a real danger to our industry—and more broadly to our way of life."

Not long afterward Mikhail Gorbachev appeared onstage and received a standing ovation. Here was the man who'd ended the Cold War, who'd brought political freedom to hundreds of millions, who'd opened vast new markets. At the age of sixty-nine Gorbachev looked remarkably unchanged from his appearance during the Reagan years. His hair was white, but he seemed vigorous and strong, still capable of running a mighty empire. He spoke quickly in Russian and then waited patiently for the translator to catch up. His delivery was full of energy and passion. "I like America," Gorbachev said with a broad smile. "And I like American people." He wanted to give the audience a sense of what was happening in Russia today. Few people in the United States seemed to care much about events in Russia, a dangerous state of affairs. He asked the crowd to learn about his country, to form partnerships and make investments there. "You must have a lot of money," Gorbachev said. "Send it to Russia."

A few minutes into Gorbachev's speech, the audience began to lose interest. He had badly misjudged the crowd. His speech might have been a success at the Council on Foreign Relations or at the United Nations General Assembly, but at the Grand Ballroom of the Mirage it was a bomb. As Gorbachev explained why the United States must strongly support the policies of Yevgeny Primakov (the Russian prime minister who was fired not long afterward) row after row of eyes began to glaze. He earnestly asked why there was "some kind of a dislike of Primakov that is widespread in this country," unaware that few Americans knew who Yevgeny Primakov was and even fewer cared about him, one way or the other. I counted at least half a dozen people seated near me in the Grand Ballroom who fell asleep during Gorbachev's speech. The executive right beside me suddenly awoke in the middle of a long anecdote about how the Mongol invasion had affected the Russian character in the Middle Ages. The executive seemed startled and unaware of his surroundings, then glanced at the podium for a moment, felt reassured, and drifted back to sleep, his chin resting flat on his chest.

Gorbachev sounded like a politician from a distant era, from a time before sound bites. He was serious, long-winded, and sometimes difficult to follow. His mere presence at the Mirage was far more important to this crowd than anything he said. The meaning hit me as I looked around at all the fast food executives, the sea of pinstriped suits and silk ties. In ancient Rome, the leaders of conquered nations were put on display at the Circus. The symbolism was unmistakable; the submission to Rome, complete. Gorbachev's appearance at the Mirage seemed an Americanized version of that custom, a public opportunity for the victors to gloat—though it would have been even more fitting if the fast food convention had been down the road at Caesar's Palace.

As a Soviet leader, Mikhail Gorbachev never learned when to leave the stage, a flaw that led to his humiliating defeat in the election of 1996. He made the same mistake in Las Vegas; people got up and left the Grand Ballroom while he was still speaking. "Margaret Thatcher was a lot better," I heard one executive say to another as they headed for the door. Thatcher had addressed the previous year's Chain Operators Exchange.

The day after Gorbachev's speech at the Mirage, Bob Dylan performed at the grand opening of the new Mandalay Bay casino. And billboards along the interstate announced that Peter Lowe's Success 1999 was coming to Las Vegas, with special appearances by Elizabeth Dole and General Colin Powell.

An Empire of Fat

For most of the twentieth century, the Soviet Union stood as the greatest obstacle to the worldwide spread of American values and the American way of life. The collapse of Soviet Communism has led to an unprecedented "Americanization" of the world, expressed in the growing popularity of movies, CDs, music videos, television shows, and clothing from the United States. Unlike those commodities, fast food is the one form of American culture that foreign consumers literally consume. By eating like Americans, people all over the world are beginning to look more like Americans, at least in one respect. The United States now has the highest obesity rate of any industrialized nation in the world. More than half of all American adults and about one-quarter of all American children are now obese or overweight. Those proportions have soared during the last few decades, along with the consumption of fast food. The rate of obesity among American adults is twice as high today as it was in the early 1960s. The rate of obesity among American children is twice as high as it was in the late 1970s. According to James O. Hill, a prominent nutritionist at the University of Colorado, "We've got the fattest, least fit generation of kids ever."

The medical literature classifies a person as obese if he or she has a Body Mass Index (BMI) of 30 or higher—a measurement that takes into account both weight and height. For example, a woman who is five-foot-five and weighs 132 pounds has a BMI of 22, which is considered normal. If she gains eighteen pounds, her BMI rises to 25, and she's considered overweight. If she gains fifty pounds, her BMI reaches 30, and she's considered obese.

Today about 44 million American adults are obese. An additional 6 million are "super-obese"; they weigh about a hundred pounds more than they should. No other nation in history has gotten so fat so fast.

A recent study by half a dozen researchers at the Centers for Disease Control and Prevention found that the rate of American obesity was increasing in every state and among both sexes, regardless of age, race, or educational level. In 1991, only four states had obesity rates of 15 percent or higher; today at least thirty-seven states do. "Rarely do chronic conditions such as obesity," the CDC scientists observed, "spread with the speed and dispersion characteristic of a communicable disease epidemic." Although the current rise in obesity has a number of complex causes, genetics is not one of them. The American gene pool has not changed radically in the past few decades. What has changed is the nation's way of eating and living. In simple terms: when people eat more and move less, they get fat. In the United States, people have become increasingly sedentary—driving to work instead of walking, performing little manual labor, driving to do errands, watching television, playing video games, and using a computer instead of exercising. Budget cuts have eliminated physical education programs at many schools. And the growth of the fast food industry has made an abundance of high-fat, inexpensive meals widely available.

As people eat more meals outside the home, they consume more calories, less fiber, and more fat. Commodity prices have fallen so low that the fast food industry has greatly increased its portion sizes, without reducing profits, in order to attract customers. The size of a burger has become one of its main selling points. Wendy's offers the Triple Decker; Burger King, the Great American; and Hardee's sells a hamburger called the Monster. The Little Caesars slogan "Big! Big!" now applies not just to the industry's portions, but to its customers. Over the past forty years in the United States, per capita consumption of carbonated soft drinks has more than quadrupled. During the late 1950s the typical soft drink order at a fast food restaurant contained about eight ounces of soda; today a "Child" order of Coke at McDonald's is twelve ounces. A "Large" Coke is thirty-two ounces—and about 310 calories. In 1972, McDonald's added Large French Fries to its menu; twenty years later, the chain added Super Size Fries, a serving three times larger than what McDonald's offered a generation ago. Super Size Fries have 540 calories and 25 grams of fat. At Carl's Jr. restaurants, an order of CrissCut Fries and a Double Western Bacon Cheeseburger boasts 73 grams of fat—more fat than ten of the chain's milk shakes.

A number of attempts to introduce healthy dishes (such as the McLean Deluxe, a hamburger partly composed of seaweed) have proven unsuccessful. A taste for fat developed in childhood is difficult to lose as an adult. At the moment, the fast food industry is heavily promoting menu items that contain bacon. "Consumers savor the flavor while operators embrace [the] profit margin," *Advertising Age* noted. A decade ago, restaurants sold about

20 percent of the bacon consumed in the United States; now they sell about 70 percent. "Make It Bacon" is one of the new slogans at McDonald's. With the exception of Subway (which promotes healthier food), the major chains have apparently decided that it's much easier and much more profitable to increase the size and the fat content of their portions than to battle eating habits largely formed by years of their own mass marketing.

The cost of America's obesity epidemic extends far beyond emotional pain and low self-esteem. Obesity is now second only to smoking as a cause of mortality in the United States. The CDC estimates that about 280,000 Americans die every year as a direct result of being overweight. The annual health care costs in the United States stemming from obesity now approach $240 billion; on top of that Americans spend more than $33 billion on various weight-loss schemes and diet products. Obesity has been linked to heart disease, colon cancer, stomach cancer, breast cancer, diabetes, arthritis, high blood pressure, infertility, and strokes. A 1999 study by the American Cancer Society found that overweight people had a much higher rate of premature death. Severely overweight people were four times more likely to die young than people of normal weight. Moderately overweight people were twice as likely to die young. "The message is we're too fat and it's killing us," said one of the study's principal authors. Young people who are obese face not only long-term, but also immediate threats to their health. Severely obese American children, aged six to ten, are now dying from heart attacks caused by their weight.

The obesity epidemic that began in the United States during the late 1970s is now spreading to the rest of the world, with fast food as one of its vectors. Between 1984 and 1993, the number of fast food restaurants in Great Britain roughly doubled—and so did the obesity rate among adults. The British now eat more fast food than any other nationality in Western Europe. They also have the highest obesity rate. Obesity is much less of a problem in Italy and Spain, where spending on fast food is relatively low. The relationship between a nation's fast food consumption and its rate of obesity has not been definitively established through any long-term, epidemiological study. The growing popularity of fast food is just one of many cultural changes that have been brought about by globalization. Nevertheless, it seems wherever America's fast food chains go, waistlines start expanding.

In China, the proportion of overweight teenagers has roughly tripled in the past decade. In Japan, eating hamburgers and french fries has not made people any blonder, though it has made them fatter. Overweight people were once a rarity in Japan. The nation's traditional diet of rice, fish, vegetables, and soy products has been deemed one of the healthiest in the world. And yet the Japanese are rapidly abandoning that diet. Consumption of red meat has been rising in Japan since the American occupation after World War II. The arrival of McDonald's in 1971 accelerated the shift in Japanese eating habits. During the 1980s, the sale of fast food in Japan more than doubled; the rate of obesity among children soon doubled, too. Today about one-third of all Japanese men in their thirties—members of the nation's first generation raised on Happy Meals and "Bi-gu Ma-kus"—are overweight. Heart disease, diabetes, colon cancer, and breast cancer, the principal "diseases of affluence," have been linked to diets low in fiber and high in animal fats. Long common in the United States, these diseases are likely to become widespread in Japan as its fast food generation ages. More than a decade ago a study of middle-aged Japanese men who had settled in the United States found that their switch to a Western diet doubled their risk of heart disease and tripled their risk of stroke. For the men in the study, embracing an American way of life meant increasing the likelihood of a premature death.

Obesity is extremely difficult to cure. During thousands of years marked by food scarcity, human beings developed efficient physiological mechanisms to store energy as fat. Until recently, societies rarely enjoyed an overabundance of cheap food. As a result, our bodies are far more efficient at gaining weight than at losing it. Health officials have concluded that prevention, not treatment, offers the best hope of halting the worldwide obesity epidemic. European consumer groups are pushing for a complete ban on all television advertising directed at children. In 1992 Sweden banned all TV advertising directed at children under the age of twelve. Ads have been banned from children's television programming in Norway, Belgium, Ireland, and Holland. The eating habits of American kids are widely considered a good example of what other countries must avoid. American children now get about one-quarter of their total vegetable servings in the form of potato chips or french fries. A survey of children's advertising in the European Union (EU) found that 95 percent of the food ads there encouraged kids to eat foods high in sugar, salt, and fat. The company running the most ads aimed at children was McDonald's.

McLibel

"Resist America beginning with Cola," said a banner at Beijing University in May of 1999. "Attack McDonald's, Storm KFC." The U.S. Air Force had just bombed the Chinese Embassy in Belgrade, Yugoslavia, and anti-American demonstrations were erupting throughout China. At least a dozen McDonald's and four Kentucky Fried Chicken restaurants were damaged by Chinese protesters. For some reason, no Pizza Huts were harmed. "Maybe they think it's Italian," said a Pizza Hut spokesman in Shanghai.

A generation ago American embassies and oil companies were the most likely targets of overseas demonstrations against "U.S. imperialism." Today fast food restaurants have assumed that symbolic role, with McDonald's a particular favorite. In 1995, a crowd of four hundred Danish anarchists looted a McDonald's in downtown Copenhagen, made a bonfire of its furniture in the street, and burned the restaurant to the ground. In 1996, Indian farmers ransacked a Kentucky Fried Chicken restaurant in Bangalore, convinced that the chain threatened their traditional agricultural practices. In 1997, a McDonald's in the Colombian city of Cali was destroyed by a bomb. In 1998, bombs destroyed a McDonald's in St. Petersburg, Russia, two McDonald's in suburban Athens, a McDonald's in the heart of Rio de Janeiro, and a Planet Hollywood in Cape Town, South Africa. In 1999, Belgian vegetarians set fire to a McDonald's in Antwerp, and a year later, May Day protesters tore the sign off a McDonald's in London's Trafalgar Square, destroyed the restaurant, and handed out free hamburgers to the crowd. Fearing more violence, McDonald's temporarily closed all fifty of its London restaurants.

In France, a French sheep farmer and political activist named Jose Bové led a group that demolished a McDonald's under construction in his hometown of Millau. Bové's defiant attitude, brief imprisonment, and impassioned speeches against "lousy food" have made him a hero in France, praised by socialists and conservatives, invited to meetings with the president and the prime minister. He has written a French bestseller entitled *The World Is Not for Sale—And Nor Am I!* In a society where food is a source of tremendous national pride, the McDonald's Corporation has become an easy target, for reasons that are not entirely symbolic. McDonald's is now the largest purchaser of agricultural commodities in France. Bové's message—that Frenchmen should not become "servile slaves at the service of agribusiness"—has struck a chord. During July of 2000 an estimated thirty thousand demonstrators gathered in Millau when Jose Bové went on trial, some carrying signs that said "Non à McMerde."

The overseas critics of fast food are far more diverse than America's old Soviet bloc adversaries. Farmers, leftists, anarchists, nationalists, environmentalists, consumer advocates, educators, health officials, labor unions, and defenders of animal rights have found common ground in a campaign against the perceived Americanization of the world. Fast food has become a target because it is so ubiquitous and because it threatens a fundamental aspect of national identity: how, where, and what people choose to eat.

The longest-running and most systematic assault on fast food overseas has been waged by a pair of British activists affiliated with London Greenpeace. The loosely organized group was formed in 1971 to oppose French nuclear weapon tests in the South Seas. It later staged demonstrations in support of animal rights and British trade unions. It protested against nuclear power and the Falklands War. The group's membership was a small, eclectic mix of pacifists, anarchists, vegetarians, and libertarians brought together by a commitment to nonviolent political action. They ran the organization without any formal leadership, even refusing to join the International Greenpeace movement.

A typical meeting of London Greenpeace attracted anywhere from three people to three dozen. In 1986 the group decided to target McDonald's, later explaining that the company "epitomises everything we despise: a junk culture, the deadly banality of capitalism." Members of London Greenpeace began to distribute a six-page leaflet called "What's Wrong with McDonald's? Everything they don't want you to know." It accused the fast food chain of promoting Third World poverty, selling unhealthy food, exploiting workers and children, torturing animals, and destroying the Amazon rain forest, among other things. Some of the text was factual and straightforward; some of it was pure agitprop. Along the top of the leaflet ran a series of golden arches punctuated by slogans like "McDollars, McGreedy, McCancer, McMurder, McProfits, McGarbage." London Greenpeace distributed the leaflets for four years without attracting much attention. And then in September of 1990 McDonald's sued five members of the group for libel, claiming that every statement in the leaflet was false.

The libel laws in Great Britain are far more unfavorable to a defendant than those in the United States. Under American law, an accuser must prove that the allegations at the heart of a libel case are not only false and defamatory, but also have been recklessly, negligently, or deliberately spread. Under British law, the burden of proof is on the defendant. Allegations that may harm someone's reputation are presumed to be false. Moreover, the defendant in a British court has to use primary sources, such as firsthand witnesses and official documents, to prove the accuracy of a published statement. Secondary sources, including peer-reviewed articles in scientific journals, are deemed inadmissible as evidence. And the defendant's intentions are irrelevant—a British libel case can be lost because of a truly innocent mistake.

The McDonald's Corporation had for years taken advantage of British libel laws to silence its critics. During the 1980s alone, McDonald's threatened to sue at least fifty British publications and organizations, including Channel 4, the Sunday *Times,* the *Guardian,* the *Sun,* student publications, a vegetarian society, and a Scottish youth theater group. The tactic worked, prompting retractions and apologies. The cost of losing a libel case, in both legal fees and damages, could be huge.

The London Greenpeace activists being sued by McDonald's had not written the leaflet in question; they had merely handed it to people. Nevertheless, their behavior could be ruled libelous. Fearing the potential monetary costs, three of the activists reluctantly appeared in court and apologized to McDonald's. The other two decided to fight.

Helen Steel was a twenty-five-year-old gardener, minibus driver, and bartender who'd been drawn to London Greenpeace by her devotion to vegetarianism and animal rights. Dave Morris was a thirty-six-year-old single father, a former postal worker interested in labor issues and the power of multinational corporations. The two friends seemed to stand little chance in court against the world's largest fast food chain. Steel had left school at seventeen, Morris at eighteen; and neither could afford a lawyer. McDonald's, on the other hand, could afford armies of attorneys and had annual revenues at the time of about $18 billion. Morris and Steel were denied legal aid and forced to defend themselves in front of a judge, instead of a jury. But with some help from the secretary of the Haldane Society of Socialist Lawyers, the pair turned the "McLibel case" into the longest trial in British history and a public relations disaster for McDonald's.

The McDonald's Corporation had never expected the case to reach the courtroom. The burden on the defendants was enormous: Morris and Steel had to assemble witnesses and official documents to support the broad assertions in the leaflet. The pair proved to be indefatigable researchers, aided by the McLibel Support Campaign, an international network of activists. By the end of the trial, the court record included 40,000 pages of documents and witness statements, as well as 18,000 pages of transcripts.

McDonald's had made a huge tactical error by asserting that everything in the leaflet was libelous—not only the more extreme claims ("McDonald's and Burger King are . . . using lethal poisons to destroy vast areas of Central American rainforest"), but also the more innocuous ones ("a diet high in fat, sugar, animal products, and salt . . . is linked with cancers of the breast and bowel, and heart disease"). The blunder allowed Steel and Morris to turn the tables, putting McDonald's on trial and forcing a public examination of the chain's labor, marketing, environmental, nutrition, food safety, and animal welfare policies. Some of the chain's top executives were forced to appear on the stand and endure days of cross-examination by the pair of self-taught attorneys. The British media seized upon the David-and-Goliath aspects of the story and made the trial front-page news.

After years of legal wrangling, the McLibel trial formally began in March of 1994. It ended more than three years later, when Justice Rodger Bell submitted an 800-page judgment. Morris and Steel were found to have libeled McDonald's. The judge ruled that the two had failed to prove many of their allegations—but had indeed proved some. According to Justice Bell's decision, McDonald's did "exploit" children through its advertising, endanger the health of its regular customers, pay workers unreasonably low wages, oppose union activities worldwide, and bear responsibility for the cruelty inflicted upon animals by many of its suppliers. Morris and Steel were fined £60,000. The two promptly announced they would appeal the decision. "McDonald's don't deserve a penny," Helen Steel said, "and in any event we haven't got any money."

Evidence submitted during the McLibel trial disclosed much about the inner workings of the McDonald's Corporation. Many of its labor, food safety, and advertising practices had already been publicly criticized in the United States for years. Testimony in the London courtroom, however, provided new revelations about the company's attitude toward civil liberties and freedom of speech. Morris and Steel were stunned to discover that Mc-Donald's had infiltrated London Greenpeace with informers, who regularly attended the group's meetings and spied on its members.

The spying had begun in 1989 and did not end until 1991, nearly a year after the libel suit had been filed. McDonald's had used subterfuge not only to find out who'd distributed the leaflets, but also to learn how Morris and Steel planned to defend themselves in court. The company had employed at least seven different undercover agents. During some London Greenpeace meetings, about half the people in attendance were corporate spies. One spy broke into the London Greenpeace office, took photographs, and stole documents. Another had a six-month affair with a member of London Greenpeace while informing on his activities. McDonald's spies inadvertently spied on each other, unaware that the company was using at least two different detective agencies. They participated in demonstrations against McDonald's and gave out anti-McDonald's leaflets.

During the trial, Sidney Nicholson—the McDonald's vice president who'd supervised the undercover operation, a former police officer in South Africa and former superintendent in London's Metropolitan Police—admitted in court that McDonald's had used its law enforcement connections to obtain information on Steel and Morris from Scotland Yard. Indeed, officers belonging to Special Branch, an elite British unit that tracks "subversives" and organized crime figures, had helped McDonald's spy on Steel and Morris for years. One of the company's undercover agents later had a change of heart and testified on behalf of the McLibel defendants. "At no time did I believe they were dangerous people," said Fran Tiller, following her conversion to vegetarianism. "I think they genuinely believed in the issues they were supporting."

For Dave Morris, perhaps the most disturbing moment of the trial was hearing how McDonald's had obtained his home address. One of its spies admitted in court that a gift of baby clothes had been a ruse to find out where Morris lived. Morris had unwittingly accepted the gift, believing it to be an act of friendship—and was disgusted to learn that his infant son had for months worn outfits supplied by McDonald's as part of its surveillance.

I visited Dave Morris one night in February of 1999, as he prepared for an appearance the next day before the Court of Appeal. Morris lives in a small flat above a carpet shop in North London. The apartment lacks central heating, the ceilings are sagging, and the place is crammed with books, boxes, files, transcripts, leaflets, and posters announcing various demonstrations. The place feels like everything McDonald's is not—lively, unruly, deeply idiosyncratic, and organized according to a highly complex scheme that only one human being could possibly understand. Morris spent about an hour with me, as his son finished homework upstairs. He spoke intensely about McDonald's, but stressed that its arrogant behavior was just one manifestation of a much larger problem now confronting the world: the rise of powerful multinationals that shift capital across borders with few qualms, that feel no allegiance to any nation, no loyalty to any group of farmers, workers, or consumers.

The British journalist John Vidal, in his book on the McLibel trial, noted some of the similarities between Dave Morris and Ray Kroc. As Morris offered an impassioned critique of globalization, the comparison made sense—both men true believers, charismatic, driven by ideas outside the mainstream, albeit championing opposite viewpoints. During the McLibel trial, Paul Preston, the president of McDonald's UK, had said, "Fitting into a finely working machine, that's what McDonald's is about." And here was Morris, in the living room of his North London flat, warmed by a gas heater in the fireplace, surrounded by stacks of papers and files, caring nothing for money, determined somehow to smash that machine.

On March 31, 1999, the three Court of Appeal justices overruled parts of the original McLibel verdict, supporting the leaflet's assertions that eating McDonald's food can cause heart disease and that workers are treated badly. The court reduced the damages owed by Steel and Morris to about £40,000. The McDonald's Corporation had previously announced that it had no intention of collecting the money and would no longer try to stop London Greenpeace from distributing the leaflet (which by then had been translated into twenty-seven languages). McDonald's was tired of the bad publicity and wanted this case to go away. But Morris and Steel were not yet through with McDonald's. They appealed the Court of Appeal decision to the British House of Lords and sued the police for spying on them. Scotland Yard settled the case out of court, apologizing to the pair and paying them £10,000 in damages. When the House of Lords refused to hear their case, Morris and Steel filed an appeal with the European Court of Human Rights, challenging the validity not only of the verdict, but also of the British libel laws. As of this writing, the McLibel case is entering its eleventh year. After intimidating British critics for years, the McDonald's Corporation picked on the wrong two people.

Back at the Ranch

When the first McDonald's opened in East Germany, in December of 1990, the company was unsure how American food would be received there. On opening day the McDonald's in Plauen served potato dumplings, a Vogtland favorite, along with hamburgers and fries. Today hundreds of McDonald's restaurants dot the landscape of eastern Germany. In town after town, statues of Lenin have come down and statues of Ronald McDonald have gone up. One of the largest is in Bitterfeld, where a three-story-high, illuminated Ronald can be seen from the autobahn for miles.

During my first visit to Plauen, in October of 1998, McDonald's was the only business open in the central market square. It was Reunification Day, a national holiday, and everything else was closed, the small shops selling used clothing and furniture, the pseudo-Irish pub on one corner, the pizzeria on another. McDonald's was packed, overflowing not just with children and their parents, but with teenagers, seniors, young couples, a cross-section of the town. The restaurant was brightly lit and spotlessly clean. Cheerful middle-aged women took orders behind the counter, worked in the kitchen, delivered food to tables, scrubbed the windows. Most of them had worked at this McDonald's for years. Some had been there since the day it opened. Across the street stood an abandoned building once occupied by a branch of the East German army; a few blocks away the houses were dilapidated and covered in graffiti, looking as though the Wall had never fallen. That day McDonald's was the nicest, cleanest, brightest place in all of Plauen. Children played with the Hot Wheels and Barbies that came with their Happy Meals, and smiling workers poured free refills of coffee. Outside the window, three bright red flags bearing the golden arches fluttered in the wind.

Life after Communism has not been easy in Plauen. At first there was an outpouring of great optimism and excitement. As in other East German towns, people quickly used their new liberty to travel overseas for the first time. They borrowed money to buy new cars. According to Thomas Küttler, the hero of Plauen's 1989 uprising, thoughts about Friedrich von Schiller and the freedom of their forefathers soon gave way to a hunger for Western consumer goods. Küttler is disappointed by how fast the idealism of 1989 vanished, but feels little nostalgia for the old East Germany. Under Communist rule in Plauen, a person could be arrested for watching television broadcasts from the West or for listening to American rock 'n' roll. Today in Plauen you can get dozens of channels on cable and even more via satellite. MTV is popular there, and most of the songs on the radio are in English. Becoming part of the larger world, however, has had its costs. Plauen's economy has suffered as one after another, old and inefficient manufacturing plants closed, throwing people out of work. Since the fall of the Berlin Wall, Plauen has lost about 10 percent of its population, as people move away in search of a better life. The town seems unable to break free from its past. Every year a few unexploded bombs from World War II are still discovered and defused.

At the moment, Plauen's unemployment rate is about 20 percent—twice the rate in Germany as a whole. You see men in their forties, a lost generation, too young to retire but too old to fit into the new scheme, staggering drunk in the middle of the day. The factory workers who bravely defied and brought down the old regime are the group who've fared worst, the group with the wrong skills and the least hope. Others have done quite well.

Manfred Voigt, the McDonald's franchisee in Plauen, is now a successful businessman who, with his wife, Brigitte, vacations in Florida every year. In an interview with the *Wall Street Journal*, Manfred Voigt attributed his recent success to forces beyond his control. "It was dumb luck," Voigt explained; "fate." He and his wife had no money and could not understand why McDonald's had chosen them to own its first restaurant in East Germany, why the company had trained and financed them. One explanation, never really explored in the *Wall Street Journal* profile, might be that the Voigts were one of the most powerful couples in Plauen under the old regime. They headed the local branch of Konsum, the state-controlled foodservice monopoly. Today the Voigts are one of Plauen's wealthiest couples; they own two other McDonald's in nearby towns. Throughout the former Eastern bloc, members of the old Communist elite have had the easiest time adjusting to Western consumerism. They had the right connections and many of the right skills. They now own some of the most lucrative franchises.

The high unemployment rate in Plauen has created social and political instability. What seems lacking is a stable middle ground. Roughly a third of the young people in eastern Germany now express support for various nationalist and neo-Nazi groups. Right-wing extremists have declared large parts of the east to be "foreigner-free" zones, where immigrants are not welcome. The roads leading into Plauen are decorated with signs posted by the Deutschland Volks Union, a right-wing party. "Germany for the Germans," the signs say. "Jobs for Germans, Not Foreigners." Neo-Nazi skinheads have thus far not caused much trouble in Plauen, though a black person today needs real courage to walk the city's streets at night. The opposition to American fast food voiced by many environmentalists and left-wing groups does not seem to be shared by German groups on the far right. When I asked an employee at the McDonald's in Plauen if the restaurant had ever been the target of neo-Nazis, she laughed and said there'd never been any threats of that kind. People in the area did not consider McDonald's to be "foreign."

Around the time that Plauen got its McDonald's in 1990, a new nightclub opened in a red brick building on the edge of town. "The Ranch" has an American flag and a Confederate flag hanging out front. Inside there's a long bar, and the walls are decorated with old-fashioned farm implements, saddles, bridles, and wagon wheels. Frieder Stephan, the owner of The Ranch, was inspired by photographs of the American West, but gathered all the items on the walls from nearby farms. The place looks like a bar in Cripple Creek, circa 1895. Before the fall of the Berlin Wall, Frieder Stephan was a disc jockey on an East German tourist ferry. He secretly listened to Creedance Clearwater, the Stones, and the Lovin' Spoonful. Now forty-nine years old, he is the leading impresario in Plauen's thriving country-western scene, booking local bands (like the Midnight Ramblers and C.C. Raider) at his club. The city's country-western fans call themselves "Vogtland Cowboys," put on their western boots and ten-gallon hats at night, and hit the town, drinking at The Ranch or joining the Square Dance Club at a bar called the White Magpie. The Square Dance Club is sponsored by Thommy's Western Store on Friedrich Engels Avenue. Plauen now has a number of small westernwear shops like Thommy's that sell imported cowboy boots, cowboy posters, fancy belt buckles, work shirts with snaps, and Wrangler jeans. While teenagers in Colorado Springs today could not care less about cowboys, kids in Plauen are sporting bolo ties and cowboy hats.

Every Wednesday night, a few hundred people gather at The Ranch for line dancing. Members of Plauen's American Car Club pull up in their big Ford and Chevy trucks. Others come from miles away, dressed in their western best, ready to dance. Most of them are working class, and many are unemployed. Their ages range from seven years old to seventy. If somebody doesn't know how to line-dance, a young woman named Petra gives lessons. People wear their souvenir T-shirts from Utah. They smoke Marlboros and drink beer. They listen to Willie Nelson, Garth Brooks, Johnny Cash—and they dance, kicking up their boots, twirling their partners, waving their cowboy hats in the air. And for a few hours the spirit of the American West fills this funky bar deep in the heart of Saxony, in a town that has seen too much history, and the old dream lives on, the dream of freedom without limits, self-reliance, and a wide-open frontier.   ■

NOTES:

Few West Germans are familiar with the unusual history of Plauen, though it is abundantly detailed in a number of locally published books. *Plauen: auf historischen Postkarten* (Plauen, Germany: Plauen Verlag, 1991), by Frank Weiss, uses old postcards to illustrate the history of the city during its most prosperous era. *Plauen: 1933–1945* (Plauen: Vogtländischer Heimatverlag Neupert, 1995) is an oversized book, full of photographs, that traces the effects of the Great Depression and the rise of the Nazi Party. The Allied bombing of the city is vividly documented through before-and-after photographs in *Plauen 1944/1945: Eine Stadt wird zerstört* (Plauen: Vogtländischer Heimatverlag Neupert, 1995), by Rudolf Laser, Joachim Mensdorf, and Johannes Richter. For life near the East German border, I relied on Ingolf Hermann's *Die Deutsch-Deutsch Grenze* (Plauen: Vogtländischer Heimatverlag Neupert, 1998). Plauen's 1989 uprising is chronicled in Rolf Schwanitz's *Zivilcourage: Die friedliche Revolution in Plauen anhand von Stasi-Akten* (Plauen: Vogtländischer Heimatverlag Neupert, 1998). *Plauen: Ein Rundgang Durch die Stadt* (Plauen: Milizke Verlag, 1992) gives a sense of the city after the Wall came down.

John Connelly, an assistant professor of history at the University of California, Berkeley, is one of the few American academics who has both visited and written about postwar Plauen. Professor Connelly shared his recollection of the city with me and sent me the fine article he wrote about its rebellion: "Moment of Revolution: Plauen (Vogtland), October 7, 1989," *German Politics & Society*, Summer 1990. Thomas Küttler, the hero of that uprising, told me how it unfolded and shared his thoughts about its legacy. I am grateful to Cordula Franz for help in arranging interviews in Plauen and to Sybille Unterdoifel for introducing me to The Ranch. Frieder Stephan, the owner of The Ranch, helped me fathom the local youth culture and explained his musical journey from rock to disco to country and western. Christian Pöllmann, who helps run a theater company in Plauen, as well as the German Social Union Party, gave me a strong sense of life under Communism and of the hunger for all things American. The photographer Franziska Heinze and journalist Markus Schneider helped me gather information about their home town. Siegfried Pater—filmmaker, environmentalist, and author of *Zum Beispiel McDonald's* (Göttingen:

Lamuv Verlag, 1994)—described some of McDonald's misbehavior in Germany. Barbara Distil, the curator of the Dachau Museum, spoke to me about the controversy surrounding the local McDonald's. For the history of the camp, I relied on a book that she edited with Ruth Jakusch: *Concentration Camp Dachau 1933–1945* (Brussels: Comité International de Dachau, 1978).

The Illustrated History of Las Vegas (Edison, N.J.: Chartwell Books, 1997), by Bill Yenne, conveys how the city has been radically transformed in recent years. *The Players: The Men Who Made Las Vegas* (Reno: University of Nevada Press, 1997), edited by Jack Sheehan, provides a good deal of insight into the unique culture that emerged there. Timothy O'Brien's *Bad Bet: The Inside Story of the Glamour, Glitz, and Danger of America's Gambling Industry* (New York: Times Business, 1998) explains precisely how the casinos make their money.

Much of my information on obesity comes from articles in *Science,* the *Journal of the American Medical Association,* and the *New England Journal of Medicine.* The nutritionist Jane Kirby placed many of the claims and counterclaims about diet into a calm and reasonable perspective for me. Greg Critser's "Let Them Eat Fat: The Heavy Truths about American Obesity," *Harper's,* March 2000, is a provocative essay on fast food and the poor.

My account of the McLibel trial is based on interviews with the two principals, Helen Steel and Dave Morris, and on the transcripts of the trial (which were available, along with other interesting material, at the anti-McDonald's Web site <www.mcspotlight.org>). Fanny Armstrong—the director of an excellent documentary, *McLibel: Two Worlds Collide*—was extremely helpful. John Vidal's book, *McLibel,* tells the whole, extraordinary story of the trial. The essays collected in *Golden Arches East: McDonald's in East Asia* (Stanford, Calif.: Stanford University Press, 1997), edited by James L. Watson, reveal some of the unpredictable ways in which fast food is now being embraced by other cultures.

■ *QUESTIONS FOR MAKING CONNECTIONS WITHIN THE READING* ■

1. Eric Schlosser begins "Global Realization" with a visit to Plauen, which he writes, "has been alternately punished, rewarded, devastated, and transformed by the great unifying systems of the twentieth century. . . . Plauen has been a battlefield for these competing ideologies, with their proudly displayed and archetypal symbols: the smokestack, the swastika, the hammer and sickle, the golden arches." What are the "competing ideologies" to which Schlosser refers? What do the "archetypal symbols" he mentions represent?

2. Toward the middle of "Global Realization," Schlosser describes an experience he had during a trip to Las Vegas that "revealed the strange power of fast food in the new world order." What is the "new world order," and what role does the fast-food industry have to play in it?

3. Schlosser's essay ends with a description of a bar in Plauen called "The Ranch," where he says "the old dream lives on, the dream of freedom without limits, self-reliance, and a wide-open frontier." Is the "old dream" preferable to the "illusion" that Las Vegas sells? If globalization is "the new dream," what are the goals of this dream? How does the new dream differ from the old dream?

■ *QUESTIONS FOR WRITING* ■

1. Schlosser argues that fast food "threatens a fundamental aspect of national identity: how, where, and what people choose to eat." Why are foreign nations threatened by the spread of fast food? Will nations continue to exist if the project of globalization is realized?

2. Schlosser insists that Las Vegas sells "the most brilliant illusion of all, a loss that feels like winning." McDonald's, presumably, is selling a similar illusion. What is lost when the fast-food industry succeeds? Is there anything that the consumer can do to combat this "loss that feels like winning"?

■ *QUESTIONS FOR MAKING CONNECTIONS BETWEEN READINGS* ■

1. For most of its history, McDonald's has placed a much higher premium on affordability, speed of service, and taste than on nutrition or culinary virtuosity. After half a century, however, Americans are now in a position to see that the McDonald's innovation—the industrial mass production of cooked food—has had a number of unforeseen negative consequences. How would Edward Tenner look at McDonald's, and how might his perspective on the subject differ from Schlosser's? Would you say that Americans have become more discerning and sophisticated in their eating habits than they were back in the days when restaurant fare meant burgers, fries, and milkshakes? Would you say that Americans are eating more healthily? Is the industrial mass production of cooked food inherently unhealthy? Drawing on examples from Tenner's piece, consider the adjustments that might help to make fast food into healthy food as well.

2. Any business venture involves, of necessity, both a prediction about what the future holds and an effort to create that future. As Schlosser shows, the process of globalization represents the effort to create a future where the needs and desires of the entire planet are coordinated, organized, and satisfied. With Jon Gertner's essay, "The Futile Pursuit of Happiness," in mind, one might well ask what role happiness plays in the effort to create this future. What might be the emotional consequences of pursuing the "McDonald's" version of the future? Is the effort to realize the dream of globalization driven by reason or affective miscalculation? Is it inevitable that the result of globalization will be global disappointment?

www **For additional suggestions about making connections between readings, visit the Link-O-Mat and More Sample Questions at <www.newhum.com>.**

JAMES C. SCOTT

HOW DO OPPRESSED peoples survive under repressive regimes? When oppression becomes unbearable, what makes revolution possible? At a time when governments have become awesomely powerful, and awesomely effective at controlling the behavior of the governed, is resistance a meaningful act? These are some of the questions that James C. Scott, Director of the Program in Agrarian Studies at Yale University and Sterling Professor of Political Science and Anthropology, has spent his professional life trying to answer. By working across the disciplines of political science, anthropology, ecology, and cultural studies, Scott is expressing his conviction that "the only way to loosen the nearly hegemonic grip of the separate disciplines on how questions are framed and answered is to concentrate on themes of signal importance to several disciplines."

The author of *The Moral Economy of the Peasant: Rebellion and Subsistence in Southeast Asia* (1976), *Weapons of the Weak: Everyday Forms of Peasant Resistance* (1985), *Domination and the Arts of Resistance: Hidden Transcripts* (1990), Scott has described his most recent book, *Seeing Like a State: How Certain Schemes to Improve the Human Condition Have Failed* (1997), as the result of an "intellectual detour that became so gripping" it forced him to abandon "his original itinerary altogether." Having set out to understand why the state has always cracked down so hard on nomadic peoples, Scott ended up seeing state efforts to foster sedentary lifestyles as part of a larger project of making society "legible." With this insight, *Seeing Like a State* then evolved into an exploration of the ways that state planners have tended to take "exceptionally complex, illegible, and local social practices . . . and created a standard grid whereby [these practices] could be centrally recorded and monitored."

"Behind the Official Story," the opening chapter of *Domination and the Arts of Resistance*, records Scott's abiding interest in the unruliness of the masses and his commitment to providing alternate understandings of the words and actions

---

Scott, James C. "Behind the Official Story." *Domination and the Arts of Resistance: Hidden Transcripts*. New Haven: Yale University Press, 1990. 1–16.

Initial quotation drawn from the Yale Agrarian Studies Web site; final quotation drawn from James Scott's introduction to *Seeing Like a State: How Certain Schemes to Improve the Human Condition Have Failed* (New Haven: Yale University Press, 1998).

of the disempowered. Is it possible to know the story "behind" the official story? Or is this story, which Scott terms "the hidden transcript," forever out of reach of those who are in power? By exploring questions about power in these terms, Scott invites his readers to consider the possibility that reading itself might be a form of resistance.

www   **To learn more about James Scott and popular resistance movements, please visit the Link-O-Mat at <www.newhum.com>.**

Behind the Official Story

I tremble to speak the words of freedom before the tyrant.
—CORYPHAEUS, in Euripides, *The Bacchae*

The Labourer and Artisan, notwithstanding they are Servants to their Masters, are quit by doing what they are bid. But the Tyrant sees those that are about him, begging and suing for his Favour; and they must not only do what he commands, but they must think as he would have them [think] and most often, to satisfy him, even anticipate his thoughts. It is not sufficient to obey him, they must also please him, they must harass, torment, nay kill themselves in his Service; and . . . they must leave their own Taste for his, Force their Inclination, and throw off their natural Dispositions. They must carefully observe his Words, his Voice, his Eyes, and even his Nod. They must have neither Eyes, Feet, nor Hands, but what must be ALL upon the watch, to spy out his Will, and discover his Thoughts. Is this to live happily? Does it indeed deserve the Name of Life?
—ESTIENNE DE LA BOETIE, *A Discourse on Voluntary Servitude*

And the intensest hatred is that rooted in fear, which compels to silence and drives vehemence into constructive vindictiveness, an imaginary annihilation of the detested object, something like the hidden rites of vengeance with which the persecuted have a dark vent for their rage.
—GEORGE ELIOT, *Daniel Deronda*

If the expression "Speak truth to power" still has a utopian ring to it, even in modern democracies, this is surely because it is so rarely practiced. The dissembling of the weak in the face of power is hardly an occasion for surprise.

It is ubiquitous. So ubiquitous, in fact, that it makes an appearance in many situations in which the sort of power being exercised stretches the ordinary meaning of *power* almost beyond recognition. Much of what passes as normal social intercourse requires that we routinely exchange pleasantries and smile at others about whom we may harbor an estimate not in keeping with our public performance. Here we may perhaps say that the power of social forms embodying etiquette and politeness requires us often to sacrifice candor for smooth relations with our acquaintances. Our circumspect behavior may also have a strategic dimension: this person to whom we misrepresent ourselves may be able to harm or help us in some way. George Eliot may not have exaggerated in claiming that "there is no action possible without a little acting."

The acting that comes of civility will be of less interest to us in what follows than the acting that has been imposed throughout history on the vast majority of people. I mean the public performance required of those subject to elaborate and systematic forms of social subordination: the worker to the boss, the tenant or sharecropper to the landlord, the serf to the lord, the slave to the master, the untouchable to the Brahmin, a member of a subject race to one of the dominant race. With rare, but significant, exceptions the public performance of the subordinate will, out of prudence, fear, and the desire to curry favor, be shaped to appeal to the expectations of the powerful. I shall use the term *public transcript* as a shorthand way of describing the open interaction between subordinates and those who dominate.[1] The public transcript, where it is not positively misleading, is unlikely to tell the whole story about power relations. It is frequently in the interest of both parties to tacitly conspire in misrepresentation. The oral history of a French tenant farmer, Old Tiennon, covering much of the nineteenth century is filled with accounts of a prudent and misleading deference: "When he [the landlord who had dismissed his father] crossed from Le Craux, going to Meillers, he would stop and speak to me and I forced myself to appear amiable, in spite of the contempt I felt for him."[2]

Old Tiennon prides himself on having learned, unlike his tactless and unlucky father, "the art of dissimulation so necessary in life."[3] The slave narratives that have come to us from the U.S. South also refer again and again to the need to deceive:

> I had endeavored so to conduct myself as not to become obnoxious to the white inhabitants, knowing as I did their power, and their hostility to the colored people. . . . First, I had made no display of the little property or money I possessed, but in every way I wore as much as possible the aspect of slavery. Second, I had never appeared to be even so intelligent as I really was. This all colored at the south, free and slaves, find it particularly necessary for their own comfort and safety to observe.[4]

As one of the key survival skills of subordinate groups has been impression management in power-laden situations, the performance aspect of their conduct has not escaped the more observant members of the dominant group. Noting that her slaves fell uncharacteristically silent whenever the latest news from the front in the Civil War became a topic of white conversation, Mary Chesnut took their silence as one that hid something: "They go about in their black masks, not a ripple of emotion showing; and yet on all other subjects except the war they are the most excitable of all races. Now Dick might be a very respectable Egyptian Sphinx, so inscrutably silent he is."[5]

Here I will venture a crude and global generalization I will later want to qualify severely: the greater the disparity in power between dominant and subordinate and the more arbitrarily it is exercised, the more the public transcript of subordinates will take on a stereotyped, ritualistic cast. In other words, the more menacing the power, the thicker the mask. We might imagine, in this context, situations ranging all the way from a dialogue among friends of equal status and power on the one hand to the concentration camp on the other, in which the public transcript of the victim bears the mark of mortal fear. Between these extremes are the vast majority of the historical cases of systematic subordination that will concern us.

Cursory though this opening discussion of the public transcript has been, it alerts us to several issues in power relations, each of which hinges on the fact that the public transcript is not the whole story. First, the public transcript is an indifferent guide to the opinion of subordinates. Old Tiennon's tactical smile and greeting mask an attitude of anger and revenge. At the very least, an assessment of power relations read directly off the public transcript between the powerful and the weak may portray a deference and consent that are possibly only a tactic. Second, to the degree that the dominant suspect that the public transcript may be "only" a performance, they will discount its authenticity. It is but a short step from such skepticism to the view, common among many dominant groups, that those beneath them are deceitful, shamming, and lying by nature. Finally, the questionable meaning of the public transcript suggests the key roles played by disguise and surveillance in power relations. Subordinates offer a performance of deference and consent while attempting to discern, to read, the real intentions and mood of the potentially threatening powerholder. As the favorite proverb of Jamaican slaves captures it, "Play fool, to catch wise."[6] The power figure, in turn, produces a performance of mastery and command while attempting to peer behind the mask of subordinates to read their real intentions. The dialectic of disguise and surveillance that pervades relations between the weak and the strong will help us, I think, to understand the cultural patterns of domination and subordination.

The theatrical imperatives that normally prevail in situations of domination produce a public transcript in close conformity with how the dominant group would wish to have things appear. The dominant never control the stage absolutely, but their wishes normally prevail. In the short run, it is in the interest of the subordinate to produce a more or less credible performance, speaking the lines and making the gestures he knows are expected of him. The result is that the public transcript is—barring a crisis—systematically skewed in the direction of the libretto, the discourse, represented by the dominant. In ideological terms the public transcript will typically, by its accommodationist tone, provide convincing evidence for the hegemony of dominant values, for the hegemony of dominant discourse. It is in precisely this public domain where the effects of power relations are most manifest, and any analysis based exclusively on the public transcript is likely to conclude that subordinate groups endorse the terms of their subordination and are willing, even enthusiastic, partners in that subordination.

A skeptic might well ask at this point how we can presume to know, on the basis of the public transcript alone, whether this performance is genuine or not. What warrant have we to call it a performance at all, thereby impugning its authenticity? The answer is, surely, that we cannot know how contrived or imposed the performance is unless we can speak, as it were, to the performer offstage, out of this particular power-laden context, or unless the performer suddenly declares openly, on stage, that the performances we have previously observed were just a pose.[7] Without a privileged peek backstage or a rupture in the performance we have no way of calling into question the status of what might be a convincing but feigned performance.

If subordinate discourse in the presence of the dominant is a public transcript, I shall use the term *hidden transcript* to characterize discourse that takes place "offstage," beyond direct observation by powerholders. The hidden transcript is thus derivative in the sense that it consists of those offstage speeches, gestures, and practices that confirm, contradict, or inflect what appears in the public transcript.[8] We do not wish to prejudge, by definition, the relation between what is said in the face of power and what is said behind its back. Power relations are not, alas, so straightforward that we can call what is said in power-laden contexts false and what is said offstage true. Nor can we simplistically describe the former as a realm of necessity and the latter as a realm of freedom. What is certainly the case, however, is that the hidden transcript is produced for a different audience and under different constraints of power than the public transcript. By assessing the discrepancy *between* the hidden transcript and the public transcript we may begin to judge the impact of domination on public discourse.

The abstract and general tone of the discussion thus far is best relieved by concrete illustrations of the possibly dramatic disparity between the public and the hidden transcripts. The first is drawn from slavery in the antebellum U.S. South. Mary Livermore, a white governess from New England, recounted the reaction of Aggy, a normally taciturn and deferential black cook, to the beating the master had given her daughter. The daughter had been accused, apparently unjustly, of some minor theft and then beaten while Aggy looked on, powerless to intervene. After the master had finally left the kitchen, Aggy turned to Mary, whom she considered her friend and said,

Thar's a day a-comin'! Thar's a day a-comin'! . . . I hear the rumblin ob de chariots! I see de flashin ob de guns! White folks blood is a runnin on the ground like a ribber, an de dead's heaped up dat high! . . . Oh Lor! Hasten de day when de blows, an de bruises, and de aches an de pains, shall come to de white folks, an de buzzards shall eat dem as dey's dead in de streets. Oh Lor! roll on de chariots, an gib the black people rest and peace. Oh Lor! Gib me de pleasure ob livin' till dat day, when I shall see white folks shot down like de wolves when dey come hungry out o'de woods.[9]

One can imagine what might have happened to Aggy if she had delivered this speech directly to the master. Apparently her trust in Mary Livermore's friendship and sympathy was such that a statement of her rage could be ventured with comparative safety. Alternatively, perhaps she could no longer choke back her anger. Aggy's hidden transcript is at complete odds with her public transcript of quiet obedience. What is particularly striking is that this is anything but an inchoate scream of rage; it is a finely drawn and highly visual image of an apocalypse, a day of revenge and triumph, a world turned upside down using the cultural raw materials of the white man's religion. Can we conceive of such an elaborate vision rising spontaneously to her lips without the beliefs and practice of slave Christianity having prepared the way carefully? In this respect our glimpse of Aggy's hidden transcript, if pursued further, would lead us directly to the offstage culture of the slave quarters and slave religion. Whatever such an investigation would tell us, this glimpse itself is sufficient to make any naive interpretation of Aggy's previous and subsequent public acts of deference impossible both for us, and most decidedly for Aggy's master, should he have been eavesdropping behind the kitchen door.

The hidden transcript Aggy revealed in the comparative safety of friendship is occasionally openly declared in the face of power. When, suddenly, subservience evaporates and is replaced by open defiance we encounter one of those rare and dangerous moments in power relations. Mrs. Poyser, a character in George Eliot's *Adam Bede* who finally spoke her mind, provides an illustration of the hidden transcript storming the stage. As tenants of the elderly Squire Donnithorne, Mrs. Poyser and her husband had always resented his rare visits, when he would impose some new, onerous obligation on them and treat them with disdain. He had "a mode of looking at her which, Mrs. Poyser observed, 'allays aggravated her; it was as if you was an insect, and he was going to dab his fingernail on you.' However, she said, 'your servant, sir' and curtsied with an air of perfect deference as she advanced towards him: she was not the woman to misbehave toward her betters, and fly in the face of the catechism, without severe provocation."[10]

This time the squire came to propose an exchange of pasture and grain land between Mr. Poyser and a new tenant that would almost certainly be to the Poysers' disadvantage. When assent was slow in coming, the squire held out the prospect of a longer term farm lease and ended with the observation—a thinly veiled threat of eviction—that the other tenant was well-off and would be happy to lease the Poysers' farm in addition to his own. Mrs. Poyser, "exasperated" at the squire's determination to ignore her earlier objections "as if she had left the room" and at the final threat, exploded. She "burst in with the desperate determination to have her say out this once, though it were to rain notices to quit, and the only shelter were the workhouse."[11] Beginning with a comparison between the condition of the house—frogs on the steps of the flooded basement, rats and mice coming in through the rotten floorboards to eat the cheeses and menace the children—and the struggle to pay the high rent, Mrs. Poyser let fly her personal accusations as she realized that the squire was fleeing out the door toward his pony and safety:

> You may run away from my words, sir, and you may go spinning underhand ways o' doing us a mischief, for you've got old Harry to your friend, though nobody else is, but I tell you for once as we're not dumb creatures to be abused and made money on by them as ha' got the lash i' their hands, for want o' knowing how t' undo the tackle. An if I'm th' only one as speaks my mind, there's plenty o' the same way o' thinking i' this parish and the next to 't, for your name's no better than a brimstone match in everybody's nose.[12]

Such were Eliot's powers of observation and insight into her rural society that many of the key issues of domination and resistance can be teased from her story of Mrs. Poyser's encounter with the squire. At the height of her peroration, for example, Mrs. Poyser insists that they will not be treated as animals despite his power over them. This, together with her remark about the squire looking on her as an insect and her declaration that he has no friends and is hated by the whole parish, focuses on the issue of self-esteem. While the confrontation may originate in the exploitation of an onerous tenancy, the discourse is one of dignity and reputation. The practices of domination and exploitation typically generate the insults and slights to human dignity that in turn foster a hidden transcript of indignation. Perhaps one vital distinction to draw between forms of domination lies in the kinds of indignities the exercise of power routinely produces.

Notice also how Mrs. Poyser presumes to speak not just for herself but for the whole parish. She represents what she says as the first public declaration of what everyone has been saying behind the squire's back. Judging from how rapidly the story traveled and the unalloyed joy with which it was received and retold, the rest of the community also felt Mrs. Poyser had spoken for them as well. "It was known throughout the two parishes," Eliot writes, "that the Squire's plan had been frustrated because the Poysers had refused to be 'put upon,' and Mrs. Poyser's outbreak was discussed in all the farmhouses with a zest that was only heightened by frequent repetition."[13] The vicarious pleasure of the neighbors had nothing to do with the actual sentiments expressed by Mrs. Poyser—hadn't everyone been saying the same thing about the squire among themselves for years? The content, though Mrs. Poyser may have put it with considerable folk elegance, was stale; it was saying it openly (with witnesses) to the squire's face that was remarkable and that made Mrs. Poyser into something of a local hero. The first open statement of a hidden transcript, a declaration that breaches the etiquette of power relations, that breaks an apparently calm surface of silence and consent, carries the force of a symbolic declaration of war. Mrs. Poyser had spoken (a social) truth to power.

Delivered in a moment of anger, Mrs. Poyser's speech was, one might say, spontaneous—but the spontaneity lay in the timing and vehemence of the delivery, not in the content. The content had, in fact, been rehearsed again and again, as we are told: "and though Mrs. Poyser had during the last twelve-month recited many imaginary speeches, meaning even more than met the ear, which she was quite determined to make to him the next time he appeared within the gates of the Hall Farm, the speeches had always remained imaginary."[14] Who among us has not had a similar experience? Who, having been insulted or suffered an indignity—especially in public— at the hand of someone in power or authority over us, has not rehearsed an imaginary speech he wishes he had given or intends to give at the next opportunity?[15] Such speeches may often remain a personal hidden transcript that may never find expression, even among close friends and peers. But in this case we are dealing with a shared situation of subordination. The tenants of Squire Donnithorne and, in fact, much of the nongentry in two parishes had ample personal reasons to take pleasure in his being publicly humbled and to share vicariously in Mrs. Poyser's courage. Their common class position and their social links thus provided a powerful resolving lens bringing their collective hidden transcript into focus. One might say, without much exaggeration, that they had together, in the course of their social interchange, written Mrs. Poyser's speech for her. Not word for word, of course, but in the sense that Mrs. Poyser's "say" would be her own reworking of the stories, the ridicule, and the complaints that those beneath the Squire all shared. And to "write" that speech for her, the squire's subjects had to have some secure social space, however sequestered, where they could exchange and elaborate their criticism. Her speech was her personal rendition of the hidden transcript of a subordinate group, and, as in the case of Aggy, that speech directs our attention back to the offstage culture of the class within which it originated.

An individual who is affronted may develop a personal fantasy of revenge and confrontation, but when the insult is but a variant of affronts suffered systematically by a whole race, class, or strata, then the fantasy can become a collective cultural product. Whatever form it assumes—offstage parody, dreams of violent revenge, millennial visions of a world turned upside down—this collective hidden transcript is essential to any dynamic view of power relations.

Mrs. Poyser's explosion was potentially very costly, and it was her daring—some would have said foolhardiness—that won her such notoriety. The word *explosion* is used deliberately here because that is how Mrs. Poyser experienced it:

> "Thee'st done it now," said Mr. Poyser, a little alarmed and uneasy, but not without some triumphant amusement at his wife's outbreak. "Yis, I know I've done it," said Mrs. Poyser, "but I've had my say out, and I shall be the'easier for 't all my life. There's no pleasure in living, if you're to be corked up for iver, and only dribble your mind out by the sly, like a leaky barrel. I shan't repent saying what I think, if I live to be as old as the Squire."[16]

The hydraulic metaphor George Eliot puts in Mrs. Poyser's mouth is the most common way in which the sense of pressure behind the hidden transcript is expressed. Mrs. Poyser suggests that her habits of prudence and deception can no longer contain the anger she has rehearsed for the last year. That the anger will find a passage out is not in doubt; the choice is rather between a safer but less psychologically satisfying process of "dribbl[ing] your mind out by the sly" and the dangerous but gratifying full blast that Mrs. Poyser has ventured. George Eliot has, in effect, taken one position here on the consequences for consciousness of domination. Her claim is that the necessity of "acting a mask" in the presence of power produces, almost by the strain engendered by its inauthenticity, a countervailing pressure that cannot be contained indefinitely. As an epistemological matter, we have no warrant for elevating the truth status of Mrs. Poyser's outburst over that of her prior deference. Both are arguably part of Mrs. Poyser's self. Notice, however, that as Eliot constructs it, Mrs. Poyser feels she has finally spoken her mind. Inasmuch as she and others in comparable situations feel they have finally spoken truthfully to those in power, the concept truth may have a sociological reality in the thought and practice of people whose actions interest us. It may have a phenomenological force in the real world despite its untenable epistemological status.

An alternative claim, nearly a logical mirror image of the first, is that those obliged by domination to act a mask will eventually find that their faces have grown to fit that mask. The practice of subordination in this case produces, in time, its own legitimacy, rather like Pascal's injunction to those who were without religious faith but who desired it to get down on their knees five times a day to pray, and the acting would eventually engender its own justification in faith. In the analysis that follows I hope to clarify this debate considerably, inasmuch as it bears so heavily on the issues of domination, resistance, ideology, and hegemony that are at the center of my concern.

If the weak have obvious and compelling reasons to seek refuge behind a mask when in the presence of power, the powerful have their own compelling reasons for adopting a mask in the presence of subordinates. Thus, for the powerful as well there is typically a disparity between the public transcript deployed in the open exercise of power and the hidden transcript expressed safely only offstage. The offstage transcript of elites is, like its counterpart among subordinates, derivative: it consists in those gestures and words that inflect, contradict, or confirm what appears in the public transcript.

Nowhere has the "act of power" been more successfully examined than in George Orwell's essay "Shooting an Elephant," from his days as a subinspector of police in the 1920s in colonial Burma. Orwell had been summoned to deal with an elephant in heat that had broken its tether and was ravaging the bazaar. When Orwell, elephant gun in hand, finally locates the elephant, which has indeed killed a man, it is peacefully grazing in the paddy fields, no longer a threat to anyone. The logical thing would be to observe the elephant for a while to ensure that its heat had passed. What frustrates logic for Orwell is that there are now more than two thousand colonial subjects who have followed and are watching him:

> And suddenly I realized that I should have to shoot the elephant after all. The people expected it of me and I had got to do it; I could feel their two thousand wills pressing me forward, irresistibly. And it was at this moment, as I stood there with the rifle in my hands, that I first grasped the hollowness, the futility of the white man's dominion in the East. Here was I, the white man with his gun, standing in front of the unarmed native crowd— seemingly the leading actor of the piece; but in reality I was only an absurd puppet pushed to and fro by the will of those yellow faces behind. I perceived in this moment that when the white man turns tyrant it is his own freedom that he destroys. He becomes a sort of hollow posing dummy, the conventionalized figure of a sahib. For it is the condition of his rule that he shall spend his life in trying to impress the "natives," and so in every crisis he has to do what the "natives" expect of him. He wears a mask and his face grows to fit it. . . . A sahib has got to act like a sahib; he has got to appear resolute, to know his own mind and do definite things. To come all that way, rifle in hand, with two thousand people marching at my heels, and then to trail feebly away, having done nothing—no, that was impossible. The crowd would laugh at me. And my whole life, every white man's life in the East, was one long struggle not to be laughed at.[17]

Orwell's use of the theatrical metaphor is pervasive: he speaks of himself as "leading actor of the piece," of hollow dummys, puppets, masks, appearances, and an audience poised to jeer if he doesn't follow the established script. As he experiences it, Orwell is no more free to be himself, to break convention, than a slave would be in the presence of a tyrannical master. If subordination requires a credible performance of humility and deference, so domination seems to require a credible performance of haughtiness and mastery. There are, however, two differences. If a slave transgresses the script he risks a beating, while Orwell risks only ridicule. Another important distinction is that the necessary posing of the dominant derives not from weaknesses but from the ideas behind their rule, the kinds of claims they make to legitimacy. A divine king must act like a god, a warrior king like a brave general; an elected head of a republic must appear to respect the citizenry and their opinions; a judge must seem to venerate the law. Actions by elites that *publicly* contradict the basis of a claim to power are threatening. The cynicism of the taped Oval Office conversations in the Nixon White House was a devastating blow to the public transcript claim to legality and high-mindedness. Similarly, the poorly concealed existence of special shops and hospitals for the party elites in the socialist bloc profoundly undercut the ruling party's public claim to rule on behalf of the working class.[18]

One might usefully compare forms of domination in terms of the kinds of display and public theater they seem to require. Another, perhaps even more revealing way of addressing the same question would be to ask what activities are most sedulously hidden from public view by different forms of domination. Each form of rule will have not only its characteristic stage setting but also its characteristic dirty linen.[19]

Those forms of domination based on a premise or claim to inherent superiority by ruling elites would seem to depend heavily on lavish display, sumptuary laws, regalia, and public acts of deference or tribute by subordinates. The desire to inculcate habits of obedience and hierarchy, as in military organizations, can produce similar patterns. In extreme cases display and performance dominate, as in the case of the Chinese emperor Long Qing, whose public appearances were so minutely choreographed that he became virtually a living icon deployed in rituals that risked nothing to improvisation. Offstage, in the Forbidden City, he might carouse as he wished with princes and aristocrats.[20] This may be something of a limiting case, but the attempt by dominant elites to sequester an offstage social site where they are no longer on display and can let their hair down is ubiquitous, as is the attempt to ritualize contact with subordinates so that the masks remain firmly in place and the risk that something untoward might happen is minimized. Milovan Djilas's early critique of Yugoslavia's new party elite contrasted a meaningful but secret backstage with the empty ritual of public bodies: "At intimate suppers, on hunts, in conversations between two or three men, matters of state of the most vital importance are decided. Meetings of party forums, conferences of the government and assemblies, serve no purpose but to make declarations and put in an appearance."[21] Strictly speaking, of course, the public ritual Djilas denigrates does indeed serve a purpose inasmuch as the theater of unanimity, loyalty, and resolve is intended to impress an audience. Public ritual of this kind is both real and meaningful; Djilas's complaint is rather that it is also a performance designed to conceal an offstage arena of politics that would contradict it. Dominant groups often have much to conceal, and typically they also have the wherewithal to conceal what they wish. The British colonial officials with whom Orwell served in Moulmein had the inevitable club to repair to in the evenings. There, except for the invisible Burmese staff, they were among their own, as they might have put it, and no longer strutting before the audience of colonial subjects. Activities, gestures, remarks, and dress that were unseemly to the public role of sahib were safe in this retreat.[22] The seclusion available to elites not only affords them a place to relax from the formal requirements of their role but also minimizes the chance that familiarity will breed contempt or, at least, diminish the impression their ritually managed appearances create. Balzac captures the fear of overexposure, as it now might be termed, among the Parisian magistrates of the mid-nineteenth century:

> Ah what an unfortunate man your true magistrate is! You know, they ought to live outside the community, as pontiffs once did. The world should only see them when they emerged from their cells at fixed times, solemn, ancient, venerable, pronouncing judgment like the high priests of antiquity, combining in themselves the judicial and the sacerdotal powers! We should only be visible on the bench. . . . Nowadays we may be seen amusing ourselves or in difficulties like anybody else. . . . We may be seen in drawing rooms, at home, creatures of passion, and instead of being terrible we are grotesque.[23]

Perhaps the danger that unregulated contact with the public may profane the sacred aura of judges helps explain why, even in secular republics, they retain more of the trappings of traditional authority than any other branch of government.

Now that the basic idea of public and hidden transcripts has been introduced, I will venture a few observations by way of orienting the subsequent discussion. For the study of power relations, this perspective alerts us to the fact that virtually all ordinarily observed relations between dominant and subordinate represent the encounter of the *public* transcript of the dominant with the *public* transcript of the subordinate. It is to observe Squire Donnithorne imposing on Mr. and Mrs. Poyser on all those occasions on which, prior to the explosion, she managed to keep up the pretense of being deferential and agreeable. Social science is, in general then, focused resolutely on the official or formal relations between the powerful and weak. This is the case even for much of the study of conflict, as we shall see, when that conflict has become highly institutionalized. I do not mean to imply that the study of this domain of power relations is necessarily false or trivial, only that it hardly exhausts what we might wish to know about power.

Eventually we will want to know how the *hidden* transcripts of various actors are formed, the conditions under which they do or do not find public expression, and what relation they bear to the public transcript.[24] Three characteristics of the hidden transcript, however, merit clarification beforehand. First, the hidden transcript is specific to a given social site and to a particular set of actors. Aggy's oath was almost certainly rehearsed in various forms among the slaves in their quarters or at the clandestine religious services that we know were common. Orwell's peers, like most dominant groups, would risk less from a public indiscretion, but they would have the safety of the Moulmein Club in which to vent their spleen. Each hidden transcript, then, is actually elaborated among a restricted "public" that excludes—that is hidden from—certain specified others. A second and vital aspect of the hidden transcript that has not been sufficiently emphasized is that it does not contain only speech acts but a whole range of practices. Thus, for many peasants, activities such as poaching, pilfering, clandestine tax evasion, and intentionally shabby work for landlords are part and parcel of the hidden transcript. For dominant elites, hidden-transcript practices might include clandestine luxury and privilege, surreptitious use of hired thugs, bribery, and tampering with land titles. These practices, in each case, contravene the public transcript of the party in question and are, if at all possible, kept offstage and unavowed.

Finally, it is clear that the frontier between the public and the hidden transcripts is a zone of constant struggle between dominant and subordinate—not a solid wall. The capacity of dominant groups to prevail—though never totally—in defining and constituting what counts as the public transcript and what as offstage is, as we shall see, no small measure of their power. The unremitting struggle over such boundaries is perhaps the most vital arena for ordinary conflict, for everyday forms of class struggle. Orwell noticed how the Burmese managed to insinuate almost routinely a contempt for the British, while being careful never to venture a more dangerous open defiance:

> Anti-European feeling was very bitter. No one had the guts to raise a riot, but if a European woman went through the bazaars alone somebody would probably spit betel juice over her dress. . . . When a nimble Burman tripped me up on the football field and the referee (another Burman) looked the other way, the crowd yelled with hideous laughter. . . . In the end the sneering yellow faces of the young men that met me everywhere, the insults hooted after me when I was at a safe distance, got badly on my nerves. The young Buddhist priests were the worst of all.[25]

Tactical prudence ensures that subordinate groups rarely blurt out their hidden transcript directly. But, taking advantage of the anonymity of a crowd or of an ambiguous accident, they manage in a thousand artful ways to imply that they are grudging conscripts to the performance.

The analysis of the hidden transcripts of the powerful and of the subordinate offers us, I believe, one path to a social science that uncovers contradictions and possibilities, that looks well beneath the placid surface that the public accommodation to the existing distribution of power, wealth, and status often presents. Behind the "anti-European" acts Orwell noted was undoubtedly a far more elaborate hidden transcript, an entire discourse, linked to Burman culture, religion, and the experience of colonial rule. This discourse was not available—except through spies—to the British. It could be recovered only offstage in the native quarter in Moulmein and only by someone intimately familiar with Burman culture. Nor, of course, did the Burmans know—except through the tales that servants might tell—what lay behind the more or less official behavior of the British toward them. That hidden transcript could be recovered only in the clubs, homes, and small gatherings of the colonists. The analyst in any situation like this has a strategic advantage over even the most sensitive participants precisely because the hidden transcripts of dominant and subordinate are, in most circumstances, *never in direct contact*. Each participant will be familiar with the public transcript and the hidden transcript of his or her circle, but not with the hidden transcript of the other. For this reason, political analysis can be advanced by research that can compare the hidden transcript of subordinate groups with the hidden transcript of the powerful and both hidden transcripts with the public transcript they share. This last facet of the comparison will reveal the effect of domination on political communication.

Just a few years after Orwell's stint in Moulmein a huge anticolonial rebellion took the English by surprise. It was led by a Buddhist monk claiming the throne and promising a utopia that consisted largely of getting rid of the British and taxes. The rebellion was crushed with a good deal of gratuitous brutality and the surviving "conspirators" sent to the gallows. A portion, at least, of the hidden transcript of the Burmans had suddenly, as it were, leapt onto the stage to declare itself openly. Millennial dreams of revenge and visions of just kingship, of Buddhist saviors, of a racial settling of scores of which the British had little inkling were being acted on. In the brutality of the repression that followed one could detect an acting out of the admission that Orwell struggled against and that undoubtedly found open expression in the whites only club that "the greatest joy in the world would be to drive a bayonet into a Buddhist priest's guts." Many, perhaps most, hidden transcripts remain just that: hidden from public view and never "enacted." And we are not able to tell easily under what precise circumstances the hidden transcript will storm the stage. But if we wish to move beyond apparent consent and to grasp potential acts, intentions as yet blocked, and possible futures that a shift in the balance of power or a crisis might bring to view, we have little choice but to explore the realm of the hidden transcript. ■

NOTES

1. *Public* here refers to action that is openly avowed to the other party in the power relationship, and transcript is used almost in its juridical sense (*procès verbal*) of a complete record of what was said. This complete record, however, would also include nonspeech acts such as gestures and expressions.

2. Emile Gauillaumin, *The Life of a Simple Man*, ed. Eugen Weber, rev. trans. Margaret Crosland, 83. See also 38, 62, 64, 102, 140, and 153 for other instances.

3. Ibid., 82.

4. Lunsford Lane, *The Narrative of Lunsford Lane, Formerly of Raleigh, North Carolina* (Boston, 1848), quoted in Gilbert Osofsky, ed., *Puttin' on Ole Massa: The Slave Narratives of Henry Bibb, William Wells, and Solomon Northrup*, 9.

5. *A Diary from Dixie*, quoted in Orlando Patterson, *Slavery and Social Death: A Comparative Study*, 208.

6. Ibid., 338.

7. I bracket, for the moment, the possibility that the offstage retraction or the public rupture may itself be a ruse designed to mislead. It should be clear, however, that there is no satisfactory way to establish definitively some bedrock reality or truth behind any particular set of social acts. I also overlook the possibility that the performer may be able to insinuate an insincerity into the performance itself, thereby undercutting its authenticity for part or all of his audience.

8. This is not to assert that subordinates have nothing more to talk about among themselves than their relationship to the dominant. Rather it is merely to confine the term to that segment of interaction among subordinates that bears on relations with the powerful.

9. *My Story of the War*, quoted in Albert J. Raboteau, *Slave Religion: The "Invisible Institution" of the Antebellum South*, 313.

10. *Adam Bede*, 388–89.

11. Ibid., 393.

12. Ibid., 394.

13. Ibid., 398.

14. Ibid., 388.

15. We are, I think, apt to have the same fantasy when we are bested in argument among equals or insulted by a peer. The difference is simply that asymmetrical power relations do not interfere with the declaration of the hidden transcript in this case.

16. Ibid., 395. For readers unfamiliar with *Adam Bede* who would like to know how things turned out, the squire died providentially some months later, lifting the threat.

17. *Inside the Whale and Other Essays*, 95–96.

18. Similar inequalities are not nearly so symbolically charged in Western capitalist democracies, which publicly are committed to defend property rights and make no claims to be run for the particular benefit of the working class.

19. We all recognize homely versions of this truth. It is, parents sense, unseemly to argue publicly in front of their children, especially over their discipline and conduct. To do so is to undercut the implicit claim that parents know best and are agreed about what is proper. It is also to offer their children a political opportunity to exploit the revealed difference of opinion. Generally, parents prefer to keep the bickering offstage and to present a more or less united front before the children.

20. Ray Huang, *1571: A Year of No Significance.*

21. *The New Class,* 82.

22. I suspect that it is for essentially the same reason that the subordinate staff in virtually any hierarchical organization tend to work in open view while the elite work behind closed doors, often with anterooms containing private secretaries.

23. *A Harlot High and Low [Splendeurs et misères des courtisanes],* trans. Reyner Happenstall, 505. The twentieth-century literary figure who made the masks of domination and subordination the center of much of his work was Jean Genet. See, in particular, his plays *The Blacks* and *The Screens.*

24. I overlook, deliberately for the moment, the fact that there are for any actor several public and hidden transcripts, depending upon the audience being addressed.

25. *Inside the Whale,* 91. A shouted insult seems hardly a hidden transcript. What is crucial here is the "safe distance" that makes the insulter anonymous: the message is public but the messenger is hidden.

■ *QUESTIONS FOR MAKING CONNECTIONS WITHIN THE READING* ■

1. At the opening of his essay, James Scott offers a "crude and global generalization" that he acknowledges needs further qualification: "the greater the disparity in power between dominant and subordinate and the more arbitrarily it is exercised, the more the public transcript of subordinates will take on a stereotyped, ritualistic cast." Create a chart that maps out this relationship, using one of the examples that Scott has provided: the master and the slave, the tenant and the landlord, the colonizer and the colonized. How might the behavior of the parties involved change as the disparity in power grows? How would the behavior change as the arbitrariness of the exercise of power increases?

2. Scott provides an approach to reading and understanding the elaborate performance that occurs whenever the powerful and the disempowered engage with one another. In the staging of this performance, which Scott terms "the public transcript," "[i]t is frequently in the interest of both parties," Scott maintains, "to tacitly conspire in misrepresentation." What is it, exactly, that gets misrepresented by the public transcript? How does one distinguish between acts of misrepresentation that warrant study and those that are simply acts of civility?

3. Toward the end of his essay, Scott asserts that "virtually all ordinarily observed relations between dominant and subordinate represent the encounter of the *public* transcript of the dominant with the *public* transcript of the subordinate." Provide an example from your own experience that illustrates Scott's assertion. What would it take to gain access to the "private transcripts" of those involved in your example? Does your example confirm Scott's assertion that the analyst of such situations "has a strategic advantage over even the most sensitive participants"?

■ *QUESTIONS FOR WRITING* ■

1. One might argue that in a democracy there is no distinction between the public and the hidden transcript: indeed, in the United States, the freedom of the press guarantees that readers are provided with an unending diet of revelations about the private lives of politicians and ordinary people alike. Would you say that freedom of the press and the advent of modern media serve to eliminate the distinction between the public and the private transcripts that Scott has described? In the United States, has the private transcript been made public and thereby emptied of all its power?

2. Scott is interested in promoting the development of a social science that "uncovers contradictions and possibilities, that looks well beneath the placid surface that the public accommodation to the existing distribution of power, wealth, and status often presents." What is to be gained by developing such a social science? Would it help to promote better forms of government? More effective forms of resistance?

■ *QUESTIONS FOR MAKING CONNECTIONS BETWEEN READINGS* ■

1. In "How to Tell a True War Story," Tim O'Brien insists that the story he has to tell is true, even though that story comes from O'Brien's collection *The Things They Carried,* which he explicitly labels a work of fiction. Is O'Brien providing "the public transcript" or "the hidden transcript" of what it means to go to war? If one accepts Scott's terminology, is it possible to speak definitively of "truth" and "fiction," or do all accounts become subject to the charge that their authors are interested, biased, or invested in a certain point of view? In fact, is it even possible "to tell a true war story"?

2. Susan Faludi's "The Naked Citadel" provides an opportunity to explore the explanatory power and the limits of Scott's approach to studying resistance. How does one determine who is dominant and who is subordinate at The Citadel? Which transcripts has Faludi gained access to in her research? Scott argues that, "by assessing the discrepancy *between* the hidden transcript and the public transcript we may begin to judge the impact of domination on public discourse." What does "The Naked Citadel" reveal about "the impact of domination on public discourse"?

www   **For additional suggestions about making connections between readings, visit the Link-O-Mat and More Sample Assignments at <www.newhum.com>.**

ALEXANDER STILLE

HOW WILL THE environmental problems of the twenty-first century be solved? And who will do this work? Will it be scientists? Members of the business community? Religious leaders? In "The Ganges' Next Life," Alexander Stille ['Shtē-la] shows how these questions are being answered by those who are working to clean up the Ganges River, the center of India's spiritual and commercial life. He focuses on the collaboration between Veer Bhadra Mishra, a Hindu religious leader and environmental engineer, and William Oswald, an American scientist specializing in renewable energy sources, to design a sustainable system for purifying the water that flows through the Ganges. In the process, Stille documents just how fluid the relationships between science and religion, environmentalism and capitalism, tradition and modernity can be. Stille invites his readers to consider the essential role that cross-cultural collaboration has to play in making change possible.

Stille, who writes for the *New York Times* and the *New Yorker*, specializes in Italian political culture and has covered subjects as diverse as Primo Levi's suicide, the resurgence of interest in the 1960s media theorist Marshall McLuhan, and recent efforts by sociologists to quantify happiness. He is the author of two books: *Benevolence and Betrayal: Five Italian Jewish Families under Fascism* (1993), a documentary that captures the life of Italy's Jews during the Holocaust, and *Excellent Cadavers: The Mafia and the Death of the First Italian Republic* (1995), a study of two prosecutors who sought to put an end to the Mafia's control of Sicily in the mid-1980s. *Excellent Cadavers*, which has been praised as "totally absorbing and distinctly chilling. . . . An altogether outstanding work of contemporary history," was made into a feature-length film by HBO in 1999.

www To learn more about Alexander Stille and the effort to clean up the Ganges, visit the Link-O-Mat at <www.newhum.com>.

Stille, Alexander. "The Ganges' Next Life." *New Yorker.* January 19, 1998. 58–67.

Quotation from "Barry Unsworth's Favorite Books," <http://www.randomhouse.com/nanatalese/exclusive/unsworthfavs.html>.

The Ganges' Next Life

Shortly after dawn, Veer Bhadra Mishra, a silver-haired Brahman in a traditional Indian dhoti, or loincloth, walks slowly and stiffly down a long, steep stairway from his temple in the city of Varanasi to the banks of the Ganges, as he has done almost every day of his fifty-eight years. All around him, along a seven-kilometre stretch of the river dominated by majestic, crumbling temples, palaces, and ashrams, the pageant of Indian life passes by. Tens of thousands of bathers, at eighty different ghats, or landing areas, plunge into India's holiest body of water. White-bearded ascetics raise their emaciated arms to salute the sun god; housewives in bright-colored saris toss garlands of marigolds to Mother Ganges, the river goddess; adolescent boys in G-strings do pushups, flex their muscles, and wash their bodies; naked children splash in the water; and families carry their dead to the "burning ghats" to cremate them and scatter their ashes on the river.

The tug of these traditions, some of which go back three thousand years, to the founding of Varanasi (also known as Banaras), the holiest city in India, pulls Mishra to the river, despite having suffered a broken thigh, which makes walking painful. But on this particular day, in early March, he remains on the bank, because of a nagging cold and also because of the poor quality of the water: it is filled with raw sewage, human and industrial waste, the charred remains of bodies, and animal carcasses. Normally, Mishra tries to perform five full immersions—five is an auspicious number, he explains. But even when he is feeling well he holds his nose as he puts his head in, and he no longer drinks the river water.

"There is a struggle and turmoil inside my heart," Mishra says. "I want to take a holy dip. I need it to live. The day does not begin for me without the holy dip. But, at the same time, I know what is B.O.D."—biochemical oxygen demand—"and I know what is fecal coliform." He is referring to some of the scientific indices of water pollution.

For Mishra, this struggle of the heart is particularly acute because he has a complex double identity: he is the mahant—the head—of Sankat Mochan Temple, one of the principal temples of Varanasi, and he is also a professor of hydraulic engineering at Banaras Hindu University.

As a devout Hindu, Mishra views the Ganges as a goddess, a river that, because of its divine origin, is pure and purifies all those faithful who immerse themselves in her. Just as Muslims vow to visit Mecca, it is the dream of all good Hindus to visit Varanasi and bathe in the Ganges at least once in their lives. It is said that one drop of Ganges water carried by a breeze that lands on your cheek hundreds of miles away is enough to cleanse a lifetime of sins. All Hindus seek to have their ashes scattered along the Ganges at their deaths, and it is considered particularly lucky to die in Varanasi, because from there your soul will travel straight to Heaven.

But, as a scientist, Mishra cannot forget what he knows about the condition of the river water. Up in the temple complex behind him stands a state-of-the-art laboratory where bacteria cultures are being grown in special incubators in order to measure the level of pathogens at various points along the river. In some places at Varanasi, the fecal-coliform count has been known to reach a hundred and seventy million bacteria per hundred millilitres of water—a terrifying three hundred and forty thousand times the acceptable level of five hundred per hundred millilitres.

Some five hundred million people—one out of every twelve people in the world—now live in the basin of the Ganges and its tributaries. A hundred and fourteen cities dump their raw sewage directly into the river, which starts at Nepal, in the Himalayas, flows fifteen hundred miles through India and Bangladesh, and empties into the Bay of Bengal at Calcutta. Not surprisingly, waterborne illnesses—hepatitis, amebic dysentery, typhoid, and cholera—are common killers, helping to account for the deaths of more than two million Indian children each year.

What is particularly disturbing about these numbers is that they come at the end of a ten-year government cleanup project called the Ganga Action Plan—a project that most people, even in government, concede has failed. Now the government is preparing for the second phase of the Ganga Action Plan, and Mishra is trying to keep the government from repeating its mistakes: he is pushing a new plan to save the river.

The battle to clean the Ganges is about much more than the environmental future of a river. Just as the river is a symbol of India, its cleanup is a test of India's condition fifty years after independence, and its outcome may answer some of the fundamental questions about the country's future. Will India (and other parts of the Third World) master its problems, or will it descend into a nightmarish Malthusian struggle over diminishing natural resources? Will India find creative ways to preserve its rich cultural traditions, or will it become homogenized into the new global economy? Will its ancient rituals, such as bathing in the Ganges, survive beyond the next century?

Varanasi is one of the oldest continuously occupied cities in the world, contemporary with the dynasties of ancient Egypt or Mesopotamia. But while no one sacrifices to the Egyptian sun god Ra or to Baal anymore, some sixty thousand devotees take the holy dip each day in Varanasi, lighting fires along the shores of the Ganges to Lord Shiva, the god who is believed to have caught the river in the tangled locks of his hair as it descended to earth from Heaven.

"Please consider them an endangered species, these people who still have this faith, this living relationship with the river," Mishra says with passion. "If birds can be saved, if plants can be saved, let this species of people be saved by granting them holy water."

Mishra, as the mahant of Sankat Mochan Temple, is himself the living link to one of Varanasi's most cherished legacies. He is spiritual heir to a greatly revered Hindu saint, Tulsi Das, who in the sixteenth century wrote a famous Hindi version of the Ramayana, one of the most important texts of Hinduism, originally written in Sanskrit. Mahantji, as Mishra is almost universally known in Varanasi (Indians add the suffix "ji" to a name to denote affection and respect), lives, with his family, in the house that Tulsi Das built, overlooking the Ganges and above the landing Tulsi Ghat. The house contains an original manuscript of Tulsi Das's Ramayana and a pair of the saint's wooden sandals. Mishra's position as mahant, which has been passed from father to son in his family for many generations, accords him a semidivine status among the disciples of Tulsi Das. As Mishra is speaking about things like biomass and biogas, a steady stream of worshippers stop by to touch his feet—a traditional sign of respect in India.

Mishra wears his status lightly. He is a person of exquisite courtesy and genuine warmth, without a hint of arrogance or self-regard. He has a handsome tan face, dark-brown eyes, an elegant head of white hair with a shock of black in the center, and a gray mustache. If his lower body is slow and awkward, from his broken thigh, his face is highly mobile and expressive, as if to underscore the Hindu belief that the body is but an imperfect vessel for the noble spirit. He smiles easily and laughs a lot, frequently at himself. He jokes about his "throne room"—the name his Western friends have teasingly given a room where he receives guests. It is in fact a modestly decorated room on the ground floor of his house, in which a large wooden platform covered with mattresses provides the mahant a place to sit cross-legged or lean back on a cushion. He dresses almost invariably in nothing but a lightblue dhoti—a single swath of cotton that wraps around his waist and covers his shoulders like a toga—and generally goes barefoot. The one exception is when he lectures at the university: then he puts on a pair of loafers and a brown Western-style suit, in which he looks somewhat ill at ease.

In 1982, after years of speaking out about the deteriorating condition of the river, Mishra founded, with two other engineers from Banaras Hindu University, the Sankat Mochan Foundation, a private secular organization dedicated to cleaning the Ganges. This has taken Mishra far from the traditional, religious role of mahant and brought him into contact with politicians in New Delhi, American State Department officials, and environmentalists and scientists around the world. Overcoming a certain amount of criticism and ridicule among some Hindus in Varanasi, he has travelled to places like Sydney, New York, and San Francisco in order to attend water-resource conferences and explore alternative waste technologies. Like India itself on the eve of the millennium, Mishra is trying to incorporate what is best from the West in order to preserve the Hindu traditions that he loves.

*   *   *

In his attempt to clean the Ganges, the mahant finds himself teamed with a seeming unlikely partner—William Oswald, an emeritus professor of engineering at Berkeley, who is a gray-haired seventy-eight-year-old with elephantlike ears, two hearing aids, an impish smile, and an earthy sense of humor. On being told that the Hindus believed that they would go straight to Heaven if they died in Varanasi, Oswald replied, "They'll get there a lot faster if they go in that water."

Mishra and Oswald were brought together by Friends of the Ganges, a San Francisco–based group of environmentalists who have been working closely with the Sankat Mochan Foundation to help find a solution to Varanasi's water-pollution problems.

Oswald is the pioneer of a kind of "back to the future" approach to modern urban waste, called Advanced Integrated Wastewater Pond Systems, in which sewage is treated in a carefully engineered series of natural algae ponds. Waste decomposes naturally in water through a combination of microbial fermentation and photosynthesis. It works like this: In a pond, bacteria grow on sewage and, in the process, decompose it into its elements—carbon, nitrogen, hydrogen, oxygen, etc. Algae in the pond assimilate these nutrients and, as their green biomass grows, produce oxygen through photosynthesis. Algae are the most efficient producers of oxygen on the planet: they supply more than one and a half times their weight in oxygen, and are the largest single source of atmospheric oxygen in the air we breathe. The oxygen that algae produce sustains the aquatic life of a pond or a river; fish both feed on algae and breathe the oxygen that algae produce; bacteria also use the oxygen to keep the process of decomposition going in a self-sustaining cycle of creation and decay.

Oswald is to algae what Michael Jordan is to basketball. When he and I first met, in Delhi, he excused himself in advance for not remembering my name: "For every new person's name I learn, I forget the name of an alga." Back in the late sixties, at the request of the United States Air Force's space program, Oswald invented something called the Algatron—a system for growing algae in space to provide oxygen for astronauts. Although it has been tried out only on mice in a California laboratory, Oswald proved, in principle, that you could create a self-sustaining ecosystem in a weightless environment. In his view, algae are among the great unacknowledged heroes of the planet. Algae and bacteria have a symbiotic relationship that performs miracles in converting toxic or disease-carrying waste into oxygen, new plant life, and valuable protein for other forms of life to feed on.

Oswald's system is not a utopian environmentalist's fantasy. Before the age of mechanical treatment plants, ponds were one of the primary means of taking care of sewage. They are cheaper than mechanical treatment plants and clean wastewater more thoroughly, but they generally require more land. As a result, most major United States cities have switched to mechanized plants in recent decades, relegating pond systems to smaller cities and towns—some seventy-five hundred of them throughout the United States.

Oswald has devoted his life to devising pond systems that improve on nature's by handling waste in an accelerated fashion while using less space. He has created a system that moves water, by means of gravity and paddle wheels, through a linked sequence of ponds, each with its own special environment, meant to encourage a particular kind of waste treatment. The first group of ponds are dug very deep, in order to create a dark, sunless environment without oxygen, where anaerobic bacteria decompose the heavier solid wastes. The second group are shallow, so that all the water is exposed to sunlight in order to encourage algae to grow through photosynthesis and kill off harmful bacteria. The third ponds are deep, still ponds, in which the algae settle and can be easily "harvested," to be fed to pigs or chickens, or else left in the water for fish farming. In the final phase, the water passes into large, reservoirlike ponds from which it will be reused in irrigation.

This technology appears ideally suited to India, one of whose most abundant resources is sunlight. And it seems fitting that the scientific key to the modern problems of Varanasi, one of India's most ancient cities, could be one of the most ancient and also one of the simplest life-forms: algae.

In 1994, Mishra travelled to Northern California and visited three pond systems built by Oswald. Last summer, Earl Kessler, a member of the State Department's Agency for International Development, or AID, sent a delegation as well. Kessler was sufficiently impressed to commission both Oswald and Mishra's Sankat Mochan Foundation to prepare a feasibility study for a waste-pond system at Varanasi. Last spring, Oswald and his partner, Bailey Green, an acquaintance of mine, were scheduled to fly to India in order to complete the study and try to win Indian government support for the plan, and I decided to accompany them.

When we arrived, Mishra and two of his close colleagues at the foundation presented the American engineers with a surveyor's map they had prepared of the area where the ponds would be constructed, with carefully traced markings for ground elevation and soil composition. Oswald and Green have proposed a system of thirty-two ponds in a dried-up river channel near the island of Dhab, downstream from Varanasi. They spread the map on a table in a guesthouse overlooking a grassy lawn where a colored tent and a marigold-festooned stage were decked out for the foundation's annual festival of *dhrupad*—the most ancient form of Indian classical music—which was to begin later that evening.

As they pored over the map, Oswald worried about possible hitches in the successful completion of the pond project, which, if it should be carried out, would be the largest of his career. "Are you sure that a dike that is seventy-five metres above sea level will be high enough for the monsoon?" he asked. During the last thirty years, Oswald had seen many ambitious pond projects in the Third World evaporate for a host of technical, political, and financial reasons.

But, after fifteen years of work, the mahant was anxious that the project's momentum not be slowed by nettlesome details. "We will show that Dr. Oswald's pond system can work even in India," he said grandly.

"I don't want to be a hero," responded Oswald the pragmatist. "I just want to be right."

The musicians outside began to tune up their instruments, and the conversation about the soil composition of the proposed pond site continued to the drone of sitars. The musicians played until six-thirty in the morning, and as we lay under our mosquito nets later that night ancient ragas ran through our waking and sleeping thoughts.

The following afternoon, we set off by boat down the Ganges to examine the site where the ponds would be constructed. There were about twenty of us on a long, flat, beat-up wooden boat with a put-put motor and a canvas sheet stretched over us for protection against the midday sun. Besides us visitors and the mahant, the passengers were mostly volunteers from the Varanasi area, devotees of the temple who also donated their time to the Clean the Ganges campaign. (The foundation can afford only two full-time staff members. Its laboratory was provided through the efforts of the Swedish chapter of Friends of the Ganges, and one of Mishra's household servants doubles as a laboratory assistant.)

Because Tulsi Ghat is at the far south end of Varanasi, the trip took us in slow motion past the entire city. The ghats rise up dramatically out of the water, at the top of tall stairways, and so serve as a kind of two-way theatre: people on the ghats observe the activity on the river below, while those passing by in boats observe the doings of people up above.

Although Varanasi is the chief center of Hindu learning and culture, almost every religious practice and every region of India are represented along the river. There is a ghat for the Dandi Panth ascetics and a ghat leading to a temple surrounded by erotic Nepalese sculptures. There are pagodalike ghats reminiscent of southern India, and fortresslike ghats, which recall the Mogul conquerors of the north. Some ghats are old and are built of sombre, earth-colored stone; others are made of modern concrete and are painted white, yellow, pink, red, or green.

Along with all the different religious practices, all the different forms of pollution along the Ganges were similarly evident. There were ghats where herds of water buffalo cooled off in the water. At others, washerwomen rinsed out their laundry on the shore while a rainbow of colored saris lay drying on the steps. Hinduism contains many rituals of purification and hygiene, including a prohibition against using soap in the Ganges, which is widely ignored.

After a few minutes, we slowly passed the first of the burning ghats. At all hours of the day and night, the funeral pyres burn on the shore, with family members circling the fire and saying prayers. When the firewood has been consumed, the remains of the dead are consigned to the river to begin their journey from this world to the next, but in some cases the bodies may not have been fully consumed. On the average, about forty thousand traditional funerals are performed on the banks of the Ganges at Varanasi each year. In addition, about three thousand other dead bodies—those of people too poor to afford a funeral—and about nine thousand dead cattle are tossed into the river annually. As part of the government's Ganga Action Plan, close to twenty-nine thousand turtles were released at Varanasi a few years ago, in the hope that they would consume any decomposing body parts. But the turtle farm is now empty, and there are no turtles in the river. Many people suspect that they were poached for food.

The government cleanup, however, did include the building of an electric crematorium at one of the two main burning ghats, in order to cut back on the traditional funerals. The program seems to be working, for the lines in front of the brick crematorium are much longer than the ones in front of the firewood sellers. This, in Mishra's view, is an instance of India's adaptability: "The reasons are economic," he explained. "A traditional funeral today will cost between fifteen hundred and two thousand rupees, and the charge for the electric crematorium is seventy rupees."

The traditional forms of Indian life visible along the shores of the Ganges— the funeral pyres, the water buffalo, the washerwomen—are not the principal source of pollution at Varanasi. Looking closely, even along the bathing ghats you can see large sewage pipes draining directly into the river. The city's trunk sewer, which was built by the British in 1917, is strained beyond capacity. As recently as fifty years ago, the population of Varanasi was just over a quarter million; now it is a million four hundred thousand, and growing.

Upon leaving Varanasi, we reached the point where the Varuna River meets the Ganges, and there the surface of the water was bubbling like soup on a low flame—raw sewage turning into methane gas. Just a mile or so up the Varuna is a huge new pumping station, which is supposed to transport Varanasi's sewage to a large treatment plant a few miles downstream. Able to handle but a fraction of the city's two hundred million litres of sewage per day, the plant pumps the sewage of Varanasi up several hundred yards, only to dump the bulk of it into the Varuna, where it then travels back to the Ganges.

A few miles farther downstream, there was a sudden explosion of algae blooms, in such unnatural quantities that for several hundred yards the Ganges took on the unhealthy appearance of a swamp. It is here that the Indian government has placed its treatment plant, but the plant only performs what in the waste business is called "primary treatment"—the equivalent of going through just the first of Oswald's four ponds. Because the plant's "cleaned" effluent is still full of sewage and harmful bacteria, it, together with the hot Indian sun, stimulates the growth of far more algae than the natural resources of the river can absorb. As they decompose they consume, rather than create, oxygen, putting a strain on the marine life of the river. This condition shows up when the oxygen level of the water is tested in a laboratory: biological oxygen demand, or B.O.D., is one of the principal measures of water pollution. Where pollution places a high demand on oxygen, less is available for fish and other organisms.

The central government, in New Delhi, has recently spent about a hundred and fifty million dollars building Western-style high-technology wastewater plants along the Ganges, like the one we just passed, which are particularly ill-suited to Indian conditions. The treatment facilities run on electricity, and when the power goes out—as happens several times a day in many Indian cities—they stop operating. Similarly, the plants become overwhelmed during the monsoon season and simply shut down. Even when they are working, the facilities are so expensive and so difficult to operate that many of the cities say they cannot afford to maintain them.

In Varanasi, sewage is backing up into people's toilets or forming fetid puddles in their yards and in the streets. Local residents became so enraged about a year ago that they forced a city water engineer to stand for several hours in a pool of sewage in order to better acquaint him with the problem.

After decades of supporting this type of expensive, high-technology project, the United States State Department is now a proponent of "sustainable technology"—projects like Oswald's ponds, which cost less, use little electricity, and can be maintained with relatively little training by local people. (The pond system designed for Varanasi is estimated to cost between ten and sixteen million dollars, as opposed to twenty-five million for the city's mechanized treatment plant, which handles only a quarter to a third as much waste.)

In 1985, the government in New Delhi also adopted Western waste-treatment technology without considering the radically different ways that people use the rivers in India. It is still common in Europe for sewage-treatment plants to discharge partly cleaned effluent into rivers, but the inhabitants of London and Paris would not dream of bathing in or drinking out of the Thames or the Seine. "They have made such blunders," the mahant said. "It is like a theme park of failed technology."

Although our trip downriver to the island of Dhab was only about ten miles long, it took us nearly five hours, because the boat kept running aground. With each successive stop, more members of our party were out in the river pushing the boat and fewer of us were in it. The small Western contingent was calculating the probability of catching some dread tropical disease if it was forced to take an unanticipated holy dip to reach shore.

The Ganges is generally a mile wide throughout its course, but it becomes shallow in the dry months leading up to the summer monsoon. The problem has grown worse in recent years as more and more river water has been diverted for irrigation. Throughout our journey, we saw large pipes sucking water out of the Ganges toward distant fields. While India has twenty percent of the world's people, it has only four percent of the world's fresh water. With its population approaching a billion, the country is scheduled to overtake China as the world's most populous nation, and its future growth could mean mass starvation. Some three hundred million Indians are already classified as "Food Insecure"—a bad monsoon away from starvation.

Under these circumstances, wars over water—a prospect that haunts the twenty-first century—have already become a reality in India. India and Bangladesh have come close to breaking off diplomatic relations over the use of Ganges water. And in 1994 the Indian state of Haryana simply diverted a sizable portion of New Delhi's water supply, claiming it needed the water for irrigation. The struggle for water can only get worse as India's growing urban population demands Western standards of plumbing. The seventeen five-star hotels of New Delhi consume eight hundred thousand litres of water daily—enough to fulfill the requirements of a million three hundred thousand slum dwellers, who have no plumbing whatever. And as the number of flush toilets increases so will the amount of sewage.

As I was contemplating the prospect of ecological Armageddon during our on-again, off-again voyage in the shallow waters of the Ganges, we heard the distant sound of a brass band. A large crowd was massed on the banks of the island of Dhab, and, even though it was nearly sunset and they had been waiting all afternoon, they greeted the arrival of the Sankat Mochan Foundation and its Western guests with triumphal music and wild jubilation.

Dhab is one of the pockets of rural India that have been largely left out of the past fifty years of development: it has no electricity and no year-round bridge to the mainland. About ten miles long, Dhab, with a population of forty thousand, has a curious geographical configuration: it is an island during the rainy season and a tenuous part of the mainland the rest of the year. As the course of the Ganges gradually shifted over centuries toward the southeast, it exposed a former channel to the north of the island, which can be crossed during the drier months of the year but still floods during the summer. This wide former river channel is sandy and infertile, and has no proper road. It is here that the Sankat Mochan Foundation would like to put its system of wastewater ponds. The plan also involves building three main roads across the dikes of the ponds to connect Dhab to the mainland—roads that cable could be laid in, providing the electric spark that would connect the people of Dhab to the rest of the world.

Amid cries of "Hail to the gods!" we climbed up the banks of a shore thick with eagerly waiting crowds, who were waving painted banners and were ready to hand us armfuls of carefully stitched flower wreaths. So we proceeded slowly, in cars sent ahead by the foundation, stopping at every village cluster for a new celebration. Again and again, there were bands and painted banners, and entire canopies of marigolds. At each stop, mothers sent their children forward to touch our feet, lay on wreaths, and say prayers.

It was dark before we reached our final stop and the main ceremony, in which we were invited to eat a sticky orange sweet and drink some lemon tea. The mahant and the elected chiefs of the villages read a declaration. The people of Dhab stated their support for the Oswald pond project. The declaration ended with the fervent hope that this good deed would bring them *mukti* and *bhukti*—liberation in the next life and happiness in this one.

The wild sense of expectation and hope on the island—the sense that the pond project would instantly transform people's lives for the better—was both moving and sobering. While there is a legitimate worry about the levelling effect of every remote outpost's plugging into the world grid, Dhab's desire to be part of the wider world is palpable and overpowering. On a clear night, villagers on certain parts of the island can see the lights of a distant railroad yard. They stand and watch this bright symbol of the world they yearn to be a part of—a world of lights, power tools, modern appliances, and, of course, television.

"Our moral responsibility is now very great," the mahant said as we set off for Varanasi amid final cheers.

The next ten days back at Tulsi Ghat were filled with activity on various fronts. The foundation members were trying to set up a series of high-level seminars in which to present the American engineers and their plan to local officials, including the mayor of Varanasi; to technocrats at the Water Commission in Lucknow, the capital of the state of Uttar Pradesh, the region in which Varanasi lies; and to national ministers, politicians, and environmental activists at a major conference in New Delhi. Oswald and Green were working day and night with their pencils and calculators, as they drew up a new set of site-specific engineering plans and came up with precise figures on the money and the land that would be needed to build the pond system. Staff members and volunteers of the foundation were trying to track down things like the cost of moving a ton of earth in Varanasi.

Also during those ten days a stream of special visitors passed through the mahant's "throne room": engineers, village chiefs, politicians, local bureaucrats, university professors—anyone thought to have access to some important decision-making body. In between meetings, the mahant was on his cordless phone, lining up support and making sure that people who had promised to attend a particular meeting would actually show up.

The day after we returned from the island, Mishra received a phone call from a member of the Indian parliament representing Varanasi, who was eager to hear about the trip. The people of Dhab had evidently become so disappointed with the traditional politicians that they would no longer receive them. It seemed that the mahant had inadvertently uncovered a small political gold mine—a unified group of approximately twenty-five thousand highly motivated voters. As a result, the mahant found himself in the role of power broker—a role in which he felt some discomfort. "We are not political people, and it is still not clear to me what we should do with this consensus," he explained to me, as we sat in the throne room overlooking the Ganges.

And yet perhaps the only way to realize the pond project is through judiciously applied political pressure. "We have to have a more effective way to influence the politicians and harness the support we have built," Mishra said. So far, the political work appears to be paying off. The foundation has succeeded in winning the support of both the central government in New Delhi and the municipal government of Varanasi. The final obstacle to building the ponds remains the state government of Uttar Pradesh.

In the midst of all this engineering, organizing, and politicking, life at Tulsi Ghat continued as if it were a medieval village within the city. Devotees trooped through at all hours to worship at one of several pagodalike shrines in the courtyard. Sanskrit students passed through on their way to a school that the temple runs. Behind Mishra's house is an arena with a round corrugated-tin roof, in which each morning young men practiced a traditional form of Hindu wrestling. Sacred cows also wandered through, while goats walked into the shrines to eat the flowers that worshippers had left for the gods.

While this ritual-filled life moved at the stately pace of the Ganges, the activity of the Sankat Mochan Foundation marched to the high-pitched squeal of the fax machine. Mishra himself shuttled between these two worlds, finding time, despite long meetings and conferences, to keep up his religious duties, from his holy dip at dawn to the closing ceremonies at the temple, which sometimes did not end until midnight. Somewhere in between, he and I managed to have a series of conversations about his own double role as holy man and environmental activist, and about his own curious blend of science and Hinduism. "Even in my wildest dreams, I would not have thought that something like this would happen in my life," the mahant said, with a burst of laughter. Nothing in Mishra's early life prepared him for a life of science and political activism. "My father and my grandfather had the traditional education, which means Sanskrit and wrestling and music," he said. "There was no reason to deviate." In 1952, Mishra's father died, and Mishra, only fourteen, had the role of mahant thrust upon him. His destiny seemed even more fixed. "From that time onward, there would be a distance between me and the other people," he said, rather ruefully. "Because of traditional respect, even old people would come and touch my feet to pay respect, so there was no intimate interaction. My life was very protected."

When Mishra reached the age of seventeen, however, he made a radical and unprecedented move: he enrolled at Banaras Hindu University: "I don't know why this happened," he said, his voice rising with genuine perplexity. "In my family, I am the first person to go to the university." When he got there, his path became even more unusual: he started taking science courses. "Why I studied physics, chemistry, and mathematics, I don't know. Why I became a civil engineer with a specialty in hydraulics, I don't know. I can now see this as a scheme of the god."

Although there are no other known cases of someone's combining the vocation of mahant and that of civil engineer, it seems typical of India's uncanny ability to preserve its culture while surviving countless foreign occupations and absorbing new influences, from the Persians and the Islamic Mogul conquerors to the departure of the British, in 1947. The Indian writer Gita Mehta, in her latest book "Snakes and Ladders," tells a story that sums up this quality of Indian culture very well:

> There were two men who were considered the holiest in India, one called the Diamond-Hard Ascetic and the other called the Field of Experience. The Diamond-Hard Ascetic challenged his rival to a duel to prove that he was the holiest of all. I have become so hard through countless austerities, he said, that you can strike me with a sword of steel. And indeed the sword bounced off him. When he took the sword to the Field of Experience, it simply went through him, at which point the Ascetic conceded that the other man was holier.

The Field of Experience is India: seeming to offer no resistance, it is nevertheless impregnable. Other traditional societies—like China, Burma, and nations governed under strict Islamic law—preserve themselves by steeling themselves against the outside world, but they may become much more vulnerable as they begin to open up. India is a wide-open society, through which numerous armies have marched, and yet it remains remarkably itself.

India's economy, which has been frequently written off, came to life as a result of a policy of liberalization started in 1991. Growing at the rate of six percent a year ever since, India has been enjoying a boom similar to China's, but it has done so while remaining the world's largest democracy. Though its problems, in their scale, are almost unimaginable, so are its assets. It has more poor people than any other country in the world, but it also has a huge well-educated middle class. More than a hundred million Indians speak English, the lingua franca of the computer world, which is more than the number of speakers of English in Great Britain, Australia, and New Zealand combined. It is not an accident that software developers have turned to India for highly skilled software engineers. Half a world away, computer companies in Silicon Valley send their work problems to technicians in Bangalore, and those technicians work on them all day while the people in California sleep. Bill Gates arrived in Delhi while I was there, and his arrival was accorded the pomp of Queen Victoria's Diamond Jubilee during the days of Raj.

"These things—satellite television, this Internet surfing—are with us whether we like it or not," Mishra says. "They are means. They can be used in a beautiful way. It is as if you were riding a lion—you should be strong enough to tame the lion, or it will eat you." In keeping with that spirit, the Sankat Mochan Foundation is believed to be the first group in Varanasi to sign up for an E-mail and Internet connection.

This extremely open attitude toward the outside, however, has—so far, at least—in no way lessened the country's intense religiosity. To a remarkable degree, Indians have adapted new technology to their own traditional purposes. When Indian television broadcast a movie version of the Ramayana, many Indian families moved their sets up onto their household altars and worshipped before them. Some observers might be scandalized by this, but these people were not worshipping the television; they were worshipping their gods. In Varanasi, on the night celebrating the wedding anniversary of the gods Shiva and Parvati, I saw numerous shrines to Shiva elaborately decorated with flashing electric lights, pulsing to the beat of Indi-pop disco music. To Western eyes, these shrines, built around an ancient phallic symbol and decked out like entrances to Las Vegas night clubs, seemed sacrilegious and surreal, but ordinary Indians were clustered around them in devout worship, just as they would have been a generation or a millennium ago.

"I think in India this lion will be tamed!" Mishra said, with a delighted laugh, when I mentioned the disco shrine.

The mahant is also convinced that science and religion have to mesh if the Ganges is to be saved. The Western approach, based on fear of a possible ecological disaster, will not work, he said. "If you go to people who have a living relationship with Ganga and you say, 'Ganga is polluted, the water is dirty,' they will say, 'Stop saying that. Ganga is not polluted. You are abusing the river.' But if you say 'Ganga is our mother. Come and see what is being thrown on the body of your mother—sewage and filth. Should we tolerate sewage being smeared on the body of our mother?' you will get a very different reaction, and you can harness that energy."

One attraction of the Oswald pond system is that it seems to combine modern science with traditional Hindu ideas, relying mainly on the self-cleansing properties of nature. Indeed, there is a curious parallel between Oswald's descriptions of the self-sustaining ecology of a pond system and certain traditional Hindu beliefs about the fundamental nature of the universe. "All living organisms fit into one of three categories," Oswald explained to me. "Either they are producers, like algae and other plants that create oxygen, or they are consumers, like cows, which eat plants, or human beings, who eat plants and cows, or they are decomposers, like fungi, which dispose of things when they're dead." Hinduism, in its mythopoetic description of the universe, may have intuited something similar. Mishra told me, "There are three gods: Brahma, the creator, Vishnu, the sustainer, and Shiva, the god who provides us happiness in this world, which is decaying every day."

When I pointed out the analogy to Mishra, he seemed fascinated. "What did Professor Oswald say when you mentioned this?" he asked. I told him that Oswald had replied, with humor, "I'll leave that to your literary imagination. If I go back to California talking about Lord Shiva, they'll put me in a straitjacket."

Mishra, however, sees no necessary contradiction between the mythological and the scientific. Indeed, the practice of harnessing the metaphors of Hindu mythology to create a new environmental ethos is common in India. Even secular magazines, like *India Today,* invoke Lord Krishna's love of the forest in writing about the need for protection against the denuding of the Indian landscape. "With the Clean the Ganges campaign," Mishra says, "a meaning has been given to my religious background and to my scientific background. If both these backgrounds were not there, probably I would not have done this." He concludes by saying, "Life is like a stream. One bank is the Vedas"—the earliest Hindu Sanskrit texts—"and the other bank is the contemporary world, which includes science and technology. If both banks are not firm, the water will scatter. If both banks are firm, the river will run its course." ∎

■ QUESTIONS FOR MAKING CONNECTIONS WITHIN THE READING ■

1. Why does Mishra value the Ganges? Why does Oswald? Why does Stille?

2. Describing governmental efforts to clean up the Ganges, Mishra says, "They have made such blunders. It is like a theme park of failed technology." Chart out all the efforts Stille describes that have been made to clean up the Ganges. Why does Mishra see these as examples of "failed technology" rather than, say, a "failed politics" or even a "failed world view?"

3. At one point while he is moving down the Ganges River, Stille finds himself "contemplating the prospect of ecological Armageddon." What is "ecological Armageddon" exactly? Why might the failure to clean up the Ganges matter to anyone who doesn't live on its banks?

■ QUESTIONS FOR WRITING ■

1. Stille is intrigued by Mishra's "complex double identity" and spends much of the essay trying to make sense of how Mishra can be both a devout Hindu and a scientist at the same time. Stille seems surprised that

Mishra can maintain such an identity. What is a "complex double identity," exactly? Why is Mishra able to maintain his? Does everyone have one? Or only a few people? What other types of identity are there?

2. In his discussion of efforts to clean up the Ganges, Stille declares that "wars over water—a prospect that haunts the twenty-first century—have already become a reality in India." Is it possible that there could be struggles—if not wars—over water in the United States this century? To respond to this question, you might begin by finding out where the water you drink at your school and at your home comes from. Where does this water go? How is it cleaned?

■ *QUESTIONS FOR MAKING CONNECTIONS BETWEEN READINGS* ■

1. In Michael Pollan's essay, "Playing God in the Garden," we learn about the efforts multinational agricultural corporations are making to genetically modify the food chain, a project that they justify, in part, in the name of better feeding the world's inhabitants. In "The Ganges' Next Life," we learn how religious practice, the population explosion, and governmental incompetence have combined to contaminate the Ganges River. Should science be working to provide the means for the human population to continue to increase? Is feeding the world objectively good? Does it matter if this project is motivated by reason, spirituality, or hopes for financial gain?

2. One could argue that William Oswald has developed a new and unique approach to cleaning up water, one that rejects centralized, high-tech installations in favor of solutions that "cost less, use little electricity, and can be maintained with relatively little training by the local people." Can we say the same, however, about what Mishra has done—that his approach is also "new and unique"? Some people might argue that the changes Mishra has made are merely a matter of style—dressing up Oswald's approach in the clothing of traditional Indian religion. But how might Virginia Postrel reply to this accusation? In what ways might changes in the "style" of technology play a key role in cleaning up the Ganges?

www **For additional suggestions about making connections between readings, visit the Link-O-Mat and More Sample Assignments at <www.newhum.com>.**

GREGORY STOCK

GREGORY STOCK, the Director of the Program on Medicine, Technology and Society at the University of California, Los Angeles School of Medicine, is a scientist, educator, and entrepreneur. Stock is a vocal and enthusiastic supporter of using genetic technology to alter human DNA to select for desired traits. Interestingly, Stock does not believe that limits should be placed on the characteristics we should be allowed to select for; he advocates the manipulation of genetic material to gain "enhanced" results ranging from better health to increased strength, intelligence, and attractiveness. Stock argues that genetic choice technology is not simply a possibility but an inevitability, and for that reason, he believes that we should begin to think seriously about how to deal with the swift and dramatic changes that will come to human reproduction in the immediate future. In "The Enhanced and the Unenhanced," he writes: "The enormous collective project of conscious human evolution has begun."

Stock's vision is not merely a practical one; implicit in his argument is a philosophy that reinterprets the concepts of nature, life, and humanity. In fact, Stock does not view "human-directed" technology and nature as separate spheres. Rather, he argues that humans are a part of the natural world, as are the technologies we create. Furthermore, Stock feels that the development of germinal choice technology is "the ultimate expression and realization of our humanity" rather than a threat to what is "human within us." While Stock supports the results of these technologies, he acknowledges that there is still considerable thinking to be done about how the changes to human reproduction will unfold, and he urges us to take part in the conversation as a society. But he shifts the parameters of the conversation away from the hypothetical and theoretical and into the realm of the practicable. As he observes, "My view is that we don't have

Stock, Gregory. "The Enhanced and the Unenhanced." *Redesigning Humans: Our Inevitable Genetic Future.* Boston: Houghton Mifflin, 2002. 176–201.

Biographical information drawn from <http://www.greatertalent.com/bios/stock.shtml> and <http://www.kurzweilai.net/bios/frame.html?main=/bios/bio0189.html>. Closing quotation drawn from the Salon.com interview with Gregory Stock, <http://research.arc2.ucla.edu/pmts/salon.htm>.

the wisdom to understand these technologies yet. . . . You wait to see how people actually use them. You keep an eye on them."

www To learn more about Gregory Stock and the germinal choice technology, please visit the Link-O-Mat at <www.newhum.com>.

■ ■

The Enhanced and the Unenhanced

Gradually, the truth dawned on me: that Man had not remained one species, but had differentiated into two distinct animals: that my graceful children of the Upperworld were not the sole descendants of our generation, but that this bleached, obscene, nocturnal Thing, which had flashed before me, was also heir to all the ages.

—*H. G. Wells,* The Time Machine, *1895*

As we move into an era of advanced germinal choice, children conceived with these technologies will necessarily intermingle with those with more haphazard beginnings. But how they will relate to one another in the long run is no more clear than whether a gulf will ultimately widen between them, partitioning humanity into the enhanced and the unenhanced.

The answers depend on which enhancements become feasible, their cost, who has access to them, who adopts them, and the nature of competing enhancements for adults. All this is as yet uncertain, but we can begin to discern some of the critical choices we will face. At so early a point in the development of GCT (germinal choice technology), identifying the policies that will serve us best is difficult, but spotting some that would serve us poorly is easy.

I have argued that germinal choice technology will offer us significant benefits and we will use the technology to acquire them. Moreover, the first wave of technologies offering substantive new human reproductive choices may be only a decade away. In-depth genetic testing, sophisticated preimplantation genetic diagnosis, egg banking, improved *in vitro* fertilization, and cloning are poised to transform our reproductive choices, while progress in genomics and with highly targeted pharmaceuticals will work in parallel by altering our perceptions of our genetic potentials, vulnerabilities, and handicaps. A decade or so beyond this first wave, a few rudimentary germline modifications may appear in special situations. And another decade beyond, more sophisticated and powerful germline manipulations may begin supplementing sophisticated genetic screenings and adult interventions. This timeline is little more than a guess, but whether substantive GCT enhancement arrives in ten years or fifty, the social and ethical challenges it brings will be similar.

A closer look at the possibility of overlapping effects of embryo screening procedures and early germline engineering suggests that preimplantation genetic diagnosis will likely be potent enough to provide significant human enhancement in addition to disease screening. Consider what would happen if parents wishing to enrich for a trait that is substantively shaped by genetics were to create a hundred healthy embryos, test them . . . and implant the one most predisposed toward that trait.

If such embryos could be selected, for example, for the gene variants responsible for a large portion of the genetic contribution to high IQ[1], the average score of children selected in this way might be nearly 120[2], well above the average score of 100 found in the general population and higher than nearly 9 out of 10 people. Moreover, this shift would take place in a single generation and use a proven medical procedure.

Such sophisticated embryo selection would be just as much a human enhancement as germline engineering. Indeed, no one would later be able to tell whether the lab had selected an embryo or modified one to obtain a particular genome. Here is another case where, if we continue to focus on the theological implications of laboratory procedures rather than on the results they bring, we will greatly weaken our attempt to deal with the approaching challenges.

To imagine that progress in germinal choice technology is irrelevant to the health of adults not planning high-tech parenthood is tempting, since the fateful meeting of sperm and egg that brought us into being is now beyond reach. Our lives, however, may be linked more directly to the arrival of advanced germinal choice than we might think. Adult enhancement, to the extent that it is feasible, rests on the same scientific foundations as embryo selection and will probably become available around the same time. The importance of nuclear transfer techniques to both reproductive cloning and regenerative medicine is no coincidence; such intersections will occur again and again.

Keeping in mind that genetic enhancement may be only a first step in humanity's coming journey of self-transformation adds valuable perspective to discussions of GCT. Fusion of human and machine in this century may be unlikely, but eventually the two may begin to join in important ways. If they do, the philosophical questions provoked by the coexistence of enhanced and unenhanced humans will arise once again. The future debate would not be about the displacement within our biological selves of the natural by the made, however, but about the displacement of the biological by the machine.

This could make today's battles over mere biological enhancement seem quaint, because whatever these future humans may have become, they would have to grapple not merely with enhancement but with moving beyond biology itself.

The Enhanced

When bioethicists use the term "enhancement," they usually must confront the problem of defining normal human functioning, because they wish to differentiate between therapy and actual enhancement.[3] The committee of the American Association for the Advancement of Science that considered germline policy in year 2000, for example, concluded that although "the use of IGM [inherited genetic modifications] to prevent and treat clear-cut diseases in future generations is ethically justifiable . . . IGM should be used only for cases which are clearly therapeutic." But such distinctions become arbitrary for such goals as retarding aging, which would be both an enhancement of our vitality and a therapy for age-related decline—in effect, a *therapeutic enhancement.*

I see nothing wrong with enhancement per se, so I use the term to mean any augmentation of attributes or overall functioning, whether or not it moves a person beyond our sense of normal human functioning. Abstract judgments about the value of particular characteristics and whether they relate to disease will tell us no more about how people will use germinal choice technology than they've told us about the use of cosmetic surgery or drugs. To see the future of GCT, we need to be more pragmatic and acknowledge that people want to be healthier, smarter, stronger, faster, more attractive. Enhancements are those modifications that people view as largely beneficial and that serve their goals. Virtually by definition, people seek such modifications.

A useful way of analyzing potential embryo enhancements is to categorize them by two measures: the degree to which the altered quality is health-related, and the magnitude of the embodied changes. Targeted traits will range from those that are clearly health-related—risks for heart disease, diabetes, or severe depression—to those that touch health less directly, such as obesity, and those that are largely cosmetic and idiosyncratic—hair color, musical talent, height, curiosity. We all would want our children to be at low risk for leukemia, but we might disagree about how tall or outgoing we'd like them to be.

We may best gauge the extent of a modification by comparing it to the typical range of human functioning in that realm. At one extreme are restorations of lost capacities—hearing for the deaf or improved immune response for those with compromised immune systems. In the middle are improvements that make people a little smarter, stronger, or taller, and that lift the underperformers to average level, and the average up to elite perfor-mance. At the other extreme are enhancements that carry a person beyond the normal human range, exceeding even today's elite performers—super-human endurance, intellect, strength, or vitality.

Enhancements with different effects will present us with very different social, moral, and political questions. Many people, for example, have no problem with enhancements that are health related and that improve sub-normal attributes—we generally call them therapies. Enhancements of idio-syncratic traits are more troubling because they can seem subjective and frivolous, though we know that those who seek cosmetic surgery often view it as critical to their mental health. But enhancements that would take us to elite or superhuman levels give most people cause for concern.

What is essential to realize about such interventions is that as the degree of enhancement rises, so will the technical difficulties involved. I cannot overemphasize this, because it is central to the future trajectory of human enhancement technology. Less extreme improvements will be much easier to accomplish and will even be available through embryo screening proce-dures, which do not manipulate genes.[4] So initially GCT will offer less to those seeking superhuman performance than to those trying to avoid ge-netic impairments or improve some area of low or average performance. Widespread use of GCT would almost certainly raise average performance levels and improve health in coming generations, as well as narrow the spread between those with higher and lower potentials. This leveling does not arise from any imposed restriction on the technology. It flows directly from the step-by-step nature of technological advance, the greater complex-ity of more extreme enhancements, and people's tendency not to subject their children to unnecessary risks. Moreover, if adult enhancements be-come broadly available, they will lead to a similar flattening of the distribu-tion of individual endowments.

Ridley Scott's 1982 film *Blade Runner,* like most science fiction, portrays genetic engineering as creating superhuman powers. The film's "replicants" are superior to mere mortals in most ways, but the tradeoff for their powers is extreme: after four years, they collapse and die. Roy, a replicant who re-turns to Earth looking for a way to escape his fate, crushes to death his cre-ator, Tyrell, who tells him that it cannot be: "The light that burns twice as bright burns half as long. And you have burned so very very brightly, Roy. . . . Revel in your time."

Such imagery disregards the immensity of the challenge of designing superhuman performance. Dog breeding illustrates the problem. Over thou-sands of years, emphasis on any one characteristic has brought tradeoffs with others. By amplifying specific wolf traits, we have bred specialist ca-nines, not created superwolves. The saluki runs faster than any wolf. The bloodhound follows a scent better. The springer spaniel flushes game better. The toy poodle certainly is no superwolf. In their 1965 book *Genetics and the*

Social Behavior of the Dog, John Paul Scott and John Fuller articulated it this way: "It is inconceivable that any particular domestic breed could compete with wolves under natural conditions. . . . A wolf is a rugged and powerful animal adapted to life under a variety of adverse conditions. Consequently, no one of his behavioral capacities can be developed to a high degree. . . . The idea that natural selection will produce a super-man or super-animal of any sort is an unobtainable myth."[5]

We have seen too much progress in the intervening decades to be so sure that genetic engineering cannot create superior humans, but we are far from that goal. If the task were easy, natural evolution would have done it already. No such difficulty will keep us from improving average or below-average performance. All we have to do is copy nature. To give an embryo the genetics to achieve an adult height of eight feet without grave health problems would be an immense challenge; to achieve a height of six feet would not.

As GCT becomes increasingly potent, we will face tough personal decisions about what is best for our children and what risks and tradeoffs we will accept for them. There will be no simple answers. Our personalities and values will shape our attitudes. We will probably agree that certain types of manipulation are wrong, just as we agree that certain parental behaviors constitute abuse, and we will agree that certain enhancements exist that any responsible parent would make, just as we generally agree that kids should enhance their immunity by getting vaccinations. But there will also be passionate disagreements, and these cases will be very difficult to regulate.

Let's return to the example of the deaf parents who wish to have a deaf child. Germinal choice technology will make it possible, and as hard as it may be for someone with normal hearing to accept, preventing these parents from doing so would be dangerously close to coercive eugenics that targets the disabled. As long as deaf parents rely on embryo selection, stopping them from selecting an embryo destined to develop into a deaf child is tantamount to making them destroy that embryo.

The coming choices will force us to confront our attitudes about what constitutes a meaningful life, our responsibilities to others, our prejudices, and what we mean when we say that all potential lives are equal and deserve protection. In essence, we will soon have to face, in concrete human terms, the implications of our philosophies about human diversity.

Humans and Posthumans: Our Evolutionary Future

Humanity's manipulation of canine evolution has produced a wide range of breeds and served as an unwitting pilot project for our coming manipulation of our own evolution.[6] In the early phases of human self-modification, the social constraints will be entirely different from those of canines, and the methods much more sophisticated, but scientists no doubt will encounter some of the same biological limits and possibilities.

Two critical questions that come up are whether this process will fragment humanity into independent breeds—future human Saint Bernard and dachshund analogs—and if so, whether they will persist and evolve into separate *posthuman* species.

First let's look at the idea of speciation. Despite the dramatically different shapes, sizes, and dispositions of dogs, *Canis familiaris* is still a single species.[7] Reproductive isolation is central to speciation. Different species cannot interbreed under normal conditions. Such isolation is unlikely to occur in future human subpopulations. Not only will our offspring remain in close physical proximity, unless and until humans migrate out into the vast seas of space, but genomics and advanced reproductive technologies are breaching the barriers to genetic exchange even among different species. If scientists in Oregon can already give a jellyfish gene to a primate, surely we will continue to be able to exchange genes with one another.

In addition, species are biological forms that persist, averaging some four million years before extinction, according to the fossil record. If we succeed in progressively modifying our biology by altering our genes and supplementing our chromosomes, however, changes will be ongoing and new variants will emerge within a span of generations or centuries. Such posthumans could hardly be called "species."

Although even the concept of species may cease to be meaningful as reproduction shifts to the laboratory, the issue of whether the human community will eventually fragment into persistent independent groups remains. The only constant in a future of rapid biological manipulation would be evolutionary change itself. What could unite us in this future would be our common participation in this fluid, self-directed process rather than any transitory similarities in form. Seen in this light, strange as future humans may become if germline manipulation achieves its promise, they will still remain *human*.

In the past, the reproductive isolation needed to generate even the modest biological differences among human groups has required geographical or cultural separation. Both, however, are greatly diminishing because of increased individual mobility, modern communications, and softening cultural rigidities—trends likely to deepen despite strong opposition. Traditional Darwinian evolution now produces almost no change in humans and has little prospect of doing so in the foreseeable future. The human population is too large and entangled, and selective pressures are too localized and transitory.

In the future, however, the rapid technology-driven process of genetic design may achieve meaningful group-specific changes without reproductive isolation. With genetic refinements accumulating in the laboratory instead of in biological lineages, groups of individuals bound only by a common commitment to some specific enhancement could serve as a virtual test bed for refining genetic alterations. The spread of gene modules would not be by reproductive success but by reputation, word of mouth, even advertising. In essence, mimetic rather than biological mechanisms will drive the penetration of genes in the human population.[8]

The underlying source of this profound shift in the evolutionary process is the external storage and manipulation of human genes. As the genetic constructs we provide our children are increasingly explored, maintained, and refined in laboratories, working their way into our hearts and our children's bodies by public relations and persuasion rather than sex, the cultural processes hitherto shaped by our biology will turn the tables and remold our biology.

The consequences of a similar externalization some five thousand years ago give a hint of the tremendous implications of the coming genetic breakthroughs. The development of writing allowed knowledge—which hitherto had been stored only biologically and passed imperfectly from one fragile brain to another—to be captured physically and copied as needed.[9] The result was the accumulation, refinement, and spread of knowledge to an extent otherwise impossible. Civilization rests upon this.

Our genetics has been similarly constrained. Evolution, for all its awesome constructions, is ultimately a vast tale of trial and error—and a slow and cautious one for a large organism like us. Random change is more likely to be deleterious than beneficial, so modifications must prove themselves over many generations. But while nature has eons, you and I do not.

As researchers gather and correlate human genetic profiles and adult human attributes, they will be able to assemble and interpret information about the effects of various clusters of genes. When they identify favorable combinations, they will preserve them outside our bodies—in tissue cultures, in freezers, and on computers—and we will pass them on to our children if we choose to. We will make mistakes. But so do random variation and natural selection. The enormous collective project of conscious human evolution has begun.

The Tensions of Living Together

As we gain conscious control over our biology, we will transform the range of what is human by expanding our diversity. Whether this diversification of the human form and character will isolate us from one another and make us truly separate is uncertain. Here I refer not to physical isolation, though that might well occur, but to a separation of our spirits, our purposes, and our biological identities. Dogs and cats, for example, are distinct and live among us, but they are our pets. If groups of future humans come to see each other as different, will they be able to remain on an equal footing?

Such changes to whole populations will require widespread germinal choice, of course, but a gradual transition to laboratory conception will likely follow the arrival of comprehensive embryo screening and advanced IVF, as parents come to view this as protection for their children. Even those uninterested in enhancement may start to see it as reckless and primitive to conceive a child without prior genetic testing.

With the advent of germline engineering, however, human artificial chromosomes will probably render laboratory conception obligatory rather than optional. The union of egg and sperm from two individuals with different numbers of chromosomes or different sequences of genes on their extra chromosomes would be too unpredictable with intercourse. But laboratory conception may not be a burden because such parents will probably want the most up-to-date chromosome enhancements anyway.

This move from bedroom to laboratory conception is one that future humans are unlikely ever to reverse, because they will not want to discard the benefits residing on their artificial chromosomes. This change seems dramatic, but it is not as big a leap as it might initially seem. Laboratory conception is just one more step down the path we took long ago when our distant ancestors embraced fire, clothing, and other early technologies, beginning a cultural process that has continually deepened our connection with and dependence on technology.

In the future, laboratory-mediated conception may seem no more foreign than medically assisted birth does today. In 1900, few thought of giving birth in a hospital as "natural"; only 5 percent of births took place there.[10] Today, in the United States, almost all births do, and some 30 percent are by cesarean section, a frequently avoidable procedure that is nonetheless readily accepted.

How germinal choice technology affects our future will hinge on who has access to it as well as on what it offers. If the technology is available to large numbers of people, it is unlikely to give rise to a narrow elite.

Regulatory and healthcare policies will be important factors in determining how broadly available GCT becomes, but the nature of the technology itself may play a more critical role. Whether GCT is a free healthcare benefit or is for sale on the open market, the more complex and individualized the technology, the more expensive and less widely available it will be. With healthcare plans the costly procedures are rationed; on the open market, only the affluent can afford them.

Different technological approaches will likely lead to procedures with different costs.[11] To alter specific genes in place in an embryo's genome, for example, would be expensive because it would require a customized research effort for each embryo. Artificial chromosomes, on the other hand, might allow cheap enhancement for the many, because robotic devices could load them with a tailored package of off-the-shelf gene modules, and validate and test them before injecting them into embryos. So government policies that encourage research to refine artificial chromosomes and other technology platforms suited to widely available GCT might push development in this direction.

An altogether different strategy is to focus on access to the technology by attempting to control its clinical use. Such an approach poses a significant risk because it leads to categorical bans that, as previously discussed, will reserve the technology for narrow segments of society. Provision of free universal access to major aspects of GCT would align better with our ideals of equal opportunity for children and might be surprisingly affordable. If the price of a full GCT procedure could be kept down to, say, $6,000 a baby, this would be roughly equal to the average yearly expenditure on a student in public school in the United States.

As GCT begins to offer parents truly meaningful possibilities, our regulatory policies will have significant consequences for society. The first important choice we face will be our handling of advanced PGD, IVF, and egg banking. If tests to screen for almost all genetic diseases, for example, become available, but primarily to the affluent, such disorders will turn into diseases of the disadvantaged. Our policies will become even more crucial when we can screen embryos for genetic potentials.

As society moves closer to becoming a meritocracy, the most talented from all ethnicities and backgrounds will intermingle, form partnerships, and mate with similarly talented and successful others. Over time, this self-sorting will tend to divide society, increasingly distancing the more gifted from the less. Narrowly limited genetic screening and enhancement technology would accelerate such divisions and reinforce privilege, whereas broadly available technology would counteract them.

Not long ago, restricting access to education was one way of reinforcing class divisions, but we work so hard now to provide every child with the education to reach his or her potential that this repartitioning of society by talent and intellect, rather than by family and status, is already well under way in many countries. In the United States, the student bodies at elite institutions are ethnically and culturally more diverse than ever, but they are drawn from a narrow segment of the population. In 1990, Yale and Harvard together enrolled 1 in 400 of all freshmen at four-year colleges, but that included 1 in 10 of the small number of students scoring above 700 on the verbal portion of the Scholastic Aptitude Test, or SAT.[12] This aggregation of an intellectual elite at the top universities is a new phenomenon. In 1950, such schools were ten times less selective when it came to standardized tests.

Kids soon learn how competitive the world is and where their talents do and do not lie. We have all been through this. If we were astute, lucky, or found good mentors, we ended up doing what we were best at. Some of our aptitudes emerged from our experiences; others—those innate talents that come so naturally we may take them for granted—came straight from our biology. People without the special talents and attributes that our society values—those who are clumsy, inarticulate, unattractive, slow-witted; those who would find it wonderful just to be average—are at a great disadvantage. Their hopes and aspirations may have always matched their lesser potentials, but more likely their dreams had to shrink one disappointment at a time.

Perhaps a mother who is unattractive remembers what it was like to suffer the teasing of her classmates and recalls her struggle for acceptance. Perhaps a father who was short and weak recalls being picked on as a boy. Perhaps a young man remembers watching others easily answer questions he could not fathom and thinks back on how humiliating it was to be dropped to the "slow" group. Maybe a young woman wanted to be a writer, but could never bring any magic to the words she wrote. These wounds heal, but they do not go away. Saying that we all have special, different talents and need to find them is too glib. Think about that person who was not bright or athletic or musically gifted, who felt lucky just to get by.

We have no choice, of course, but to play the hand we are dealt. But at the same time, we strive to protect our children and give them the breaks we never had: the education we couldn't afford, the family stability we wanted, the wealth we dreamed of, the guidance we needed. Society applauds these efforts but will be wary of parents who try to help their children through genetic interventions. Safety aside, though, why shouldn't we try to give our future children the talents we did not have or eliminate deficiencies that held us back? If we could make our baby smarter, more attractive, a better athlete or musician, or keep him or her from being overweight, why wouldn't we?

One social problem that might attend germinal choice technology, if it really can give our children raw talents, would be that such enhanced abilities would soon be less special. As in Garrison Keillor's Lake Wobegon, all the children would be above average. To the extent that talent and good health are heritable, children of some parents have an edge. Show me the brilliant intellectual who does not expect his child to be near the top of the class, the sports superstar who does not expect his child to have athletic gifts. Such kids may not turn out to be the smartest or the most talented, but they will probably do fairly well. Their genetics is not the whole story, but it is important. There is a reason adopted children tend to resemble their biological parents more than their adoptive ones: life does not start from scratch each generation; it takes from the past.

With the completion of the sequencing of the human genome, it has become fashionable to make a point of saying that we differ from one another in only 1 in 1,000 of our DNA bases. We are 99.9 percent the same as our

fellow humans, whoever they may be. This statement is reassuring and politically correct, but misleading. We only have to look around us to see the
extraordinary differences among us. Biological diversity is real. We come in
a multitude of shapes and sizes. We have distinct personalities and temperaments. We possess various talents and vulnerabilities. We draw much of this
from our genetic constitutions.

How can this be when our genetics are 99.9 percent the same? We see
the answer when we realize that our DNA sequence is about 98.5 percent the
same as a chimpanzee's, perhaps 85 percent the same as a mouse's. Open up
a mouse and you find a heart, lungs, intestines, bones, nerves, muscles. Mice
are close cousins to us. And when it comes simply to having homologous
genes rather than exact DNA sequences, the similarity between all life is
even clearer. Some 98 percent of the mouse's genes are ours too, 60 percent
of the fruit fly's, and more than 25 percent of those of a banana.[13] All life has
cells. These cells divide in the same ways. They regulate their DNA and
manage their metabolism and cellular communication in the same ways.
They have the same basic biochemistry. Our genetic similarities come from
the fundamentals we all share. Of course you and I are nearly the same. We
are both animals, both vertebrates, both primates—both humans. The differences between us are subtle, but that doesn't mean we shouldn't care about
them. A difference of 1 in 1,000 bases between any two people is not trivial,
even though it is much less than the difference between, say, two chimpanzees. It amounts to 3 million differing bases in their individual genomes.
Sure, the vast majority will be scattered through the so-called junk DNA between their genes, and of the 150,000 or so differences in their actual genes,
most will be neutral and not lead to any functional differences. But a single
base can be the difference between vibrant health and early death. Parkin-
son's disease comes from a single changed base. So do sickle cell anemia and
hemophilia. A single base difference can make the fingers on a person's
hands resemble toes, or cause mental retardation.

We do not yet know what percentage of two people's genes differ in
meaningful ways, but a good guess is around 10 to 20 percent—several
thousand genes.[14] Moreover, because our major competitors for just about
everything in life are other people, we are fine-tuned by evolution to be
highly sensitive to the minute distinctions among us. We don't care that we
are all mammals, all primates. These are givens. We care about our differences. All people might look pretty much the same to a space alien or a mosquito—or even an evolutionary biologist—but not to a coach trying to build
a winning sports team or to someone looking for a mate.

As we untangle our genes and learn to select and alter them, some parents will want to give their children endowments they themselves could
only dream of. If such interventions become commonplace, the result will be
revolutionary, because it will be a major step toward equalizing life's possibilities. The gifted of today ultimately may not welcome such a leveling, be-

cause it would diminish the edge their children enjoy and make society very competitive, even for the best endowed.

If GCT enhancements prove feasible, eventually the mass of humanity will seize the power to enrich its children's natural endowments. Strong voices will oppose this, but most of the warnings about the danger of eugenics and the threat of lab-built humans will come from people with the most to lose—the well-endowed elite. Surely theirs are the children who would ultimately suffer from the arrival of a genetic bazaar where all parents can obtain equivalent talents and potentials for their children.

Today's intellectual elite might not want to live in a world as aggressive, competitive, and uncontrolled as the one that would emerge from universal access to potent germinal choice technologies, so their distaste for the technology may deepen once its true implications become clear.[15] Such resistance would be reminiscent of earlier elites who liked society the way it was and tried to protect their privileged position. The wellborn of an earlier time were right to fear the political reforms that broke down class divisions. Now a new elite may wince, because if the God-given gifts of talent and intelligence that have raised them above the throng are suddenly laid out for everyone else, their future would not be so secure.

The concern about preserving the ideals of an egalitarian society and preventing the creation of a genetic elite that inspires many of the philosophical objections to GCT among intellectuals is ironic, both because they themselves are among the elite and because any enduring effort to block these technologies will restrict access to them, compounding rather than alleviating genetic advantages.[16]

To look at the possible implications of advanced germinal choice technology more concretely, let's imagine a best-case scenario: science and policy combine to make germinal enhancement widely available, relatively commonplace, and largely under the control of individual parents.

In such a society, many parents might shun GCT, but others would embrace it enthusiastically. With time, people's genetics would become a manifestation of their parents' values and predilections. Initially, the differences between the enhanced and the unenhanced would be only statistical, in that those with enhancements would tend to outperform many, but not all, of those without enhancements. But as the technology grew more potent, less overlap would exist between the two populations, and as this became clear to parents, many of the children of those who had shunned the technology would likely enhance their own children, to keep them from being at a disadvantage.

A similar story would be played out globally, as countries that initially blocked GCT gradually felt compelled to amend or repeal their laws and accept it. Access to advanced technology typically flows from national wealth, but adoption of GCT may hinge more on the religious and cultural traditions in particular regions. Some of the richest nations could easily be the most resistant to the technology. Eventually, however, they probably will have no choice. What, after all, would a country that bans advanced embryo diagnosis do if other nations were to embark on popularly supported eugenic programs aimed at dramatically raising the average IQ of their next generation?

Breeds Apart

As we move from embryo selection to direct germline enhancement, one might imagine that devising artificial chromosomes that can enhance one embryo as effectively as another would ensure that humanity would not split into separate breeds, since future parents, whatever their own particular genetic endowments, would be able to select their children's genetic modules from an expanding common library of enhancements.[17]

Enabling couples to give their future children genetic predispositions differing from their own, however, does not necessarily mean that they would. Our experiences, associations, and natures circumscribe our values and attitudes. Parents with general competencies might well consider such balance good for their children, while parents with narrow, highly specialized talents might see greater specialization as preferable.

As we increasingly manifest our aptitudes, temperaments, and philosophies in our children through our decisions about their genetic makeup, a self-reinforcing channeling of human lineages will likely develop. Family names once denoted family professions that persisted for generations. The Cooks, Fishers, Smiths, Taylors, and Bakers of the world could no doubt uncover the corresponding trades among their ancestors. Perhaps in the future, clusters of genetic predispositions, lifestyles, and philosophical orientations will arise that are equally persistent. Families of musicians, politicians, therapists, scientists, and athletes would not be locked in by social constraints and limited opportunities, however, but by tight feedback between genetic selection and the values, philosophies, and choices that both author that selection and flow from it. Such future human specialization might be far deeper than that which has occurred historically. Maintaining it would require an ongoing cycle of renewed choices that couples, at least theoretically, could break when they decided to have children, but most probably would not.

Ideally, the resulting partitioning of the social landscape would proceed according to individual predispositions and desires rather than some preexisting template imposed on unwilling populations. But the possibilities of abuse by governments or individual parents who breed children for their own purposes should rightly give us pause. We must remember, though, that tyranny and child abuse require no advanced technology, and whether either would be changed much by the presence of germinal choice is highly debatable.

Even disregarding outright abuse, scenarios of human design are jarring, if not frightening, because they evoke troubling images of freakish human forms. While we should not dismiss such images entirely, neither should we allow them to grow in our minds to the point where they oversimplify and distort a future landscape whose complicated topography is not yet defined. Rare, special attributes such as photographic memory or extraordinary athletic ability may become both more extreme and more commonplace, but that does not mean they will be grotesque. As for the fear that parental choices might become too uniform, children would be as unique as they are now. The multiplicity of individual experience molds an infinity of expression from our genes, even if they have been chosen.

Despite the occasional exception, as in the case of parents who select deafness, when we are able to choose our offspring's genetic predispositions, we will probably opt to avoid most of the genetic disabilities and vulnerabilities that afflict us today. In this limited sense, early applications of preimplantation genetic diagnosis will narrow human diversity, but the polio vaccine did as much and brought few complaints.[18] And as sophisticated embryo screening and germline manipulation begin to enrich enhancement possibilities, no doubt clusters of attributes will be reinforced, which in time will expand diversity.

Today, when that rare combination of genetic and environmental factors comes together to create genius in one of its many guises, the combination usually disappears in the next generation. This happens because contributing environmental influences do not recur and because genetic constellations dissipate during genetic recombination. In the future, parents not only might preserve key aspects of such genetic influences through embryo selection, they might also have the knowledge and the means to push those talents even further, by creating environments that reinforce them and by refining chromosomal additions.

What aspects of themselves people will want to boost or moderate is hard to say. But taken together, their choices will have a powerful effect on society. Children's biological predispositions will come to reflect parental philosophies and attitudes, and thus children will manifest the ethos and values that influence their parents. Consider gender. Many couples would make different choices about the attributes of boys and girls. Thus, GCT might translate cultural attitudes about gender into the biology of children. If a society believes that women are (or should be) more empathetic and supportive, and boys more aggressive and independent, then whether or not these gender specificities are true now is not as important as the likelihood that they will gradually become true.

Because our notions of personal identity are specific to particular cultures and times, purely cultural distinctions could become more embedded in our genetics and may increase the biological differences among human populations. Each culture assigns its own value to traits such as calmness, obedience, and curiosity. To the extent that genes can influence these differences, GCT might reinforce them.

Many social commentators today complain about the homogenization of culture, brought on by global commerce and communications. The arrival of advanced, widespread germinal choice technology may counteract that trend by allowing people to infuse some of their cultural differences into the biology of their children. In a mixed cultural environment like that in America, of course, these effects would be played out on a national stage. Current debates about whether some of the differences among ethnic and racial groups are cultural or biological will soon become irrelevant, given the coming interdependence of the two. In any event, once we can fashion our children's biological predispositions, many cultural and personal influences will feed directly into biology.

Enhancement will be not a single dimension of change but a wide range of modification and augmentation, superimposed on the broad distribution of naturally occurring human qualities, so distinguishing between the enhanced and the unenhanced will initially be difficult, if not impossible. But germinal choice will eventually become so commonplace that the question won't even be interesting, especially given that potent quasi-medical pharmaceutical enhancements for adults will probably also become widespread. If so conservative a group as the Amish are willing to seek gene therapy, virtually no one will forgo drug, technological, and genetic enhancement once it is safe, reliable, beneficial, and perhaps even fashionable.

In the future, humanity will be an ever-shifting mélange of those who are biologically unaltered, those with improved health and longevity, and those with sundry other enhancements. In essence, we and our children increasingly will be reflections of our personal philosophies and values. Where today we sculpt our minds and bodies using exercise, drugs, and surgery, tomorrow we will also use the tools that biotechnology provides.

We cannot say what powers future humans will assume, what forms they will take, or even if they will be strictly biological, but we can be certain of one predisposition they will have. They will be committed to the process of human enhancement and self-directed evolution.[19] This we know, because without this commitment they would lag behind and be displaced by those who are more aggressive in this regard.

But the immediate cultural landscape wrought by germinal choice and biological manipulation will be more familiar than we might think. We are used to enormous human diversity. An anorexic eighty-pound fashion model, a four-hundred-pound sumo wrestler, a tiny svelte gymnast, and a towering basketball center are very different from one another. So may be their lives and passions—or those of a deaf-mute and a concert pianist, for that matter. We also are used to enormous technological gulfs between people: the vision and hearing of those with and without televisions and telephones differ greatly.

Whether our differences today are primarily the result of genetics, culture, technology, or education, they are real and they permeate our lives. Many of us revel in the giant and diverse human aggregations that are our modern cities; others simply cope with them. The enhancements brought by germinal choice will not soon sweep us into a realm so alien that we could detect the change on a stroll through a crowd but the changes will affect us profoundly.

The biggest challenge will be our changing image of ourselves. At the outset I said that these new technologies would force us to examine the very question of what it means to be human. As we follow the path that germline choice offers, we are likely to find that being human has little to do with the particular physical and mental characteristics we now use to define ourselves, and even less to do with the methods of conception and birth that are now so familiar. Adjusting to new possibilities in these areas will be hard for many of us, because it will demand a level of tolerance and acceptance that until now has been the exception rather than the rule. But perhaps the drama of the shift will itself ease the change by capturing our attention and forcing us into new patterns of relationship. Until now, to accept each other we often have had to pretend that we are all the same, but maybe when we see that we are all different and unequal—increasingly so—we will learn to accept our differences.

As we move into the centuries ahead, our strongest bond with one another may be that we share a common biological origin and are part of a common process of self-directed emergence into an unknowable future. Seen in this light, the present differences among us are trivial, because we are companions in transition and are likely to remain so.

Perhaps this state of transition is what has always defined us. The mechanisms of change were different in previous eras, but the culturally and technologically driven process of becoming that which we are not, of changing the world around us and our own selves, is not new—only the pace and depth of change are truly unprecedented.

A World Aborning

To some, the coming of human-directed change is unnatural because it differs so much from any previous change, but this distinction between the natural and the unnatural is an illusion. We are as natural a part of the world as anything else is, and so is the technology we create. As we consciously transform ourselves, we will become no less human than we became tens of thousands of years ago when we embarked upon a course of self-domestication and began, quite unconsciously, to self-select for the human qualities that enable us to live and work together effectively.[20] That we are uneasy about what lies ahead is not surprising. The arrival of GCT signals a diffuse and unplanned project to redesign ourselves. But it is neither an invasion of the inhuman, threatening that which is human within us, nor a transcendence of our human limits. Remaking ourselves is the ultimate expression and realization of our humanity. We would be foolish to believe that this future is without peril and filled only with benefits, that these powerful technologies will not require wisdom to handle well, or that great loss will not accompany the changes ahead. We are beginning an extraordinary adventure that we cannot avoid, because, judging from our past, whether we like it or not this *is* the human destiny.

It brings to mind the advertisement that Sir Ernest Shackleton, the renowned British explorer, placed in 1912 when he was recruiting a team for an expedition to cross the icy Antarctic continent on foot: "Men wanted for hazardous journey. Small wages. Bitter cold. Long months of complete darkness. Safe return doubtful. Honour and recognition in case of success."[21]

Some five thousand people responded to his call. Shackleton selected twenty-seven and began the journey. Their ship became frozen in place just off the Antarctic coast and was later crushed by the ice, but after a harrowing and nearly unbelievable two-year ordeal, they all returned safely. Shackleton looked back on it in his diary: "In memories we were rich. We had pierced the veneer of outside things. We had suffered, starved and triumphed, groveled down yet grasped at glory, grown bigger in the bigness of the whole. We had seen God in His splendors, heard the text that nature renders. We had reached the naked soul of man."

Our journey into our own biology is very different. The endeavor is collective rather than individual, its course encompasses centuries rather than years, there will be no return, and the voyage is as spiritual as it is physical. But we too are entering uncharted territory. We too will no doubt face adversity. And the destination may prove less important than the journey itself. As we pierce the veneer of inside things, we too may reach the naked soul of man.

We have created artificial intelligence from the inert sand at our feet through the silicon revolution, we are moving out into space from the thin planetary patina that hitherto has held all life, we are reworking the surface of our planet and shaping it to suit us. These developments will transform the world we inhabit. Amid all this, could we really imagine that we ourselves would somehow remain unchanged? Or that we would want to? If we were to succeed in turning back from the path of self-modification now opening before us, we would not be pleased with the result, because ultimately we would find ourselves in a world so different from the one that spawned us that we would feel estranged and adrift. Adaptable as we are, to remain at home in the world we are forming, we will have to adjust ourselves to cope with it.

At the end of the nineteenth century, visionary biologists imagined a bleak human future. Our very successes, by softening natural selection and saving those who would otherwise die young, seemed to ensure that the human species would slowly deteriorate. Germinal choice technology frees us from this fate, but it brings other, more immediate threats.

As we enter into advanced reproductive technology, we would do well to recall the Nazi concentration camps. Eugenics, as practiced in the first half of the past century, attests to the horrors of governmental abuse, and although Germany was the most egregious case, it was not alone. In the 1920s, the eugenics movement, which was often called "race hygiene," was centered in the United States and Great Britain, and included adherents in Poland, France, Italy, Scandinavia, Japan, and Latin America. Many of these programs were voluntary, but some were not.[22]

Some say that if we do not learn from history, we risk repeating it, but the challenge is always to understand what history is telling us. The lessons of past eugenic abuse do not concern technology, biology, or human reproduction, but nationalism, totalitarian regimes, individual freedom, and tyranny. Government abuse is what we must fear, not germinal choice technology. GCT is not a weapon, and the chaos of countless individual genetic choices by individual parents is not a threat, especially if the choices are circumscribed by modest oversight. Some push for uniform global policies, but these raise specters of the same governmental abuses that history warns us about.[23] Far better that we find our way in this coming journey by trial and error—cautious, informed trial, of course, and as little error as possible—but trial and error nonetheless.

There is no way we can permanently forgo these enhancement technologies if they prove robust and useful. Those who would shun healthier constitutions and extended lifespans might hope to remain the way they are, linked to a human past they cherish. But future generations will not want to remain "natural" if that means living at the whim of advanced creatures to whom they would be little more than intriguing relics from an abandoned human past.

What is occurring now is no less than a birth. The occasion may prove messy and painful, but it carries the wonder of new life and new possibilities, the promise of growth and achievement. Humanity has been building toward this moment for tens of thousands of years. Conception took place long ago when we first chipped stone tools and used fire. Quickening came with early agriculture, writing, and the formation of larger human communities. Now the contractions are forceful and rapid. The head is beginning to show. Will we suddenly lose our nerve because of the realization that life will change forever and because we can barely guess the character of this child of our creation? I hope not. We cannot push the head back, and we risk doing ourselves grievous harm if we make the attempt. We may not like the future we are creating, so vastly will it ultimately differ from our present. Yet our descendants—those beings who are the product of today's crude beginnings at unraveling our biology—will be unable to imagine living without the many enhancements that we will make possible for them.

A thousand years hence, these future humans—whoever or whatever they may be—will look back on our era as a challenging, difficult, traumatic moment. They will likely see it as a strange and primitive time when people lived only seventy or eighty years, died of awful diseases, and conceived their children outside a laboratory by a random, unpredictable meeting of sperm and egg. But they will also see our era as the fertile, extraordinary epoch that laid the foundation of their lives and their society. The cornerstone will almost certainly be the reworking of human biology and reproduction. To me, being here, not only to witness but to participate in this unprecedented development, is an amazing privilege. But we are so much more than observers and architects of these changes; we are also their objects.

Public policies about germinal choice technology will be effective only to the extent that they are prescient enough to elicit technology that succeeds in promoting future research and development. Whether DNA chips, advanced *in vitro* fertilization, and human artificial chromosomes will provide the foundation for germinal choice or whether some other cluster of technologies will fill that role remains to be seen. In either case, we will work toward embryo screening and other germline procedures that are either cheap and accessible to everyone or expensive and accessible to only a few.

If there is a window of opportunity for government to influence the future path of these technologies, it is unlikely to last for long. Only a few countries now have the capacity to realize them. If these nations move toward workable GCT and responsible strategies for using the resulting reproductive procedures, they may shape the basic approaches that become dominant. If they restrict the development of GCT and simply continue probing the fundamentals of our biology, unknown others will take the critical early steps and determine the shape of GCT for the immediate future.

The great challenge is not how we handle cloning, embryo selection, germline engineering, genetic testing, genetically altered foods, or any other specific technology. We will muddle through as we always have. Unlike nuclear weapons, these technologies will be forgiving; they carry no threat of imminent destruction to multitudes of innocent bystanders. The crucial question is whether we will continue to embrace the possibilities of our biological future or pull back and relinquish their development to braver souls in more adventurous nations of the world.

Many European countries have already made a provisional decision in this regard. In part because of their sensitivity over the eugenic abuses of the past, they are forgoing these technologies and trusting others to forge them. I suspect that this stance on so central an element of our future will be temporary, but in any event, Europe will have a decade to mull over the matter before GCT emerges in a serious way.

As I see it, the coming opportunities in germinal choice technology far outweigh the risks. What is more, a free-market environment with real individual choice, modest oversight, and robust mechanisms to learn quickly from mistakes is the best way both to protect us from potential abuses and to channel resources toward the goals we value.   ∎

NOTES

1. Predispositions for high IQ—and other cognitive attributes, for that matter—may be among the most complex of human traits. Though single-gene mutations have been implicated in various substantial diminutions of cognitive functioning, no specific genes have yet been found that account for even a few percentage points of variation in IQ among people with average and above-average scores. Current bioinformatic studies are too primitive—too small and crude—to identify combinations of alleles that together will raise IQ or to identify rare individual alleles that do. If researchers have so far failed to identify any strong single-gene contributions, this does not mean that combinations of genes will exert no strong effects, that there are no rare alleles that exert significant effects, or that no way will be found to manipulate relevant biochemical pathways. But if embryo selection for the main components of the heritable contribution to high IQ proves possible, this would still not usher in a genetic supermarket where parents could fill a shopping cart with multiple enhancements. Even without inherent biological tradeoffs among traits, finding the right gene combinations would require the screening of huge numbers of embryos.

2. This estimate assumes that IQ is only 50 percent heritable in typical environments (which is at the low end of current estimates; see, for example, Steen, 1999, pp. 113–35) and that only half of the total genetic variance is within individual families. The top embryo—selected on genetic criteria alone—would on average become an adult who tested at 118. By comparison, the top 1 percent of children have IQs of about 138.

3. See Parens, 1998. "The use of IGM": See Frankel and Chapman, 2000, p. 42.

4. Say IQ turned out to be very complex, shaped by twenty key genes and hundreds of others with minor influences. No doubt there would be many genes or small clusters of genes that when mutated cause nutritional problems or otherwise disrupt normal brain development, resulting in diminished intelligence. PKU (phenylketonuria) is one such condition described by Paul (1998, p. 178), and it is relatively straightforward to repair. But the task of improving on a rare combination of genes that contribute to genius would be far more difficult and demand greater caution about unseen tradeoffs.

5. See Scott and Fuller, 1974, pp. 403, 411.

6. See Vila et al., 1997, and Wayne, 1993. Although the oldest archaeological evidence of the association between dogs and people dates back only about 14,000 years, mitochondrial sequencing suggests that dogs branched off from gray wolves around 135,000 years ago. (Gray wolves had branched off from coyotes and foxes 5 to 10 million years earlier.) It is possible that dogs did not diverge anatomically from wolves until humans began to inhabit agricultural centers and impose stronger selective pressures. Few dog breeds can be traced back more than a few thousand years, and most have appeared only in the past few centuries. This may seem a short time, but a single breeder's hand can direct their evolution for thirty or more dog generations,

whereas our evolution, with so few generations encompassed by any single human lifetime, must be directed by larger social and cultural forces.

In a forty-year domestication experiment on foxes, Russian breeders, using modern methods, selected for a single trait: tameness. This, they believe, is the common trait that all human domestication has selected, and it produced aspects of doglike morphology, coat color variability, size changes, tail changes, and such. See Trut, 1999. www.blarg.net/~critter/dogfamily/ancientdog_3.htm.

7. When researchers compared a hundred different genetic markers from ninety-six dog breeds, they couldn't distinguish one breed from another. This means that the differences are much more fine-grained, encompassing relatively small numbers of genes. These differences may give us great insight into the potential for directing human evolution. Certainly, such efforts have been relatively easy with dogs and foxes. (Personal communication, Jasper Rine, University of California at Berkeley.) Biological forms that persist: See Raup, 1991, p. 108.

8. See Blackmore, 1999.

9. See Stock, 1993, p. 85.

10. See Wertz and Wertz, 1989.

11. See Capecchi, 2000. $6,000 a baby: The cost of a viable pregnancy by IVF for a thirty-year-old woman without serious fertility problems is now about $12,000. Assuming savings from new technology, IVF that is routine, massive numbers of procedures, and automated GCT, the lower figure is not outlandish; it costs about the same amount to order a strain of knock-out mice from a laboratory.

12. See Cook and Frank, 1991.

13. These figures are not precise, since we don't even know the exact number of human genes, but they are in the ballpark. For a good general discussion of the human genome, see the *Nova* interview with Eric Landers, the director of the Center for Genome Research at the Whitehead Institute: www.pbs.org/wgbh/nova/genome/deco_lander.html. The differences between us: We are a young species, all coming from a population of a few tens of thousands of people that existed 100,000 years ago in Africa. Because this founder population was so small and recent, the differences between two humans are perhaps a quarter as great as those between two chimpanzees.

14. This would include the coding regions of genes, which determine the sequences of the protein or proteins each gene specifies, and the non-coding regions, which regulate the expression of the genes. Together these account for perhaps 5 percent of the human genome.

15. While some people fear that GCT will be narrowly held and therefore lead to a genetic elite, others fear that the multitudes will have access to GCT and make pathological or at least unwise choices. And some people fear both. For example, Sheldon Krimsky, a professor at Tufts University, writes, "The availability of eugenic techniques in reproduction to a minority of affluent people will support the 'geneticization' of a society, enabling an aristocracy with so-called proper genes to use it to their class advantage." This suggests that such choices would be of value. But elsewhere in the same essay, he suggests that "offering people the opportunity to choose the phenotype of a child will result in psychosocial pathologies, including deeper class and racial divisions within society" (Krimsky, 2000). Apparently, only the elite would have the sense to use the technology to their benefit.

16. The so-called War on Drugs provides a cautionary tale for GCT. This war has filled our jails, corrupted swaths of law enforcement and government, made criminals out of many otherwise law-abiding citizens, and funneled enormous resources into the hands of criminals. But many supporters of it contend that legalization would be far worse, because it would bring about greater use of drugs and destroy countless lives. Duke and Gross (1994) presents an excellent argument against the War on Drugs.

17. Were enhancements based on changes to our 46 existing chromosomes rather than on replaceable artificial chromosomes, each generation would have to build on the changes made by the previous one, so family lineages would progressively accumulate benefits and diverge from one another. In essence, everyone's genetic choices about their offspring would be circumscribed by the past decisions of their ancestors.

18. The screening out of genetic vulnerabilities would no doubt also result in fewer individuals whose afflictions bring about uncommon achievements—the manic depressive who writes great literature, the physically impaired artist who creates great works of art. In any event, in the future many such afflictions will be increasingly blunted by improved medical treatment.

19. Campbell (1995) explores the concept of self-directed evolution at length. He calls it "regenerative evolution" and believes that small groups of future humans, highly committed to self-evolution, will outstrip humanity as a whole, leaving it far behind. In his view, how humanity responds to GCT is irrelevant, because small founder groups will be at the heart of any future evolutionary change.

20. This process mirrors our domestication of dogs, cats, livestock, and crops. By selecting for those qualities that bring these species into our lives, we have transformed them, and we have transformed ourselves through a similar process of self-selection. Our transformation has been primarily cultural, but it has almost certainly had a biological component: selection for the traits that allow survival in the altered world we have been creating.

21. See Worsley, 1931.

22. Kevles (1995) provides an in-depth look of the origins of the eugenics movement. The mainstream movement was largely oriented toward voluntarism and relied on education, contraception, and moral injunction. Eugenic ideas were so commonly accepted that a 1937 poll in *Fortune* magazine showed 63 percent of Americans endorsing the compulsory sterilization of habitual criminals and 66 percent in favor of sterilizing "mental defectives." In 1939, Hermann Muller, who later won the Nobel Prize and helped found the "genius" sperm bank in San Diego, published a "Genetics Manifesto" with twenty-two other scientists asserting that it should be "an honor and a privilege, if not a duty, for a mother, married or unmarried, or for a couple, to have the best children possible, both in upbringing and genetic endowment."

23. See Macer, 2000.

■ *QUESTIONS FOR MAKING CONNECTIONS*
WITHIN THE READING ■

1. The last paragraph of Stock's reading begins with these words: "As I see it, the coming opportunities in germinal choice technology far outweigh

the risks." Do you feel that Stock's argument fully supports this claim? Conversely, would you say that he has done an adequate job of giving the risks "equal time" with the benefits?

2. Much of the debate over genetic technology has focused on the issue of cloning. Does Stock's focus on genetic choice technology as opposed to cloning make his job as a spokesperson easier or more difficult? Can Stock's argument for genetic choice technology be applied to cloning as well? Can his argument be used to justify technological changes of every kind? If you feel that his argument could be used to justify every change, is that a strength or a weakness?

3. What does Stock mean in this passage:

> Today's intellectual elite might not want to live in a world as aggressive, competitive, and uncontrolled as the one that would emerge from universal access to potent germinal choice technology, so their distaste for the technology may deepen once its true implications become clear.

Why would the world that Stock foresees be more "aggressive, competitive, and uncontrolled" than it is right now? What would elites have to fear from such a world? If our society creates a free market in genetic technology, are we likely to see more, or less, equality? Will we see more, or less, peace and security? If everyone gets smarter and stronger, what might be the result?

▪ QUESTIONS FOR WRITING ▪

1. Questions related to genetic technology can be viewed from many perspectives—scientific, ethical, historical, religious, economic, political, and pragmatic. What perspectives does Stock tend to adopt? How does his choice of perspectives shape the conclusions he reaches?

2. How does Stock's proposal differ from the practice of eugenics in Nazi Germany? Does it matter if individuals rather than governments make decisions about the genetic modification of future generations? Do you agree that individuals are less likely than governments to withhold access to genetic technologies? Should *anyone* have the right to change the genetic make-up of the coming generation?

▪ QUESTIONS FOR MAKING CONNECTIONS BETWEEN READINGS ▪

1. Stock assumes that genetic technologies can be made widely, or even universally, available. Does William Greider paint a picture of American social life that lends credence to Stock's assumptions? Would a free market

in genetic technology assure that everyone could take advantage of ᴖ technological advances? How might the market in these technologies ᴖ protected or controlled to make certain that everyone would be able to compete equally for these benefits? Should such market protections be introduced?

2. Stock's discussion of genetic technology focuses on enhancing the conventional physical and mental powers of individuals. He appears to be less interested in the psychological effects that might follow from such "enhancements." Starting with Martha Stout's discussion of the way the brain processes traumatic events, weigh the advantages and disadvantages of genetic changes that might eliminate our innate tendency to dissociate ourselves from painful events. Could it be that the fugue state Stout describes has a survival advantage? Is it possible that the desire to redesign human beings is a product of a dissociated state of mind? Would a person less alienated from the world really want to enhance human beings as they now exist?

www **For additional suggestions about making connections between readings, visit the Link-O-Mat and More Sample Assignments at <www.newhum.com>.**

MARTHA STOUT

WHAT IS SANITY? Are "normal" people always dependably sane, or could it be said that we experience sanity only as a temporary, fluctuating state? After witnessing a traumatic event, have you ever spent time in a state that is not exactly sane, a state of either frantic agitation or numbness, withdrawal, and distraction? These are the questions that Martha Stout, a Clinical Instructor in Psychology at Harvard Medical School and a Clinical Associate at the Massachusetts General Hospital, pursues in *The Myth of Sanity: Divided Consciousness and the Promise of Awareness* (2002). Drawing on more than twenty years' experience working with patients who have suffered psychological trauma, Stout uses her case studies to show that the ability to dissociate from reality, which functions as a life-preserving defense mechanism during times of stress in childhood, can develop into a way of life that leads to emotional detachment and prolonged disengagement with the world. In the most extreme cases, this dissociative behavior can lead individuals to black out for extended periods of time or to develop multiple personalities in order to contend with life's many demands.

In seeking to establish a continuum that extends from the everyday experience of spacing out to the more traumatic experience of being shell-shocked, Stout invites her readers to recognize just how common the experience of dementia, or "self-shifting," can be. The patients Stout focuses on have been forced to come to terms with the extreme forms this dementia can take, and, with her help, they come to see the meaning of their own lives as something they must continually work to construct. In jargon-free prose, Stout tells the stories of her patients' struggles for and with sanity, revealing in each case how buried or missing memories of the past serve to disrupt and distort the experience of the present.

www **To learn more about Martha Stout and dissociative identity disorder, please visit the Link-O-Mat at <www.newhum.com>.**

Stout, Martha. "When I Woke Up Tuesday Morning, It Was Friday," in *The Myth of Sanity: Divided Consciousness and the Promise of Awareness.* New York: Penguin Books, 2002. 15–43.

Biographical information drawn from <http://www.prweb.com/releases/2002/3/prweb34520.htm>.

■ ■

When I Woke Up Tuesday Morning, It Was Friday

"The horror of that moment," the King went on, "I shall never, never forget!"

"You will, though," the Queen said, "if you don't make a memorandum of it."

—Lewis Carroll

Imagine that you are in your house—no—you are *locked* in your house, cannot get out. It is the dead of winter. The drifted snow is higher than your windows, blocking the light of both moon and sun. Around the house, the wind moans, night and day.

Now imagine that even though you have plenty of electric lights, and perfectly good central heating, you are almost always in the dark and quite cold, because something is wrong with the old-fashioned fuse box in the basement. Inside this cobwebbed, innocuous-looking box, the fuses keep burning out, and on account of this small malfunction, all the power in the house repeatedly fails. You have replaced so many melted fuses that now your little bag of new ones is empty; there are no more. You sigh in frustration, and regard your frozen breath in the light of the flashlight. Your house, which could be so cozy, is tomblike instead.

In all probability, there is something quirky in the antiquated fuse box; it has developed some kind of needless hair trigger, and is not really reacting to any dangerous electrical overload at all. Should you get some pennies out of your pocket, and use them to replace the burned-out fuses? That would solve the power-outage problem. No more shorts, not with copper coins in there. Using coins would scuttle the safeguard function of the fuse box, but the need for a safeguard right now is questionable, and the box is keeping you cold and in the dark for no good reason. Well, probably for no good reason.

On the other hand, what if the wiring in the house really is overloaded somehow? A fire could result, probably will result eventually. If you do not find the fire soon enough, if you cannot manage to put the fire out, the whole house could go up, with you trapped inside. You know that death by burning is hideous. You know also that your mind is playing tricks, but thinking about fire, you almost imagine there is smoke in your nostrils right now.

So, do you go back upstairs and sit endlessly in a dark living room, defeated, numb from the cold, though you have buried yourself under every blanket in the house? No light to read by, no music, just the wail and rattle of the icy wind outside? Or, in an attempt to feel more human, do you make things warm and comfortable? Is it wise to gamble with calamity and howling pain? If you turn the power back on, will you not smell nonexistent smoke every moment you are awake? And will you not have far too many of these waking moments, for how will you ever risk going to sleep?

Do you sabotage the fuse box?

I believe that most of us cannot know what we would do, trapped in a situation that required such a seemingly no-win decision. But I do know that anyone wanting to recover from psychological trauma must face just this kind of dilemma, made yet more harrowing because her circumstance is not anything so rescuable as being locked in a house, but rather involves a solitary, unlockable confinement inside the limits of her own mind. The person who suffers from a severe trauma disorder must decide between surviving in a barely sublethal misery of numbness and frustration, and taking a chance that may well bring her a better life, but that feels like stupidly issuing an open invitation to the unspeakable horror that waits to consume her alive. And in the manner of the true hero, she must choose to take the risk.

For trauma changes the brain itself. Like the outdated fuse box, the psychologically traumatized brain houses inscrutable eccentricities that cause it to overreact—or more precisely, *mis*react—to the current realities of life. These neurological misreactions become established because trauma has a profound effect upon the secretion of stress-responsive neurohormones such as norepinephrine, and thus an effect upon various areas of the brain involved in memory, particularly the amygdala and the hippocampus.

The amygdala receives sensory information from the five senses, via the thalamus, attaches emotional significance to the input, and then passes along this emotional "evaluation" to the hippocampus. In accordance with the amygdala's "evaluation" of importance, the hippocampus is activated to a greater or lesser degree, and functions to organize the new input, and to integrate it with already existing information about similar sensory events. Under a normal range of conditions, this system works efficiently to consolidate memories according to their emotional priority. However, at the extreme upper end of hormonal stimulation, as in traumatic situations, a breakdown occurs. Overwhelming emotional significance registered by the amygdala actually leads to a *decrease in hippocampal activation,* such that some of the traumatic input is not usefully organized by the hippocampus, or integrated with other memories. The result is that portions of traumatic memory are stored not as parts of a unified whole, but as isolated sensory images and bodily sensations that are not localized in time or even in situation, or integrated with other events.

To make matters still more complex, exposure to trauma may temporarily shut down Broca's area, the region of the left hemisphere of the brain that translates experience into language, the means by which we most often relate our experience to others, and even to ourselves.

A growing body of research indicates that in these ways the brain lays down traumatic memories differently from the way it records regular memories. Regular memories are formed through adequate hippocampal and cortical input, are integrated as comprehensible wholes, and are subject to meaning-modification by future events, and through language. In contrast, traumatic memories include chaotic fragments that are sealed off from modulation by subsequent experience. Such memory fragments are wordless, placeless, and eternal, and long after the original trauma has receded into the past, the brain's record of it may consist only of isolated and thoroughly anonymous bits of emotion, image, and sensation that ring through the individual like a broken alarm.

Worse yet, later in the individual's life, in situations that are vaguely similar to the trauma—perhaps merely because they are startling, anxiety-provoking, or emotionally arousing—amygdala-mediated memory traces are accessed more readily than are the more complete, less shrill memories that have been integrated and modified by the hippocampus and the cerebral cortex. Even though unified and updated memories would be more judicious in the present, the amygdala memories are more accessible, and so trauma may be "remembered" at inappropriate times, when there is no hazard worthy of such alarm. In reaction to relatively trivial stresses, the person traumatized long ago may truly *feel* that danger is imminent again, be assailed full-force by the emotions, bodily sensations, and perhaps even the images, sounds, smells that once accompanied great threat.

Here is an illustration from everyday life. A woman named Beverly reads a morning newspaper while she sits at a quiet suburban depot and waits for a train. The article, concerning an outrageous local scandal, intrigues her so much that for a few minutes she forgets where she is. Suddenly, there is an earsplitting blast from the train as it signals its arrival. Beverly is painfully startled by the noise; her head snaps up, and she catches her breath. She is amazed that she could have been so lacking in vigilance and relaxed in public. Her heart pounds, and in the instant required to fold the newspaper, she is ambushed by bodily feelings and even a smell that have nothing whatever to do with the depot on this uneventful morning. If she could identify the smell, which she never will, she would call it "chlorine." She feels a sudden rigidity in her chest, as if her lungs had just turned to stone, and has an almost overpowering impulse to get out of there, to run.

In a heartbeat, the present is perceptually and emotionally the past. These fragments of sensation and emotion are the amygdala-mediated memories of an afternoon three decades before, in Beverly's tenth summer, when, walking home from the public swimming pool, she saw her younger sister skip into the street and meet an immediate death in front of a speeding car. At this moment, thirty years later, Beverly *feels* that way again.

Her sensations and feelings are not labeled as belonging to memories of the horrible accident. In fact, they are not labeled as anything at all, because they have always been completely without language. They belong to no narrative, no place or time, no story she can tell about her life; they are free-form and ineffable.

Beverly's brain contains, effectively, a broken warning device in its limbic system, an old fuse box in which the fuses tend to melt for no good reason, emphatically declaring an emergency where none now exists.

Surprisingly, she will probably not wonder about or even remember the intense perceptual and emotional "warnings," because by the next heartbeat, a long-entrenched dissociative reaction to the declared emergency may already have been tripped in her brain, to "protect" her from this "unbearable" childhood memory. She may feel strangely angry, or paranoid, or childishly timid. Or instead she may feel that she has begun to move in an uncomfortably hazy dream world, far away and derealized. Or she may completely depart from her "self" for a while, continue to act, but without self-awareness. Should this last occur in a minor way, her total experience may be something such as, "Today when I was going to work, the train pulled into the station—the blasted thing is so loud!—and the next thing I remember, it was stopping at my stop." She may even be mildly amused at herself for her spaciness.

Most of us do not notice these experiences very much. They are more or less invisible to us as we go about daily life, and so we do not understand how much of daily life is effectively spent in the past, in reaction to the darkest hours we have known, nor do we comprehend how swampy and vitality-sucking some of our memories really are. Deepening the mire of our divided awareness, in the course of a lifetime such "protective" mental reactions acquire tremendous *habit strength*. These over-exercised muscles can take us away even when traumatic memory fragments have not been evoked. Sometimes dissociation can occur when we are simply confused or frustrated or nervous, whether we recognize our absences or not.

Typically, only those with the most desperate trauma histories are ever driven to discover and perhaps modify their absences from the present. Only the addictions, major depressions, suicide attempts, and general ruination that attend the most severe trauma disorders can sometimes supply motivation sufficiently fierce to run the gauntlet thrown down by insight and permanent change. On account of our neurological wiring, confronting past traumas requires one to reendure all of their terrors mentally, in their original intensity, to feel as if the worst nightmare had come true and the horrors had returned. All the brain's authoritative warnings against staying present for the memories and the painful emotions, all the faulty fuses, have to be deliberately ignored, and in cases of extreme or chronic past trauma, this process is nothing short of heroic.

It helps to have an awfully good reason to try, such as suffocating depression or some other demonic psychological torment. Perhaps this is a part of the reason why philosophers and theologians through the centuries have observed such a strong connection between unbearable earthly sorrow and spiritual enlightenment, a timeless relationship that psychologists have mysteriously overlooked.

In order to appreciate what psychological trauma can do to the mind, and to a life, let us consider an extreme case of divided awareness, that of a woman whose psyche was mangled by profound trauma in her past, and who came to me for treatment after several serious suicide attempts. Her story is far grimmer than any most of us will ever know, and the consequent suffering in her adult life has been nearly unsurvivable. And yet, should one meet her on the street, or know her only casually, she would seem quite normal. In fact, one might easily view her as enviable. Certainly, when looking on from a distance, nothing at all would appear to be wrong, and much would be conspicuously right.

Julia is brilliant. After the *summa cum laude* from Stanford, and the full scholarship at the graduate school in New York, she became an award-winning producer of documentary films. I met her when she was thirty-two, and an intellectual force to be reckoned with. A conversation with her reminds me of the *New York Review of Books,* except that she is funnier, and also a living, breathing human being who wears amethyst jewelry to contrast with her electric auburn hair. Her ultramarine eyes gleam, even when she is depressed, giving one the impression, immediately upon meeting her, that there is something special about her. She is, however, soft-spoken and disarming in the extreme. She does not glorify, does not even seem to notice, either her prodigious intelligence or her beauty.

Those same blue eyes notice everything, instantly, photographically. The first time she walked into my office, she said, "Oh how nice. Did you get that little statue in Haiti? I did a kind of project there once. What a spellbinding place!"

She was referring to a small soapstone figurine, the rounded abstraction of a kneeling man, that I had indeed purchased in Port-au-Prince, and that sat on a shelf parallel to my office door. She had not glanced back in that direction as she came in, and must have captured and processed the image in a microsecond of peripheral perception.

"That's very observant," I said, whereupon she directed at me a smile so sparkling and so warm that, for just the barest moment, her lifelong depression cracked and vanished from the air around her, as if it had been nothing but a bubble. The radiance of her momentary smile caused me to blink, and I knew exactly then, even before the first session began, that if she would let me, I would do everything I could to keep this particular light from going out.

At a moment's notice, Julia can speak entertainingly and at length about film, music, multicultural psychology, African politics, theories of literary criticism, and any number of other subjects. Her memory for detail is beyond exceptional, and she has the storyteller's gift. When she is recounting information, or a story, her own intellectual fascination with it gives her voice the poised and expertly modulated quality of the narrator of a high-budget documentary about some especially wondrous endangered animals, perhaps Tibetan snow leopards. She speaks a few astutely inflected sentences, and then pauses, almost as if she is listening—and expects you to be listening—for the stealthy *crunch-crunch* of paws on the snow's crust.

Curious about this, I once asked her whether she were an actress as well as a filmmaker. She laughed, and replied that she could do first-rate narrative voice-overs, if she did say so herself, but had not a smidgen of real theatrical ability. In fact, she said, sometimes the people she worked with teased her good-naturedly about this minor chink in her armor.

At my first session with her, when I asked her why she had come to therapy, she spent thirty minutes telling me in cinematic detail about her recent attempt to kill herself, by driving to an isolated Massachusetts beach at three A.M. on a Tuesday in late January, and lying down by the surf. By so doing, she sincerely expected not to be found until well after she had frozen to death. Taking her omniscient narrator tone, intellectually intrigued by the memory, she described the circumstances of her unlikely accidental rescue by a group of drunken college students, and then spent the second thirty minutes of our hour together likening this near-death experience to the strangely impersonal distance from story one can achieve on film with certain authorial camera moves.

"By then, I was floating above myself, looking down, sort of waiting. And I know I couldn't actually have seen those kids, but I *felt* that I did. Over the sound of the waves, I don't think you can really *hear* footsteps in the sand, but still . . ."

And I strained to hear the *crunch-crunch.*

Therapy is a frightening thing, and people do not often seek it out because they are only mildly unhappy. In my work, and because of the high-risk individuals who are referred to me, it is not unusual for me to hear stories of attempted suicide from people I have only just met. I have come almost to expect such accounts, in fact.

At our second session, and in exactly the same tone she had used to describe her suicide attempt, Julia began by giving me an interesting account of her new project on the life of a promising writer who had died young, reportedly of a rare blood disease he had contracted in western China. After about fifteen minutes of this, I stopped her, and explained that I wanted to know something about her, about Julia herself, rather than about Julia's work. Seeing the blank expression come over her face, I tried to provide her with some nonthreatening guidance. I asked her some general, factual questions about her childhood.

And at that second session, this is what the articulate, intellectually gifted Julia remembered about her own childhood: An only child, she knew that she had been born in Los Angeles, but she did not know in which hospital. She vaguely remembered that when she was about ten, her parents had moved with her to another neighborhood; but she did not remember anything about the first neighborhood, or even where it was. Though she did not know for sure, she assumed that the move must have taken place because her parents had become more prosperous. She remembered that she had a friend in high school named Barbara (with whom "I must have spent a lot of time"), but she could not remember Barbara's last name, or where Barbara had gone after high school. I asked Julia about her teachers, and she could not remember a single one of them, not from grade school, not from middle school, not from high school. She could not remember whether or not she had gone to her high school prom or her high school graduation. The only thing she seemed to remember vividly from childhood was that when she was about twelve, she had a little terrier dog named Grin, and that her mother had Grin put to sleep when he needed an expensive stomach operation.

And that was all she remembered of her childhood, this successful thirty-two-year-old woman with the cinematic mind. And it took forty-five minutes for her to pull out that much from the dark, silent place that housed her early memories. She could not remember a single holiday or a single birthday. At thirty-two, she could swim, read, drive a car, and play a few songs on the piano. But she could not remember learning any of these skills.

Insufficient memory in the context of an adequate intellect, let alone a gifted one, is the next observation—right after the extraordinary understatement and humor—that causes me to become suspicious about a patient's past.

At our third session, she asked me an astonishing question, but also, really, the obvious question: "Do other people remember those things, about their teachers, and going to their graduation, and learning to drive, and so on?" When I told her that, yes, they usually do remember, at least to a much greater degree than she did, she reverently said, "Wow," and then she was quiet for a few minutes. Finally, she leaned forward a little and asked, "So what's wrong with me?"

Cautiously, because I knew what I had to say might at first sound preposterous or worse to Julia, I said, "I'm wondering about early traumatic experiences in your life. Even when someone's cognitive memory is perfectly good, as yours is, trauma can disrupt the memory in emotional ways."

Julia thought I was way off base; or at least the part of her that collected amethyst jewelry, made award-winning films, and talked about camera angles thought I was way off base. Another part of Julia, the part that kept trying to commit suicide, the part that prevented her from moving back to Los Angeles as her career demanded, the part that sometimes made her so sleepy during the middle of an ordinary day that she had to be driven home, that part kept her coming back to therapy for the next six years. During those six years, step by step, Julia and I cast some light on what had happened to her. She agreed to be hypnotized; she began to remember her dreams; she acknowledged her faint suspicions. She even traveled back to Los Angeles, to talk with distant relatives and old neighbors.

What we eventually discovered was that, when she was a child, Julia had lived in a house of horrors, with monsters jumping out at her without warning and for no apparent reason, except that Julia had come to assume, as abused children do, that she must be a horrible person who deserved these punishments. By the time she was school age, she had learned not to cry, because tears only encouraged her parents to abuse her further. Also, she had lost any inclination whatsoever to let anyone know what was going on. Telling someone and asking for help were concepts foreign to her despairing little soul. The thought that her life might be different had simply stopped occurring to her.

And soon, in a sense, she had stopped telling even herself. When the abuse began, she would "go somewhere else"; she would "not be there." By this, she meant that her mind had learned how to dissociate Julia's self from what was going on around her, how to transport her awareness to a place far enough away that, at most, she felt she was watching the life of a little girl named Julia from a very great distance. A sad little girl named Julia was helpless and could not escape; but psychologically, Julia's self could go "somewhere else," could be psychologically absent.

Simply put, Julia did not remember her childhood because she was not present for it.

All human beings have the capacity to dissociate psychologically, though most of us are unaware of this, and consider "out of body" episodes to be far beyond the boundaries of our normal experience. In fact, dissociative experiences happen to everyone, and most of these events are quite ordinary.

Consider a perfectly ordinary person as he walks into a perfectly ordinary movie theater to see a popular movie. He is awake, alert, and oriented to his surroundings. He is aware that his wife is with him and that, as they sit down in their aisle seats, she is to his right. He is aware that he has a box of popcorn on his lap. He knows that the movie he has come to see is entitled *The Fugitive,* and that its star is Harrison Ford, an actor. As he waits for the movie to begin, perhaps he worries about a problem he is having at work.

Then the lights in the theater are lowered, and the movie starts. And within twenty-five minutes, he has utterly lost his grasp on reality. Not only is he no longer worried about work, he no longer realizes that he has a job. If one could read his thoughts, one would discover that he no longer believes he is sitting in a theater, though in reality, he is. He cannot smell his popcorn; some of it tumbles out of the box he now holds slightly askew, because he has forgotten about his own hands. His wife has vanished, though any observer would see that she is still seated four inches to his right.

And without moving from his own seat, he is running, running, running—not with Harrison Ford, the actor—but with the beleaguered fugitive in the movie, with, in other words, a person who does not exist at all, in this moviegoer's real world or anyone else's. His heart races as he dodges a runaway train that does not exist, either.

This perfectly ordinary man is dissociated from reality. Effectively, he is in a trance. We might label his perceptions as psychotic, except for the fact that when the movie is over, he will return to his usual mental status almost instantly. He will see the credits. He will notice that he has spilled some popcorn, although he will not remember doing so. He will look to his right and speak to his wife. More than likely, he will tell her that he liked the movie, as we all tend to enjoy entertainments in which we can become lost. All that really happened is that, for a little while, he took the part of himself that worries about work problems and other "real" things, and separated it from the imaginative part of himself, so that the imaginative part could have dominance. He *dissociated* one part of his consciousness from another part.

When dissociation is illustrated in this way, most people can acknowledge that they have had such interludes from time to time, at a movie or a play, reading a book or hearing a speech, or even just daydreaming. And then the out-of-body may sound a little closer to home. Plainly stated, it is the case that under certain circumstances, ranging from pleasant or unpleasant distraction to fascination to fear to pain to horror, a human being can be psychologically absent from his or her own direct experience. We can go somewhere else. The part of consciousness that we nearly always conceive of as the "self" can be not there for a few moments, for a few hours, and in heinous circumstances, for much longer.

As the result of a daydream, this mental compartmentalization is called distraction. As the result of an involving movie, it is often called escape. As the result of trauma, physical or psychological, it is called a dissociative state. When a hypnotist induces dissociation, by monotony, distraction, relaxation or any number of other methods, the temporary result is called an hypnotic state, or a trance. The physiological patterns and the primary behavioral results of distraction, escape, dissociative state, and trance are virtually identical, regardless of method. The differences among them seem to result not so much from how consciousness gets divided as from how often and how long one is forced to keep it divided.

Another recognizable example of how consciousness can be split into pieces has to do with the perception of physical pain. On the morning after seeing *The Fugitive*, our moviegoer's wife is working frenetically to pack her briefcase, eat her breakfast, get the kids off to school, and listen to a news report on television, all at the same time. She is very distracted. In the process of all this, she bashes her leg soundly against the corner of a low shelf. Yet the woman is not seemingly aware that she has injured herself. That night, as she is getting ready for bed, she notices that she has a large colorful bruise on her right thigh. She thinks, "Well, now, I wonder how I did that."

In this case, a person was distracted, and the part of her consciousness that would normally have perceived pain was split apart from, and subjugated to, the part of her consciousness that was goal-directed. She was not there for the direct experience of her pain. She was somewhere else (the briefcase, the breakfast, the kids, the news). And because she was not there, she does not remember the accident.

The direct experience of physical pain can be split off in cases of much more serious injury as well. Most of us have heard stories along the lines of the parent who, with a broken leg, goes back to the scene of an accident and wrenches open a mangled car door with her bare hands in order to rescue her child. Less valorous, I myself remember my car being demolished by a speeding limousine. My knee was injured, but I felt no pain just after the crash, was more or less unaware of my body at all. My first thought before being dragged out of my car was to peer into the rearview mirror and inspect my teeth, and to decide that everything must be okay because there were no chips in them. And then there are the war stories about maimed infantrymen who have had to flee from the front line. All such circumstances affect memory in fascinating ways. Note, for example, that when veterans get together, they often laugh and tell war stories as though those times had been the best of their lives.

Agony that is psychological can be dissociated, too. While she was being abused, Julia developed the reaction of standing apart from herself and her situation. She stopped being there. Certainly, some parts of her consciousness must have been there right along. She could watch her parents, even predict their moods. She could run and hide. She could cover her injuries. She could keep her parents' secrets. But the part of her consciousness that she thinks of as her self was not there; it was split off, put aside, and therefore in some sense protected. And because her self had not been there, her self could not remember what had happened to her during much of her childhood.

What does this feel like, not being able to remember whole chapters of one's own life? I have asked many people this question, Julia among them. As usual, her answer was obvious and startling at the same time.

"It doesn't feel like anything," she answered. "I never really thought about it. I guess I just assumed, sort of tacitly assumed, that everyone's memory was like mine, that is to say, kind of blank before the age of twenty or so. I mean, you can't see into someone else's mind, right? All you can do is ask questions, and it never even occurred to me to ask anybody about this. It's like asking, 'What do you see when you see blue?' First of all, you'd never think to ask. And secondly, two people can agree that the clear blue sky is blue, but does the actual color blue look the *same* to both of them? Who knows? How would you even ask that question?

"Of course, every now and then I'd hear people talking about pin-the-tail-on-the-donkey, or some other thing about a little kid's birthday, and I'd wonder how they knew that. But I guess I just figured their memory was especially good, or maybe they'd heard their parents talk about it so much that it seemed like a memory.

"The memories I did have seemed like aberrations, like pinpoints of light in a dark room, so vague that you're not really sure whether you're seeing them or not. Certainly, there was nothing like a continuous thread of memory that linked one part of my life to another.

"Really it wasn't until you started asking me questions about my teachers and so forth that I ever even had any serious questions about my memory. After you started asking, I asked a couple of other people, just out of curiosity, and I began to realize that other people really do have childhood memories, and some of them are pretty vivid. I was surprised.

"What can I tell you? It just never occurred to me to wonder about it before. It felt like . . . it felt like nothing."

She shrugged. Most people shrug. They are genuinely surprised, and at a loss.

Now the conspicuous question to ask Julia was, "All this time that you've been so unhappy, all the times you've tried to end your life, what did you think was causing all that misery?"

"I thought I was crazy," she answered.

This is easy enough to understand. Imagine a simple and, relatively speaking, innocuous example. Imagine that someone, call her Alice, leaves work early one day and goes to the oral surgeon to have her two bottom wisdom teeth extracted. The extractions go well; the doctor packs the gums with cotton and sends Alice home. On the way home, for some fictitious reason, let us say magic moonbeams, Alice completely loses her memory of the visit to the oral surgeon. She now assumes that she is driving directly home from work, as she does on most days. After she gets home, she is okay for a while, but gradually the anesthetic wears off, and she begins to experience a considerable amount of pain in her mouth. Soon the pain is too strong to ignore, and she goes to the bathroom mirror to examine the situation. When she looks into her mouth, she discovers that there are wads of cotton in there. And when she takes the cotton out, she discovers that two of her teeth are missing, and she is bleeding!

Alice is now in the twilight zone. The ordinary experience of having her wisdom teeth pulled has turned into a situation that makes her feel insane. One or two more of such experiences, and she would be convinced.

Childhood trauma creates a particularly bewildering picture. Observe normal children at play, and you will realize that children are especially good at dissociating. In the interest of play, a child can, in a heartbeat, leave himself behind, become someone or something else, or several things at once. Reality is even more plastic in childhood. Pretend games are real and wonderful and consuming. It is clear to anyone who really looks that normal children derive unending joy from their superior ability to leap out of their "selves" and go somewhere else, be other things. The snow is not cold. The body is not tired, even when it is on the verge of collapse.

Because children dissociate readily even in ordinary circumstances, when they encounter traumatic situations, they easily split their consciousness into pieces, often for extended periods of time. The self is put aside and hidden. Of course, this reaction is functional for the traumatized child, necessary, even kind. For the traumatized child, a dissociative state, far from being dysfunctional or crazy, may in fact be lifesaving. And thanks be to the normal human mind that it provides the means.

This coping strategy becomes dysfunctional only later, after the child is grown and away from the original trauma. When the original trauma is no longer an ongoing fact of life, prolonged dissociative reactions are no longer necessary. But through the years of intensive use, the self-protective strategy has developed a hair trigger. The adult whom the child has become now experiences dissociative reactions to levels of stress that probably would not cause another person to dissociate.

The events that are most problematic tend to be related in some way to the original trauma. However, human beings are exquisitely symbolic creatures, and "related" can reach unpredictable and often indecipherable levels of abstraction and metaphor. A long shadow from a city streetlight can remind someone of the tall cacti on the Arizona desert where his father used to threaten to "feed" him to the rattlesnakes. An innocent song about the wind in the willow trees can remind someone else of the rice fields that were a part of her childhood's landscape in Cambodia. A car backfiring on Beacon Street in Boston can remind yet another person of that spot on the trail where his eighteen-year-old platoon mate exploded six feet in front of him.

And so for the adult who was traumatized as a child, the present too has a kind of mercurial quality. The present is difficult to hold on to, always getting away.

In Julia's case, though she had not questioned her poverty of memory for the past, she had begun to suspect even before she came into therapy that she was losing time in the present. Probably this is because there are more external reality checks on the present than there are on the past. From other people—and from radio, television, the Internet, date books—there are ongoing reminders of the present time of day, and day of the week. Markers of time in the past are less immediate, and sooner or later most dates and chronologies for the past begin to feel amorphous to us all. It is hardly amazing that one should have forgotten something that happened twenty years ago. But if a person lets on that she has no memory of an important event that occurred this very week, friends and associates are unlikely to let such a lapse go unremarked.

At one of her early sessions with me, Julia announced, "When I woke up Tuesday morning it was Friday."

"Pardon?"

"When I woke up this morning it was Tuesday, and then I discovered that it was Friday for everybody else."

"How do you mean?"

"Well, the last thing I remember before waking up this morning was having dinner Monday night. So I thought it was Tuesday. And then I went in to work, and some sponsors were there that I was supposed to meet with on Friday. So I asked my assistant what was up, and she said, 'You wanted to meet with these people this morning, remember?' And I said, 'No. I wanted to meet with them on Friday.' She looked at me, and said, 'Today is Friday, Julia.'

"I finessed. I laughed and said, 'Of course. That's terrible. No more late nights for me. Pretty soon I'll be forgetting my name. Ha, ha.' But it isn't funny. This happens a lot. I just lose time. Hours, days. They're gone, and I don't know what I've done or where I've been or anything else.

"I've never told anyone this before. It's embarrassing. Actually, it's terrifying.

"I don't understand any of it, but the thing I understand the least is that apparently I go about my business during these times, and nobody notices any difference in me. At least, no one ever says anything. After the meeting this morning, I realized that on Tuesday, Wednesday, and Thursday, I must have done a mountain of editing. There it was, all finished. I did a good job, even. And I don't remember a bloody thing."

During this confession, I saw Julia cry for the first time. Quickly, though, she willed her tears under control, and wanted me to tell her about a word she had heard me use the previous week, "dissociative." She questioned me as if the issue were a strictly academic one for her, which it clearly was not. I gently steered her back to the subject of herself and her week.

"Where did you have dinner Monday night?"

"What? Oh. Dinner Monday night. I had dinner at the Grill 23 with my friend Elaine."

"Was it a nice time?" I continued to question.

"I think so. Yes, I think it was okay."

"What did you and Elaine talk about, do you remember?"

"What did we talk about? Let's see. Well, I think we talked about the film a bit. And we talked about the waiter. Very cute waiter." She grinned. "And we probably spent the longest time talking about Elaine's relationship with this new guy, Peter. Why do you ask?"

"You said the dinner was the last thing you remembered before you woke up this morning. I thought it might be important. What did Elaine say about Peter?"

"Well, she said she's madly in love, and she said she wanted me to meet him because she thought we'd have a lot to talk about. He's from L.A., too."

"You and Peter are both from L.A. What else did you and Elaine say about L.A.?"

Julia looked suddenly blank, and said, "I don't remember. Why? Do you really think something about the place where I grew up scares me enough that just talking about it blasts me into never-never land for three days? That really can't be, though. I mean, I talk about L.A. a lot to people."

"I think it's possible that something during the dinner scared you enough to make you lose yourself for a while, although we'll never know for sure. Obviously, talking about L.A. doesn't always do that, but maybe there was something in that particular conversation that reminded you of something else that triggered something in your mind, something that might seem innocuous to another person, or even to you at another time. But as I say, we'll never know for sure."

"That's frightening. That's awful. It's like I'm in jail in my own head. I don't think I can live this way anymore."

"Yes, it's very frightening. I suspect it's been very frightening for a long time."

"You got that right."

Julia's knowledge of her own life, both past and present, had assumed the airy structure of Swiss cheese, with some solid substance that she and her gifted intellect could use, but riddled with unexplained gaps and hollows. This had its funny side. A few months later, when she had gained a better acceptance of her problem, she came in, sat down, and said in a characteristically charming way, "How do you like my new bracelet?"

"It's beautiful," I replied. "I've always admired your amethyst jewelry. When did you get that piece?"

"Who knows?"

She grinned at me again, and we both laughed.

The somewhat old-fashioned term for Julia's departures from herself during which she would continue to carry out day-to-day activities is "fugue," from the Italian word *fuga,* meaning "flight." A dissociative state that reaches the point of fugue is one of the most dramatic spontaneously occurring examples of the human mind's ability to divide consciousness into parts. In fugue, the person, or the mind of the person, can be subdivided in a manner that allows certain intellectually driven functions to continue—rising at a certain time, conversing with others, following a schedule, even carrying out complex tasks—while the part of consciousness that we usually experience as the "self"—the self-aware center that wishes, dreams, plans, emotes, and remembers—has taken flight, or has perhaps just darkened like a room at night when someone is sleeping.

The departures of fugue are related to certain experiences in ordinary human life that are not generated by trauma. For example, similar is the common experience of the daily commuter by car who realizes that sometimes she or he arrives back at home in the evening without having been aware of the activities of driving. The driving was automatically carried out

by some part of the mind, while the self part of the mind wa
dreaming, or listening to the radio. The experience is th
home without remembering the process of the trip. If one
minute and complex decisions and maneuvers involved in
ordinary event is really quite remarkable.

Clinical fugue differs from common human experience not so mu
kind as in degree. Fugue is terror-driven and complete, while the more recognizable condition is the result of distraction, and relatively transparent.
As fugue, the car trip example would involve a driver who failed to remember not just the process of the trip, but also the fact that there had been a trip,
and from where. Far beyond distraction, the more remarkable dissociative
reaction of fugue would have been set off by something—an event, a conversation, an image, a thought—that was related, though perhaps in some
oblique and symbolic way, to trauma.

Not all traumatized individuals exhibit outright fugue. For some people, stressful events trigger a demifugue that is less dramatic but in some
ways more agonizing. Another of my patients, Lila, refers to her experience
as "my flyaway self":

"I had an argument with the cashier at the Seven-Eleven store. I gave
him a twenty and he said I gave him a ten. He wouldn't give me my other
ten dollars back. The way he looked at me—it was just the way my stepfather used to, like I was stupid, like I was dirt. I knew he wasn't really my
stepfather, but all the feelings were there anyway. After a minute, I just
couldn't argue about it. I left without my money, and by the time I got back
home, my flyaway self thing had started. Once it starts, it's like there's absolutely nothing I can do about it. I'm gone, and there's nothing I can do
about it."

"What does it feel like?"

"Oh boy. I don't know how to describe it. It's just . . . it's just really
awful. I don't know . . . everything around me gets very small, kind of unreal, you know? It's my flyaway self, I call it. It feels like . . . my spirit just
kind of flies away, and everything else gets very small—people, everything.
If it were happening now, for example, you would look very small and far
away, and the room would feel kind of unreal. Sometimes even my own
body gets small and unreal. It's awful. And when it happens, I can't stop it. I
just can't stop it."

What Lila describes as her "flyaway self" is in some respects similar to
the derealization that most people have known occasionally, usually under
passing conditions of sleep deprivation or physical illness. One temporarily
has the sense of looking at the world through the wrong end of a telescope:
everything looks small and far away, though one knows intellectually that
these same things are just as close and life-sized as ever.

Imagine being forced to live lengthy segments of your life in this state.
Imagine that you were falling inexorably into it, to remain there for a week

more at a time, because of events such as an unpleasant argument with a stranger at a convenience store. As bad as this would be, the situation for someone like Lila is incalculably worse, because for her the phenomenon has its origins in trauma.

Another of my patients offered a specific image, and for me an indelible one, to describe the same dissociative condition. Forty-nine-year-old Seth, like Julia, is successful, educated, and visually talented, and his disquieting description reflects his aptitudes. At the beginning of this particular therapy session, he had been telling me about a startling encounter, at a company softball game, with another person lost in the dissociated space with which he himself was all too familiar.

"I knew exactly where she was," said Seth.

"What does it feel like?" I asked. "Can you tell me what it feels like when you're there? How do you change?"

"I don't change. It's not that I change. *Reality* changes. Everything becomes very small, and I exist entirely inside my mind. Even my own body isn't real."

Indicating the two of us and the room around us, he continued, "Right now, this is what's real. You're real. What we're saying is real. But when I'm like that, the office is not real. *You're* not real anymore."

"What is real at those times?" I asked.

"I don't know exactly. It's hard to explain. Only what's going on in my mind is real. I'll tell you what it feels like: I feel like I'm dog-paddling out in the ocean, moving backwards, out to sea. When I'm still close enough to the land, I can sort of look way far away and see the beach. You and the rest of the world are all on the beach somewhere. But I keep drifting backwards, and the beach gets smaller, and the ocean gets bigger and bigger, and when I've drifted out far enough, the beach disappears, and all I can see all around me is the sea. It's so gray—gray on gray on gray."

"Is there anything out in the ocean with you?" I asked.

Seth replied, "No. Not at that point. I'm completely alone, more alone than you can imagine. But if you drift out farther, if you go all the way out to where the bottom of the sea drops off to the real abyss part, then there are awful things, these bloodthirsty sea creatures, sharks and giant eels and things like that. I've always thought that if something in the real world scared me enough, I'd drift out and out to past the dropping-off part, and then I would just be gobbled up, gone—no coming back, ever.

"When I'm floating out in the middle of the sea, everything else is very far away, even time. Time becomes unreal, in a way. An hour could go by that seems like a day to me, or four or five hours could go by, and it seems like only a minute."

Some extreme trauma survivors recognize that they are dissociative, and others do not recognize this. Many times, an individual will realize at some point in adulthood that she or he has had a lifelong pattern of being "away" a grievously large portion of the time.

During the same session, Seth described his own situation in this way:

"Actually, when I was a child, I don't know how much time I spent away like that. I never thought about it. It was probably a lot of the time, maybe even all the time. It just *was.*"

"You mean it was your reality, and so of course you never questioned it, any more than any other child questions his reality?"

"Right. That's right. That was when I was a child. And most of the time it still happens automatically, bang, way before I know it's coming; but in here now, sometimes, there's this brief moment when I know I'm about to go away, but I still have time to try to keep it from taking over. Emphasis on *try.*"

"How do you do that?" I asked.

"By concentrating. By trying with everything I've got to concentrate on you, and what you're saying, and on the things around me in the office here. But then there's physical pain, too. My eyes hurt, and I know I could make myself feel better if I shut them. But I try not to. And I get this thing in my stomach, which is the hardest thing to fight. There's this pain that feels like I just swallowed a whole pile of burning coals, this torture feeling that beams out from my stomach to the rest of my body; sooner or later, it just takes me over."

He grimaced and put a fist to his breastbone.

When Seth said this about pain in his stomach, I remembered, as I had remembered during descriptions by many, many others, that there is a common Japanese term, *shin pan,* inexactly translated as "agitated heart syndrome," referring to a great pain between the chest and the stomach, just under the solar plexus. *Shin pan,* a condition as real within Eastern medicine as is cataract or ulcer or fractured fibula within Western medicine, is a pain of the heart that does not involve the actual physical organ. In our culture, we consider such a thing—a "heartache," if you will—to be poetry at most. We do not understand that much of the rest of the world considers it to be quite real.

I said to Seth, "It must be frightening to be out in the ocean like that."

"Actually, it's not," he replied. "The abyss part, with the sharks and all, that's frightening. But for most of my life it was really no more frightening than the things that were on the beach, no more frightening than reality, I guess is what I'm saying. So floating in the middle of the ocean was really the best place, even though I guess that sounds strange. Also, being there takes care of the physical pain; there's no more pain when I'm there. It's just that now, I mean lately, the beach, where you are, and everything else, sometimes it makes me wish I could maybe be there instead. I guess you could say that now, at least sometimes, I want to live."

I smiled at him, but he looked away, unsure of what he had just proposed.

Referring back to Seth's softball team acquaintance, whose dissociative episode had begun our discussion, I said, "It must be strange to be with another person when you know she's drifting away in an ocean just like you do sometimes."

"Yes, it's very strange."

"How did you know she was drifting? Did she tell you?"

"No. She didn't tell me. She didn't say anything at all about being dissociated. She was just standing around with us, talking about these incredible things, horrible things from her past, without any emotion, without any reaction to them. She played well that day, actually, but she won't remember any of it, that's for sure."

"You mean," I asked, "another person, besides you, might not have known she was dissociated?"

"Absolutely. I'm sure someone else might not have known at all. It's just that I looked at her, and I saw me. It was like talking to somebody who didn't have a soul."

"You mean her soul was somewhere else?"

"Yes, I guess so. Her soul was somewhere else," Seth said.

After a brief silence, he turned the discussion back to his own life: "The other day, my wife was trying to talk to me about something really important that happened when the twins were born. Doesn't matter what it was; what matters is that I had no idea what she was talking about. I didn't have a clue. It wasn't a dim memory. It wasn't anything. I didn't have that memory because I wasn't there."

"You weren't there, but your wife didn't know that at the time?" I asked.

"No, she didn't know that at all. But you know, most of the time when she and I are making love, and I'm not there, she doesn't know it even then."

"You mean, someone can be that close to you, and still not know?"

"Yes."

At that moment I thought, and then decided to say aloud, "That's so sad."

A single tear skimmed down Seth's cheek. He wiped it quickly with the back of his hand, and said, "I'm sorry, it's just that, well, when I think about it, I realize that, really, I've missed most of my own life."

He stopped and took a deep breath, and I wondered whether he might have to dissociate just to get through this experience in my office.

I asked, "Are you here now, at this moment?"

"Yes, I think so. Yes."

There was another pause, and then with more emotion in his voice than he was usually able to show, he said, "It's so hard, because so much of the time when I'm here, what you're seeing is not what I'm seeing. I feel like such an impostor. I'm out in my ocean, and you don't know that. And I can't tell you what's going on. Sometimes I'd really like to tell you, but I can't. I'm gone."

Seth's description of his inner life makes it wrenchingly clear that the traumatized person is unable to feel completely connected to another person, even a friend, even a spouse. Just as limiting, perhaps even more limiting, is such a person's disconnection from his or her own body. You will recall that Lila's "flyaway self" owned a body that was only "small and unreal," and that when Seth was in his ocean, his mind was separated from his physical self. I began this chapter with Julia, the brilliant producer of documentary films, and as it happens, about a year into her treatment, an event occurred that well illustrates the survivor's trauma-generated dissociation from the body itself, or more accurately, from those aspects of mind that inform one of what is going on in the body.

One morning just after the workday began, Julia's assistant, a gentle young woman who was quite fond of her boss, noticed that Julia was look-ing extremely pale. She asked how Julia was feeling, and Julia replied that she thought her stomach was a little upset, but other than that she was sure she was fine. Ten minutes later, walking down a corridor, Julia fell to the floor, and by the time the panic-stricken assistant came to her aid, she was unconscious. An ambulance arrived and rushed Julia to the Massachusetts General Hospital, where she underwent an immediate emergency appen-dectomy. Her life was in danger, and the situation was touch-and-go for a while, because her infected appendix had already ruptured and severe peri-tonitis had resulted. She survived, however, and during her recovery, when she was well enough to see me again, she recounted a postsurgery conver-sation with her doctor.

"The doctor kept asking me, 'Didn't you feel anything? Weren't you in pain?' I told her my stomach had been upset that morning, but I didn't re-member any real pain. She said, 'Why didn't you call me?' I guess she just couldn't believe that I really hadn't felt any pain. She said that I should have been in agony by the previous night, at the very latest. She kept saying 'agony.' But I didn't feel it. I swear to you I didn't feel any pain, much less agony."

"I believe you," I said to Julia.

"Well, I don't think she did. I guess a ruptured appendix involves a lot of pain for most people."

"Yes. Yes it does," I replied, trying to disguise some of my own astonish-ment.

"I know I've tried to kill myself intentionally, more than once, so maybe this sounds crazy—but I don't want to die one day just because I'm confused."

"What do you mean?" I asked.

"I don't want to die because I can't feel anything. I don't want to end up dead because I can't feel what's going on in my body, or because I can't tell the difference between that psychosomatic pain I'm always getting in my chest and some honest-to-God heart attack."

Julia said "psychosomatic," but I was thinking *shin pan*, again.

"You know how we talk about my tendency to be dissociative? Well do you think I dissociate from my body too? Because if that's what I'm doing, then it's the illusion from hell. I mean, if it's supposed to save me, it's not working. In fact, it's going to kill me one day. And even if it doesn't kill me, what's the use of living if I can't feel anything? Why should I be alive when I lose big parts of my life? I mean, really, how can you care about anything if you can't even know the truth about yourself? If you keep losing yourself?"

I said, "I think that's one of the best questions I've ever heard."

"You do? You mean you agree with me about how I can't really care about living if I keep losing myself?"

"I said that's one of the best *questions*. I didn't say I knew the answer."

"Oh boy, you're cagey," she said, and grinned. "So okay, how do I find the answer?"

"Well you know, you could try to remember. We could try hypnosis, for one thing."

I believed that Julia might be ready to bring up the lights in the cold, dark house of her past.

"Yes, so you've said. And the idea scares the hell out of me." There was a substantial pause before she continued. "The idea scares the hell out of me, but I think I have to do it anyway."

"Why do you have to?"

"Because I want to know. Because I want to live."

"So, let's do it?" I asked.

"Let's do it," Julia said.   ■

■ QUESTIONS FOR MAKING CONNECTIONS WITHIN THE READING ■

1. Drawing on the information Stout provides, discuss the relations between the mind—in particular the memory—and the brain. Why are traumatic memories generally inaccessible? When Stout refers to "our divided awareness," what does she mean? Is it possible for awareness to become undivided? If such a state can be achieved at all, can it ever become permanent, or is "dividedness" an inescapable feature of consciousness itself?

2. Explain the difference between dissociation and ordinary distraction. What is it about Julia's lapses of memory that qualifies them as examples of dissociation? Are there significant differences between Julia's lapses and Seth's? Has Seth devised ways of coping that have proven more successful than Julia's?

3. In her discussion of Seth, Stout makes a reference to the condition known as *shin pan*, a term taken from Asian medicine. Does this reference bring something new to our understanding that the term "heartache" does not? Is Stout just showing off her knowledge of Eastern culture, or is she trying to get us to rethink our own attitudes about the importance of emotions?

■ *QUESTIONS FOR WRITING* ■

1. The title of Stout's book is *The Myth of Sanity: Divided Consciousness and the Promise of Awareness.* Now that you have read one chapter from her book, why do you think she refers to sanity as a "myth"? What does she mean by "the promise of awareness"? How might "awareness" differ from "sanity"?

2. Julia and Seth both qualify as extreme cases of dissociation, but their experiences may also shed some light on ordinary consciousness. Taking Stout's essay as your starting point, and drawing also on your own experience, discuss the nature of consciousness. Does the mind operate like a camcorder, or is awareness more complex and less continuous than the images stored in a camcorder's memory?

3. Can people ever know reality, or are we trapped within our own mental worlds? If memory shapes our perceptions from moment to moment, then would you say that experience can ever teach us anything new? If memory is unreliable, then what are the implications for self-knowledge? Is the ancient adage "Know Thyself" actually an invitation to wishful thinking?

■ *QUESTIONS FOR MAKING CONNECTIONS BETWEEN READINGS* ■

1. Could our contemporary relation to the natural world be described as dissociated? Is it possible that an entire society can suffer from dissociation? Has David Abram described a society that is, in Stout's sense of the term, *dissociated* from sensuous experience? Are the steps Abram prescribes for restoring our connections to the natural environment comparable to the kind of therapeutic program Stout supports for improving the lives of her patients? Can a society become "healthy," or is this a project that only individuals can embark on?

2. In what ways does Oliver Sacks's discussion in "The Mind's Eye" confirm, complicate, or contradict Stout's claims about trauma and its consequences? Although Sacks is concerned with adaptations to blindness and not emotional trauma, both authors explore the ways the mind compensates for losses and injuries of one kind or another. Are Julia and Seth in some ways comparable to the blind men and women Sacks describes?

www **For additional suggestions about making connections between readings, visit the Link-O-Mat and More Sample Assignments at <www.newhum.com>.**

DEBORAH TANNEN

DEBORAH TANNEN BECAME interested in cross-cultural communication after she graduated from college in 1966 and taught English in Greece for two years. After earning a master's degree in English from Wayne State University and teaching writing in the United States for a few years, Tannen decided to pursue a doctorate in linguistics at Berkeley. It was just Tannen's luck that the first linguistics institute she attended focused on language in a social context. "Had I gone another summer," Tannen has said, "it's quite likely I would have concluded linguistics was not for me."

Tannen is currently University Professor on the faculty of the linguistics department at Georgetown University. Tannen, who has published sixteen books and more than eighty-five articles and is the recipient of four honorary doctorates, is best known as the author of *You Just Don't Understand: Women and Men in Conversation* (1991), which is credited with bringing gender differences in communication style to the forefront of public awareness. This book was on the *New York Times Bestsellers* list for nearly four years, including eight months as number one, and has been translated into twenty-five languages.

"The Roots of Debate in Education and the Hope of Dialogue" is drawn from one of Tannen's most recent books, *The Argument Culture* (1998), which examines the social, political, and emotional consequences of treating discussions as battles to be won or lost. Tannen's goal in this work is to get her readers to notice "the power of words to frame how you think about things, how you feel about things, how you perceive the world. The tendency in our culture to use war metaphors so pervasively, and to frame everything as a metaphorical battle, influences how we approach each other in our everyday lives."

www **To learn more about Deborah Tannen and styles of argumentation, visit the Link-O-Mat at <www.newhum.com>.**

Tannen, Deborah. "The Roots of Debate in Education and the Hope of Dialogue." *The Argument Culture: Moving from Debate to Dialogue.* New York: Random House, 1998. 256–290.

Biographical information from Deborah Tannen's home page <http://www.georgetown.edu/tannen/> on the Georgetown University Web site; quotation Deborah Tannen, interview by Michael Toms <http://www.newdimensions.org/article/tannen.html>. "Agreeing to Disagree: The Culture of Argument in America." *New Dimensions World Broadcasting Network.*

The Roots of Debate in Education and the Hope of Dialogue

The teacher sits at the head of the classroom, feeling pleased with herself and her class. The students are engaged in a heated debate. The very noise level reassures the teacher that the students are participating, taking responsibility for their own learning. Education is going on. The class is a success.

But look again, cautions Patricia Rosof, a high school history teacher who admits to having experienced that wave of satisfaction with herself and the job she is doing. On closer inspection, you notice that only a few students are participating in the debate; the majority of the class is sitting silently, maybe attentive but perhaps either indifferent or actively turned off. And the students who are arguing are not addressing the subtleties, nuances, or complexities of the points they are making or disputing. They do not have that luxury because they want to win the argument—so they must go for the most gross and dramatic statements they can muster. They will not concede an opponent's point, even if they can see its validity, because that would weaken their position. Anyone tempted to synthesize the varying views would not dare to do so because it would look like a "cop-out," an inability to take a stand.

One reason so many teachers use the debate format to promote student involvement is that it is relatively easy to set up and the rewards are quick and obvious: the decibel level of noise, the excitement of those who are taking part. Showing students how to integrate ideas and explore subtleties and complexities is much harder. And the rewards are quieter—but more lasting.

Our schools and universities, our ways of doing science and approaching knowledge, are deeply agonistic. We all pass through our country's educational system, and it is there that the seeds of our adversarial culture are planted. Seeing how these seeds develop, and where they came from, is a key to understanding the argument culture and a necessary foundation for determining what changes we would like to make.

Roots of the Adversarial Approach to Knowledge

The argument culture, with its tendency to approach issues as a polarized debate, and the culture of critique, with its inclination to regard criticism and attack as the best if not the only type of rigorous thinking, are deeply rooted in Western tradition, going back to the ancient Greeks.[1] This point is made by Walter Ong, a Jesuit professor at Saint Louis University, in his book

Fighting for Life. Ong credits the ancient Greeks[2] with a fascination with adversativeness in language and thought. He also connects the adversarial tradition of educational institutions to their all-male character. To attend the earliest universities, in the Middle Ages, young men were torn from their families and deposited in cloistered environments where corporal, even brutal, punishment was rampant. Their suffering drove them to bond with each other in opposition to their keepers—the teachers who were their symbolic enemies. Similar in many ways to puberty rites in traditional cultures, this secret society to which young men were confined also had a private language, Latin, in which students read about military exploits. Knowledge was gleaned through public oral disputation and tested by combative oral performance, which carried with it the risk of public humiliation. Students at these institutions were trained not to discover the truth but to argue either side of an argument—in other words, to debate. Ong points out that the Latin term for school, *ludus,* also referred to play or games, but it derived from the military sense of the word—training exercises for war.

If debate seems self-evidently the appropriate or even the only path to insight and knowledge, says Ong, consider the Chinese approach. Disputation was rejected in ancient China as "incompatible with the decorum and harmony cultivated by the true sage."[3] During the Classical periods in both China and India, according to Robert T. Oliver, the preferred mode of rhetoric was exposition rather than argument. The aim was to "enlighten an inquirer," not to "overwhelm an opponent." And the preferred style reflected "the earnestness of investigation" rather than "the fervor of conviction." In contrast to Aristotle's trust of logic and mistrust of emotion, in ancient Asia intuitive insight was considered the superior means of perceiving truth. Asian rhetoric was devoted not to devising logical arguments but to explicating widely accepted propositions. Furthermore, the search for abstract truth that we assume is the goal of philosophy, while taken for granted in the West, was not found in the East, where philosophy was concerned with observation and experience.

If Aristotelian philosophy, with its emphasis on formal logic, was based on the assumption that truth is gained by opposition, Chinese philosophy offers an alternative view. With its emphasis on harmony, says anthropologist Linda Young, Chinese philosophy sees a diverse universe in precarious balance that is maintained by talk. This translates into methods of investigation that focus more on integrating ideas and exploring relations among them than on opposing ideas and fighting over them.

Onward, Christian Soldiers

The military-like culture of early universities is also described by historian David Noble, who describes how young men attending medieval universities were like marauding soldiers: The students—all seminarians—roamed the streets bearing arms, assaulting women, and generally creating mayhem. Noble traces the history of Western science and of universities to joint origins in the Christian Church. The scientific revolution, he shows, was created by religious devotees setting up monastery-like institutions devoted to learning. Early universities were seminaries, and early scientists were either clergy or devoutly religious individuals who led monklike lives. (Until as recently as 1888, fellows at Oxford were expected to be unmarried.)

That Western science is rooted in the Christian Church helps explain why our approach to knowledge tends to be conceived as a metaphorical battle: The Christian Church, Noble shows, has origins and early forms rooted in the military. Many early monks[4] had actually been soldiers before becoming monks. Not only were obedience and strict military-like discipline required, but monks saw themselves as serving "in God's knighthood," warriors in a battle against evil. In later centuries, the Crusades brought actual warrior-monks.

The history of science in the Church holds the key to understanding our tradition of regarding the search for truth as an enterprise of oral disputation in which positions are propounded, defended, and attacked without regard to the debater's personal conviction. It is a notion of truth as objective, best captured by formal logic, that Ong traces to Aristotle. Aristotle regarded logic as the only trustworthy means for human judgment; emotions get in the way: "The man who is to judge would not have his judgment warped by speakers arousing him to anger, jealousy, or compassion. One might as well make a carpenter's tool crooked before using it as a measure."[5]

This assumption explains why Plato wanted to ban poets from education in his ideal community. As a lover of poetry, I can still recall my surprise and distress on reading this in *The Republic* when I was in high school. Not until much later did I understand what it was all about.[6] Poets in ancient Greece were wandering bards who traveled from place to place performing oral poetry that persuaded audiences by moving them emotionally. They were like what we think of as demagogues: people with a dangerous power to persuade others by getting them all worked up. Ong likens this to our discomfort with advertising in schools, which we see as places where children should learn to think logically, not be influenced by "teachers" with ulterior motives who use unfair persuasive tactics.

Sharing Time: Early Training in School

A commitment to formal logic as the truest form of intellectual pursuit remains with us today. Our glorification of opposition as the path to truth is related to the development of formal logic, which encourages thinkers to regard truth seeking as a step-by-step alternation of claims and counterclaims.[7] Truth, in this schema, is an abstract notion that tends to be taken out of context. This formal approach to learning is taught in our schools, often indirectly.

Educational researcher James Wertsch shows that schools place great emphasis on formal representation of knowledge. The common elementary school practice of "sharing time" (or, as it used to be called, "show-and-tell") is a prime arena for such training. Wertsch gives the example of a kindergarten pupil named Danny who took a piece of lava to class.[8] Danny told his classmates, "My mom went to the volcano and got it." When the teacher asked what he wanted to tell about it, he said, "I've always been taking care of it." This placed the rock at the center of his feelings and his family: the rock's connection to his mother, who gave it to him, and the attention and care he has lavished on it. The teacher reframed the children's interest in the rock as informational: "Is it rough or smooth?" "Is it heavy or light?" She also suggested they look up "volcano" and "lava" in the dictionary. This is not to imply that the teacher harmed the child; she built on his personal attachment to the rock to teach him a new way of thinking about it. But the example shows the focus of education on formal rather than relational knowledge—information about the rock that has meaning out of context, rather than information tied to the context: Who got the rock for him? How did she get it? What is his relation to it?

Here's another example of how a teacher uses sharing time to train children to speak and think formally. Sarah Michaels spent time watching and tape-recording in a first-grade classroom. During sharing time, a little girl named Mindy held up two candles and told her classmates, "When I was in day camp we made these candles. And I tried it with different colors with both of them but one just came out, this one just came out blue and I don't know what this color is." The teacher responded, "That's neat-o. Tell the kids how you do it from the very start. Pretend we don't know a thing about candles. OK, what did you do first? What did you use?" She continued to prompt: "What makes it have a shape?" and "Who knows what the string is for?" By encouraging Mindy to give information in a sequential manner, even if it might not seem the most important to her and if the children might already know some of it, the teacher was training her to talk in a focused, explicit way.

The tendency to value formal, objective knowledge over relational, intuitive knowledge grows out of our notion of education as training for debate. It is a legacy of the agonistic heritage. There are many other traces as well. Many Ph.D. programs still require public "defenses" of dissertations or dissertation proposals, and oral performance of knowledge in comprehensive exams. Throughout our educational system, the most pervasive inheritance is the conviction that issues have two sides, that knowledge is best gained through debate, that ideas should be presented orally to an audience that does its best to poke holes and find weaknesses, and that to get recognition, one has to "stake out a position" in opposition to another.

Integrating Women in the Classroom Army

If Ong is right, the adversarial character of our educational institutions is inseparable from their all-male heritage. I wondered whether teaching techniques still tend to be adversarial today and whether, if they are, this may hold a clue to a dilemma that has received much recent attention: that girls often receive less attention and speak up less in class.[9] One term I taught a large lecture class of 140 students and decided to take advantage of this army (as it were) of researchers to answer these questions. Becoming observers in their own classrooms, my students found plenty of support for Ong's ideas.

I asked the students to note how relatively adversarial the teaching methods were in their other classes and how the students responded. Gabrielle DeRouen-Hawkins's description of a theology class was typical:

> The class is in the format of lecture with class discussion and participation. There are thirteen boys and eleven girls in the class. In a fifty-minute class:
> Number of times a male student spoke: 8
> Number of times a female student spoke: 3
> . . . In our readings, theologians present their theories surrounding G-D, life, spirituality and sacredness. As the professor (a male) outlined the main ideas about the readings, he posed questions like "And what is the fault with /Smith's/ basis that the sacred is individualistic?" The only hands that went up were male. Not one female <u>dared</u> challenge or refute an author's writings. The only questions that the females asked (and all female comments were questions) involved a problem they had with the content of the reading. The males, on the other hand, openly questioned, criticized, and refuted the readings on five separate occasions. The three other times that males spoke involved them saying something like: "/Smith/ is very vague in her theory of XX. Can you explain it further?" They were openly argumentative.[10]

This description raises a number of fascinating issues. First, it gives concrete evidence that at least college classrooms proceed on the assumption that the educational process should be adversarial: The teacher invited students to criticize the reading. (Theology, a required course at Georgetown, was a subject where my students most often found adversarial methods—interestingly, given the background I laid out earlier.) Again, there is nothing inherently wrong with using such methods. Clearly, they are very effective in many ways. However, among the potential liabilities is the risk that women students may be less likely to take part in classroom discussions that are framed as arguments between opposing sides—that is, debate—or as attacks on the authors—that is, critique. (The vast majority of students' observations revealed that men tended to speak more than women in their classes—which is not to say that individual women did not speak more than individual men.)

Gabrielle commented that since class participation counted for 10 percent of students' grades, it might not be fair to women students that the agonistic style is more congenial to men. Not only might women's grades suffer because they speak up less, but they might be evaluated as less intelligent or prepared because when they did speak, they asked questions rather than challenging the readings.

I was intrigued by the student's comment "/Smith/ is very vague in her theory of XX. Can you explain it further?" It could have been phrased "I didn't understand the author's theory. Can you explain it to me?" By beginning "The author is vague in her theory," the questioner blamed the author for *his* failure to understand. A student who asks a question in class risks appearing ignorant. Prefacing the question this way was an excellent way to minimize that risk.

In her description of this class, Gabrielle wrote that not a single woman "dared challenge or refute" an author. She herself underlined the word "dared." But in reading this I wondered whether "dared" was necessarily the right word. It implies that the women in the class wished to challenge the author but did not have the courage. It is possible that not a single woman *cared* to challenge the author. Criticizing or challenging might not be something that appealed to them or seemed worth their efforts. Going back to the childhoods of boys and girls, it seems possible that the boys had had more experiences, from the time they were small, that encouraged them to challenge and argue with authority figures than the girls had.

This is not to say that classrooms are more congenial to boys than girls in every way. Especially in the lowest grades, the requirement that children sit quietly in their seats seems clearly to be easier for girls to fulfill than boys, since many girls frequently sit fairly quietly for long periods of time when they play, while most boys' idea of play involves at least running around, if not also jumping and roughhousing. And researchers have pointed out that some of the extra attention boys receive is aimed at controlling such physical exuberance. The adversarial aspect of educational traditions is just one small piece of the pie, but it seems to reflect boys' experiences and predilections more than girls'.

A colleague commented that he had always taken for granted that the best way to deal with students' comments is to challenge them; he took it to be self-evident that this technique sharpens their minds and helps them develop debating skills. But he noticed that women were relatively silent in his classes. He decided to try beginning discussion with relatively open questions and letting comments go unchallenged. He found, to his amazement and satisfaction, that more women began to speak up in class.

Clearly, women can learn to perform in adversarial ways. Anyone who doubts this need only attend an academic conference in the field of women's studies or feminist studies—or read Duke University professor Jane Tompkins's essay showing how a conference in these fields can be like a Western shoot-out. My point is rather about the roots of the tradition and the tendency of the style to appeal initially to more men than women in the Western cultural context. Ong and Noble show that the adversarial culture of Western science and its exclusion of women were part and parcel of the same historical roots—not that individual women may not learn to practice and enjoy agonistic debate or that individual men may not recoil from it. There are many people, women as well as men, who assume a discussion must be contentious to be interesting. Author Mary Catherine Bateson recalls that when her mother, the anthropologist Margaret Mead, said, "I had an argument with" someone, it was a positive comment. "An argument," to her, meant a spirited intellectual interchange, not a rancorous conflict. The same assumption emerged in an obituary for Diana Trilling, called "one of the very last of the great midcentury New York intellectuals."[11] She and her friends had tried to live what they called "a life of significant contention"—the contention apparently enhancing rather than undercutting the significance.

Learning by Fighting

Although there are patterns that tend to typify women and men in a given culture, there is an even greater range among members of widely divergent cultural backgrounds. In addition to observing adversarial encounters in their current classrooms, many students recalled having spent a junior year in Germany or France and commented that American classrooms seemed very placid compared to what they had experienced abroad. One student, Zach Tyler, described his impressions this way:

> I have very vivid memories of my junior year of high school, which I spent in Germany as an exchange student. The classroom was very debate-oriented and agonistic. One particular instance I remember well was in physics class, when a very confrontational friend of mine had a heated debate with the teacher about solving a problem. My friend ran to the board and scribbled out how he would have solved the problem, completely different from the teacher's, which also gave my friend the right answer and made the teacher wrong.
>
> STUDENT: "You see! This is how it should be, and you are wrong!"
> TEACHER: "No! No! No! You are absolutely wrong in every respect! Just look at how you did this!" (He goes over my friend's solution and shows that it does not work.) "Your solution has no base, as I just showed you!"
> STUDENT: "You can't prove that. Mine works just as well!"
> TEACHER: "My God, if the world were full of technical idiots like yourself! Look again!" (And he clearly shows how my friend's approach was wrong, after which my friend shut up.)

In Zach's opinion, the teacher encouraged this type of argument. The student learned he was wrong, but he got practice in arguing his point of view.

This incident occurred in high school. But European classrooms can be adversarial even at the elementary school level, according to another student, Megan Smyth, who reported on a videotape she saw in her French class:

> Today in French class we watched an excerpt of a classroom scene of fifth-graders. One at a time, each student was asked to stand up and recite a poem that they were supposed to have memorized. The teacher screamed at the students if they forgot a line or if they didn't speak with enough emotion. They were reprimanded and asked to repeat the task until they did it perfectly and passed the "oral test."

There is probably little question about how Americans would view this way of teaching, but the students put it into words:

> After watching this scene, my French teacher asked the class what our opinion was. The various responses included: French schools are very strict, the professor was "mean" and didn't have respect for the students, and there's too much emphasis on memorization, which is pointless.

If teaching methods can be more openly adversarial in European than American elementary and high schools, academic debate can be more openly adversarial there as well. For example, Alice Kaplan, a professor of French at Duke University, describes a colloquium on the French writer Céline that she attended in Paris:

> After the first speech, people started yelling at each other. "Are you suggesting that Céline was fascist!" "You call that evidence!" "I will not accept ignorance in the place of argument!" I was scared.[12]

These examples dramatize that many individuals can thrive in an adversarial atmosphere. And those who learn to participate effectively in any verbal game eventually enjoy it, if nothing else than for the pleasure of exercising that learned skill. It is important to keep these examples in mind in order to avoid the impression that adversarial tactics are always destructive. Clearly, such tactics sometimes admirably serve the purpose of intellectual inquiry. In addition to individual predilection, cultural learning plays a role in whether or not someone enjoys the game played this way.

Graduate School as Boot Camp

Although the invective Kaplan heard at a scholarly meeting in Paris is more extreme than what is typical at American conferences, the assumption that challenge and attack are the best modes of scholarly inquiry is pervasive in American scholarly communities as well. Graduate education is a training ground not only for teaching but also for scientific research. Many graduate programs are geared to training young scholars in rigorous thinking, defined as the ability to launch and field verbal attacks.

Communications researchers Karen Tracy and Sheryl Baratz tapped into some of the ethics that lead to this atmosphere in a study of weekly symposia attended by faculty and graduate students at a major research university. When they asked participants about the purpose of the symposia, they were told it was to "trade ideas" and "learn things." But it didn't take too much discussion to uncover the participants' deeper concern: to be seen as intellectually competent. And here's the rub: To be seen as competent, a student had to ask "tough and challenging questions."

One faculty member commented, when asked about who participated actively in a symposium,

> Among the graduate students, the people I think about are Jess, Tim, uh let's see, Felicia will ask a question but it'll be a nice little supportive question.[13]

"A nice little supportive question" diminished the value of Felicia's participation and her intelligence—the sort of judgment a student would wish to avoid. Just as with White House correspondents, there is value placed on asking "tough questions." Those who want to impress their peers and superiors (as most, if not all, do) are motivated to ask the sorts of questions that gain approval.

Valuing attack as a sign of respect is part of the argument culture of academia—our conception of intellectual interchange as a metaphorical battle. As one colleague put it, "In order to play with the big boys, you have to be willing to get into the ring and wrestle with them." Yet many graduate students (and quite a few established scholars) remain ambivalent about this ethic, especially when they are on the receiving rather than the distribution end. Sociolinguist Winnie Or tape-recorded a symposium at which a graduate student presented her fledgling research to other students and graduate faculty. The student later told Or that she left the symposium feeling that a truck had rolled over her. She did not say she regretted having taken part; she felt she had received valuable feedback. But she also mentioned that she had not looked at her research project once since the symposium several weeks before. This is telling. Shouldn't an opportunity to discuss your research with peers and experts fire you up and send you back to the isolation of research renewed and reinspired? Isn't something awry if it leaves you not wanting to face your research project at all?

This young scholar persevered, but others drop out of graduate school, in some cases because they are turned off by the atmosphere of critique. One woman who wrote to me said she had been encouraged to enroll in graduate school by her college professors, but she lasted only one year in a major midwest university's doctoral program in art history. This is how she described her experience and her decision not to continue:

> Grad school was the nightmare I never knew existed. . . . Into the den of wolves I go, like a lamb to slaughter. . . . When, at the end of my first year (masters) I was offered a job as a curator for a private collection, I jumped at the chance. I wasn't cut out for academia—better try the "real world."

Reading this I thought, is it that she was not cut out for academia, or is it that academia as it was practiced in that university is not cut out for people like her. It is cut out for those who enjoy, or can tolerate, a contentious environment.

(These examples remind us again of the gender dynamic. The graduate student who left academia for museum work was a woman. The student who asked a "nice little supportive question" instead of a "tough, challenging one" was a woman. More than one commentator has wondered aloud if part of the reason women drop out of science courses and degree programs is their discomfort with the agonistic culture of Western science. And Lani Guinier has recently shown that discomfort with the agonistic procedures of law school is partly responsible for women's lower grade point averages in law school, since the women arrive at law school with records as strong as the men's.)

The Culture of Critique: Attack in the Academy

The standard way of writing an academic paper is to position your work in opposition to someone else's, which you prove wrong. This creates a need to make others wrong, which is quite a different matter from reading something with an open mind and discovering that you disagree with it. Students are taught that they must disprove others' arguments in order to be original, make a contribution, and demonstrate their intellectual ability. When there is a need to make others wrong, the temptation is great to oversimplify at best, and at worst to distort or even misrepresent others' positions, the better to refute them—to search for the most foolish statement in a generally reasonable treatise, seize upon the weakest examples, ignore facts that support your opponent's views, and focus only on those that support yours. Straw men spring up like scarecrows in a cornfield.

Sometimes it seems as if there is a maxim driving academic discourse that counsels, "If you can't find something bad to say, don't say anything." As a result, any work that gets a lot of attention is immediately opposed. There is an advantage to this approach: Weaknesses are exposed, and that is surely good. But another result is that it is difficult for those outside the field (or even inside) to know what is "true." Like two expert witnesses hired by opposing attorneys, academics can seem to be canceling each other out. In the words of policy analysts David Greenberg and Philip Robins:

> The process of scientific inquiry almost ensures that competing sets of re-sults will be obtained. . . . Once the first set of findings are published, other researchers eager to make a name for themselves must come up with differ-ent approaches and results to get their studies published.[14]

How are outsiders (or insiders, for that matter) to know which "side" to be-lieve? As a result, it is extremely difficult for research to influence public policy.

A leading researcher in psychology commented that he knew of two young colleagues who had achieved tenure by writing articles attacking him. One of them told him, in confidence, that he actually agreed with him, but of course he could not get tenure by writing articles simply supporting someone else's work; he had to stake out a position in opposition. Attacking an established scholar has particular appeal because it demonstrates origi-nality and independence of thought without requiring true innovation. After all, the domain of inquiry and the terms of debate have already been established. The critic has only to say, like the child who wants to pick a fight, "Is not!" Younger or less prominent scholars can achieve a level of at-tention otherwise denied or eluding them by stepping into the ring with someone who has already attracted the spotlight.

The young psychologist who confessed his motives to the established one was unusual, I suspect, only in his self-awareness and willingness to ar-ticulate it. More commonly, younger scholars, or less prominent ones, con-vince themselves that they are fighting for truth, that they are among the few who see that the emperor has no clothes. In the essay mentioned ear-lier, Jane Tompkins describes how a young scholar-critic can work herself into a passionate conviction that she is morally obligated to attack, because she is fighting on the side of good against the side of evil. Like the reluctant hero in the film *High Noon*, she feels she has no choice but to strap on her holster and shoot. Tompkins recalls that her own career was launched by an essay that

> began with a frontal assault on another woman scholar. When I wrote it I felt the way the hero does in a Western. Not only had this critic argued *a, b,* and *c,* she had held *x, y,* and *z!* It was a clear case of outrageous provocation.[15]

Because her attack was aimed at someone with an established career ("She was famous and I was not. She was teaching at a prestigious univer-sity and I was not. She had published a major book and I had not."), it was a "David and Goliath situation" that made her feel she was "justified in hit-ting her with everything I had." (This is analogous to what William Safire describes as his philosophy in the sphere of political journalism: "Kick 'em when they're up.")[16]

The claim of objectivity is belied by Tompkins's account of the spirit in which attack is often launched: the many motivations, other than the search for truth, that drive a critic to pick a fight with another scholar. Objectivity would entail a disinterested evaluation of all claims. But there is nothing disinterested about it when scholars set out with the need to make others wrong and transform them not only into opponents but into villains.

In academia, as in other walks of life, anonymity breeds contempt. Some of the nastiest rhetoric shows up in "blind" reviews—of articles submitted to journals or book proposals submitted to publishers. "Peer review" is the cornerstone of academic life. When someone submits an article to a journal, a book to a publisher, or a proposal to a funding institution, the work is sent to established scholars for evaluation. To enable reviewers to be honest, they remain anonymous. But anonymous reviewers often take a tone of derision such as people tend to use only when talking about someone who is not there—after all, the evaluation is not addressed to the author. But authors typically receive copies of the evaluations, especially if their work is rejected. This can be particularly destructive to young scholars just starting out. For example, one sociolinguist wrote her dissertation in a firmly established tradition: She tape-recorded conversations at the company where she worked part-time. Experts in our field believe it is best to examine conversations in which the researcher is a natural participant, because when strangers appear asking to tape-record, people get nervous and may change their behavior. The publisher sent the manuscript to a reviewer who was used to different research methods. In rejecting the proposal, she referred to the young scholar "using the audiotaped detritus from an old job." Ouch. What could justify the sneering term "detritus"? What is added by appending "old" to "job," other than hurting the author? Like Heathcliff, the target hears only the negative and—like Heathcliff—may respond by fleeing the field altogether.

One reason the argument culture is so widespread is that arguing is so easy to do. Lynne Hewitt, Judith Duchan, and Erwin Segal came up with a fascinating finding: Speakers with language disabilities who had trouble taking part in other types of verbal interaction were able to participate in arguments. Observing adults with mental retardation who lived in a group home, the researchers found that the residents often engaged in verbal conflicts as a means of prolonging interaction. It was a form of sociability. Most surprising, this was equally true of two residents who had severe language and comprehension disorders yet were able to take part in the verbal disputes, because arguments have a predictable structure.

Academics, too, know that it is easy to ask challenging questions without listening, reading, or thinking very carefully. Critics can always complain about research methods, sample size, and what has been left out. To study anything, a researcher must isolate a piece of the subject and narrow the scope of vision in order to focus. An entire tree cannot be placed under a microscope; a tiny bit has to be separated to be examined closely. This gives critics the handle of a weapon with which to strike an easy blow: They can point out all the bits that were not studied. Like family members or partners in a close relationship, anyone looking for things to pick on will have no trouble finding them.

All of this is not to imply that scholars should not criticize each other or disagree. In the words of poet William Blake, "Without contraries is no progression."[17] The point is to distinguish constructive ways of doing so from nonconstructive ones. Criticizing a colleague on empirical grounds is the beginning of a discussion; if researchers come up with different findings, they can engage in a dialogue: What is it about their methods, data, or means of analysis that explains the different results? In some cases, those who set out to disprove another's claims end up proving them instead—something that is highly unlikely to happen in fields that deal in argumentation alone.

A stunning example in which opponents attempting to disprove a heretical claim ended up proving it involves the cause and treatment of ulcers. It is now widely known and accepted that ulcers are caused by bacteria in the stomach and can be cured by massive doses of antibiotics. For years, however, the cure and treatment of ulcers remained elusive, as all the experts agreed that ulcers were the classic psychogenic illness caused by stress. The stomach, experts further agreed, was a sterile environment: No bacteria could live there. So pathologists did not look for bacteria in the stomachs of ailing or deceased patients, and those who came across them simply ignored them, in effect not seeing what was before their eyes because they did not believe it could be there. When Dr. Barry Marshall, an Australian resident in internal medicine, presented evidence that ulcers are caused by bacteria, no one believed him. His findings were ultimately confirmed by researchers intent on proving him wrong.[18]

The case of ulcers shows that setting out to prove others wrong can be constructive—when it is driven by genuine differences and when it motivates others to undertake new research. But if seeking to prove others wrong becomes a habit, an end in itself, the sole line of inquiry, the results can be far less rewarding.

Believing as Thinking

"The doubting game" is the name English professor Peter Elbow gives to what educators are trained to do. In playing the doubting game, you approach others' work by looking for what's wrong, much as the press corps follows the president hoping to catch him stumble or an attorney pores over an opposing witness's deposition looking for inconsistencies that can be challenged on the stand. It is an attorney's job to discredit opposing witnesses, but is it a scholar's job to approach colleagues like an opposing attorney?

Elbow recommends learning to approach new ideas, and ideas different from your own, in a different spirit—what he calls a "believing game." This does not mean accepting everything anyone says or writes in an unthinking way. That would be just as superficial as rejecting everything without thinking deeply about it. The believing game is still a game. It simply asks you to give it a whirl: Read *as if* you believed, and see where it takes you. Then you can go back and ask whether you want to accept or reject elements in the argument or the whole argument or idea. Elbow is not recommending that we stop doubting altogether. He is telling us to stop doubting exclusively. We need a systematic and respected way to detect and expose strengths, just as we have a systematic and respected way of detecting faults.

Americans need little encouragement to play the doubting game because we regard it as synonymous with intellectual inquiry, a sign of intelligence. In Elbow's words, "We tend to assume that the ability to criticize a claim we disagree with counts as more serious intellectual work than the ability to enter into it and temporarily assent."[19] It is the believing game that needs to be encouraged and recognized as an equally serious intellectual pursuit.

Although criticizing is surely part of critical thinking, it is not synonymous with it. Again, limiting critical response to critique means not doing the other kinds of critical thinking that could be helpful: looking for new insights, new perspectives, new ways of thinking, new knowledge. Critiquing relieves you of the responsibility of doing integrative thinking. It also has the advantage of making the critics feel smart, smarter than the ill-fated author whose work is being picked apart like carrion. But it has the disadvantage of making them less likely to learn from the author's work.

The Socratic Method—Or Is It?

Another scholar who questions the usefulness of opposition as the sole path to truth is philosopher Janice Moulton. Philosophy, she shows, equates logical reasoning with the Adversary Paradigm, a matter of making claims and then trying to find, and argue against, counterexamples to that claim. The result is a debate between adversaries trying to defend their ideas against counterexamples and to come up with counterexamples that refute the opponent's ideas. In this paradigm, the best way to evaluate someone's work is to "subject it to the strongest or most extreme opposition."[20]

But if you parry individual points—a negative and defensive enterprise—you never step back and actively imagine a world in which a different system of ideas could be true—a positive act. And you never ask how larger systems of thought relate to each other. According to Moulton, our devotion to the Adversary Paradigm has led us to misinterpret the type of argumentation that

Socrates favored: We think of the Socratic method as systematically leading an opponent into admitting error. This is primarily a way of showing up an adversary as wrong. Moulton shows that the original Socratic method—the *elenchus*—was designed to convince others, to shake them out of their habitual mode of thought and lead them to new insight. Our version of the Socratic method—an adversarial public debate—is unlikely to result in opponents changing their minds. Someone who loses a debate usually attributes that loss to poor performance or to an adversary's unfair tactics.

Knowledge as Warring Camps

Anne Carolyn Klein, an American woman who spent many years studying Tibetan Buddhism, joined a university program devoted to women's studies in religion. It was her first encounter with contemporary feminist theory, which she quickly learned was divided into two warring camps. In one camp are those who focus on the ways that women are different from men. Among these, some emphasize that women's ways are equally valid and should be respected, while others believe that women's ways are superior and should be more widely adopted. Both these views—called "difference feminism"—contrast with those in the other camp, who claim that women are no different from men by nature, so any noticeable differences result from how society treats women. Those who take this view are called "social constructionists."[21]

Klein saw that separating feminist theory into these two camps reflects the Western tendency to rigid dichotomies. Recalling how Buddhist philosophy tries to integrate disparate forces, she shows that there is much to be gained from both feminist views—and, in any case, both perspectives tend to coexist within individuals. For example, even though the constructionist view of gender has won ascendancy in academic theory (that's why we have the epithet "essentialist" to describe those who hold the view that is in disfavor but no commonly used epithet to sneer at the constructionist view), "feminists still struggle to recognize and name the commonalities among women that justify concern for women's lives around the world and produce political and social alliances." Klein asks, "Why protest current conditions unless the category 'women' is in some way a meaningful one?"[22] She shows, too, that the very inclination to polarize varied views of women and feminism into two opposing camps is in itself essentialist because it reduces complex and varied perspectives to simplified, monolithic representations. This also makes it easy to dismiss—and fight about—others' work rather than think about it.

Reflecting this warring-camps view, journalist Cynthia Gorney asked Gloria Steinem, "Where do you stand in the current debate that the feminist world has divided into 'equity' feminism versus 'difference' feminism—

about whether women are to be treated like men or as different from men?" This question bears all the earmarks of the adversarial framework: the term "debate" and the separation of a complex domain of inquiry into two opposed sides. Steinem responded:

> [*Sighs.*] Of course, you understand that I've turned up in every category. So it makes it harder for me to take the divisions with great seriousness, since I don't feel attached to any of them—and also since I don't hear about the division from women who are not academics or in the media. The idea that there are two "camps" has not been my experience. The mark to me of a constructive argument is one that looks at a specific problem and says, "What shall we do about this?" And a nonconstructive one is one that tries to label people. "Difference" feminist, "gender" feminist—it has no meaning in specific situations.[23]

In this short comment, Steinem puts her finger on several aspects of the argument culture. First, she identifies academics and journalists as two groups that have a habit of—and a stake in—manufacturing polarization and the appearance of conflict. Second, she points out that this view of the world does not describe reality as most people live it. Third, she shows that polarizing issues into "a debate" often goes along with "labeling" the two sides: Lumping others together and sticking a label on them makes it easy to ignore the nuances and subtleties of their opinions and beliefs. Individuals are reduced to an oversimplification of their ideas, transformed into the enemy, and demonized.

False dichotomies are often at the heart of discord.

Question the Basic Assumption

My aim is not to put a stop to the adversarial paradigm, the doubting game, debate—but to diversify: Like a well-balanced stock portfolio, we need more than one path to the goal we seek. What makes it hard to question whether debate is truly the only or even the most fruitful approach to learning is that we're dealing with assumptions that we and everyone around us take to be self-evident. A prominent dean at a major research university commented to me, "The Chinese cannot make great scientists because they will not debate publicly." Many people would find this remark offensive. They would object because it generalizes about all Chinese scientists, especially since it makes a negative evaluation. But I would also question the assumption that makes the generalization a criticism: the conviction that the only way to test and develop ideas is to debate them publicly. It may well be true that most Chinese scientists are reluctant to engage in public, rancorous debate. I see nothing insulting about such a claim; it derives from the Chinese cultural norms that many Chinese and Western observers have documented. But we also know that many Chinese have indeed been great scientists.[24] The falsity of the dean's statement should lead us to question whether debate is the only path to insight.

Consensus Through Dissension?

The culture of critique driving our search for knowledge in the scientific world of research is akin to what I have described in the domains of politics, journalism, and law. In those three institutions, an increasingly warlike atmosphere has led many people already in those professions to leave, and many who would have considered entering these professions in the past are now choosing other paths. Those who remain are finding it less fun; they don't look forward to getting up and going to work in the same way that they and others used to. And in all these areas, raised voices and tempers are creating a din that is drowning out the perhaps more numerous voices of dialogue and reason. In law, critics of the principle of zealous advocacy object on the grounds of what it does to the souls of those who practice within the system, requiring them to put aside their consciences and natural inclinations toward human compassion— just what some among the press say about what aggression journalism is doing to journalists.

Forces affecting these institutions are intertwined with each other and with others I have not mentioned. For example, the rise of malpractice litigation, while prodding doctors to be more careful and providing deserved recompense to victims, has also made the doctor-patient relationship potentially more adversarial. At the same time, physicians are finding themselves in increasingly adversarial relationships with HMOs and insurance companies—as are the patients themselves, who now need the kind of advice that was offered under the headline "When Your HMO Says No: How to Fight for the Treatment You Need—and Win."[25]

People in business, too, report an increasingly adversarial atmosphere. There are, of course, the hostile takeovers that have become common, along with lawsuits between companies and former employees. But there is also more opposition in the day-to-day doing of business. A man who works at a large computer company in Silicon Valley told me that he sees this daily. Disagreement and verbal attack are encouraged at meetings, under the guise of challenging assumptions and fostering creativity. But in reality, he observes, what is fostered is dissension. In the end, the company's ability to do business can be threatened. He has seen at least one company virtually paralyzed by trying to seek consensus after assiduously stirring up dissension.

Who Will Be Left to Lead?

If this seems to describe an isolated phenomenon in a particular industry, take note: A comparable situation exists in our political life. The culture of critique is threatening our system of governance. Norman Ornstein, a political analyst at the American Enterprise Institute, articulates how.[26]

Ornstein offers some astonishing statistics: Between 1975 and 1989, the number of federal officials indicted on charges of public corruption went up by a staggering 1,211 percent. During the same period, the number of non-federal officials indicted doubled. What are we to make of this? he asks. Does it mean that officials during that decade were far more corrupt than before? Not likely. Every systematic study, as well as all anecdotal evidence, suggests just the opposite: Public officials are far less corrupt now; fewer take bribes, get drunk in the middle of their duties, engage in immoral conduct, and so on.

What we have is the culture of critique. The press is poised to pounce on allegations of scandal, giving them primacy over every other kind of news. And the standards by which scandals are judged have declined. Allegations make the news, no matter where they come from, often without proof or even verification. (Remember the ruckus that accompanied reports that planes were forced to circle and travelers were delayed while President Clinton got a haircut on Air Force One in the Los Angeles airport?[27] And that George Bush did not know what a supermarket scanner was? Both turned out to be false.) Political opponents seize on these allegations and use them to punish or bring down opponents. The sad result is that laws designed to improve ethics have not improved ethics at all. Instead, they have made government almost impossible. Allegations trigger long investigations that themselves damage reputations and suggest to the public that terrible things are going on even when they aren't.

Prosecutors, too, are part of the web, Ornstein continues. In the past, an ambitious prosecutor might set out to snare a criminal on the FBI's ten most wanted list. Now the temptation is to go after a senator or cabinet member—or a vice president. That's where attention is paid; that's where the rewards lie.

The threat is not only to those at the highest levels of government but to public servants at every level. I spoke to someone prominent in the arts who was invited to join a federal commission. But first there was a questionnaire to fill out—pages and pages of details requested about the prospective nominee's personal, professional, and financial life. Special request was made for anything that might be embarrassing if it became public. The person in question simply declined the invitation.

The artist I spoke to typified a situation Ornstein described: It is becoming almost impossible to get qualified people to serve in public positions, from the highest executive nominations to part-time or even honorary appointments. Leaving private life for public service has always required personal sacrifice: Your family life is disrupted; you take a pay cut. But now those contemplating such a move must be willing to make an even greater sacrifice: putting their personal reputation at risk. Instead of enhancing reputations, going into public services now threatens them, whether or not the officials have done anything to be ashamed of.

Disruption of family life is intensified, too, by the inordinate delay, Ornstein explained. While a nominee waits to be confirmed, life goes on hold: A spouse's job is in limbo; children await a change in schools; houses must—but can't—be found or rented or bought or sold. What is causing the delays to become so much more protracted than they were before? Every step in the process: Presidents (and their staffs) must take much more time in choosing potential nominees, to make absolutely sure there is nothing in their lives or backgrounds that could embarrass not just the nominee but the president. Once people are selected, the FBI takes weeks or months longer than it used to for background checks, because it too wants to make sure it is not embarrassed later. Finally, the nomination goes to the Senate, where political opponents of the president or the nominee try to go for the jugular on ethics charges.

The result of all these forces is a much smaller pool of qualified people willing to consider public service, long periods when important posts are left vacant, a climate of suspicion that reinforces public doubts about the ethics of people in government, and real disruption in the running of our country.

We have become obsessed with the appearance of impropriety, as Peter Morgan and Glenn Reynolds show in a book with that title. Meanwhile, real impropriety goes unnoticed. We have to ask, as Ornstein does, whether the price we're paying to have pristine individuals fill every public post is worth what we're getting—and he (like Morgan and Reynolds) doubts that what we're getting is less impropriety.

The Cost in Human Spirit

Whatever the causes of the argument culture—and the many causes I have mentioned are surely not the only ones—the most grievous cost is the price paid in human spirit: Contentious public discourse becomes a model for behavior and sets the tone for how individuals experience their relationships to other people and to the society we live in.

Recall the way young boys on Tory Island learned to emulate their elders:

> All around milled little boys imitating their elders, cursing, fluffing, swaggering, threatening. It was particularly fascinating to see how the children learned the whole sequence of behavior. Anything that the men did, they would imitate, shouting the same things, strutting and swaggering.[28]

Tory Island may be an especially ritualized example, but it is not a totally aberrant one. When young men come together in groups, they often engage in symbolic ritual displays of aggression that involve posturing and mock battles. Without pressing the parallel in too literal a way, I couldn't help thinking that this sounds a bit like what journalists and lawyers have observed about their own tribes: that the display of aggression for the benefit of peers is often more important than concrete results.

Consider again law professor Charles Yablon's observation that young litigators learn to value an aggressive stance by listening to their elders' war stories about "the smashing victories they obtained during pretrial discovery in cases which ultimately were settled." Litigators

> derive job satisfaction by recasting minor discovery disputes as titanic struggles. Younger lawyers, convinced that their future careers may hinge on how tough they *seem* while conducting discovery, may conclude that it is more important to look and sound ferocious than act cooperatively, even if all that huffing and puffing does not help (and sometimes harms) their cases.[29]

Against this background, recall too the observations made by journalists that their colleagues feel pressured to ask tough questions to get peer approval. Kenneth Walsh, for example, commented that "it helps your stature in journalism" if you ask challenging questions because that way "you show you're tough and you're independent." Just as litigators trade war stories about how tough they appeared (whether or not that appearance helped their client), Walsh points out that a journalist who dares to challenge the president takes on a heroic aura among his peers. He recalled a specific incident to illustrate this point:

> Remember Brit Hume asking the question . . . about the zigzag decision-making process of President Clinton? And of course President Clinton cut off the questions after that one question because he felt it was not appropriate. That's what we all remember about the Ruth Bader Ginsburg period, is that Brit asked that question.[30]

Let's look at the actual exchange that earned Brit Hume the admiration of his peers. President Clinton called the press conference to announce his nomination of Judge Ruth Bader Ginsburg to the Supreme Court. After the president introduced her, Judge Ginsburg spoke movingly about her life, ending with tributes to her family: her children, granddaughter, husband, and, finally, her mother, "the bravest and strongest person I have known, who was taken from me much too soon." Following these remarks, which moved listeners to tears, journalists were invited to ask questions. The first (and, as it turned out, also the last) asked by correspondent Hume was this:

The withdrawal of the Guinier nomination, sir, and your apparent focus on Judge Breyer and your turn, late, it seems, to Judge Ginsburg, may have created an impression, perhaps unfair, of a certain zigzag quality in the decision-making process here. I wonder, sir, if you could kind of walk us through it and perhaps disabuse us of any notion we might have along those lines. Thank you.

This question reminded everyone—at the very moment of Judge Ginsburg's triumph and honor—that she was not the president's first choice. It broke the spell of her moving remarks by shifting attention from the ceremonial occasion to the political maneuvers that had led up to the nomination—in particular, implying criticism of the president not from the perspective of substance (whether Judge Ginsburg would make a good Supreme Court Justice) but strategy (the decision-making process by which she was chosen). Remarking, "How you could ask a question like that after the statement she just made is beyond me," the president closed the event.

The answer to how Brit Hume could have asked a question like that lies in Walsh's observation that journalists value a display of toughness. In this view, to worry about Judge Ginsburg's feelings—or those of the viewing audience—would be like an attorney worrying about the feelings of a witness about to be cross-examined. But public ceremonies play a role in the emotional lives not only of participants but also of observers, an enormous group in the era of television. Viewers who were moved by Judge Ginsburg's personal statement shared in the ceremony and felt connected to the judge and, by implication, to our judicial system. Such feelings of connection to public figures whose actions affect our lives is a crucial element in individuals' sense of community and their feeling of well-being. Breaking that spell was harmful to this sense of connection, contributing a little bit to what is often called cynicism but which really goes much deeper than that: alienation from the public figures who deeply affect our lives and consequently from the society in which we live.

In this sense, the valuing of the appearance of toughness is related to another theme running through all the domains I discussed: the breakdown in human connections and the rise of anonymity. Lieutenant Colonel Grossman points out that this, too, was one of many ways that the experience of serving in Vietnam was different for American soldiers than was the experience of serving in previous wars. Remember my Uncle Norman, who at the age of eighty-seven was still attending annual reunions of the "boys" he had served with in World War II? This was possible because, as Grossman describes, soldiers in that war trained together, then went to war and served together. Those who were not killed or wounded stayed with the group until they all went home together at the end of the war. No wonder the bonds they forged could last a lifetime. Vietnam, in contrast, was a "lonely war" of individuals assigned to constantly shifting units for year-long tours of duty (thirteen months for Marines). Grossman's description is graphic and sad:

In Vietnam most soldiers arrived on the battlefield alone, afraid, and without friends. A soldier joined a unit where he was an FNG, a "f——ing new guy," whose inexperience and incompetence represented a threat to the continued survival of those in the unit. In a few months, for a brief period, he became an old hand who was bonded to a few friends and able to function well in combat. But then, all too soon, his friends left him via death, injury, or the end of their tours. . . . All but the best of units became just a collection of men experiencing endless leavings and arrivals, and that sacred process of bonding, which makes it possible for men to do what they must do in combat, became a tattered and torn remnant of the support structure experienced by veterans of past American wars.[31]

Though this pattern is most painful in this context, it parallels what we have seen in all the other domains of public dialogue. Recall attorney Susan Popik's observation "You don't come up against the same people all the time. That encouraged you to get along with them because you knew that in six months, you would be across the table from them again."[32] Recall journalists' lamenting that the present White House press corps is a large group, often unknown to aides and leaders, kept at a distance from the leaders they are assigned to cover: confined in a small room, in the back of the president's plane, behind ropes at public events. Contrast this with the recollections of those old enough to remember a small White House press corps that had free run of official buildings and lots of private off-the-record meetings with public officials, including the president and first lady, so that they actually got to know them—as people. And recall departing Senator Heflin's regret about the decline of opportunities for legislators of opposing parties to socialize, which led to friendships developed "across party and ideological lines" that "led to more openness and willingness to discuss issues on a cordial basis" and to finding "common ground." We could add the demise of the family doctor who came to your home, replaced by an overworked internist or family practitioner—if not an anonymous emergency room—and, if you're unlucky enough to need them but lucky enough to get to see them, a cadre of specialists who may not talk to each other or even much to you, or surgeons who may spend hours saving your life or limb but hardly ever see or speak to you afterward.

In all these domains, wonderful progress has been accompanied by more and more anonymity and disconnection, which are damaging to the human spirit and fertile ground for animosity.

Getting Beyond Dualism

At the heart of the argument culture is our habit of seeing issues and ideas as absolute and irreconcilable principles continually at war. To move beyond this static and limiting view, we can remember the Chinese approach to yin and yang. They are two principles, yes, but they are conceived not as irreconcilable polar opposites but as elements that coexist and should be brought into balance as much as possible. As sociolinguist Suzanne Wong Scollon notes, "Yin is always present in and changing into yang and vice versa."[33] How can we translate this abstract idea into daily practice?

To overcome our bias toward dualism, we can make special efforts not to think in twos. Mary Catherine Bateson, an author and anthropologist who teaches at George Mason University, makes a point of having her class compare *three* cultures, not two.[34] If students compare two cultures, she finds, they are inclined to polarize them, to think of the two as opposite to each other. But if they compare three cultures, they are more likely to think about each on its own terms.

As a goal, we could all try to catch ourselves when we talk about "both sides" of an issue—and talk instead about "all sides." And people in any field can try to resist the temptation to pick on details when they see a chance to score a point. If the detail really does not speak to the main issue, bite your tongue. Draw back and consider the whole picture. After asking, "Where is this wrong?" make an effort to ask "What is right about this?"— not necessarily *instead,* but *in addition.*

In the public arena, producers can try to avoid, whenever possible, structuring public discussions as debates. This means avoiding the format of having two guests discuss an issue, pro and con. In some cases three guests—or one—will be more enlightening than two.

An example of the advantage of adding a third guest was an episode of *The Diane Rehm Show* on National Public Radio following the withdrawal of Anthony Lake from nomination as director of central intelligence. White House Communications Director Ann Lewis claimed that the process of confirming presidential appointments has become more partisan and personal.[35] Tony Blankley, former communications director for Newt Gingrich, claimed that the process has always been rancorous. Fortunately for the audience, there was a third guest: historian Michael Beschloss, who provided historical perspective. He explained that during the immediately preceding period of 1940 to 1990, confirmation hearings were indeed more benign than they have been since, but in the 1920s and the latter half of the nineteenth century, he said, they were also "pretty bloody." In this way, a third guest, especially a guest who is not committed to one side, can dispel the audience's frustration when two guests make opposite claims.

Japanese television talk shows provide a window on other possibilities. Sociolinguist Atsuko Honda compared three different current affairs talk shows televised in Japan. Each one presents striking contrasts to what Americans take for granted in that genre. (The very fact that Honda chose to compare three—not two—is instructive.) The Japanese shows were structured in ways that made them less likely to be adversarial. Within each structure, participants vigorously opposed each other's ideas, yet they did so without excessively polarizing the issues.

Consider the formats of the three shows: *Nichiyoo Tooron (Sunday Discussion)* featured a moderator and four guests who discussed the recession for an hour. Only the moderator was a professional news commentator; two guests were associated with research institutes. The two other shows Honda examined concerned Japanese involvement in a peacekeeping mission in Cambodia. *Sunday Project* featured three guests: one magazine editor and two political scientists; the third show was a three-and-a-half-hour discussion involving fourteen panelists sitting around an oval table with a participating studio audience composed of fifty Japanese and Cambodian students. Viewers were also invited to participate by calling or faxing. Among the panelists were a history professor, a military analyst, a movie director, a scholar, a newscaster, and a legislator.

It is standard for American shows to provide balance by featuring two experts who represent contrasting political views: two senators or political consultants (one Republican, one Democrat), two journalist commentators (one on the left, one on the right), or two experts (one pro and one con). These Japanese shows had more than two guests, and the guests were identified by their expertise rather than their political perspectives. Another popular Japanese show that is often compared to ABC's *Nightline* or PBS's *Jim Lehrer News Hour* is called *Close-up Gendai*.[36] Providing thirty minutes of nightly news analysis, the Japanese show uses a format similar to these American TV shows. But it typically features a single guest. Japanese shows, in other words, have a wide range of formats featuring one guest or three or more—anything but two, the number most likely to polarize.

The political talk shows that Honda analyzed included many disagreements and conflicts. But whereas moderators of American and British talk shows often provoke and stoke conflict to make their shows more interesting, the Japanese moderators—and also the other guests—expended effort to modulate conflicts and defuse the spirit of opposition, but not the substance of disagreement. One last example, taken from Honda's study, illustrates how this worked.

In the long discussion among fourteen panelists, a dispute arose between two: Shikata, a former executive of the Japanese Self-Defense Forces, supported sending these forces to Cambodia. He was opposed by Irokawa, a historian who believed that the involvement of these forces violated the Japanese constitution. This exchange comes across as quite rancorous:

SHIKATA: Why is it OK to send troops to the protecting side but not OK to the protected side?
IROKAWA: Because we have the Japanese Constitution.
SHIKATA: Why is it so, if we have the Constitution?

IROKAWA: Well, we have to abide by the Constitution. If you don't want to follow the Constitution, you should get rid of your Japanese nationality and go somewhere else.

These are pretty strong words. And they were accompanied by strong gestures: According to Honda, as Shikata posed his question, he was beating the table with his palms; as Irokawa responded, he was jabbing the air toward Shikata with a pen.

Yet the confrontation did not take on a rancorous tone. The television cameras offered close-ups of both men's faces—smiling. In Japanese and other Asian cultures, smiling has different connotations than it does for Americans and Europeans: It tends to express not amusement but embarrassment. And while Shikata and Irokawa smiled, other panelists rushed to add their voices—and everyone burst out laughing. The laughter served to defuse the confrontation. So did the loud cacophony of voices that erupted as several panelists tried to speak at once. When individual voices finally were distinguished, they did not take one side or the other but tried to mediate the conflict by supporting and criticizing both sides equally. For example, Ohshima, a movie director, said:

OHSHIMA: I think that both parties overestimate or underestimate the realities for the sake of making a point.

Atsuko Honda found this to be typical of the televised discussions she analyzed: When a conspicuous conflict arose between two parties, other participants frequently moved in with attempts to mediate. In this way, they supported the Japanese ideal of avoiding winners and losers and helped everyone preserve some measure of "face." This mediation did not prevent varying views from being expressed; it resulted in different kinds of views being expressed. If two sides set the terms of debate and subsequent comments support one side or the other, the range of insights offered is circumscribed by the original two sides. If the goal instead is to mediate and defuse polarization, then other panelists are more likely to express a range of perspectives that shed nuanced light on the original two sides or suggest other ways of approaching the issue entirely.

Moving from Debate to Dialogue

Many of the issues I have discussed are also of concern to Amitai Etzioni and other communitarians. In *The New Golden Rule,* Etzioni proposes rules of engagement to make dialogue more constructive between people with differing views. His rules of engagement are designed to reflect—and reinforce—the tenet that people whose ideas conflict are still members of the same community.[37] Among these rules are:

- Don't demonize those with whom you disagree.
- Don't affront their deepest moral commitments.
- Talk less of rights, which are nonnegotiable, and more of needs, wants, and interests.
- Leave some issues out.
- Engage in a dialogue of convictions: Don't be so reasonable and conciliatory that you lose touch with a core of belief you feel passionately about.

As I stressed [. . .] earlier [. . .], producers putting together television or radio shows and journalists covering stories might consider—in at least some cases—preferring rather than rejecting potential commentators who say they cannot take one side or the other unequivocally. Information shows might do better with only one guest who is given a chance to explore an idea in depth rather than two who will prevent each other from developing either perspective. A producer who feels that two guests with radically opposed views seem truly the most appropriate might begin by asking whether the issue is being framed in the most constructive way. If it is, a third or fourth participant could be invited as well, to temper the "two sides" perspective.

Perhaps it is time to reexamine the assumption that audiences always prefer a fight. In reviewing a book about the history of *National Geographic*, Marina Warner scoffs at the magazine's policy of avoiding attack. She quotes the editor who wrote in 1915, "Only what is of a kindly nature is printed about any country or people, everything unpleasant or unduly critical being avoided."[38] Warner describes this editorial approach condescendingly as a "happy-talk, feel-good philosophy" and concludes that "its deep wish not to offend has often made it dull." But the facts belie this judgment. *National Geographic* is one of the most successful magazines of all time—as reported in the same review, its circulation "stands at over 10 million, and the readership, according to surveys, is four times that number."

Perhaps, too, it is time to question our glorification of debate as the best, if not the only, means of inquiry. The debate format leads us to regard those doing different kinds of research as belonging to warring camps. There is something very appealing about conceptualizing differing approaches in this way, because the dichotomies appeal to our sense of how knowledge should be organized.

Well, what's wrong with that?

What's wrong is that it obscures aspects of disparate work that overlap and can enlighten each other.

What's wrong is that it obscures the complexity of research. Fitting ideas into a particular camp requires you to oversimplify them. Again, disinformation and distortion can result. Less knowledge is gained, not more. And time spent attacking an opponent or defending against attacks is not spent doing something else—like original research.

What's wrong is that it implies that only one framework can apply, when in most cases many can. As a colleague put it, "Most theories are wrong not in what they assert but in what they deny."[39] Clinging to the elephant's leg, they loudly proclaim that the person describing the elephant's tail is wrong. This is not going to help them—or their readers—understand an elephant. Again, there are parallels in personal relationships. I recall a man who had just returned from a weekend human development seminar. Full of enthusiasm, he explained the main lesson he had learned: "I don't have to make others wrong to prove that I'm right." He experienced this revelation as a liberation; it relieved him of the burden of trying to prove others wrong.

If you limit your view of a problem to choosing between two sides, you inevitably reject much that is true, and you narrow your field of vision to the limits of those two sides, making it unlikely you'll pull back, widen your field of vision, and discover the paradigm shift that will permit truly new understanding.

In moving away from a narrow view of debate, we need not give up conflict and criticism altogether. Quite the contrary, we can develop more varied—and more constructive—ways of expressing opposition and negotiating disagreement.

We need to use our imaginations and ingenuity to find different ways to seek truth and gain knowledge, and add them to our arsenal—or, should I say, to the ingredients for our stew. It will take creativity to find ways to blunt the most dangerous blades of the argument culture. It's a challenge we must undertake, because our public and private lives are at stake.   ■

NOTES

1. This does not mean it goes back in an unbroken chain. David Noble, in *A World Without Women*, claims that Aristotle was all but lost to the West during the early Christian era and was rediscovered in the medieval era, when universities were first established. This is significant for his observation that many early Christian monasteries welcomed both women and men who could equally aspire to an androgynous ideal, in contrast to the Middle Ages, when the female was stigmatized, unmarried women were consigned to convents, priests were required to be celibate, and women were excluded from spiritual authority.

2. There is a fascinating parallel in the evolution of the early Christian Church and the Southern Baptist Church: Noble shows that the early Christian Church regarded women as equally beloved of Jesus and equally capable of devoting their lives to religious study, so women comprised a majority of early converts to Christianity, some of them leaving their husbands—or bringing their husbands along—to join monastic communities. It was later, leading up to the medieval period, that the clerical movement gained ascendancy in part by systematically separating women, confining them in either marriage or convents, stigmatizing them, and barring them from positions of

power within the church. Christine Leigh Heyrman, in *Southern Cross: The Beginnings of the Bible Belt,* shows that a similar trajectory characterized the Southern Baptist movement. At first, young Baptist and Methodist preachers (in the 1740s to 1830s) preached that both women and blacks were equally God's children, deserving of spiritual authority—with the result that the majority of converts were women and slaves. To counteract this distressing demography, the message was changed: Antislavery rhetoric faded, and women's roles were narrowed to domesticity and subservience. With these shifts, the evangelical movement swept the South. At the same time, Heyrman shows, military imagery took over: The ideal man of God was transformed from a "willing martyr" to a "formidable fighter" led by "warrior preachers."

3. Ong, *Fighting for Life,* p. 122. Ong's source, on which I also rely, is Oliver, *Communication and Culture in Ancient India and China.* My own quotations from Oliver are from p. 259.

4. Pachomius, for example, "the father of communal monasticism . . . and organizer of the first monastic community, had been a soldier under Constantine" and modeled his community on the military, emphasizing order, efficiency, and military obedience. Cassian, a fourth-century proselytizer, "'likened the monk's discipline to that of the soldier,' and Chrysostom, another great champion of the movement, 'sternly reminded the monks that Christ had armed them to be soldiers in a noble fight'" (Noble, *A World Without Women,* p. 54).

5. Aristotle, quoted in Oliver, *Communication and Culture in Ancient India and China,* p. 259.

6. I came to understand the different meaning of "poet" in Classical Greece from reading Ong and also *Preface to Plato* by Eric Havelock. These insights informed many articles I wrote about oral and literate tradition in Western culture, including "Oral and Literate Strategies in Spoken and Written Narratives" and "The Oral/Literate Continuum in Discourse."

7. Moulton, "A Paradigm of Philosophy"; Ong, *Fighting for Life.*

8. The example of Danny and the lava: Wertsch, *Voices of the Mind,* pp. 113–14.

9. See David and Myra Sadker, *Failing at Fairness.*

10. Although my colleagues and I make efforts to refer to our students—all over the age of eighteen—as "women" and "men" and some students in my classes do the same, the majority refer to each other and themselves as "girls" and "boys" or "girls" and "guys."

11. Jonathan Alter, "The End of the Journey," *Newsweek,* Nov. 4, 1996, p. 61. Trilling died at the age of ninety-one.

12. Kaplan, *French Lessons,* p. 119.

13. Tracy and Baratz, "Intellectual Discussion in the Academy as Situated Discourse," p. 309.

14. Greenberg and Robins, "The Changing Role of Social Experiments in Policy Analysis," p. 350.

15. These and other quotes from Tompkins appear in her essay "Fighting Words," pp. 588–89.

16. Safire is quoted in Howard Kurtz, "Safire Made No Secret of Dislike for Inman," *The Washington Post,* Jan. 19, 1994, p. A6.

17. I've borrowed the William Blake quote from Peter Elbow, who used it to open his book *Embracing Contraries.*

18. Terence Monmaney, "Marshall's Hunch," *The New Yorker,* Sept. 20, 1993, pp. 64–72.

19. Elbow, *Embracing Contraries,* p. 258.

20. Moulton, "A Paradigm of Philosophy," p. 153.

21. Social constructionists often deride the ideas of those who focus on differences as "essentialist"—a bit of academic name-calling: it is used only as a way of criticizing someone else's work: "Smith's claims are repugnant because they are essentialist." I have never heard anyone claim, "I am an essentialist," though I have frequently heard elaborate self-defenses: "I am not an essentialist!" Capturing the tendency to use this term as an epithet, *Lingua Franca,* a magazine for academics, describes "essentialist" as "that generic gender studies *j'accuse!*" See Emily Nussbaum, "Inside Publishing," *Lingua Franca,* Dec.–Jan. 1977, pp. 22–24; the quote is from p. 24.

22. Klein, *Meeting the Great Bliss Queen,* pp. 8–9.

23. Cynthia Gorney, "Gloria," *Mother Jones,* Nov.–Dec. 1995, pp. 22–27; the quote is from p. 22.

24. See, for example, Needham, *Science and Civilization in China.*

25. Ellyn E. Spragins, *Newsweek,* July 28, 1997, p. 73.

26. This section is based on an interview with Ornstein. See also Ornstein's article, "Less Seems More."

27. The story behind the haircut story is told by Gina Lubrano, "Now for the Real Haircut Story . . . ," *The San Diego Union-Tribune,* July 12, 1993, p. B7. That the supermarket scanner story was not true was mentioned by George Stephanopoulos at a panel held at Brown University, as reported by Elliot Krieger, "Providence Journal/Brown University Public Affairs Conference," *The Providence Journal-Bulletin,* Mar. 5, 1995, p. 12A.

28. Fox, "The Inherent Rules of Violence," p. 141.

29. Yablon, "Stupid Lawyer Tricks," p. 1639.

30. Kenneth Walsh made this comment on *The Diane Rehm Show,* May 28, 1996.

31. Grossman, *On Killing,* p. 270.

32. Susan Popik made this comment on the *U.S. Business Litigation* panel.

33. Suzanne Wong Scollon: Personal communication.

34. Mary Catherine Bateson: Personal communication.

35. At the time of this show, Ms. Lewis was deputy communications director.

36. Yoshiko Nakano helped me with observations of *Close-up Gendai.*

37. Etzioni, *The New Golden Rule,* pp. 104–106. He attributes the rule "Talk less of rights . . . and more of needs, wants, and interests" to Mary Ann Glendon.

38. Marina Warner, "High-Minded Pursuit of the Exotic," review of *Reading National Geographic* by Catherine A. Lutz and Jane L. Collins in *The New York Times Book Review,* Sept. 19, 1993, p. 13.

39. I got this from A. L. Becker, who got it from Kenneth Pike, who got it from . . .

REFERENCES

Elbow, Peter. *Embracing Contraries: Explorations in Learning and Teaching* (New York and Oxford: Oxford University Press, 1986).

Etzioni, Amitai. *The New Golden Rule: Community and Morality in a Democratic Society* (New York: Basic, 1996).

Fox, Robin. "The Inherent Rules of Violence." In *Social Rules and Social Behaviour,* Peter Collet, ed. (Totowa, N.J.: Rowman and Littlefield, 1976), pp. 132–49.

Greenberg, David H., and Philip K. Robins. "The Changing Role of Social Experiments in Policy Analysis." *Journal of Policy Analysis and Management* 5:2 (1986), pp. 340–62.

Grossman, Dave. *On Killing: The Psychological Cost of Learning to Kill in War and Society* (Boston: Little, Brown, 1995).

Havelock, Eric A. *Preface to Plato* (Cambridge, Mass.: Belknap Press, Harvard University Press, 1963).

Heyrman, Christine Leigh. *Southern Cross: The Beginnings of the Bible Belt* (New York: Knopf, 1997).

Kaplan, Alice. *French Lessons: a Memoir* (Chicago: University of Chicago Press, 1993).

Klein, Anne Carolyn. *Meeting the Great Bliss Queen: Buddhists, Feminists, and the Art of the Self* (Boston: Beacon Press, 1995).

Kurtz, Howard. *Hot Air: All Talk, All the Time* (New York: Times Books, 1996).

Moulton, Janice. "A Paradigm of Philosophy: The Adversary Method." In *Discovering Reality,* Sandra Harding and Merrill B. Hintikka, eds. (Dordrecht, Holland: Reidel, 1983), pp. 149–64.

Needham, Joseph. *Science and Civilization in China* (Cambridge, England: Cambridge University Press, 1956).

Noble, David. *A World Without Women: The Christian Culture of Western Science* (New York and Oxford: Oxford University Press, 1992).

Oliver, Robert T. *Communication and Culture in Ancient India and China* (Syracuse, N.Y.: Syracuse University Press, 1971).

Ong, Walter J. *Fighting for Life: Contest, Sexuality, and Consciousness* (Ithaca, N.Y.: Cornell University Press, 1981).

Ornstein, Norman J. "Less Seems More: What to Do About Contemporary Political Corruption." *The Responsible Community* 4:1 (Winter 1993–94), pp. 7–22.

Tompkins, Jane. "Fighting Words: Unlearning to Write the Critical Essay." *Georgia Review* 42 (1988), pp. 585–90.

Tracy, Karen, and Sheryl Baratz. "Intellectual Discussion in the Academy as Situated Discourse." *Communication Monographs* 60 (1993), pp. 300–20.

Wertsch, James V. *Voices of the Mind: A Sociocultural Approach to Mediated Action* (Cambridge, Mass.: Harvard University Press, 1991).

Yablon, Charles. "Stupid Lawyer Tricks: An Essay on Discovery Abuse." *Columbia Law Review* 96 (1996), p. 1618–44.

▪ *QUESTIONS FOR MAKING CONNECTIONS WITHIN THE READING* ▪

1. In the course of her argument Deborah Tannen refers to "our adversarial culture," "the culture of critique," and to maleness, logic, formalism, and polarization. She refers as well to the customs and discourses of Western religion and science, and to contemporary educational practices. Define these terms and explain how they fit together. What is the relation between logic and aggression, religion and science, and ancient Greece and the education offered by our universities?

2. In what ways has the "boot camp" model shaped your own educational experience? In an actual boot camp, is it the drill sergeant alone who cre-

ates the tension, or does everyone collaborate in creating and sustaining an atmosphere of rivalry and violence? How about in the case of schooling: In what ways do the students themselves actively collaborate in making the classroom into a "camp"? In what ways does the system—the culture and the institutions of schooling—reinforce these behaviors?

3. In the section entitled "Getting Beyond Dualism," Tannen describes the dynamics of three Japanese television programs, which she offers as examples of a less agonistic style of public discussion. What features distinguish these programs from comparable discussions in the U.S. media and in places like the classroom? Does disagreement have a different significance in the context of Japanese culture? When people disagree in Western settings, what might be at stake? What values and outcomes matter the most? In the Japanese context, what values and outcomes are most significant? How might an American misunderstand the Japanese programs?

■ *QUESTIONS FOR WRITING* ■

1. University professors routinely study communities and institutions outside the university, and they are often quite critical of what they discover there, but the university itself is seldom the object of comparable scrutiny. In what ways—if any—does the culture of critique stifle inquiry and thwart constructive change within the university itself? If Tannen is correct in her estimations, then would it be fair to say that the advancement of knowledge is only one of the university's many goals and perhaps not even the most important one? What might the other goals be?

2. The university in the United States is a unique institution in many ways. For one thing, all faculty above the level of assistant professor have lifetime employment and cannot be dismissed except for gross dereliction of duty. Most public universities receive automatic funding from state coffers. Many private universities have enormous endowments, sometimes in the billions of dollars. And most professors are shielded from any assessment of their effectiveness as teachers, except through course evaluations. In what ways does the university's unique situation contribute to the persistence of the culture of critique? What about the media? Do the media also contribute to the persistence of this culture?

■ *QUESTIONS FOR MAKING CONNECTIONS BETWEEN READINGS* ■

1. Was the attack on the World Trade Center and the Pentagon an act of war or a crime? What difference does the choice of words make in describing this—or any other—act of violence? Drawing on the work of Tannen and Mary Kaldor, discuss the relationship between the terms we use to

describe acts of violence and the ways we elect to respond to acts of violence. Would changing the words we use and the ways we use them create new options for responding to violence, or are such concerns a luxury during times of great danger?

2. How does Malcolm Gladwell's discussion of the dynamics of social change confirm, contradict, or complicate Tannen's argument? Does Gladwell's account suggest that social change is decided by the strongest argument? Does debate even play a significant role? If public debate and rational deliberation have a marginal influence, why does the university place so high a premium on them? Have professors depicted the social world in ways that are flattering to themselves? In what ways is this depiction both accurate *and* inaccurate?

www For additional suggestions about making connections between readings, visit the Link-O-Mat and More Sample Assignments at <www.newhum.com>.

EDWARD TENNER

EDWARD TENNER HAS been called a "philosopher of everyday technology." His principal concern is the way that human beings interact with the products of technological innovation. In exploring these interactions, Tenner takes a very expansive view, and his thinking brings together subjects as diverse as agriculture, antibiotics, automobiles, chairs, shoes, football helmets, and computer software. Tenner's studies of technological development have led him to conclude that innovation often produces—at least in the short term—unintended negative consequences. These negative consequences, which Tenner calls technology's "revenge effects," sometimes actually make life *less* safe, convenient, and efficient than before the inventions came into being. As he puts it, "A small change to solve a minor problem may create a larger one." Moreover, he notes that the risk of technology's revenge effects has only been intensified by the ubiquity of computer software in modern life.

Revenge effects unfold around us every day—in the form of traffic jams, for example, and as online spam. But Tenner is intrigued and inspired by the way that people have responded with creativity to these problems. Revenge effects are unintended—that much is true—but our efforts to improve the quality of life need not be self-defeating. As Tenner puts it, "human culture, not some inherent will of the machine, has created most revenge effects," and for this reason, he argues that we must not lose sight of our capacity to change and adapt. As the pace of innovation accelerates, Tenner considers one question to be especially important for any reflection on the best course for the future: "How can we break out of ruts and change our thinking?"

Tenner's educational and professional background is eclectic. In addition to *Why Things Bite Back* (1996), Tenner is also the author of *Our Own Devices: How*

Tenner, Edward. "Another Look Back, and a Look Ahead." *Why Things Bite Back: Technology and the Revenge of Unintended Consequences.* New York: Knopf, 1996. 254–277.

Biographical information drawn from Edward Tenner's home page <http://www .edwardtenner.com/>. Quotes drawn from the Princeton University Web site <http://www .princeton.edu/pr/pwb/02/1021/3a.shtml>, the NPR interview with Tenner <http:// www.npr.org/programs/science/archives/1998/jul/980711.science.html>, and from *Why Things Bite Back.*

Technology Remakes Humanity (2003). He is currently a writer, speaker, and technology consultant, and was formerly employed as the science editor at Princeton University Press. He is the recipient of a Guggenheim fellowship and has been affiliated with Princeton's Institute for Advanced Study and the Jerome and Dorothy Lemelson Center for the Study of Invention and Innovation at the National Museum of American History.

www   **To learn more about Edward Tenner and the revenge effect, please visit the Link-O-Mat at <www.newhum.com>.**

Another Look Back, and a Look Ahead

"Doing Better and Feeling Worse." This phrase from a 1970s symposium on health care is more apt than ever, and not only in medicine. We seem to worry more than our ancestors, surrounded though they were by exploding steamboat boilers, raging epidemics, crashing trains, panicked crowds, and flaming theaters. Perhaps this is because the safer life imposes an ever-increasing burden of attention. Not just in the dilemmas of medicine but in the management of natural hazards, in the control of organisms, in the running of offices, and even in the playing of games there are, not necessarily more severe, but more subtle and intractable, problems to deal with.

To investigate why disasters should lead to improvement, and improvement should paradoxically foster discontent, it might help to look at three areas of technology we have not considered before: timekeeping, navigation, and motorization. The automobile first presented an acute problem—collisions—but its success reduced that difficulty while adding to it another, less easily soluble one—congestion. And the recent history of motoring also suggests a paradox of safety, that the better-made and less dangerous motor vehicles become, the greater are the burdens on the operator. The prognosis for revenge effects is hopeful: we will probably keep them under control. By replacing brute force with finesse, concentration with variety, and heavy traditional materials with lighter ones, we are already starting to overcome the thinking and habits that led to many revenge effects. Technology, too, is evolving and responding. The one thing we will not be able to do is avoid the endless rituals of vigilance.

In one example after another, revenge has turned out to be the flip side of intensity. The velocity of twentieth-century transportation and warfare produces trauma on an unprecedented scale, which in turn calls for equally intensive care; but the end result may be chronic brain damage that is beyond medical treatment. Intensive antibiotic therapy has removed the horror of some of the nineteenth century's most feared infections, yet it has also promoted the spread of even more virulent bacteria. Massive shielding of beaches from the energy of waves has deflected their intensity to other shores or robbed these beaches of replenishing sand. Smoke jumpers have suppressed small forest fires but have thereby helped build reservoirs of flammable materials in the understory for more intense ones. Towering smokestacks have propelled particulates at great velocity higher into the atmosphere than ever before—to the dismay of residents over an ever wider radius. Intensive chicken-pig-duck agriculture in China has rushed new influenza virus strains into production, for distribution internationally by the increasingly dense and speedy world network of commercial aircraft. Accelerating processor speed has multiplied computer operations without necessarily reducing costs to programmers, system managers, and end users. Rigid molded ski boots have helped prevent ankle and tibia fractures at the cost of anterior cruciate ligament injuries. And what are so-called pests but intensified life forms? Most of these animals and plants are unusually robust, prolific, and adaptive. The animals are mobile and the plants spread rapidly. Fire ants, Africanized bees, starlings, melaleuca go about their business single-mindedly. Even the dreamy-looking eucalyptus is capable of burning intensely to propagate itself—taking entire neighborhoods with it. And when intensity is a genuine protection against catastrophe, it may fail to address and even complicates persistent low-level problems.

We have learned the limits of intensiveness. What next? In the near time, intensification is still working. Human health and longevity have improved in most places and by most measures. As we have seen, people may feel sicker today because they are more likely to survive with some limitation or chronic illness. But they really are better off. It is hard to disagree with optimists like Leonard Sagan and Aaron Wildavsky when they point to the benefits of growth. Fortunately, every prediction of global famine and misery has failed—so far.

The second argument for optimism is humanity's success in digging deeper and looking harder for old resources and substituting new ones. In the crucible of technological change, shortages produce surpluses and crises yield alternatives. When the biologist Paul Ehrlich lost a bet with the economist Julian Simon on future prices of a bundle of commodities selected by Ehrlich—they dropped between 1980 and 1990, costing Ehrlich $576.06—the transaction seemed to bear out Simon's argument that inexhaustible human ingenuity would find a way around apparent shortages. Market forces appear to impose conservation and encourage discovery more efficiently than legislation generally can. We have seen how the feared hardwood shortage of the early twentieth century never happened, much to the dismay of Jack London and other hopeful eucalyptus growers. Of course, this analysis has revenge effects of its own for market economics: if constraint helps make us so much more clever, why should the state not prod the infinitely creative human mind with more taxes and restrictions? Heavy taxes on fossil fuels should, by the same logic, do wonders for conservation and alternative energy sources.[1]

When it comes to interpreting the last hundred years, the optimists have the upper hand. The future is another matter. Optimists counter projections of global warming, rising sea levels, population growth, and soil depletion with scenarios of gradual adjustment and adaptation. If the crisis of life in the oceans is the problem, then fish farming is the answer. A true optimist sees a silver lining even in the destruction of rain forests and wilderness: there may be much less acreage, but more and more people will be able to travel and see it. In terms of this strange anthropocentric, utilitarian calculus there will actually be more *available* forest and wilderness. As for soil depletion, genetic engineering and new methods of cultivation will presumably let us cope; the world can probably support a population of ten billion or more. (In 1994 it stood at 5.6 billion.) Optimists and pessimists disagree not so much on what is attainable, but on how long it will *be* attainable. What the first group welcomes as a successful adaptation the second belittles as a stopgap. Optimists and pessimists curiously agree that crisis is good for us, but for different reasons. Pessimists welcome emergency as a violent cure for profligacy. Optimists welcome it as an injection of innovatory stimulus.

The Ambiguity of Disaster

One reason for optimism is that disaster is paradoxically creative. It legitimizes and promotes changes in rules—changes that may be resisted as long as the levels of casualties remain "acceptable" prior to a disaster that leads to change. More important, disasters mobilize the kind of ingenuity that technological optimists believe exists in unlimited supply. Of course, new disasters may themselves be unintended consequences of prior solutions. It is uncertain whether, at least in developed countries, the incidence of new catastrophes is gradually declining or not. Should disasters be considered as waves that remain constant in amplitude, damped, or amplified? The unanswerable question about technological revenge effects is whether we are really learning. Even tragedies like Chernobyl and Bhopal are ambiguous as forewarnings. Are they just the most recent in an ongoing series that will strike again in Western Europe and North America, where matters are far less secure than their leaders admit? Or will they spark environmental consciousness and vigilance in the former Soviet bloc and the developing world? It is too soon to say, but there is excellent evidence that great disasters do have long-term reverse revenge effects.

The first great modern stimulus from disaster may have been the defeat of the Spanish Armada in 1588. The economic historian David Landes has speculated that this greatest setback in the history of Spain was what led its king Philip III to offer a perpetual pension of 6,000 ducats to "the discoverer of the longitude" when he ascended the throne ten years later. (Landes is not sure, however, what method would have kept the surviving ships from their fate on the rocks of Ireland and the Orkney Islands.) In France the Duc d'Orléans made a comparable offer. From Galileo to Newton, most of the giants of the scientific revolution of the late sixteenth and seventeenth centuries, with or without prizes in mind, joined the search. None of these thinkers produced a practical astronomical system, yet the shipwrecks and prizes did have other substantial benefits. The sociologist Robert K. Merton has suggested how many advances in mathematics, astronomy, mechanics, and magnetism could be traced to the vast losses that Spain and other maritime powers had suffered.[2]

It took a further disaster to complete the paradoxical work: the wreck of three ships from the fleet of Admiral Sir Clowdesley Shovell in 1707 on the Scilly Isles off the west coast of England, killing almost two thousand sailors. (The admiral reportedly struggled ashore, only to be murdered for his magnificent ring.) Today we know that bad geography, charts, and compasses, and poor navigation, complicated by fog and unpredictable currents, were mainly to blame. To contemporaries, though, the lesson was a new urgency in the search for a way to determine longitude at sea. Of course, a valid method would in turn make possible more accurate printed aids to navigation. The question of longitude was not immediately supported officially; only seven years later, in 1714, was an Act of Parliament passed, offering up to £20,000—at least $1 million in today's purchasing power—for a method of determining longitude on an oceangoing vessel.[3]

Entrepreneurs and cranks had been at work on solutions ever since the wreck, proposing lines of ships somehow "anchored" in mid-ocean, telepathic goats, and even dogs communicating through a "sympathetic powder" said by its promoters to relay sensations from an animal on land to one at sea after having been sprinkled on both. But the prize, after more than another decade had passed, attracted the attention of the gifted clockmaker John Harrison, who built a chronometer that met the specifications of the act. The steps and the time it took him to refine his timepiece (along with the fact that he did not secure payment of his claims until 1773, when he was eighty) are not the point here. What matters is that the magnitude of the Scilly Isles wreck eventually justified the great reward offered.

The earlier prizes contributed indirectly to the Act of Parliament. It was Newton, who had long worked on the problem, whose recommendation was essential for the act's passage. Only in hopes of the new prize did Harrison and other leading craftsmen abandon their normal clientele for a largely speculative project that had frustrated the scientific elite of Europe for decades. The search for longitude may represent the first great public high-technology program. In its costs and benefits it became one of the most successful. Anything like it would almost certainly have been long delayed in the absence of a spectacular new disaster.[4]

It took another two hundred years for a single marine disaster to have an international impact comparable to that of the Scilly Isles wreck. This was the sinking of the *Titanic*, pride of the White Star Line, on April 14, 1912. The ship's tragic end was memorialized not only as an enormous loss of life and property—over fifteen hundred passengers and crew perished, including the captain—but also as a cautionary tale. Some of its perceived lessons were social, the image of the frivolous rich fiddling as the world was about to burn, or even escaping in lifeboats as the poor drowned in steerage. Even the failure of other ships to respond to its distress calls has been blamed on the priority given by radio operators to the social cables of their first-class passengers. But in the long run, the dangers of technological pride rather than class conflict seemed to be the message of this disaster. Even more than the loss of the three English ships two centuries earlier, the sinking of the *Titanic* immediately became what risk analysts now call a *signal event*—one that reveals an ominous and previously underestimated kind of danger.[5]

The problem was not mainly in the operation of the ship's systems, useless though some of the lifeboat mechanisms turned out to be. Even though White Star officials never claimed the ship was actually unsinkable, the captain and crew acted with inappropriate confidence, steaming at high speed through waters notorious for sea ice. After the *Titanic* hit the iceberg, the same confidence in the ship's safeguards delayed, with tragic consequences, the implementation of rescue procedures that could have reduced casualties immeasurably. (Her officers doubtless had faith in the owners' stringent design specifications, but marine archaeologists now believe that the vessel's steel plates did not meet these standards.) Belief in the safety of the ship became the greatest single hazard to the survival of its passengers, greater than the icebergs themselves. In fact, crews of other nearby vessels that might have rescued passengers believed the *Titanic*'s distress flares could only mean some celebration, not an emergency.

Less known is how important the *Titanic* disaster was in solving what had been a serious problem for international navigation: the prevalence of sea ice in the ocean lanes of the world's most active and lucrative route, the North Atlantic. The wreck had precedents: in the 1880s over fifty passenger ships reported sea ice damage in and around the Grand Banks off the Newfoundland coast where the *Titanic* later went down; fourteen of them had sunk. It was the loss of the *Titanic* that led not only to new regulations requiring lifeboat space for all passengers and crew, but to a series of international conferences on the Safety of Life at Sea (SOLAS) beginning in 1913. The International Ice Patrol, established in 1913, now uses aerial surveillance, satellite images, and radio-equipped oceanographic drifter buoys. The biggest bergs even have their own radio transmitters. Ships possess advanced radar systems. It would require extraordinary negligence for a captain to let an iceberg sink a ship.[6]

At least for passengers embarking in the United States, an ocean cruise now appears extraordinarily safe. From 1970 to 1989, only two of over thirty million passengers died in accidents involving cruise ships operating out of the United States, despite a number of collisions and fires. Each generation of ships meets higher standards. SOLAS new specifies a maximum thirty-minute evacuation time for cruise ships. Only one ship has ever sunk after hitting an iceberg since the *Titanic,* and that was in 1943, when the Ice Patrol was discontinued during the Second World War.[7]

Both tragedies and their consequences illustrate the engineer and historian Henry Petroski's point that a great disaster is often the best stimulus for new engineering ideas. Two things have changed, though, since the early eighteenth century. The growth of engineering as a profession has made a new type of error possible, as Petroski has also shown: overconfidence in the safety of a new design, the defects of which too often remain hidden until some new disaster occurs. But there is also a second type of error: failure to observe the repeated rituals that safe operation of advanced technology entails. The higher potential speed of steamships required (and requires) more rather than less care. The larger number of passengers and crew required (and requires) more careful drills and inspection of equipment. It is still difficult for a prospective passenger to tell how well trained a crew may be to handle an emergency. We know some technology has a built-in demand for care, a maintenance compulsion. But there is always a hidden catch of technological improvement: the need for enhanced vigilance that we have already seen in medicine, in environmental modification, in the translocation of plants and animals, in electronic systems, and even in some aspects of athletics.[8]

At this point in the history of technology we can draw a fundamental lesson from an unexpected source, the law of negligence. In a number of important articles, the legal scholar Mark Grady correlates better and safer technology with the number of lawsuits for malpractice and personal injury. During the centuries when bleeding, purging, and mercury compounds (as we have seen) hastened the deaths of many of the West's elite, legal action against the physicians who pursued these remedies was rare. The public did not hold doctors in awe; neither did they really expect heroic remedies to work. In fact, it was precisely because they doubted the scientific basis of contemporary treatments that a malpractice suit had little point.

According to Grady, "the first negligence explosion occurred during the 1875–1905 period. In that time of industrial revolution, claims increased by fully 800%, and the negligence rule did not change significantly. When machines abound, negligence claims increase. Put differently, a doctor who forgot to perform a modern fetal health procedure could not have been liable in 1960, before the procedure was invented." On this view, a dialysis machine reduces the risk of kidney failure in nature but adds a new risk: that physicians and technicians operating the machines under their supervision may fail to make safe connections, test the hemodialytic solution, or observe all the other precautions of good practice. Anyone who has watched the pilot and copilot of a common two-engine commuter aircraft carry out their extensive preflight procedures, flipping through pages in a printed notebook as they read their scripts, has been struck by the number of precautions that a long-accepted and well-developed technology imposes.[9]

By the standards of its day, the *Titanic* was a ship relatively high in what Grady calls "durable precautions," the safety hardware that popular opinion supposed made it unsinkable. It is true that size, luxury, and speed had higher priority than safety in her design—but she had the latest in communications and damage-containment equipment. Grady's analysis suggests, though, that the very presence of these measures increased the importance of "nondurable precautions"—all the things an officer or crew member must remember to do—in keeping the ship afloat. The flow of messages on the ship's radio demanded constant attention: did a given message warrant immediate transmission to the bridge? Once the captain was aware of it, did it necessitate a change of speed or course? And with lifeboats come other questions. Have they been inspected regularly? Does each crew member know his or her part in supervising a possible abandonment? If a major marine loss occurs, it is the way an emergency plan is carried out, not physical safeguards alone, that will determine whether or not it becomes a disaster for human life.

Here is where the difference between early and industrial technology becomes telling. The captain of a seventeenth-century oceangoing ship needed excellent navigation skills, and the management of cargo, ballast, and rigging were already arts for specialists. Some captains and pilots of Renaissance and early modern Europe had superb intuition which let them achieve amazing feats of "dead reckoning": the estimation of position from relatively crude measurements of last position, direction, and speed. A gifted mariner could go beyond the limits of the technology of the day. Yet because of the difficulty of measuring longitude, compounded by the other defects of instruments, disaster could happen to the best of seafarers. That is why Sir Clowdesley Shovell still got an overbearing tomb by Grinling Gibbons in Westminster Abbey after his catastrophic end. (On the other hand, Joseph Addison ridiculed it as "the figure of a beau, dressed in a long periwig, and reposing himself upon velvet cushions under a canopy of state," and deplored that it commemorated only his demise and not his victories.) The better and the safer technology becomes, the more we presume human error when something goes seriously wrong. If it is not the error of the captain or crew, it is one of the engineers or designers of equipment, or of executives and their maintenance policies.[10]

The Automobile and Revenge Effects

Intensity—disaster—precaution—vigilance: the cycle appears on land as well as at sea. The rise of motoring shows this more clearly than the transformation of sailing, but in a different way. . . . [N]ineteenth-century railroad accidents were the first of a new type of technological disaster unknown in the eighteenth century. Historians of technology have long pointed out the importance of indignation over early railroad tragedies in developing the first complex control systems in American business, not to mention safety hardware like signals and air brakes. But there is an equally interesting side to the intensification of transportation by the railroad: the rise of automobile transport. Casualties from car accidents occur as a steady series of small disasters, not the few-but-great wrecks involving trains and steamships. The automobile invited chronic catastrophes. Indignation built more slowly.[11]

The growing capacity of the nation's railroad network had an unforeseen consequence that few scholars have noted—chaos in the horse-drawn city. Nearly every passenger journey or freight shipment began and ended with a horse-drawn vehicle or a horse, at least until cable cars and electric trolleys spread late in the century. Even the physical size of horses increased throughout the nineteenth century, to move the heavier loads and serve the larger populations of European and American cities. By the 1880s, massive Percherons were a familiar sight on American streets. Teamstering already was a crucial trade, and the number of horses for every teamster was growing. Local delivery by horse could cost nearly as much as hundreds of miles by rail. Today's Budweiser Clydesdales, a magnificent public relations asset, are the heritage of yesterday's logistical nightmares.[12]

Herds of horses multiplied. Even after cable and electric power had begun to replace horse traction for streetcars, horses were everywhere. The Fiss, Doerr, and Carroll horse auction mart on East 24th Street in New York drew up to a thousand buyers and boasted its own seven-story, block-long stable. New York City's horses alone produced over 300 million pounds of manure annually; stables accumulated tens of thousands of cubic feet for months at a time. In fact, as we have seen, one imported pest, the English sparrow, thrived on the bounty of grain in horse droppings. Repeated horse epidemics—technically epizootics—paralyzed commerce and interfered with firefighting. Despite limitation of their workdays to four hours, horses died after only a few years of service, usually in the middle of the street, up to fifteen thousand a year in New York. Dust from powdered horse manure helped spread tuberculosis and tetanus. As railroads grew safer, the horse-drawn city became more dangerous.[13]

Less remembered today than the sanitary problems caused by horses were the safety hazards they posed. Horses and horse-drawn vehicles were dangerous, killing more riders, passengers, and pedestrians than is generally appreciated. Horses panicked. In frequent urban traffic snarls, they bit and kicked some who crossed their path. Horse-related accidents were an important part of surgical practice in Victorian England and no doubt in North America as well. In the 1890s in New York, per capita deaths from wagons and carriage accidents nearly doubled. By the end of the century they stood at nearly six per hundred thousand of population. Added to the five or so streetcar deaths, the rate of about 110 per million is close to the rates of motor vehicle deaths in many industrial countries in the 1980s. On the eve of motorization, the urban world was not such a gentle place.[14]

The automobile was an answer to disease and danger. In fact, private internal-combustion transportation was almost utopian. The congested tenements of the center city spread dirt and disease. Dispersing people into the green suburbs was a favorite theme of city reformers. Progressive mayors supported the extension of horsecars and then trolleys. But at least on city stretches, these had an unpleasant intensity of their own. In 1912 the *Los Angeles Record* found their air "a pestilence . . . heavy with disease and the emanations from many bodies. . . . A bishop embraced a stout grandmother, a tender girl touched limbs with a city sport. . . ." And hard-pressed straphangers objected to allegedly high fares, reckless drivers, and rude conductors.[15]

Automobiles may have begun as rich people's toys, but thanks largely to Henry Ford, they soon came to represent independence *from* the rich: from railroad interests, traction (streetcar) companies, center-city landlords. By the 1950s and the 1960s, the automotive industry had come to represent big business at its most arrogant, but motorization won because it rallied so many small businesses. Diffuse interests were its political strength. Motoring did not benefit only car manufacturers and petroleum producers and refiners. It enriched tens of thousands of small businesses: trucking companies, suburban developers, construction contractors, dealers and parts retailers, service station operators. Of course, as Clay McShane and other urban historians before him have documented, road improvement was not really populist, or uniformly popular. It did change the nature of the street, but to the disadvantage of residents. The roadway ceased to be a gathering place and became a thoroughfare. Many neighborhoods resisted asphalt paving, and children even stoned passing cars. Still, motoring showed the political advantages of spreading benefits to many small and medium-sized interests.[16]

In spite of clear damage to urban greenery and space, using roads to help disperse people in private suburban houses remained not just a popular but a politically correct idea for a long time, and not only in America. Franklin D. Roosevelt thought that spreading population would lower the cost of government and directly reduce the expense of urban services. One radical planner, Carol Aronovici, wrote in 1932: "Let the old cities perish so that we may have great and beautiful cities." Aronovici called for "a thorough emancipation of the suburban communities from the metropolis" that was threatening to "suck their very physical existence into the body politic of decayed and corrupted political organization." (More than sixty years later, these same towns—now aging demographically and economically— are beginning to make common cause with the old central cities against the flight of businesses and residents to the sprawling outer suburbs.)[17]

At virtually the same time a school of Soviet planners called the "disurbanists" were dreaming of dispersing their own overcrowded urban masses into new settlements amid the fields and forests by building new road networks. A distinguished visitor, the French architect Le Corbusier, summed up the mood in his book *La Ville Radieuse* (1930):

> People were encouraged to entertain an idle dream: "The cities will be part of the country; I shall live 30 miles away from my office under a pine tree; my secretary will live 30 miles away from it too, in the other direction, under another pine tree. We shall both have our own car. We shall use up tires, wear out road surfaces and gears, consume oil and gasoline. All of which will necessitate a great deal of work . . . enough for all. . . ."[18]

It is almost as though postwar American suburbia was the realized fantasy of Soviet planners. Or, more accurately, the victory of motorization was an unintended consequence of an international decentralizing mood. As Kenneth Jackson has pointed out, even the *Bulletin of the Atomic Scientists* embraced dispersion of cities in a 1951 special issue, "Defense Through Decentralization." It promoted satellite cities and low-density suburbs in which former urbanites could be housed more safely for the duration of the Cold War.[19]

Automobiles and road systems promoted an old technological utopia, the community of private villas. Automobiles also have an immense advantage over railroads and trolleys: they make it possible to go directly from one outlying point to another. America never had an integrated national or even regional transportation network as European countries did. Its trains and even some of its urban transport systems were run by competing corporations. Nostalgic admirers of railroad transportation forget how many trips required completing two sides of a triangle, sometimes with hours of waiting between them. K. H. Schaeffer and Elliot Sclar, transportation analysts, exposed these shortcomings trenchantly in *Access for All*. A trip of fourteen miles from the small town of New Washington, Ohio, to its county seat could take all day by rail, even when train travel was at its peak. And New Washington's two depots were a half mile apart.[20]

Usually, motorization bought space rather than time. Ivan Illich wrote in 1974: "The typical American spends over 1,600 hours a year (or thirty hours a week or four hours a day including Sundays) in his car. This includes the time spent behind the wheel, moving or stopped, the hours of work needed to pay for it and for gasoline, tires, tolls, insurance, fines, and taxes. . . . For this American it takes 1,600 hours to cover a year total of 6,000 miles, four miles per hour. This is just as fast as a pedestrian and slower than a bicycle."[21]

In fact, the greatest surprise of motoring was the speed at which traffic clogged the roads, including freeways and other limited-access highways built to relieve congestion. When the Washington Beltway was dedicated in 1964, the governor of Maryland, who cut the ribbon on its last segment, called it "a road of opportunity." The federal highway administrator compared it to a wedding ring. The *Washington Post* declared that "the stenographer in Suitland will be able to get to the Pentagon without finding the day ruined almost before it begins." Twenty-two years later, another *Post* correspondent reported: "The dream turned to nightmare. The Great Belt tightened to the point where right now it resembles nothing less than a noose around the communal neck. . . . We could die on the Beltway and rot until vultures pick clean our bones." London's counterpart, the M25, had already exceeded its projected traffic for the year 2001 by the late 1980s, only three years after completion. Surprisingly, even states like Kentucky, Missouri, Nebraska, South Carolina, Tennessee, and Texas classify more than half their interstate highway mileage as congested. And mature suburbs of large cities have become so traffic-choked that the American Automobile Association itself has moved its headquarters from Fairfax County, Virginia, to Florida.[22]

There are social reasons for this recongestion: not just two-commuter families but the multiple motorized errands that suburban living demands. Saturday afternoons may be the most crowded times of all. Traffic engineers, applied mathematicians, and economists have also discovered that expanding old routes and adding new ones may actually increase travel time. An enlarged bridge will redirect traffic that had been taking a longer route around it, but unless it is substantially larger, it will be just as slow. New highways also may increase total travel time for all travelers when they draw traffic from alternative rail systems. And the ultimate recongesting effect is called Braess's Paradox, in honor of a pioneering investigator of the subject. Where each of two congested routes has a bottleneck, adding what appears to be a shortcut between them may actually increase travel time for everyone. The reason: the new, "direct" road actually funnels traffic through *both* the old bottlenecks. Thanks to quirks of driver psychology, even common operations like merging traffic can produce equally counterproductive results. Because motorists tend to close up spaces to discourage entering cars from cutting in front of them, especially when these attempt to enter from other roads, mysterious traffic jams can appear a mile or more from the actual merge. Because spaces are tight, a driver decelerating slightly at the head of a clump can unwittingly induce one following motorist after another to brake a bit harder. And when congestion reaches a certain maximum roadway capacity, the flow of cars falls so sharply that traffic engineers recognize (but still can't fully explain) a "breakdown." What appears rational to an individual driver becomes irrational for the motoring population and for society. Recongesting turns out to be a form of recomplicating, of creating a machine of parts coupled in poorly understood ways.[23]

What is interesting technologically about this new congestion is its unexpectedly positive side. It has helped make driving safer than anyone thought it would ever be. Congestion may be a chronic negative side effect of mobility, but safety is a positive outcome of congestion. There is a school of thought that denies that driving or anything else can ever be made safer. This is called risk homeostasis. The phrase means simply that people unconsciously seek a certain level of hazard. They compensate for "dangerous" conditions by driving more cautiously—and offset safety measures by taking more risks. The geographer John G. U. Adams looked into the accident rate of England's "adventure playgrounds," loosely supervised assortments of high wooden ladders and platforms that offer "opportunities to test skills appropriate to chimpanzees." They are visibly more dangerous than "fixed equipment" playgrounds with their smooth surfaces and rubberized matting. Yet insurance companies quote lower liability rates for the adventure playgrounds, and the secretary of the National Playing Fields Association has written that "the accident rate is lower than in orthodox playgrounds since hooliganism which results from boredom is absent." Adams and others (mainly social scientists) have argued conversely that seat belts, by making drivers feel more secure, actually cause more pedestrian casualties even as they reduce motorist injuries.[24]

Few traffic engineers accept risk homeostasis as a principle, or the seat belt as an instance of it. In fact, as Leonard Evans, a physicist and safety researcher, argues, some safety measures save more lives than we might have predicted, but others may actually increase casualties. The fifty-five-mile-per-hour speed limit reduced deaths more than anyone had expected. Seat belts met expectations. Studded tires, improved acceleration, and antilock braking systems (ABS) have a moderate benefit, though there is some evidence that ABS-equipped drivers may have as many crashes as those not similarly equipped, or perhaps even more. New traffic signals seem to have a neutral effect. So do strict inspections. And surprisingly, zebra stripes and flashing lights at crossings actually increase pedestrian injuries significantly. (That does not mean they are useless. As another leading traffic specialist, Frank Haight, has put it, the benefit of some safety measures is fair access rather than safety. They give pedestrians not absolute protection from reckless motorists but the welcome ability to cross roads that would otherwise be almost impassable.) Changing any single piece of hardware, or any law, may or may not have the desired effect.[25]

It isn't only safer equipment, then, that has brought down the rate of deaths per million passenger-miles. In fact, cause and effect might be reversed. Only when drivers start giving up speed and price to protection do manufacturers start selling safer cars. And that seems to depend on the amount of driving. The British mathematician and traffic engineer R. J. Smeed had that most remarkable gift, the ability to point out an obvious pattern that others had missed. In 1949, Smeed began to plot the relationship between fatalities per vehicle and vehicles per capita. What he found then, and what he and others have noticed ever since, is that more driving makes fatal accidents less likely per mile driven.[26]

In the late 1960s, for example, the nations with the highest fatality rates were developing countries with few private automobiles per capita. Even today within Europe, the riskiest countries are those on the periphery, like Portugal, where automobile ownership is still twenty years or more behind England or Germany. John Adams, while dissenting from Smeed's conclusions about the reasons for greater safety, found that later data supported Smeed's original 1949 paper.[27]

Smeed's observations point to a very complex process: a set of technological, legal, and social changes that more general driving brings. Countries with few roads, wide-open spaces, and few vehicles may be dangerous to motorists' health. A colleague once recalled from her childhood in Iran that on long stretches of country road, chauffeurs raced toward each other in the center, playing a local variation of chicken. Visibility was excellent, but there were no lane-dividing stripes. One driver *nearly* always turned off; the point was to wait long enough to maintain one's honor. What in the United States are adolescent rites may elsewhere be the serious contests of middle-aged men.

Early motorization's mix of human, animal, and motor power can be equally fatal. In India in the early 1980s, there were seventy-five road deaths a day, half as many as in the United States, which had forty times as many vehicles. Twenty times more people were killed in accidents than in floods. In 1989, more than a thousand died on the Grand Trunk Road from New Delhi to Calcutta alone. Uniquely Indian, or Third World? Not at all. Early in the century, New York also had a mix of animal-drawn vehicles, automobiles, streetcars, bicycles, and pedestrians, and saw casualties double during the earliest driving boom.[28]

Congestion leads to demands for limited-access roads that in turn promote safer high-speed driving. U.S. national statistics also suggest that the most dangerous roads are straight, two-lane desert highways, with the worst being the notorious U.S. 66 near Gallup, New Mexico. One study of motor-vehicle crash mortality found a hundredfold variation; in Esmeralda County, Nevada, the death rate was 558 per 100,000, while in Manhattan it was 2.5.[29] In hilly country with old roads and many new drivers, the results are similar. Whereas the United States had 248 deaths per million vehicles in 1989, Britain 248, and the Netherlands 236, Portugal had 1,163. The Portuguese-based writer Robert D. Kaplan has written of drivers on the twisting and crumbling Sintra-Lisbon highway: "Instead of going slow, they race along . . . passing on curves at night, with the ease and tranquillity of a blind person reading Braille."[30] Yet these same people are impeccably courteous pedestrians and have passed stiff written tests requiring a three-month course. The gentle Malaysians, mostly teetotaling Muslims, also reflect the spirit of early motorization. Malaysian drivers "love to pass on blind curves or approaching hills," wrote one visiting American. "They routinely ride up on each other's tails, going 50, 60, 70 miles an hour, then impertinently flash their headlights."[31]

The traffic congestion of highly motorized countries poses a chronic rather than an acute health menace. Road safety statistics do not reflect the health consequences of vehicle emissions. A car that covers ten miles in thirty minutes of rush-hour crawl produces three and a half times the hydrocarbons of one that takes eleven minutes at off-peak hours. Idling engines produce three hundred times as much carbon monoxide as those running freely. While automotive emissions were reduced by 76 to 96 percent from 1967 to 1990, the number of cities with hazardous ground-level ozone increased to over one hundred by the late 1980s. Estimates of the health and agricultural damage done by carbon monoxide and smog range from $5 billion to $16 billion per year. All of these are serious chronic consequences, but they don't alter the fact that riding in a motor vehicle has become far safer.[32]

There is an unexpected discipline in the apparently more dangerous congested road. Interstates and other limited-access highways would not be feasible without a minimum traffic volume. Density forces slower and more uniform speeds. It also makes possible greater police supervision, better rescue services, and easier access to emergency treatment facilities. The safest part of the New Jersey Turnpike is the crowded metropolitan portion north of New Brunswick; the more rural South Jersey section has twice its accident rate. And much of the reason is that congestion compels vigilance. The chairman of the Turnpike Authority explained: "[I]n the north . . . there is so much going on, you're pumping adrenaline just to stay on top of it. We're keeping you alert up here. Down there you're dozing." In fact, as Albert O. Hirschman has pointed out, proper driving is actually easier in the city than in the country. "The city traffic requires greater technical mastery, but this increase in the difficulty of driving is outweighed by the fact that intense traffic helps [the driver] in the task of focusing his attention."[33]

In spite of countless incidents of violence on the highway, in spite of all our experiences to the contrary, mature motorization seems to engender (relatively) more courteous and disciplined behavior, "collective learning" in Leonard Evans's phrase, or, as the *Washington Post*'s Malcolm Gladwell puts it, "driving under the influence of society."[34]

A spokesman from the Insurance Institute for Highway Safety reports that while safety-related advertising once appeared to harm sales by substituting fear for fantasy, "safety is only second to quality and well ahead of price in the consumer's mind."[35] We are far from the free spirits of early motoring, of Booth Tarkington's George Amberson Miniver, of Kenneth Grahame's Mr. Toad, "the terror, the traffic-queller, the Lord of the lone trail, before whom all must give way or be smitten into nothingness and everlasting night."[36] Or, as the columnist Richard Cohen has written, "Jay Gatsby never dreamed of gridlock."[37]

Conservation of Catastrophe?

Marine navigation and motoring alike seem to argue for optimism, for the idea that intensification can be tamed, in fact that disasters are self-correcting. Society learns. Progress, that long-despised concept, comes in by the back door. The point is not that disasters continue, but that on balance and by most measures, people continue to be better off. Unfortunately for technological optimism, things are not quite so simple.

The *Titanic*'s sinking has been moralized so much that we have to remember the incident would have turned out much differently had her plates not fractured. No one had tested (and possibly no one could have tested) metal for the kind of brittle fracture her hull experienced. Even if the crew had been able to evacuate every passenger safely, the loss of the ship would have been one of the greatest material disasters of peacetime marine history.

The disturbing fact about the accident is that we can never be completely confident of the behavior of any new material as part of a complex system. Splinters from fiber-optic cables, to take just one case, can pose serious health risks for telephone workers (and especially for self-taught laypeople) who have to cut and splice them. Yet it is rare to see this problem mentioned in most discussions of networking.

Software adds another dimension to complexity. . . . [T]he risk of fatal bugs in life-critical systems can be [very high]. Malfunction in software control of processes is also less likely to produce the warning signals familiar in the mechanical world—heat, noise, color change, vibration. A system crash may be much more sudden. It is harder to achieve what engineers call "graceful degradation."

The historian of science Michael S. Mahoney has observed that computers do not eliminate artisans but reintroduce them in the new guise of programmers. Recomplication has made software so bulky that only teams of programmers can write it, yet talented programmers are individualists who do not usually work efficiently as part of a team. This affects not only operating systems and applications software for desktop computers, but the code that runs everything from aircraft navigation to automotive fuel injection and medical equipment. As John Shore, a software engineer, has pointed out, vigilance works well for mechanical systems; high-rise elevators need constant maintenance, but they rarely injure people. Software requires maintenance, too, but this makes it less rather than more reliable. Every feature that is added and every bug that is fixed adds the possibility of some new and unexpected interaction between parts of the program. A small change to solve a minor problem may create a larger one. The technical writer Lauren Wiener has noted that the repeated paralysis of local and regional telephone systems in 1991 resulted from only a few changed lines in the millions of lines of code that drove call-routing computers. A meaningful test of the revisions would have taken thirteen weeks.[38]

Catastrophic risk will stay with us because more rather than less of life is likely to depend on complex software. Intelligent vehicle-highway systems (IVHS) may someday squeeze more capacity out of existing limited-access roads. Individual vehicles under electronic control would join formations called platoons. These convoys could be spaced more tightly than today's normal traffic. And they could control some of our daily highway nightmares, such as the tailgater, the lane jumper, and the sleepless trucker. But if software or communication or even a lead vehicle's tire failed, the results could be catastrophic. If we add the dependence of government, banking, and commerce on global electronic networks that in turn depend on software, a revival of catastrophic errors cannot be ruled out. (And the critics of IVHS insist that electronically controlled roads will soon be recongested anyway.)[39]

Even more serious than hidden risk may be displaced risk. The safety of one technology has a way of creating danger in another. Our current successes may be preparing us for failures where we least expect them. . . . [G]ood hygiene left the well-scrubbed children of the middle and upper classes more susceptible to polio than the dirty kids of the poor. . . . Mirko D. Grmek [has suggested] that success in suppressing bacterial infection indirectly promoted the rise of AIDS and other new viral infections by leaving a niche for virulent pathogens.

If hidden risk is the concern of the liberal, distrustful of corporate assurances of safety through technology, displaced risk is the objection of the conservative to regulation. And conservative skepticism is directed less often at technologies themselves than at attempts to limit, regulate, or impose them. Requiring parents to place their infants in (paid-for) child carrier seats on airlines instead of carrying them on their laps may lead more families to drive instead of fly. Since aircraft are safer than highways, the argument runs, the rule may injure more infants than would have been hurt in the air. Pesticide-free fruit and vegetables at high prices may be more harmful to public health, by reducing consumption by the poor, than cheap produce with pesticide residues would have been. Taking this line of thought to an extreme, one British researcher has even found that male physicians who quit smoking tend to offset their health gains with higher rates of alco-holism, accidents, and suicide. (Not surprisingly, tobacco industry sources supported this study.)[40]

Like hidden risks, displaced risks appear impossible to rule out of any proposed change. The natural and social worlds interact in too many poorly understood ways. Risk analysts call these unexpected effects Type III errors. (A Type I error is an unnecessary preventive step, like evacuating a coastline when storm warnings turn out to be a false alarm, or delaying the approval of a lifesaving drug. A Type II error is a decidedly harmful action like releas-ing a drug that turns out to have lethal side effects.) When strict directives on meat radiation after the Chernobyl meltdown of 1986 destroyed the Lapp reindeer-meat economy, as a recent report of the Royal Society pointed out, the unexpectedness of the result made it a Type III rather than a Type I error. Many market-oriented risk analysts like Aaron Wildavsky urge resilience and gradual responses to unforeseen consequences as they occur, rather than attempts to calculate and balance all possible results. The report of the Royal Society points to clearly organized schools of "anticipationism" and "resilientism." Resilience often turns out to be an excellent policy, provided the phenomena cooperate and appear distinctly and gradually on the horizon.[41]

In the real world, few trends emerge without ambiguity, beyond a rea-sonable doubt, before precious time is lost. It is now more than 150 years since the eccentric French utopian socialist Charles Fourier predicted that the increasing cultivation of the earth would bring about higher tempera-tures and eventually a melting of the polar icecap. While Fourier's scientific credentials were dubious—he thought the northern seas would become "a sort of lemonade" and humanity would move about on "antilions" and get their fish from "antisharks"—he was on to something. In fact, at about the same time, another Frenchman, coincidentally also named Fourier (the physicist Jean-Baptiste), discovered that the earth's atmosphere maintains the planet's warmth by trapping heat. As early as a hundred years ago, the Swedish geochemist Svante Arrhenius speculated on a possible increase of up to 6 degrees C. in air temperature if industrial carbon dioxide emissions continued to grow. Yet even now, the science we need most gives us not the precision we want but a set of possible tempos and consequences. We want numbers, but instead our best models give us ranges. We want a truth that will apply to the whole globe, or at least to our own continent, and face the likelihood of patchy local change. We want an idealized eighteenth-century celestial mechanics to rule our world, but we find only probabilistic models.[42]

We can't even count on conditions continuing to drift slowly. As Stephen Jay Gould and others have often reminded us, steep rather than gradual natural change is the norm, and it is extremely hard to predict the future state of a complex system even without the added imponderables of human culture and behavior. Well before climate became an issue, human culture (including technology) set off bizarre chains of cause and effect. The fashion for feathers and entire dead birds on women's hats in the late nineteenth century devastated whole species; but it also drew women and men into bird preservation movements that outlived the fad. The early automobile spread its own nemesis, the puncture weed with its tire-killing spiked seedpods. Decades after safer and puncture-resistant tubeless tires appeared, this technology unexpectedly abetted another pest: the Asian tiger mosquito, a vector for dengue fever, which traveled the Pacific in recycled tires and now enjoys an extended breeding season in water that collects in tire dumps. We have already seen how cleaning up European harbors probably helped spread tenacious zebra mussels to North America. Yet motorization also helped reduce the population of European sparrows.

Anyone correctly predicting these sequences well in advance would have seemed a crank or an alarmist. In fact, most of the greatest changes of the twentieth century simply did not occur to the nineteenth-century imagination. Air war and weapons of mass destruction were outstanding exceptions, and even these were logical extensions of pre-1900 sieges and bombardments. Otherwise the human ability to envision something truly new, good *or* bad, is surprisingly limited. Late-twentieth-century personal computers are radically different not just from nineteenth-century analytical engines and mechanical calculators but even from those (far slower) behemoths, the postwar data processors of the von Neumann era. High European mortality in tropical Asia and Africa did not prepare the Western mind for the emergence of AIDS and other "new" viruses—nor for the influenza epidemic of 1918.

Extrapolation doesn't work, because neither nature nor human society is guaranteed to act reasonably. Some things like computer processor power and data storage get better and cheaper more quickly than the optimists expected; on the other hand, the tasks that they are supposed to perform, like machine translation, turn out to be more difficult than most people had thought. What is almost a constant, though, is that the real benefits usually are not the ones that we expected, and the real perils are not those we feared. What prevail are sets of loosely calculable factors and ranges of outcomes, with no accepted procedure for choosing among them. And since we have seen that it is impossible to rid any computer models of bugs, we have no assurance that reality will not be well beyond our projected range in either direction. Instead of the malice of the isolated object, we face ever more complicated possible linkages among systems of objects.

It is impossible, then, to prove that large-scale disasters will not reassert themselves in North America and the rest of the developed world, that we will not intensify not only our chronic problems but our acute ones. William H. McNeill has a telling phrase for this possibility: the Conservation of Catastrophe. Just as engineers will continue to explore the bounds of a "safe" bridge design, test pilots will "push the envelope," regional planners will overrate the capacity of roads to evacuate a hurricane zone, and engineers will disregard all they have learned about O-rings. We can even find analogies in the realm of finance: the New Deal's precautions against the bank failures of the Depression created institutions that helped promote the wave of savings-and-loan bankruptcies of the 1980s. International electronic networks for communication and commerce make new kinds of disasters possible, as localized malfunctions now have unprecedented opportunities for spreading. If the postal carriers of one city start hoarding or discarding mail, it is a major problem but no immediate threat to the system's integrity. If a network node were to go wrong in some unforeseen way, worldwide systems could fail before the cause was even identified.

The real question is not whether new disasters will occur. Of course they will. It is whether we gain or lose ground as a result. It is whether our apparent success is part of a long-term and irreversible improvement in the human condition or a deceptive respite in a grim and open-ended Malthusian pressure of human numbers and demands against natural limits. It is whether revenge effects are getting worse or milder. I think, but cannot prove, that in the long run they are going to be good for us. And I would like to suggest why.

Retreating from Intensity

Revenge effects reached their peak in the hundred years between the 1860s and the 1960s, during the very acme of technological optimism. Clobbering nature into submission united North Americans and Europeans, Communists and Republicans. Explosives, heavy machinery, agriculture, and transportation seemed at last to be fulfilling the injunction of Genesis 1:28 to "fill the earth and subdue it." Soviet citizens named their children for Henry Ford and his tractors. Contemporaries thought they were living at the beginning of an era of open-ended change; but it is also clear that few of them reckoned with the tendency of nature to strike back. Although (as the historian Douglas Weiner has documented) Friedrich Engels himself wrote of how nature "avenges" humanity against exploitation, the Eastern Bloc kept subjugating its part of the planet until the bitter end.[43]

The real meaning of Communism's collapse had less to do, in fact, with collectivism than with a fixation on intensity that continued through the Gorbachev years. Officially the regime campaigned to conserve materials. But it also set output goals by weight, not performance. Industrial quotas, meted out in metric tons, were filled with heavy stuff—sometimes incredibly sturdy, more often simply bad. The alleged Soviet boast of producing the world's largest microchips may be apocryphal, but Marshall I. Goldman, an economist who visited the USSR often, noticed an exceptional proportion of office typewriters with unnecessary extra-long carriages.[44]

The Soviet fixation on goals by gross weight and volume was only an extreme case of the pathology of intensity: the single-minded overextension of a good thing. We should keep in mind that the West went through even more serious crises of intensification. Potatoes, a great benefit for the European popular diet, were genetically vulnerable when grown from a single strain and used as a primary source of nutrition by the very poor. Yet terrible as the Irish potato famine of the 1840s was, nothing like it has recurred. The crash of the French raw silk industry in the 1850s, so important for Louis Pasteur's career, also showed how dangerous it could be for so many families to link their economic fate to a single organism.

It is curious how many resource-rich nations and regions have faltered because they relied too strongly on exploiting only one or two sources of natural wealth. The Mississippi delta, the deserted mining towns of the Rockies, and the desolate coal patches of the Pennsylvania anthracite country all have their counterparts overseas: Sicily, the Ukraine, and Argentina as former world breadbaskets, Romania and Azerbaijan as fabled energy reserves, Zaire and Siberia as gold vaults, the Ruhr as ironworks. The nature of the resource does not seem to matter. Nor do colonialism or foreign rule, though absentee ownership may. It was wealth that became an enemy of a vital diversity. On the other side, resource-poor islands and formerly isolated regions like Switzerland, Japan, Taiwan, and Singapore have become the twentieth century's economic stars.[45]

Of course, it is too optimistic to say that we have overcome the perils of intensity. We have already seen how "rationalized" forestry in England and Scotland has helped turn the familiar ground squirrel of North America into a significant woodland pest. The science writer Matt Ridley has described how even in Tory England, state-promoted conversion of "unproductive" downland to wheat fields and ancient forests to conifer plantations had endangered butterflies and other native wildlife and plants. In Spain and Portugal, the ancient *dehesas* of mixed cork oak and holm oak in a setting of grain and grasslands have also been threatened by clearance for Euro-subsidized crops. Elsewhere, clear-cut forestry and overfishing continue. The greatest risk of any new natural technology, especially a genetic one, is not a superpest. It is an apparently harmless organism or chemical that begins as a stunning success and displaces alternatives in the marketplace. Making anything so hardy and productive is like announcing a huge prize for the first naturally selected pests and parasites. Sooner or later there will be a big winner.[46]

All this hardly means that science or technology has overintensified life, or that traditional agriculture was always environmentally benign. In the Mediterranean and elsewhere, preindustrial agriculture could devastate as well as foster diversity; it is hard to imagine any biologically engineered organism as catastrophic in the wild as the otherwise useful and endearing goat. And technologies can follow a number of alternative paths, depending on the assumptions and interests of those who develop and support them. Technologies can help preserve old genetic resources, evaluate new crops, reduce the quantity of pesticide and herbicide applications, consume less water. In other words, they can diversify and *de*-intensify. This implies a new balance between public and market-driven research, since (as the geneticist Richard C. Lewontin and others have shown) commercial research necessarily neglects natural, nonpatentable varieties of organisms that would be in the public domain after the first sale.

In agriculture, the retreat from intensity means forgoing applications of heavy fertilizer in favor of planting complementary crops in the same fields, increasing both productivity and resilience. In medicine, the retreat from intensity demands a shift away from the heavy reliance on a handful of antibiotics. In business computing, it implies a heavy dose of skepticism about the functional value of "more powerful" new releases of both hardware and software. It also suggests doubts as to whether higher workloads and longer days always yield more profit; sometimes it even calls for deliberately slowing or interrupting the pace of work. In sports, it provokes a harder look at whether stiffer and more powerful equipment necessarily makes for a better game. The retreat from intensification does not necessarily require giving it up; it does mean subjecting it to much greater scrutiny.

It isn't enough, of course, to modify intensity. Reducing revenge effects demands substituting brains for stuff. And the record of human ingenuity in making brainpower do the work of energy and raw materials is impressive. Balloon-frame houses, the invention of anonymous carpenters on the nearly treeless prairies of the nineteenth-century American Midwest, became famous for their durability as well as their economy. In our own time the cheapest electronic computers available today from any discount store can calculate many times faster than the room- and building-size arrays of relays and vacuum tubes of the industry's pioneer days. Steel is lighter and stronger, yet certain plastics are lighter and stronger than steel. Automobiles now weigh less and use less gasoline per mile. A CD weighs a fraction of an LP, and a CD player is lighter and more compact than a conventional turntable. New mathematical algorithms allow the same information to be stored on smaller disks—or more information on the same size disk.

The engineer Robert Herman, the technology analyst Jesse H. Ausubel, and their associates argue that technological change exerts powerful forces both for increasing and for reducing the amount of energy and other resources used. Electronic storage can reduce the consumption of paper, but . . . it can also multiply it. Lighter goods may heighten rather than diminish the need for materials if they are marketed or treated as throwaways rather than durables. (Thick, returnable glass bottles may, for example, demand less intense use of energy and other resources than even recyclable aluminum.) In fact, as Herman and Ausubel have suggested, lighter and more efficient automobiles promote resource-consuming if dispersed suburban living and thus materialization. Nuclear power generation begins with low-weight raw materials but ends with vast contaminated structures that probably can never be reused.[47]

What appears to be a technological question—how much of anything we really need—is in the end a social one. It is the size and appearance of a yard or a lawn or a house, the taste for (or repudiation of) meat, and so forth. Often what is most crucial, and most uncertain, is not invention and discovery but taste and preference. The open question, raised during the upheavals of the 1970s and then forgotten during the boom of the 1980s, is whether cultural change can lead to new preferences that will in turn relieve humanity's pressure on the earth's resources. Human culture, not some inherent will of the machine, has created most revenge effects. Without the taste for silk, there would have been no gypsy moths in North America. Without the preference for detached housing, there would still be congestion, perhaps, but more economical congestion. Without the love of oceanside living, shore erosion yes, but no social disruption.

Even more promising than diversification and dematerialization is an attitude that has not yet found its rightful name. It is the substitution of cunning for the frontal attack, and it is not new. It began with immunization against smallpox—as we have seen, a folk practice long before Edward Jenner introduced it to medicine—and continued with the vaccines of the late nineteenth and twentieth centuries.

Finesse means abandoning frontal attacks for solutions that rely on the same kind of latent properties that led to revenge effects in the first place. Sometimes it means ceasing to suppress a symptom. In medicine, finesse suggests closer attention to the evolutionary background of human health and illness, to the positive part that fever plays, for example, in fighting infection. At other times, finesse means living with and even domesticating a problem organism. As we have seen, researchers like Stanley Falkow and Paul Ewald have suggested a kind of evolutionary compromise with what are now lethal bacteria and viruses, turning them into common but harmless companions. In the office, finesse means producing more by taking more frequent breaks and conveying more information by, for example, limiting rather than multiplying color schemes. In construction, finesse means allowing skyscrapers to sway slightly in the wind instead of bracing them to resist it. On the road, finesse means a calmer approach to driving, improving the speed and economy of all drivers by slowing them down at times when impulse would prompt accelerating. It can mean moving more traffic by metering access to some roads and even closing off others. (Some German analysts have written of the "softening," *Besänftigung*, of traffic.) Diversification, dematerialization, and finesse are far from a rejection of science.

To the contrary, it is science that points us away from crude reductionism and counterproductive brute force toward technologies that improve human life. But the improvement has a cost.

As the Red Queen said in *Through the Looking-Glass,* we are no longer in the "slow sort of country" where running gets one somewhere: "Now, *here,* you see, it takes all the running you can do, to keep in the same place. If you want to get somewhere else, you must run at least twice as fast as that!" And in fact the alternatives to the intensified, revenge-prone modes of earlier technology seem to take nearly all the running we can do. Even the optimistic report of the Council for Agricultural Science and Technology (CAST) makes clear that most of our agricultural research goes to "maintenance," that is, to keeping the gains we have made: dealing with deteriorating water quality and increasing costs, and offsetting "biological surprises like the appearance of more virulent pests." The same could probably be said of many medical efforts. Similarly, the power of personal computer hardware seems driven by the need to compensate for the way that more elaborate interfaces and features slow the fundamentals of performance.[48]

Technological optimism means in practice the ability to recognize bad surprises early enough to do something about them. And that demands constant monitoring of the globe, for everything from changes in mean temperatures and particulates to traffic in bacteria and viruses. It also requires a second level of vigilance at increasingly porous national borders against the world exchange of problems. But vigilance does not end there. It is everywhere. It is in the random alertness tests that have replaced the "dead man's pedal" for train operators. It is in the rituals of computer backup, the legally mandated testing of everything from elevators to home smoke alarms, routine X-ray screening, securing and loading new computer-virus definitions. It is in the inspection of arriving travelers for products that might harbor pests. Even our alertness in crossing the street, second nature to urbanites now, was generally unnecessary before the eighteenth century. Sometimes vigilance is more of a reassuring ritual than a practical precaution, but with any luck it works. Revenge effects mean in the end that we will move ahead but must always look back just because reality is indeed gaining on us.   ∎

NOTES

1. John Tierney, "Betting on the Planet," *New York Times Magazine,* 2 December 1990, 52.

2. David S. Landes, *Revolution in Time: Clocks and the Making of the Modern World* (Cambridge, Mass.: Harvard University Press, 1983), 103–13; Robert K. Merton, *Science, Technology, and Society in Seventeenth-Century England* (New York: Harper Torchbooks, 1970 [1938]), 167–77.

3. Derek Howse, *Greenwich Time and the Discovery of the Longitude* (Oxford: Oxford University Press, 1980), 44–72.

4. David S. Landes, *Revolution in Time: Clocks and the Making of the Modern World* (Cambridge, Mass.: Harvard University Press, 1983), 103–13, 144–57.

5. See Paul Slovic, "Perception of Risk," *Science,* vol. 236, no. 4799 (17 April 1987), 280–85; and Paul Slovic, "Perception of Risk: Reflections on the Psychometric Paradigm," in Sheldon Krimsky and Dominic Golding, eds., *Social Theories of Risk* (Westport, Conn.: Praeger, 1992), 117–52.

6. John P. Eaton and Charles A. Haas, *Titanic: Triumph and Tragedy* (New York: Norton, 1987), 310–11; Edward Bryant, *Natural Hazards* (Cambridge: Cambridge University Press, 1991), 68.

7. James T. Yenckel, "How Safe Is Cruising?," *Washington Post,* 11 August 1991, E6.

8. See Henry Petroski, *To Engineer Is Human: The Role of Failure in Successful Design* (New York: St. Martin's Press, 1985).

9. Mark F. Grady, "Torts: The Best Defense Against Regulation," *Wall Street Journal,* 3 September 1992, A11; Mark F. Grady, "Why Are People Negligent? Technology, Nondurable Precautions, and the Medical Malpractice Explosion," *Northwestern University Law Review,* vol. 82 (Winter 1988), 297–99, 312. See also Grady's review of Paul C. Weiler's *Medical Malpractice on Trial,* "Better Medicine Causes More Lawsuits, and New Administrative Courts Will Not Solve the Problem," *Northwestern University Law Review,* vol. 86 (Summer 1992), 1068–81.

10. On seventeenth-century navigation, see Landes, *Revolution in Time,* 105–11; Carla Rahn Phillips, *Six Galleons for the King of Spain* (Baltimore: Johns Hopkins University Press, 1986), 129–34. On Shovell's tomb: Margaret Whitney, *Sculpture in Britain, 1530 to 1830* (Baltimore: Penguin, 1964), 58. There is probably more to late-nineteenth- and early-twentieth-century litigation than Grady acknowledges: the deference shown by judges and juries of the time toward elite defendants in tort liability cases. To name just three other notorious cases, the industrialists' club that maintained the dam that broke and caused the Johnstown flood in 1889 (2,200 dead), the owners of the *General Slocum,* which caught fire in New York Harbor in 1904 (1,021 dead), and the proprietors of the Triangle Shirtwaist Factory, which burned with 145 dead, escaped civil and criminal action. Even with Astors, Wideners, and Guggenheims among the *Titanic* passengers and the victims' families, the final settlement with the White Star Line was minuscule by late-twentieth-century standards: $663,000 (£136,701) on total claims of $16,804,112 (£3,464,765). See Eaton and Haas, *Titanic,* 277–79.

11. James C. Beniger, *The Control Revolution: Technological and Economic Origins of the Information Society* (Cambridge, Mass.: Harvard University Press, 1986), 221–26 and references.

12. Clay McShane, *Down the Asphalt Path: The Automobile and the American City* (New York: Columbia University Press, 1994), 42–45.

13. Christopher Gray, "Who Holds the Reins of Fate of a 1907 Horse-Auction Mart?" *New York Times,* 8 November 1987, Real Estate, 14; McShane, *Asphalt Path,* 51–54.

14. Daniel Pool, *What Jane Austen Ate and Charles Dickens Knew* (New York: Simon & Schuster, 1993), 250–51; McShane, *Asphalt Path,* 46–50; for a summary of modern fatalities, Leonard Evans, *Traffic Safety and the Driver* (New York: Van Nostrand Reinhold, 1991), 3.

15. Scott L. Bottles, *Los Angeles and the Automobile: The Making of the Modern City* (Berkeley: University of California Press, 1987), 22.

16. On powers and interests in highway building, see Mark H. Rose, *Interstate: Express Highway Politics, 1941–1956* (Lawrence: University Press of Kansas, 1979).

17. Mark S. Foster, *From Streetcar to Superhighway: American City Planners and Urban Transportation, 1900–1940* (Philadelphia: Temple University Press, 1981), 143–45; "Onwards and Outwards," *Economist,* vol. 333, no. 7885 (15 October 1994), 31.

18. Cited in Anatole Kopp, *Town and Revolution: Soviet Architecture and City Planning, 1917–1935* (New York: Braziller, 1970), 173. The Disurbanists (or Deurbanists) actually had in mind the relocation of urban functions along great highways, not the present American suburban pattern.

19. Kenneth Jackson, *Crabgrass Frontier: The Suburbanization of the United States* (New York: Oxford University Press, 1985), 249.

20. K. H. Schaeffer and Elliot Sclar, *Access for All: Transportation and Urban Growth* (Baltimore: Penguin, 1975), 40–44.

21. Ivan Illich, *Energy and Equity* (New York: Harper & Row, 1974), 18–19.

22. Ibid., 95–96; David Remnick, "Berserk on the Beltway," *Washington Post Magazine*, 7 September 1986, 66ff, 95; "Urban Freeways, Interstates in a Jam," *USA Today*, 18 September 1989, 10A; John F. Harris, "Auto Club, Citing Traffic, to Shut Fairfax Office," *Washington Post*, 1 October 1986.

23. Richard Arnott and Kenneth Small, "The Economics of Traffic Congestion," *American Scientist*, vol. 82, no. 5 (September–October 1994), 446–55; Bob Holmes, "When Shock Waves Hit Traffic," *New Scientist*, vol. 142, no. 1931 (25 June 1994), 36–40.

24. "Risk Homeostasis and the Purpose of Safety Regulation," *Ergonomics*, vol. 31, no. 4 (1988), 408–9.

25. Evans, *Traffic Safety*, 287–90; Haight remarks in telephone interview, October 1991.

26. R. J. Smeed and G. O. Jeffcoate, "Effects of Changes in Motorisation in Various Countries on the Number of Road Fatalities," *Traffic Engineering and Control*, vol. 12, no. 3 (July 1970), 150–51.

27. John Adams, "Smeed's Law and the Emperor's New Clothes," in Leonard Evans and Richard C. Schwing, eds., *Human Behavior and Traffic Safety* (New York: Plenum Press, 1985), 195–96, 235–37.

28. William K. Stevens, "When It Comes to Highway Chaos, India is No. 1," *New York Times*, 26 October 1983, A2; Steve Coll, " 'Road Kings' Truck Across India," *Washington Post*, 28 October 1989, A1; McShane, *Asphalt Path*, 174–77.

29. "Drivin' My Life Away," *Scientific American*, vol. 257, no. 2 (August 1987), 28, 30; Susan P. Baker, R. A. Whitefield, and Brian O'Neill, "Geographic Variations in Mortality from Motor Vehicle Crashes," *New England Journal of Medicine*, vol. 316, no. 22 (28 May 1987), 1384–87.

30. "In Portugal, Wheels of Misfortune," *New York Times*, 22 July 1990, Travel, 39.

31. Deborah Fallows, "Malaysia's Mad Motorists," *Washington Post*, 10 July 1988, C5.

32. James J. MacKenzie, Roger C. Dower, and Donald D. T. Chen, *The Going Rate: What It Really Costs to Drive* (Washington: World Resources Institute, 1992), 13.

33. Angus Kress Gillespie and Michael Aaron Rockland, *Looking for America on the New Jersey Turnpike* (New Brunswick, N.J.: Rutgers University Press, 1989), 114–15; Albert O. Hirschman, *The Strategy of Economic Development* (New Haven, Conn.: Yale University Press, 1958), 134, 143–45. Hirschman also points out that "a road that is not traveled is likely to deteriorate sooner than one that has to support heavy traffic: the former will surely be neglected whereas there is some hope that the latter will be maintained." Because bituminous surfaces show deterioration early, they may be more suitable for less-traveled roads in developing countries than gravel would be. They don't degrade gracefully, as electrical engineers put it; they demand attention.

34. "How Driving Under the Influence of Society Affects Traffic Deaths," *Washington Post*, 2 September 1991, A3.

35. Charles Stile, "N.J. Drivers Yielding to Safety," *Trenton Times,* 15 September 1991, A1.

36. Kenneth Grahame, *The Wind in the Willows* (New York: Charles Scribner's Sons, 1961), 121.

37. "Jay Gatsby Never Dreamed of Gridlock," *Trenton Times,* 19 November 1991, A18.

38. Michael S. Mahoney, personal communication; John Shore, "Why I Never Met a Programmer I Could Trust," *Communications of the ACM,* vol. 31, no. 4 (April 1988), 372; Wiener, *Digital Woes,* 99–100.

39. For the most useful recent summary of the vast literature on road issues, see the special issue of *CQ Researcher,* vol. 4, no. 17 (6 May 1994), 385–408.

40. P. N. Lee, "Has the Mortality of Male Doctors Improved with the Reductions in Their Cigarette Smoking?" *British Medical Journal,* 15 December 1979, 1538–40.

41. *Risk: Analysis, Perception, and Management* (London: Royal Society, 1992), 155–59, 138–42.

42. See Jonathan Beecher, *Charles Fourier: The Visionary and His World* (Berkeley: University of California Press, 1987), 338–41; Spencer Weart, "From the Nuclear Frying Pan into the Global Fire," *Bulletin of the Atomic Scientists,* vol. 48, no. 5 (June 1992), 18–27.

43. See Douglas R. Weiner, *Models of Nature* (Bloomington: University of Indiana Press, 1988), 195, for Engels's article "The Role of Labor in the Transformation from Ape to Man" as a rallying point for Soviet conservationists. Their opponents insisted that Engels meant only abusive capitalist development, not dialectically informed socialist intervention.

44. On early Soviet production quotas and the technological conservatism they encouraged, see Kendall E. Bailes, *Technology and Society Under Lenin and Stalin* (Princeton, N.J.: Princeton University Press, 1978), 350; Marshall I. Goldman, *What Went Wrong with Perestroika* (New York: Norton, 1991), 87; Marshall I. Goldman, *Gorbachev's Challenge* (New York: Norton, 1987), 123–24. Let those who have never used a Pentium computer to compose a yard-sale announcement cast the first stone.

45. The superiority of knowledge and the proper work ethic to wealth in resources became a watchword of 1980s reformers. Nathan Glazer's "Two Inspiring Lessons of the 1980s," *New York Times,* 24 December 1989, Review, 11, even suggests that some resources like the agricultural lands of Europe and Japan with their heavily subsidized surplus crops are becoming "a positive burden to economic success."

46. Matt Ridley, "Butterflies Fall Victim to Man's Interfering Hand," *Sunday Telegraph,* 17 July 1994, 32; Malcolm Smith, "Science: Live the High Life and Save the Wildlife," *Independent,* 30 May 1994, 19.

47. Robert Herman, Siamak A. Ardekani, and Jesse H. Ausubel, "Dematerialization," *Technological Forecasting and Social Change,* vol. 38 (1990), 333–47.

48. Lewis Carroll, *Through the Looking-Glass,* in *The Complete Works of Lewis Carroll* (New York: Modern Library, n.d. [1896 edn.]), 164; "How Much Land Can Ten Billion People Spare for Nature?," Council for Agricultural Science and Technology Task Force Report 121 (February 1994), 26.

■ *QUESTIONS FOR MAKING CONNECTIONS*
WITHIN THE READING ■

1. First, define and explain one of Tenner's key terms, such as "revenge effects," "intensiveness," "technological optimists," "signal event,"

"homeostasis," "complex system," "recomplication," "extrapolation," "intensity," or "finesse." Next, try to connect the key term that you have chosen with the other key terms. Finally, develop a key term of your own that names an event or process Tenner describes but does not himself name.

2. On the basis of your reading of "Another Look Back, and a Look Ahead," would you describe Tenner as a "technological optimist"? How can anyone claim to be an optimist about technology if it is, as Tenner concedes, "extremely hard"—and perhaps even impossible—"to predict the future state of a complex system even without the added imponderables of human culture and behavior"? Is it possible that technological innovation will reach a point of diminishing returns, when the costs of innovation, or the dangers, outweigh the potential benefits? Does Tenner ever consider this possibility?

3. In what ways does Tenner's discussion of new technologies confirm his belief that progress "comes in by the back door"? To what degree does technological change take place in response to people's needs and their conscious choices? To what degree does technology shape those needs and choices? On the basis of Tenner's examples, would it be fair to say that technology has a life of its own that no one can control, or would such a claim be an exaggeration?

■ *QUESTIONS FOR WRITING* ■

1. The last two centuries have brought about technological change on a scale and at a pace that nobody in any prior age could have imagined. In fact, the pace of change has grown so quickly that we expect innovations to outstrip our predictions. Under these conditions, will it ever be possible to say "no" to technology? Many people believe, for example, that the automobile has diminished the quality of American life in many ways—by polluting the air and allowing suburban sprawl to gobble up the countryside, and by depopulating cities and erasing the local cultures of towns and neighborhoods. Perhaps the most remarkable thing about cars is the rapidity of their development—too rapid, perhaps, for anyone to stop and weigh the consequences. If technology now exceeds human control, do we need to rethink the trust we place in it?

2. How has Tenner's account changed the way you think about technology? Ordinarily, we view technology in a number of different lights: as a neutral instrument or tool; as a miraculous gift; as a specialized pursuit, far removed from human feelings; as a form of knowledge synonymous with science; as a Frankensteinlike monster; as an extension of the market-

place. In what ways does Tenner complicate and perhaps even contradict these commonsense ways of viewing technology? Is it naive to think that we have created technology simply to make our lives better and easier? Does technology express an aspect of ourselves we ordinarily overlook? Other than comfort and security, what satisfactions do we derive from its creation?

■ *QUESTIONS FOR MAKING CONNECTIONS BETWEEN READINGS* ■

1. Tenner assures us, in spite of all the complications, that progress "comes in by the back door." In making this claim he seems to believe that a self-correcting process will usually operate, with "intensity" followed by "disaster," which produces "precaution" and finally "vigilance." Is this argument confirmed, extended, complicated, or refuted by Relman and Angell's account of the pharmaceutical industry's procedures for developing and marketing new drugs? Does the need for regulation and monitoring show that financial considerations can derail technology's ususal self-correcting tendencies? Are financial considerations sometimes at odds with the development of scientific knowledge in general?

2. Both Tenner and Steven Johnson in his essay, "The Myth of the Ant Queen," ask their readers to reconsider the role of technological innovation in the rise of contemporary society. Would both authors agree that it makes sense to be a "technological optimist"? Or would they say that technological optimism is just an expression of wishful thinking—a hope that things will turn out well when they actually might not? Does it make sense to think that the "emergent systems" Johnson describes tend to find solutions automatically, even when the people or life-forms involved remain blissfully unaware? Or is it essential that we recognize and consciously attempt to solve the problems we have created?

www **For further suggestions about making connections between readings, visit the Link-O-Mat and More Sample Assignments at <www.newhum.com>.**

ROBERT THURMAN

ROBERT THURMAN, ONE of the first Americans to be ordained as a Tibetan Buddhist monk, is often considered to be the most prominent and influential expert on Buddhism in the United States today. A scholar, translator, activist, and lecturer, Thurman began his explorations into Buddhism in his early twenties when he traveled to India on a "vision quest" and ended up becoming a student of the Dalai Lama. Upon returning to the United States, Thurman wanted to continue his studies and become an academic because, in his own words, "The only lay institution in America comparable to monasticism is the university." Thurman is currently the Jey Tsong Khapa Professor of Indo-Tibetan Buddhist Studies at Columbia University and the president of Tibet House, a nonprofit organization dedicated to the study and preservation of Tibetan culture.

Infinite Life (2004) is the latest in a series of books that Thurman has written on Buddhism. Chief among his goals in this text is to guide laypeople into their first explorations of the Buddhist concept of selflessness. The ultimate goal of the lessons that Thurman offers his readers is to impart a deeper sense of interconnectedness, a process that is meant to reduce the negative feelings individuals hold about themselves and to increase the positive feelings they have for others. In so doing, Thurman seeks to show that the happiness guaranteed by America's founders "should be ours and that there are methods for discovering which happiness is really reliable and satisfying, and then securing that in an enduring way without depriving others."

www **To learn more about Robert Thurman and Buddhism in America, please visit the Link-O-Mat at <www.newhum.com>.**

Thurman, Robert. "Wisdom." *Infinite Life*. Riverhead Books, Penguin, 2004. 49–71.

Biographical information drawn from <http://www.bobthurman.com/site.html> and <http://literati.net/Thurman/index.htm>. Initial quote taken from <http://literati.net/Thurman/index.htm>; closing quote from <http://www.bobthurman.com/site.html>.

Wisdom

Preamble: Selflessness

At one point in the early 1970s, after I'd gotten my Ph.D. and started teaching Buddhism, I went back to visit my old teacher, the Mongolian lama Geshe Wangyal. We were working on a project to translate a Buddhist scientific text from the Tibetan. We were six or seven people gathered around a kitchen table, and Geshe-la began to talk about the inner science of Buddhist psychology, the Abhidharma. He was reading us a few verses about the insight of selflessness, the deep release of becoming unbound, when I began to feel a little dizzy, even nauseous. It was a funny feeling. It felt slightly like a vibration spinning in my head. The vibration came not from Geshe-la, but from this ancient tradition. It was as though my habitual mind couldn't quite find traction. I realized that if I fought it, the sensation would only get more nerve-wracking and I would only feel more nauseous. So I didn't fight it. Instead, I let go and relaxed, and soon I was able to orient myself in another way, away from my "self." I felt like I was slowly but surely loosening my self-centered perspective on life and the world. In a useful way, a strengthening way, I was beginning to experience the great Buddhist mystery that is the selflessness of subjects and objects.

The Buddha based his psychology on his discovery of actual and ultimate reality. This he called "selflessness" and "voidness," or "emptiness." Some people love these words from the moment they hear them, but others are frightened by them. People often ask me, "Why did Buddha have to be such a downer? Obviously nirvana is a happy, cheerful state. So why didn't he just call it 'bliss' or something? Why did he have to label the reality he discovered with negative words such as 'voidness,' 'emptiness,' and 'selflessness'?" When people respond negatively to these terms, it's often because they're worried that the words imply they are going to die, disappear, or go crazy in their attempts to seek enlightenment. And that's exactly why the Buddha called reality by those names. He did it on purpose, to liberate you! Why? Because the only thing that's frightened by the word "selflessness" is the artificially constructed, unreal, and unrealistic self. That self is only a pretend self, it lacks reality, it doesn't really exist. That pseudo-self seems to quiver and quake because the habit that makes it seem real wants to keep its hold on you. So if you're seeking happiness and freedom, then you should want to scare the heck out of your "self"—you want to scare it right out of your head!

Actually, *it* is constantly scaring the heck out of *you*. Your "self" is always busy terrorizing you. You have a terrorist in your own brain, coming out of your own instincts and culture, who is pestering you all the time. "Don't relax too much," it is saying, "you'll get stepped on. A bug will bite you. Someone will be nasty to you. You'll get passed by, abused, sick. Don't be honest. Pretend. Because if you're honest, they'll hurt you." And it's ordering you, "Be my slave. Do what I tell you to do. Keep me installed up here at this very superficial level of the brain where I sit in my weird Woody Allen–type cockpit. Because I'm in control." Your falsely perceived, fixated, domineering self is precisely what's getting between you and a fulfilling life.

Early on, some of the Western psychologists who were beginning to learn from the Buddhist tradition—members of the transpersonal and other movements—came up with the idea that the relationship between Buddhist and Western psychology is this: "Western psychology helps somebody who feels they are nobody become somebody, and Buddhist psychology helps somebody who feels they are somebody become nobody." When I first heard this, I was at an Inner Science conference with the Dalai Lama. Everybody laughed, applauded, and thought it was a great insight. The Dalai Lama just looked at me and kind of winked and was too polite to say anything. I started to jump up to make a comment, but he stopped me. He told me to be quiet and let all of them ponder it for a few years until they realized the flaw in their thinking. Because of course that idea is not even remotely correct.

The purpose of realizing your own selflessness is not to feel like you are nobody. After he became enlightened, the Buddha did not sit under a tree drooling, and saying "Oh, wow! I'm nobody!" Think about it: If he just "became nobody," if he escaped from the world through self-obliteration, then he wouldn't have been able to share so many teachings here on earth, to work for the good of all beings for years and years, long after he achieved nirvana. He would've just stayed in his "nobody" state and forgotten about all of us poor humans busy suffering through our miserable lives.

The reason why we sometimes think that the goal of Buddhism is just "to become nobody" is that we don't understand the concept of selflessness. "Selflessness" does not mean that we are nobody. It does not mean that we cease to exist. Not at all. There is no way you can ever "not exist," just as you cannot become "nothing." Even if you go through deep meditation into what is called "the realm of absolute nothingness," you will still exist. Even if you are so freaked out by a tragedy, such as losing your only child, that you try to end your existence completely, you will still exist. I have a healthy respect for tragedy. We do have terrible tragedies. Personally, I don't bear misfortune well; it knocks me out. But there is no way to become nobody. Even if you were to succeed in killing yourself, you will be shocked when you awaken to disembodied awareness, out-of-body but still a somebody, a ghostly wraith who wishes he hadn't just done that. And a terribly unfortunate living person who has been so brutalized that he blanks out who he was in a seemingly impenetrable psychosis is still somebody, as everybody else around him knows.

Our mind is so powerful that it can create a state of absolute nothingness that seems totally concrete. Thousands of yogis in the history of India and a few mystics in the West have entered such a state of nothingness. But no one can stay there forever, and it is not where you want to be.

Have you ever had a minor experience of nothingness? I've had it in the dentist's chair with sodium pentothal, because I used to eat a lot of sweets and not brush my teeth as a youngster so I had to have teeth pulled. They give you this knockout anesthetic, and if you are a hard-working intellectual, you are tired of your mind, so you think, "Oh great, I'm going to be obliterated for a little while." You're really pleased, and you feel this little buzz, and you're just about to get there. You're going to experience nothingness, a little foretaste of the nihilistic notion of nirvana! But suddenly the nurse is shaking you awake saying, "You've been slobbering in that chair long enough. Get out of here." It's over. You started to pass out, wanting to be gone, but now you're suddenly back with no sense of having been gone at all! And that's what it is like in the state of absolute nothingness. It's like being passed out in the dentist's chair. There's no sense of duration of time. But eventually you wake up, totally disoriented with a nasty headache, and you never even got to enjoy the oblivion.

So we can never become nothing, as appealing as that may sound to those who are addicted to the idea of nothingness after death. We are always somebody, even though we are selfless in reality. We are just different sorts of "somebodies" than we used to be. "Realizing your selflessness" does not mean that you become a nobody, it means that you become the type of somebody who is a viable, useful somebody, not a rigid, fixated, I'm-the-center-of-the-universe, isolated-from-others somebody. You become the type of somebody who is over the idea of a conceptually fixated and self-created "self," a pseudo-self that would actually be absolutely weak, because of being unrelated to the reality of your constantly changing nature. You become the type of somebody who is content never to be quite that sure of who you are—always free to be someone new, somebody more.

That's the whole point of selflessness. If you don't know exactly who you are all the time, you're not sick, you're actually in luck, because you're more realistic, more free, and more awake! You're being too intelligent to be stuck inside one frozen mask of personality! You've opened up your wisdom, and you've realized that "knowing who you are" is the trap—an impossible self-objectification. None of us knows who we really are. Facing that and then becoming all that we can be—astonishing, surprising, amazing—always fresh and new, always free to be more, brave enough to become a work in progress, choosing happiness, open-mindedness, and love over certitude, rigidity, and fear—this is realizing selflessness!

I never met the late, great comedian Peter Sellers, except splitting my sides in laughter while watching some of his movies, especially the *Pink Panther* series. I know he had his ups and downs in his personal life, though you can't believe all the things you hear from the tabloids. But I did read a quote from him, or maybe from his psychiatrist, that he was deeply troubled and distressed because he suffered from "not knowing who he really was." He would get into his roles as an actor so totally, he would think he was the person he was playing, and he couldn't find himself easily as his "own" person. So he suffered, feeling himself "out of control" in his life. When I read this, my heart went out to him. I imagined his psychiatrist sternly telling him he had better calm down and track himself down, and put a lid on his ebullient sense of life, leading him on and on in self-absorption in therapy under the guise that he was going to "find himself" once and for all. I, feeling a bit more freed by having awakened to even the tiniest taste of selflessness, wanted to cry out to Peter Sellers, "Stop suffering by thinking your insight is confusion! Don't listen to the misknowing and even fear your freedom! Learn to surf the energy of life that surges through your openness! You have discovered your real self already, your great self of selflessness, and that openness is what enables you to manifest the heart that shines through your work and opens the hearts of your audiences. Your gift is to release them into laughter, itself a taste of freedom! Why be confused and feel your great gift is something wrong?" But I didn't know him so I could not tell him what I'm telling you. But our lives are infinite and I will be telling his ongoing life-form one of these days, whether I recognize him or not!

The Buddha was happy about not knowing who he was in the usual rigid, fixed sense. He called the failure to know who he was "enlightenment." Why? Because he realized that selflessness kindles the sacred fire of compassion. When you become aware of your selflessness, you realize that any way you feel yourself to be at any time is just a relational, changing construction. When that happens, you have a huge inner release of compassion. Your inner creativity about your living self is energized, and your infinite life becomes your ongoing work of art.

You see others caught in the suffering of the terminal self-habit and you feel real compassion. You feel so much better, so highly relieved, that your only concern is helping those constricted other people. You are free to worry about them because, of course, they are having a horrible time trying to know who they are and trying to be who they think they should be! They are busy being ripped apart by the great streams of ignorance, illness, death, and other people's irritating habits. So they suffer. And you, in your boundless, infinitely interconnected, compassionate state, can help them.

This is the other crucial point about selflessness: It does not mean that you are disconnected. Even nirvana is not a state of disconnection from the world. There is no way to become removed from yourself or from other beings. We are ultimately boundless—that is to say, our relative boundaries are permeable. But we are still totally interconnected no matter what we do. You cannot disappear into your own blissful void, because you are part of everyone and they are part of you. If you have no ultimate self, that makes you free to be your relative self, along with other beings. It's as if your hand represents the universe and your fingers represent all beings. Each of your fingers can wiggle on its own, each can operate independently, just as each being has its own identity. And yet your fingers are part of your hand. If your hand did not exist, your fingers would not exist. You are one of many, many fingers on the hand that is all life.

To my surprise and delight, I learned recently that even some Western psychologists are now beginning to study and understand the harm done by self-centered thinking. The psychologist Dr. Larry Scherwitz conducted a study about type A people—the aggressive, loud, annoying types, like me. Scientists used to think that type As died younger because of their fast-paced, stressful lives. But this new study reveals that, in fact, some of us type A people are not going to die of a heart attack that soon after all. The type Bs out there, the mild-mannered, quiet, inward-focused types, might find this worrisome! We may stay around for years bothering them, because it turns out that the type A personality is not a risk factor for coronary heart disease or other stress-related health problems. It turns out that some people, like me, though we freak out all the time, are not always that stressed. Some of us actually enjoy being this way.

What is the real risk factor, then? Scherwitz and his colleagues reanalyzed the data and conducted some new studies. They discovered, by analyzing the speech patterns of type As and type Bs, that the high risk of heart disease and stress-related illness is correlated with the *amount of self-reference* in people's speech—the amount of self-preoccupation, self-centeredness, and narcissism. "Me, me, I, I, my, my, mine, mine. My golf course, my country club, my job, my salary, my way, my family, my religion, my shrine, my guru, my, my, mine." The more "I, me, my, and mine" there is in their speech—"mine" most of all—the more likely they are to succumb to stress, to keel over because their bodies revolt against that pressure of self-involvement. Whereas even though some people can be aggressive, annoying, loud, and seemingly "stressed," if their overall motivation is altruistic and they don't pay too much attention to themselves, they live longer. And the quiet type Bs who are also more concerned about others, not necessarily out of any altruistic religious inklings, but just naturally not paying much attention to themselves, tend to live longer, too.

I find this study amazing. I was with the Dalai Lama when he heard about the results. He was intrigued and very pleased. "Oh, really?" he said.

"Let me see that paper. In Buddhist psychology, we also have this idea that obsessive self-preoccupation—possessiveness and selfishness and self-centeredness—is life's chief demon!"

Let us explore the problems created by this demon of self-preoccupation, the ways in which it causes us suffering. We will then practice a fundamental meditation in which we look for the fixated self and find that it does not, after all, exist. Once we have freed ourselves from the constricting habit of always thinking that we are the center of the universe, we will experience our first taste of the boundless joy and compassion that is infinite life.

Problem: Misknowledge and Self-Preoccupation

One of the hardest things we have to do on a regular basis is to admit that we are wrong. We stubbornly insist that we're right in situations where we're not quite sure if we are, and even when we sense that we've slipped. How much more indignant do we become when we feel certain that we're right and someone has the gall or the stupidity to challenge us? In this case, we feel an absolute imperative to jump up and trumpet our rightness. If we still cannot get others to agree with us, we soon become self-righteous and then outraged.

Believe it or not, the fact that we struggle so much with being wrong is of tremendous importance to our task of awakening to the reality of selflessness. We should examine our habit of needing to be right carefully to see why it feels so good.

Being right means that the world affirms us in what we think we know. "Knowing" something is a way of controlling it, being able to put it in its proper place in relation to us so that we can use it effectively. As Dharmakirti, the seventh century Indian philosopher, said, "All successful action is preceded by accurate knowledge." So knowledge is power, in the sense that it empowers us to act successfully. Misknowledge, misunderstanding a situation, is weakness, in the sense that our actions may fail in their aim, backfire, or have unintended consequences. Knowledge is security, in that we know our vulnerabilities and can avoid harm. Misknowledge is danger, in that we don't know what others might do to us or what traps may await us. We therefore feel powerful and secure when we're right, weak and vulnerable when we're wrong.

Viewed in this context, being right seems like a struggle for survival, a drive to win. It's natural for us to cling to that feeling, even when we have not investigated the reality around us because we don't really want to know if we are wrong. We think that finding ourselves in the wrong means a loss of power and safety, forgetting that actually *it is the only way* for us to discover what is truly right and truly wrong, thereby gaining real power and real safety. When we pretend, we focus our attention on appearing to be right no matter what the reality, we distract ourselves from being awake to what really is going on, and so place ourselves at a disempowering disadvantage.

In light of this simple analysis, what lies at the center of our constant need to assure our rightness and, therefore, our power and security? Is it not the certainty that "I am"? Does not the strong sense of "I am" seem absolutely right, unquestionable, in fact? Every self-identification, judgment, and impulse beginning with "I am"—"I am me," "I am American," "I am human," "I am male," "I am right," "I am sure," "I am angry"—seems natural, undeniable, imperative. As such, we are habitually driven to obey in feelings, thoughts, words, and deeds whatever comes from within the inexhaustible fountain of I am's, I think's, I want's, I love's, I hate's, and I do's. "I" is the absolute captain of our ship, the agent of our fate, the master of our lives.

When apes or bulls or mountain goats snort and paw the ground and then charge head first at one another, we interpret their behavior as an "I" versus "I" contest, sometimes to the death. Similarly, the imperative issuing from our "I" can be so adamant, so unchallengeable, that we human beings, too, will sacrifice our lives. Just think of the nature of such statements as follows, when the "I" is aligned with country, church, God, family, race, gender, or species: "I am a patriot!" "I am a Protestant!" "I am a Catholic!" "I am a Christian!" "I am a Muslim!" "I am a believer!" "I am an atheist!" "I am white!" "I am a male!" "I am human!" In these situations, the "I" exercises tremendous power over us, and can often lead us to our death.

The "I," the ego-self seemingly absolutely resident in the heart of our being, is the one thing of which we each are absolutely certain, which we will die for, which we will kill for, which we will obey slavishly and unquestioningly throughout our lives. We are so accustomed to our habitual sense of self that we consider even the slightest absence of it—a moment of derangement, a loss of consciousness in fainting or deep sleep, a disorienting distraction of passion or terror, a dizzying state of drunkenness or drug-intoxication, a psychological or neurological disorder—absolutely terrifying. We can't imagine our lives without our "I" as a constant, demanding presence.

What is shocking and difficult for most Westerners to accept is that the Buddha discovered that this most certain knowledge of the "self" is actually "misknowledge"—a fundamental misunderstanding, a delusion. And what's more, he realized that this discovery was the key to liberation, the gateway to enlightenment. When he saw the false nature of the "I," he emitted his "lion's roar," pronouncing the reality of selflessness, identitylessness, voidness. This was his *Eureka!* moment, his scientific breakthrough, his insight into reality, from whence has flowed for thousands of years the whole philosophical, scientific, and religious educational movement that is Buddhism. Identifying this habitual, certain self-knowledge as the core misknowledge allowed the Buddha to give birth to wisdom, truth, and liberating enlightenment.

But the Buddha knew perfectly well that it would do no good to simply order people to accept his declaration of selflessness as dogma and cling to it as a slogan or creed. The instinctual entanglement of human beings within the knot of self-certainty is much too powerful to be dislodged in this way, selflessness at first too counterintuitive to be acknowledged as truth. No, the Buddha realized, people must discover their real nature for themselves. So he made his declaration of selflessness not a statement of fact but rather a challenge to inquiry.

"I have discovered selflessness!" the Buddha announced. "I have seen through the reality of the seemingly solid self that lay at the core of my being. This insight did not destroy me—it only destroyed my suffering. It was my liberation! But you need not believe me. Discover the truth for yourself. Try with all your might to verify this 'self' you feel is in there, to pin it down. If you can do that, fine, tell me I'm wrong and ignore whatever else I may have to say. But if you fail to find it, if each thing you come up with dissolves under further analysis, if you discover, as I did, that there is no atomic, indivisible, durable core 'self,' then do not be afraid. Do not recoil or turn away. Rather, confront that emptiness and recognize it as the doorway to the supreme freedom! See through the 'self' and it will release you. You will discover that you are a part of the infinite web of interconnectedness with all other beings. You will live in bliss from now on as the relative self you always were; free at long last from the struggle of absolute alienation, free to help others find their own blessed freedom and happiness!"

Though in this paraphrase of his core teaching the Buddha offers us much encouragement, the challenge remains its central thrust. "You think you're really you? Don't just accept that blindly! Verify whether or not your 'self' is actually present within you. Turn your focused attention to it and explore it. If it's as solid as it seems, then it should be solidly encounterable. If you can't encounter it, then you must confront your error."

The great philosopher Descartes made a grave error when he thought he discovered in his fixed subjective self the one certain thing about existence. After demolishing the entire universe of observable things with hammer blows of systematic doubt, he was unable to give even a tiny tap to collapse this sense of self! And so he set down as the basis for his entire philosophy the famous proposition, "I think, therefore I am!"

Believe it or not, in his deep exploration for the "self," Descartes almost took another path that would have led him to enlightenment. He got very close to discovering that he could not find the "self" he felt to be so absolutely present. After intensively dissecting appearances, drilling through layer upon layer of seeming certainties, he came out with nothing that he could hold onto as the "self." But then he made the tragic mistake. Instead of accepting his selflessness, he instead said to himself, "Ah! Well, of course

I cannot find the self. It is the self that is doing the looking! The 'I' is the subject and so it cannot be an object. Though I cannot find it, still my knowledge that it is the absolute subject cannot be doubted. It confirms its existence by doubting its existence. *Cogito ergo sum!* Of this I can remain absolutely certain."

Why was this mistaken? His logic sounds plausible enough at first. It is, after all, a clever way out of the dilemma of looking for something you are sure is there but cannot find. But what's wrong with it? Let's say that I am looking for a cup. I find it, so I can be certain that the cup exists. I look for my friend and find her, so I can be certain she's there. I look for my glasses, I do not find them—so I proclaim certainty that they are there? No—I go get another pair because I acknowledge I've lost them. I look for my oh-so-familiar "I," and I cannot find it! Why would I think it's there, then? Because I've arbitrarily put it in the category of "things that are there only when I can't find them"? No, when I can't find it, it's rather more sensible that I must give up the sense of certainty that it's there. I feel it's there when I don't look for it, but as soon as I look for it with real effort, it instantly eludes discovery. It seems always to be just around the next corner in my mind, yet each time I turn around to seize it, it disappears. And so I must slowly come to accept the fact that it may not be there after all.

Put another way, imagine that you are walking through the desert when, far off on the horizon, you see an oasis. Yet when you get closer, it disappears. "Aha!" you think to yourself. "A mirage." You walk away. Miles later, you turn around and look back. There's the oasis again! Do you feel certain that the water is there now? No, on the contrary you feel certain that it is only a mirage of water. In the same way, when you look for the "self" and don't find it, you must accept that it is merely a mirage. Your solid self-sense is only an illusion.

Had Descartes persisted and found the door to freedom in his selflessness, as the Buddha did, then instead of proclaiming, "I think, therefore I am," he might have said, "Even though I can find no concrete, fixated 'self,' I still can think. I still seem to be. Therefore I can continue to be myself, selflessly, as a relative, conventional, but ultimately unfindable being."

Whenever you decide to try a particular yoga recommended in this book, the crucial first step is always deciding to make the change. You must begin by accepting the fact that your habitual conceptions could be wrong. If, for example, you live with the delusion that it is just fine to remain addicted to nicotine, that three packs of cigarettes a day puts you in optimal operating condition, then there is no way you will successfully complete a yoga to quit smoking. Likewise, in this crucial quest of the self, the presumed core of your self-addiction, you must first convince yourself through empirical observation that the way you hold your self-identity—the constricted feeling of being wrapped around a solid, independent core—is uncomfortable and disabling.

Why should you even care if the rigid "self" that you believe in so strongly really exists or not? Our self feels most real when we are right and righteous, when we are wrongly or unfairly challenged. And it also seems unique, completely separate from everyone and everything else in the universe. This separateness can feel like freedom and independence when we are in a good mood. But when we are in trouble, lonely or angry, under pressure or dissatisfied, this separateness feels like isolation, alienation, unfair treatment, or deprivation. When we are wholly gripped by fury, the searing energy that wants to attack a target picks our "I" up like a mindless tool and flings us at the other person. It is so disconnected that it even disregards our sense of self-protection, making us take actions that injure us, ignore injuries undergone, and even harm others with no regard for the consequences. There is no more powerful demonstration of our strong sense of being an independent entity than when we give ourselves over completely to anger.

When we look around at others, we see that they are just as alienated from us as we are alienated from them. As we want things from them, they want things from us. As we reject them, they seem to reject us. We don't love them, so how can we expect them to love us? And yet they are endless, while "I" am just one. So I am badly outnumbered. I feel threatened. I can never get enough, have enough, or be enough. I will inevitably lose the me-versus-all-of-them struggle in the long run.

We can, of course, experience moments of unity with other beings, through falling in love, or having a child, for example. When we do, we experience tremendous relief—for a moment, there are two of us teamed up against all the others together. We have an ally. But unfortunately those moments are too rare, and they do not last long before the old self-isolation reemerges. Even lovers can turn into adversaries, couples often seek divorce, and children recoil from their parents, who in turn reject them.

This alienation caused by the presumed independent, absolute self was why the Buddha saw its illusion as the source of human suffering. The situation of feeling that it's always "the self versus the world," with the self as the long-term loser, is unsatisfactory and untenable. When we recognize the inevitable nonviability of our self-centered reality, it motivates us to engage in the quest for the true nature of the self. It makes it existentially essential for us to pause in our headlong rush through life and turn within, to verify whether the "self" really exists as we feel it does.

We can take great encouragement from the fact that the Buddha told us we could escape from our suffering. Still, we cannot merely accept someone else's report. No one else can do the job of replacing misunderstanding with understanding for us. We must look at reality and verify for ourselves whether our habitual sense of having a fixed self or the Buddha's discovery of selflessness is ultimately true. In this way, we can begin to transform the self-preoccupation that causes chronic suffering into the insightful, gradual opening and letting go of the self that is, paradoxically, so self-fulfilling. We want to be happy, but ironically we can only become happier to the extent that we can develop an unconcern for our "self." This process is long and gradual, though you will experience frequent breakthrough moments that will thrill you and motivate you to continue.

Before we actually engage in the meditation practice used to discover the true nature of the self, we must set up our parameters in practical, clear terms. When we look through a darkened house for a misplaced key, we first remember what the key looks like, and then we search for it carefully, room by room, turning lights on as we go. We use a flashlight to look under beds and in hidden corners. When we have looked everywhere exhaustively and not found it, we decide we've missed it somehow, so we go back and repeat the process. However, after one or two searches of this kind, we come to a decisive conclusion that the key is not in the house. We know we could continue looking endlessly, but that would be impractical. So we decide to proceed accordingly with our lives.

In the case of the quest for the self, we will look through all the processes of our body and mind that we can find and investigate them thoroughly. Our physical systems, sensational feelings, conceptual image bank, emotional energies, and consciousness itself constitute the house through which we will search. There are also various vaguely defined areas such as "spirit" and "soul" that, like a dusty attic or dank cellar, we may feel the need to explore. It is easy to get lost in these murky, dank, and oft-forgotten quarters of the mind. So we must get a clear picture of what we want to find ahead of time. And most important, we must set some limits to the exercise, since practically speaking we cannot continue to search indefinitely.

At this point you should search through the house of your body-mind-spirit a few times with great concentration and systematic thoroughness, with my help and the help of many experts who have guided me through this practice. If, during this process, you find a "self," then enjoy it to the full. If, however, as I suspect will be the case, you do not find what stands up solidly as your "real self" by the end of the process, then you will have to live with the fact that there is no such thing. You will need to make the practical decision to turn from seeking the "self" to explore instead the ramifications of being a relative self without any absolute underpinning.

This commitment to practicality in your quest for the self is of great importance at the outset and will have a significant impact on the success of the endeavor. Once you have made the commitment in your own mind, you may begin.

Practice: Trying to Find Your "I"

You are now prepared to deepen your understanding of your selflessness. You will be looking at yourself introspectively, trying to grasp exactly what your essence is. When you do this practice well, you will begin to feel your-self dissolving, just as I did at my mentor Geshe-la's house many years ago. You will start realizing—gradually and also suddenly, in spurts—that you can't find this mysterious "self." Your strong feeling of having an absolute "I" is maddeningly elusive when you try to pin it down precisely.

. . . In looking for your "self," start with your body. Ask yourself, "Am I my body?" In order to answer this question, you must define your body. It is composed at least of your five sense organs, right? Your skin and sensitive inner surfaces constitute the touch organ, then you have your eyes for sight, your nose for smell, your ears for hearing, and your tongue for taste. So first let's explore all of your senses together, your sensory system.

Identify the sound sense. What do you hear—a dog barking, a phone ringing, music playing, or perhaps just the sound of your own breathing? Now notice the visual field. You are reading words on the page. What else do you see? What are the images on the edge of your peripheral vision? How about smell? Perhaps you smell the scent of incense burning, or of musty wood. Do you taste anything: something you ate a while ago, tea you drank, or just the taste of your own mouth? The tactile field is everything touching your skin, including other parts of your skin touching your skin. Your hand may be resting on your knee, for example. Your bottom is touch-ing a pillow. Just identify all the sensations, the textures, smells, tastes, sounds, and sights.

Now notice your internal sensations, like the breakfast in your tummy. You might have a slight pain in your back or your knee. Maybe your foot is falling asleep, and you're annoyed because there's a slightly painful sensa-tion there. You might have a pleasurable sensation in some part of you that is feeling good if, for example, you worked out yesterday or had a massage.

Recognize that for each of these sensations you are experiencing, you are receiving data from the outside world. The sensations are not all coming from your own body. So your body is not just inside your skin; your body is both your organs and the field of all incoming sense objects. It's everything you are seeing and hearing and smelling and tasting and touching. It's the chair or pillow you're sitting on. The words you are reading on this page. The incense drifting into your nostrils. If you look at one sensation, you re-alize that you are sharing your material body with the outside world. Say, for example, you are looking at light bouncing off a table. That light is a part of your shared sensory system, and therefore part of your body, too.

So already you have begun to expand your self-definition, just by look-ing at your five senses. Suddenly you are not just something that sits there inside your skin. You are your environment as well. Your body interfuses with the outside world that you perceive with your senses. All of our bodies are totally overlapping, all the time. Do you see? And when you think, "this is 'me' over here inside this skin," you are unrealistically thinking that "I" am not connected to others through the sense perceptions that we have in common. But you are connected, even before you talk to them or think anything about them, through your shared environment.

Now you can move to the next level of analysis of the self, which exists at the level of your mind. First is the sensational system, the feelings of pleasure, pain, and numbness associated with sense perceptions of sights, sounds, smells, tastes, textures, and mental sense inner objects. When you experience these six kinds of objects, you react as pleased, irritated, or indifferent. Mentally inventory your sensations at the moment, and notice how you react at this basic feeling level. Notice that this heap of sense-reactions has no self-core within it.

Next is your conceptual system, your ideas, mental maps, and internal images. You have a picture of yourself as you exist in the world. You have a concept of yourself as human, not animal. You have a picture of yourself as male or female. You have a body image, and an image of each part of your body. You have a concept of your identity as a teacher, a manager, a doctor, or whatever. You have a concept of yourself as successful or as a failure. Inventory this mass of ideas and images and notice that you have whole clouds of pictures and concepts. But is this incredibly chaotic mass of images and words and diagrams and maps and so forth that is your conceptual system the real "you"? Your perception of yourself changes all the time, depending on your mood, whom you're with, or what you're doing. Sometimes you think, "I'm a high-powered executive," whereas other times you think, "I'm just a tiny speck on a tiny planet of six billion people." So surely your conceptual system cannot be your "self." The "you" self is not any of these ideas, since it seems to be the entity that is noticing all of them.

At the fourth level of analysis, find your emotional system. You are constantly reacting to all of these images and notions. Right now, you're probably feeling a bit irritated with me. You're thinking to yourself, "Why is he making me do this? Why doesn't he just crack a joke? Let's have some fun. What is this terrible business of exploring the self, 'discovering selflessness'? How is this helping me?" And so on and so forth. You're feeling annoyed and anxious and confused. Or maybe you're just feeling bored. Anyway, your emotions are there in your mind, always functioning, but always changing. You can take a peek at them now, as they swirl around in your heart and head, and you can see that they are not fixed. You are not defined by your emotions. They are not the elusive "self" you're seeking.

Lastly, turn your attention to your consciousness system. It is the most important system of all. You see at once how it is a buzzing, blooming, swirling mass of subtle energies. Nothing is fixed, nothing stable within it. With your mental consciousness, you hop from one sense to another. You analyze your ideas, you focus internally on your emotions and thoughts, and you can even focus on being thought free. Your consciousness aims itself at being free of thought by the thought of being free of thought. How strange! As you inventory your consciousness, don't allow yourself to rest with a bare awareness, but go a bit deeper—explore further with your analytic attention. Ask yourself, "Who is this supposedly rigid 'self'? Is it the same self right now as the one who woke up grumbling this morning, preparing that cup of coffee, rushing to get ready, quickly brushing its teeth? Is it the same self who was born a tiny, unaware, helpless infant years ago? Who is the 'me' who knows my name, who knows what I want, where I am, and what I'm doing? Who is the 'me' who knows I'm an American, who knows I'm a—whatever: a Buddhist or a Christian or an atheist? Where is that person now? Where is that absolute, unchanging structure?" You can see how your self-consciousness is a buzzing, blooming, swirling mass of confusion—nothing is fixed, nothing stable within it. You can barely remember what you did yesterday morning—I can't remember at all at my age! So how can you possibly have a rigid self? See how releasing these sorts of thoughts can be! . . .

The deepest stage of awareness comes when your consciousness begins to turn inward to gaze upon itself. At first it thinks, "I now know that these sensory, mental, and emotional systems looming before me are not the 'self,' they are not 'me.' But the awareness that looks at them, that contemplates and investigates them, that is my 'self.' " And yet you soon discover that you are mistaken even in this conclusion. The moment you begin to examine your own conscious mind, you engage in a whirling, internal dervish-dance where your awareness spins round and round upon itself. This contemplation can be dizzying, nauseating, painful, and even a bit frightening, as the felt "self" disappears and evades its own attention. You can never catch it, even as you become more experienced at this meditation and come back to this place again and again. Time and again you will feel frustrated by your continued failure to come up with a result. Yet you must not lose heart. You must remember that looking for your "self" is the most important thing you can ever do in your evolutionary development. You must keep faith that you are on the brink of a quantum leap; you are so close to awakening.

As you enter into this confusing realm of spinning self-seeking, be careful not to make the mistake Descartes made by withdrawing from it all with some sort of decision about "you" being the subject and therefore not any sort of findable object. Also, be careful not to fall into the nihilistic trap of withdrawing from the spinning by deciding that all is nothing after all and so naturally the self-sense is an illusion. Keep whirling upon your "self" as long as you feel absolutely there is a self to whirl upon, to look at, to catch. Put your full truth-seeking, analytic energy into the drive to find it.

Eventually, you will experience a gradual melting process. The whirling will slowly dissolve without fear: you won't shrink back in terror of falling into an abyss-like void because you are already overcoming your self-addiction. You control the tendency to shrink back in terror of falling into a looming void by your drilling, whirling energy of awareness itself. You dissolve your fearing subject, the object for which you are feeling fear, and the imagined nothingness that only the pseudo–self-addiction wants you to fear. However fully you feel such processes at first, what happens to you is that, as you begin to melt, your drive intensity lessens, you feel buoyed by a floating sensation coming from within your nerves and cells, from within your subjectivity as well as your object-field. At some point, you lose your sense of self entirely, as if you were a field of open space. Like Neo and his colleagues in the movie *The Matrix* when they entered one of the computer-generated training fields, you will find yourself standing in a blank white space—except in your case, in this transcending moment, you break free from your "digital residual self-image." You will be only the blank white space, a bare awareness of yourself as a boundless entity. Dissolving into this space, you'll feel intense bliss, a sense of extreme relief.

When you first melt into the spacious experience of freedom, it is enthralling, like emerging from a dark cave into infinite light. You feel magnificent, vast, and unbound. If you inadvertently fall into this state unprepared by arriving there too quickly, you may be tempted to think that you have arrived at the absolute reality, and this is a bit of a danger. You might think, feeling it nonverbally at this stage, that you've conquered the differentiated universe and realized its true "nothingness," experiencing it as such a profound and liberating release that you never again want any contact with the real world. Remember, however, that nothingness is not your ultimate goal—you are not trying to escape reality, but to embrace it. If you reach this space of release gradually through the repeated whirling of your self turning upon itself, then you'll be able to enjoy the vastness and magnificence without losing awareness that it is only another relational condition. You'll realize that the great emptiness is ultimately empty of itself; it is not reality, either.

Since you *are* the void, you do not need to remain in the void, and your original self-sense slowly reemerges within the universe of persons and things. But you are aware that it is not the same "self" you had before—it is forever different, now become infinite and unbound. You have changed. You now perceive your "self" consciously, living with it yet maintaining an educated distance from it. You are like one of the characters in *The Matrix*, present and active as real being, yet at the same time realizing that the apparent reality that surrounds you is only illusory. All that was apparent becomes transparent.

One of the most significant changes you will notice upon discovering your selflessness is that your sense of being separate from everyone else has now eroded. Your new awareness enables you to perceive others as equal to yourself, a part of you, even. You can see yourself as they see you, and experience empathically how they perceive themselves as locked within themselves. You have arrived at the doorway to universal compassion, and it frees you from being locked away behind a fixed point-of-awareness and opens you to a sort of field awareness wherein others are really just the same as you while simultaneously relationally different. Through the sense of sameness, you feel their pains as if they were your own: when they hurt, you hurt. Yet through the sense of relational difference and balanced responsibility, you naturally feel moved to free them from their pains, just as you move automatically to eliminate your own pains. When your hand is burned by a hot pothandle, you react at once to pull away from the heat, you plunge it into cold water, you rush to find ice. You respond instinctively to remove the pain. You don't consider it a selfless act of compassion for your hand. You just do it through your neural connection to your hand. Your new open awareness feels others' hands through a similar sense of natural connection.   ■

■ *QUESTIONS FOR MAKING CONNECTIONS*
WITHIN THE READING ■

1. Choose one important term from Thurman's essay, such as "nirvana," "nothingness," "emptiness," "enlightenment," "meditation," "compassion," "ignorance," "self," "happiness," and "freedom." Then, by tracing Thurman's use of the term throughout the chapter, offer your own explanation of its meaning. Definitions for all of these terms may be found in a dictionary but here you are being asked to explain the meaning of the term as Thurman uses it. You might even contrast Thurman's use of the term to more commonplace understandings. "Ignorance," for example, has a special significance in the context of Buddhist thought. How does it differ from "ignorance" as we normally define it?

2. Instead of discussing the soul, Thurman focuses on the mind. How is "mind" different from "soul"? What are some of the broader implications of Thurman's attention to the mind instead of the soul? If the mind is transformed, can the essence of the person remain somehow immune to change? Conversely, if a person's mental habits and perceptions remain unchanged, is it possible to imagine that the essence of the person has still been altered somehow? We might ordinarily think of each person as endowed with an individual soul, but is the mind individualized in the same way? Where is the mind located, according to Thurman? Is it the same as the brain?

3. Thurman speaks about "enlightenment" instead of "redemption" or "salvation." How does "enlightenment" differ from "salvation"? What are the differences between Thurman's emphasis on the experience of "selflessness" and the famous Greek dictum, "Know thyself"? Could selflessness qualify as a form of self-knowledge? Could it qualify as a form of redemption or salvation?

■ *QUESTIONS FOR WRITING* ■

1. Buddhism is often studied on the college level in courses offered by philosophy and religion departments. Judging from Thurman's account, however, would you say that Buddhism can best be defined as a philosophy? Would you say that Buddhism might best be defined as a religion? Or, judging from Thurman's account, would you say that Buddhism has some elements in common with science, which is based on empirical observation? Would you say that it is in some ways closer to a science than to a religion or a philosophy?

2. What are the social and political implications of Thurman's argument? How would the cultivation of "wisdom" as he describes it affect people in a competitive, consumption-oriented society like our own? Is Thurman's brand of meditation compatible with democracy and the idea that all of us are equal? How might the cultivation of wisdom influence the current political climate? Would the climate become less adversarial? Less driven by rigid ideology? Or would people who cultivate wisdom simply wash their hands of politics?

■ *QUESTIONS FOR MAKING CONNECTIONS BETWEEN READINGS* ■

1. In "When I Woke Up Tuesday Morning, It Was Friday," Martha Stout describes forms of "divided" or "dissociated" consciousness that are produced by severely traumatic events. One of Stout's patients, whom she calls "Julia," becomes so dissociated from the here and now that whole days never get recorded in Julia's memory. After rereading Stout's analysis of dissociation, decide whether or not the form of meditation that Thurman describes might help someone like Julia. Is it possible that meditation as Thurman describes it could actually *produce* dissociation in healthy people? What aspects of meditation might be most helpful to people like Julia? Is it possible that dissociation is actually more widespread than most people even realize? Is trauma really necessary to produce severely divided consciousness, or do certain features of contemporary life help to produce it—television, commercial radio, video games, and movies?

2. In what ways is reading like the practice of meditation? To explore this question, draw primarily on Azar Nafisi's chapter from *Reading Lolita in Tehran*. At a key moment in her account, Nafisi makes this observation:

> Whoever we were—and it was not really important what religion we belonged to, whether we wished to wear the veil or not, whether we absorbed certain religious norms or not—we had become the figment of someone

else's dreams. A stern ayatollah, a self-proclaimed philosopher-king, had come to rule our land.

How, according to Nafisi, can the reading of fiction help us throw off the veils—literal and virtual—that others have imposed on us? Does reading as she describes involve its own form of mental cultivation, comparable in some ways to the meditational practice Thurman describes? Does reading allow Nafisi and her students to experience a form of "selflessness"? How can we tell the difference between the veils imposed on us and the persons we really are? Is it possible that "selflessness" allows us to create an identity of our own?

www   **For additional suggestions about making connections between readings, visit the Link-O-Mat and More Sample Assignments at <www.newhum.com>.**

FRANS DE WAAL

FRANS DE WAAL [de Vaal] began his work on the link between human and primate behavioral patterns in 1975 with a six-year project studying the world's largest captive colony of chimpanzees at the Arnhem Zoo in the Netherlands. De Waal discussed the initial results of his research into how primates resolve conflict in *Chimpanzee Politics* (1982) and has since published a series of books that seek to further establish the continuum of conciliatory and aggressive behavioral patterns that link humans and primates: *Peacemaking Among Primates* (1989), *Good Natured: The Origins of Right and Wrong in Humans and Other Animals* (1996), and *Bonobo: The Forgotten Ape* (1997).

Originally trained as a zoologist and ethologist in the Netherlands, de Waal is currently the C. H. Candler Professor of Primate Behavior at Emory University and director of the Living Links Center at the Yerkes Regional Primate Research Center in Atlanta, Georgia. The goal of the Living Links Center is to study the four extant breeds of great apes—the bonobos, chimpanzees, gorillas, and orangutans—that connect humans to our primate relatives. By exploring these links, de Waal and his colleagues hope "to reconstruct human evolution, pinpoint the differences and similarities between humans and apes, and educate the public about apes and promote their well-being and conservation." By insisting primates have a "culture" that they learn through observation, de Waal sees himself as challenging both the humanities and the social sciences, which have assumed a sharp distinction between humans and animals, and the sciences, which have depicted humans as "taking over the world by means of aggression." In "Survival of the Kindest" and "Down with Dualism," two chapters drawn from de Waal's most recent book, *The Ape and the Sushi Master: Cultural Reflections by a Primatologist* (2001), de Waal offers an alternate understanding of the relationship between primates and humans. As de Waal explained in a

de Waal, Frans. "Survival of the Kindest" and "Down with Dualism." *The Ape and the Sushi Master: Cultural Reflections by a Primatologist.* New York: Basic Books, 2001. 315–335, 337–357.

Biographical information drawn from the Living Links Center's Web site <http://www.emory.edu/LIVING_LINKS/>; quotations from Frans de Waal, interview by Ira Flatow, "Science Friday," National Public Radio, 1 June 2001 <http://search.npr.org/cf/cmn/cmnpd01fm.cfm?PrgDate=06/01/2001&PrgID=5>.

recent interview, it is by studying the compassionate and altruistic behavior of the bonobo and the other great apes that we can gain access "to a side of ourselves that the textbooks have put under the table."

www **To learn more about Frans de Waal and the study of primates, visit the Link-O-Mat at <www.newhum.com>.**

■ ■

Selections from
The Ape and the Sushi Master

Survival of the Kindest

Of Selfish Genes and Unselfish Dogs

"How selfish soever man may be supposed, there are evidently some principles in his nature, which interest him in the fortune of others, and render their happiness necessary to him, though he derives nothing from it, except the pleasure of seeing it."
—Adam Smith, 1759

"Altruism may arise in the chimpanzee, in some modest degree, where there has been no training in generosity. On any reasonable view, this requires reinterpretation of the traditional hedonistic, law-of-effect view of human nature and human motivation."
—Donald Hebb, 1971

The most absurd animal exhibit I have ever seen was at a small zoo in Lop Buri, Thailand. Two medium-sized dogs shared a cage with three full-grown tigers. While the tigers cooled their bodies in dirty water, the dogs moved around, hopping unconcernedly over the huge striped heads that rested on the concrete rim of the pool. The dogs were walking snacks, but the tigers evidently failed to perceive them as such.

I learned that one of the dogs had raised the tiger cubs along with her own puppy, and that the whole family had happily stayed together. The mother was said to be top dog over everyone else.

The tigers were no pushovers, though. They silently stalked the three-year-old son of my hosts when he strolled by the cage, their yellow eyes glued to the boy, ready to pounce if some miracle removed the bars holding them back. In the forest, a member of the same species once roared at the boy's father, a tall German primatologist, making his blood curdle, and permanently changing his perspective on the risk factors of his job.

A couple of meters from this exhibit stood a statue depicting combat between a tiger and an eagle, both of them larger than life. The eagle seemed to be trying to scratch out the tiger's eyes with its talons, an implausible encounter because the two animals normally don't get in each other's way. But it was a dramatic rendition of the ubiquitous struggle for existence, the cutthroat competition between organisms over limited resources, or, as Tennyson immortalized it, "nature, red in tooth and claw."

Both the statue and the cage with tigers and dogs presented artificial situations, but with conflicting messages. While the animals demonstrated how well teeth and claws can be held under control, the statue arrogantly declared: "Who cares what you actually see in nature? This is how it works!" Unintentionally, the zoo thus offered grounds for reflection on observed versus theorized nature.

The incredible sacrifice of the mother dog in rearing three tigers falls under the biological definition of altruism—that is, she incurred a serious cost for the benefit of others. She didn't do it for herself, her family, or even her species, so why did she do it? What energy she must have put into raising three giant animals so totally unlike herself! The difference in size was every bit as large as that between, say, a tiny hedge sparrow and the enormous cuckoo nestling she is raising. But the hedge sparrow had been tricked by an egg similar to her own, whereas it is hard to imagine that a dog is unable to tell a tiger cub from a puppy by sight, let alone smell.

Biologists often explain altruism by so-called kin selection. Kindness towards one's kin is viewed as a genetic investment, a way of spreading genes similar to one's own. Assisting kin thus comes close to helping oneself. Sacrifices on behalf of kin are pervasive, from honey bees that die for their colony by stinging intruders to birds—such as scrub jays—that help their parents raise a nest full of young. Humans show the same bias toward kin, giving rise to expressions such as "Blood is thicker than water." No wonder awards for heroism are rarely bestowed on those who have saved members of their own family.

The bitch of our story qualifies as a heroine, though, since she gave tender loving care and nourishing milk to individuals that could not possibly be her relatives. Kin selection, therefore, cannot explain her behavior. The alternative hypothesis is the "You scratch my back, I'll scratch yours" argument, where the help is directed to someone willing to repay the service. In my own work, I have tested this idea by recording grooming sessions among chimpanzees at the Yerkes Primate Center's Field Station, near Atlanta, after which I watched food sharing among the same apes. I found that if chimpanzee A had groomed B in the morning, A's chances of getting food from B in the afternoon were greatly improved. All parties stand to gain in such an economy of exchange.

Could this account for the dog's behavior? It might be argued that the cats repaid her by not devouring her, but such altruism-by-omission is a bit of a stretch. It certainly doesn't explain the mother's generosity. Had she simply rejected the cubs, she would not have had to contend with them as dangerous adults to begin with. Clearly, she got little or nothing out of the whole deal.

Does this mean that the evolutionary paradigm is fundamentally flawed? The answer depends on how broad or narrow a vision of evolution one embraces. The above theories explain cooperation reasonably well, but they do not apply—and do not need to apply—to each and every single instance. The beauty of unnatural arrangements, such as placing tiger cubs on a dog's nipples, is that they expose the disjunction between motive and function. The original *function* of maternal care is obviously to raise one's own offspring, but the *motivation* to provide such care reaches beyond that function. The motivation has become strong and flexible enough to reach out to other young, even those of other species, regardless of what is in it for the mother. Motives often acquire lives of their own. As a result, they do not always neatly fit biology's dominant metaphors, which emphasize ruthless competition.

The Spider and the Fly

Anyone who has seen the film *Il Postino* (The Postman) realizes the extraordinary lure of the metaphor. The apprentice poet of the movie learns to offer a fresh look at the world through carefully selected analogies. Shy at first, he soon relishes the poet's proverbial "license" to transform reality, which helps him greatly in wooing the opposite sex.

People are animists by nature, always interpreting reality in their own image. It starts early when children freely ascribe inner lives to clouds, trees, dolls, and other objects. This tendency is commercially exploited with pet rocks, chia pets, and Tamagotchi, which show remarkably little resemblance to the usual recipients of human love.[1] The phenomenon is not even limited to our species; chimpanzees, too, care for imaginary young. Richard Wrangham observed a six-year-old juvenile, Kakama, carry and cradle a small wooden log as if it were a newborn. Kakama did so for hours on end, one time even building a nest in a tree and putting the log into it on its own. Kakama's mother was pregnant at the time. The field-worker notes: "My intuition suggested a possibility that I was reluctant, as a professional skeptical scientist, to accept on the basis of a single observation: that I had just watched a young male chimpanzee invent and then play with a doll in possible anticipation of his mother giving birth."[2]

Scientists are not immune to the urge to project needs and desires onto inanimate objects. Unfortunately for us, however, we lack the license of the poet and the innocence of the child. Metaphors are used in science to great effect and advantage, but also at great peril. Taken literally, they often ob-scure the truth. This lot befell the well-known "struggle for existence" view of the natural world. It kept generations of biologists from recognizing the shared interests among individuals and species even though Charles Dar-win—always wiser than his followers—had warned in *The Origin of Species:* "I use the term Struggle for Existence in a large and metaphorical sense in-cluding dependence of one being on another."[3]

In chemistry and physics, metaphors are common, as when we say that elements are "attracted" to each other (not to mention that they "like" each other), or when we use concepts such as "force" and "resistance." Anthro-pomorphic interpretations are attempts to make sense of the world around us. In modern biology, this has led to the characterization of genes as "self-ish" and of organisms as "adapting" to their environment. Genes are said to be our rulers, and to strive for their own replication. But really, all that is going on is that genes, a mere batch of DNA molecules, replicate at different rates depending on the success of the traits that they produce. Rather than doing the selecting themselves, genes are *being* selected. Adaptation, too, is a blind and passive process resulting from the elimination of less successful forms. All of this is known to every biologist, but we are unable to resist in-fusing evolution with direction and intent.

It is only a small step from calling genes selfish to slapping the same label onto the carriers of those genes: plants, animals, and people. Thus, according to George Williams, one of the world's leading evolutionary biologists, "natural selection maximizes short-sighted selfishness."[4] He thus extends the utilitarian language of his discipline to the domain of motivation. This is a slippery extrapolation, because the selfishness of genes is entirely metaphorical—genes have no self, hence cannot possibly be selfish—whereas animals and people do qualify for the literal appli-cation.

Thus, the concept of "selfishness" has been plucked from the English language, robbed of its vernacular meaning, and applied outside of the psy-chological domain where it used to belong. It is now often used as if it were a synonym for "self-serving," which of course it is not. Selfishness implies the *intention* to serve oneself, hence knowledge of what one stands to gain. Without such knowledge, selfishness is a much more problematic concept than many evolutionary thinkers realize. A vine may serve its own interests by overgrowing and suffocating a tree, but since plants lack intentions and knowledge they cannot possibly be selfish except in a rather meaningless sense.

The question then becomes whether animals and people possess the knowledge to act selfishly. In nature, the future is mostly hidden behind a veil of ignorance. The spider builds her web in order to catch flies and the squirrel hides nuts to get through the winter, but it is unlikely that spiders and squirrels do so knowingly. This would require previous experience, whereas even the youngest, most naïve spiders and squirrels weave webs and store nuts. They have no clue how useful their actions will turn out to be. Both species would have become extinct long ago if it were otherwise. And these are only the simplest examples I can think of. Many behavioral functions are much harder to recognize. The stallion fights at great risk against other stallions so as to claim a harem of mares and sire offspring with them, but it would be ridiculous to suggest that the stallion himself knows how a victory might affect his reproductive chances. For this, he would need to know the relation between sex and procreation, an understanding yet to be demonstrated in any nonhuman animal.

Even human behavior doesn't necessarily depend on awareness of its results. The healthy appetites of children and pregnant women, for instance, serve their need for growth. It would be a mistake, however, to assume that these individuals eat out of a desire to grow: hunger does the trick. Motivations follow their own rules, fulfill their own goals, and require their own set of explanations.

Instead of the piecemeal evolution of individual acts—such as bite, scratch, flee, lick, or nurse—natural selection has produced entire psychologies that orchestrate a species' whole repertoire of behavior. Animals weigh choices, absorb information, learn which behavior yields rewards, and solve problems intelligently, and they do all of this within a framework of natural tendencies that have proven their value over the ages. Genes are definitely part of the equation, but to say that animals are nothing but machines controlled by genes is like saying that a Rembrandt is nothing but fabric and paint, or that a brain is a mere collection of neurons. While not incorrect, such statements miss by a mile the higher levels of organization.

Returning to our mother dog, it is easy to recognize in her behavior a complex psychology shaped by a long history of reliance of maternal care. The tendency to feed and clean dependent young is well established for excellent reasons. At the same time, the entrenched nature of the tendency makes it vulnerable to exploitation, as when people gave the dog tiger cubs to raise. Not that this matters much to the mother. From an evolutionary perspective, care for non-offspring may be maladaptive, but from a psychological perspective, it remains entirely authentic and fitting behavior for the species. Another dog, at Beijing Zoo, recently acted as wet nurse for three snow-leopard cubs whose mother had abandoned them.[5]

And so, the dog at the Thai zoo really hadn't done anything unusual, nothing that a good canine wouldn't or shouldn't do. Her behavior did provide a stark reminder, though, of how narrow a portrayal of nature the nearby statue offered. The statue was intended to show selection at work, but could not begin to convey the variety of outcomes evolution has produced. Paradoxically, harsh selection processes have led to some amazingly cooperative species with character traits such as loyalty, trust, sympathy, and generosity.

The Midwife Bat

Before we now conclude that animals and people can be truly unselfish, we need to subject the terms "altruism" and "kindness" to the same scrutiny as was just applied to "selfishness." Here, too, we risk confusion: functional altruism—in which one individual gains from another's actions—does not necessarily rest on intended kindness, in which someone else's well-being is the goal.

When a blue jay gives alarm shrieks for a red-tailed hawk gliding around the corner, does he do so in order to warn others? All potential prey of the hawk take immediate action, and thus profit from the jay's alert, whereas the jay takes enormous risks, telling the hawk, in effect: "Here I am!" On the surface, this seems an act of unmitigated altruism. The critical question remains, however, whether the jay cared about the others: did he even realize the wider impact of his calls?

There exist many examples of altruism in which awareness of what the behavior means to others is questionable. This is especially true for social insects, which sacrifice themselves on a massive scale for their colony and queen. Many other animals help each other find food and water, avoid predation, raise offspring, and so on. Only a few of the largest-brained animals, however, seem to operate with a solid understanding of how their behavior affects others. When these animals go out of their way to help others without any clear benefits for themselves, it is possible that the other's welfare is their goal. I am thinking, for example, of how Binti Jua, the lowland gorilla at Chicago's Brookfield Zoo, scooped up and gently transported an unconscious boy who had fallen into her enclosure. Binti followed a chain of action no one had taught her, resulting in the boy's rescue.[6]

In another incident, a British tourist was protected by dolphins in the Gulf of Akaba off the Red Sea. While cavorting with dolphins, the man was attacked by sharks. When his companions on the vessel heard his screams, they thought at first it was a joke, until they saw blood stain the water. Three dolphins surrounded the injured victim, leaping up and smacking the water with their tails and flippers, and successfully kept the sharks at bay.[7]

In my work on the evolution of morality, I have found many instances of animals caring for one another and responding to others' distress. For example, chimpanzees will approach a victim of attack, put an arm around her and gently pat her back, or groom her. These reassuring encounters, termed *consolations*, are so predictable that my students and I have recorded hundreds of instances.[8] In monkeys, on the other hand, consolation has never been demonstrated. On the contrary, monkeys often avoid victims of aggression. Our closest relatives, the anthropoid apes, thus seem more empathic than monkeys. Apes may be able to perceive the world from someone else's perspective, and hence understand what is wrong with the other, or what the other needs.

Nadie Ladygina-Kohts noticed similar empathic tendencies in her young chimpanzee, Yoni, whom she raised in Moscow at the beginning of the twentieth century. Kohts, who analyzed Yoni's behavior in the minutest detail, discovered that the only way to get him off the roof of her house (much more effectively than by holding out a reward) was to appeal to his feelings of concern for her:

> If I pretend to be crying, close my eyes and weep, Yoni immediately stops his plays or any other activities, quickly runs over to me, all excited and shagged, from the most remote places in the house, such as the roof or the ceiling of his cage, from where I could not drive him down despite my persistent calls and entreaties. He hastily runs around me, as if looking for the offender; looking at my face, he tenderly takes my chin in his palm, lightly touches my face with his finger, as though trying to understand what is happening, and turns around, clenching his toes into firm fists.[9]

In previous books, such as *Good Natured* (1996), I have amassed other examples in support of this empathic capacity in the chimpanzee and its closest relative, the bonobo. For instance, an adult daughter brought fruit down from a tree to her aging mother, who was too old to climb. In another instance, juveniles interrupted their rambunctious play each time they got close to a terminally sick companion. There is also the report of an old male leading a blind female around by the hand, and of an ape who released a damaged bird by climbing to the highest point of a tree, spreading the bird's wings, and sending it off through the air. This individual seemed to have an idea of what kind of assistance might be best for an injured bird. There exist ample stories of this sort about apes that suggest a capacity to assist others insightfully.

But even though apes may be special in this regard, we cannot exclude similar capacities in other animals. A well-documented instance of possible altruism concerns a very different species: Rodrigues fruit bats in a breeding colony in Florida, studied by Thomas Kunz, a biologist at Boston University.[10] By chance, Kunz witnessed an exceptionally difficult birthing process in which a mother bat failed to adopt the required feet-down position. Instead, she continued to hang upside-down. Taking on a midwife role, another female spent no less than two and a half hours assisting the inexperienced mother. She licked and groomed her behind, and wrapped her wings around her, perhaps so as to prevent the emerging pup from falling. She also repeatedly fanned the exhausted mother with her wings. But what amazed the biologist most was that the helper seemed to be *instructing* the mother: the mother adopted the correct feet-down position only after the helper had done so right in front of her. On four separate occasions the helper adopted the correct position in full view of the mother—a position normally used only for urination or defecation, which the helper didn't engage in—and each time the mother followed the helper's example.

It looked very much as if the midwife bat was aware of the difficulties the mother's unorthodox position was causing, and that she tutored the mother to do the right things. If she indeed monitored the effects of her actions and deliberately strove for a successful delivery, the helper's behavior was not just functionally but also intentionally altruistic. When the pup was finally born, it climbed onto its mother's back assisted by head-nuzzling from the helper female.

We easily recognize such helping tendencies, because they are prominent in our own species. This is abundantly clear when people crawl into smoking ruins to save others, such as during earthquakes and fires. Given our talent for risk assessment, there can be nothing inadvertent about such behavior. When Lenny Skutnik dove into the icy Potomac River in Washington, D.C., to rescue a plane-crash victim, or when European civilians sheltered Jewish families during World War II, incredible risks were taken on behalf of complete strangers. Even if reward comes afterward in the form of a medal or a moment on the evening news, this is of course never the motive. No sane person would willingly risk his life for a piece of metal or five minutes of televised glory. The decision to help is instantaneous and impulsive, without much time to think. When fugitives knock on the door, one determines there and then whether to take them in.

But even if many heroic acts escape traditional biological explanations in terms of "short-sighted selfishness," this doesn't make the underlying tendencies counterrevolutionary. More than likely, the helping responses of dolphins, gorillas, or people toward strangers in need evolved in the context of a close-knit group life in which most of the time such actions benefited relatives and companions able to repay the favor. The impulse to help was therefore never totally without survival value to the one showing the impulse. But, as so often, the impulse became dissociated from the consequences that shaped its evolution, which permitted it to be expressed even when payoffs were unlikely. The impulse thus was emancipated to the point where it became genuinely unselfish.

Depressed Rescue Dogs

The animal literature is filled with examples of normal behavior under unusual circumstances. Followed by a single file of goslings, Konrad Lorenz demonstrated the tendency of these birds to imprint on the first moving object they lay their eyes on. He thus permanently confused their sense of species-belonging. Niko Tinbergen saw stickleback fish in a row of tanks in front of his laboratory window, in Leiden, make furious territorial displays at the mail delivery van in the street below. At the time, Dutch mail vans were bright red, the same color as the male stickleback's underbelly during the breeding season, and the fish mistook the van for an intruder of their own species.

Artificial situations sometimes help us see more clearly how behavior is regulated. When goslings do the normal thing, following their mom around all day, one might think that they share our exalted view of motherhood. We are quickly disabused of this notion, however, when they follow a bearded zoologist with equal devotion. And when sticklebacks defend their territory, we might think that they want to keep competitors out, whereas in reality they are only reacting to a species-typical red flag. What animals really are after is not always evident, and tinkering with conditions is a way to find out.

For altruistic behavior, an informative context is that of rescue dogs. Trainers tap into the inborn tendency of these cooperative hunters to come to each other's aid. Time and again, dogs demonstrate this ability spontaneously towards their human "pack members." An example is the occasion on which a rottweiler and golden retriever crawled side by side on their bellies toward their master, who had broken through the ice on a frozen lake. The heavy man managed to grab their collars, one in each hand, upon which both dogs inched backward, pulling him out.[11]

Rescue dogs are trained to perform such responses on command, often in repulsive situations, such as fires, that they would normally avoid unless the entrapped individuals are familiar. Training is accomplished with the usual carrot-and-stick method. One might think, therefore, that the dogs perform like Skinnerian rats, doing what has been reinforced in the past, partly out of instinct, partly out of a desire for tidbits. If they save human lives, one could argue, they do so for purely selfish reasons.

The image of the rescue dog as a well-behaved robot is hard to maintain, however, in the face of their attitude under trying circumstances with few survivors, such as in the aftermath of the bombing of the Murrah Federal Building in Oklahoma City. When rescue dogs encounter too many dead people, they lose interest in their job regardless of how much praise and goodies they get.

This was discovered by Caroline Hebard, the U.S. pioneer of canine search and rescue, during the Mexico City earthquake of 1985. Hebard recounts how her German shepherd, Aly, reacted to finding corpse after corpse and few survivors. Aly would be all excited and joyful if he detected human life in the rubble, but became depressed by all the death. In Hebard's words, Aly regarded humans as his friends, and he could not stand to be surrounded by so many dead friends: "Aly fervently wanted his stick reward, and equally wanted to please Caroline, but as long as he was uncertain about whether he had found someone alive, he would not even reward himself. Here in this gray area, rules of logic no longer applied."[12]

The logic referred to is that a reward is just a reward: there is no reason for a trained dog to care about the victim's condition. Yet, all dogs on the team became depressed. They required longer and longer resting periods, and their eagerness for the job dropped off dramatically. After a couple of days, Aly clearly had had enough. His big brown eyes were mournful, and he hid behind the bed when Hebard wanted to take him out again. He also refused to eat. All other dogs on the team had lost their appetites as well.

The solution to this motivational problem says a lot about what the dogs wanted. A Mexican veterinarian was invited to act as stand-in survivor. The rescuers hid the volunteer somewhere in a wreckage and let the dogs find him. One after another the dogs were sent in, picked up the man's scent, and happily alerted, thus "saving" his life. Refreshed by this exercise, the dogs were ready to work again.[13]

What this means is that trained dogs rescue people only partly for approval and food rewards. Instead of performing a cheap circus trick, they are emotionally invested. They relish the opportunity to find and save a live person. Doing so also constitutes some sort of reward, but one more in line with what Adam Smith, the Scottish philosopher and father of economics, thought to underlie human sympathy: all that we derive from sympathy, he said, is the pleasure of seeing someone else's fortune. Perhaps this doesn't seem like much, but it means a lot to many people, and apparently also to some big-hearted canines.

Under certain conditions and for certain species, therefore, we can drop the customary quotation marks around "altruism." At least in some cases, we seem to be dealing with the genuine article: a good deed done *and* intended.

Apples and Oranges

It is not hard to see why biologists call the problems they deal with multi-layered. At the evolutionary level a behavior may be self-serving; at the psychological level it may be kind and unselfish; and at yet another level it may be best understood by the effects of hormones on certain brain areas. Similarly, from the performer's perspective a behavior may be a mere reflex or fully deliberate, yet this matters little to the recipient, who mainly cares about whether the behavior helps or harms him.

When we freely jump from one level or perspective to another we run the risk of forgetting to keep our language straight. For example, nature documentaries now customarily discuss animal behavior in the shorthand of evolutionary biology ("The croaking frog advertises his genetic superiority to potential mates"), making us forget that animals know nothing about the genetic story. Even worse is that scientists who operate on one level sometimes can't stand another level's idiom, and vice versa. This explains why some flinch at the same behavior being called selfish. In fact, both may be right within their respective frameworks.

If one biologist's apples are another's oranges, this obviously creates a communication problem. We usually resolve the difficulty by asking whether someone is talking at the "proximate" (direct causation) or "ulti-mate" (adaptive value) level, but this distinction has never caught on outside of biology. The tension between the two is forever there, however. The mother dog who raises tiger cubs is at once extraordinarily generous and doing what her genes, based on millions of years of self-service, nudge her to do. By following her natural impulses, she illustrates the contradictions that lend so much richness to evolutionary accounts that we will never be done mining their meaning.

Down with Dualism!

Two Millennia of Debate About Human Goodness

"We approve and we disapprove because we cannot do otherwise. Can we help feeling pain when the fire burns us? Can we help sympathizing with our friends? Are these phenomena less necessary or less powerful in their consequences, because they fall within the subject sphere of experience?"

—Edward Westermarck, 1912

Edward Westermarck's writings, including those about his journeys to Morocco, kept me busy as I leaned back in a cushy seat on a jet from Tokyo to Helsinki. More comfortable than a camel, I bet! I was on my way to an international conference in honor of the Swedish-Finn, who lived from 1862 until 1939, and who was the first to bring Darwinism to the social sciences.

His books are a curious blend of dry theorizing, detailed anthropology, and secondhand animal stories. He gives the example of a vengeful camel that had been excessively beaten on multiple occasions by a fourteen-year-old "lad" for loitering or turning the wrong way. The camel passively took the punishment, but a few days later, finding itself unladen and alone on the road with the same conductor, "seized the unlucky boy's head in its monstrous mouth, and lifting him up in the air flung him down again on the earth with the upper part of the skull completely torn off, and his brains scattered on the ground."[1]

I don't know much about camels, but stories of delayed revenge abound in the zoo world, especially about apes and elephants. We now have systematic data on how chimpanzees punish negative actions with other negative actions—a pattern called a "revenge system"—and how if a macaque is attacked by a dominant member of its troop it will turn around to redirect aggression against a vulnerable, younger relative of its attacker.[2] Such behavior falls under what Westermarck called the "retributive emotions," but for him "retributive" went beyond its usual connotation of getting even. It included positive tendencies, such as gratitude and the repayment of services. Depicting the retributive emotions as the cornerstone of human morality, Westermarck weighed in on the question of its origin while antedating modern discussions of evolutionary ethics, which often take the related concept of reciprocal altruism as their starting point.[3]

That Westermarck goes unmentioned in the latest books on evolutionary ethics, or serves only as a historic footnote, is not because he paid attention to the wrong phenomena or held untenable views about ethics, but because his writing conveyed a belief in human goodness. He felt that morality comes naturally to people. Contemporary biologists have managed to banish this view to the scientific fringes under the influence of the two Terrible Toms—Thomas Hobbes and Thomas Henry Huxley—who both preached that the original state of humankind, and of nature in general, is one in which selfish goals are pursued without regard for others. Compromise, symbiosis, and mutualism were not terms the Toms considered particularly useful, even though these outcomes are not hard to come by in both nature and human society.

Are we naturally good? And if not, whence does human goodness come? Is it one of our many marvelous inventions, like the wheel and toilet training, or could it be a mere illusion? Perhaps we are naturally bad, and just pretend to be good?

Every possible answer to these questions has been seriously advocated by one school of thought or another. I myself have struggled with the question of human nature, contrasting the views of present-day biologists—from whom an admission of human virtue is about as hard to extract as a rotten tooth—with the belief of many philosophers and scientists, including Charles Darwin, that our species moderates its selfishness with a healthy dose of fellow-feeling and kindness. Anyone who explores this debate will notice how old it is—including, as it does, explicit Chinese sources, such as Mencius, from before the Western calendar—so that we can justifiably speak of a perennial controversy.

Westermarck Beats Freud

In a stately building on a wintry, dark Helsinki day, not far from his childhood home, we discussed Westermarck's brave Darwinism, which was initially applauded but soon opposed by contemporary big shots such as Sigmund Freud and Claude Lévi-Strauss. Their resistance was so effective that the Finn has been largely forgotten.

His most controversial position concerned incest. Both Freud and many anthropologists were convinced that there would be rampant sex within the human family if it were not for the incest taboo. Freud believed that the earliest sexual excitations and fantasies of children are invariably directed at close family members, while Lévi-Strauss declared the incest taboo the ultimate cultural blow against nature—it was what permitted humanity to make the passage from nature to culture.

These were high-flown notions, which carried the stunning implication that our species was somehow predestined to free itself of its biological shackles. Westermarck didn't share the belief that our ancestors started out with rampant, promiscuous sex over which they gained control only with great difficulty. He instead saw the nuclear family as humanity's age-old reproductive unit, and proposed that early association within this unit (such as normally found between parent and offspring and among siblings) kills sexual desire. Hence, the desire isn't there to begin with. On the contrary, individuals who grow up together from an early age develop an actual sexual *aversion* for each other. Westermarck proposed this as an evolved mechanism with an obvious adaptive value: it prevents the deleterious effects of inbreeding.

In the largest-scale study on this issue to date, Arthur Wolf, an anthropologist at Stanford University, spent a lifetime examining the marital histories of 14,402 Taiwanese women in a "natural experiment" dependent on a peculiar Chinese marriage custom. Families used to adopt and raise little girls as future daughters-in-law. This meant that they grew up since early childhood with the family's son, their intended husband. Wolf compared the resulting marriages with those arranged between men and women who did not meet until their wedding day. Fortunately for science, official household registers were kept during the Japanese occupation of Taiwan. These registers provide detailed information on divorce rates and number of children, which Wolf took as measures of, respectively, marital happiness and sexual activity. His data supported the Westermarck effect: association in the first years of life appears to compromise marital compatibility.[4]

These findings are especially damaging to Freud, because if Westermarck is right then Oedipal theory is wrong. Freud's thinking was premised on a supposed sexual attraction between members of the same family that needs to be suppressed and sublimated. His theory would predict that unrelated boys and girls who have grown up together will marry in absolute bliss, as there is no taboo standing in the way of their primal sexual desires. In reality, however, the signs are that such marriages often end in misery. Co-reared boys and girls resist being wed, arguing that they are too much like brother and sister. The father of the bride sometimes needs to stand with a stick by the door during the wedding night to prevent the two from escaping the situation. In these marriages, sexual indifference seems to be the rule, and adultery a common outlet. As Wolf exclaimed at the conference, Westermarck may have been less flamboyant, less self-assured, and less famous than any of his mighty opponents; the fundamental difference was that he was the only one who was right!

A second victim is Lévi-Strauss, who built his position entirely on the assumption that animals lead disorderly lives in which they do whatever they please, including committing incest. We now believe, however, that monkeys and apes are subject to exactly the same inhibitory mechanism as proposed by Westermarck. Many primates prevent inbreeding through migration of one sex or the other. The migratory sex meets new, unrelated mates, while the resident sex gains genetic diversity by breeding with immigrants. In addition, close kin who stay together avoid sexual intercourse. This was first observed in the 1950s by Kisaburo Tokuda in a group of Japanese macaques at the Kyoto Zoo. A young adult male who had risen to the top rank made full use of his sexual privileges, mating frequently with all of the females except for one: his mother.[5] This was not an isolated case; mother-son matings are strongly suppressed in all primates. Even in the sexy bonobos, this is the one partner combination in which intercourse is rare or absent. Observation of thousands of matings in a host of primates, both captive and wild, has demonstrated the suppression of incest.

The Westermarck effect serves as a showcase for Darwinian approaches to human behavior because it so clearly rests on a *combination* of nature and nurture: it has a developmental side (learned sexual aversion), an innate side (the way early familiarity affects sexual preference), a cultural side (some cultures raise unrelated children together and others raise siblings of the opposite sex apart, but most have family arrangements that automatically lead to sexual aversion among relatives), a likely evolutionary reason (suppression of inbreeding), and direct parallels with animal behavior. On top of this comes the cultural *taboo*, which is unique for our species. An unresolved issue is whether the taboo merely serves to formalize and reinforce the Westermarck effect or adds a substantially new dimension.

That Westermarck's integrated view was underappreciated at the time is understandable, as it flew in the face of the Western dualistic tradition. What is less understandable is why these dualisms remain popular today. Westermarck was more Darwinian than some contemporary evolutionary biologists, who are best described as Huxleyan.

Bulldog Bites Master

In 1893, before a large audience in Oxford, Huxley publicly tried to reconcile his dim view of the nasty natural world with the kindness occasionally encountered in human society. Huxley realized that the laws of the physical world are unalterable. He felt, however, that their impact on human existence could be softened and modified if people kept nature under control. Comparing us with the gardener who has a hard time keeping weeds out of his garden, he proposed ethics as humanity's cultural victory over the evolutionary process.[6]

This was an astounding position for two reasons. First, it deliberately curbed the explanatory power of evolution. Since many people consider morality the essence of our species, Huxley was in effect saying that what makes us human is too big for the evolutionary framework. This was a puzzling retreat by someone who had gained a reputation as "Darwin's

Bulldog" owing to his fierce advocacy of evolutionary theory. The solution that Huxley proposed was quintessentially Hobbesian in that it stated that people are fit for society only by education, not nature.

Second, Huxley offered no hint whatsoever where humanity could possibly have unearthed the will and strength to go against its own nature. If we are indeed born competitors who don't care one bit about the feelings of others, how in the world did we decide to transform ourselves into model citizens? Can people for generations maintain behavior that is out of character, like a bunch of piranhas who decide to become vegetarians? How deep does such a change go? Are we the proverbial wolves in sheep's clothing: nice on the outside, nasty on the inside? What a contorted scheme!

It was the only time Huxley visibly broke with Darwin. As aptly summarized by Huxley's biographer, Adrian Desmond: "[He] was forcing his ethical Ark against the Darwinian current which had brought him so far."[7] Two decades earlier, in *The Descent of Man*, Darwin had stated the continuity between human nature and morality in no uncertain terms. The reason for Huxley's departure has been sought in his suffering at the cruel hand of nature, which had just taken his beloved daughter's life, and in his need to make the ruthlessness of the Darwinian cosmos palatable to the general public. He could do so, he felt, only by dislodging human ethics, declaring it a cultural innovation.

This dualistic outlook was to get an enormous respectability boost from Freud's writings, which throve on contrasts between the conscious and subconscious, the ego and superego, Eros and Death, and so on. As with Huxley's gardener and garden, Freud was not just dividing the world in symmetrical halves: he saw struggle everywhere! He explained the incest taboo and other moral restrictions as the result of a violent break with the freewheeling sexual life of the primal horde, culminating in the collective slaughter of an overbearing father by his sons. And he let civilization arise out of a renunciation of instinct, the gaining of control over the forces of nature, and the building of a cultural superego. Not only did he keep animals at a distance, his view also excluded women. It was the men who reached the highest peaks of civilization, carrying out tortuous sublimations "of which women are little capable."[8]

Humanity's heroic combat against forces that try to drag us down remains a dominant theme within biology today. Because of its continuity with the doctrine of original sin, I have characterized this viewpoint as "Calvinist sociobiology."[9] Let me offer a few illustrative quotations from today's two most outspoken Huxleyans.

Declaring ethics a radical break with biology, and feeling that Huxley had not gone far enough, George Williams has written extensively about the wretchedness of Mother Nature. His stance culminates in the claim that human morality is an inexplicable accident of the evolutionary process: "I account for morality as an *accidental* capability produced, in its boundless *stupid-*

ity, by a biological process that is normally opposed to the expression of such a capability" (my italics). In a similar vein, Richard Dawkins has declared us "nicer than is good for our selfish genes," and warns that "we are never allowed to forget the narrow tightrope on which we balance above the Darwinian abyss." In a recent interview, Dawkins explicitly endorsed Huxley: "What I am saying, along with many other people, among them T. H. Huxley, is that in our political and social life we are entitled to throw out Darwinism, to say we don't want to live in a Darwinian world."[10]

Poor Darwin must be turning in his grave, because the world implied here is totally unlike what he himself envisioned. Again, what is lacking is an indication of how we can possibly negate our genes, which the same authors at other times don't hesitate to depict as all-powerful. Thus, first we are told that our genes know what is best for us, that they control our lives, programming every little wheel in the human survival machine. But then the same authors let us know that we have the option to rebel, that we are free to act differently. The obvious implication is that the first position should be taken with a grain of salt.

Like Huxley, these authors want to have it both ways: human behavior is an evolutionary product except when it is hard to explain. And like Hobbes and Freud, they think in dichotomies: we are part nature, part culture, rather than a well-integrated whole. Their position has been echoed by popularizers such as Robert Wright and Matt Ridley, who say that virtue is absent from people's hearts and souls, and that our species is potentially but not naturally moral.[11] But what about the many people who occasionally experience in themselves and others a degree of sympathy, goodness, and generosity? Wright's answer is that the "moral animal" is a fraud: "[T]he pretense of selflessness is about as much part of human nature as is its frequent absence. We dress ourselves up in tony moral language, denying base motives and stressing our at least minimal consideration for the greater good; and we fiercely and self-righteously decry selfishness in others."[12]

To explain how we manage to live with ourselves despite this travesty, theorists have called upon self-deception and denial. If people think they are at times unselfish, so the argument goes, they must be hiding the selfish motives from themselves. In other words, all of us have two agendas: one hidden in the recesses of our minds, and one that we sell to ourselves and others. Or, as philosopher Michael Ghiselin concludes, "Scratch an 'altruist,' and watch a 'hypocrite' bleed." In the ultimate twist of irony, anyone who doesn't believe that we are fooling ourselves, who feels that we may be genuinely kind, is called a wishful thinker and thus stands accused of fooling himself![13]

This entire double-agenda idea is another obvious Freudian scheme. And like a UFO sighting, it is unverifiable: hidden motives are indistinguishable from absent ones. The quasi-scientific concept of the subconscious conveniently leaves the fundamental selfishness of the human species intact despite daily experiences to the contrary.[14] I blame much of this intellectual twisting and turning on the unfortunate legacy of Huxley, about whom evolutionary biologist Ernst Mayr didn't mince any words: "Huxley, who believed in final causes, rejected natural selection and did not represent genuine Darwinian thought in any way. . . . It is unfortunate, considering how confused Huxley was, that his essay [on evolutionary ethics] is often referred to even today as if it were authoritative."[15]

Moral Emotions

Westermarck is part of a long lineage, going back to Aristotle and Thomas Aquinas, which firmly anchors morality in the natural inclinations and desires of our species. Compared to Huxley's, his is a view uncompounded by any need for invisible agendas and discrepancies between how we are and how we wish to be: morality has been there from the start. It is part and parcel of human nature.

Emotions occupy a central role in that, as Aristotle said, "Thought by itself moves nothing." Modern cognitive psychologists and neuroscientists confirm that emotions, rather than being the antithesis of rationality, greatly aid thinking. They speak of emotional intelligence. People can reason and deliberate as much as they want, but if there are no emotions attached to the various options in front of them, they will never reach a decision or conviction.[16] This is critical for moral choice, because if anything, morality involves strong convictions. These don't—or rather can't—come about through a cool Kantian rationality; they require caring about others and powerful gut feelings about right and wrong.

Westermarck discusses, one by one, a whole range of what philosophers before him used to call the "moral sentiments." He classifies the retributive emotions into those derived from resentment and anger, which seek revenge and punishment, and those that are more positive and prosocial. Whereas in his time there were few good animal examples of the moral emotions—hence his occasional reliance on Moroccan camel stories—we know now that there are many parallels in primate behavior. Thus, he discusses "forgiveness," and how the turning of the other cheek is a universally appreciated gesture: we now know from our studies that chimpanzees kiss and embrace and that monkeys groom each other after fights.[17] Westermarck sees protection of others against offenders resulting from "sympathetic resentment"; again, this is a common pattern in monkeys and apes, and in many other animals, who stick up for their friends, defending them against attackers. Similarly, the retributive kindly emotions ("desire to give pleasure in return for pleasure") have an obvious parallel in what biologists now label reciprocal altruism, such as providing assistance to those who assist in return.[18]

When I watch primates, measuring how they share food in return for grooming, comfort victims of aggression, or wait for the right opportunity to get even with a rival, I see very much the same emotional impulses that Westermarck analyzed. A group of chimpanzees, for example, may whip up an outraged chorus of barks when the dominant male overdoes his punishment of an underling, and in the wild they form cooperative hunting parties that share the spoils of their efforts. Although I shy away from calling chimpanzees "moral beings," their psychology contains many of the ingredients that, if also present in the progenitor of humans and apes, must have allowed our ancestors to develop a moral sense. Instead of seeing morality as a radically new invention, I tend to view it as a natural outgrowth of ancient social tendencies.

Westermarck was far from naïve about how morality is maintained; he knew it required both approval and negative sanctions. For example, reflecting on an issue that today we might relate to developments taking place in South Africa's Truth and Reconciliation Commission, he explains how forgiveness prohibits revenge but not punishment. Punishment is a necessary component of justice, whereas revenge—if let loose—only destroys. Like Adam Smith before him, Westermarck recognized the moderating role of sympathy: "The more the moral consciousness is influenced by sympathy, the more severely it condemns any retributive infliction of pain which it regards as undeserved."[19]

The most insightful part of his writing is perhaps where Westermarck tries to come to grips with what defines a moral emotion as moral. Here he shows that there is much more to these emotions than raw gut feeling. In analyzing these feelings he introduces the notion of "disinterestedness." Emotions, such as gratitude and resentment, directly concern one's own interests—how one has been treated or how one wishes to be treated—and hence are too egocentric to be moral. Moral emotions, in contrast, are disconnected from one's immediate situation: they deal with good and bad at a more abstract, disinterested level. It is only when we make general judgments of how *anyone* ought to be treated that we can begin to speak of moral approval and disapproval. This is an area in which humans go radically farther than other primates.[20]

Westermarck was ahead of his time, and he went well beyond Darwin's thinking on these matters. In spirit, however, the two were on the same line. Darwin believed that there was plenty of room within his theory to accommodate the origins of morality, and he attached great importance to the capacity for sympathy. He by no means excluded animals from this view: "Many animals certainly sympathize with each other's distress or danger."[21] He has been proven right; laboratory experiments on monkeys and even rats have shown powerful vicarious distress responses. The sight of a conspecific in pain or trouble often calls forth a reaction to ameliorate the situation. These reactions undoubtedly derived from parental care, in which vulnerable individuals are tended with great care, but in many animals they stretch well beyond this situation, including relations among unrelated adults.[22]

Darwin did not see any conflict between the harshness of the evolutionary process and the gentleness of some of its products. As discussed in the previous chapter with regard to the distinction between motive and function, all one needs to do is make a distinction between how evolution operates and the actual psychologies it has produced. Darwin knew this better than anyone, expressing his views most clearly when he emphasized continuity with animals even in the moral domain. In *The Descent of Man*, he takes exactly the opposite position of those who, like Huxley, view morality as a violation of evolutionary principles: "Any animal whatever, endowed with well-marked social instincts, the parental and filial affections being here included, would inevitably acquire a moral sense or conscience, as soon as its intellectual powers had become as well developed, or nearly as well developed, as in man."[23]

The *Ke* Willow

There is never much new under the sun. Westermarck's emphasis on the retributive emotions, whether friendly or vengeful, reminds one of Confucius' reply to the question whether there is any single word that may serve as prescription for all of one's life. Confucius proposed "reciprocity" as such a word. Reciprocity is also, of course, the crux of the Golden Rule ("Do unto others as you would have them do unto you"), which remains unsurpassed as a summary of human morality.

A follower of the Chinese sage, Mencius, wrote extensively about human goodness during his life, from 372 to 289 B.C.[24] Mencius lost his father when he was only three, and his mother made sure he received the best possible education. The mother is at least as well known as her son, and still serves as a maternal model to the Chinese for her absolute devotion.

Called the "second sage" because of his great influence, Mencius had a revolutionary bent in that he stressed the obligation of rulers to provide for the common people. Recorded on bamboo clappers and handed down to his descendants and their students, his writings show that the debate about whether we are naturally moral, or not, is ancient indeed. In one exchange, Mencius reacts against Kaou Tsze's views, which are strikingly similar to Huxley's gardener and garden metaphor: "Man's nature is like the *ke* willow, and righteousness is like a cup or a bowl. The fashioning of benevolence and righteousness out of man's nature is like the making of cups and bowls from the *ke* willow."[25]

Mencius replied:

> Can you, leaving untouched the nature of the willow, make with it cups and bowls? You must do violence and injury to the willow, before you can make cups and bowls with it. If you must do violence and injury to the willow, before you can make cups and bowls with it, *on your principles* you must in

the same way do violence and injury to humanity in order to fashion from it benevolence and righteousness! Your words alas! would certainly lead all men on to reckon benevolence and righteousness to be calamities.

Evidently, the origins of human kindness and ethics were a point of debate in the China of two millennia ago. Mencius believed that humans tend toward the good as naturally as water flows downhill. This is also evident from the following remark, in which he seeks to exclude the possibility of a double agenda on the grounds that the moral emotions, such as sympathy, leave little room for this:

> When I say that all men have a mind which cannot bear to see the suffering of others, my meaning may be illustrated thus: even nowadays, if men suddenly see a child about to fall into a well, they will without exception experience a feeling of alarm and distress. They will feel so, not as a ground on which they may gain the favor of the child's parents, nor as a ground on which they may seek the praise of their neighbors and friends, nor from a dislike to the reputation of having been unmoved by such a thing. From this case we may perceive that the feeling of commiseration is essential to man.

Mencius' example is strikingly similar to both the one by Westermarck ("Can we help sympathize with our friends?") and Smith's famous definition of sympathy ("How selfish soever man may be supposed to be . . ."). The central idea underlying all three statements is that distress at the sight of another's pain is an impulse over which we exert no control: it grabs us instantaneously, like a reflex, leaving us without the time to weigh the pros and cons. Remarkably, all of the alternative motives that Mencius considers occur in the modern literature, usually under the heading of reputation building. The big difference is, of course, that Mencius rejects these explanations as too contrived given the immediacy and force of the sympathetic response. Manipulation of public opinion is entirely possible at other times, he says, but not at the moment a child falls into a well.

I couldn't agree more. Evolution has produced species that follow genuinely cooperative impulses. I don't know whether people are, deep down, good or evil, but I do know that to believe that each and every move is selfishly calculated overestimates human mental powers, let alone those of other animals.[26]

Interesting additional evidence comes from child research. Freud, B. F. Skinner, and Jean Piaget all believed that the child learns its first moral distinctions through fear of punishment and a desire for praise. Like Huxleyan biologists who see morality as culturally imposed upon a nasty human nature, they conceived morality as coming from the outside, imposed by adults upon a passive, naturally selfish child. Children were thought to adopt parental values to construct a superego, the moral agency of the self. Left to their own devices, like the children in William Golding's *Lord of the Flies*, they would never arrive at anything even close to morality.

Already at an early age, however, children know the difference between moral principles ("Do not steal") and cultural conventions ("No pajamas at school"). They apparently appreciate that the breaking of certain rules distresses and harms others, whereas the breaking of other rules merely violates expectations about what is appropriate. Their attitudes don't seem to be based purely on reward and punishment. Whereas pediatric handbooks still depict young children as self-centered monsters, we know now that by one year of age they spontaneously comfort people in distress, and that soon thereafter they begin to develop a moral perspective through interactions with other members of their species.[27]

Rather than being nicer than is good for our genes, we may be just nice enough. Thus, the child is not going against its own nature by developing a caring, moral attitude, and civil society is not like an out-of-control garden subdued by a sweating gardener. We are merely following evolved tendencies.

How refreshingly simple!   ■

NOTES FOR "SURVIVAL OF THE KINDEST"

1. In the 1975 Christmas season, millions of Americans spent five dollars each to purchase ordinary rocks as pets. The rocks were sold in boxes with air holes and came with a manual explaining how to train the rock to roll over, to play dead, and to protect its owner. Tamagotchi is a popular Japanese electronic gadget that mimics a chick. It eats, sleeps, defecates, gets cranky, and beeps for attention. If the owner does not take care of it, Tamagotchi dies.

2. Wrangham and Peterson (1996). Playing with "dolls" is not unusual in nonhuman primates. I have seen young chimpanzees in captivity act the same as Kakama with a piece of cloth or a broom. A wild mountain gorilla was seen to pull up a mass of soft moss, which she carried and held like an infant under her chest, cuddling and "nursing" it (Byrne, 1995).

3. Darwin (1859).

4. Quoted from an interview by Roes (1998).

5. Also, let us not forget that many people volunteer to adopt children—some even kidnap newborns from the maternity ward—following urges that evidently transcend genetic self-interest.

6. See Chapter 1 ("The Whole Animal").

7. Reported in *The Jerusalem Post*, July 26, 1996.

8. De Waal and Aureli (1996).

9. Ladygina-Kohts (in press).

10. Kunz and Allgaier (1994).

11. Jewell (1997).

12. Whittemore and Hebard (1995).

13. Whittemore and Hebard (1995).

NOTES FOR "DOWN WITH DUALISM"

1. Westermarck (1912).

2. de Waal and Luttrell (1988) and Aureli et al. (1992).

3. For recent debate about evolutionary ethics, see the *Journal of Consciousness Studies*, vol. 7 (1–2), edited by L. D. Katz (2000).

4. Wolf (1995). Others before him studied marriages in Israeli kibbutzim and found that children do not have sexual intercourse, let alone marry unrelated children of the opposite sex with whom they have grown up in the same peer group (reviewed by Wolf, 1995).

5. Tokuda (1961–62).

6. Huxley (1894).

7. Desmond (1994).

8. Freud (1913, 1930).

9. de Waal (1996a). See also Flack and de Waal (2000).

10. Williams quoted in Roes (1998), Dawkins in *Times Literary Supplement* (November 29, 1996), and Dawkins in another interview by Roes (1997). The profound irony, of course, is that contrary to Dawkins's warning against a Darwinian world, such a world is eminently more livable than a Huxleyan one, which is devoid of natural moral tendencies. Dawkins seems almost a reincarnation of Huxley in terms of both combativeness (e.g., Dawkins, 1998) and his departure from Darwinism. Such notions as that we are survival machines, that we are born selfish and need to be taught kindness, and especially that morality and biology are miles apart were alien to Darwin yet typical of Huxley. Darwin never looked at any life form as a machine. He had a Lorenz-like rapport with animals and didn't shy away from attributing intentions and emotions to them. Crist (1999) discusses at length Darwin's anthropomorphism, which has irritated some scholars, but confirms that those with an integrated view of nature don't necessarily have a problem with it (see also Chapter 1, "The Whole Animal"). Given their differences of opinion, Darwin couldn't resist referring, in his final letter to Huxley, to the latter's depiction of all living things (including humans) as machines: "I wish to God there were more automata in the world like you." (Cited in Crist, 1999).

11. In view of their cynical positions, the titles of the books by Wright (*The Moral Animal*) and Ridley (*The Origins of Virtue*) don't exactly cover their message (Wright, 1994; Ridley, 1996).

12. Wright (1994).

13. Sober and Wilson (1998) write about this accusation: "We feel we should address a criticism that is often leveled at advocates of altruism in psychology and group selection in biology. It is frequently said that people endorse such hypotheses because they *want* the world to be a friendly and hospitable place. The defenders of egoism and individualism who advance this criticism thereby pay themselves a compliment; they pat themselves on the back for staring reality squarely in the face. Egoists and individualists are objective, they suggest, whereas proponents of altruism and group selection are trapped by a comforting illusion."

14. Ideas about the subconscious and its evolutionary *raison d'être* have been around since Badcock (1986) and Alexander (1987). The first explicitly sought to provide Freudian-Darwinian solutions to the "problem" of altruism.

15. Mayr (1997).

16. Damasio (1994).

17. Aureli and de Waal (2000).

18. Westermarck lists moral approval as a kind of retributive kindly emotion, hence as a component of reciprocal altruism. These views antedate discussions about "indirect

reciprocity" and reputation building in the modern literature on evolutionary ethics (e.g., Alexander, 1987).

19. Smith (1759).
20. These reflections by Westermarck parallel Smith's (1759) idea of an "impartial spectator."
21. Darwin (1871).
22. Reviewed by Preston and de Waal (in press).
23. Darwin (1871).
24. This makes Mencius a contemporary of Aristotle—born 384 B.C. in Greece—the first and foremost Western philosopher to root morality in human biology (Arnhart, 1998).
25. All quotations are from Mencius (372–289 B.C.), *The Works of Mencius.*
26. See Chapter 10 ("Survival of the Kindest"), which also contains the full quotation from Smith.
27. Killen and de Waal (2000).

REFERENCES

Alexander, R. A. (1987). *The Biology of Moral Systems.* New York: Aldine de Gruyter.

Arnhart, L. (1998). *Darwinian Natural Right: The Biological Ethics of Human Nature.* Albany, N.Y.: SUNY Press.

Aureli, F., Cozzolino, R., Cordischi, C., and Scucchi, S. (1992). Kin-oriented redirection among Japanese macaques: An expression of a revenge system? *Animal Behaviour* 44: 283–291.

Aureli, F., and de Waal, F. B. M. (2000). *Natural Conflict Resolution.* Berkeley: University of California Press.

Badcock, C. R. (1986). *The Problem of Altruism: Freudian-Darwinian Solutions.* Oxford, England: Blackwell.

Crist, E. (1999). *Images of Animals: Anthropomorphism and Animal Mind.* Philadelphia: Temple University Press.

Damasio, A. R. (1994). *Descartes' Error: Emotion, Reason, and the Human Brain.* New York: Putnam.

Darwin, C. (1964 [1859]). *On the Origin of Species.* Cambridge, Mass.: Harvard University Press.

Darwin, C. (1981 [1871]). *The Descent of Man, and Selection in Relation to Sex.* Princeton, N.J.: Princeton University Press.

Dawkins, R. (1998). *Unweaving the Rainbow: Science, Delusion and the Appetite for Wonder.* New York: Houghton Mifflin.

Desmond, A. (1994). *Huxley: From Devil's Disciple to Evolution's High Priest.* New York: Perseus.

Flack, J. C., and de Waal, F. B. M. (2000). "Any animal whatever": Darwinian building blocks of morality in monkeys and apes. *Journal of Consciousness Studies* 7 (1–2): 1–29.

Freud, S. (1989 [1913]). *Totem and Taboo.* New York: Norton.

Freud, S. (1989 [1930]). *Civilization and Its Discontents.* New York: Norton.

Huxley, T. H. (1989 [1894]). *Evolution and Ethics.* Princeton, N.J.: Princeton University Press.

Jewell, D. (July 14, 1997). Brave hearts. *People.*

Killen, M., and de Waal, F. B. M. (2000). The evolution and development of morality. In F. Aureli and F. B. M. de Waal (eds.), *Natural Conflict Resolution*, pp. 352–372. Berkeley: University of California Press.

Kunz, T. H., and Allgaier, A. L. (1994). Allomaternal care: Helper-assisted birth in the Rodrigues fruit bat, *Pteropus rodricensis. J. Zool., London* 232: 691–700.

Ladygina-Kohts, N. N. (in press). *Infant Chimpanzee and Human Child* (F. B. M. de Waal, ed.). New York: Oxford University Press.

Mayr, E. (1997). *This is Biology: The Science of the Living World.* Cambridge, Mass.: Belknap.

Mencius (372–289 B.C.). *The Works of Mencius.* English transl. Gu Lu. Shanghai: Shangwu Publishing House.

Preston, S. D., and de Waal, F. B. M. (in press). The communication of emotions and the possibility of empathy in animals. In *Altruistic Love: Science, Philosophy, and Religion in Dialogue.* Oxford, England: Oxford University Press.

Ridley, M. (1996). *The Origins of Virtue.* London: Viking.

Roes, F. (1998). A conversation with George C. Williams. *Natural History* 5: 10–15.

Smith, A. (1937 [1759]). *A Theory of Moral Sentiments.* New York: Modern Library.

Sober, E., and David Wilson, D. S. (1998). *Unto Others: The Evolution and Psychology of Unselfish Behavior.* Cambridge, Mass.: Harvard University Press.

Tokuda, K. (1961–62). A study of sexual behavior in the Japanese monkey. *Primates* 3(2): 1–40.

de Waal, F. B. M. (1996a). *Good Natured.* Cambridge, Mass.: Harvard University Press.

de Waal, F. B. M., and Aureli, F. (1996). Consolation, reconciliation, and a possible cognitive difference between macaque and chimpanzee. In A. E. Russon, K. A. Bard, and S. T. Parker (eds.), *Reaching into Thought: The Minds of the Great Apes*, pp. 80–110. Cambridge, England: Cambridge University Press.

de Waal, F. B. M., and Luttrell, L. M. (1988). Mechanisms of social reciprocity in three primate species: symmetrical relationship characteristics or cognition? *Ethology and Sociobiology* 9: 101–118.

Westermarck, E. (1912). *The Origin and Development of the Moral Ideas*, vol. 1. London: Macmillan.

Whittemore, H., and Hebard, C. (1995). *So That Others May Live.* New York: Bantam.

Wolf, A. P. (1995). *Sexual Attraction and Childhood Association: A Chinese Brief for Edward Westermarck.* Stanford, Calif.: Stanford University Press.

Wrangham, R. W., and Peterson, D. (1996). *Demonic Males: Apes and the Evolution of Human Aggression.* Boston: Houghton Mifflin.

Wright, R. (1994). *The Moral Animal; The New Science of Evolutionary Psychology.* New York: Pantheon.

■ *QUESTIONS FOR MAKING CONNECTIONS WITHIN THE READING* ■

1. In "Survival of the Kindest," Frans de Waal distinguishes between "functional altruism" and "intended kindness." In "Down with Dualism," he looks at the difference between "emotions" and "moral emotions." Using

examples from your own experience, define these key terms. What relationships do you see between these terms? Is altruism, for example, "an emotion"?

2. Why does de Waal find the animal exhibit in Lop Buri to be "absurd"? What kind of animal exhibit would best represent his understanding of the essential characteristics that have governed evolution in the animal kingdom?

3. What evidence does de Waal present to support his belief that nature is governed by "survival of the kindest"? How does his evidence differ from the evidence offered by those who believe that nature is governed by "survival of the fittest?"

▪ QUESTIONS FOR WRITING ▪

1. De Waal concludes "Survival of the Kindest" with a description of the animal kingdom that is bound to shock some readers: he describes dogs who became "depressed" when exposed to a great deal of death; he discusses a strategy meant to help the dogs recover their "emotional investment" in helping others; finally, he concludes with the assertion that there are species of animals who intend to do good deeds. What would change if de Waal were right? That is, what would the consequences be if de Waal's account of the evolutionary value of kindness replaced the dominant account of evolution as the arena of "survival of the fittest"? Is de Waal's revision of the evolution narrative simply an academic matter, or does it have social, cultural, and spiritual ramifications?

2. As de Waal sees it, Westermarck's ideas were ignored because they "flew in the face of the Western dualistic tradition." What is this tradition, and why would one want to work in some other tradition? What is de Waal's relationship to this tradition? If those who live in the West can't escape or avoid this tradition, what other relationships might they have to it?

▪ QUESTIONS FOR MAKING CONNECTIONS BETWEEN READINGS ▪

1. "Down with Dualism" concludes with de Waal's assertion "that distress at the sight of another's pain is an impulse over which we exert no control." In "The Wreck of Time," Annie Dillard reflects on major events in the last millennium, including great tragedies that involved the deaths of untold numbers of innocent victims. Do the stories that Dillard has to tell support de Waal's argument about nature or Huxley's? If "moral emotions" are part of the genetic make-up of humans, then how can we account for the

disasters that Dillard describes? And how do we account for the fact that some, perhaps including Dillard, feel so little distress at learning about the pain others have experienced?

2. In making his argument for an alternate explanation of the evolutionary process, de Waal relies on the work of Edward Westermarck, who believed that "human goodness" is part of our genetic make-up. De Waal suggests that instead of encouraging ever more ruthless competition, the process of evolution also engenders forms of life that, surviving by means of cooperation, develop correspondingly altruistic emotions. De Waal suggests, moreover, that many different species have developed altruistic sensibilities, not only human beings but also chimpanzees and dogs. If de Waal and Westermarck are correct, how does one account for the problems on the job that Greider describes in "Work Rules"? If evolution has counterbalanced "survival of the fittest" with "survival of the kindest," are we destined—sooner or later—to develop a "moral economy"? If not, then is it possible that our economic system is pushing us into modes of behavior that violate our basic biological nature?

www **For additional suggestions about making connections between readings, visit the Link-O-Mat and More Sample Assignments at <www.newhum.com>.**

ACKNOWLEDGMENTS

p. 1   The "Ecology of Magic," from THE SPELL OF THE SENSUOUS by David Abram, copyright © 1996 by David Abram. Used by permission of Pantheon Books, a division of Random House, Inc.

p. 25   From WRITING WOMEN'S WORLDS: Bedouin Stories by Lila Abu-Lughod. Copyright © 1992 The Regents of the University of California. Used by permission.

p. 55   Excerpt from A HISTORY OF GOD by Karen Armstrong, copyright © 1993 by Karen Armstrong. Used by permission of Alfred A. Knopf, a division of Random House, Inc.

p. 78   Reprinted from Jonathan Boyarin, "Waiting for a Jew: Marginal Redemption at the Eighth Street Shul," in BETWEEN TWO WORLDS: Ethnographic Essays on American Jewry, edited by Jack Kugelmass. Chapter copyright © 1988 by Jonathan Boyarin. Copyright © 1988 by Cornell University. Used by permission of the publisher, Cornell University Press.

p. 101 "A World on the Edge" from WORLD ON FIRE: HOW EXPORTING FREE MARKET DEMOCRACY BREEDS ETHNIC HATRED AND GLOBAL INSTABILITY by Amy Chua, copyright © 2003, 2004 by Amy Chua. Used by permission of Doubleday, a division of Random House, Inc.

p. 120 "The Wreck of Time" by Annie Dillard, Harper's Magazine, January 1998. Copyright © 1998 Annie Dillard. Reprinted by permission of the author.

p. 130 "The Naked Citadel" by Susan Faludi. Copyright © 1994 by Susan Faludi. First appeared in THE NEW YORKER. Reprinted by permission of the author and the Sandra Dijkstra Literary Agency.

p. 166 Copyright © 2003 by The New York Times Co. Reprinted with permission.

p. 178 From THE TIPPING POINT by Malcolm Gladwell. Copyright © 2000, 2002 by Malcolm Gladwell. By permission of Little, Brown and Company, Inc.

p. 196 "What Does the Dreaded 'E' Word *Mean,* Anyway?" by Stephen Jay Gould, Natural History, January 2000. Copyright The American Museum of Natural History, 2000. Reprinted by Rhonda S. Shearer, Art Science Research Laboratory, Inc., New York, New York.

p. 212 Reprinted with the permission of Simon & Schuster Adult Publishing Group, from THE SOUL OF CAPITALISM by William Greider. Copyright © 2003 by William Greider. All rights reserved.

p. 233 "Second Proms and Second Primaries: The Limits of Majority Rule" by Lani Guinier, Boston Review, Oct/Nov, 1992. Copyright © 1992 Lani Guinier. Used with permission.

p. 247 "The Myth of the Ant Queen" is reprinted with the permission of Scribner, an imprint of Simon & Schuster Adult Publishing Group, from EMERGENCE: THE CONNECTED LIVES OF ANTS, BRAINS, CITIES AND SOFTWARE by Steven Johnson. Copyright © 2001 by Steven Johnson.

p. 267 "Beyond Militarism" by Mary Kaldor presented at the Nobel Peace Prize Centennial Symposium in Oslo, December 2001. Reprinted by permission of the Nobel Institute and the author. All rights reserved.

p. 285 From INTO THE WILD by Jon Krakauer. Copyright © 1996 by Jon Krakauer. Used by permission of Villard Books, a division of Random House, Inc.

AUTHOR AND TITLE INDEX